RALLY! RALLY! RALLY!

TO MEN OF COLOR!

AUTHORITY HAS BEEN RECEIVED TO RAISE

A REGIMENT

OF

MEN OF COLOR

FOR 100 DAYS

Rally, Men of Color, at Once for Your Country

Arm for the Defence of your Homes! Enroll yourselves for the Emergency. A Regiment ought to be Raised within TWO DAYS. Chester and Delaware Counties will send Three Companies—Bucks and Montgomery will do as well. What will Philadelphia do?

COL. TAGGART

Late Colonel 12th Regiment Pennsylvania Reserves, will command, and the Officers will be the Graduates of the Military Board at Washington.

$50 CITY BOUNTY

Will be Paid each Man. Come, then, to Head-quarters,

No. 1210 CHESTNUT STREET

AND ENROLL YOUR NAMES.

U. S. Steam-Power Book and Job Printing Establishment, Ledger Buildings, Third and Chestnut Streets, Philadelphia.

Like Men of War

Like Men of War

BLACK TROOPS IN THE CIVIL WAR
1862–1865

NOAH ANDRE TRUDEAU

CASTLE BOOKS

This edition published in 2002 by

CASTLE BOOKS
A division of Book Sales, Inc.
114 Northfield Avenue
Edison, New Jersey 08837

Published by arrangement with

Little, Brown and Company, (Inc.)
1271 Avenue of the Americas
New York, New York 10020

Library of Congress Cataloging-in-Publication Data
Trudeau, Noah Andre.
        Like men of war : Black troops in the Civil War, 1862-1865 / by
Noah Andre Trudeau.
                p.   cm.
        Includes bibliographical references (p.) and index.
        1. United States—History—Civil War, 1861-1865—Participation,
        Afro-American. 2. Afro-American soldiers—History—19th century.
        I. Title.
E540.N3T78   1998   97-15380
973.7'41—DC21

ISBN: 0-7858-1476-0

Text design by Robert Lowe

Printed in the United States of America

FOR
George W. Williams and Joseph T. Wilson,
who showed the way,
Dudley Taylor Cornish and James M. McPherson,
who set the standard,
Edwin S. Redkey and Joseph T. Glatthaar,
who followed with distinction

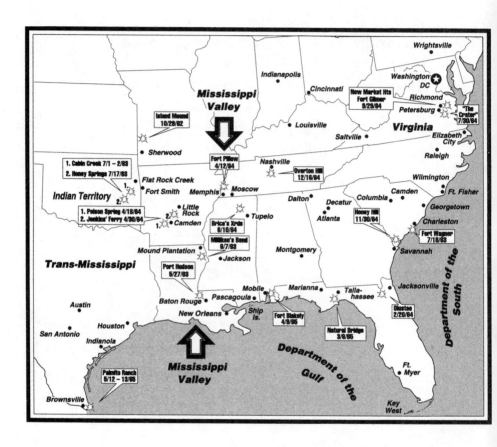

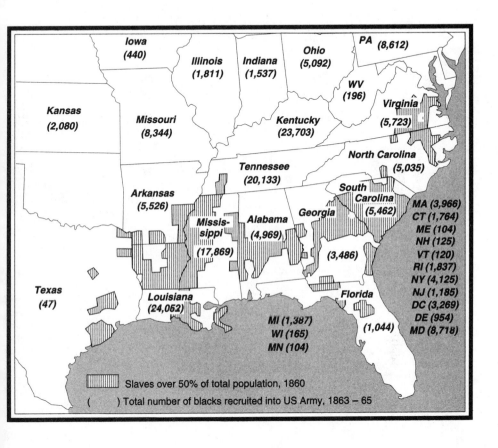

State	Value
Iowa	(440)
Illinois	(1,811)
Indiana	(1,537)
Ohio	(5,092)
PA	(8,612)
WV	(196)
Kansas	(2,080)
Missouri	(8,344)
Kentucky	(23,703)
Virginia	(5,723)
North Carolina	(5,035)
Tennessee	(20,133)
Arkansas	(5,526)
South Carolina	(5,462)
Mississippi	(17,869)
Alabama	(4,969)
Georgia	(3,486)
Texas	(47)
Louisiana	(24,052)
Florida	(1,044)
MI	(1,387)
WI	(165)
MN	(104)
MA	(3,966)
CT	(1,764)
ME	(104)
NH	(125)
VT	(120)
RI	(1,837)
NY	(4,125)
NJ	(1,185)
DC	(3,269)
DE	(954)
MD	(8,718)

▨ Slaves over 50% of total population, 1860

( ) Total number of blacks recruited into US Army, 1863 – 65

Contents

List of Maps   *xiii*

Picture List   *xvii*

Preface   *xix*

Author's Note   *xxiii*

Part One: 1861–1862

1. "A Liberating Army"   3

Part Two: 1863

2. "Will They Fight?"   23

Interlude: "The Power of Fear"   60

3. "The Old Flag Never Touched the Ground"   63

Interlude: "The Question of Pay"   91

4. "The Question That Negroes Will Fight Is Settled"   94

Part Three: 1864

5. "Amid a Storm of Bullets"   121

6. "You Are Fighting against Your Master"   156

7. "With Wild, Exultant Cheers"   182

8. "On to Richmond!"   201

Interlude: "This Disgraceful Distinction"   252

9. "I Am Ready to Die for Liberty"   256

10. "Saved the Colors"   283

Interlude: "A Practice Justified by No Rule of War"   310

11. "Into the Very Mouth of Death"   313

12. "Captain, I Am Wounded; What Shall I Do?"   334

Part Four: 1865

13. "Ye's Long Been A-coming"   353

Interlude: "We Want Black Commissioned Officers"   373

14. "Our Errand through the State"   375

15. "The Negro Will Fight & Fight Bravely"   396

Interlude: "Their Enthusiam Was Said to Be . . . Remarkable"   409

16. "Babylon Is Fallen"   415

Interlude: "Nothing Has So Shocked Us So Much"   433

17. "That Winds Up the War"   435

Part Five: 1865–1938

18. "This Good Work Is Only Begun"   455

Chapter Notes   471

Bibliography   495

Acknowledgments   531

Index   533

List of Maps

———◦———

(Black troops in Combat: Major Battlefields and Regions)   *vi*

(Black troops: Total Numbers Recruited and Areas of Greatest
    Slave Populations)   *vii*

Island Mound, October 29, 1862/Burnside's Expedition,
    February 6–April 26, 1863   4

Louisiana Native Guards, September 1862–June 1863   30

The Lower Mississippi   36

Port Hudson, May 27, 1863 (Union Assaults)   39

Port Hudson, May 27, 1863 (Attack by the Louisiana
    Native Guards)   42

Milliken's Bend, June 7, 1863   52

The Jacksonville Campaign, March 1863   65

Charleston Harbor and Nearby Islands/Hilton Head to Charleston   75

Assault on Wagner, July 18, 1863   79

Fort (Battery) Wagner, July 18, 1863   83

1863 (Wrightsville/Mound Plantation/Cabin Creek/Wolf River
    Bridge/Elizabeth City Expedition)   96

Honey Springs, July 17, 1863   107

The Florida Expedition, February 1864   130

Eastern Florida, 1864   131

Olustee, February 20, 1864   138

Olustee, 2:00 P.M.	140
Olustee, 3:00 P.M.	141
Olustee, 4:30 P.M.	146
Olustee, 4:30–6:30 P.M.	149
Fighting Forrest, March–July 1864	162
Fort Pillow, April 12, 1864	164
Brice's Cross Roads, June 10, 1864	174
The Red River Campaign/Arkansas, 1864	184
Poison Spring, April 18, 1864/Jenkins' Ferry, April 30, 1864	187
On to Richmond!, February–March 1864	202
The Overland Campaign, May–June 1864	210
Spotsylvania, May 15, 1864/Bermuda Hundred Campaign, May 1864	213
Wilson's Wharf, May 24, 1864/Baylor's Farm, June 15, 1864	218
Petersburg, June 15, 1864	223
The Crater, July 30, 1864	237
(The Crater) 6:30 A.M./8:30 A.M.	240
James Island, July 2, 1864	259
1864 (Watie-Gano Raid/Asboth's Expedition/Georgia, 1864)	264
Saltville, October 2, 1864	272
(New Market Heights, September 29, 1864) 5:30 A.M./7:00 A.M.	288
September 29, 1864/Fort Gilmer	295
October 27, 1864	302
Hatch's Expedition, November 1864	317
(Honey Hill) November 29, 1864	319
(Honey Hill) November 30, 1864, A.M.	321
(Honey Hill) November 30, 1864, Noon	325
(Honey Hill) November 30, 1864, 1:30 P.M.	327
(Tennessee) November–December 1864	336
Nashville, December 15–16, 1864	339
(Nashville) December 15, 1864/December 16, 1864	342
Charleston, February 1865	355
Ft. Fisher, 1865/February 11/Forks Road, February 20	361
Natural Bridge, March 6, 1865	368
Potter's Raid, April, 1865	377
Boykins Mill, April 18, 1865/4:00 P.M.	392
Mobile Campaign, March–April 1865/April 9	400

(Appomattox Campaign: Odyssey of the Confederacy's Only Black
    Military Unit)   412
Richmond, April 3, 1865   417
Roads to Appomattox/April 2/April 9   429
Palmito Ranch, May 11–12, 1865   441
Palmito Ranch, May 13, 1865   448
Policing the Peace, May 1865   457
Texas Campaign, 1865–1867   459

Picture List

(Between pages 232 and 233)

——◦——

1st Regiment South Carolina Infantry (A.D.)
The Attack on Fort (Battery) Wagner
Battery Wagner, the Morning after the Assault
Wild's North Carolina Raid
Jacksonville Road near Olustee
The Fort Pillow Massacre
Major Booth's Redoubt at Fort Pillow
Company E, 4th USCT
Private William H. Johnson, 23rd USCT, Executed at Petersburg
The Crater
Officers and Men of the 1st USCT
The Dutch Gap Canal
Boyd's Landing, on the Broad River, in South Carolina
Grahamville Road near Honey Hill
A Detail from the 107th USCT
55th Regiment Massachusetts Infantry (Colored) Enters Charleston
Looking toward the Confederate Position at Boykins Mill
Monument at Boykins Mill
Black Troops Mustering Out in Little Rock in 1865
A Portion of the 5th USCT

Preface

———◇———

IT is curious how time and distance provide clarity about some things. I had written about the Overland Campaign of 1864 (*Bloody Roads South,* 1989) because the subject fascinated me; I had undertaken to tell the story of the struggle for Petersburg, Virginia (*The Last Citadel,* 1991), because it was something that deserved the attention. Only after the latter did I realize that I had been writing a trilogy all along, and that the subject of my next book project (*Out of the Storm,* 1994) was as obvious as it was inevitable. In much the same way, I had been touching upon the topic of black soldiers from the very beginning. Rarely center stage, they were nevertheless a steady presence in those three books. Now I recognize that the seed had been growing there all along.

When I first began to consider the prospect of writing a single-volume history of Civil War black troops in combat, I had to determine whether it was a story that *could* be told. The accounts I was familiar with regarding their actions were, in nearly every case, penned by white officers who served in black regiments. Most often missing from the equation was any testimony from the rank and file. Since my approach to writing campaign or battle narratives draws heavily upon firsthand accounts, this posed a seemingly insurmountable problem. The turning point came when I encountered a collection of letters written by black Civil War soldiers, edited by Edwin S. Redkey. This book, *Grand Army of Black Men,* was a revelation in every sense of the word. Suddenly, voices I had feared could not be found were speaking to me of their hopes, aspirations, problems, and combat experiences. Redkey's principal sources were two Civil War–era black newspapers, New York's *Anglo-African* and Philadelphia's *Christian Recorder.* A tip from Donald Yacovone at the Massachusetts Historical Society led me to Harvard's Houghton Library, where I procured a microfilm containing a complete run of the *Anglo-African* from 1861 through 1865. In that way, some 125 letters from black soldiers came into my possession. Around that same time I was able to contact Redkey himself, who generously turned over to me typescripts of letters he had prepared but not used in his book, gleaned from the *Christian Recorder, The Liberator,* and other newspaper sources. Now it was not only possible to write a combat history of black troops in the Civil War, but, I realized, very necessary.

There had already been a number of fine works written about black troops in the Civil War, most notably Dudley Taylor Cornish's *The Sable Arm* (1956) and Joseph T. Glatthaar's *Forged in Battle* (1990). The former explored the social/political background of the decision to raise black regiments and provided a lively overview of their service. The latter investigated the command relationship between the white officers and their African American soldiers. Each briefly treated some of the military actions involving these units, but they were not the primary focus. I hope that this volume will complement the excellent coverage provided by those two, and that through the combination there may emerge a more complete picture of the black military experience in the Civil War.

Attractive and important though the black soldier letters that I obtained from the newspapers of the era were, there was, it is clear, a high degree of self-selection involved in their publication. Most of the 180,000 African Americans who wore Union blue were ex-slaves, and precious few of them entered the service knowing how to read or write. To add some of those other voices to the mix, I relied heavily on service and pension records on file at the National Archives in Washington. Searching these records was not unlike panning for gold: I had to examine a good many to extract the few nuggets I have used in my text. Nonetheless, I believe that the effort was worth it. While the accounts contained in these files are almost always transcripts of interviews made by white pension agents, the words and images that emerge have a powerful authenticity. Add to this the bits and pieces gathered from manuscript archives, a handful of published primary materials, and numerous official documents (most not published), and you have the building blocks upon which this work rests.

Deciding what actions to write about was both easy and difficult. African American troops took part in some 449 separate engagements; only an enclyclopedia could have covered all of them. The relatively few major engagements (including Port Hudson, Olustee, Petersburg, and Fort Blakely) were obvious selections, but the fact remains that the overwhelming majority of combats involving black troops were much smaller affairs, often no more than a slight skirmish or minor outpost scrap. My selection was thus a balancing act of sorts, between those actions for which minimal primary black accounts were available and those that provided some broad geographic representation.

I should mention here that the words used to describe each of those combats are not fanciful inventions. Several key sources often used by writers on the Civil War (e.g., the *Official Records,* Dyer's *Compendium,* and Fox's *Regimental Losses in the Civil War*) apply certain measurement standards to the naming of combats, which I have also used. The criteria include the number of troops engaged, the size of the action in space and time, and casualties. According to this information, a combat is classified as an "action," "skirmish," "engagement," "battle," "affair," and so on. While it may be politic for a local history to refer to a particular combat as a "battle," a more balanced evaluation might well settle for the term "skirmish."

In every case, I have tried to let the evidence speak for itself. I did not feel that I could fully trust either white Northern accounts or white Southern ones. Each had a distinct agenda: Union officers were often anxious to build up the performance of the black soldiers, while Confederates were equally determined to tear it down. Whenever possible, I sought black soldier accounts as the benchmark against which to measure the other material. Where no such accounts were available, I assembled as much hard data as I could (especially casualty lists) in order to gauge the intensity of a struggle. In approaching the subject in this way, I discovered that some famous reports of black soldier actions are unsupported by the facts. Accounts of vicious hand-to-hand combat at Port Hudson on May 27, for instance, repeatedly quoted in postwar histories, must be dismissed as almost total fiction for lack of any primary materials or supporting data.

The actions of black troops in the Civil War require no validation from me, nor are they well served by broadly generalized statements based on biased material. It is my hope that by providing an honest and carefully researched account of their combat experiences, I may in some way help these soldiers tell their own story.

Author's Note

————◁○▷————

ANY study of black troops in the Civil War must grapple with the confusing evolution of the naming conventions used to designate their units. At first, the cognomen followed the pattern applied to white regiments, with one significant addition. As each regiment was organized, it joined the service with a state name and number. Yet from the very beginning, African American units were seen as "different," so nearly every one entering the rolls bore an additional qualifier, either "A.D." (African Descent) or "Colored." Starting late in 1863, the U.S. War Department changed all this, redesignating most of the black units already in service as "United States Colored Troops," or USCT. In this way, for instance, the 1st North Carolina Colored, which fought under that name at Olustee in 1863, also participated in the Honey Hill campaign in 1864 as the 35th USCT. To further complicate matters, there was an interim phase during which some outfits acquired a second or even a third redesignation before the final USCT number was applied. For clarity's sake, rather than utilize a unit's ultimate designation throughout my text, I have decided to use the name it had *at the time it fought in the action described.* Thus, in the chapter regarding Olustee, you will read about the 1st North Carolina Colored, while in that about Honey Hill, the 35th USCT is cited; again, both names refer to the same body of men.

While I realize that this approach may cause some confusion, my wish to preserve and honor the self-identity of these units compelled me to adopt this system.

With the addition of that caveat, readers already used to my way of referencing units will find the same set of rules applied here as in my previous books. My preference is to refer to units above the regimental level (i.e., corps, divisions, brigades) by the names of their commanders (e.g., Dwight's division), though in many instances I have also followed the Union habit of simply numbering these units (e.g., Twenty-fifth Corps, Ninth Corps, Fourth Division). References to white regiments are always made by number and state—for example, 24th Massachusetts, or 4th Mississippi.

One purpose of my previous books was to provide a comprehensive accounting of the combat experiences of both sides involved in the engagements covered. This time, however, my focus is on one side alone, so I have drawn upon Confederate and other Union accounts only when needed to support the narrative. While I have relied on these other sources to make certain that my exposition of a particular action is as "correct" as possible in regard to the facts, the point of view presented is almost always that of the black soldiers engaged.

The essential battle tactic of this era was to maneuver the long, usually four-abreast marching columns into two (or often three, with the third serving as a reserve) lines of battle, with as many rifles as possible facing the enemy. Regimental and national flags were generally placed in the center of a regimental front, with either end of this extended line's being the flank. Geographic descriptions are always given from the point of view of the side under discussion, unless otherwise noted.

I have again used my variable rule on spelling in order to eliminate the qualifier *sic* from the text. Where a particular spelling seems to me to convey a vivid sense of character, I have preserved the original; otherwise, I have exercised some judicious editorial cleaning-up of manuscript passages. Where a place-name exists in several variants, I have explained my choice in a footnote at the first occurrence of the name.

Finally, in this book I have for the first time used footnotes to identify quotation sources. Uncovering many of these sources was a journey of joyous discovery for me; by readily identifying them, I hope to encourage others to explore some of the same paths.

Part One

1861–1862

Chapter One

"A Liberating Army"

———◇———

Skirmish at Island Mound, Missouri, October 29, 1862

FROM a distance, the marching column seemed insignificant amid the empty, rolling countryside of western Missouri. The military force, perhaps 250 men altogether, moved rapidly but cautiously, the soldiers knowing they were in enemy territory. The month was October, the year 1862.

Already the simmering tensions of decades had propelled the nation into large-scale combat at Bull Run, Wilson's Creek, Pea Ridge, Fort Donelson, Shiloh, the Virginia Peninsula, and Antietam. The scope may have been smaller along the Kansas-Missouri border, but even there, men were killing each other over the same principles and passions that drew many thousands into death grapples in places that later generations would deem hallowed ground.

This particular column, marching under the United States flag, had left Fort Lincoln, in eastern Kansas, on Sunday, October 26. It comprised detachments from five companies of a singular regiment, with one section under Captain Richard G. Ward and the other led by Captain Henry C. Seaman, who was also in overall command. They were to break up a party of Rebel guerrillas reportedly operating along the Osage River, in Bates County, Missouri.

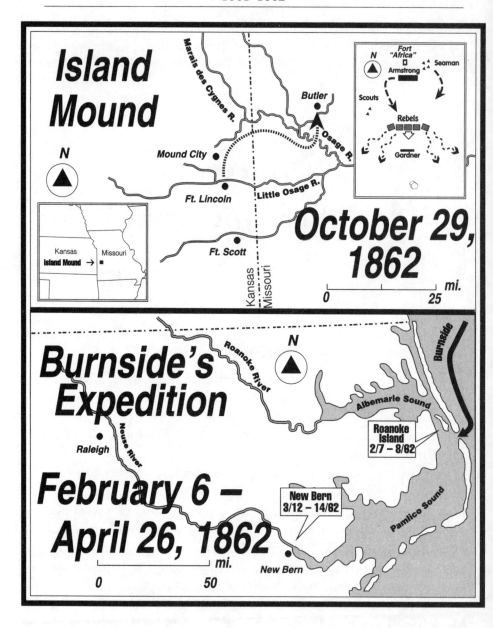

The enlisted men in this force were black soldiers belonging to the 1st Kansas (Colored) Volunteer Infantry, a state regiment not yet under Federal control. The presence of armed black men was not unusual—African Americans had been fighting along this portion of the frontier from the very beginnings of the conflict—but such men had yet to see action as a unit. All that was about to change, however.

The column covered some twenty miles on its first day out of Fort Lincoln, reaching Dickey's Crossing (or Dickies Ford) on the Osage at two o'clock in the afternoon of October 27. "Shortly after crossing the stream," Captain Ward reported, "we were made aware of the presence of the enemy in force by their scouts and by information from citizens." Pushing ahead another three miles toward the home of a local resident named Toothman, said to be a "notorious rebel," the black men entered a region dotted with large earthen mounds, the vestiges of an ancient Indian civilization. Once at Toothman's, the expedition erected slight barricades and camped for the night. (Perhaps to acknowledge the large black presence in this operation, some of the men began to refer to their encampment as "Fort Africa.")[1]

The officers pondered their situation. From the intelligence gathered, they reckoned that the enemy's strength was greater than anticipated, so two couriers were sent off to bring back reinforcements from Forts Lincoln and Scott, while a third headed for the friendly settlement of Paoli.

Tuesday, October 28, passed with both sides' observing each other at long range and engaging in what Captain Ward termed "desultory skirmishes." The next day, despite a strong suspicion that the enemy had been reinforced, it was decided to risk a party of fifty men to forage for salt and cornmeal. To provide a diversion, a second force of sixty men under Captains Andrew J. Armstrong and Andrew I. Crew moved toward the enemy's camp on Osage Island. Two miles from Fort Africa, Armstrong's group ran into mounted Rebels, who taunted the black men as they deployed into a skirmish line with cries of "Come on you d----d niggers." Musketry crackled across the prairie; men fell as sharpshooters found their mark. The diversionary force returned to Fort Africa, where Armstrong claimed to have knocked seven Confederates from their saddles, with no fatalities to his own group.[2]

Some of the enemy now pressed the camp, driving in the pickets. Captain Ward worried that the Rebels were "concentrating troops behind the mound south of us." A small detail under Lieutenant Joseph Gardner, sent out to regain the picket line and gauge the Confederates' strength, chased a few mounted Rebels over the mound.

The firing became very sharp almost immediately after Gardner and his men disappeared from view. A support force of twenty more men hustled out to aid them, followed by Captain Armstrong and his sixty soldiers. Ward soon learned that Gardner and his group were holed up in a house about eight hundred yards south of the mound, to which they were now preparing to return. He ordered Armstrong to cover this movement, but when Gardner's men began their retreat, they were charged by a large number of mounted enemy troops and backed into a small ravine on the north slope of the mound. Here they made a stand. "I have witnessed some hard fights," Captain Ward later recalled, "but I never saw a braver sight than that hand-ful of brave men fighting. . . . Not one surrendered or gave up a weapon."[3]

Armstrong's party now entered the fray, with the captain "yelling to his men to follow him, and cursing them for not going faster." For a few minutes the prairie literally blazed as the Rebels, finding them-selves outflanked by other Federal units coming from Fort Africa, set the grass on fire to cover their withdrawal. At times the combat was hand-to-hand, and savage. A Cherokee black named John Six Killer shot two of the enemy, bayoneted a third, and clubbed down a fourth before being mortally wounded himself. Then the Rebels were gone, and the sounds of battle were reduced to the groans of the wounded and dying. When reinforcements arrived the next day, a pursuit of the enemy was begun, but there was no further contact.

Eight Union men lay dead, and eleven wounded. Corporal Joseph Talbot and Privates Marion Barber, Samuel Davis, Henry Gash, Thomas Lane, Allen Rhodes, and John Six Killer had fallen in this first unit action by black troops. Also dead was one of the white offi-cers, Captain Crew, shot by the Rebels after refusing to surrender. The enemy's losses were later put at some fifteen to fifty killed, with as many wounded. According to one of the Confederate leaders, "The black devils fought like tigers . . . not one would surrender, though they had tried to take a prisoner." This fight, officially deemed merely a "skirmish," was sometimes referred to as "Toothman's Mound" or, more often, "Island Mound." Recognizing the symbolic importance of this engagement, Leavenworth's radical abolitionist newspaper, misleadingly named the *Daily Conservative,* crowed, "It is useless to talk any more of negro courage. The men fight like tigers, each and every one of them, and the main difficulty was to hold them well in hand."[4]

For Frederick Douglass, the bombardment of Fort Sumter launched a campaign of violence aimed squarely at the heart of the slave-owning Confederacy. "The cry now is for war, vigorous war, war to the bitter end," he told readers of the *Douglass Monthly* in May 1861. Douglass, himself an escaped slave, was one of the most prominent and eloquent figures in the U.S. abolitionist movement. "From the first," he would later write in his autobiographical *Life and Times,* "I, for one, saw in this war the end of slavery; and truth requires me to say that my interest in the success of the North was largely due to this belief."[5]

While openly advocating the enlistment of blacks in the military, Douglass also acknowledged that any African Americans in uniform would be assailed on two sides—by the Confederacy and its slave owners before them and by the pervasive racism of the North behind. As U.S. citizens flocked to the colors after Fort Sumter, Douglass proclaimed a key precondition for black participation: "Nothing," he said, "short of an open recognition of the Negro's manhood, his rights as such to have a country equally with others, would induce me to join the army in any capacity."[6]

Douglass's admonitions went unheard, however, amid the pounding drums and blaring trumpets of war. Hundreds of Northern free blacks joined the rush to defend the Union, giving no thought to any possible political agenda. In Boston, a rally at the Twelfth Baptist Church resolved that Massachusetts blacks were "ready to stand by and defend the Government with 'our lives, our fortunes, and our sacred honor.'" Black militia units began forming in Providence, New York, Cincinnati, Philadelphia, and elsewhere. In the nation's capital, a frontier explorer named Jacob Dodson offered the services of "300 reliable colored free citizens" to protect the city.[7]

A sixty-five-year-old black from Pottsville, Pennsylvania, Nicholas Biddle, made himself a member of the local artillery company and joined its march to defend Washington. When a secessionist mob in Baltimore hurled stones at the volunteers, one struck Biddle in the face; though shaken and bloodied by the incident, he remained with the unit, one of the first to answer the call to arms.

Hardly had the initial heady enthusiasm settled down, though, before state and Federal governments proclaimed a war policy that pointedly excluded African Americans. Washington's *National Intelligencer* explained on October 8, 1861, "The existing war has no direct relation to slavery. It is a war for the restoration of the Union under the existing Constitution." Responding to Jacob Dodson's proposal to organize a black unit in Washington, the Secretary of War declared, "I have to say that this Department has no intention to call into the service of the Government any colored soldiers." The various militia groups were ordered to disband, some even threatened with arrest as "disorderly gatherings." "We want you d----d niggers to keep out of this," patriotic blacks were told by the Cincinnati police. "This is a white man's war."[8]

In much the same way as their Northern counterparts, if with a very different allegiance, Southern African Americans also responded to the outside threat against their world. Even before the storm sparked by Fort Sumter, several of Charleston's free blacks informed state officials, "Our attachments are with you, our hopes of safety & protection from you. Our allegiance is to So. Ca. and in her defense, we are willing to offer up our lives, and all that is dear to us." Southern newspapers were soon filling their columns with reports of assistance on the part of free blacks. In Petersburg, Virginia, those who helped build fortifications at Norfolk were presented with a Confederate flag and assured that they would "reap a rich reward of praise, and merit, from a thankful people." On the other side of the Confederacy, at Vicksburg, Mississippi, a black veteran of the War of 1812 promised $500 and contributed a horse to the local cavalry company. Between these two points were many other places where Southern African Americans lent public support to the nascent Confederacy.[9]

What can account for this seeming paradox? Leaving aside the obvious possibility of coercion, it must be noted that because the issue of black equality was not yet incorporated in the North's war goals, many individual African Americans still viewed the conflict in regional terms. In both of America's previous wars, Southern blacks had responded when outside forces threatened their communities, and few in 1861 could have predicted that the fighting would last as long, or spread as widely, as it ultimately did. For a few, too, the onset of war offered financial and social opportunities. Some of those who stepped forward no doubt believed that by doing so they would improve their standing once the brief unpleasantness was over.

Just as in the North, black military units began organizing, in places such as Charleston, Nashville, Memphis, Augusta, and Montgomery, and as far away as Fort Smith, Arkansas. Here, too, white authorities rejected such efforts—perhaps sharing the Northern leaders' desire to keep the slavery issue off the table, but more likely fearing the effect that the presence of any group of armed black men might have on the much larger slave population. Nat Turner's brief but fierce rebellion was only thirty years in the past, and the earlier slave uprisings of Denmark Vesey and Gabriel still retained nearly as strong a grip on the public memory.

Yet the complex pageant of Southern society could take unusual and unexpected turns with the inclusion of Louisiana and New Orleans. This unique region, whose rich culture was infused with influences from France, Spain, and Africa, had fewer taboos against arming blacks than did the rest of the South. When, on May 22, 1861, the all-black Planche Guards unit was organized, it enjoyed both the sanction and the support of the New Orleans city government. By the end of May, a sufficient number of companies had formed that the state governor appointed a colonel and lieutenant colonel to command what was now styled the Regiment of Free Men of Color. Before year's end there would be fourteen companies in all (about 440 men) in what became known as the Native Guards, Louisiana Militia. Also willing to help the state in its crisis were two smaller militia units raised on Isle Brevelle in Natchitoches Parish. In neither case would these militia companies find even lukewarm support from the Confederate government. What arms they had were personal weapons; their uniforms were come by at their own expense; and they were assigned solely to rear-echelon duties. Yet all of these Native Guard companies would still be serving under the Louisiana Confederate flag when the Union invasion fleet appeared off the mouth of the Mississippi in early 1862.

All such voluntary activity, it must be noted, applied only to the 21,667 free blacks of military age (according to the 1860 census) residing in the South. The situation was very different for the 668,956 eligible male slaves, who had no say whatsoever regarding their part in the unfolding events. Most were put to work erecting fortifications around vital manufacturing and population centers, or building defenses at key strategic points. Others marched to war as personal servants of their masters or were pressed into service as cooks, teamsters, hospital attendants, or members of railroad work gangs. Many more were placed on production lines for the Confederate war industry.

This extensive use of forced black labor had the unintended effect of magnifying the slavery issue for Northern policymakers as Federal armies began to confront the problem. The Union enclaves that were soon established along the Atlantic and Gulf coasts posed a direct challenge to the rigid Southern slave-control system. Running away had always been an option for a slave, though the massive net of laws, enforcement, and terror imposed on the black population by white authorities discouraged all but a relative handful from choosing it. And indeed, at first it seemed as if this "war" between North and South would change nothing: slaves had been confirmed in their status as property by the United States Supreme Court, and some Federal officers believed it their duty to enforce all U.S. laws on the books—including those governing fugitive slaves. Yet even as those Union officers were returning runaways to their masters, others were finding creative ways to avoid doing so.

In late May 1861, three escaped slaves showed up at Fortress Monroe, a Union stronghold on the tip of Virginia's Peninsula, claiming they had been forced by their master to dig a Confederate battery position. It happened that the officer commanding this post—indeed, in charge of the entire Department of Virginia—was a Massachusetts lawyer and politician turned general named Benjamin Franklin Butler. Like his colonial namesake, Butler possessed a seemingly limitless stock of shrewd ingenuity.

When a Confederate officer presented himself and demanded that this human property be returned under existing laws, Butler refused. He argued that because in this case the blacks had been employed against the U.S. Government, they had become legitimate contraband of war and thus fair game for confiscation. Butler would later lay claim to being the first to utilize the term "contraband" in this context; in fact, the evidence is a bit murky on that point, though it is certainly true that through his act he established a precedent that other, likeminded Union officers were quick to follow. Suddenly the small Federal enclaves began to attract a growing number of male slaves and their families. Butler's fateful action was further legitimized on August 8, when the U.S. Congress authorized the seizure of all Southern property used "in aid of the rebellion"—a definition that specifically included slaves. From his editorial pulpit, Frederick Douglass issued a strident call to "Let the slaves and free colored people be called into service, and formed into a liberating army."[10]

One of the few blacks—determined individuals all—who had contrived to beat the system by serving in a white unit, George E. Stephens was a Philadelphia cabinetmaker signed on to cook for the colonel of the 26th Pennsylvania. Late in 1861, he watched in horror as a young Maryland slave who had reached the Union encampments near Bladensburg was restored to his owner; the fifteen-year-old was not classified as contraband because he came from a so-called loyal slave state. "We resort to another method now," Stephens informed the readers of New York's black newspaper, the *Anglo-African*. "We hurry the panting fugitive to the Virginia side, and urge him to enter the Federal lines from that direction." Stephens later became a member of the famous 54th Massachusetts and would be commissioned a first lieutenant by war's end.[11]

Another black who crossed the color barrier was William Henry Johnson, who, as a member of the 8th Connecticut, was present at Bull Run. He did not sugar-coat the truth about the conditions faced by the soldiers, telling the readers of Boston's black newspaper *Pine and Palm*, "We were driven like so many sheep into Washington, disgraced and humiliated." Regarding the arming of blacks en masse, Johnson asked and answered the question, "Shall we do it? Not until our rights as men are acknowledged by the government in good faith."[12]

The 8th Connecticut went ashore on Roanoke Island on February 7, 1862, as part of an operation to establish a Federal position in North Carolina as far south as New Bern on the Neuse River. The 8th did not play an active role at first, but Johnson was nonetheless able to inform his readers that Roanoke Island's blacks were "jubilant at the success of the Stars and Stripes."[13]

As crowds of contrabands made their way into this new Union zone, Johnson proclaimed that the "abolition of slavery is rapidly progressing South—it is in the natural course of events, and must be; for wherever the Federal Army goes, the so-called master dies, and the slaves, once chattels, are transformed into men!" On March 14, the 8th Connecticut took part in the assault on New Bern; the regiment's colonel afterward praised his men for their "commendable coolness and bravery." "Many brave souls have been sent to their last account," Johnson scribbled early in the day. At day's end, with the cheers of his victorious comrades still ringing in his ears, he hoped that the Confederates had got the message: "If it does not satisfy them that Uncle Sam is in earnest, and that *Old Abe* does not mean to split them like *rails,* we will give them another turn, and this time near *Richmond.*" Soon after this engagement, Johnson received a medical discharge from the 8th.[14]

Throughout the first year of the war, Abraham Lincoln carefully resisted any official effort to arm blacks. He did, however, acknowledge the validity of the "contraband" policy in instructions sent to Brigadier General Thomas W. Sherman, who, in the process of establishing a Federal perimeter around Port Royal, South Carolina, was taking in large numbers of runaway slaves. Sherman's guidelines read, "You will employ such persons in such services as they may be fitted for—either as ordinary employees, or, if special circumstances seem to require it, in any other capacity, with such organization (in squads, companies, or otherwise) as you may deem most beneficial to the service; this, however, not being a general arming of them for military service."[15]

Had Lincoln in 1861 desired to enlist blacks into the military, he could readily have claimed the authority under a broad interpretation of existing laws. But the need for such radical action was simply not apparent—at least, not yet. The contraband issue remained a small matter; volunteer recruitment was still sufficient, as overall Union casualties remained low and Federal columns had yet to seriously penetrate the Confederacy. All this began to change, though, in 1862. Union successes in the West brought more slave regions under U.S. control, and the awful carnage suffered that year created a ferocious need for more men. Congress responded by passing the Second Confiscation Act and the Militia Act, which broadened the President's powers to use black men in military service. Lincoln still was not ready to move on this issue, but the entire discourse was about to be transformed through the unauthorized actions of two men: General Sherman's successor in South Carolina and a radical senator from Kansas.

There was something grand, terrible, and Old Testament about James H. Lane—at once a social radical, a master political opportunist, a visionary, a demagogue, and an unscrupulous stone-cold killer who more than earned the sobriquet of "Grim Chieftain." In the prewar struggle known as Bloody Kansas, Lane, thanks as much to adroit self-promotion as to actual events, emerged alongside James Montgomery, Charles Jennison, and John Brown as a leading violent abolitionist. Well before national war erupted, mounted raiders from Kansas (commonly known as jayhawkers) destroyed Missouri farms and "liberated" slaves. Most of these ruthless men hardly noticed the difference when their own fight became a backdrop for the larger conflict. By then James H. Lane had been elected to the U.S. Senate.

In winter and summer Lane could be seen garbed in overalls, a calfskin vest, and a heavy bearskin overcoat. Yet when he spoke, in the words of one who heard him, "His extraordinary eloquence thrills like the blast of a trumpet." Recruitment for his armed bands was equal-opportunity and color-blind. In 1861, a reporter describing a unit organized under Lane's authority carefully noted that alongside a "doughty and white cavalier rode an erect, well-armed and very black man: his figure and bearing were such that, without any other distinguishing character, he would still have been a marked man." On October 3, Lane, sent back to Kansas by Lincoln to raise volunteer regiments, declared that "confiscation of slaves and other property which can be made useful to the Army should follow treason as the thunder peal follows the lightning flash."[16]

Thanks to the Second Confiscation Act and the Militia Act, Senator Lane came to Kansas armed with the legal authority—or so he believed—to raise a black regiment. In August he appointed abolitionists James M. Williams and Henry C. Seaman to recruit one. (Lane would later claim to have received verbal permission from Lincoln for his actions.) Utterly unperturbed by stated government policy, Lane wired Washington on August 5, "I am receiving negroes under the late act of Congress. Is there any objection? . . . Soon have an army." Even after Secretary of War Edwin M. Stanton replied that "regiments of persons of African descent can only be raised upon express and special authority of the President, [who] has not given authority to raise such troops in Kansas," Lane blithely continued to recruit blacks.[17]

"Give them a fair chance," he told reluctant whites, "put arms in their hands, and they will do the balance of the fighting in this war." Many "volunteers" were swept into the ranks by jayhawking raids into Missouri, while others were given little choice by the Grim Chieftain, who told them, "We don't want to threaten, but we have been saying that you would fight, and if you don't fight we will make you."[18]

Lane later testified that it took him four months' worth of public relations to sell the idea to the "anti-slavery" people of his state, and that even then the troops had to drill out of sight to avoid a white backlash. Lane was warned by a newspaper writer to keep the black soldiers away from the white ones, because "with one exception, there is not a Kansas regiment from which they would not have as much to fear as from the rebels." Yet he would not be turned from his purpose. Although it would not be formally recognized by the Federal government until January 13, 1863, the 1st Kansas (Colored) Volunteer Infantry was in the field and in action by the fall of 1862.[19]

Lane routinely ignored or ran over anyone who stood in his way. Even before the 1st Kansas (Colored) took shape, one who ran afoul of him was the sixty-year-old commander of the Western Department, Major General David Hunter. Complaining to a fellow department commander in February 1862, Hunter angrily itemized everything that had been authorized and sent to him intended solely for the "forces under General J. H. Lane." Concluded Hunter, "In fact, I may say that, so far as Washington was concerned, the Kansas Senator would seem to have effectively 'jayhawked' out of the minds of the War Department any knowledge or remembrance of the general commanding this department." A month after penning this note, Hunter transferred to the newly designated Department of the South, which embraced the small coastal areas that had been secured to protect Federal blockading fleet anchorages in South Carolina, Georgia, and northeast Florida. Suddenly, and with no forewarning, he began to act just like Jim Lane.[20]

Hunter realized that his eighteen thousand men were necessarily widely dispersed to guard the abandoned Sea Island cotton plantations. He had little prospect of being sent reinforcements, but there was one source of manpower that he *could* tap: escaped slaves. On April 13, 1862, he proclaimed that all "persons of color lately held to involuntary service by enemies of the United States . . . are hereby confiscated and declared free." He took another fateful step less than a month later. "From the beginning," he would later write in his own defense, "I urged upon the government, in the strongest terms, the enlistment of Negro troops, the former slaves of the rebels, not only as adding to the number and efficiency of our own forces, but chiefly on account of its depriving the enemy of just so much labor in their fields, and compelling them to send an equal number of white men to do the necessary cultivation."[21]

Matching actions to words, Hunter in April enlisted the help of a minister named Abram Murchison in organizing what was called the First South Carolina Volunteer Regiment. (This was five months before Jim Lane undertook a similar effort in Kansas.) Determined to succeed, Hunter embarked on a recruitment program that verged on outright impressment. Edward L. Pierce, a Treasury Department official who supervised the government's use of ex-slaves to run abandoned plantations, complained loudly of Hunter's tactics. Black males of military age, Pierce charged, "were taken from the fields without being allowed to go to their houses even to get a jacket." According to a Northern teacher who assisted the former slaves, "None wished to volunteer." Another instructor observed that many blacks actually feared being taken from their plantations, "as they think it is a trap to get able-bodied [men] and send them to Cuba to sell." Said Pierce, "Sometimes whole plantations, learning what was going on, ran off to the woods for refuge."[22]

Black men caught in these sweeps ended up at Hilton Head, where they were given uniforms (dark-blue coats with red pants) and drilled by squads and companies. No arms were supplied, and their "military" duties consisted largely of manual labor for the Quartermaster's Department. Although the Lincoln administration had quickly quashed Hunter's emancipation proclamation, it remained ambivalent about the "First South Carolina." According to Hunter, "I made repeated efforts, in vain, to get this Regiment recognized and paid by the Government. . . . I could get no reply approving or disapproving my conduct in this matter."[23]

In June, an angry Kentucky congressman asked Hunter if it was true that he had raised a regiment of fugitive slaves, and if he had done so with the government's approval. In his written reply, Hunter sarcastically informed the congressman that "no regiment of 'fugitive slaves' has been or is being organized in this department. There is, however, a fine regiment of persons whose late masters are 'fugitive rebels.'" As to the second point, Hunter claimed that War Department guidelines issued to his predecessor provided him with all necessary justification.[24]

Hunter's widely circulated response had the practical effect of placing the question of black combat enlistment squarely in the midst of the national dialogue. Yet even with the passage of the Second Confiscation and Militia acts, which quickly followed Hunter's actions, Lincoln was not ready to commit himself. He would bend the government's policy to allow officers to arm blacks for purposes of self-defense, but he drew the line at making them full-fledged soldiers. Hunter lacked the Grim Chieftain's resolute determination, and his actions in South Carolina were given much wider press coverage than were Lane's in Kansas. Morale in the "First South Carolina" began to deteriorate once it became clear that Hunter could neither pay nor equip the unit. Desertions increased to the point that white guards were stationed around the black camps to prevent more men from leaving. On August 10, 1862, David Hunter informed the War Department that he had disbanded the First South Carolina Volunteer Regiment, though he kept on his best company for guard duty on St. Simon's Island. Hunter took a leave of absence from his department on September 3, the great experiment seemingly at an end.

In 1855, Abraham Lincoln had described to a friend his personal response to slavery, saying, "I confess I hate to see the poor creatures hunted down and caught and carried back to their stripes and unrequited toil; but I bite my lips and keep quiet."[25]

Throughout the whirl of 1861, Lincoln remained steadfastly silent on the issues of freeing the slaves and arming black men. So ominous was his silence that one black leader, the Reverend J. P. Campbell, could assert that the President "has no quarrel whatever with the south, upon the slavery question." Events seemed to support Campbell's observation. When a Union general, the popular John C. Fremont, proclaimed that Missouri's slaves were now free, Lincoln disavowed him. The editor of the *Anglo-African* was quick to condemn Lincoln's repudiation of Fremont, "which hurls back into the hell of slavery the thousands in Missouri rightfully set free by the proclamation of Gen. Fremont." After also suppressing David Hunter's emancipation edict, Lincoln was censured by the editor of a black San Francisco newspaper. Said the *Pacific Appeal,* "We fear the Administration is pursuing a course detrimental to the best interests of the country, and encouraging the Rebels in their efforts to overthrow the Union, and perpetuate slavery."[26]

Early in July 1862, Lincoln began working on a document of some importance that he kept secret even from those closest to him: a presidential declaration emancipating the slaves in Confederate territory. Still hoping to avoid having to take such a drastic step, Lincoln first attempted to resolve the issue through a U.S. Government program calling for compensated, gradual emancipation. A trial program was actually enacted for the District of Columbia under which slave owners were paid a set value for their property, but when Lincoln met with representatives from the still-loyal border states, he found them unwilling to consider such an arrangement. The U.S. senator from Kentucky said, "I regard the whole thing, so far as the slave states are concerned, as full of arsenic, sugar-coated."[27]

Even as Lincoln was struggling to conceive a policy, events elsewhere were pushing the process of change. In South Carolina, the military governor of David Hunter's Department of the South, a well-regarded brigadier general named Rufus Saxton, asked to arm a black security force to protect the various plantations in the Beaufort District. His request was granted. No mention was made of turning the blacks into U.S. soldiers; all that happened was that some five thousand black laborers entered the Quartermaster's service and were provided with the means to defend themselves. Nothing in the orders that Saxton received from the Secretary of War suggested that a line had been crossed, but nevertheless, for the first time, a U.S. military field commander was authorized to arm and equip a unit of black men:

> In view of the small force under your command and the inability of the Government at the present time to increase it, in order to guard the plantations and settlements occupied by the United States from invasion and protect the inhabitants thereof from captivity and murder

by the enemy, you are also authorized to arm, uniform, equip, and receive into the service of the United States such number of volunteers of African descent as you may deem expedient, not exceeding 5,000, and may detail officers to instruct them in military drill, discipline, and duty, and to command them.[28]

Throughout this period, citizens and newspapers around the country debated the issue. "Certainly we hope we may never have to confess to the world that the United States Government has to seek an ally in the negro to regain its authority," worried the *Milwaukee Sentinel*. In Iowa, the *Dubuque Times* ridiculed the prospect of having black men help in a white man's war: "The idea of calling on *him* . . . to fight our battles . . . is not only a confession of our own weakness and cowardice . . . but . . . the last outcropping of a local insanity." Countered an Ohio abolitionist newspaper, "Let us have a new programme, and at the head of it, *colored regiments*." "We don't want to fight side and side with the nigger," wrote a white New York soldier. "We think we are a too superior race for that." Yet another white enlisted man, writing in 1862 from Virginia, observed, "I thought I hated slavery as much as possible before I came here, but here, where I can see some of its workings, I am more than ever convinced of the cruelty and inhumanity of the system." "For my part," declared a U.S. officer in South Carolina, "I make bold to say that I am not so fastidious as to object to a negro being food for powder and I would arm every man of them." Looking back at 1862 from the vantage point of 1863, *Harper's Weekly* concluded, "The bulk of the people of the United States entertained a notion that it was unworthy of a civilized or a Christian nation to use in war soldiers whose skin was not white."[29]

On July 21, 1862, Lincoln shared his emancipation document with his cabinet. He had decided to free the slaves in those states that should remain in rebellion as of January 1, 1863. Missing from this first draft was any mention of arming the freed slaves, but when the Emancipation Proclamation was officially released, that September, it stipulated that they might be "received into the armed services of the United States to garrison forts, positions, stations, and other places and to man vessels of all sorts in said service."[30]

The Emancipation Proclamation removed all practical limitations on the recruitment of African American men into the armed services.

Soon blacks would be entering combat in fully authorized military units, and the consequences of their actions would be profound. Frederick Douglass made the significance of this clear in an address he gave in 1863, soon after several newly raised black regiments had participated in large-scale fighting: "Once let the black man get upon his person the brass letters U.S.; let him get an eagle on his button, and a musket on his shoulder, and bullets in his pocket, and there is no power on earth or under the earth which can deny that he has earned the right of citizenship in the United States."[31]

January 1, 1863, was a "cloudy, but not disagreeable" day at Fort Scott, Kansas, home to the 1st Kansas (Colored) Volunteer Infantry. A little past one in the afternoon, the men marched in a dress parade by companies, stacked arms, and then took their places at tables "which in the form of a parallelogram, were set in front of Headquarters." Everyone sang the "Star-Spangled Banner," and then the speeches began, marking the first official day of the Emancipation Proclamation.

Captain Ethan Earle of Company F led off with some appropriate comments, after which Lieutenant A. T. Sholes gave "three cheers and a tiger" for President Lincoln. Next to speak was the commander of Fort Leavenworth, who predicted that "before many months roll over our heads, the official reports of some of our Generals down South will electrify the land with the details of battle wherein colored men will be mentioned favorably as having fought and bled for their country."

A hymn written for the event was sung, and then Colonel James M. Williams, commanding the 1st Kansas, rose. Speaking with all the flowery effusion expected of serious orators of that day, Williams observed that the efforts of blacks under arms "will be no mere struggle for conquest, but a struggle for their own freedom, a determined and, as I believe, irresistible struggle for the disenthralment of a people who have long suffered oppression and wrong at the hands of our enemies."

Another hymn followed, after which a white Arkansan refugee praised Western soldiers and a second original song was presented. Then the regimental adjutant stepped forward to read aloud the second paragraph of the Emancipation Proclamation:

> That on the first day of January, in the year of our Lord one thousand eight hundred and sixty-three, all persons held as slaves within any

19

State, or any designated part of a State, the people whereof shall be in rebellion against the United States, shall be then and thenceforward, and forever, free; and the Executive government of the United States, including the military and naval authority thereof, will recognize and maintain the freedom of such persons, and will do no act or acts to repress such persons, or any of them, in any efforts they make for their actual freedom.

"Now, boys," said the adjutant, pointing to the Stars and Stripes, "do you understand that? It means that you may 'hunt, shoot, and destroy' every rebel slaveholder in the land, and that flag . . . and all under it shall not hinder but aid you in such righteous retribution." His remarks were met with what was described as "tumultuous cheering."

Speaking next, Captain William D. Mathews, commanding Company D, said, "Today is a day for great rejoicing with us. As a thinking man I never doubted this day would come. . . . Now is our time to strike. Our own exertions and our own muscle must make us men. If we fight we shall be respected. I see that a well-licked man respects the one who thrashes him." (Mathews, a black man from Maryland, would not be confirmed in his rank by the U.S. War Department.) A verse of "Dixie," with appropriately changed lyrics, followed. Then the regiment's surgeon made a few observations, and the adjutant stepped forward to deliver the keynote address, in which he extolled the service of blacks in America's War for Independence and in the War of 1812.

According to a reporter's account of this entire affair, "The John Brown song, with its stirring 'Hallelujah Chorus,' was then sung by the entire regiment with thrilling effect, and the festivities terminated with nine cheers for 'A Free Union and its President Abraham Lincoln,' which were given with a will and vim that made the welkin ring. So celebrated the Freedmen of Missouri—now soldiers of the Union—the never-to-be-forgotten New Year's Day in 1863."[32]

Part Two

1863

Chapter Two

"Will They Fight?"

——◁◇▷——

THE Battle of Baton Rouge had been a near thing for the Union. On August 5, 1862, a Confederate strike force of about twenty-five hundred men, led by Major General John C. Breckinridge, had attacked the town, which was defended by a Federal complement of equal size under Brigadier General Thomas Williams. At day's end the Stars and Stripes still flew, though nearly two hundred lay dead and corrupting. The shock waves from this action reached all the way to New Orleans, where Major General Benjamin F. Butler suddenly became very concerned about his ability to hold the lower Mississippi valley.

There was no middle ground when it came to Benjamin F. Butler. "He is by all odds the most shocking and disreputable looking man I ever clapped my eyes on," declared a young officer in a black regiment who saw Butler in 1864. The chaplain of another black regiment first encountered Butler as he roundly cursed his mired horse. "The General looks just like his picture," wrote the cleric. "A great big swearing-domineering man." Butler's war service had been varied, to say the least: after suppressing the efforts of secessionist Marylanders to gain control of their state, and then stumbling into one of the earliest Union battlefield defeats at Big Bethel, the seemingly indefatigable officer had wangled his way into commanding the Union army that occupied New Orleans on April 26. Taking the Crescent City proved easier than keeping it, however, and Butler's rule of the region had been controversial. Among the worst of his problems was the small size of the force (about eighteen thousand men) with which he was to control the parishes around New Orleans and, at the same time, generate some offensive activity.[1]

Two months before the fight at Baton Rouge, Butler had been visited by the black officers of the now-disbanded Native Guards, Louisiana Militia. They and their men had refused to evacuate the city when the Union troops arrived, most instead choosing to return to their homes to see what the Federal occupation would bring. "The officers of that company," Butler later related to the Secretary of War, "called upon . . . the question of the continuance of their organization and to learn what disposition they would be required to make of their arms; and in color, nay, also in conduct, they had more the appearance of white gentlemen than some of those who have favored me with their presence claiming to be the 'chivalry of the South.'"[2]

To Butler they explained that most had joined the militia unit in fear of retaliation if they failed to do so. When they had said their piece, he sent them home without committing himself to their cause. The issue of what to do with these blacks and others who were flocking to his outposts was a vexing one for the man who, in 1859, had exclaimed to Bay State voters, "What nonsense to talk of enlisting Negroes in the militia! Would they chalk the black soldiers or blacken the white recruits?" Butler also believed that blacks were inherently "horrified of firearms." But soon after arriving in the Crescent City, he wrote that the "question now pressing me is the state of negro property here and the condition of the negroes as men."[3]

Butler's attitude toward blacks was changing, always guided by his canny reading of political currents and tempered by a narrowly legalistic interpretation of the issues. His decision regarding contrabands was not the act of an abolitionist; he had simply found a course of action that made it possible for him to confiscate the property of owners who were in rebellion. It followed from that same line of reasoning that if the slave owners took the oath of allegiance, he would return their human property without hesitation. How far Butler was from any pure abolitionist principles is evidenced by his dealings with one of his activist subordinates, Brigadier General John W. Phelps.

The English correspondent William Howard Russell remembered Phelps as a "tall, saturnine, gloomy, angry-eyed sallow man, soldier-like, too, and one who places John Brown on a level with the great martyrs of the Christian world." Butler put Phelps in charge of Camp Parapet, one of the key defensive stations outside New Orleans, specifying in his instructions, "You will cause all unemployed persons, black and white, to be excluded from your lines." This order was incomprehensible to Phelps, who could not partake in the inhumanity of turning away fugitive slaves. Butler soon learned that not only was Phelps welcoming runaways into his lines, he was also sending out squads to urge nearby slaves to escape. On July 30, 1862, Phelps sent Butler a request for "arms, accouterments, clothing, camp and garrison equipage, etc., for three Regiments of Africans which I propose to raise for the defense of this point."[4]

Phelps's message crossed in transit one from Butler ordering him to employ contraband labor to clear fields of fire and erect entanglements around Camp Parapet. Phelps penned a reply that same day in which he icily refused "to become the mere slave driver which you propose."[5]

Writing to his wife on August 2, Butler summed up the situation: "Phelps has gone crazy. He is organizing the negroes into regiments and wants me to arm them. . . . I told him he must set the negroes to work and not drill them, and he thereupon has resigned. I have sent the whole matter to the President." Three days later, Confederate General Breckinridge's men came screaming out of the morning mists outside Baton Rouge, and this palpably real threat to his military department set the wheels turning in Butler's always motile mind. "I had written to Washington for reinforcements," he later testified to Congress, "but they replied that they could not give me any, though they wrote that I must hold New Orleans at all hazards." Butler pondered the problem and came up with a solution that, like his earlier "contraband" policy, would have great repercussions for black Americans. Since the Federal government could not supply him with the white troops he needed, declared Butler, "I would enlist all the colored troops I could from the free negroes." On August 14, he wrote to the Secretary of War, "I am going to use the men of the free colored

ـrigade of whom you have heard; they have been used by our enemies whose mouths are shut and they will be loyal."[6]*

Butler believed that his action was entirely different from what Phelps had been attempting. Whereas Phelps wanted to arm slaves, Butler was merely reactivating a state militia unit manned by loyal New Orleans citizens who happened to be *gens de couleur libre*. He had already recruited one white regiment from disaffected Louisiana militiamen, and to reach out to this new group was only to extend an existing policy. The resignation of the troublesome General Phelps was accepted on August 21.

Like most whites of his day, Butler had a limited appreciation of the capabilities of black soldiers. That October, he actively dissuaded a Connecticut officer from seeking command of a black regiment. Recounting his conversation with Butler, the officer wrote his parents that the "colored troops will probably be kept near [New Orleans] and used to garrison unhealthy positions; they will be called on for fatigue duty, such as making roads, building bridges and draining marshes; they will be seldom put into battle, and will afford small chance of distinction."[7]

Even as these events were taking place, other actions were also occurring in Louisiana that were to play a significant role in the combat history of black units. On August 15, an advance party from Breckinridge's force entered Port Hudson, a small town some twenty-five miles above the capital. Located on a steep bluff at a point where the Mississippi River veers nearly 90 degrees, Port Hudson was the perfect location at which to block further Union river movement from New Orleans. It provided a southern anchor for a critical 110-mile span of the river crowned on its northern end by the citadel city of Vicksburg. By controlling this stretch, the Rebels could keep open a vital supply line to the western Confederacy via the Red River, which entered the Mississippi forty miles above Port Hudson.

Making ample use of slave labor, the Confederates began to erect a series of river batteries and protecting earthworks that the undermanned Butler could do nothing to prevent. On August 21, to the accompaniment of widespread looting and property destruction, he even pulled his troops out of Baton Rouge in order to tighten up the defen-

---

*Butler's "shut-mouthed" enemies were the Louisiana Confederate officials who had allowed the Native Guards to muster in the first place. Butler was confident that having permitted this to happen, they would not be able to object to his doing the same thing.

sive perimeter around the Crescent City. As a part of this beefing-up of the New Orleans defenses, Butler called out the Native Guards.

On September 27, 1862, the 1st Regiment Louisiana Native Guards was formally mustered into the United States Army—the first all-black regiment to enter U.S. service during the Civil War. Although Butler had taken pains in all his communications with Washington to emphasize that its rank and file were all free men, he had been careful to leave open substantial loopholes in his definition of the term. In a September 24 letter to Treasury Secretary Salmon P. Chase, Agent G. S. Denison observed that Butler's representatives were recruiting three classes of free men: "[1st.] Those who have received freedom from their owners. 2nd. Those who are made free by the present military courts. 3rd. All who come in from the enemy's lines." Added Denison wryly, "You see this includes almost all colored people."[8]

According to Joseph T. Wilson, who joined the 2nd Regiment Louisiana Native Guards soon after the 1st had been mustered, "The first regiment's line officers were colored, and the field officers were white." Captain Spencer H. Stafford became the colonel of the 1st. His black officers were Captains Andre Cailloux, Edward Carter, George R. Case, Edgard Davis, John Depass, Joseph Follin, James H. Ingraham, Alcide Lewis, James Lewis, Henry L. Rey, Charles Sentmanat, and Louis A. Snaer, and Lieutenants Alfred Bourgeau, Charles Butler, John Crowder, Emile Detiege, Octave Fog, Louis D. Lanien, Victor Lavigne, Jules Mallet, Joseph L. Montieu, Morris W. Morris, Ehurd Moss, Oscar Orillion, Paul Paree, Eugene Rapp, Hyppolite St. Louis, Louis A. Thibaut, and Charles Warfield. Noted Treasury Agent Denison, "The company officers of this first Reg't are educated men, and each speaks at least two languages." Added a newspaper correspondent, "I found . . . that I was conversing with men of no ordinary knowledge and mental capacity."[9]

The 2nd Regiment Louisiana Native Guards mustered into Federal service on October 12, followed on November 24 by the 3rd, marking these the second and third black military units to enter the U.S. Army. Nathan W. Daniels was assigned to command the 2nd, and John A. Nelson the 3rd. Recalled Joseph T. Wilson, "The second, like the first, had all colored line officers; the third was officered regardless of color." All three were based at Camp Strong Station, about four miles north of New Orleans, where they were armed and given basic training. Here Colonel Stafford took overall charge of the three regiments, while Major Chauncey Bassett assumed command of the 1st. According to an observer close to Butler, "Better soldiers never shouldered arms. They were zealous, obedient and intelligent. No men in the Union army had such a stake in the contest as they. Few understood it as well as they."[10]

The median age in these regiments was twenty-eight, and the average height five-foot-six. Most of those in the 1st Regiment practiced skilled trades—they were bricklayers, carpenters, plasterers, shoe-makers, and cigar-makers—while many in the 3rd were farmers or field hands who hailed from the state's Teche District. It was a highly motivated group: the three regiments combined lost only fifty-one men to desertion in the first three months of service, despite the fact that the units were stationed close to home and subject to a steady stream of racial harassment. Francis E. Dumas, a major in the 2nd Regiment, explained his enlistment by saying, "I only wish . . . my boy may stand in the street equal to a white boy when the war is over."[11]

Even within the laissez-faire culture of New Orleans, racism was ever present. Writing to the newspaper *L'Union* on October 16, Captain Henry L. Rey of the 1st Regiment reported, "When our soldiers visit the city, the insolent regards of the rebels are fixed upon them; they put on a sneering air; and sometimes have the impudence to cut jokes about them, the villains! . . . They say that our regiment will not fight. . . . Mr. Editor, come and visit our camp. . . . You can . . . see the enthusiasm of the negro soldiers, and at the parade you can see, crossed in the glittering sun, a thousand white bayonets, held by black, yellow or white hands." Eight days after Captain Rey penned his letter, a reporter for the *New York Tribune* watched as the 1st Regiment passed through New Orleans. "They both marched and looked well," he wrote. "They were dispatched to the Algiers side of the river, for some duty, I presume," he added.[12]

This "duty" involved participation in a large-scale offensive operation organized by Butler to drive Confederate forces away from the Bayou Lafourche region immediately west of the city. Two strong columns were to descend upon the district from the north (via Donaldsonville) and west (using the Atchafalaya River), while a third, moving out from Algiers, was to follow the line of the Opelousas and Great Western Railroad toward Brashear City, repairing the route as it went. It was to this third group that the 1st Regiment Louisiana Native Guards was assigned; it soon had the 2nd to support it.

Although the regiment was entering a combat zone, the duties it undertook consisted solely of railroad repair work. The men were nevertheless kept under close scrutiny, for no one was sure how these raw black troops would perform. There was noticeable relief in Treasury Agent Denison's tone when he reported at the close of the campaign that the "two colored regiments . . . have done well, and accomplished all that has been given them to do." The absence of any fighting meant that the black units had yet to face the real test, however. In a November letter to the *New Orleans Daily Delta,* Captain James H. Ingraham of the 1st Regiment endeavored to assure the paper's readers that the men were "still anxious . . . to show the world that the latent courage of the African is aroused." While the 1st Regiment spent the remainder of the year on outpost duty in the Lafourche area, the 3rd was employed in the district to harvest the sugar crop, as the 2nd protected the railroad closer to New Orleans.[13]

The next event of significance for these pioneer black units came on December 14, when Butler was abruptly relieved of his command by Lincoln and replaced by Major General Nathaniel P. Banks. Like Butler, Banks was a politician-turned-general whose base of operations was Massachusetts. As Speaker of the U.S. House, he had injected moderation and fairness into the bitter debates on slavery that had shook Congress before the war. Also like Butler, Banks had been quickly promoted by President Lincoln to a high military rank for reasons that had more to do with his political clout and potential influence on recruitment than on his military ability. Just how unskilled Banks was in the arts of the soldier was demonstrated in 1862 when he opposed "Stonewall" Jackson in the Shenandoah Valley and performed poorly. Why Lincoln chose Banks to replace Butler has been a matter of endless speculation, but it is certainly true that by the end of 1862, Butler had become a political liability in a state that Lincoln hoped might be cajoled into rejoining the Union, while Banks was much less abrasive. Tragically for the Native Guards, however, Banks was profoundly skeptical of their military value.

Both Butler and Banks faced local authorities worried that the presence of black troops would be disruptive to the general African American population. Toward the end of the Lafourche operation,

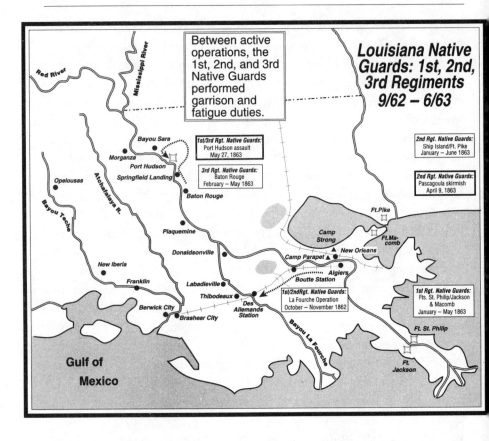

Between active operations, the 1st, 2nd, and 3rd Native Guards performed garrison and fatigue duties.

Louisiana Native Guards: 1st, 2nd, 3rd Regiments 9/62 – 6/63

1st/3rd Rgt. Native Guards: Port Hudson assault May 27, 1863

3rd Rgt. Native Guards: Baton Rouge February – May 1863

2nd Rgt. Native Guards: Ship Island/Ft. Pike January – June 1863

2nd Rgt. Native Guards: Pascagoula skirmish April 9, 1863

1st/2ndRgt. Native Guards: La Fourche Operation October – November 1862

1st Rgt. Native Guards: Fts. St. Philip/Jackson & Macomb January – May 1863

Red River

Mississippi River

Bayou Sara
Morganza
Port Hudson
Springfield Landing
Opelousas
Atchafalaya R.
Baton Rouge
Bayou Teche
New Iberia
Franklin
Berwick City
Brashear City
Plaquemine
Donaldsonville
Labadieville
Thibodeaux
Des Allemands Station
Camp Strong
Camp Parapet
New Orleans
Algiers
Boutte Station
Ft. Pike
Ft. Macomb
Ft. St. Philip
Ft. Jackson
Bayou La Fourche

Gulf of Mexico

the field commander, Bridgadier General Godfrey Weitzel, reported to Butler that thanks to the presence of the 1st and 2nd Louisiana Native Guards in that region, "symptoms of servile insurrection are becoming apparent." Butler's response was to chide his commander for overreacting. Whatever unrest was occurring, Butler reasoned, was due not to the presence of the two Native Guards regiments, but rather to the general "arrival of United States troops, carrying, by the act of Congress, freedom to this servile race." The following December, when white planters told General Banks that having black troops in their area would only exacerbate tensions after the Emancipation Proclamation went into effect, the Union officer promptly scattered the three regiments throughout his department. On Christmas Eve, seven companies of the 2nd Regiment boarded transports that would ferry them to Ship Island, off the Mississippi state coast, where they would guard military convicts and POWs, while the remaining three companies were posted to Fort Pike. A few weeks later, the 1st Regiment was split into detachments assigned to Fort Jackson (four companies), Fort St. Philip (four companies), and Fort Macomb (two companies). The 3rd Regiment was meanwhile spread out to protect the sugar plantations.[14]

The stresses on the men themselves were especially strong at this time. As Colonel Stafford complained in late February, "The protection promised to families is not given; wives and mothers of the soldiers are locked up in the Police Jail and Parish Prison for 'safe keeping,' because they do not happen to have 'free papers' or a 'protection' or a 'pass' signed by some white man." According to the record of the 1st Regiment Louisiana Native Guards for January 1863, "The conduct of the men at Forts St. Philip and Jackson, while enduring insults and discomforts, is evidence of their discipline and devotion to the cause in which they are engaged." Colonel Stafford petitioned General Banks on January 3, asking that the dispersed regiments be brigaded together and sent into action. He was certain, he said, that "when tried, they will not be found wanting."[15]

This sentiment was echoed by Lieutenant George R. Case of the 1st Regiment, who avowed that a native black Louisiana unit would fight better than a white one from the East because "a regiment composed of men with their heads turned toward home cannot fight as well as those who take up arms for freedom, and who have nothing else to fight for."[16]

Skirmish at Pascagoula, Mississippi, April 9, 1863

Banks's banishment of the 2nd Regiment to Ship Island did not prevent it from entering combat. While the unit was stationed there, its commander, Colonel Nathan W. Daniels, received orders to raid the Mississippi town of Pascagoula, and, in Daniels's words, to "capture Confederate troops said to be in possession of the place in small force." On April 6, 1863, he took two companies of the 2nd—about 180 men in all—aboard the steam transport *General Banks,* and the following morning steamed to a rendezvous with the U.S. gunboat *John P. Jackson,* which was to provide fire support for the landing. It was an unfortunate set of circumstances for Daniels, whose men had tangled with sailors from the latter vessel while at Ship Island.[17]

At 9:00 A.M. on April 9, Daniels landed his party on the East Pascagoula wharf and, as he noted in his diary, "took possession of the hotel, hoisted the American colors upon the cupola and threw out pickets." The enemy reaction was swift. "I myself saw them from the cupola of the hotel," said Daniels, "coming down the Mobile road in heavy force with banners waving, cutlasses flailing, evidently intending to make an immediate attack." The Rebel squadrons were soon pressing hard, cutting off some of the outposts, who nonetheless wrote Daniels, "fought on bravely and succeeded after long fighting in getting to their companies." Daniels put the enemy's number at at least three hundred cavalry and infantry, assisted by some local citizens. As the fighting spread into the early afternoon, he determined that more Confederates were on their way.[18]

One section of Daniels's command fell back to the wharf and was ferried aboard the *General Banks,* only to be quickly ordered back ashore to cover a general withdrawal and to clean out a nest of Rebel sharpshooters inside the Federal perimeter. No sooner had this detachment clambered onto the wharf than the *Jackson,* which had contributed little to the defense up to this point, "unfortunately and perhaps designedly" (in Daniels's words) threw a shell that landed among the black soldiers. In his after-action report, Daniels noted that this friendly fire had killed four of his men and seriously wounded five more. Up to this time, several hours of skirmishing with the Confederates had cost him only two killed and five slightly wounded.[19]

Finally, at around two in the afternoon, Daniels withdrew. He had angry words with the officer commanding the *Jackson,* but that was as far as the matter went. In a more detailed accounting, completed on April 11 but not included in the *Official Records,* Daniels concluded:

> Great credit is due to the troops engaged, for their unflinching bravery and steadiness under this their first fire, exchanging volley after volley with the coolness of veterans; and for their determined tenacity in maintaining their position, and taking advantage of every success that their courage and valor gave them; and also to their officers, who were cool and determined throughout the action, fighting their commands against five times their numbers, and confident throughout of success,—all demonstrating to its fullest extent that the oppression which they have heretofore undergone from the hands of

their foes, and the obloquy that had been showered upon them by those who should have been friends, had not extinguished their manhood, or suppressed their bravery, and that they had still a hand to wield the sword, and a heart to vitalize its blow.[20]

Among those singled out for praise was Major Francis E. Dumas, who served in order to make it possible for his child to stand equal to a white after the war.

Even before this action involving the 2nd Regiment, General Banks was moving to purge the 3rd of its black officers. The incident that sparked this action had taken place at Baton Rouge, which Federal forces had reoccupied against meager opposition on December 17. A black assigned to be officer of the day, in attempting to give orders to the white guard unit, had been met with a flat refusal of the men to, in the words of a newspaper reporter, "acknowledge a negro their superior." Banks summoned all the black officers of the 3rd to report to him in New Orleans, where he heard their grievances. When the officers returned the next day for his decision, he told them they had best resign because the Federal government would not recognize their rank. Faced with the alternative of a humiliating dismissal, all sixteen signed a letter of resignation and returned to Baton Rouge to find that their replacements had already been appointed. Their resignations were never made public. As these officers protested in a vain appeal filed with the War Department in May, "So secretly was [the matter] conducted that officers of other Colored Regiments are not aware that we have resigned." They realized that Banks had tricked them.[21]

About a month after Banks engineered this officer purge of the 3rd Regiment, Robert H. Isabelle, a 2nd Lieutenant in the 2nd Regiment, also resigned, saying: "When I joined the United States army I did so with the sole object of laboring for the good of the Union, supposing that all past prejudice would be suspended for the good of our country . . . but after five or six months' experience I am convinced that the same prejudice still exist[s]."[22]

Whatever his personal feelings, Nathaniel P. Banks was an astute political survivor who could recognize when the wind had changed. After the Emancipation Proclamation was issued, he began to view black soldiers in a remarkably different light, on March 20 going so far as to organize a black regiment of engineers who would be assigned to dig trenches, erect fortifications, and perform general manual labor. Once it became inevitable that the government would enlist more blacks into the service, Banks swallowed enough of his prejudice to issue an order, on May 1, authorizing the "organization of a corps d'armee of colored troops, to be designated as the 'Corps d'Afrique.'" He limited the size of each full black regiment to five hundred men (half as many as in a white regiment) and announced that these units would be commanded by the "best officers" of his army. Banks kept the size of the regiments small because he believed that African Americans were "a race unaccustomed to military service"; and since he was pressing all the black officers to resign, those who remained to command these new regiments would be white.[23]

In mid-April there arrived in New Orleans one Brigadier General Daniel Ullmann, a New York politician and veteran of service during the Peninsula Campaign in Virginia, who carried a brief directly from Lincoln to raise a brigade of four regiments of black "Louisiana volunteer infantry." Ullmann soon found his efforts sabotaged by Banks's people. One of his representatives was prevented from recruiting by the Provost Marshal of St. Bernard Parish, who told him that "God had made the black to work on sugar and cotton, and not to be soldiers." "My officers were met with difficulties at every step," Ullmann wrote, still angry twenty years after the war. "With a few very honorable exceptions, the whole mass of the officers, not only of the regular army, but where we did not expect it, of the volunteers, had an implacable prejudice which led them to say and do many foolish things." (Writing to his wife after learning of Ullmann's appointment, Banks said, "The government has sent out a poor man who will make us all the trouble he can.") Ullmann's recruitment and training had not yet produced any results by the time the 1st and 3rd Louisiana Native Guards entered combat.[24]

Assault on Port Hudson, Louisiana, May 27, 1863

Throughout his tenure as commander of the Department of the Gulf, General Banks had been bedeviled by the problem of Port Hudson. The Confederates had steadily improved their position there, so that it now represented a major obstacle to Union advances either by water or by land. On the evening of March 14, 1863, Rear Admiral David Farragut led a procession of seven ships (six of them lashed together in pairs) in a maximum effort to run the gauntlet of Port Hudson's guns. The firing began at 11:20 P.M., and for the next ninety minutes the stretch of the Mississippi fronting the Rebel citadel was a seething arena of hissing shells and gut-wrenching explosions. When dawn came, only the first two ships of Farragut's command had made it through; of the others, one was sunk, and most of the rest badly damaged. Banks, who was supposed to demonstrate against Port Hudson's land side, had failed to do so.

On March 20, Banks's army began a two-day pull back to Baton Rouge. The commander resolved to ignore the thorny problem represented by Port Hudson in the faint hope that the two Federal vessels that had managed to run its gauntlet might yet cut its supply line, and thus force its evacuation. Banks now sent some of his command into the western section of the state, known as the Teche country. His purpose seems to have been threefold: to break up any Confederate detachments operating in that region; to gather supplies; and to establish direct communications with U. S. Grant, who was just beginning the most decisive phase of his long campaign against Vicksburg. It took a good while for messages to pass between the two men, making it impossible for them effectively to coordinate their blows against the bookended bastions. At first, Grant informed Banks that he intended to send down twenty thousand men to help capture Port Hudson, but by the time Banks acknowledged this communication and moved some units to establish contact on the Red River, Grant was too heavily engaged in fighting for Vicksburg to spare any troops; in fact, in a dispatch written on May 10, he asked *Banks* to send *him* some men. Lacking sufficient transportation to fulfill this request, Banks determined to use his forces to eliminate the Port Hudson problem once and for all. On May 20, he began to concentrate every accessible unit for his campaign against Port Hudson.

With the 2nd Regiment Louisiana Native Guards off on Ship Island, only the 1st and 3rd regiments were available. The 1st had been moved up to Baton Rouge and placed alongside the 3rd. It was a tense time for the two black units: the 3rd was now minus all its black officers, and those in the 1st must have wondered when it would be their turn. Nor had there been any cessation of racial incidents. On May 13, a detail from the 1st on a wood-cutting assignment was stopped at the picket line by a white officer who would not

let the men pass. Colonel Spencer H. Stafford, commanding the 1st, came roaring out of camp in response and loudly pronounced the entire white brigade "a set of God damn thieves." The machinery of military justice descended swiftly on Stafford, who was charged with "conduct to the prejudice of good order and military discipline," tried, convicted, and dismissed. Lieutenant Colonel Chauncey J. Bassett now took over the 1st. On May 20, he received orders to "hold his regiment in readiness to move at a moment's notice."[25]

From May 21 to 25, the 1st and 3rd Regiments moved toward Port Hudson, usually in the rear of the Union columns. The weather was hot, the roads were dusty, and there was little good water to be had. Detachments from the 3rd had at least one run-in with a squad of marauding Rebels. On May 23, the black regiments reached the main body of white troops that now ringed Port Hudson. Then, on May 25, the Native Guards marched from the Union left to the extreme right, "a hard long tramp." Banks's plan was to attack the Confederate position from every direction, so troops all along the perimeter spent May 26 preparing their approach. For the black soldiers, this meant protecting an engineering detail from the 42nd Massachusetts as it successfully threw up a pontoon bridge across Big Sandy Creek, to replace a wood structure burned by the Confederates. A Bay State soldier who watched them thought the black soldiers performed this task "in a cool, collected manner."[26]

A correspondent for the *New York Times,* riding with General Banks's entourage, passed the Native Guards this day as they respectfully saluted their commanding officer. The reporter voiced the question of many in the army when he asked aloud, "Will they fight?"[27]

It is difficult to assess the morale and combat readiness of the 1st and 3rd Louisiana Native Guards at this point, and it would be wrong to assume that one regiment was necessarily a mirror of the other. The enlisted men of the 3rd had seen all of their black officers purged in a callous manner that could only have exacerbated the inherent distrust former slaves harbored toward white authorities. An officer from the 52nd Massachusetts, writing to the *New Orleans Daily True Delta* after the Port Hudson assault, asserted that there was no bond of confidence between the officers and the men of the regiment.

The 1st, in contrast, still retained its black officers, who eagerly anticipated a battle that would vindicate them in the eyes of the world. Before any race of people could be considered "worthy" of full partnership in the rights and riches of a nation, it was necessary for its members to display certain qualities, the most important of which was manhood. When the newspaperman asked, "Will they fight?" he was really wondering, "Will they show courage?" The history, experiences, and direct testimony of the black officers of the 1st Louisiana suggest that they knew very well the nature of the test confronting them, and that they were determined to meet the challenge. "I do not intend to resign . . . ," declared Lieutenant John H. Crowder, in Company K of the regiment. "[As] long as there is a button to hold to I will hold it."[28]

This spirit was exemplified by Captain André Cailloux of Company E, 1st Regiment Louisiana Native Guards, a figure of importance in New Orleans society, an ex-slave honored as a fine horseman and boxer, and a man who celebrated the purity of his African lineage by referring to himself as the "blackest man in America." Cailloux was devoted to his men. Another inspiring figure in the 1st was Color Sergeant Anselmas Planciancois. In one of his last acts with the regiment, Colonel Stafford presented the men with their flags and exhorted the color guard never to surrender them; it is said that Planciancois replied, "Colonel, I will bring back these colors in honor or report to God the reason why."[29]

As he spread out his thirty thousand men to embrace Port Hudson, Banks placed his right wing under Brigadier General Godfrey Weitzel. Weitzel's forces were in turn organized into two divisions, with the one holding the extreme right commanded by Brigadier General William Dwight, Jr. Three brigades made up Dwight's division: two white ones consisting largely of New England and New York regiments, and one comprising the 1st and 3rd Native Guards, a detachment of the white 1st Louisiana Cavalry, and a pair of guns from the 6th Massachusetts Artillery. Colonel John A. Nelson of the 3rd Native Guards commanded this last brigade, ceding leadership of his regiment to Lieutenant Colonel Henry Finnegass.

General Dwight had served in the East with the 70th New York, and been wounded and captured at the Battle of Williamsburg in 1862. A hard drinker with a penchant for shady financial dealings, Dwight had asked for the black regiments to be put under him. Writing to his mother on the night of May 26, he noted, "I have had the negro Regts. longest in the service assigned to me, and I am going to storm a detached work with them. You may look for hard fighting, or for a complete run away." Dwight went on to stress how important

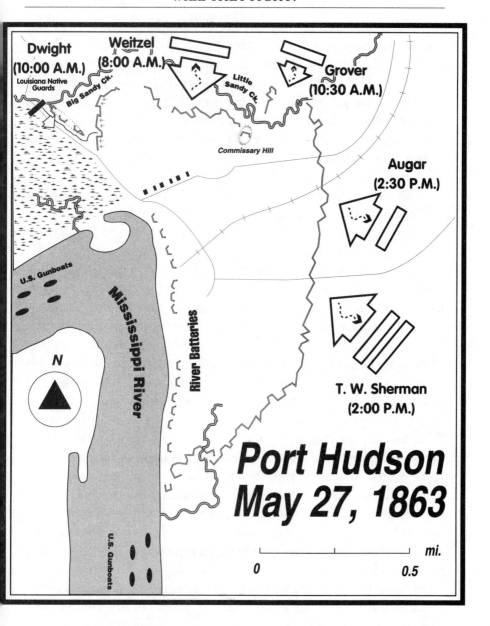

the performance of the black troops in the coming fight would be. "The negro will have the fate of his race on his conduct," he wrote. "I shall compromise nothing in making this attack, for I regard it as an experiment."[30]

The grand assault Banks envisaged for the morning of May 27 was not clearly mapped out for his subordinate commanders, nor did they carry out their actions on this day with any apparent reference to each other. The Confederate position was generally in the shape of a half-circle, with its lines bowing eastward; the numerous ravines that coursed through the area dictated a defense built upon strong points, with every bit of high ground well posted. The uneven terrain meant it would be difficult to maintain or control the long lines of battle used in the attack formations.

The day began with a bombardment of the Confederate position by the Federal artillery, opening at 5:30 A.M. and lasting for about an hour. The U.S. naval vessels in the river drew within range and began firing at 7:00, adding another hour's worth of shelling to the offensive mix.

The right wing, under Weitzel, was the first to engage Port Hudson's main defenses. Between 7:00 and 8:00 A.M., Weitzel's white troops pressed forward in a series of assaults against a key Confederate position known as Commissary Hill. The Federal formations were thinned by the hard terrain and the heat, as many men dropped out of the advance and into the protective folds of nearby ravines. Only a handful of the troops that began the advance actually managed to reach the edge of the Rebel works, and these few lacked the strength to break through, so the combat quickly became a deadly stalemate. With his way blocked along the line of Little Sandy Creek, Weitzel looked to his extreme right to relieve the pressure on his center.

Brigadier General Dwight, who according to some accounts was drunk this day, had not bothered to reconnoiter his sector. He seems to have assumed that because the Telegraph Road led directly from his flank into the town, the route was clear. Dwight confidently assured Colonel Nelson that this approach represented the "easiest way into Port Hudson."[31]

In fact, the truth was quite the opposite: the road ran out into a floodplain for a distance of about half a mile from Big Sandy Creek, then abruptly veered up a steep bluff that constituted the main Confederate position. Once they passed over the creek, troops moving along the Telegraph Road would be under fire both from artillery on the bluff and from river batteries farther south. Even worse, the Confederates had dug a series of rifle pits along a thin piece of high ground running parallel to the road, which would allow them to rake the flank of any body of troops moving below. This outerwork was manned on May 27 by sixty men drawn from the 39th Mississippi and the 9th Louisiana Partisan Ranger Battalion. Six companies of the 39th (about three hundred men) occupied the main position, providing support to six cannon. Nature had also improved the Rebel position: the Mississippi was running near its crest, so a pool of backwater covered the ground west of the road, serving further to compress any potential attacking line. Instead of being the "easiest way into Port Hudson," the route assigned to the black troops was a nearly impossible one.

Sometime before 10:00 A.M., six companies from the 1st Regiment and nine from the 3rd crossed the pontoon bridge and filed into a grove of willow trees just south of the road. Here they formed into lines of battle. The two guns from the 6th Massachusetts also came over, unlimbered after crossing the bridge, and challenged the six guns on the steep bluff. It was no contest; the Yankee gunners got off just one round before their position was smothered in counterfire. With two men down and three horses killed, the Bay Staters quickly pulled back across the creek.

Captain Cailloux moved among the ranks of the 1st Regiment's color guard, steadying the men with words of encouragement in both French and English. Then, at 10:00 A.M., the two ranks of the 1st Regiment emerged from the willows and pressed down the road toward the bluff. They were supported by two more ranks of men from the 3rd, making about a thousand altogether joining in the attack. The first two hundred yards were covered at a quick time, as enemy sharpshooters on the ridge extracted a deadly toll. It was probably in this phase of the action that Captain Cailloux was hit in the left arm, a shattering blow that paralyzed the limb. The leading ranks now entered the Rebel artillery's killing zone, and the six cannon unleashed a torrent of shells against the first wave of black soldiers at four hundred yards, staggering the line. Sergeant Planciancois never knew what hit him: a shell blew off the top of his head, splattering brains and gore over the flag he had vowed to defend to the death. Up to this point the men of the 1st Regiment had held together. A lieutenant in Company F later confessed that he had "entertained some fears as to their pluck" but added that he "had none now. . . . Valiantly did the heroic descendants of Africa move forward, cool as if marshaled for dress parade."[32]

41

If there was any hesitation at all in that first wave of men, it was only momentary. Captain Cailloux, his bloody left arm hanging useless at his side, led a surge that carried them to within two hundred yards of the main line, point blank for the artillery and for the enemy riflemen. Cailloux was hit again, and killed. The 1st Regiment, its battle lines disordered by the charge and the carnage, managed to fire one volley before reeling back in confusion; the fragile cohesion of the 3rd Regiment could not hold together under the rush of fleeing men, and everyone retreated into the willows.

While officers worked to re-form the ranks, two further attempts were made to take the enemy position. In one, a detachment from the 3rd Regiment tried to wade through the backwater to get close enough to rush the Rebels, but it was stopped by a pool of water eight feet deep and forty wide. A few reckless soldiers swam this obstacle; most were shot down once they emerged into the open. Another group tried to clamber up to the rifle pits that flanked the road but was enfiladed by the river batteries and swept off the steep slope.

Command and control of Nelson's brigade fell apart. The colonel sent an aide to General Dwight to inform him that the attack had failed and that the regiments had suffered heavy losses. "Charge again," Dwight ordered the startled aide, "and let the impetuosity of the charge counterbalance the paucity of numbers." Colonel Nelson dutifully sent instructions to Lieutenant Colonels Bassett and Finnegass to renew the assault. Then, to Nelson's surprise, Finnegass came to him with a series of insignificant requests that only wasted time. When Nelson insisted that he return to prepare his regiment to attack, Finnegass refused. By now, the tenor of Dwight's instructions had taken a turn for the bizarre. "Tell Colonel Nelson to keep charging as long as there is a corporal's guard left," the records show he said. "When there is only one man left, let him come to me and report."[33]

The blatant refusal by Finnegass to renew the effort, and a gut feeling that any further attack would be futile, moved Nelson to his own act of insubordination. Recognizing that Dwight was monitoring the action by its noise alone, Nelson had his men step up their rate of fire while holding their position in the willows. At more than six hundred yards' distance, there was little that a rifle could hit, but the noise would convince Dwight that his suicidal orders were being obeyed.

So as the other portions of Banks's army launched fierce but fruitless assaults from the east and southeast against the Port Hudson defenses, the black troops fired their guns at an out-of-range target, all the while enduring a steady shelling and sniping that cost them casualties throughout the afternoon. Despite this bloody and terrifying initiation into the "manhood" of combat, the spirit of these soldiers was unbowed. According to a reporter from the *New Orleans Era,* "There were several instances of wounded returning to the field after their wounds had been dressed, and fighting with their comrades the balance of the day." One soldier nursing a bad leg injury held his place until he had exhausted all the bullets in his cartridge box, explaining, "I guess I can gib'em some more yet." George R. Sanders, a hospital steward for the 3rd Regiment, later wrote that the men "maid three charges and held thire ground."[34]

Darkness at last ended the fighting at Port Hudson. At no point had the Confederate defenses been broken. Banks later reported 293 of his men killed, 1,545 wounded, and 157 missing. Confederate casualties for all categories totaled between 250 and 275. The losses suffered by the two Native Guard regiments remain a matter of speculation: accounts in some newspapers, especially those with an abolitionist agenda, put them as high as 600, though most authorities eventually settled on 37 killed, 155 wounded, and 116 missing. Among the dead was young Lieutenant John H. Crowder of Company K, whom death saved from the shame of forced resignation. Of all the Union units engaged this day, only one white regiment saw more of its men killed than the 1st. Banks now decided to mount a siege, though he would try once more on June 14 to storm the bastion—an action in which the Native Guards were to be held in reserve.

The May 27 attack by the two Native Guard regiments sounded a clarion call throughout the land. Stories of the black troops' unflinching advance spread along the army grapevine, growing with each retelling. A Wisconsin soldier who would later serve in a black regiment wrote his father that the "negroes fought like devils, they made five charges on a battery that there was not the slightest chance of their taking, just (as their officers said) to show our boys that they *could* and *would* fight." In another letter about the events of May 27, a soldier in the 156th New York said of the Native Guards, "They charged and re-charged and didn't know what retreat meant. They lost in their two regiments some four hundred men as near as I can learn. This settles the question about niggers not fighting well. They, on the contrary, make splendid soldiers and are as good fighting men as any we have." "A race of serfs stepped up to the respect of the world," exclaimed a Massachusetts soldier, "and commenced a national existence."[35]

Even General Banks got swept up in the moment. "They fought splendidly," he wrote to his wife; he expressed much the same sentiment in his official report. In its editorial column of June 11, written after Banks's report was made public, the *New York Times* declared, "This official testimony settles the question that the negro race can fight with great prowess. . . . It is no longer possible to doubt the bravery and steadiness of the colored race when rightly led."[36]

The immediate aftermath of the fight was a bitter one for the Native Guards, however. They were denied a truce to bury their dead,* so the body of valiant Captain Cailloux (already picked over by scavengers) had to lie rotting until Port Hudson surrendered, on July 9, after word was received of Vicksburg's capitulation five days earlier to Grant. Starvation and hopelessness had accomplished at the Port Hudson garrison what force of arms could not. Cailloux's body was taken to New Orleans for a hero's funeral, but the fate of the surviving black officers was neither pleasant nor honorable, as Banks continued to remove them. He instituted an examining board to test their fitness to command, even as he refused to pay them, citing a government policy prohibiting black officers. Adding to the insult, the white members of the board were often junior in rank to the blacks being tested, and several stood to gain through promotion should the senior officers fail. Six members of the 1st Regiment resigned for medical reasons before mid-August, and Banks's board rejected three more. When thirteen of the officers passed the rigid tests, Banks had five of them transferred to a new regiment in the Corps d'Afrique. Four of the five, feeling betrayed by this move, chose to resign; the fifth officer, Lieutenant Oscar Orillion, was killed in a slight action near Jackson, Louisiana.

The daily pattern of racist abuse would cut down the eight officers who remained with the 1st, one at a time. When Captain Joseph Follin resigned in February 1864, he complained that "prejudices are so strong against colored officers, that . . . they cannot [endure] with honor to themselves." Just one man, Louis A. Snaer, managed to hold his commission until the end of the war.

---

*Southern accounts indicate that it was the Yankee General Banks who "did not deem it worth while to bury the colored troops," while Northern sources condemn the Confederates. Given the strongly positive tone of Banks's personal and official correspondence regarding the action of the black troops, the former explanation hardly seems plausible.

Similar waves of prejudicial action also continued to wear away at the black officer cadre of the 2nd Regiment, until only one, Charles Sauvenet, remained. Morale suffered in all three regiments. Shortly after the next-to-last black officer left the 1st Regiment, fifty enlisted men deserted.[37]

The white officers commanding these regiments did not fare much better. Colonel Stafford was dismissed following his court-martial, though his discharge was changed to an honorable one in later years. Colonel Daniels of the 2nd Regiment resigned after failing to rebuke an aide who insulted the wife of a naval officer. Colonel Nelson likewise resigned, in August 1863, and Lieutenant Colonel Finnegass was dishonorably discharged.

The history of the black regiments in the Mississippi Valley was already entering a new phase even as the 1st and 3rd Regiments were proving their mettle at Port Hudson. Brigadier General Ullmann's recruiting efforts were beginning to pay off with a new generation of units (all officered by whites) designated the Corps d'Afrique. The Native Guards were folded into this organization on June 6 and renamed the 1st, 2nd, and 3rd Regiments of Infantry of the Corps d'Afrique. This designation would hold until 1864, when the three would be renamed once more, this time becoming the 73rd, 74th, and 75th Regiments, United States Colored Troops, or USCT.

For the first but not the last time in this war, the question of whether or not black troops would fight had been asked, and answered by deeds in the affirmative. Ten of the former officers of the 3rd Native Guards actually petitioned General Banks for permission to recruit for a new regiment. In their statement, these black soldiers vowed, "If the world doubts our fighting give us A chance and we will show them what we can do."[38]

Action at Milliken's Bend, Louisiana, June 7, 1863

Rear Admiral David D. Porter was grim-faced as he stepped from his flagship *Black Hawk* onto the riverbank at Milliken's Bend, which was covered with the bloody debris of recent, bitter fighting. Porter passed through what had been a regimental encampment and came to a long levee that had served as an outer defense wall. There he saw what he later described as "quite an ugly sight." A long ditch dug along the inside slope of the barrier was literally lined with dead black soldiers—"mostly shot on the top of the head," Porter observed. Picking his way past these corpses, he reached the top of the levee and looked beyond to where there "lay an equal number of rebels, stinking in the sun." There had been a "desperate" engagement at this place, made remarkable by the fact that the black troops that had fought here were, for the most part, untrained. Green they may have been, but as Porter took pains to note in his report, the black soldiers "stood at their post like men."[39]

Events leading to the action at Milliken's Bend had begun on May 21 outside Vicksburg, where Major General Ulysses S. Grant was improving the logistical support for his military operations. When he launched this campaign with a surprise crossing of the river below Vicksburg, he allowed his supply line to stretch precariously along the west bank of the Mississippi, with key depots located at Young's Point, Milliken's Bend, and Lake Providence. This remained his primary route for supplies until his siege of the Rebel defenders within Vicksburg freed him to open up a more direct supply link via the Yazoo River. Once that link was completed, on May 21, the importance of the west-bank depots diminished, as did Grant's need to station front-line combat troops there. These areas thus became recruiting centers and training camps for a number of black regiments being raised by one of the unsung heroes of the effort to create African American military units: Brigadier General Lorenzo Thomas.

Nearly sixty years old, Thomas was a desk man from the East, where he had served in the office of the adjutant general. If he had any personal opinion on the issues regarding black units, he kept them to himself. There is evidence that Secretary of War Stanton's decision to put Thomas in charge of recruiting Mississippi Valley blacks was based less on an appreciation of that officer's qualifications than on a simple desire to get rid of a holdover from a previous regime. "The subject was new to me," Thomas would later admit, "and I entered upon the duty by no means certain of what I might be able to effect."[40]

Thomas was given authority not only to recruit enlisted men but also to appoint white officers to command them. The old bureaucrat took to the stump like a born-again preacher. He arrived in Columbus, Kentucky, on April 2 to begin his western journey. "I am here to raise as many regiments of blacks as I can," Thomas told the audiences of white soldiers he met. "I am authorized to give commissions, from the highest to the lowest, and I desire those persons who are earnest in the work to take hold of it." By April 18, just three weeks after commencing his recruiting tour, Thomas had authorized the raising of ten black regiments.[41]

Among those won over by Thomas's orations was an Ohio soldier named Jacob Bruner. Writing to his wife on April 9, Bruner said:

> Thomas is direct from Washington, clothed with the fullest authority to commission officers to take charge of negro companies and regiments. Uncle Abe has at last sensibly concluded to arm the darkey and let him fight. They are not to be placed by the side of the white soldiers but is to be organized into companies, regiments and brigades by themselves with white officers. This is considered the master stroke of policy and this produced a most cheering and beneficial result among the soldiers. . . . I think the slavery question which has puzzled our fathers for fifty years is now being solved.[42]

Bruner was commissioned a first lieutenant in the 9th Regiment Louisiana Infantry (African Descent). Soon after initially gathering at Vicksburg on May 1, the regiment was posted to Milliken's Bend, where it joined two companion units, one organized on May 16 as the 1st Regiment Mississippi Infantry (A.D.), and the other mustered in on May 23 as the 11th Regiment Louisiana Infantry (A.D.). The enlisted ranks for all three regiments were filled by former slaves from the region.

If the somewhat embellished memoirs of the 9th's Lieutenant David Cornwell can be believed, the recruitment process was a mixture of earnest entreaties (which produced few new men) and outright chicanery (which brought in many more). After watching his captain exhort a group of former plantation slaves without success, Cornwell returned the next day accompanied by his formidable regimental sergeant, Jack Jackson, known as Big Jack. The newly liberated laborers crowded around the large noncom, who soon had them formed into a line and marching down the road. With Cornwell surreptitiously cutting out the old and infirm from the pack, Big Jack led his innocent procession back toward the army camp, picking up additional marchers at every plantation stop. Once in camp, the men were lined up in front of the astonished captain and, in a ceremony few of them understood, sworn in as soldiers in the U.S. Army.

"From that time on," Cornwell later recalled, "Jack and I attended to the recruiting, and we had only to find the darkey to get the recruit." "As fast as we get them we clothe them from head to foot in precisely the same uniform that 'our boys' wear, give them tents, rations, and blankets and they are highly pleased and hardly know themselves," wrote Lieutenant Bruner on April 28.[43]

The men who entered the enlisted ranks of these regiments were, for the most part, field hands and farmers. Of the eighty-one in Company A of the 11th Regiment Louisiana Infantry (A.D.), more than half (fifty-four) were under the age of thirty, with another six in their forties. The younger men came from Louisiana or Mississippi, while some of the older ones listed their birthplace as Virginia or Kentucky. Among those who joined the regiment were Sharper Jordan, a private in Company D who had helped care for his mother after the family was emancipated; Sergeant Henry H. Hunter (Company C), who had married as a slave, with the consent of his owner, and lived together with his wife, as was the custom of that time; and Private Wesley Foster, also in Company D, a nineteen-year-old described as "short in stature and stoutly built." Foster had a friend in the regiment named Captain Lemons, who had lived on a neighboring plantation. As Lemons later remembered, "There was so many things new and exciting that we did not have much [time to] talk about home affairs."[44]

Other events leading to the June 7 fight at Milliken's Bend stemmed from the efforts of the Confederate military leaders of the Trans-Mississippi Department (representing the states of Missouri, Arkansas, Texas, modern Oklahoma, and western Louisiana) to disrupt Grant's Vicksburg campaign. There was a serious difference of opinion within the Trans-Mississippi military high command as to the best way to stop Grant. Major General Richard Taylor, in charge of the District of West Louisiana, wanted to move all available forces against New Orleans, reasoning that this would compel Banks to lift his siege of Port Hudson and thus free its defenders to reinforce Vicksburg. Taylor's superior, Lieutenant General Edmund Kirby Smith, disagreed. He favored striking at the Union supply depots strung along the west bank of the Mississippi River, thus forcing Grant to either abandon his operation or face starvation.

Kirby Smith's plan prevailed, and Taylor was put in charge of carrying it out. On June 5 he arrived in Richmond, Louisiana, situated about ten miles west of Young's Point and fifteen miles southwest of Milliken's Bend. With him was a division of Texas infantry commanded by Major General John G. Walker, consisting of three brigades. Taylor had in hand a scouting report on the Federal westbank depots, which claimed that "the line was guarded by convalescents and some negro troops; no danger was anticipated." Instead of concentrating against each of the three depots in turn, Taylor decided on a more ambitious plan calling for simultaneous strikes on June 7 at Young's Point, Milliken's Bend, and Lake Providence. A detached unit located near Lake Providence was assigned that target, while one of Walker's brigades was ordered to take Young's Point and a second given Milliken's Bend, with the third brigade held as a reserve. To Brigadier General Henry E. McCulloch, who was to capture Milliken's Bend, Taylor gave verbal orders "to engage the enemy before day and carry his works at the point of the bayonet."[45]

The three Federal depots were part of the District of Northeastern Louisiana, under the command of Brigadier General Elias S. Dennis, whose headquarters were at Young's Point. Operational control of Milliken's Bend was vested in Colonel Hermann Lieb, commanding the 9th Regiment Louisiana Infantry (A.D.). Taylor's concentration at Richmond had not gone unnoticed by Dennis, who, late on June 5, ordered Colonel Lieb to reconnoiter that area. He sent Lieb a detachment from the 10th Illinois Cavalry, to which Lieb added another 250 men from his 9th Regiment. Lieb's footsoldiers left camp at 2:00 A.M. on June 6, joining the cavalry about three miles down the road. Reaching a bridge and a fork in the road, the groups divided, with the cavalry moving toward Young's Point while the infantry pressed on to Richmond. Three miles farther on, the black soldiers came upon some Rebel outposts, causing Lieb, worried about a possible ambush, to retrace his steps. His men had just recrossed the bridge when a cloud of dust heralded the return of the Illinois troopers, who shouted that enemy riders were right behind them. Lieb had already readied his men for a fight, something that was welcomed by at least one cavalryman. Trooper F. W. Sedgwick remembered how he and his comrades

came in sight of a line of men in bright new blue uniforms, who soon opened fire on "our friends the enemy." They supposing it a large force for our support, ceased their all-too-friendly advances on us. When we had time to look well at our men in blue, we discovered they had black faces. I had been raised an Abolitionist, yet was opposed to the plan of arming negroes before that day, but I can tell you of one who became a sudden convert right then and there, perfectly willing that negroes should have as good a right to be shot as myself.[46]

Having discovered that the enemy was in strength at Richmond, Lieb immediately began organizing a defense of Milliken's Bend, petitioning General Dennis for reinforcements. Dennis sent Lieb a detachment of 130 men from the 23rd Iowa, who came on the U.S. gunboat *Choctaw*. Since the white troops had traveled without their camp equipment, it was decided to let them spend the night of June 6 on the gunboat. The two hundred men from the 10th Illinois Cavalry had meanwhile retired to their camp a few miles south of Milliken's Bend, where they would remain until after the fighting had ended.

Lieb's position at Milliken's Bend was a strong one. Because the river was running low, the steep bank (about fifteen feet from its upper edge to the water) provided a natural earthwork for the Federals. A six-foot-high levee had been constructed about 150 yards west of the bank, creating an outer defensive point. Lieutenant Cornwell remembered that the levee was "sufficiently wide at the top for a wagon road, with a gradual[ly] sloping side, say of about 25 degrees." The fields surrounding the landing area were intersected by a series of thick hedges known as bois d'arc, sporting wicked thorns that would break up any troop formation. There was a hundred-foot gap in the hedge on the left of the Union line where some of the brush had been chopped down by mistake on June 6, but the line's flanks were anchored by heavy timber and drainage ditches. Lieb doubled his pickets and sent out a squad of mounted infantry to give early warning of the enemy's approach.[47]

The officers serving in the three black regiments faced the prospect of a fight with mixed emotions. Lieutenant Cornwell's grim assessment was that there was "nothing for it but to sell out at the highest market price." Lieutenant Colonel Cyrus Sears of the 11th Regiment worried about the fact that his men had been issued their arms only sixteen days earlier: "All veterans, at least, must know how inadequate were sixteen days to recruit, muster, organize, arm, equip, drill—in short to make soldiers of *any* material, under *any* circumstances."

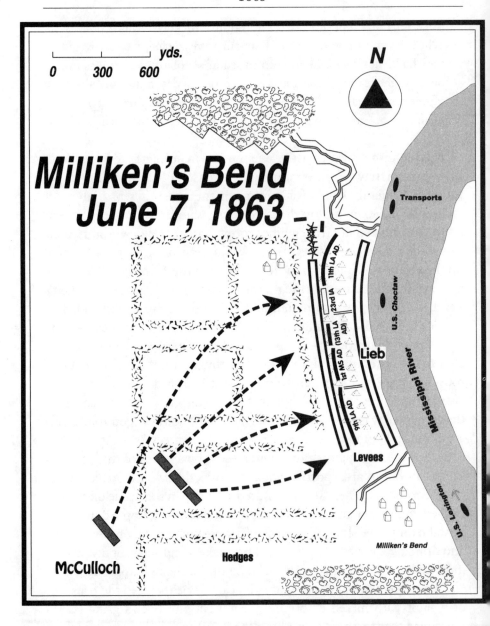

Incredibly, the men of the 1st Regiment Mississippi Infantry (A.D.) had received their weapons only the day before, on June 6, and as dawn rose on June 7, few in the ranks had even fired them once.[48]

At 2:00 A.M., Colonel Lieb ordered his units to stand to behind the levee. Holding the extreme left were the 285 men of the 9th Regiment Louisiana Infantry (A.D.); next to them were placed the 153 just-armed members of the 1st Regiment Mississippi Infantry (A.D.). In his unpublished report, Colonel Lieb indicated that the next body of men in line constituted the 13th Regiment Louisiana Infantry (A.D.), a regiment that nowhere appears on the Federal rolls and an identification that was later disputed by at least one officer present at the fight.* On the right of these black recruits was a gap that was to be filled by the 23rd Iowa soldiers once they got off the *Choctaw*. Holding down the right side of the line was the 11th Regiment Louisiana Infantry (A.D.).

Timing was critical for the success of Taylor's attack on the Federal position at Milliken's Bend. Since the day promised to be a hot one, Taylor was anxious to begin and end fighting early. Stretching the combat into the afternoon could also expose his troops to the Federal gunboats, which were sure to come quickly once word of the action spread.

McCulloch's Texans left Richmond at 7:00 P.M. on June 6. At about 3:00 A.M., his mounted advance reached Lieb's outposts. The Federals let the horsemen approach to within a few yards before opening fire; the surprised Rebel troopers tumbled back against the head of the infantry column, which began to shoot at the hapless riders. McCulloch deployed his leading infantry unit into a line of battle and drove the Federal outposts back to the first line of hedgerows, where the Union troops were reinforced by skirmishers whose combined fire sufficed to stop the thin screen preceding McCulloch's first unit. It was around 4:00 A.M. when the Confederate general fully deployed his brigade for the assault. Lieutenant Cornwell of the 9th marveled at this display of the Rebel commander's offensive power: "His front covered the field from hedge to hedge, double rank, elbow to elbow. They . . . had the appearance of a brigade on drill."[49]

Colonel Lieb afterward reported that

> the enemy advanced on the left of our line, throwing out no skirmishers in front, with a strong force of cavalry on his right flank, marching in close column by division until within three-fourths of a mile of our works.

*The 13th Regiment Louisiana Infantry (A.D.) never completed its organization. Under special orders issued on July 6, the men recruited for it were assigned to the 1st Regiment Mississippi Infantry (A.D.).

My men were ordered to withhold their fire until the enemy were within musket shot; and the first volley was delivered when they were within that range, which made them waver and recoil; a number running in confusion to the rear, the balance pushing on with intrepidity, soon reaching the levee, where a charge was ordered by their leaders, when they came madly on with the cries—kill the d----d Abolitionists, spare the Niggers. Our men being unaccustomed to the use of Muskets, some having had but two days' drilling, the most proficient not more than three weeks', the enemy succeeded in getting up to our works, a number of them on top of the [levee] . . . before many of our men succeeded in reloading their pieces, while many of them (Austrian Rifles) failed to fire.

A desperate hand to hand fight of several minutes duration then ensued.[50]

The 9th Regiment was the first struck. The hedgerow funneled the attackers through the openings, according to McCulloch's report, "never . . . more than half a company" at a time. After passing through these entanglements, the men re-formed into small groups that then rushed the levee. This dissipated the surge of the assault and gave the black defenders some small advantage, except on the extreme left, where there was no such obstacle, the hedgerow having been cut down. Recalled Lieutenant Cornwell, "I had seen the weakness of the men at the levee and ordered my men to keep their loads and not shoot a man, if he could bayonet him; and not to pull off his gun until the muzzle was against a rebel." As the Confederate tide began to slip around the left flank, Cornwell excitedly forgot the proper command to give, and instead shouted to his company, "Now bounce them Bullies." Further toward the center of the line, the levee's flat top was the stage for hand-to-hand combat as black man grappled with white. Said Cornwell, "The yelling, cutting and slashing for ten or fifteen minutes was terrible." The sergeant known as Big Jack laid into a group of Texans, in Cornwell's words "smashing in every head he could reach." Cornwell called to his men to fall back to the inside slope of the work, but Big Jack was too full of fury to heed the command. He clambered to the top of the levee just as the Confederate flankers fell back. "On the other side they were yelling, 'Shoot that big nigger, shoot that big nigger,' while Jack was daring the whole gang to come up there and fight him. Then a bullet reached his head and he went full length on the levee."[51]

Nearby were Captain Matthew M. Miller and Company I of the regiment. "I narrowly escaped death once," he wrote right after the fight. "A rebel took deliberate [aim] at me with both barrels of his gun and the bullets passed so close to me that the powder that remained on them burned my cheek. Three of my men who saw him aim and fire thought that he wounded me each fire. One of them was killed by my side, and he fell on me, covering my clothes with his blood, and before the rebel could fire again I blew his brains out with my gun." Lieutenant Cornwell's luck ran out at about this time, when he spotted a Rebel drawing a bead on him and yelled to one of his soldiers to shoot the Johnny. "He was too slow and the fellow plugged me," recollected Cornwell. "The ball shattered the bone of my right arm at the shoulder."[52]

According to the record of the 1st Regiment Mississippi Infantry (A.D.), "Many of the severely wounded voluntarily returned to the ranks after washing their wounds. One soldier whose jaw was so severely shattered that utterance was impossible would not leave his post, until peremptorily ordered by his commander to the rear. He soon died from the effects of his wound."[53]

The attacking wave roiled along the levee to the point where the detachment of the 23rd Iowa had only just stepped into position. Said an Iowa soldier,

Both sides used their bayonets with effect. One member of the regiment and a rebel met and at the same instance plunged their bayonets into one another. . . . Another rebel ran his bayonet through one of our men, and another of our men knocked his brains out with the butt of his musket. . . . [The] negroes . . . stood much better than I supposed they would, being so green in the business, but they fired too high, and exposed themselves too much, as they would fire and then keep their heads in danger to watch the effect of their shots.

A historian of the Iowa regiment would later write that "white and black indiscriminately and without order, fought for dear life." Next engaged was the 11th Regiment. Lieutenant Colonel Sears, who led the men of the 11th this day, described the action as a "hot little scrap," adding, "No doubt fighting has seldom been more strenu-ous." He claimed that the "enemy fought us under the skull, coffin and cross bones (black) flag."[54]

During the brutal close-in combat along the levee, some of the white officers in the Louisiana (A.D.) regiments lost their nerve and scrambled back to the riverbank. General McCulloch observed that the "white or true Yankee portion ran like whipped curs almost as soon as the charge was ordered." Lieutenant Colonel Sears confirmed that Colonel Edwin W. Chamberlain, commanding the 11th Regiment, remained aboard one of the vessels in the river during the battle (for which dereliction he was afterward allowed to resign), but avowed that otherwise, "Each and every line officer did his duty nobly."[55]

The Texans finally managed to assemble enough men around the Federal left to open a devastating enfilade fire. This peeled the de-fenders off the levee's inner wall and forced the Federals back to the river. In some places, squads of black soldiers retreated under disci-pline; in others, they fled in terror. A Texas soldier, writing home the next day, admitted that the blacks had "fought desperate," while the official history of Walker's Division says that "bayonets were crossed, and muskets clubbed, and the struggle indeed became a close and deadly one." General McCulloch allowed that the charge of his brigade "was resisted by the negro portion of the enemy's force with considerable obstinacy." This assessment was seconded by one of his men, who recalled, "After some hard fighting, [the black soldiers] were driven to the water's edge."[56]

A question lingers about the actions of the 23rd Iowa once the levee line was breached. The white officers of the Louisiana (A.D.) regiments were unanimous in their contention, as reported by Colonel Lieb, that the "23rd Iowa Infantry left the field soon after the enemy had gained possession of the levee, headed by their Colonel, and were seen no more." Captain Miller of the 9th declared that the men of the 23rd "all fled before our right fell back." Contradicting this, however, was the insistence of Captain W. M. Little of the 23rd that "not a man flinched in the regiment till he was ordered to fall back," and that "we had to fall back to the river bank." Another Iowan, Robert W. Henry, part of a detail from the 26th Iowa that got hooked up with the 23rd, wrote that the Confederates "outnumbered us largely and we gave way, back to the river bank was our next and only hope. . . . On they came with a yell, we reached the bank and turned on them, but few pieces were loaded yet we halted them. . . . On the bank the niggers were doing well. We done our best."[57]

Ironically, the Federal retreat had two effects that served further to blunt the momentum of the Confederate attack. First, the abandoned encampment area slowed down the Rebels, whose discipline suffered as the weary, hungry men stopped to plunder the tents. Second, the Union fallback opened a field of fire for the gunboat *Choctaw*, which was soon dropping shells amid the milling Confederates. Because the warship was firing blind, with little more than some amateur spotting provided by a few Louisiana (A.D.) officers on shore, the actual destructive results of this bombardment were minimal, but the prospect of charging the naval guns was nonetheless daunting to the Rebel field officers. To compound the problem, the *Choctaw* was soon joined by a second gunboat, the *Lexington*.

The lower river level meant that the *Choctaw*'s gunners had a hard time shooting over the riverbank, and slammed some friendly fire into the Federal ranks. According to Lieutenant Colonel Sears of the 11th Regiment, "I know the shots from [our gunboats] . . . did kill and wound some of our men . . . from the fact that I was very unpleasantly spattered with blood, brains and flesh of one of our men, who there had his head shot off from one of the gunboats. I shall never forget that our navy did some real execution at Milliken's Bend."[58]

Confederate General McCulloch pulled his men back behind the captured levee and decided he needed reinforcements. But before he received a reply from General Walker, his men sighted the *Lexington* steaming into range. That was enough. Loading all his wounded into ambulances, McCulloch retreated toward Richmond around midday. He had covered only a short distance when he met General Walker coming up with the reserve; after a quick consultation, the two men agreed that victory was out of the question. The action at Milliken's Bend was over. In his postwar memoir, Richard Taylor provided a bitter summary of the entire operation: "As foreseen, our movement resulted, and could result, in nothing," he declared.[59]

Of the fifteen hundred Confederates engaged in the action, McCulloch reported 44 killed, 131 wounded, and 10 missing. On the Union side, the price paid by the 9th Regiment was 63 killed and 100 wounded; in the 1st Regiment Mississippi Infantry (A.D.), it was 2 killed and 21 wounded; and in the 11th Regiment, 23 killed and 112 wounded. The detachment from the 13th Regiment filed no report of its casualties. Writing more than fifty years after the fighting, Captain Little of the 23rd Iowa put his losses at 25 killed and 43 wounded, which approaches the calculation of the Iowa adjutant general of 23 killed and 41 wounded. Of the eleven hundred Federals engaged at Milliken's Bend, almost four hundred were casualties of some kind. Among these was Colonel Lieb, wounded early in the fight, and Sergeant Big Jack and Lieutenant Jacob Bruner, both killed. Other enlisted men who died in this engagement were Sharper Jordan, Henry H. Hunter, and Wesley Foster. Jordan was one of two sons lost to the war by Lucinda Montgomery, who afterward stated with some pride that both had died "fighting for their liberties."[60]

The triple strike envisioned by General Taylor proved to be an attempt to do too much with too little. The brigade assigned to tackle Young's Point never even bothered to contest the issue once its commander counted three Federal gunboats in the river; the force advancing on Lake Providence met stronger resistance earlier than anticipated, and after skirmishing for most of the day, it, too, withdrew. The only real effort by the military powers of the Trans-Mississippi to contest the Union siege of Vicksburg was at an end. The starved, surrounded citadel would finally surrender on July 4.

The actions of the black soldiers at Milliken's Bend soon came to the attention of a general who was to assume even greater responsibilities in the Union effort than he already shouldered. In his brief note covering General Dennis's official report of this engagement, Ulysses S. Grant said, "In this battle most of the troops engaged were Africans, who had but little experience in the use of fire-arms. Their conduct is said, however, to have been most gallant, and I doubt not but with good officers they will make good troops."[61]

For the first time in a battle, black prisoners were taken by the Rebels. When informed of this circumstance, General Kirby Smith wrote to Richard Taylor, "I hope this may not be so, and that your subordinates . . . may have recognized the propriety of giving no quarter to armed negroes and their officers." A week or so after Milliken's Bend, Grant received the interrogation report of a Confederate deserter who claimed to have seen a mass hanging of the captured blacks. Grant wrote at once to Taylor, who strongly denied that any such event had taken place. "I am now truly glad to hear your denial," Grant wrote in response. Although no record has emerged regarding the fate of the blacks captured at Milliken's Bend, it seems most likely that they would have been reabsorbed into the slave system and disappeared into the maw of that society.[62]

News of the positive performance of the black troops at Milliken's Bend spread across the country. Said Captain Miller of the 9th Regiment in a letter that was widely reprinted, "I never more wish to hear the expression, 'The niggers won't fight.'" Charles Dana, who represented the War Department in Grant's operation, wrote to Edwin Stanton that the "sentiment [in] . . . regard to the employment of negro troops has been revolutionized by the bravery of the blacks in the recent Battle of Milliken's Bend. Prominent officers, who used in private to sneer at the idea, are now heartily in favor of it." Word of this affair had a chilling effect on the other side. "It is hard to believe that Southern soldiers—and Texans at that—have been whipped by a mongrel crew of white and black Yankees," wrote one Kate Stone in her journal. "There must be some mistake." A Louisiana lady named Sarah L. Wadley noted in her private diary, "It is terrible to think of such a battle as this, white men and freemen fighting with their slaves, and to be killed by such a hand, the very soul revolts from it, O, may this be the last."[63]

In the report of his activities for the year 1863, Brigadier General Lorenzo Thomas tallied thirty-two separate units that had been organized during the period in the Mississippi Valley region, a total enlistment of 20,800 men. With pardonable pride, he reported that the "majority of the freedmen manifest a partiality for the military service, and are undoubtedly happy and contented in their position in the Army." In his conclusion he stated, "It is to be presumed that as our armies advance the number of our colored organizations will be largely increased." Sarah Wadley's wish that the fighting between black and white at Milliken's Bend might be the last would not be granted.[64]

Interlude

"The Power of Fear"

————◇————

TERROR was the glue that bound together the Southern slave system. A North Carolina planter, writing in 1802, said it was a "pity that [it is] agreeable to the nature of things [that] Slavery and Tyranny must go together and that there is no such thing as having an obedient and useful Slave, without the painful exercise of undue and tyrannical authority." In 1849, a writer for *De Bow's Review* asserted, "We have to rely more and more on the power of fear. . . . We are determined to continue [as] masters, and to do so we have to draw the rein tighter and tighter day by day to be assured that we hold them in complete check." Whites who assisted slaves in rebelling against or fleeing their owners could expect a merciless response. It was death for a North Carolina citizen to hide a runaway slave; in Alabama, any white conspiring with blacks "shall be punished with death, whether such rebellion or insurrection be made or not."[1]

It was by these terms that on August 21, 1862, the C.S. War Department declared Major General David Hunter and Brigadier General John W. Phelps "outlaws." If captured, they were to be held "for execution as a felon at such time and place as the President [i.e., Jefferson Davis] shall order." By the time Major General Benjamin F. Butler was added to the list, the Confederate proscription had been considerably broadened. Butler himself was personally condemned,

60

any slaves caught armed and in uniform were to be punished by state authorities as their laws allowed, and all white officers taken prisoner were to be transferred to state authority for trial (and presumably execution) for inciting insurrection. Subsequent actions by the C.S. Congress and president further refined these punishments as 1863 brought more black Union regiments into the field.[2]

"The Black Flag order of the Confederacy [i.e., on the execution of prisoners] was a godsend to the colored regiments," recalled the commander of the 2nd Kansas (Colored) Volunteer Infantry. "Every officer and every soldier knew that it meant the bayonet, with no quarter, whenever and wherever they met the enemy." "The officers of the colored regiments at this time had every incentive to do the utmost within their power to make the men good soldiers," wrote one such officer. "Their own personal safety was dependent on the fighting qualities of their men, more than in white regiments."[3]

By mid-1863 the Lincoln administration felt it could no longer be silent in the face of unanswered Confederate threats that jeopardized the recruitment process. In a July 31 proclamation, the President vowed "that for every soldier of the United States killed in violation of the laws of war, a rebel soldier shall be executed; and for every one enslaved by the enemy or sold into slavery, a rebel soldier shall be placed at hard labor on the public works, and continued at such labor until the other shall be released and receive the treatment due to a prisoner of war." A rhetorical balance of terror had at last been achieved.[4]

The actual practice of Confederate forces in the field was considerably less extreme than advocated by the directives spilling out of Richmond. Captured white officers from black regiments were for the most part handled as prisoners of war, though sometimes as second-class ones. Efforts were made to return ex-slave prisoners to their owners, though it remains unclear how often this happened or how many men were affected. Perhaps the most tragic fate awaited free blacks captured in arms, a group that was usually held apart from exchanges.

Southern refusals to treat captured black soldiers as prisoners of war contributed to the breakdown of the prisoner-exchange system in 1863. The arrangement had worked well enough at first, following protocols established in a cartel negotiated in 1862, but when Confederate officials began to omit blacks from their exchange lists, Union officals had to confront the matter. Secretary of War Edwin

Stanton succinctly summarized the matter in a memorandum dated November 17, 1863:

> It is known that the rebels will exchange man for man and officer for officer, except blacks and officers in command of black troops. These they absolutely refuse to exchange. This is the point on which the whole matter hinges. Exchanging man for man and officer for officer, with the exception the rebels make, is a substantial abandonment of the colored troops and their officers to their fate, and would be a shameful dishonor to the Government bound to protect them. When they agree to exchange all alike there will be no difficulty.[5]

The two parties remained divided on this issue until well into 1864. In the interim, thousands of captured soldiers on both sides languished in inadequate prison camps.

Ironically, the "power of fear" used by Southern whites now turned against them. The nightmare image of armed black men began to dominate their thoughts and the way they viewed their once-secure world. An observer writing from Selma, Alabama, in July 1863 noted that the notion of "the 'faithful slave' is about played out. They are the most treacherous, brutal, and ungrateful race on the globe."[6]

Chapter Three

"The Old Flag Never Touched the Ground"

————◦◦◦————

Two strains of sturdy New England lineage crossed briefly on July 4, 1863, in the South Carolina coastal village of Beaufort. One man was infused with a certainty of purpose akin to religious conviction; the other was driven by a nagging sense of duty and a tragic sense of self-destiny. Both men were products of New England's intellectual hothouse. The writings of Emerson, Hawthorne, and Thoreau were not unknown to them, nor were the fiery antislavery sentiments of William Lloyd Garrison and Wendell Phillips. For one of these two, the abolitionist message was the stuff of crusade; for the other, it was a troubling tug on the conscience.

Each had seen more of the world than most Americans, but both had stepped forward when civil war erupted. Thomas Wentworth Higginson was forty, Robert Gould Shaw twenty-six. Colonel Higginson commanded an outfit of former slaves, the 1st Regiment South Carolina Infantry (A.D.), while Colonel Shaw led a unit consisting largely of northern free blacks, the 54th Regiment Massachusetts Infantry (Colored).

Whereas Higginson's unit was based near Beaufort, Shaw's was only stopping there on its way to Georgia's St. Simon's Island. The two men met by chance and had dinner together. Shaw instantly sensed the zealot in Higginson, later writing, "I never saw any one

63

who put his whole soul into his work as he does." Higginson, for his part, observed, "I should have known Shaw anywhere by his resemblance to his kindred, nor did it take long to perceive that he shared their habitual truthfulness and courage." Shaw was equally taken with his like-spirited fellow New Englander: "I was very much impressed with his open-heartedness & purity of character," he declared.[1]

Differing experiences put a gulf between the two. Higginson had been with his regiment since late 1862 and had led it on a number of operations; Shaw's men had yet to see any action at all, a prospect that left doubts in the young colonel's mind. "For instance," related Higginson,

> *he admitted the mere matter of courage to be settled, as regarded the colored troops, and his whole solicitude bore on this point,—Would they do as well in line-of-battle as they had already done in more irregular service, and on picket and guard duty? Of this I had, of course, no doubt, nor, I think, had he; though I remember his saying something about the possibility of putting them between two fires in case of need, and so cutting off their retreat. I should never have thought of such a project, but I could not have expected him to trust them as I did, until he had been actually under fire with them.[2]*

The two parted, never again to meet. For one, the path of military service with black troops would bring wide recognition in life, but obscurity afterward; for the other, the same path would lead to immortality.

Occupation of Jacksonville, Florida, March 10–30, 1863

All day Sunday, March 8, the steamers *Boston* and *Burnside* lay anchored at the mouth of the St. John's River, awaiting the arrival of the armed transport *John Adams* to proceed inland. On board the two vessels were nearly a thousand men of the 1st and 2nd Regiments South Carolina Infantry (A.D.), as well as muskets for as many more again. The pause in the operation injected a dull interlude into what had been a steady build-up of tension for Colonel Thomas W. Higginson. Only three days earlier, he had received orders to capture

Jacksonville, direct from Brigadier General Rufus Saxton, Military Governor, Department of the South, headquartered at Beaufort.

Saxton had "reliable information that there are large numbers of able-bodied negroes in that vicinity who are watching for an opportunity to join us." Further, he was confident that the "entire State of

Florida can be rescued from the enemy, and an asylum established for persons from other States who are freed from bondage by the proclamation of freedom, from which they can never be driven."[3]

While waiting for the *Adams* to arrive, Higginson spent part of the time gazing across the "sultry mouth of that glassy river," watching the antics of the great pelicans and examining the bodies of those birds shot by his equally bored soldiers. His regiment had accreted around the nucleus of the sole company that remained when David Hunter terminated his experiment in black recruitment. Higginson, whose abolitionist credentials were beyond question, had been helping to organize a volunteer white company when Saxton offered him the newly re-formed 1st South Carolina. After some soul-searching, the young captain accepted and joined his regiment in November 1862.

Higginson would never forget his first impressions of his new command: "They looked black enough to satisfy the most exacting abolitionist; there seemed hardly a mulatto among them, and these were, indeed, scarce in the regiment." A student of the history of slave insurrections, Higginson asked his men why there had been so few such rebellions in the South. "They always made the same answer," he remembered, "that they had neither the knowledge, nor the weapons, nor the mutual confidence to make any such attempt successful."[4]

"It needs but a few days to show the absurdity of distrusting the military availability of these people," he wrote shortly after taking charge. "To learn drill, one does not want a set of college professors; one wants a squad of eager, active, pliant school-boys; and the more childlike these pupils are the better. . . . They are simple, docile, and affectionate almost to the point of absurdity." Prior to this Florida expedition, Higginson had led detachments in small-scale raids along South Carolina's coastal rivers; now he and the full regiment were embarked on an expedition of considerably greater magnitude.[5]

The *John Adams* arrived late on Monday, March 9. At 2:00 A.M. on March 10, the flotilla moved up the St. John's toward Jacksonville. Also along were the *Norwich* and the *Uncas*, a pair of small U.S. Navy gunboats detached from blockade duties. The enlarged expedition reached Jacksonville at 8:00 A.M.

This was the third time Union forces had entered the city, but the first for African American troops. The black soldiers came ashore at both the upper and the lower ends of the town: Higginson led a party of the 1st onto the upper wharf, while Colonel James Montgomery and his men from the 2nd took the lower one. Wrote a correspondent,

> Col. Higginson jumped ashore, followed by Capt. [George] Dolly's company—the men scrambling off as best they could, neglecting, in their eagerness, to avail themselves of the gang-plank. They immediately formed in marching order, and started on the double quick for the railroad depot. The remainder of the force soon followed, part of it advancing to the outskirts of the town and blocking all approaches. This movement was executed with such promptness that the first knowledge of the invasion only came to the townspeople when they saw the black soldiers marching past their dwellings.

Recalled Higginson, "The pretty town was our own without a shot." There was a slight skirmish involving one of the gunboats later that day at the edge of Jacksonville, but a few shells fired in the general direction of the Rebels served to quiet them down.[6]

A black woman named Susie King, who traveled with the 1st South Carolina as its laundress, was present on the second day of the occupation when a Confederate force estimated at five hundred men tested the black soldiers. According to King, several Federals were wounded or killed in an ambush by a group of whites in blackface. Also this day, a large detachment of mounted Southerners encountered some 250 men from the 2nd South Carolina, who, wrote a reporter, unleashed a "volley which threw them into confusion, and [the Federals] immediately advanced upon their disordered ranks before they had time to recover."[7]

Higginson quickly set about improving the town's defenses. Streets were barricaded, pickets were regularly rotated to suggest there were a great many troops on hand, and the little gunboats were kept on visible patrols. One particular incident gave Higginson a profound insight into the racial tensions that existed in the South. As he recalled it, "The spot was pointed out to me where two of our leading men had seen their brothers hanged by Lynch law; many of them had private wrongs to avenge." Susie King soon discovered that Jacksonville's white residents "were bitterly against our people and had no mercy or sympathy for us." On March 17, Higginson agreed to allow women and children to evacuate the town if they so wished.[8]

As the occupation continued, Higginson found himself on the horns of a dilemma. His recruitment efforts had so far been unsuccessful because virtually all the able-bodied black men in town had been run off into the countryside by their owners. With only a thousand men on hand, he was unable to follow them into the interior, and each day brought fresh casualties. On March 18, some members of Company K of the 1st South Carolina were surprised by a party of Rebels. "Although this had been the first fire that many of them had ever been under, not a man flinched but returned the fire with the coolness of veteran soldiers," noted a company officer.[9]

On March 20, the 6th Connecticut arrived to reinforce Higginson's command, followed two days later by detachments from the 8th Maine. "This increased my command to four regiments," Higginson later wrote. "Skirmishing had almost ceased. . . . We were safe from any attack by a small force. . . . All looked bright." When a Federal chaplain offered Sabbath services, the large congregation consisted of "white and black soldiers, navy and army officers and civilians." March 23 marked the arrival of Colonel John D. Rust of the 8th Maine, who assumed overall command.[10]

That same day, the Confederates began shelling the town with a thirty-two-pounder rifled cannon mounted on a railroad car that had been moved within range along the Atlantic and Gulf Central tracks. The slow bombardment continued for twenty-four hours. A few buildings were struck, and some civilians were frightened, but no one was injured. In one of the lighter moments of the whole affair, Higginson led two hundred men out to capture what had been reported to be a Rebel camp of twenty-two tents. Upon close approach, however, it was found instead to be "a solitary farmhouse,—where the family-washing had been hung out to dry!"[11]

March 25 brought an action of considerably greater scale and symbolism as Higginson led a reconnaissance force west of Jacksonville along the railroad to Four-mile Station. His command consisted of five companies from the 8th Maine, four from the 6th Connecticut, and a portion of the 1st South Carolina. As they left the town limits, the regiments deployed with the 8th on the right, the 6th on the left, and the 1st in between. The Federals brought a surprise with them—a ten-pound Parrott cannon mounted on a handcar.

Higginson was exhilarated. "The mounted Rebel pickets retired before us through the woods, keeping usually beyond range of the skirmishers, who in a long line—white, black, white—were deployed transversely," he remembered. "For the first time I saw the two colors fairly alternate on the military chessboard; it had been the object of much labor and many dreams, and I liked the pattern at last."[12]

The units halted at a railroad bridge near Four-mile Station. Some of the soldiers began destroying the structure, while others wrecked sections of the track bed. By now the Rebels had hustled up their railroad gun. "Suddenly there came a sharp puff of . . . smoke that seemed like a forked tongue," observed Higginson, "and then a hollow report, and we could see a great black projectile hurled into the air, and falling a quarter of a mile away from us." The shell caused some casualties in the 8th Maine. The Yankee gun returned fire, the smaller-caliber Federal piece barking its defiance of the deeper-throated Confederate weapon. The men quickly adapted to the enemy's cannon, and in the 1st South Carolina at least, the soldiers "shouted with childish delight over every explosion." The Union men now began to fall back, ripping up track as they went, so that the pursing Rebel railroad gun soon ran out of rail. Higginson's expedition returned to Jacksonville without further incident.[13]

The presence of so many African American troops in such a large Southern town did not go unnoticed throughout the Confederacy. A writer for the *Savannah Republican* took a bellicose posture, noting, "We only hope that the enemy will take it into their heads to concentrate their entire force of 'American citizens of African descent' at Jacksonville. . . . [Their owners] will then have some prospect of recovering their stolen property, provided they can be got far enough from the gun-boats to be caught. The idea of their doing any serious fighting against white men is simply ridiculous."[14]

A day after Higginson's action, Colonel Montgomery led a riverborne raiding party to the town of Palatka. He met with slight opposition and returned the same evening with $3,000 worth of confiscated cotton and thirty recruits for his regiment. Colonel Higginson was busily preparing further inland raids when orders came, on March 28, to evacuate all the troops to Hilton Head. It was a doleful procession that took to the boats on the morning of March 29; in addition to the soldiers, there were some fifty Unionist families that, having openly declared their allegiance during the occupation, now faced retribution. Also coming, recalled a white soldier, were "large numbers of negroes . . . fearing to be left behind."[15]

"While the evacuation was taking place several fires were lit," reported Colonel Rust, "a portion of them undoubtedly by secessionists; these fires were not confined to the lines of any regiment." "The Sixth Connecticut charge it upon the Eighth Maine and the Eighth Maine hurl it back upon the Sixth Connecticut," noted a correspondent. One of the Maine soldiers, pausing in the town to accomplish a little selective looting, saw "some negro troops setting fires and from their songs and shouting they appeared to be having a good time." Although Colonel Higginson eloquently denied that his troops took part in the conflagration, it is a difficult claim to sustain: at least one company of the 1st South Carolina came from Florida, and within the slave culture, arson was such a common form of resistance that many antebellum Southern criminal codes mandated a death sentence for the crime. It stretches credulity to imagine that none—particularly among those with "private wrongs to avenge"—would have resorted to the torch. Higginson did later admit that some of his men "were excited by the spectacle, and sang and exhorted without ceasing."[16]

The fruits of this expedition were considerably more meager than General Saxton had anticipated. It appears that the Federal haul of recruits was less than fifty, with the expedition itself costing around ten killed and perhaps twice that many wounded. Nevertheless, Higginson believed that the 1st South Carolina's performance represented a turning point for black military units:

There is no doubt that for many months the fate of the whole movement for Colored soldiers rested on the behavior of this one regiment. A mutiny, an extensive desertion, an act of severe discipline, a Bull Run panic, a simple defeat, might have blasted the whole movement for arming the blacks. . . . Col. [Milton B.] Littlefield says that [Treasury] Secretary [Salmon P.] Chase told him the Cabinet at Washington kept their whole action in regard to enlisting colored troops waiting to hear from us in Florida, and when the capture of Jacksonville was known, the whole question was regarded as settled, the policy avowed, and Adjutant General [Lorenzo] Thomas sent out on his mission. This is, I think, the best expression of the importance of our action that has yet occurred.[17]

Assault on Fort Wagner,* South Carolina, July 18, 1863

The 54th Regiment Massachusetts Infantry (Colored) was a unit touched by destiny. "Every black man and woman," declared the *Anglo-African,* "feels a special interest in the success of this regiment." It was the creation of the Bay State's fervent abolitionist governor, John A. Andrew, who, after receiving the authorization to raise a black regiment on January 15, 1863, immediately sought out the best and brightest young Massachusetts men (white, of course) to command it. In a January 30 letter to a parent of one of those candidates, Andrew made it clear that the 54th would be no ordinary outfit:

> I am about to raise a Colored Regiment in Massachusetts. This I cannot but regard as perhaps the most important corps to be organized during the whole war . . . ; and therefore I am very anxious to organize it . . . [as] a model for all future Colored Regiments. I am desirous to have for its officers, . . . young men of military experience, of firm Anti-Slavery principles, ambitious, superior to a vulgar contempt of color, and having faith in the capacity of Colored men for military service.[18]

Andrew's letter was addressed to Francis G. Shaw, whose son, Robert, was a captain in the 2nd Massachusetts. Andrew wanted young Shaw to be colonel of the 54th, fully foreseeing the manifold weights that would come to rest on his shoulders. "With my deep conviction of the importance of this undertaking in view of the fact that it will be the first Colored Regiment to be raised in the Free States, and that its success or failure will go far to elevate or to depress the estimation in which the character of the Colored Americans will be held throughout the World, the command of such a Regiment seems to me to be a high object of ambition for any officer," Andrew declared.[19]

---

*Technically, the design of Wagner was that of a battery and not that of a fort. A fort is defended on all sides, while Wagner's plans specified a low-lying breastwork for the rear wall. Although it is referred to in almost every Southern account as Battery Wagner, I have opted to use the designation of Fort, which predominates in the Union texts.

Robert Gould Shaw initially rejected Andrew's offer. "If I had taken it," he explained to his sister, "it would only have been from a sense of duty; for it would have been anything but an agreeable task." But after a few days' reflection, he changed his mind. The more he thought about it, the more convinced he became that the "undertaking will not meet with so much opposition as was at first supposed." Shaw had also warmed to the higher purpose of the whole enterprise—"to prove that a negro can be made a good soldier."[20]

Since the small black population of Massachusetts could not of itself fill the 54th's ranks, a phalanx of dedicated recruiters spread throughout the North to help realize the governor's dream. Working under the direction of abolitionist George L. Stearns, this group included Frederick Douglass, who proclaimed, "Action! Action! not criticism, is the plain duty of this hour. Words are now useful only as they stimulate to blows." Fitting deed to word, his two sons, Charles and Lewis, were the first to enlist from New York.[21]

The 54th Massachusetts took shape at Camp Meigs, in the town of Readville, outside of Boston. Many who enlisted felt an enthusiasm akin to that at the start of a crusade. A black cabinetmaker from Philadelphia named George E. Stephens observed in a letter to the *Anglo-African* that the 54th would "reflect honor to our race, and . . . has become the representative of men of color in the North." James Henry Gooding, recruited from a New England whaler, wrote to the *New Bedford Mercury* in early March to assert, "Our people must know that if they are ever to attain to any position in the eyes of the civilized world, they must forgo comfort, love, fear, and above all, superstition, and fight for it. . . . Consider that on this continent, at least, their race and name will be totally obliterated unless they put forth some effort now to save themselves."[22]

On May 28, the full regiment marched through Boston on its way to the steamships that would carry it to the front. "All along the route," recalled an officer with the regiment, "the sidewalks, windows, and balconies were thronged with spectators, and the appearance of the regiment caused repeated cheers and waving of flags and handkerchiefs." After stopping briefly at Hilton Head and Beaufort, South Carolina, the 54th sailed south to St. Simon's Island, where Colonel Shaw reported to Colonel James Montgomery.[23]

A graduate of the Kansas school of jayhawking, Montgomery embraced "conceptions of foraging," according to Thomas W. Higginson, that were "rather more Western and liberal than mine." To Lieutenant John W. M. Appleton of the 54th, he was "not a soldierly looking man, but very pleasant and easily approached." His discipline could be severe: on one occasion, Appleton recalled, a black deserter was tried by Montgomery, found guilty, and shot two hours later. For his part, Shaw, while greatly admiring both Montgomery's energy and his utter devotion to the cause, decried his terrorist methods. "He never drinks, smokes or swears," wrote Shaw, "& considers that praying, shooting, burning and hanging are the true means to put down the Rebellion."[24]

Shaw got a bitter taste of Montgomery's war-making on June 11, when he took eight companies of the 54th on a raid with the 2nd Regiment South Carolina Infantry (A.D.) to the river town of Darien, Georgia. "The 2nd South Carolina were the first to land and the 54th followed," recorded Sergeant Stephens for the *Anglo-African.* "Cattle, sheep, pigs, poultry, and many things of use and comfort were secured. One rebel was killed by a shell, and the only persons we saw were one old colored woman and two whites, who requested to be left behind. When we left at sundown the whole town was enveloped in flames." "The town of Darien is now no more," Corporal Gooding told the *New Bedford Mercury.* "The flames could be distinctly seen from the camp on the Island from three o'clock in the afternoon till daylight the next morning."[25]

Shaw was appalled by Montgomery's savagery in torching the town, and felt that the honor of the 54th had been sullied by its association in the affair. "The reasons he gave me for destroying Darien were, that the Southerners must be made to feel that this was a real war, and that they were to be swept away by the hand of God, like the Jews of old," Shaw wrote after returning to St. Simon's. "In theory, it may seem all right to some, but when it comes to being made the instrument of the Lord's vengeance, I myself don't like it." Even though he liked Montogmery personally and even admired him, Shaw vowed that if he was sent on another such expedition, he would "refuse to obey his orders in that respect."[26]

On July 8, the 54th was told to prepare for rapid movement. By the next day, the regiment was anchored off Folly Island, South Carolina, where it joined the effort to capture Charleston under Brigadier General Quincy A. Gillmore. After a number of naval and army units moved up the Stono River on June 9 to threaten Confederate positions on James Island, Gillmore launched his main thrust on June 10, sending twenty-five hundred men from Folly Island to attack the Rebel-held Morris Island, which controlled the entrance to Charleston Harbor. Gillmore's troops cleared the lower end of the island in a day of sharp fighting; all that prevented a complete conquest was a sand-and-log fortification that stretched across the island's narrow northern end. Originally known as the Neck Battery, it had been renamed in late 1862 to honor Lieutenant Colonel Thomas M. Wagner, killed defending Charleston. What the Rebels called Battery Wagner would have to be taken before Gillmore could control Morris Island.

Following the successes of July 10, no one on Gillmore's staff imagined that Wagner would be able to stand up against an attack made the next day by three regiments. When the Federals charged forward, however, they found Wagner's defenses ready. Of the 185 men in the leading Union unit, only eighty-eight were on hand when the roll was called afterward, and the Confederate flag still waved defiantly above Wagner's ramparts. General Gillmore, a devout believer in the power of artillery, immediately laid plans for a bombardment that he confidently expected would pound the battery into impotence. He predicted that when ground troops next approached Wagner, they would merely be handling mop-up operations.

It was around noon on July 11 when the 54th finally came off its transports to join the forces operating on James Island, now in position on the island's southwestern corner. An armed camp had been established on Sol Legare's Island, which was immediately adjacent to James Island and linked to it by Rivers and Grimball's causeways. On the evening of July 15, the picket line covering these crossings was taken over by the 54th Massachusetts. The men filed into position along the marshlands that separated the islands, unaware that the Confederates were planning a counterstroke aimed at capturing the 10th Connecticut, now posted in an exposed camp near Grimball's Landing.

Three companies of the 54th were picketing on the morning of July 16 when three hundred Confederate troops came storming across Rivers Causeway. Bitter fighting ensued as the Rebels, some yelling that they would take no prisoners, overran several outposts. Sergeant Joseph D. Wilson of Company H, who had often vowed to

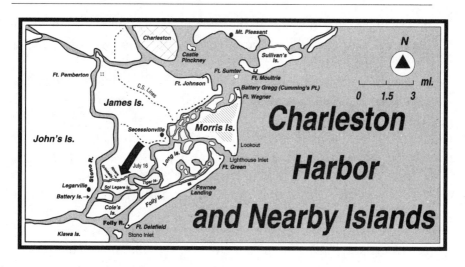

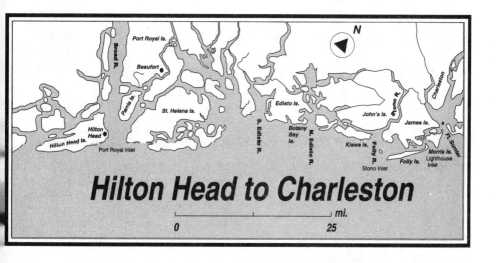

his comrades that he would never be taken alive, was true to his word. Another sergeant, Peter Vogelsang, was cornered and shot in the chest by a Rebel officer who would not let him surrender. Captain Cabot J. Russel was saved from a sword-wielding rider when Private Preston Williams parried the stroke and shot the man. Although pressed back by sheer force of numbers, Shaw's three companies bought enough time for the 10th Connecticut to withdraw to a point of safety, and for the rest of the Union force to turn out. Once the Confederates realized that the prize was gone, they withdrew across Grimball's Causeway.

For the first time in the Charleston campaign, black troops had fought white, and white anger knew no bounds. According to a South Carolina surgeon who was present, several blacks were "literally shot down while on their knees begging for quarter and mercy." A Charleston reporter accompanying the expedition mused that it was a "nice question whether [the blacks] are to be regarded as belligerents or outlaws." Several members of the 54th who fell into the enemy's hands were later found either bound and shot or bayoneted. In his next letter to the *New Bedford Mercury,* Corporal Gooding declared proudly, "We did our duty as men should." Losses in the 54th were fourteen killed, eighteen wounded, and thirteen missing.[27]

By now, word had reached the 54th of the failed assault on Wagner. Talking on the night of July 16 with his second-in-command, Lieutenant Colonel Edward N. Hallowell, Robert Shaw said he would volunteer the 54th to lead if there should be another assault. He also confessed to having a presentiment that he would fall in the regiment's first major action. When Hallowell urged Shaw to shake off the feeling, the young colonel replied, "I will try."[28]

At 9:00 P.M. on July 16, the men and officers of the 54th Massachusetts were lined up in marching order. In the midst of a lightning storm and heavy rain, the soldiers moved out, following a route marked for them by military engineers. They passed through wet, wooded lanes; crossed marshes on narrow, mud-slicked footbridges; and slogged through huge pools of heavy mud. At about 5:00 A.M. on July 17, they halted, directly across from Folly Island. The storm had passed, and the day was hot; there was little cover for the men, and promised rations did not appear.

Here the soldiers remained until evening, when, once more in the rain, they were ordered to board the transport *General Hunter.* Lacking a wharf, the troops were ferried to the vessel in longboats, thirty men at a time. Finally, at 9:00 A.M. on July 18, the steamer reached Pawnee Landing on Folly Island. "Officers and men were cheerful," noted Lieutenant Appleton. "Colonel Shaw and his staff sat on a stretcher. A few officers were grouped on a couple of rubber blankets and the men lounged in a long irregular line." According to Captain

Luis F. Emilio, "Firing at the front had been heard from early morning, which toward noon was observed to have risen into a heavy cannonade."[29]

Brigadier General Quincy Gillmore brought every possible gun into action against Wagner. His engineers had placed four batteries on the Union-controlled end of Morris Island, holding fourteen siege mortars, eleven 4.2-inch Parrotts, six three-inch Parrotts, four three-inch ordnance rifles, and two twelve-pounders. Gilmore also pressed the U.S. Navy into service, meeting with Rear Admiral John A. Dahlgren, who agreed to an all-out effort. "I thought the General not too sanguine," Dahlgren recalled, "and he added that he depended on my vessels." The naval officer provided the bombardment power of five monitors and the ironclad frigate *New Ironsides*.[30]

The land artillery began firing at 9:00 A.M., joined ninety minutes later by the navy's guns. To anyone watching the torrent of ordnance delivered on the target, Gillmore's earlier confidence would not have seemed misplaced. Large gouts of sand rose in the air from direct hits, a latticework of craters spread across the facing slopes of the earthwork, and the explosions of shells landing within the enclosure seemed almost continuous. It did not appear possible that anyone could survive the bombardment.

Gillmore's previous success had been against the masonry walls of Fort Pulaski, outside Savannah, Georgia, where his heavy guns had shattered the stonework into deadly fragments. Here, however, the sand-and-log construction of Wagner dissipated the force of the explosions and limited the damage. A few guns were dismounted, and all wooden structures were swept away, but most of the garrison was safely, if uncomfortably, crammed into a sunken shelter or bombproof. Of the approximately 1,620 men stationed in Wagner, only eight were killed during the cannonade, and twenty wounded. As per Gillmore's plan, the barrage ended shortly after sunset. Once the Federal bombardment had lifted, Wagner's defenders came to life: artillerymen scraped sand away from their pieces and loaded them with canister—deadly antipersonnel rounds that scattered golf-ball-sized lead pellets like a shotgun blast—while infantrymen took up firing positions along the parapets. Well before the first columns of Union troops appeared before Rebel Wagner, its defenders were set to meet them.

After landing on Folly Island, the men of the 54th marched until they reached Lighthouse Inlet. Late in the day, the regiment was ferried across the inlet and assembled on Morris Island at 5:00 P.M. to await orders. Colonel Shaw learned that one of his long-standing requests had been granted: the 54th was to be temporarily attached to a front-line brigade in Brigadier General Truman Seymour's division, commanded by an officer whom Shaw greatly admired, Brigadier General George C. Strong. Shaw hurried to Strong's headquarters, where he was informed that an attack on Wagner would take place in just a few hours. "You may lead the column, if you say 'yes,'" Strong told Shaw. "Your men, I know, are worn out, but do as you choose." Shaw turned to his adjutant with instructions for Lieutenant Colonel Hallowell to bring up the 54th.[31]

Controversy surrounds the selection of the 54th Massachusetts to lead the Wagner assault. A *New York Tribune* correspondent later testified that he personally overheard Generals Gillmore and Seymour discuss sacrificing the 54th in the forthcoming attack, but this story stands alone against the weight of evidence. Gillmore was confident—as events would prove, *too* confident—that the intense shelling had incapacitated the fort's defenders. As he later admitted in his official report, "The truly formidable character of Fort Wagner . . . [was] very much underestimated." Gillmore actually went so far as to suggest to Seymour that only a single brigade would be needed to occupy the fort, but the division commander opted to deploy all his units. The order in which the units would advance was left to Seymour and his brigade commanders. "It was believed that the Fifty-fourth was in every respect as efficient as any body of men," stated Seymour afterward. "It was one of the strongest and best officered, there seemed to be no good reason why it should not be selected for this advance. This point was decided by General Strong and myself."[32]

Seymour's three brigades moved into jump-off positions at dusk. Strong's brigade led the way, with the 54th forming up in an open area between the flank of the forward battery and the water's edge—perhaps sixteen hundred yards from Fort Wagner. An Ohio officer who watched the black troops dress their ranks reflected that their very presence on the battlefield symbolized the end of the Rebel way of life. Southerners, he believed, "knew that soldiers never made slaves." As the men moved up, their unfurled flags, targeted by Rebel

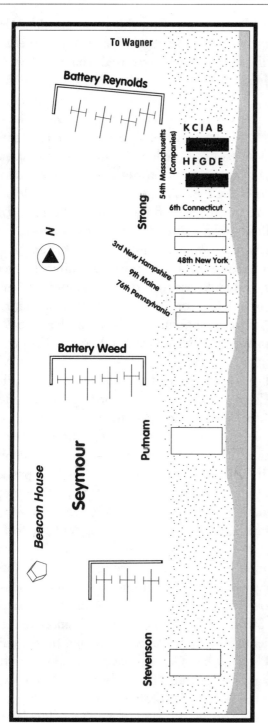

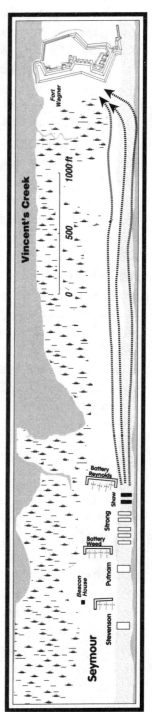

gunners on James Island, drew a few solid shots that bounded dangerously close. Instinctively the flag-bearers began to roll up the standards, until Captain William H. Simpkins realized what was happening. "Unfurl those colors!" he growled, and once more the flags shook free.[33]

The dry part of Morris Island was relatively narrow, so the deployment of the 54th took the form of two wings of two ranks apiece, the right directly in front of the left. A short distance behind the 54th were two supporting regiments, the 6th Connecticut and the 48th New York. The other regiments in Strong's brigade made up a third section of attacking troops; behind them came a brigade commanded by Colonel Haldimand S. Putnam, a combat veteran who did not share Gillmore's view that Wagner would be a pushover. "I told the general," Putnam related to one of his aides right after the meeting, "I did not think we could take the fort so, but Seymour overruled me; Seymour is a devil of a fellow for dash." To another officer, Putnam muttered darkly, "We are all going into Wagner like a flock of sheep." Behind Putnam was Brigadier General Thomas G. Stevenson's brigade.[34]

The men of the 54th were told to lie down where they were; they waited like that for perhaps thirty minutes. According to Lieutenant Garth W. James of Company C, "A long stretch of sandy beach lay between the advanced lines of Gillmore's guns and the parapets of this redoubtable fortress. . . . For . . . thirty yards or so the beach was level, then alternate drifts and mounts of sand confronted the passage onward." "I shall go in advance with the National flag," Shaw told his second-in-command. "You will keep the State flag with you; it will give the men something to rally round. We shall take the fort or die there! Good-bye!"[35]

Remembered Corporal Gooding, "Gen. Strong rode up . . . [and] asked us if we would follow him into Fort Wagner. Every man said, yes —we were ready to follow wherever we were led." Addressing the men lined up with Sergeant Stephens, Strong pointed to Wagner and said, "Take that battery." Lieutenant Appleton was standing by the color company with Colonel Shaw when General Strong stopped, pointed to the standard-bearer, and called out, "If this man should fall, who would lift the flag and carry it on?" According to Appleton, "Colonel Shaw . . . took a cigar out of his mouth, and said quietly, 'I will.'"[36]

Lieutenant James, whose brothers Henry and William were noted writers, was feeling quite keyed up. "We have the most magnificent chance to prove the value of the colored race now," he told Lieutenant Appleton. In his excitement, James accidentally discharged his revolver into the ground, drawing a baleful glare from Colonel Shaw. "I would not have had that happen for anything," James remarked sheepishly.[37]

Sergeant James C. Hewett of Company K recalled, "While lying here Captain Sim[p]kin[s] said 'Boys this flag must go in that Fort tonight; boys will you go as far as due?' The question was unanimously answered, 'Yes!'" Hewett then overheard another soldier say, "Captain if you lead us, lead us right." Sixteen-year-old Alexander H. Johnson, the regiment's drummer, later wrote that Shaw wore "a short jacket, no sash" this evening, though Captain Emilio was equally certain that "a fine narrow silk sash was wound round his waist beneath the jacket." The usually reserved Shaw was uncharacteristically emotional on this occasion. "Now I want you to prove yourselves men," he told his troops, adding that the eyes of thousands would record what they did in the attack.[38]

There was nothing fancy about the assault plan. There would be no advance parties, no subterfuge; it would be a straight-ahead charge with bayonets. The men would press forward with their guns loaded but not capped to fire—standard procedure when the desire was for the men to maintain the momentum of their rush and not pause to shoot.

It was about 7:45 P.M. when Shaw walked to the front and center of the leading wing of the 54th and called the men to attention. "Move in quick time until within a hundred yards of the fort," he said, "then double quick and charge." He then gave the order, "Forward." The double lines moved out at the prescribed speed of 110 paces per minute.[39]

Recollected Captain Emilio, "With Colonel Shaw leading, sword in hand, the long advance over three quarters of a mile of sand had begun, with wings closed up and company officers admonishing their men to preserve the alignment. Guns from Sumter, Sullivan's Island, and James Island began to play upon the regiment." Sergeant Lewis Douglass, one of Frederick's sons, advanced with Company F. He later wrote that "not a man flinched although it was a trying time. Men fell all around me. A shell would explode and clear a space of twenty feet, our men would close up again."[40]

Men staggered as they crossed through shell craters. A short distance from the eerily silent Wagner, a section of marsh narrowed the beach even further, forcing the right-hand units to swing out until they were knee-deep in the ocean, while some of those on the left had to queue and wait for space to be cleared before they could continue. Once past this choke point, the regiment was only a hundred yards from its objective. Remembered one of Wagner's defenders, "The stillness was ominous and oppressive. Then came a few stirring words, addressed by the Federal officers to the troops; they responded with loud and prolonged huzzas, and breaking into a full run they rushed gallantly upon the fort." For Sergeant Stephens, there was something curiously incongruous about this "cheering as if [we were] going on some mirthful errand." The waiting ended for both sides as the fort's defenders opened fire.[41]

Sergeant Douglass never forgot the moment when a "perfect hail of shot and shell" smashed into the men; Sergeant Stephens noted that "jets of flame darted forth from every corner and embrasure." Lieutenant James W. Grace of Company A remembered the effect of that first enemy volley, "mowing our men down by the hundreds. This caused us to fall back a little, but we soon made another rush to the works, where we received another tremendous discharge of musketry, and also grape and canister." Captain Emilio wrote that "in a moment Wagner became a mound of fire vomiting shot and shell," while Sergeant Hewett observed that the enemy's gunners and riflemen were "doing terrible execution." "Such a murderous fire I hope never to see again," exclaimed Lieutenant Richard Jewett. "It mowed down the ranks like grass before a scythe." Said Captain George Pope of Company I, "Just after . . . the Confederates opened fire . . . it was a mad rush to the fort."[42]

When Sergeant William H. Carney reached the Rebel rifle pits in front of Wagner, he found the national flag lying on the ground, its bearer shot down. Carney grabbed the colors without a thought, splashed across the moat, and began to scramble up the fort's sloping wall. The "grape, canister, and hand-grenade[s]—came in showers," he recalled. Lieutenant Appleton declared that the "shock and rattle of the canister upon the persons and arms of the men could be distinctly heard."[43]

Groups of black soldiers, no longer in any formation, somehow pushed into the battery itself. Lieutenant Appleton was among them. "Now bayonets, musket-butts, and the officers' revolvers come into

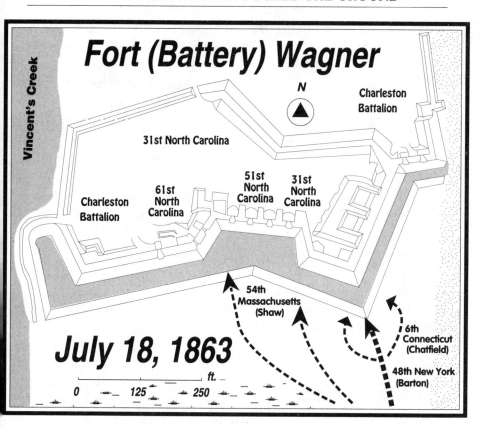

play. A mass of faces, lighted by red flashes, look up at us from the interior of the fort. Around the guns a surging, struggling mass of men are almost near enough to touch," he later recorded. Another who made it to the top of the wall was Sergeant Stephens. "Men all around me would fall and roll down the slope into the ditch," he recalled. "I had my sword-sheath blown away while on the parapet of the Fort," Lewis Douglass wrote afterward. "Swept down like chaff, still our men went on and on." Colonel Shaw stood exposed on the top of the parapet, using his sword to wave to his men to come on. Sergeant Stephens heard him call out, "Come on, men! Follow me!" Then Shaw was down, shot in the chest.[44]

"When the men saw their gallant leader fall," Corporal Gooding wrote, "they made a desperate effort to get him out, but they were either shot down, or reeled in the ditch below." Captain Emilio met one "brave fellow, with his broken arm lying across his breast," who was using his good hand to pass cartridges to an officer blazing away with a musket. Another man, "tired of the enforced combat," ignored warnings by climbing to the top of the wall, where he recklessly exposed himself. Remembered Emilio, "In a moment his dead body rolled down again." Sergeant Carney held his position on the slope of Wagner's wall, keeping the Stars and Stripes up and waving. "In this position I remained quite a while," he wrote years later, "still thinking that there were more to come, and that we had captured the fort."[45]

With officers falling all around him, command devolved to Captain Emilio. He looked into the darkness for the supporting regiments; not seeing them, he ordered a retreat, even though, as he said, "the enveloping fire was as dangerous and deadly [to retreat into] as to advance."[46]

What Emilio had missed in all the confusion was the passage of the 6th Connecticut and 48th New York, which had attacked the ocean side of the fort even as the 54th was striking the center. Here, too, the fighting was savage, with a few members of the 54th also taking part. There was a fatal delay in the time it took General Strong to lead forward the next three supporting regiments. These units were hung up at the narrow choke point, now jammed with wounded and frightened men, black and white, heading back toward the rear. Strong finally bulled his way through and brought his men to attack at the same spot the 54th had tried earlier. These troops were no more successful, however, and while organizing his men to fall back, Strong himself was badly wounded.

Captain Emilio and most of what remained of the 54th Massachusetts retreated to a "point where men were encountered singly or in small squads," and there he began to re-form the regiment. Among those passing through this makeshift line was Sergeant William H. Carney, who had been painfully wounded in the hip after saving the national flag. Carney recalled that as he reached his comrades, he "tried to hurrah; in fact, I did hurrah, and the boys hurrahed for the flag that had been brought back to them and the man that brought it. I said to them, 'Let us go back to the fort.' And the officer in charge said, 'Sergeant, you have done enough; you are badly wounded, you had better keep quiet,' or words to that effect; when I replied: 'I have only done my duty, the old flag never touched the ground.'" For his actions this day, Sergeant Carney would become the first African American soldier to be awarded the Medal of Honor.[47]

The Union tragedy this day was not over. Even as Strong's men were reeling back, Putnam's brigade came forward. Putnam had at first refused Strong's orders to advance, but then he received a command from General Seymour that he could not ignore. His four regiments formed into a great column, with Putnam on horseback leading his men toward Wagner's seaward side. Confederate artillery blasted the formation, wounding General Seymour and sending his men sprawling. The Federal tide again surged into the fort, where the fighting was now hand-to-hand. Several squads from the 54th that were still inside the fort joined in the melee. "The foe are scarce a musket's length from us," wrote Lieutenant Appleton. "They ply us with bullets and hand-grenades." Chaos reigned; at one point, a line of Federals volleyed into the black troops. Sergeant Stephens was among those who cried out, "Don't fire on us we are the Fifty-fourth." Putnam was killed as he tried to rally his men. Disorganized packets of Yankee troops continued to stumble out of the cauldron that was Fort Wagner; Sergeant Stephens staggered back with Putnam's men. "The line of retreat seemed lit with infernal fire," he recollected, "the hissing bullets and bursting shells seemed angry demons." Before being wounded, General Seymour had told Stevenson's brigade to support Putnam, but General Gillmore, suddenly apprehensive about a Rebel counterattack, canceled the orders. The assault on Wagner, which had lasted slightly more than three hours, was over.[48]

The suffering, however, was far from ended. "Dozens of our wounded were drowned," Sergeant Stephens told the *Anglo-African*. "The tide was low when we made the charge, and before we could secure our dead and wounded the tide came up, and such as could not crawl away were drowned." Others were killed when panicked ambulance drivers ran over them in the darkness. General Stevenson's men did good service by helping to retrieve some of the wounded; a few even scrambled up to Wagner's moat to succor the injured. One member of the 54th whom they could not reach was Captain Cabot J. Russel, who had been saved by Private Preston Williams on July 16.

According to a soldier in Wagner's garrison, "He was alive during the night, and frequently called for water, but died before morning." Private Williams was himself wounded.[49]

Dawn revealed a ghastly scene before Wagner. According to one survivor, "[The] dead and dying were literally piled in heaps." A Charleston newspaper claimed that the black soldiers "received no tender treatment during the skirmish," and went on to note that the "marsh in one place was thick with their dead bodies." A Rebel gunner observed that "numbers of both white and black were killed on top of our breastworks as well as inside. . . . The negroes were as fine-looking a set as I ever saw—large, strong, muscular fellows." The carnage inflicted by the artillery especially impressed a Confederate officer who viewed the mangled bodies, recording "in many instances brains here, a leg there; sometimes a head without a body and sometimes a body without a head."[50]

Six days after the assault, Corporal Gooding summarized matters for the readers of the *New Bedford Mercury*: "We have . . . learned by the flag-of-truce boat that Colonel Shaw is dead—he was buried in a trench with 45 of his men! . . . The regiment is hardly fit for service in the field at present for want of officers. Capts. [Cabot] Russell* and [William H.] Simpkins have never been heard of since the memorable night of the 18th. All the other company commanders are so severely wounded that it is feared some of them will never be able to resume the field again." The 54th lost 256 men, of whom 9 were killed, 147 wounded, and 100 missing—most of these last killed as well. Every unit involved in the attack suffered grievous casualties, for a total of 246 killed, 890 wounded, and 391 taken prisoner. General Strong, struck in the thigh by a rifle ball, was evacuated to New York City, where he died of infection on July 30. Confederate losses were much lower: 36 killed, 133 wounded, and 5 captured.[51]

Many of the injured Federals were sent to Beaufort. According to a Christian worker who was there when they arrived, "The wounded of the Fifty-fourth Massachusetts came off from the boat first; and, as those sad evidences of bravery and patriotism of the colored man passed through the lines of spectators, every heart was melted with

*i.e., Russel

tenderness and pity. We will vouch for it . . . that no word of scorn or contempt for negro soldiers will ever be heard from any who beheld that spectacle." A doctor who treated the black soldiers remembered, "The only thing that sustained us was the patient endurance of those stricken heroes lying before us, with their ghastly wounds[,] cheerful & courageous, many a poor fellow sighing that his right arm was shattered beyond hope of striking another blow for freedom!"[52]

More than any other action up to that time, the assault of the 54th Massachusetts on Fort Wagner stood as a mighty proof that the black man *would* fight. "In that terrible battle," wrote Frederick Douglass, "under the wing of night, more cavils in respect of the quality of Negro manhood were set at rest than could have been during a century of ordinary life and observation." Judge Advocate General of the U.S. Joseph Holt ventured that the "tenacious and brilliant valor displayed by troops of this race at Port Hudson, Milliken's Bend, and Fort Wagner has sufficiently demonstrated to the President and to the country the character of service of which they are capable." A Union officer in Virginia who would later enlist in a black regiment declared, "I have changed my opinion of the negroes as soldiers, since they showed themselves so efficient at the storming of Fort Wagner, and I honor any man who will take command of a body of them against all prejudice." In an editorial that appeared at war's end, the *New York Tribune* asserted,

> It is not too much to say that if this Massachusetts Fifty-fourth had faltered when its trial came, two hundred thousand colored troops for whom it was a pioneer would never have been put into the field, or would not have been put in for another year, which would have been equivalent to protracting the war in 1866. But it did not falter. It made Fort Wagner such a name to the colored race as Bunker Hill has been for ninety years to white Yankees.[53]

Young Robert Gould Shaw became the stuff of legend. His death in battle, perfectly epitomizing the ideals of selfless idealism and sacrifice, was the subject of poems by Ralph Waldo Emerson and James Russell Lowell, whose "Memoriae Positum, R.G.S." thundered:

> *Right in the van,*
> *On the red rampart's slippery swell,*
> *With heart that beat a charge, he fell*
>
> *Foeward, as fits a man;*
> *But the high soul burns on to light men's feet*
> *Where death for noble ends makes dying sweet.*[54]

Shaw's martyrdom was further enhanced when Confederate authorities refused to return his body, stating that he had been buried in a mass grave with his black enlisted men. There was open discussion throughout the North about securing Shaw's remains, but on August 24 his father ended the speculation with a public letter to General Gillmore in which he declared that a "soldier's most appropriate burial-place is on the field where he has fallen."[55]

The treatment of the black soldiers of the 54th taken prisoner in the July 16 skirmish on Sol Legare's Island and at Wagner provided a bitter coda to this action. Confederate policy stipulated that former slaves were to be returned to bondage; what was unclear was what should be done with free blacks captured in uniform. To recognize such men as soldiers was to deny everything the Confederacy proclaimed about African Americans. Languishing in harsh captivity while various branches of the South Carolina and Richmond governments batted the problem back and forth, the black POWs remained nonpersons until December 1864, when they reverted to the Confederate army. They were shipped to the military prison at Florence, South Carolina, and subsequently transferred to a series of other holding centers as Federal advances made the old ones untenable. Sometime in early March 1865, those who had survived imprisonment were at last set free.

The morning of July 19, 1863, was probably the lowest moment in the history of the 54th Massachusetts. Captain Emilio, now the senior surviving and unwounded officer, would recall that those "who had wandered to other points during the night continued to join their comrades until some four hundred men were present." Colonel Milton S. Littlefield of the as-yet-unorganized 4th Regiment South Carolina Infantry (A.D.) was temporarily assigned to command the 54th, an appointment that would last until October, when Edward N. Hallowell, wounded in the Wagner assault, returned from his convalescence to take over.[56]

Corporal Gooding spoke to the morale of the men in a letter penned on August 3. "Our boys have got over their depression of spirit somewhat, caused by the fall of so many of their companions, in the dawning of a speedy victory," he noted. "They are all in hopes of another 'good time' before going into Charleston, but they would a *leetle* rather have it on a fair field, with no odds. Charging is good when you have a fair sight; but they all agree that Wagner is a hot place."[57]

The campaign against Charleston now settled into a siege operation as General Gillmore began the tedious process of extending his entrenchments closer and closer to Wagner. In these efforts, which required much physical labor, black troops would be heavily employed. Four days after Gooding wrote his letter, Sergeant Stephens described conditions at the front for the *Anglo-African*. "This Morris Island is the most desolate heap of sand-hills I ever saw. It is so barren that you cannot find so much as a gympson weed growing. Our situation is almost unbearable. During the day the sun is intensely hot, and this makes the sand hot, so we are sandwiched between the hot sun and the hot sand."[58]

The oppressive heat was not the only danger stalking the men, however, as Corporal Gooding made clear on August 9. "The sickly season has now about commenced; daily we hear the muffled drum, accompanied by the shrill, shrieking tones of the fife, which tells us that the 'fell destroyer, Death' is near. Three times yesterday the plaintive notes . . . were played passing our camp. . . . Our own regiment, too, lost one yesterday." Each day Gillmore's siege trenches zigzagged closer and closer to Wagner; finally, on September 7, the Confederates abandoned the place, along with nearby Battery Gregg. "All hands are satisfied," declared Gooding on September 9, "and all feel that they are well repaid for disappointments and toil, and that each and every man reflect[s] credit and glory on the old flag, which waves defiantly at the gates of rebeldom."[59]

Gillmore's heavy guns now ranged freely over Charleston and against Fort Sumter, but still the proud city would not yield. Operations entered a prolonged period of stasis, as Sergeant Stephens explained to the *Anglo-African*'s readers in an October 3 letter. "The siege of Charleston drags its slow length. Morris Island can never be retaken by the enemy. Fifty thousand men could be swept away in fifty minutes by our guns. Our fatigue parties are somewhat annoyed by the rebel shells but our labor progresses. . . . The health of our regiment is bad. We average one hundred and fifty sick per day, caused no doubt by excessive fatigue duty." Added Corporal Gooding at about this time, "How long we are doomed to this monotonous state of affairs, I can't presume to say; the army has done about all in its power to do in this mode of attack on Charleston and are now putting the captured works in a state of defense."[60]

The men also faced other, unexpected dangers, as Sergeant Joseph H. Barquet related on November 18:

> One day last week, after the cold northeast wind had left us, as usual, and in duty bound as one of the fatigue, we turned up the beach to Wagner. At dinner hour we went to the well to drink, one of our men espied a bright piece of metal near the well. . . . We dug the monster out of his hiding place and it proved to be a two hundred pound torpedo [i.e., land mine], capped, cocked and loaded. For a long time, or since our possession of Wagner, hundreds of men and teams have quenched their thirst here, with no knowledge of this infernal iron devil's presence.[61]

The end of 1863 found the men of the 54th Massachusetts tested and ready. Something of their spirit was conveyed in a letter written by David Walker to the *Christian Recorder* on January 15:

> When I enlisted in this regiment it was not to secure the paltry wages that was offered, but it was that I might be one of the many that have come out to fight for the elevation of a down-trodden and oppressed race. Since then I have passed through some tight-places. . . . I felt that I was doing my duty, so I feared nothing. . . . We have shown ourselves to be men thus far, and shall always strive to do so. . . . As for myself, I am further from my home than I ever was before. When I left it was my intention to assist all I could in making a foundation for the building up of my race. . . . I cannot say where the 54th may yet go. But wherever we are, whatever may be our fate, we shall always try and be an honor to the race we represent.[62]

Interlude

"The Question of Pay"

———◦———

WHEN, on August 25, 1862, Secretary of War Edwin Stanton authorized Brigadier General Rufus Saxon to organize five thousand "volunteers of African descent," he also warranted that the men would be "entitled to and receive the same pay and rations as are allowed by law to volunteers in the service." Stanton was undoubtedly sincere in his intention, but unfortunately, he lacked the legal authority to make good on his promise. When he sought the opinion of his chief lawyer, William Whiting, the answer he got was not the one he wanted to hear. The only edict passed by Congress empowering the Secretary of War to raise black regiments was the Militia Act of July 17, 1862, which was quite specific regarding pay: it permitted recruits to receive "ten dollars per month and one ration, three dollars of which monthly pay may be in clothing." (Comparable pay for a white soldier was thirteen dollars per month, which included the three-dollar clothing allowance.) It made no difference that the act had been written with the intent to recruit army laborers, not soldiers; according to Whiting, a black man in uniform was a black man in uniform. Nor did rank affect the determination, so a sergeant was entitled to no more pay than a private.[1]

However clothed in the provisions of law, the actual implementation of this policy aroused deep and painful feelings among the ranks

91

of the newly raised black regiments. George E. Stephens, first a cook in the white 26th Pennsylvania and then a sergeant in the 54th Regiment Massachusetts Infantry (Colored), was outspoken on this issue. Writing to New York's *Anglo-African* newspaper on August 22, 1863, he reported:

> There is quite a stir in the camp of the 54th just at this moment caused by an attempt . . . to pay us off with the paltry sum of $10 per month, the amount paid to contrabands. . . . Only one company consented to take this sum. The rest of the regiment are highly incensed at the idea that after they have been enlisted as Massachusetts soldiers, and been put into the active service of the United States government, they should be paid off as the drafted ex-slaves are. The non-commissioned officers are to be paid the same as the privates.[2]

Stephens's next comment on the matter came on September 19:

> The question of pay continues to be the topic of conversation and correspondence. . . . There may be some reason for making a distinction between armed and unarmed men in the service of the government, but when the nationality of a man takes away his title to pay it becomes another thing. Suppose a regiment of Spaniards should be mustered into the service of the United States, would Congress have to pass a special law to pay Spaniards? . . . Does not the deed of muster secure the services and even life of the man mustered into the service to the government? And does not this same deed of muster give a man title to all pay and bounties awarded to soldiers bearing arms?[3]

In a personal effort to resolve this question, and after appeals to Washington had failed, Massachusetts Governor John A. Andrew convinced his legislature to make up the pay difference for the 54th and 55th Regiments Massachusetts Infantry (Colored).* However, in his humanitarian rush to right a financial wrong, Andrew overlooked the moral issue at the heart of the matter, a point not missed by Corporal James Henry Gooding of the 54th when he wrote to the *New Bedford Mercury* on November 21:

---

*In addition to these two, a black Massachusetts cavalry regiment would be organized in mid-1864.

[We are] not surprised at the solicitude of the Governor to have us paid what we have so dearly earned, nor would we be surprised if the State would cheerfully assume the burden; but the Governor's recommendation clearly shows that the General Government don't *mean* to pay us, so long as there is a loophole to get out of it, and that is what surprises us, a government that won't recognize a difference between volunteers in good faith, and a class thrown upon it by the necessities of war. . . . A man who can go on the field counts, whether he be white or black, brown or grey; and if Massachusetts don't furnish the requisite number, why she must submit to a draft. But, we as soldiers, cannot call in question the policy of the government, but as men who have families to feed, and clothe, and keep warm, we must say, that the *ten* dollars by the greatest government in the world is an unjust distinction to men who have only a black skin to merit it. To put the matter on the ground that we are not soldiers would be simply absurd, in the face of the existing facts. A soldier's pay is $13 per month, and Congress has nothing to do but to acknowledge that we *are* such —it needs no further legislation. To say even, we were *not* soldiers and pay us $20 would be injustice, for it would rob a whole race of their title to manhood.[4]

As the year 1863 ended, the pay issue remained unresolved—a simmering cauldron of distrust between the black men and the U.S. Government, which would boil over into outright mutiny in the ranks during the pivotal year of the war, 1864.

Chapter Four

"The Question That Negroes Will Fight Is Settled"

———◁◦▷———

Skirmish at Wrightsville, Pennsylvania, June 28, 1863

IT was June 1863, and the great Confederate Pennsylvania raid was under way. Spreading ahead of Robert E. Lee's men were thousands of panic-stricken refugees telling exaggerated tales of terror and mayhem. Cities not even presumed to be in danger began to mobilize. On June 15, Governor Andrew W. Curtin called "upon the people of Pennsylvania capable of bearing arms to enroll themselves in military organizations."[1]

Within two days, a company of black citizens was organized in Philadelphia and dispatched to Harrisburg, only to return not twenty-four hours later: Major General Darius Couch, a veteran rushed from the Army of the Potomac to coordinate the state's defenses, had turned them away. Although he cited a provision in the militia laws as justification, the truth was that the idea of African American soldiers had yet to be accepted by most Eastern officers. Governor Curtin was equally unhappy about the company's presence, reportedly warning the men "to keep very quiet, lest a democratic convention, then in session, should have its attention drawn to the fact of black soldiers being in town."[2]

George L. Stearns, only just appointed Recruiting Commissioner for U.S. Colored Troops in Pennsylvania, questioned Couch's decision. In response, War Secretary Stanton instructed Couch to accept all volunteer troops *"without regard to color,"* but at the same time, he cautioned Stearns not to encourage the formation of black units, as it would be "well to avoid all controversy." Nevertheless, a number of all-black companies did organize to defend the Keystone State. One came from the town of Columbia, located on the eastern bank of the Susquehanna River, some thirty-five miles south of Harrisburg. When the tocsin sounded on June 27 to summon all able-bodied citizens to arms, about 175 men turned out and formed up into four companies, three white and one black. During the night, Columbia's men marched across the great covered bridge over the Susquehanna and reported to Colonel Jacob G. Frick in Wrightsville, directly across the river.[3]

Built in 1824, the Columbia span was said to be the largest covered bridge in the world: measuring 5,620 feet from shore to shore, it was wide enough to accommodate both rail and wagon traffic. For several days now, the bridge had been choked with panicked civilians, who had to queue and wait to cross since the gatekeeper was determined to collect tolls from everyone seeking passage. Not until one of the Yankee officers charged with defending the town located the bridge company's president and persuaded him to declare a fare moratorium was the traffic jam at last cleared up.

Pennsylvania's black citizens had a powerful incentive to join the mass exodus, having learned that bands of C.S. partisan rangers, fanning out from Lee's line of march, were gathering up healthy blacks and sending them south under guard. It did not matter whether they had been born free or into slavery: the color of their skin was the sole determining factor. According to a reliable chronicler in one of the affected villages, "These poor creatures . . . sought concealment in the growing wheat fields about the town. Into these the [Rebel] cavalrymen rode in search of their prey, and many [blacks] were caught— some after a desperate chase and being fired at."[4]

Although these activities occurred without any sanction from the Confederate high command, it is difficult to believe that the hierarchy was unaware that this was happening. Fortunately, some blacks managed to escape from their captors, while others were liberated by courageous whites who boldly overpowered the guards. The evidence

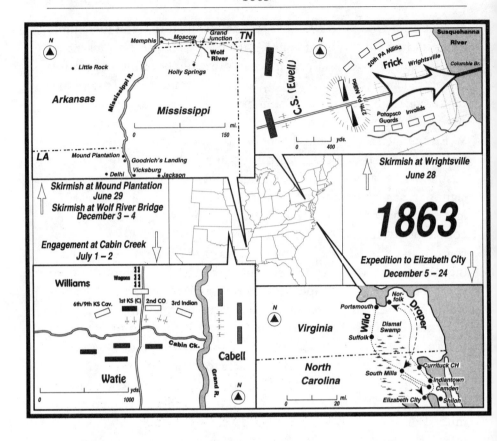

suggests that at least fifty Pennsylvania blacks were sent into slavery, an action that contributed nothing to Lee's military objectives.

Even as these depredations were taking place, Confederate Lieutenant General Richard S. Ewell's Second Corps was approaching the Susquehanna River, its target Harrisburg. One brigade was diverted and sent south to the Columbia bridge at Wrightsville, giving Colonel Frick less than a day to prepare Wrightsville's defenses. Frick selected some high ground on the main road west of the town that he thought offered defensive possibilities, but when he asked the Columbia volunteers to help dig trenches, the three white companies refused and marched home. Only the black men set down their guns and began to shovel up the dirt. They were still at it when, at 5:30 P.M. on June 28, Rebel skirmishers appeared in the distance. The blacks dropped their tools, picked up their guns, and integrated into the ranks of the 27th Pennsylvania Militia.

The Confederate commander carefully maneuvered his men into a commanding position, brought up his field pieces, and shortly after 6:00 P.M. began a slow bombardment. Special attention was paid to the entrenched strong point west of town, where one hissing shell took the head off a black minuteman posted in the hastily constructed trenches.

Realizing that his outnumbered militia stood no chance against Lee's veterans, Frick had his men retreat to the east side of the Susquehanna. Then, according to plan, he set off an explosion designed to drop just one of the bridge spans into the river. The powder ignited, but the section was only damaged, not destroyed. When the colonel ordered the blackened portion to be set afire, the flames roared out of control, and soon the entire mile-long bridge was blazing. Soldiers and civilians on both sides kept the conflagration from spreading to the shore, but the once-magnificent Columbia Bridge was a smoking ruin. After spending the night in Wrightsville, the Confederates marched off, following new orders directing them back toward Gettysburg.

It is unclear whether the Rebel brigadier intended to seize the span or to wreck it to prevent its use by Federal reinforcements, but in either case, the brief though spirited defense offered by the militiamen from York and Lancaster counties made the question moot. For once, the larger issues of racial politics fell away as black Pennsylvanians stood alongside their white neighbors to defend their homes.

In his after-action report, Colonel Frick paid tribute to these forgotten participants of the Gettysburg campaign: "Justice compels me to make mention of the excellent conduct of the company of negroes from Columbia. After working industriously in the rifle-pits all day, when the fight commenced they took their guns and stood up to their work bravely. They fell back only when ordered to do so."[5]

Skirmish at Mound Plantation, Louisiana, June 29, 1863

Nothing in the West Point curriculum had prepared Major General Ulysses S. Grant for the thorny problem he had to solve in the midst of his Vicksburg campaign. The first inklings of it came following the advance he undertook, beginning on November 2, 1862, to gain control of the crucial supply point of Grand Junction, near the Mississippi border. Grant's military operation was a success, but his movement punctured the fragile bubble of a vast system of slave-dependent plantations spread throughout the region. Suddenly, and in unprecedented numbers, whole black communities began to tramp into the Union lines seeking freedom, presenting Grant with the prospect of thousands of extra mouths to feed. "Orders of the government prohibited the expulsion of the negroes from the protection of the army, when they came in voluntarily," he later explained. "Humanity forbade allowing them to starve. . . . There was no special authority for feeding them unless they were employed as teamsters, cooks and pioneers [i.e., laborers] with the army; but only able-bodied young men were suitable for such work. . . . The plantations were all deserted, the cotton and corn were ripe: men, women and children above ten years of age could be employed in saving these crops."[6]

To put his idea into practice, Grant turned to the chaplain of an Ohio regiment, John Eaton. Before long, Eaton's first "contraband camp" was up and running. Housing was provided there, the sick were treated, and schools were established. Healthy black males were organized into work gangs to harvest the plantation crops, and paid wages that helped fund the enterprise. As Grant pressed deeper into Mississippi's cotton belt, the need for such camps increased. Further assistance came from Washington early in 1863 when Brigadier General Lorenzo Thomas arrived with full authority to "make ample provision for the negro." While Eaton remained in Tennessee to supervise his camps, Thomas operated in the new territories being opened up by Grant's men.[7]

Thomas quickly appointed three commissioners to manage the defense and day-to-day operations of abandoned plantations located along the west bank of the Mississippi River between Milliken's Bend and Lake Providence. At first, white units were deployed to protect these enclaves, but Thomas was simultaneously engaged in raising black regiments intended to fulfill that function. Among the units organized at this time was the 1st Regiment Arkansas Infantry (African Descent), whose first commander, an ardent abolitionist from New York, wrote a marching song for his men to sing to the tune of "John Brown's Body." One of its verses seemed especially pertinent:

We have done with hoeing cotton, we have done with hoeing corn,
We are colored Yankee soldiers, now, as sure as you are born;
When the masters hear us yelling, they'll think it's Gabriel's horn,
As we go marching on. [8]

Almost as soon as the companies of the 1st Arkansas (A.D.) were filled, they were posted to the various plantations along the river. On June 7, 1863, with the rest of the regiment headquartered at Goodrich's Landing, Companies E and G were sent off to Mound Plantation, so named for the large Indian-made hillock on the property. Here they remained until June 29, when circumstances thrust them into harm's way.

On that day, the defenders of Mound Plantation fell victim to yet another attempt by the head of the Rebel Trans-Mississippi Department, Lieutenant General Edmund Kirby Smith, to disrupt Grant's Vicksburg campaign. Kirby Smith saw the swath of Union-operated plantations along the western side of the Mississippi River as his best chance to cause trouble for Grant without challenging him directly, as he knew that strikes on these targets would likely not induce the Federal to alter his plans. To carry out his mission, Kirby Smith put together a combined infantry-cavalry force of about three thousand men.

Included in this raiding party was the 12th Texas Cavalry, already notorious for its harsh treatment of blacks: reports had surfaced following an 1862 raid by the regiment on a Union supply train that a number of refugee slaves traveling with the wagons had been murdered. The 12th had yet to face black troops in combat, and the officer commanding its brigade did not relish the prospect. "I would not give one of my brave men for the whole of them," he declared. [9]

On June 28, the infantry columns linked up with the cavalry brigade, and almost immediately, combat patrols began moving purposefully toward the U.S. Treasury–operated plantations. It was a black family's terror: little more than six months after joyously receiving the freedom conferred by the Emancipation Proclamation, ex-slaves were being rounded up—men, women, and children—and herded into long coffles that would eventually return them to their owners.

Early on June 29, the 12th Texas, in concert with the 19th Texas Cavalry, approached the post at Mound Plantation manned by Companies E and G of the 1st Arkansas (A.D.). One Rebel officer described it as "the most peculiar looking mound I ever saw," while another—identified for the readers of Houston's *Weekly Telegraph* only as "Soldat"—painted this word-picture of the site:

> The mound stands about the center of one of the finest plantations, several thousand acres in the heart of the most magnificent valley the world contains. It rises in a constant form to the height of about one hundred feet, and at the top is about forty feet square. On this Mound was a newly constructed fort. . . . The fort was not yet finished up on this high mound. There were two others near the base of the large one, but they were comparatively insignificant. There was dug a rifle pit some two and a half or three feet deep, with the dirt thrown up on the outside so as to form a light breastwork.[10]

The soldiers defending the mound had made their position a difficult one to assail, loosening the soil of the steep slope so that the only firm route to the top was a narrow path well covered by riflemen. Although the Federals lacked artillery, they had hauled up several large logs that could be rolled down to crush any attacking party. Most of the black troops had taken station inside this fort when the first detachments of Texas cavalry and artillery appeared at the edge of the woods, about a mile away. If the black soldiers were firm in their determination to resist, however, the same could not be said of their white officers. "Soldat" continued:

> Immediately forming the line of battle as they came out, they dashed up to the Mound. . . . At a distance of about eight hundred yards they halted, whilst the battery opened on the fort, and a body of sharpshooters was sent to occupy one of the smaller mounds. These had [exchanged] a few rounds with the garrison, when Col. [William Henry] Parsons sent up a flag demanding the unconditional surrender of the fort; and at the instant this demand was made, by his order the infantry deployed from the wood and formed line of battle ready to do his bidding. The Federal commander seeing this, and seeing himself completely in our power, surrendered on the terms that the *white officers* should be treated as prisoners of war. For the negro soldiers no reservation was made. . . . The garrison then marched down, grounded their arms, and were turned over to the infantry.[11]

After Mound Plantation, the rounding-up of black field hands and the pillaging of their homes continued until the Rebels reached Lake

Providence, where they were finally turned back by a fully aroused Federal garrison supported by gunboats. Behind the raiders, U.S. naval vessels landed troops who surveyed the destruction. According to a navy officer accompanying the soldiers, "In passing by the negro quarters on three of the burning plantations we were shocked by the sight of the charred remains of human beings. . . . No doubt they were the sick negroes whom the unscrupulous enemy were too indifferent to remove."[12]

It is estimated that some two thousand blacks were forced to march back into slavery as a result of this raid. At Mound Plantation, the 113 black soldiers and three white officers taken into captivity faced a harsh reception from the 12th and 19th Texas Cavalry regiments. "I think those with uniforms and arms should share the fate ordered by Col. Parsons when he told the boys to charge them," wrote a member of the 12th, "which was to kill them." The Texas infantry force that next took custody of the black prisoners included several units that had fought at Milliken's Bend. According to a private in the 22nd Texas, about "12 or 15" of the African American soldiers were killed before the POWs even reached the holding area.[13]

This last admission provides Southern confirmation of testimony supplied after the war by several black survivors of the ordeal. Following their capture at Mound Plantation, the prisoners were hurried off at a brutal pace, with several of their number being viciously clubbed to death when they lagged behind. Lewis Bogan, a private in the 1st Arkansas (A.D.), recalled an occasion on which the weary procession was allowed to stop "to get something to eat and the alarm was given, 'The Yankees are coming' & they started us along again and I was very tired & fell [out] & Jim [Albert, another member of the regiment,] helped me up; when one of the rebel guards, a soldier, told Jim to let go of me & another [prisoner] . . . gave out just then & they shot him." "I know we were threatened with hanging & killing every minute & we were pretty badly scared," remembered another private, Charles Bogan. Several in the regiment sustained serious injuries from other such unprovoked beatings in the course of this forced march.

Some of the soldiers vividly recalled a particularly poignant aspect of the episode. Besides the 1st Arkansas (A.D.) POWs, the ragged procession included women and children snatched from the U.S. Treasury plantations. "The rebels marched us on a run," recollected

William Harris of the regiment. "The Yankees were after us to take us back and one of the [Confederate] officers said we damned niggers never should go back alive if they could help it. They made us carry the children of the contrabands from the plantations so they would not be left in the hands of the Yankees." "They made us carry the children," seconded Lewis Bogan, "and if we gave out they would hit us with their muskets or anything they had in their hands."[14]

One of the Rebel guards, a Texas trooper in the mournful procession wending its way along the steamy dirt roads leading back toward Confederate territory, never forgot the "hushed hum of the busy voices of the men—the deep sobs of the female and childish portion of the negro captives."[15]

When the men at last arrived at the POW pens set up near Delhi, some were put to work digging fortifications, while others became cooks, and at least one was appropriated as a body servant for a Texas officer. The captured black soldiers, treated not as military prisoners but rather as runaway slaves, were scattered throughout the Trans-Mississippi, with some being sent to Shreveport, others to Little Rock, and the unluckiest among them to Texas. Those sent to prison compounds instead of labor camps suffered neglect and maltreatment. According to Private Charles Fremont, a number of his comrades froze to death in a Texas stockade in early 1864; both of Fremont's feet were severely frostbitten. William H. H. Freeman, another private, attested to the fact that the diarrhea prevalent in the camps was responsible for additional deaths.

Vicksburg surrendered to Grant on July 4, 1863. The raids ordered by Kirby Smith, devoid of any real strategic purpose, added nothing to the Confederacy's ledger save for a few thousand unfortunate human beings restored to the clutches of slavery. Yet even as the lamentations of these victims grew faint in the distance, the marching song of the 1st Arkansas (A.D.) was being adapted by new black regiments, who joined their voices to the growing chorus:

They will have to pay us wages, the wages of their sin,
They will have to bow their foreheads to their colored kith and kin,
They will have to give us house-room, or the roof shall tumble in!
As we go marching on.[16]

Skirmish near Sherwood, Missouri, May 18, 1863
Engagement at Cabin Creek, Indian Territory, July 1–2, 1863
Engagement near Honey Springs, Indian Territory, July 17, 1863

It was in the rough-and-tumble arena of the Western theater of operations that the 1st Kansas (Colored) Volunteer Infantry spent its Civil War tour of duty. There was little glory, honor, or fame to be found in the fighting here, only the certainty that the struggle would be a life-or-death contest. On January 13, 1863—less than two weeks after the rank and file had welcomed the Emancipation Proclamation—six companies of the 1st Kansas (Colored) were formally mustered into the United States service, making this the fourth black regiment to cross that barrier. It took a while longer for the 1st Kansas (Colored) to raise its remaining companies and reach full strength, but these tasks were accomplished by May 2. Almost at once, the men were marched south from Fort Scott to Baxter Springs in southeastern Kansas. Here, according to the outfit's official history, "the work of drilling the regiment was vigorously pursued."[17]

On May 18, a foraging party consisting of twenty-five men from the 1st Kansas (Colored) and twenty from the white 2nd Kansas Battery were attacked near Sherwood, Missouri. A relief force under Colonel James Williams arrived the next day. "I visited the scene of this engagement the morning after its occurrence," reported Williams, "and for the first time beheld the horrible evidences of the demoniac spirit of these rebel fiends in their treatment of our dead and wounded. Men were found with their brains beaten out with clubs, and the bloody weapons left by their sides, and their bodies most horribly mutilated." Captain John R. Graton, a line officer in the relief column, learned that a large Rebel force had been able to surprise the Federals. In a letter to his wife, he explained further, "The artillery boys and our officers, being mounted, were able to get out of the way, but the black boys being on foot had to take it, and most of them were killed."[18]

Continued Graton, "In coming to the scene of action we found eleven black boys lying where they were shot down." The bodies, earlier stripped of clothing and belongings by their killers, were laid inside a nearby house that had been abandoned by its owners and ransacked by Williams's men. A Federal patrol brought in a civilian whom someone recognized as a released prisoner from Fort Scott;

this identification, plus the newly issued U.S. Government shoes he was wearing, constituted enough evidence for Williams to condemn the man. Said Graton, "The Colonel had him marched into the house and shot, his body placed upon the pile and the house burned."[19]

On discovering that a number of local civilians had aided the Rebels, Williams "directed that the region of the country within a radius of five miles from the scene of the conflict should be devastated." "It is pretty hard," Captain Graton admitted to his wife, "but war is serious business."[20]

Along the Kansas–Indian Territory border, this war of brother against brother had taken on an unexpected dimension as different factions of the Five Civilized Nations (Seminole, Creek, Cherokee, Chickasaw, and Choctaw) chose sides. Following a bloody year of raid and counterraid in 1862, Union forces had gained enough of an upper hand by early 1863 to seize Fort Gibson, which gave them control over much of the Indian Territory. Regaining that post now became a principal objective of Confederate Trans-Mississippi strategy in the region.

Because it lay well beyond the main Federal outposts, Fort Gibson could be supplied only by wagon trains that were staged at Baxter Springs and then moved south, crossing the Broad River at a ford near Cabin Creek. The wide-open landscape made it impossible for either side to mask its intentions for very long. The Confederates, who were gathering strength just across the Arkansas River from Fort Gibson, knew when the supplies were coming, and the Federal observers could likewise detect any move to intercept them. In late June, Colonel Williams, at Baxter Springs, learning of one such impending Rebel attack, called out the 1st Kansas (Colored) and marched after the just-departed wagons. Privates Charles Clark, Samuel Moore, Randall Garland, and Andrew Sanders of the 1st Kansas (Colored) headed into this engagement under a cloud: earlier caught trying to desert, they had asked to join the expedition in hopes of mitigating their sentences.

Williams's column soon caught up with the train, which was already being guarded by the 2nd Colorado, the 3rd Indian (sent up from Fort Gibson), and companies from the 9th and 14th Kansas Cavalry regiments. As this party proceeded south, Williams was notified that the Confederates, under Cherokee Colonel Stand Watie, were waiting in a good position along the east-west-running Cabin Creek. Word also came of a second C.S. force on the eastern side of the north-south-running Grand River; only the fact that the river was running at flood levels kept the two groups from combining against the Union supply train.

Williams decided to attack the enemy units at Cabin Creek before they could be reinforced. On July 1, the 1st Kansas (Colored), backed by artillery, cleared the Rebel pickets off the creek's northern bank. Because this stream was also flowing at a high level, Williams was forced to postpone his next move until July 2, when he pushed his infantry up to the bank to occupy the enemy's full attention while he swung his cavalry around their flank. Once the troopers had splashed across, the footsoldiers pressed the whole line, forcing the Confederates to fall back. Declining to pursue them, the Federals gathered up their casualties, recorded as three killed and thirty wounded, with nine of the latter coming from the ranks of the 1st Kansas (Colored). For Privates Clark, Moore, Garland, and Sanders, the fight was a redemption: the men "behaved gallantly," reported Colonel Williams, who reduced their punishment to the loss of a month's pay plus five dollars. The extent of the Southern casualties was unknown, though as a 1st Kansas (Colored) officer noted, "A dead man or horse occasionally floated down past Ft. Gibson for several days." The supply train and its escort reached their destination on July 5.[21]

A *New York Tribune* correspondent observed that the

> rude mountain men and miners of the Second Colorado were, while on the march, inclined to sneer at the "niggers"; but now, after the exhibition they witnessed of their courage, are emulous of according them full credit. . . . One black sergeant, serving with the skirmishers, was severely wounded in the leg, a ball passing through the calf. He bound it up to stop the blood and maintained his place, loading and firing steadily, till severely wounded in the hand. Even then he did not return to camp, till, as he phrased it, "Dat da hand got so mighty stiff I'ze couldn't use it."

This was the first combat action in which the entire 1st Kansas (Colored) was engaged.[22]

Although Colonel Watie's force withdrew to the supply depot at Honey Springs, inside the Indian Territory, the Rebels were not yet ready to give up on capturing Fort Gibson. The units posted east of the Broad River, which after failing to link up with Watie had retired into Arkansas, were now directed to countermarch to rendezvous with the colonel's men at Honey Springs.

Major General James G. Blunt commanded Fort Gibson. Once he learned that the enemy's Arkansas wing was on the move, he decided to strike first, even though it would mean using flatboats to get his soldiers over the rain-swollen Arkansas River—a hair-raising prospect for the men. According to one of the teamsters involved in the operation, "The boat was an open flat with no railing around it, and some perverse mule would now and then get frightened at the water or something else, and go to backing away from the gunwale on one side and probably crowd some other mule or himself over the opposite gunwale into the water." An attempt to ford some of the wagons across cost the life of 1st Kansas (Colored) teamster Henry Sepping, who was drowned in the effort. One witness recalled that Sepping "never left his saddle-mule, and as he sunk out of sight was still jerking the lead-line to try to steer his team to the shore." Despite these setbacks, Blunt established a secure base on the southern side shortly after midnight on July 16. He had brought along all his available units, organized into two brigades. The 1st Kansas (Colored) was part of the First Brigade, which also included the 2nd Indian Regiment, a battalion of the 6th Kansas Cavalry, and some artillery —the entire force numbering about forty-five hundred men.[23]

It was just after daylight on July 17 when Blunt found the enemy (approximately three thousand strong) posted in a mile-and-a-half-long line of battle stretched across the northern side of Elk Creek, positioned to protect the Honey Springs depot in their rear. As the Federals hurried to engage the Rebels, the men passed through a heavy rain that provided many an opportunity to refill canteens that had been drained during the hard night march. The rain also soaked the gunpowder on both sides, but it was worst for those Confederates who were using an inferior Mexican mixture that the water turned into a useless paste. Blunt deployed his men along a ridge facing the enemy's line, placing the First Brigade on the Union right, with the left of the 1st Kansas (Colored) resting on the Honey Springs road. The Second Brigade made up Blunt's left flank. A teamster present recalled, "So cool and unconcerned did Blunt and his officers take it, . . . I began to doubt that there was any rebel force of consequence in front of us at all." There was such a force, however, and at around

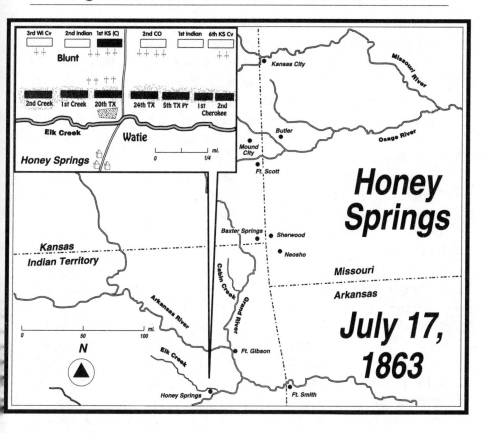

10:00 A.M., Blunt's men moved from their ridge toward Elk Creek. Before the 1st Kansas (Colored) stepped off, Colonel Williams exhorted the men, "I want you all to keep cool, and not fire until you receive the command; in all cases aim deliberately and below the waist." A teamster who tried to follow the troops with his wagon was told that a battle was coming, and warned, "Hell'll be turned loose here directly!"[24]

The combat began with skirmishing and long-distance shelling. "It was a very hot day," noted an observer, "and our soldiers had stripped themselves of everything in the way of clothing and equipment that could be dispensed with. . . . I noticed that . . . the 1st Kans. (colored—Col. Williams's), about the center of the line, had even taken off their shirts, and their black skins glistened in the sun." Then, as the Federal cannon raised their elevations, the First and Second brigades advanced. The two lines of battle now faced off in the toughest kind of Civil War combat, a steady exchange of volleys. "The rattle of musketry and artillery was incessant," Blunt wrote about this phase of the action, which lasted about two hours. Facing the black Kansas soldiers were white Texans from the 20th and 24th regiments. When Colonel Williams was seriously wounded, Lieutenant Colonel John Bowles took over the 1st Kansas (Colored).[25]

Extant sources do not agree on what happened next. An unidentified Union force (it may have been either a lost squad of cavalry or a portion of the 2nd Indian) briefly masked the front of the 1st Kansas (Colored) and then fell back. The Rebels opposite, believing it was the black regiment that was retreating, pressed forward, coming within twenty-five yards of the Federal troops before the 1st Kansas (Colored) unleashed a killing volley. This was the turning point of the fight. The Rebel regiment was shattered, and this in turn collapsed the center of the Confederate line, causing all of it to retreat. When the Union forces aggressively followed the Rebels across Elk Creek, the retirement became a rout, and the Federals soon had possession of Honey Springs, with many of its supplies intact. Some of the fleeing Rebel units spread their panic to the troops marching over from Arkansas, who consequently did an about-face. Confederate casualties were 134 killed or wounded and 47 taken prisoner; the Union loss was 17 killed and 60 wounded. The share paid by the 1st Kansas (Colored) was 2 killed and 30 wounded.

When the fighting was over, General Blunt located Colonel Williams in the field hospital. The wounded officer's first question was, "General, how did my regiment fight?" "Like veterans, most gallantly," Blunt replied. To which Williams rejoined, "I am ready to die, then." Williams's wound was not mortal, however, and he would soon be back with his men. Writing in his official report, General Blunt noted that the "First Kansas (Colored) particularly distinguished itself. . . . Their coolness and bravery I have never seen surpassed." In a private letter finished at about the same time, Blunt declared, "The question that negroes will fight is settled." A white Federal involved in the fighting made the point more colloquially when he wrote, "I never believed in niggers before, but by Jasus, they are hell for fighting."[26]

Skirmish at Wolf River Bridge, near Moscow, Tennessee, December 3–4, 1863

The "contraband camps" established in Tennessee to house the flood of slave refugees provided a ready pool for the recruitment of black troops, which began there in earnest in June 1863. During that month, two African American infantry regiments were organized at La Grange, Tennessee: the 1st and 2nd Regiments Tennessee Volunteers (African Descent).

The manner in which these men were recruited was described by an officer who would eventually command the 1st Tennessee (A.D.):

> The plan for *"persuading"* recruits while it could hardly be called the shot-gun policy was equally as convincing, and never failed to get the "recruit." The negroes were held as property by their masters, and were appropriated as such, along with mules and horses, which were put in the same list and confiscated as a "military necessity." The cavalry of the division was continually employed as scouts and skirmishers, and almost daily brought into camp hundreds of animals and negroes as spoils. The former were used in replenishing the army and increasing its effectiveness for the summer campaign, and the latter were turned over to . . . recruiting agents.[27]

Most of the men who filled the ranks of the 1st and 2nd Tennessee (A.D.) were illiterate, so there is scant primary record of their experiences. The early interactions between the white officers and black enlisted men represented a cultural shock of the first order. To white eyes, the ex-slaves were childlike, thoughtless, and primitive; social acts that in the black community had great importance seemed frivolous to the white officers, one of whom noted of the west Tennessee recruits, "Their singing, praying, and shouting in camp had to be arrested, sometimes, at the point of the bayonet."[28]

Adding to the tension was the isolation felt by many of the white officers. "To be completely ostracized by Southrons mattered little and could be endured," wrote one. "But to be slighted, snubbed, and often openly insulted by white volunteers, or censured by friends and loved ones at home, was, to say the least, very discouraging." Somehow the recruits were organized, the men drilled in the rudiments of military maneuvers, and the units put into active service. For most of those raised in Tennessee, this meant guarding strategic points, supply lines, and contraband camps.[29]

All this was a mere backdrop to larger military events in the region, climaxing November 23–25 with the breakout of the Union forces besieged at Chattanooga. Even as Southern troops retreated into Georgia, however, Confederate efforts were under way to recruit rank and file from the white populations of Tennessee and Kentucky. This assignment was handed to Major General Nathan B. Forrest, who on December 2 moved with a small body of men into west central Tennessee. To help cover the movement, Forrest's immediate superior, Major General Stephen D. Lee, led a wrecking expedition along the Memphis and Charleston Railroad. A short distance east of Moscow, Tennessee, the rail line crossed the Wolf River via a bridge deemed by Federal officials to be "a structure of much importance." Its defense was the responsibility of the 2nd Tennessee (A.D.), commanded by Colonel Frank A. Kendrick.[30]

Kendrick made preparations to meet the Rebels. His men rendered a nearby wagon bridge impassable by pulling up its floor planks and replacing them only for "legitimate and authorized crossing." At 3:00 P.M. on December 3, the pickets guarding this span were engaged by scouts from Stephen Lee's raiders, who faded away once two companies of black troops gingerly crossed the plankless structure to reinforce their comrades. Sensing that this action presaged an attack by the main body of the enemy, Kendrick kept his regiment on full alert.[31]

Help for Kendrick was on the way, in the form of a mounted brigade commanded by Colonel Edward Hatch. The 6th Illinois Cavalry was the first on the scene, reaching the bridge at 1:30 P.M., December 4. It was decided to send a reconnaissance party to investigate smoke rising over the nearby town of La Fayette, so the planks were laid to enable the 6th Illinois and a portion of the 9th Illinois cavalry to move forward. The troopers rode only a short distance toward La Fayette before stumbling into an ambush. Colonel Kendrick immediately ordered two of his black companies over the wagon bridge to occupy the rifle pits that had been dug across the road; at the same time, he sent across two more to protect the railroad span.

"Very shortly after the firing began the cavalry, which had crossed the bridge, retreated in much disorder," Kendrick later reported. "The enemy now made a desperate attempt to force a passage of the [wagon] bridge, but his impetuous charges were met by the steady and effective fire of the companies [I had] posted." Another enemy column now moved against the railroad bridge, "but all their attempts were bravely and successfully resisted." Colonel Hatch arrived with the bulk of his brigade, only to be shot and severely wounded, leaving in charge Kendrick, who promptly reinforced his black companies with white troopers armed with fast-firing breachloading carbines. The Rebels, realizing that their grab for the Wolf River bridges was destined to fail, began to withdraw at 4:10 P.M.[32]

Kendrick's losses were three killed and twelve wounded. He tallied twenty-two enemy bodies left behind, though an officer in the 2nd Tennessee (A.D.), writing the next day, claimed that the regiment had buried thirty. The same officer counted "no less than forty dead horses on the field of battle." Strategically speaking, a bridge had been saved and a Rebel raid cut short, though Forrest had been able to establish himself in Tennessee, where he would continue to gather recruits (many dragooned in a manner that was strikingly similar to the way some of the western Tennessee blacks had been "volunteered") until the pressure of converging Federal columns forced him out of the state in late December.

This little operation boosted the stature of Tennessee's black regiments. "I must say a word for the colored soldiers," wrote a 2nd Tennessee (A.D.) officer on December 5. "No troops ever fought better than that portion . . . that were engaged in yesterday's conflict." Another officer in the regiment noted that the "white troops were greatly prejudiced against the colored troops and their officers, manifestly so among the cavalry, and it continued until they saw that they would fight." On December 17, Major General Stephen A. Hurlbut, in whose Sixteenth Corps the 2nd Tennessee (A.D.) served, issued General Order Number 173, stating, "The recent affair at Moscow, Tenn., has demonstrated the fact that colored troops, properly disciplined and commanded, can and will fight well, . . . they have vindicated the wisdom of the Government in elevating the rank and file of these regiments to the position of freedmen and soldiers."[33]

Expedition to Elizabeth City, North Carolina,
December 5–24, 1863

The Emancipation Proclamation represented a radical shift in thinking that left a great many senior military men uncomfortable and unhappy. One of these was Brigadier General John G. Foster, whose Department of North Carolina included all the territory won during Burnside's 1862 expedition. Hundreds of contrabands had fled into his lines, but long after the deadline of January 1, 1863, had passed, Foster had yet to authorize the raising of any black units under his command.

Pressure to change this situation came from an unexpected quarter: Massachusetts Governor John A. Andrew. The tireless abolitionist had once before looked to the manpower in Foster's contraband camps to supply his black Massachusetts regiments, but his agents had since proved so successful in filling the ranks with Northern recruits that these ex-slaves were no longer needed for this purpose. Still, the idea of doing something important with the freedmen was never far from Andrew's thoughts.

On April 1, Andrew wrote to War Secretary Stanton to urge the "detailment of some able, brave, tried and *believing* man, as a brigadier to undertake in North Carolina the organization of the colored troops." He was confident that "2500 to 5000" men could be raised, enough for a fair-sized brigade. "But it needs a *man* always for the soul of any movement. . . . And the right man is the main point." Stanton referred Andrew's letter to General Foster, who disputed the governor's estimate; it was Foster's opinion that "not more than one Regiment . . . could be raised in this Department." He indicated that following some hit-and-run attacks by Rebel bands, he had furnished arms to small groups of blacks for self-defense, "but we found they could not be trusted in any outward movement or raid probably owing to their lack of discipline." Foster worried that any black recruitment would be "antagonistic . . . to the feelings of the white troops."[34]

John G. Foster was obviously not the right man for the job; fortunately, Andrew had someone else in mind, and he wasted no time before selling his candidate to Stanton. On April 13, the adjutant-general's office issued orders to Colonel Edward A. Wild "to raise a brigade (of four regiments) of North Carolina volunteer infantry."[35]

The man who received these orders had already paid a high price for his patriotism. While serving as a captain in the 1st Massachusetts, he had fought in the Battle of Seven Pines, where his right hand had been permanently damaged by a Rebel bullet. After recovering from his wound, Wild had helped recruit the 35th Massachusetts and become its colonel; he led that regiment at the Battle of South Mountain, during which his left arm was severely injured. Himself an experienced surgeon, Wild walked two to three miles to the field hospital, where an operation that removed his arm up to the shoulder was carried out "under his own directions."[36]

His left arm gone, his right hand crippled, Wild at first doubted his ability to command black troops. "I am not the man I was a year ago," he confessed to a friend. "Still I mean to work for my country so long as I can, and . . . do what is set before me." This can-do attitude was a strong factor in Andrew's promotion of his candidacy, but even more important were Wild's own uncompromising belief in the value of black soldiers, his deep-rooted hatred of the Confederacy, and his limitless drive to persevere in the face of all obstacles. Whether or not Stanton realized it, in sending Wild (now promoted to Brigadier General of Volunteers) to North Carolina, he was not just assigning an officer to a task; he was unleashing a volcanic presence on what had up till now been a relatively placid theater of the war.[37]

Writing to General Foster, Governor Andrew described Wild as "one of the bravest men and one of the best, most accomplished and experienced officers in the Mass. Volunteer Service." While Foster may have been alarmed by Andrew's portrayal of Wild "as a man of ideas and not simply of routine," he must have been placated by his insistence that he was also "a person of the most exemplary patience and quiet though not unenthusiastic perseverance." In announcing Wild's appointment, Foster called him a "gallant and accomplished soldier and gentleman."[38]

Soon after arriving at his new post, Wild began to reconize the immensity of his task. In addition to the challenge of raising black regiments, he was given responsibility for the contraband camps. "All seem to look to me," he complained in July. "At times when I see the weak, or the false and rotten course pursued by different provost marshals, it exasperates me so."[39]

Fortunately, Wild did not embark on this crusade without help: among those joining him was a black Massachusetts recruiter named

George N. Williams. "The 'Freedmen of African descent' in this vicinity number about ten thousand," the latter informed the readers of Philadelphia's *Christian Recorder* on May 19. "They seem to be generally intelligent, and are greatly elated at the idea of being made soldiers." In a foretaste of the problems they would face, Williams told of a black orderly given the task of watching over the baggage of officers assigned to the regiment. The young man had been abused and kicked by the white quartermaster of a Rhode Island regiment. According to Williams, "For this act [the quartermaster] . . . was arrested by General Wild himself and severely punished."[40]

Recruiting for the first regiment moved rapidly forward. In a June 6 letter to the *Christian Recorder,* Williams vowed that a "terrible blow will be struck for the Union and the rights of man by Wild's Colored Brigade, terrible to the rebels that dare destroy the rights of God and humanity." Eleven days later, he put the critical questions of the day to his readers: "Is the negro not a man? Is he not capable of bearing arms? Has he not talent? Has he not courage?" Then the day finally arrived, on June 30, when the 1st Regiment North Carolina Colored Volunteers was mustered into U.S. service, Colonel James C. Beecher commanding.[41]

At the end of July, the 1st North Carolina Colored was transferred south to take part in the siege of Charleston. There it was assigned exclusively to fatigue duty, forcing the officers to conduct their military drills in the evening, *after* the men had come off a day's laboring in the hot sun. Wild and his officers endured these conditions until September, when some of Beecher's men were ordered to clean up the camps occupied by white troops. This moved Colonel Beecher to register his anger:

> Since the commencement of the war I have never before known such duty imposed upon any Regiment. . . .
>
> They have been slaves and are just learning to be men. It is a drawback that they are regarded as, and called, "d----d niggers" by so-called "gentlemen" in the uniform of U.S. officers, but when they are set to menial work doing for white regiments what those Regiments are entitled to do for themselves, it simply throws them back where they were before and reduces them to the position of slaves again.[42]

After repeated requests, an equally disgusted General Wild was allowed to return to North Carolina in October 1863 to continue his recruiting efforts. On October 28, the 2nd Regiment North Carolina Colored Volunteers was mustered into U.S. service. Also now a part of the department were several black regiments that had been raised elsewhere under direct U.S. authority. Thus from the District of Columbia came the 1st U.S. Colored Troops (USCT), and out of Camp Delaware, Ohio, the 5th USCT; the former unit was encamped outside Portsmouth, and the latter near Norfolk. In a note written at this time and printed in the *Athens* (Ohio) *Messenger,* Sergeant Milton M. Holland of the 5th explained why he was fighting: "There is a brighter day coming for the colored man, and he must sacrifice home comforts, and his blood if necessary, to speed the coming of that glorious day."[43]

On November 11, 1863, General Foster was reassigned to the Department of the Ohio, to be replaced in the Department of North Carolina by Major General Benjamin F. Butler of Louisiana fame. Suddenly, black recruitment efforts were doubled, and within a month, Butler obtained permission from the War Department to organize an African American cavalry regiment. He also ended the static role until now assigned the black units. In early December, wanting to reestablish use of the Dismal Swamp Canal and punish Rebel guerrilla bands, he authorized Wild to undertake a major raid into North Carolina. It was understood that Wild would have a free hand "to clear the country of slaves and procure recruits for his brigade."[44]

Two converging columns set out from Portsmouth and Norfolk on December 5. The former consisted of seven hundred men from the 1st USCT and four hundred from the 2nd North Carolina Colored; the latter contained 530 men from the 5th USCT and another hundred men organized from detached units belonging to the 1st North Carolina Colored and the 55th Regiment Massachusetts Infantry (Colored). General Wild rode with the Portsmouth-based column, while the Norfolk wing marched under Colonel Alonzo G. Draper. Wild expected to be met by a pair of small canal steamers for resupply, but when he reached South Mills, he learned that they had been misdirected. "We were thus obliged to live on the country for a few days," he reported afterward, "which we did, judiciously discriminating in favor of the worst rebels." A correspondent for the *New York Times* wrote that the "inhabitants being almost exclusively 'Secesh' the colored boys were allowed to forage at will along the road."[45]

Colonel Draper rendezvoused with Wild at South Mills, and the united force then marched for Elizabeth City, reaching it on December 9 and remaining for the next seven days. None of the citizens of that area had ever seen black troops before. According to an account that appeared in the *Raleigh Journal,*

> On the streets the ladies of the place were jostled by the negro troops, and had to permit them to walk by their side and converse with them, on pain of arrest and punishment for insulting "United States troops"! Any information laid by a negro against man or woman was received as conclusive evidence and brought swift punishment upon the alleged offender.* The negro ran riot during the Yankee stay in Albemarle country.[46]

During his stopover in Elizabeth City, General Wild, as he reported, "sent out expeditions, some for guerrillas, some for forage, some for firewood, which was scarce and much needed by us. Every man was constantly employed." Enemy irregulars constantly harassed the black soldiers. "They crept upon our pickets at night, waylaid our expeditions and our cavalry scouts, firing upon us wherever they could." Undaunted, Wild met terror with terror: "Finding ordinary measures of little avail, I adopted a more rigorous style of warfare; burned their homes and barns, ate up their live stock, and took hostages from their families."[47]

In one much-talked-about incident, Wild, after what he called a "drumhead court-martial," condemned to death a straggler from a Georgia regiment named Daniel Bright, who was then forced to stand on a cider barrel with a noose around his neck. According to at least one account, Wild himself knocked out the wedge from under the barrel to hang Bright, whose body was left dangling with a placard attached that read: *This guerrilla hanged by order of Brigadier-General Wild.* Wild's action was met with grim approval on the part of his black soldiers, one of whom judged him a "noble and brave man."[48]

Wild now divided his command into several columns. While some of these went directly back into Virginia via South Mills, Colonel Draper's group was first diverted to the southeast. Draper was wise to

---

*State law throughout the antebellum South forbade slaves to testify against whites in any court trial.

the deadly ways of war in the region: at his first night camp, he carefully stoked large open fires, then quietly filed his soldiers into a nearby church, where they lay in the darkness. His caution was vindicated later that night, when a group of seventy raiders drove in his pickets and fired into the well lighted but empty camp.

Draper continued his march until he reached Shiloh, then returned north, moving along the eastern edge of the Dismal Swamp. A short distance from Indiantown, his men ran into a Rebel ambush party hidden amid the swamp's boggy fringes. "We immediately returned their fire, aiming at their smoke, as we could seldom see a man," Draper later reported. While some of his men kept the enemy occupied in front, he sent a company against each of the Confederates' flanks. Observed Sergeant Holland of the 5th USCT, "The men stood nobly and faced the cowardly foe when they were hid in the swamp firing upon them. They stood like men, and when ordered to charge, went in with a yell, and came out victorious." Added Colonel Draper, "Before we could overtake them, they had escaped into the swamp, by a path familiar to them, but at that time invisible to us." Draper's loss was three killed and eight wounded; local civilians told him that the guerrillas had lost thirteen killed or wounded.[49]

After rejoining Wild's column, the Federals learned of a guerrilla camp hidden deep in the swamp and "accessible only by means of a pathway of logs laid lengthwise for a distance of about half a mile." Several bold black soldiers picked their way along this dangerous route and burned the encampment. Wild reached Norfolk on December 23, with the last of his units coming in the next day. "Several of the white cavalry told me that no soldiers have ever done as hard marching through swamps and marshes as cheerfully as we did," said Sergeant Holland with pride, "and that if they had to follow us for any length of time it would kill their horses."[50]

In the course of this expedition, Brigadier General Wild had adopted a liberal definition of what constituted a "Rebel." Loud complaints were lodged by self-proclaimed Unionists whose property had not been spared; one testified that it was possible to "trace the track of the raid for ten miles, by the turkey buzzards, feeding on the carrion made by the destruction of animal life. Union men and widows shared the same fate [as Rebel sympathizers]; all they had was taken or destroyed."[51]

Wild's raid earned him the unmixed enmity of Confederate officials. In an open letter addressed to him and published in the *Milledgeville* (Georgia) *Southern Record,* Colonel Joel R. Griffin excoriated the Federal's actions. "Probably no expedition, during the progress of the war, has been attended with more bitter disregard for the long established usages of civilization or the dictates of humanity than your late raid into the country bordering the Albemarle," declared this officer. Then, in a chilling admission of retaliation for the execution of Daniel Bright, Griffin announced that he had hung a black soldier, "Private Samuel Jones, a private of Company B. Fifth Ohio."* Once again, both sides stood poised at the edge of the abyss, but this time it was General Butler who defused the situation by refusing Wild's request to summarily execute some hostages.[52]

Wild's raid, one of the largest in scale to that date, had proved that black units could function well under pressure. A correspondent present noted that the black soldiers were "thoroughly obedient to their officers [and] performed in the enemy's country all the duties of white soldiers—scouting, skirmishing, picket duty, guard duty, every service incident to the occupation of hostile towns, and best of all, fighting."[53]

---

*Griffin had his identification wrong; the victim was actually Private Samuel Jordan of Company D, 5th USCT.

Part Three

1864

Chapter Five

"Amid a Storm of Bullets"

——◄◦►——

Three Politicians and a General: September 1863–January 1864

THE Florida Expedition of 1864 had little if anything to do with military objectives, and everything to do with personal aspirations for the White House. One of the leading candidates seeking the 1864 Republican presidential nomination was Salmon P. Chase, a onetime Ohio governor and two-time U.S. senator who had tried and failed to secure his party's nod in 1860, then joined Lincoln's cabinet as Secretary of the Treasury. Even as he managed the nation's chaotic wartime economy with acumen, the brilliant Chase looked toward the next presidential election, when, he was certain, Lincoln would falter and the Republicans would need a new standard-bearer. Opportunities to accomplish his objectives were both found and made, and as the year 1863 began to wane, Chase found himself increasingly drawn to the possibilities offered by the situation in Florida.

Since seceding from the Union, on January 10, 1861, Florida had become something of a prize that no one wanted to keep. Early on, Federal forces had seized control of strategically important naval stations—at Fort Pickens in Pensacola Harbor, at Key West, and at Fernandina, on the eastern coast, near the Georgia border—while pretty much ignoring the rest of the state. As the focus of the war subsequently shifted to Virginia and South Carolina and along the Mississippi, most of Florida's contributions to the war effort were exported there, leaving only a small number of C.S. troops on hand to protect its residents and their property. By 1863, the state's security depended more on the enemy's lack of interest than on any force organized for its defense. This created an opening that did not escape Chase's notice.

Whenever U.S. forces took over a region that had been in rebellion, they also seized all Rebel property. Anticipating precisely this situation, Congress in 1862 had passed the Direct Tax Law, which authorized the U.S. Treasury to sell any such forfeited lands. This sinecure thus fell right into the hands of Salmon P. Chase, who was empowered to appoint Direct Tax Commissioners. Once installed, these Treasury agents wielded great power in shaping the political allegiance of a region as it moved closer and closer to rejoining the Union. This was clearly on Chase's mind when, in September 1862, he appointed the three Florida Tax Commissioners, one of whom, in any day or age, could charitably have been termed a "con man."

Lyman D. Stickney was an opportunist, an adventurer, a charmer, and a man single-mindedly dedicated to his own personal aggrandizement. A lawyer from Vermont, Stickney had arrived in Tallahassee in the winter of 1861 and soon obtained a land grant through false representations. An old sloop quickly became part of the Stickney operation; it was said that he used it simultaneously to trade with Confederates on the mainland and with U.S. officials at Key West. It was during this time that Stickney sought out Chase in Washington, claiming to be a longtime Florida Unionist anxious to advance Chase's candidacy.

Stickney became Chase's most avid Florida booster, and his optimistically inflated reports regarding the state's pro-Union sentiment provided the Treasury secretary with plenty of ammunition to push for extending Federal controls there. "I look at the war under both military and political aspects," Chase told his brother-in-law in May 1863, "and it seems to me that military occupation should immediately be followed by political reconstruction, in order to secure permanent advantages."[1]

Stickney was meanwhile also cultivating a powerful military ally in the person of Major General Quincy A. Gillmore, commanding the Department of the South. In the fall of 1863, the thirty-eight-year-old Gillmore was trying to reverse the pendulum swing of his career, which had gone from bright promise to dull disappointment in less than a year. A top West Point cadet (Class of 1849) and an elite member of the U.S. Army's engineer corps, Gillmore had stepped from the shadows of anonymity at Savannah, Georgia, on April 10, 1862. Defying common wisdom of the time, which deemed masonry forts impregnable, he had designed a bombardment plan against Confederate Fort Pulaski that would usher in an impressive new generation of artillery pieces. Using a mix of high-velocity rifled cannon and powerfully explosive conical shells, Gillmore's gunners breached Pulaski's walls after just thirty hours of sustained firing. Surrender soon followed, and Captain Gillmore became a brigadier general.

His star's rise, however, had lasted only into the summer of 1863, when he failed to break through Charleston's defenses and found himself bogged down in the painfully slow incremental advances of a siege operation. Looking to other fields for glory, Gillmore found a likely candidate in Florida, thanks in part to advice he received from Salmon P. Chase's point man for that state, Lyman Stickney. On December 11, Stickney reported to Chase the gist of a "long interview" he had had with Gillmore about plans to make Florida "a free state and forever extinguish slavery within its borders. He [Gillmore] gave his cordial assent to this proposition, said he was ready and able to redeem Florida from the rebels with Colored Troops if permitted by the Government."[2]

Three days after this talk, Gillmore presented a series of options to Major General Henry W. Halleck, General-in-Chief of U.S. Armies. After admitting that the capture of Charleston was no longer a real possibility, Gillmore suggested two better objectives in which to employ his troops: the capture of Savannah, or the invasion of Florida. The goals of the second option, according to Gillmore's note, would be to "recover the most valuable portion of that State, cut off a rich source of the enemy's supplies, and increase the number [recruited] of . . . colored troops."[3]

Halleck's reply followed on December 22. While granting Gillmore the "liberty to undertake such operations in your department as you may deem best," he cautioned him not to expect any reinforcements to help him. This did not dishearten Gillmore, who soon forgot all about Savannah. On January 11, the ubiquitous Stickney ran into him on an inspection tour at Fernandina. "He takes a lively interest in Florida affairs," Stickney promptly told Chase. "Says he will cooperate in the measures I have put in action." Following up in a February 5 letter to the Treasury secretary, Stickney (after effusively describing the formation of a "free state league, or if you please, a Chase league") added that Gillmore had given him "very strong evidence indeed that he is your friend."[4]

By now the three objectives Gillmore had presented to General Halleck for the invasion had become four. The addition, in Gillmore's words, was "to inaugurate measures for the speedy restoration of Florida to her allegiance." This added political dimension reflected the entry of a new player into the Florida game, represented at Gillmore's headquarters by John Hay, who was sporting a special commission as major. Both the rank and the assignment had been handed to Hay by his boss, President Abraham Lincoln.[5]

Characteristically, Lyman Stickney had been quick to play both sides. Still representing himself as a Florida resident of long standing, he had written Lincoln a letter urging him to grant loyal Floridians the right to vote again so that they might restore the state to the Union. "I make this request with the sincerest conviction that it will contribute much, very much to the honor and glory of your administration," wheedled Stickney.[6]

Hardly had the dust settled from a December 19 pro-Chase meeting he had organized in St. Augustine when Stickney wrote to Lincoln's private secretary, John Hay. Things were moving rapidly to a point where loyal Florida might be ready to elect representatives to Congress, Stickney told Hay, suggesting that he come down to claim the state seat. Hay discussed the matter with Lincoln, who agreed that it might not be a bad idea to have someone on the scene. According to Hay, Lincoln decided to make him a "Commissioner to go to Florida and engineer the business there." The "business," of course, was politics: Lincoln hoped to prove the viability of his Proclamation of Amnesty and Reconstruction, issued December 8, which allowed Confederate states to rejoin the Union after just 10 percent of their 1860 voters took the U.S. Oath of Allegiance.[7]

On January 13, Lincoln wrote to General Gillmore. "I understand an effort is being made by some worthy gentlemen to reconstruct a loyal State government in Florida," he said. "Florida is in your department, and it is not unlikely that you may be there in person. I have given Mr. Hay a commission of major and sent him to you. . . .

He will explain . . . my general views on the subject. It is desirable for all to co-operate; but if irreconcilable differences of opinion shall arise, you are master. I wish the thing done in the most speedy way possible."[8]

The Forces Gather: January 1–February 4, 1864

Gillmore had been quietly assembling an expeditionary force at Hilton Head, South Carolina, in anticipation of a movement south. Carrying out his intention to "redeem Florida from the rebels with Colored Troops," he included several black units in the first wave of troops to land: four of the six infantry regiments initially assigned were black, and these would be joined by a second wave of four more, three white and one African American. The black units comprised a full spectrum of experience, from raw and untried new recruits to combat-tested veterans.

Fresh to the front was the 8th USCT (United States Colored Troops), a product of Camp William Penn. This mustering and training facility, located eight miles north of Philadelphia, had been established on June 26, 1863, specifically for black infantry regiments. Its very existence represented a victory over prejudice by a number of dedicated individuals, including recruiter George L. Stearns, and by the Philadelphia Supervisory Committee for Recruiting Colored Regiments, which convinced Pennsylvania's Governor Curtin to organize black state regiments.

At the end of July 1863, the 3rd USCT became the first black regiment to "graduate" from Camp William Penn (there would be ten more). Next came the 6th USCT. It was not unusual for a new regiment to begin organizing even as another was finishing its rolls; in September 1863, for example, as the 6th was nearing completion, the first officers and men were assigned to what would become the 8th USCT. Charles W. Fribley, whose previous service had been as a captain in the 84th Pennsylvania, was appointed its colonel. The men themselves soon fell into the camp's regular training routine: 5:00 A.M. reveille, followed by drilling throughout the day until taps at 10:00 P.M.

Conscripts arrived from recruiting stations located throughout Pennsylvania, even as some of the officers and men visited neighboring states to sign up more. Lieutenant Oliver W. Norton was part of a group that traveled to Delaware. "Our camp was thronged with visitors, and darkies who wanted to enlist," he wrote to his sister on

January 4. "There are hundreds of them, mostly slaves, here now, anxiously waiting for the recruiting officer." Norton was profoundly moved when many spontaneously began to sing "Rally round the Flag." "Cool as I am I found myself getting excited as I heard their songs this afternoon and saw the electrifying effect on the crowds of slaves," he recalled.[9]

On January 16, 1864, the 8th USCT completed its rolls and left Camp William Penn for New York. There the men came to the attention of James R. W. Leonard, who filed a report for the *Anglo-African:*

> The 8th Regiment, U.S. Colored Troops, from Camp Wm. Penn, Philadelphia, arrived in this city on Sunday last [January 17], and marched through Broadway to the foot of Canal Street, where transports lay waiting to convey them to Hilton Head, their place of destination. A full brass band, . . . together with a complete fife and drum corps, created in all the wildest enthusiasm, and occasioned many pious feet to stray from the sanctuary, whilst they kept step to the inspiriting Yankee Doodle.[10]

("Marching through New York was really a triumph for a radical Abolitionist like myself," proclaimed the regimental surgeon, Dr. A. P. Heichold, "and as I tramped to the tune of John Brown . . . I could not help but think that the world does move.")[11]

> The men appeared keenly alive to the importance of the hour. Bitter experience had taught many of them the value of good government, and the wisdom of making known the power of the iron black arm of this nation. Prominent amongst this class, we noticed Mr. Charles Jackson, now Orderly Sergeant, who was beaten and thrown overboard for dead during the July [1863] riots [in New York]. His keen eye and compressed lips afforded a warning to "nigger killers."
>
> As the vessel did not, as expected, head out on Sunday, I availed myself of the invitation extended by Sergeants Chas. Jackson and John C. Chambers, to visit their men on Monday morning. This visit afforded an opportunity of observing the material commanding.
>
> Col. Fribley, a small wiry man, is a gentleman of culture and has the undivided attachment of his men. . . . The [white] officers seemed proud of the men, as they justly might be, for a nobler band of patriots never carried a gun. But one incident occurred which we had

cause to regret. On Sunday, whilst the men were in line on Canal street, Noah Smith, a young private of Co. F, having been clandestinely furnished with whiskey by some of the bystanders, became ungovernable and in a fit of drunken rage, shot the first sergeant of his Co., Sergt. Duty. . . . At last accounts he was doing well. I saw the young man brought in, in charge of an Orderly upon shipboard, sullen and indifferent. "Bind his hands behind him," said the Lieutenant. "Don't be afraid of hurting him! when you get through, let him lay out on the deck. The first effort at resistance, give him the bayonet in the mouth. We'll learn him to shoot the best officer in our regiment; one meal a day will do for him!" During the whole operation he never moved a muscle—he seemed hardened past all hope. . . . "We must have strict discipline," said the Orderly. "Examples, severe examples must be made in such cases or none of us would be safe." The regiment, which numbered 800, was conveyed in two transports, and as they left the dock they rent the air with cheer after cheer to each other and their numerous friends upon the dock. The drums beat, fifes screamed, and lastly the boys broke out amidst waving of hats and handkerchiefs,

"We're off for Charleston early in the morning."[12]

The 8th was transported to Hilton Head, arriving there in mid-January. On February 2, it was given a cool once-over by a veteran of the Fort Wagner assault and a member of the now-famous 54th Regiment Massachusetts Infantry (Colored). "Some say that the 54th has a rival," wrote Corporal James Henry Gooding. "The 8th U.S. regiment is indeed a splendid organization, and I may add that no regiment in the department can boast of a more healthy-looking, martial-bearing body of men; although in the manual of arms the old 54th can't be beat."[13]

There had been few words of protest from the ranks when orders arrived on January 27 for the 54th to leave Morris Island. "No more fatigue at the front!" some of the men had shouted as the steam transports bore them away to the south, while others hopefully added, "We'll have a rest from the sound of the guns!" Whatever lay ahead, Sergeant George E. Stephens was confident that the men would, as one black orator had proclaimed during the regiment's New Year's commemoration, "strive by deeds of valor to add still more to the accumulated testimony of negro patriotism and courage."[14]

There were a fair number of new faces in the fabled 54th. One ironic result of its highly publicized attack on Fort Wagner was that Northern blacks had flocked to enlist in its ranks. So great was the press of those wanting to join, in fact, that in early February, Colonel Edward N. Hallowell tried to have the 54th redesignated a heavy artillery regiment, which would have allowed it to muster six hundred men more than the thousand-man maximum for infantry units. "This recommendation, however, bore no fruit," Captain Emilio would write in the 54th's history. Among the "new" men joining at this time was Joseph T. Wilson, who had already seen service in Louisiana with the 2nd Regiment Louisiana Native Guards.[15]

The 54th Massachusetts (Colored) and the 8th USCT were among the first units to land in Florida. Included in the follow-up wave was the 1st Regiment North Carolina Colored Volunteers, organized by Brigadier General Edward A. Wild on June 30, 1863, and commanded by Colonel James C. Beecher. Beecher's was a restless, tormented, guilt-ridden soul, somehow befitting this thirty-six-year-old son of the New England divinity Lyman Beecher. Rebellious as a boy and teenager (excelling his classmates only in "wit [low] and wickedness"), once out of college he had run away to sea and later married an older woman given to drink. Only her death in an asylum in 1863 freed him to dedicate his life to the cause of black soldiers. "I wish doubtful people at home could see my three-weeks regiment," Beecher wrote in June 1863. "They would talk less nonsense about negro inferiority. Our discipline is better than [that of] any regiment I know of."[16]

Beecher agitated constantly for the welfare of his men, fighting against the endless fatigue assignments handed out to black units and protesting the inequities of the government's pay policy to any official who would listen to him. Determined to have his regiment equipped with more up-to-date arms in time for spring campaigning, he went north on leave in early February. It was a gesture that would cost him dearly, for hardly had he left Folly Island when orders arrived for the 1st North Carolina Colored "to be in readiness to embark at the shortest possible notice." Colonel Beecher's regiment was heading into its biggest fight, but the man who had turned the slaves into soldiers would not be there to share the dangers.[17]

On February 4, Gillmore placed Brigadier General Truman Seymour in charge of the Florida expeditionary force. To those who bothered to think about it—and some did—this signified that black troops were again going into action under the same generals who had designed the July 18 Wagner assault. It was not a good omen.

Occupation of Jacksonville, Florida, February 7–July 26, 1864

Roads to Olustee: February 7–19, 1864

The first U.S. vessels in Gillmore's expedition drew near the city of Jacksonville late on the afternoon of February 7. While the gunboat *Norwich* anchored to cover the shore, the steam transport *Maple Leaf* moved purposefully toward the town's fish-market dock. On board were Companies A, B, and D of the 54th Massachusetts (Colored), under the command of Major John W. M. Appleton. "As we approached we could see the rebel pickets riding back through the town," he recalled. A correspondent who was present on the steamer reported that "just as we touched the pier some twenty or more shots were fired upon us from the Rebel pickets, who were concealed within the town. . . . No sooner than this volley from the Rebels was heard than the three companies from the Fifty-fourth Massachusetts jumped on the dock, formed in platoons, and started off on the double-quick."[18]

Not far from where the *Maple Leaf* landed, another Federal transport, the *General Hunter*, drew up to a pier carrying Companies C, F, G, H, I, and K of the 54th. Remembered Corporal Gooding, "Every man began to load without orders and rushed for the gangways to get on shore—and almost before those in command could give the necessary orders, the men were rushing pell-mell through the streets, to catch, if possible, the cowardly crew who had fired on an unarmed transport."[19]

Lieutenant Charles M. Duren led Company D, the first off the *Maple Leaf*. Duren recollected that his men "followed [the enemy pickets] . . . up as fast as possible—firing into them. They being on horseback got away, but [we] succeeded in cutting off two of them. I deployed Co. as skirmishers, and advanced cautiously, captured two men and one Horse." "There are many women and children in town," observed Major Appleton. "They receive us well enough but are terribly afraid of our colored men. We assure them that the men will not interfere with them."[20]

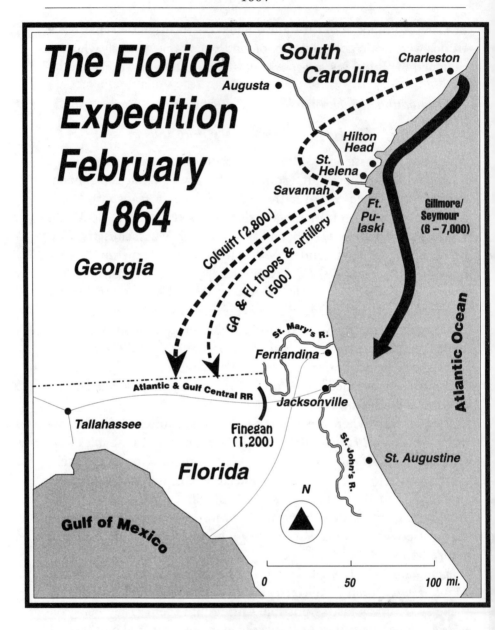

The Florida Expedition February 1864

Georgia — South Carolina — Augusta — Charleston — Hilton Head — St. Helena — Savannah — Ft. Pulaski — Gillmore/Seymour (6–7,000) — Colquitt (2,800) — GA & FL troops & artillery (500) — Atlantic & Gulf Central RR — St. Mary's R. — Fernandina — Jacksonville — Tallahassee — Finegan (1,200) — Florida — St. John's R. — St. Augustine — Atlantic Ocean — Gulf of Mexico

N

0   50   100 mi.

As the three leading companies of the 54th Massachusetts (Colored) began to clear the town, Major Appleton had a narrow escape. "While [I was] running along a street a little in advance of a squad of men, a dismounted rebel about 60 yards away laid his gun on a fence and took good aim at me. I looked up just as he fired, the ball passed close in front of me. . . . Two or three of our men fired at the Johnnie as he dodged behind a house and reached his horse I suppose." The situation had settled somewhat by the time the other companies arrived. "I am happy to say, that the 54th behaved in the most exemplary manner," observed Corporal Gooding, "not a low jest was indulged as they passed through the streets, in most cases lined with women."[21]

The 54th camped this night on the town's outskirts. Nearby was the bivouac of the 8th USCT. William P. Woodlin of the latter regiment praised the 54th for landing with "commendable celerity, capturing some six prisoners, by the time the 8th had reached their camp, just outside of the town. Two officers and four men of the rebel signal corps were also brought in that evening." The 8th's surgeon, Dr.

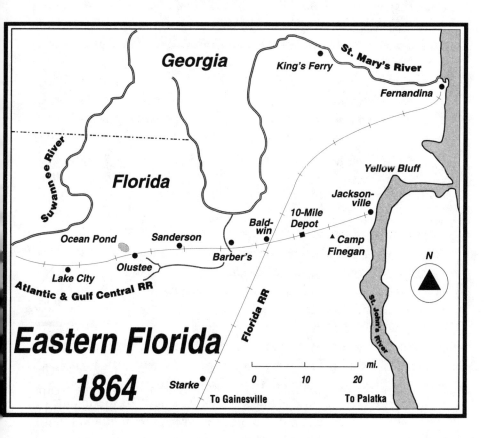

Heichold, was appalled by the sight of the devastation left in Jacksonville by the previous Federal expedition. "There were only about 20 families remaining in what was a town, I should think, of 4000 inhabitants, and they were objects of pity, and in the most wretched poverty."[22]

General Gillmore had planned this operation with great secrecy, but it was impossible to prevent watchful Confederates from guessing that something was up. The flamboyant General P. G. T. Beauregard, who bore the responsibility for the C.S. Department of South Carolina, Georgia, and Florida, lacked the troops necessary to defend every inch of the long coastline and so relied on his cool nerve, accurate intelligence gathering, and the fragile stability of the rail system to move troops quickly to threatened points. On February 8, Beauregard received a warning from his Florida commander, Brigadier General Joseph Finegan, that Union gunboats and transports were descending on Jacksonville. Already on his guard, Beauregard had been holding troops in readiness up and down the coast; now he began to issue orders that would send them southward. They could not arrive soon enough to satisfy General Finegan. At the moment when Major Appleton, Lieutenant Duren, and the three companies of the 54th Massachusetts came ashore, he had fewer than twelve hundred men under his command, and even those were widely scattered throughout the region. Once General Seymour emptied his transports, there would be nearly seven thousand Federals ready for action in eastern Florida.

It took most of Monday, February 8, to land the first wave of Union troops sent to Florida. It was nearly sundown when three columns of bluecoats set out from Jacksonville, heading due west along the Atlantic and Gulf Central Railroad line. Besides the 8th USCT, the 3rd USCT and the 2nd Regiment South Carolina Infantry (A.D.) were taking part in this phase of the operation. At around 8:00 P.M., the mounted troops in advance came into contact with Rebel pickets near the enemy's Camp Finegan. Assigning just a few men to hold the Rebels in place, the mounted force bypassed the encampment in favor of a nearby Confederate artillery park, leaving it to the infantry to deal with Camp Finegan. At about 10:00 P.M., the mounted infantry and cavalry charged into the artillery position, capturing cannon and some personnel. As the Federal footsoldiers closed in, most of the Rebel soldiers at Camp Finegan fled, abandoning a cache of equipment and supplies.

Surgeon Heichold of the 8th judged that these opening operations were carried out "in the most approved manner." His regiment reached Camp Finegan at midnight and bivouacked. "Scarcely had the men lain down and become quiet," reported one of the regiment's officers, "when there was an alarm. The companies were quickly formed, and without any confusion which might have been expected from a Regiment that had never before carried loaded muskets."[23]

The 54th Massachusetts (Colored) had been held back to garrison Jacksonville. Major Appleton, unhappy about missing the action, was chilled to the bone as the night temperature dropped toward freezing, but nevertheless, he soon got into the spirit of things. Since his lone regiment was stretched thin to cover two miles of line, he decided on a bold charade. "We built great fires and set our drum corps to them at different points to beat various tattoos. . . . The men were allowed to move about and be noisy so as to give the appearance of many troops." However, Lieutenant Duren, of Company D, was definitely not having fun. "We are roughing it, I can tell you," he wrote to his father. "Have not anything with us—living under God's sky—sleeping on the ground with a big fire at our feet. . . . Jacksonville is . . . desolate and lonely."[24]

Nearby, Corporal Gooding was composing another of his newsy letters for the readers of his hometown *New Bedford Mercury*. After describing the landing and their initially chilly reception, Gooding reflected on a slight warming of relations. "To-day those, who at first greeted us with frowns, are treating us with respect and courtesy; in fact more than we should expect to receive in some parts of the free North. And that respect is not due to the presence of an overwhelming army . . . but respect paid to men who by their deportment show that they are christianized, if not very refined." Gooding finished his letter with the conclusion of the Florida story very much up in the air. He sealed and sent his missive, which appeared in the paper's February 22 edition; by that date Gooding had been wounded in battle and captured by the enemy.[25]

For the next three days, General Seymour's expeditionary force continued to push slowly west along the railroad route. There were some sharp skirmishes, mostly between the mounted Union advance and parties of Confederate cavalry. By 6:00 P.M. on February

10, General Seymour and his men had reached Sanderson, a rail stop some forty miles west of Jacksonville. The next day his mounted infantry rode to within a short distance of Lake City, where the Yankee troopers came up against Confederates positioned behind earthworks and not disposed to move. After some desultory skirmishing, the unsupported probing units fell back to the main body at Sanderson. It rained throughout the night of February 11 and into the morning of the next day. General Seymour now resolved that he had gone too far out on a limb, so he ordered everyone—mounted or on foot—back toward Jacksonville. Seymour retraced his steps as far as the town of Barber's, where he halted and began to entrench.

Through great exertion and tireless prodding, General Finegan had, by February 11, gathered about six hundred men at Lake City. General Beauregard held up some of the troops he had promised to send at Charleston because of aggressive Federal actions on John's Island. Concluding that these movements were merely a feint to keep him from releasing the reinforcements to Finegan, Beauregard called the Union bluff, ordering a massed bombardment of Morris Island and watching with satisfaction as the various Yankee detachments all fell back. Now Beauregard felt secure enough to relinquish his hold on three and a half Georgia regiments under Brigadier General Alfred Colquitt, and soon these troops were on trains that would carry them to within a short marching distance of Lake City.

In spite of the fact that he had met only light and scattered opposition up to this point in the Florida operation, General Gillmore was worried. On February 11, he received a disquieting dispatch from his field commander, General Seymour. "The backbone of rebeldom is not here," Seymour wrote from Baldwin,

> and Florida will not cast its lot [with the Union] until more important successes elsewhere are assured. . . . I would advise that the force be withdrawn at once from the interior, that Jacksonville alone be held. . . . Many more men than you have here now will be required to support its operation, which has not been matured, as should have been

done. . . . To be thwarted, defeated, will be a sad termination to a project, brilliant thus far, but for which you could not answer, in case of mishap, to your military superiors, and Stickney and others have misinformed you.[26]

Gillmore's enthusiasm for the Florida enterprise rapidly evaporated. On February 12, he ordered Seymour to concentrate his troops "at Baldwin without delay," and the next day he told General Halleck in Washington that the "military operations in this state . . . promise to be of no great magnitude." It was now Gillmore's intention to reduce the size of the operation to just twenty-five hundred men—barely enough to fortify strong points at Jacksonville, Baldwin, and a few other places. Gillmore and Seymour met in Jacksonville on February 14 to discuss strategies and plans. Gillmore was adamant, as he later wrote, that it was "well understood [by General Seymour] . . . that no advance would be made without further instruction from me, nor until the defenses were well advanced." When General Gillmore departed for Hilton Head on February 15, he left General Seymour in charge of what was now designated the District of Florida.[27]

Despite this reversal at the top, Union operations in Florida continued to unfold as already dispatched reinforcements kept arriving. Mounted raiding parties set out from Jacksonville on February 13 and 14, headed for Gainesville, Starke, and King's Ferry. Among the new troops on the scene were the 1st North Carolina Colored* and the 55th Regiment Massachusetts Infantry (Colored), which arrived in Jacksonville between February 14 and 15.

Now established at Baldwin, the officers and men of the 54th Massachusetts (Colored) were making do. While on an errand to see the camp's commanding officer, Appleton met a local woman who was thoroughly unreconstructed in her sentiments. "Do you know you are in a terrible position young man," she said. Appleton wondered why that might be so. "Because you expect to fight here," she replied, "and if you are taken prisoner, you will surely be hung because you command nigger troops."[28]

According to the Record of Events for the 8th USCT, the regiment remained at Camp Finegan "until the afternoon of the 12th, when it

*On February 8, the 1st North Carolina Colored had been redesignated the 35th USCT, but use of that name did not become common within the regiment itself until after the fight at Olustee.

was ordered to Ten Mile Station. . . . Did picket duty here until [February] 15th when we marched to Baldwin. . . . Here we remained until the 19th the men being constantly on picket or at fatigue duty on the works." Sergeant Major Rufus S. Jones, who hailed from Pittsburgh, had a low opinion of Baldwin. "In general appearance, a person would not take it for a town in the North," he declared, "nor even disgrace the name of 'town' by applying it." Writing from Camp Finegan, Surgeon Heichold of the 8th seconded those who had found little to like in what they had seen thus far. "I don't think this land very rich," he said. "The people are a wretched, ignorant race, and a century behind the times." Lacking any personal perspective on General Gillmore, the good doctor could only indulge in a bit of naive optimism, ending his letter with the hope that when he next wrote, he would "be able to announce that the rebel army is driven out of Florida and her people free."[29]

Joining the 54th Massachusetts and the 8th USCT in the field was the 1st North Carolina Colored, which left Jacksonville on February 16 to march as far as Camp Finegan, by now renamed Camp Shaw in honor of Robert Gould Shaw. By February 17, the regiment had reached Baldwin, which was supposed to be the farthest point west of Jacksonville held by U.S. forces. However, that same day, General Seymour completely reversed himself: instead of consolidating his position, as instructed by Gillmore, he had decided to resume offensive operations.

The reinforcements long promised to General Finegan began to reach Lake City on February 12. Finegan had already started work on a strong defensive position at Olustee; writing from his Lake City headquarters on February 13, he reported that he now had "about 1,800 infantry, 450 cavalry, and two batteries, and one section of artillery." The first of General Colquitt's men, dispatched from Charleston, arrived on February 15. By the end of the day on February 18, Finegan estimated his total strength at fifty-two hundred men.

Major John Hay, the man sent to Florida by Abraham Lincoln to facilitate that state's reconstruction, sounded a warning about the officer now commanding the District. "Seymour has seemed very unsteady and queer since the beginning of the campaign," Hay noted.

"He has been subject to violent alternations of timidity and rashness, now declaring Florida loyalty was all bosh, now lauding it as the purest article extant, now insisting Beauregard was in front with the whole Confederacy & now asserting that he could whip all the rebels in Florida with a good brigade."[30]

On February 17, General Seymour wrote from Jacksonville to General Gillmore in Hilton Head, declaring that he was determined to destroy the Atlantic and Gulf Central Railroad as far west as the Suwanee River. To accomplish this, he proposed to renew the advance toward Lake City that he had halted on February 12—"All troops therefore being moved up to Barber's, and probably by the time you receive this I shall be in motion."[31]

The note dropped like a thunderbolt on General Gillmore, who received it the next day. "I . . . am very much surprised at the tone of [your letter] . . . and the character of your plans as therein stated," he wrote in reply. "As may be supposed, I am very much confused . . . and am thrown into doubt as to whether my intentions with regard to Florida matters are fully understood by you. . . . A raid to tear up the railroad west of Lake City will be of service, but I have no intention to occupy now that part of the state." Gillmore sent this reply via his chief of staff, along with orders for Seymour to halt the movement at once. But bad weather held up the officer's passage, and by the time he reached Jacksonville, the Battle of Olustee had been fought.[32]

The Battle of Olustee: February 20, 1864

Saturday dawned cool and clear. In the Union encampments surrounding Barber's, black and white soldiers cooked hurried breakfasts and prepared for the day's march. The mounted troops trotted out of camp at around 6:30 A.M., followed by Colonel Joseph Hawley's brigade (in which the 8th served), then Colonel William Barton's brigade (all white New York regiments), with Colonel James Montgomery's brigade (consisting of the 1st North Carolina Colored and the 54th Massachusetts [Colored]) last in line. "The 8th U.S. took the lead of all the colored regiments," musician William P. Woodlin recalled with pride.[33]

"The day was a most delightful one," remembered Sergeant Stephens in Company B of the 54th Massachusetts. "The springs and

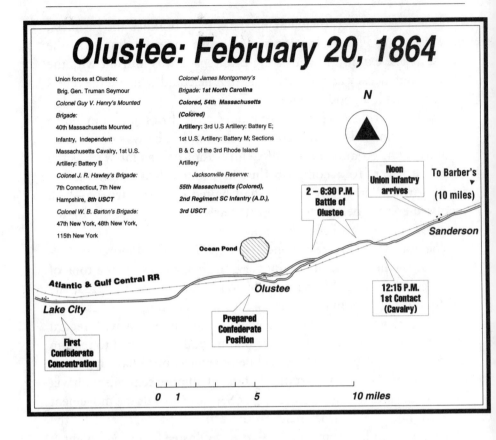

Olustee: February 20, 1864

Union forces at Olustee:

Brig. Gen. Truman Seymour

Colonel Guy V. Henry's Mounted
Brigade:

40th Massachusetts Mounted
Infantry, Independent
Massachusetts Cavalry, 1st U.S.
Artillery: Battery B

Colonel J. R. Hawley's Brigade:

7th Connecticut, 7th New
Hampshire, *8th USCT*

Colonel W. B. Barton's Brigade:

47th New York, 48th New York,
115th New York

Colonel James Montgomery's

Brigade: *1st North Carolina
Colored, 54th Massachusetts
(Colored)*

Artillery: 3rd U.S Artillery: Battery E;
1st U.S. Artillery: Battery M; Sections
B & C of the 3rd Rhode Island
Artillery

Jacksonville Reserve:

55th Massachusetts (Colored),
2nd Regiment SC Infantry (A.D.),
3rd USCT

N

Noon
Union infantry
arrives

To Barber's

(10 miles)

2 – 6:30 P.M.
Battle of
Olustee

Sanderson

Ocean Pond

Atlantic & Gulf Central RR

Olustee

12:15 P.M.
1st Contact
(Cavalry)

Lake City

Prepared
Confederate
Position

First
Confederate
Concentration

0   1   5   10 miles

rivulets along the line of march reminded us of the cool, refreshing waters at home. . . . You can see nothing but pine woods, marsh, and every five or ten miles a cluster of dilapidated, deserted huts, with no signs of agricultural thriftiness. But immense tracts of the pine-woods land are prepared for the collection of pitch. The trees are tapped, and near the roots cavities are hewn out, into which the pitch collects." Captain Luis Emilio of the 54th thought that his men were in "fine spirits" this day, an impression that was confirmed when they began to sing, "We're Bound for Tallahassee in the Morning."[34]

Not everyone in the 54th Massachusetts was in a good mood, however. Just as the men were lining up to begin the march, Major Appleton had been summoned to General Seymour's headquarters and told he was to remain behind to command a detail of the regiment assigned to Barber's. So while the rest of the 54th trooped off down the road to Lake City, Appleton resigned himself to a day of boredom.

The fast-moving mounted troops spearheading Seymour's advance reached Sanderson by around 10:00 A.M. After securing the area, the troopers kept going; they reached a point about four miles west by noon, just as the first of the Federal footsoldiers were entering the small town, where a temporary rest halt was called. Lieutenant Oliver Norton of the 8th USCT noted that the march to this point had been in "three columns, artillery in the road, flanked by the infantry on either side." "No interruption was had during the day till . . . [musket] firing was heard in front," remarked Sergeant Major Rufus Jones. "We supposed our cavalry had met a few of the enemy's pickets," explained Lieutenant Norton.[35]

The young officer's surmise was correct. Shortly after noon, the mounted infantry scrapped with a Rebel picket posted a few miles west of Sanderson. The Yankee riders had been joined by one of Hawley's infantry regiments, the 7th Connecticut, a unit that usually got special assignments because it was armed with Spencer repeating rifles. Hardly had two companies of the 7th deployed for action when the Rebel vedettes fell back, followed closely by the Federals. For perhaps four miles, the Union men pushed the Rebels along, until suddenly, at a point three miles or so east of Olustee, a more substantial enemy line of battle was seen. When informed of this, General Seymour immediately ordered Battery B of the 1st U.S. Artillery to assist the Connecticut regiment. The time was shortly after 2:00 P.M.

General Finegan's plan was to remain behind the earthworks his men had been digging near Olustee and to let the enemy come to him. To set the trap, he sent out two Georgia cavalry regiments to draw the Federals up to the prepared defenses. When the enemy seemed hesitant to take the bait, the Confederate general decided to put out more of it, sending forward three infantry regiments with a battery under the command of Brigadier General Colquitt. It was these troops that now confronted Seymour's advance, on ground that would become known as the battlefield of Olustee.

For about forty minutes, the rapid-firing veterans of the 7th Connecticut held their own against the several Confederate units before them. The footsoldiers began the action, with the Federal artillery

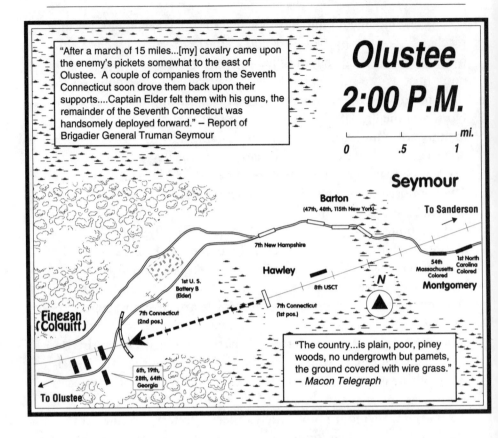

"After a march of 15 miles...[my] cavalry came upon the enemy's pickets somewhat to the east of Olustee. A couple of companies from the Seventh Connecticut soon drove them back upon their supports....Captain Elder felt them with his guns, the remainder of the Seventh Connecticut was handsomely deployed forward." – Report of Brigadier General Truman Seymour

Olustee
2:00 P.M.
mi.
0   .5   1

Seymour

Barton
(47th, 48th, 115th New York)
To Sanderson

7th New Hampshire

Hawley

1st U.S. Battery B (Elder)

8th USCT

54th Massachusetts Colored
1st North Carolina Colored

Montgomery

7th Connecticut (2nd pos.)

7th Connecticut (1st pos.)

Finegan (Colquitt)

6th, 19th, 28th, 64th Georgia

To Olustee

"The country...is plain, poor, piney woods, no undergrowth but pamets, the ground covered with wire grass." – *Macon Telegraph*

near at hand. It was one of the curious aspects of this battle that, for the most part, the Yankee cannon fought the enemy at extremely close range. "It must be borne in mind our batteries were within one hundred yards of the enemy's front," observed the reporter from the *New York Times.* "This short distance rendered it a very easy task for the rebels to pick off a man or horse at every discharge of their rifles." As more and more Rebel soldiers appeared on the field and as the Confederate lines began to overreach its own, the 7th Connecticut began to withdraw. It was nearing 3:00 P.M. when Colonel Hawley sent word for his other two regiments to come up.[36]

"The skirmishing increased as we marched, but we paid little attention to it," recalled Lieutenant Norton of the 8th USCT. "Pretty soon the boom of a gun startled us a little, but not much, as we knew our flying artillery was ahead, but they boomed again and again and it began to look like a brush." "Heavy firing was heard," recalled Sergeant Jones, "and the troops were moved forward rapidly." Racing alongside the quick-stepping ranks was the regiment's mascot, an "old white dog" that the men called Lion. The dog had been with the unit since Camp William Penn and, according to Jones, had "no objection to being among black soldiers."[37]

"An aide came dashing through the woods to us and the order was—'double quick, march!'" continued Norton. "We turned into the woods and ran in the direction of the firing for half a mile, when the head of our column reached our batteries." As Sergeant Jones saw it, "The Eighth, having been on the railroad for a short distance, was ordered to change direction to the right, and received orders to go into the fight without unslinging knapsacks, or the sergeants taking off their sashes, which caused nearly all the first sergeants to be

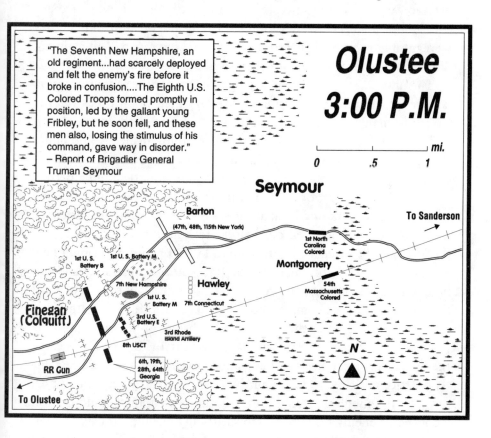

"The Seventh New Hampshire, an old regiment...had scarcely deployed and felt the enemy's fire before it broke in confusion....The Eighth U.S. Colored Troops formed promptly in position, led by the gallant young Fribley, but he soon fell, and these men also, losing the stimulus of his command, gave way in disorder."
– Report of Brigadier General Truman Seymour

killed or wounded. Only one-half the regiment was loaded, so harmless had been the estimate placed upon the enemy, that he was not looked for short of Lake City." Lieutenant Norton was within earshot when General Seymour rode up to the head of the column of black troops and called out, "Put your regiment in, Colonel Fribley."[38]

Things were beginning to happen too quickly to allow for a measured, parade-ground deployment from column into line: both of Hawley's supporting regiments would have to perform the maneuver under fire, the 7th New Hampshire taking the right wing, the 8th USCT forming the left. Hardly had the 7th New Hampshire begun the transformation when a series of catastrophes struck. First, in the confusion of the moment, Colonel Hawley gave the wrong command; he then issued two more deployment commands that only made matters worse. There were a large number of green recruits in the ranks of the veteran 7th New Hampshire, and their lack of previous battle experience, coupled with Hawley's command gaffe and the punishment they were taking from the Rebel riflemen, proved too much. The regiment dissolved in midmaneuver, the men tumbling back in disarray.

The untried 8th USCT was having to carry out the same formation change under similar conditions. "Military men say it takes veteran troops to maneuver under fire, but our regiment with knapsacks on and unloaded pieces, after a run of half a mile, formed a line under the most destructive fire I ever knew," Lieutenant Norton would declare afterward. "The 8th was formed in line of battle amid a perfect storm of bullets," reported William Woodlin of Company G, "the veteran regiments falling back at the same time, causing the battery to move to our left and open on the rebs to hold them in check." Said the 8th USCT's surgeon, Dr. Heichold, "[The] regiment being a new one and but few of the men [having] ever heard a cannon, and but little practice in loading and firing, wavered at first, but soon recovered themselves, and then commenced the struggle for life and death."[39]

With the collapse of the 7th New Hampshire on the right, and the 7th Connecticut already re-forming in the rear, the 8th USCT became the lone target of choice for the Confederates. "We have had very little practice in firing," Lieutenant Norton observed with some bitterness, "and, though they could stand and be killed, they could not kill a concealed enemy fast enough to satisfy my feelings." Surgeon Heichold watched with horror as the men of the 8th USCT "commenced dropping like leaves in autumn; still . . . here they stood . . . under one of the most terrible fires I ever witnessed." "After seeing his men murdered as long as flesh and blood could endure it, Colonel Fribley ordered the regiment to fall back slowly, firing as they went," recollected Lieutenant Norton. "As the men fell back they gathered in groups like frightened sheep, and it was almost impossible to keep them from doing so. Into these groups the rebels poured the deadliest fire, almost every bullet hitting some one. Color bearer after color bearer was shot down and the colors seized by another." "It was fearful to see horses without riders and riders without horses, shells bursting, trees crashing, batteries playing, musketry firing, regiments marching and counter-marching in such a small space," wrote Dr. Heichold.[40]

"Colonel Charles Fribley, of the Eighth, fell, mortally wounded, a short time after going into the engagement," recorded Sergeant Major Jones. A reporter for the *Philadelphia Press* put Fribley's wounding within "the first twenty minutes" of the action. Shot in the chest, Fribley was caught by one of his captains and lowered to the ground. The man who in happier days at Camp William Penn had seen the 8th USCT come into the world now gasped, "Take me out," and then died.[41]

A portion of the 8th fell back through one of the Federal batteries, whose commander pleaded for help in saving his guns. According to William Woodlin, "First Lieut. E. Lewis, Co. F, planted the Stars and Stripes by the guns and called the men to them; but such was the fierceness of the iron tempest that they . . . lost their colors." Lieutenant Lewis, with the assistance of Lieutenants Norton and Andrew F. Ely, tried to form a line to protect the battery, but the officers saw their efforts undone when one of the frantic artillery horses careened through their hasty formation. "The fire from the enemy now became so destructive we could not keep our men in line," Lewis later reported. Although he did not touch the flag again, it appears that *someone* from the regiment grasped it: an officer of the battery long remembered the "color bearer, a large, powerful man [who] . . . stood there manfully and bravely to the last."[42]*

Fribley's death further disordered the 8th USCT, but the regiment did not scatter as had the 7th New Hampshire. "We were without a

---

*After the battle, there would be an acrimonious exchange of newspaper letters between artillerymen who claimed that the blacks had abandoned the cannon to the enemy and African American soldiers who were equally adamant that they had done all in their power to save them.

commander," related Lieutenant Norton, "and every officer was doing his best to do something, he knew not what exactly." An artilleryman recalled seeing "many wounded colored soldiers appearing suddenly in front and on my left, without muskets, and it appeared as if they had been lying down and taken the first opportunity to get to the rear. Some of the infantry, while facing the enemy and firing wildly, did not show fear, nor did I see any of them absolutely run off, but groups of them huddled together and did nothing, and many were in this position shot, while they seemed unconscious that they were hit."[43]

Fate and circumstance divided up the wounded into those who would somehow make it to the rear and those who would be left behind. Private Lewis Thomas of Company C took a musket ball in the thigh; two comrades and Sergeant Jonathan T. Band helped carry him to safety. Not so lucky were Sergeant Horace Wheaton of Company C, Corporal Aaron Smith of Company A, and Private William Scott of Company D. Wheaton was wounded, left behind, and taken after the battle to Tallahassee, where he died following amputation surgery. The ball that struck Aaron Smith in the breast coursed through his right lung and lodged near his spinal column; he, too, was taken to Tallahassee after capture, and had his wound treated there. He then suffered a dismal odyssey as Confederate authorities shipped him first to Andersonville, Georgia, and after that to Salisbury, North Carolina. He would survive the war. For Private Scott, the result of his capture would be death at Andersonville, on July 4.

Enemy fire also chewed its way down the chain of command, until Captain Romanzo C. Bailey was the senior man remaining. As he afterward reported, "Seeing that a regiment at least of the enemy was moving down the railroad to again attack our left, and knowing that our ammunition was exhausted, I took the responsibility to withdraw the regiment from the field, moving by the right flank and in good order." The time was nearing 4:30 P.M.; the ordeal of the 8th USCT had lasted nearly ninety minutes.[44]

With the battle spreading in size and intensity, General Finegan considered his options: he could either order the troops already engaged to retreat to the defensive positions at Olustee Station or reinforce them further and fight the engagement where it was. In fact, Finegan really had no choice at all, and any thoughts he may have had of defending the prepared position were soon forgotten. Beginning at around 3:30 P.M., he began sending more of his units to join those under Colquitt. Also sent forward was a weapon that had been used against the previous Federal incursion: a large-caliber artillery piece mounted on a railroad car. However, in this instance the effect of the gun was more imagined than real, for, as a Northern reporter noted, "The shells passed over the heads of our men."[45]

Colonel James Montgomery's brigade of two black regiments was about six miles to the east when the fighting erupted. Reported a correspondent with the expedition, "When it became evident that our men were having hot work in front, [Montgomery] sent his adjutant, Lt. Loveridge, forward for orders, but without waiting for his return, he moved forward with the 54th Massachusetts [leading]." According to Sergeant Stephens of the 54th, "When [we were] within about three miles of the field of battle, an aide came riding up to the Colonel of the 54th Massachusetts, saying, 'For God's sake, Colonel, double-quick, or the day is lost.'" Remembered Captain Emilio, "In a few moments the regiment was moving at the double-quick, urged on by the heavier sound of battle. When the pace began to tell on the men, knapsacks, blankets, and even haversacks were cast away to lighten the load." "The road was sandy," recalled Private Joseph T. Wilson, "and the men often found their feet beneath the sand, but with their wonted alacrity they sped on up the road, the 54th leading in almost a locked running step, followed closely by the 1st North Carolina."[46]

General Seymour reacted to the collapse of the 7th New Hampshire by putting all the New York regiments of Barton's brigade into the right side of his line. When the 8th USCT fell back, the New Yorkers stretched to cover that gap as well. A deceptive lull spread over the fighting as ammunition stocks ran low on both sides: since the Rebel source of supply was close at hand, everyone knew the respite would be only temporary. Once their ammunition had been replenished, and bolstered by the fresh troops brought by Finegan (who now assumed command), the Confederates prepared to finish the day's action. Seymour's only hope was that his reserve—Montgomery's two black regiments—could buy him enough time to extricate his little army.

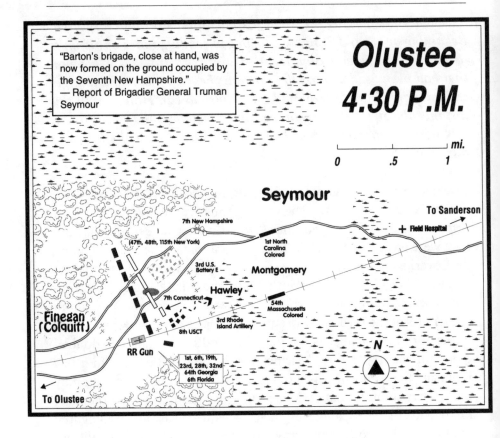

"Barton's brigade, close at hand, was now formed on the ground occupied by the Seventh New Hampshire."
— Report of Brigadier General Truman Seymour

Olustee 4:30 P.M.

"Nearing the battleground, resounding with cannon-shots and musketry, the dispiriting scene so trying to troops about to engage, of hundreds of wounded and stragglers, was encountered," noted Captain Emilio. "All sorts of discouraging shouts met the ear as the regiment speeded onward as, 'We're badly whipped!' 'You'll all get killed.'" Private Wilson would never forget how the regiment's band chimed in as the men dropped their knapsacks, "mingling its soul-stirring strains with the deafening yells of the charging columns, right, left, and from the rebel center."[47]

A reporter on the scene wrote that the 54th Massachusetts (Colored) went in first, "with a cheer." Captain Emilio vividly recollected the bitter edge to the blacks' battle cry: "Three cheers for Massachusetts and seven dollars a month!" "At the most critical juncture, just as the rebels were preparing for a simultaneous charge along the whole line, and they had captured [some of] our artillery and turned it upon us, Col. Jas. Montgomery, Col. Hallowell and Lieut.-Col. [Henry N.] Hooper [both of the 54th] formed our line of battle on right by file into line," remembered Sergeant Stephens. "As the men came into line they opened fire."[48]

Sergeant James Hewett, of Company K, recalled that "solid shot and bursting shells were making havoc among the tree tops, scattering limbs and splinters in all directions." One of the heavy branches struck Private Henry Wilson of Company A, who had already been shot in the side; somehow Wilson made it out and survived the battle. "Victims of the struggle began to come to the rear," continued Sergeant Hewett, who saw "a wounded man, with his musket in one hand and the other shattered by a Minie ball; [and] here came a man wounded through the neck, and from the copious stream of blood that was flowing from his wound, I [was] . . . sure that his time on earth was short."[49]

Even as Colonel Hallowell "mounted the stump of a tree some fifty feet in rear of his center to oversee his men and the position," one of his company officers impulsively led a rank of men forward toward some of the enemy's guns. Hallowell, however, was not going to have the integrity of his line compromised, so he ordered the officer to return, which he did. Sergeant Stephens distinctly recalled another soldier who, in his excitement, ran out toward the enemy from the line of battle, fired his gun, and then raced back to reload. "Shortly this man . . . fell, shot through the head," said Stephens. The men of the 54th also had to contend with Rebel snipers posted in the trees. A "few volleys brought them down," Captain Emilio noted grimly.[50]

The thunder of the cannon and the ear-pounding rattle of massed musketry were too much for Private Thomas Jackson of Company A, who began to act strangely after the battle and eventually had to be sent to an asylum in Washington, where he died. His comrades were certain that it was Olustee that destroyed his sanity, because "previous thereto he was perfectly sound and free from any defect."[51]

A special correspondent for the *Philadelphia Press* reported that the 1st North Carolina Colored entered the battle "with a yell on the double-quick, cheered by the 47th [New York, of Barton's brigade] as it passed." "What we saw made our blood run cold," said a sergeant in the 1st. "Everywhere, men were staggering out of the forest, faces blackened, dripping with blood and sweat, dragging themselves and their wounded comrades to safety." "The men behaved most gallantly, and never wavered, but stood their ground manfully, and even drove the left of the line," recorded the *New York Herald*'s Oscar G. Sawyer. Lieutenant Colonel William N. Reed, commanding the 1st in place of the absent Colonel Beecher, was shot and mortally wounded soon after the regiment entered the action. Captain J. S. Croft took over, later recalling, "We went in, in double column, closed in mass and deployed under fire, eliciting from all observers the warmest praises, by the performance of the movement and then line when formed." "No regiment went into action more gallantly, fought more desperately, or did better execution than the 1st North Carolina (colored) troops," declared another reporter. One of the white soldiers succored by the arrival of the 1st wrote that the "colored troops went in grandly, and they fought like devils." Glancing over from his position in the 54th Massachusetts (Colored), Private Joseph T. Wilson noted the terrible punishing being endured by the North Carolina soldiers. "Men fell like snowflakes," he later wrote.[52]

Plummeting tree limbs also took a toll on the 1st North Carolina Colored. One crashed down on Private William H. Harrison of Company A, severely bruising his arm; another struck Private David Simpson of the same company, rendering his right arm stiff for the rest of his life. The *Herald*'s Oscar Sawyer saw another member of the regiment, "terribly wounded by a musket ball through both cheeks, and bleeding in torrents from his wounds, mouth and nose, but shouting aloud through his swollen lips, dripping with blood, 'Shree Shreers for Union! Gimmum'll Gimmum'll!' [He] went to the extreme rear, yelling in his broken style the same old rallying cry of 'Gimmum'll.'"[53]

General Seymour's only thought now was to save his small army from annihilation. Behind a shield provided by Montgomery's two black regiments, his mounted infantry, and the seemingly indefatigable 7th Connecticut, the rest of the expeditionary force began to retreat. There was little calm or orderly about the movement. In their haste, the Federals left behind, in addition to many wounded, five cannon, sixteen hundred small arms, four hundred sets of accouterments, and 130,000 rounds of ammunition. They also abandoned the fantasy that Florida could be forcibly led back into the Union. Among the wounded from the 54th Massachusetts was Corporal James Henry Gooding; the ex-sailor, sometimes poet, and faithful correspondent to the *New Bedford Mercury* wound up in Andersonville, where he would die that July.

"And it was a sorrowing spectacle to see our little army, so hopeful and so gallant, in such precipitate retreat after a battle of four short hours," reflected Sergeant Stephens of the 54th. "Our retreat was steady and cool," an officer in the 1st North Carolina Colored avowed. "After retreating a few paces, we 'about faced' and gave three cheers for the flag, which all the time had been waving, while the enemy's was twice shot down. When the right arm of our color sergeant was broken, he knelt down and held up the dear old flag with his left until relieved."[54]

Private Edward D. Washington in Company B of the 54th Massachusetts afterward recollected how his unit commander rallied the men with the cry, "Give it to them, my brave boys! Give it to them!"

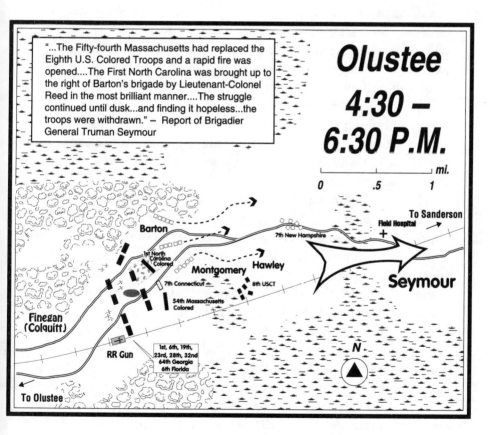

"...The Fifty-fourth Massachusetts had replaced the Eighth U.S. Colored Troops and a rapid fire was opened....The First North Carolina was brought up to the right of Barton's brigade by Lieutenant-Colonel Reed in the most brilliant manner....The struggle continued until dusk...and finding it hopeless...the troops were withdrawn." – Report of Brigadier General Truman Seymour

Olustee
4:30 –
6:30 P.M.

"As I turned around," Washington said, "I observed Col. E. N. Hallowell standing with a smile upon his countenance, as though the boys were playing a small game of ball." "When we came out of the fight [I] had felt so much care and responsibility that when the order came to fall back—I was perfectly exhausted, faint, and entirely worn out," wrote Lieutenant Charles Duren of Company D. When the actual moment came for the regiment to retreat, Colonel Montgomery urged each man to "take care of himself." This may have been Kansas-style, but it was not the way things were done in Massachusetts: Lieutenant Colonel Hooper told his color sergeant to stand fast with the flag, and helped by other officers and men, he rallied the portion of the regiment nearest him to lead it properly off the field.[55]

A number of wounded black soldiers were saved from an even more onerous fate by the stern resolve of the 8th USCT's Surgeon Heichold. According to Sergeant Major Jones, the doctor made certain that the blacks were loaded first on the ambulances, and the whites let aboard only if there was room. "Some one thought the white troops should be brought away also, but Dr. H. said: 'I know what will become of the white troops who fall into the enemy's possession, but I am not certain as to the fate of the colored troops.'" Heichold himself related that he "saw at an early stage of the fight that we would be whipped, and went round among our wounded and told them, as many as could get away, to start for Barber['s], and then started the ambulance crowded full."[56]

The Federals retreated that night all the way back to Barber's. Sergeant Stephens of the 54th remembered their passing through Sanderson: "Wounded men lined the railroad station, and the roads were filled with artillery, caissons, ammunition and baggage wagons, infantry, cavalry and ambulances." Looming out of the darkness was a sparse but fresh line of battle, commanded by Major Appleton of the 54th, who had come forward from Barber's when he was relieved, at about dusk. "It was a long line to the railroad and my command was small but all the time there streamed by on the road groups of retreating soldiers," Appleton recalled. "I drew my pistol, ordered the non-commissioned officers to assist, and drove into my line every man that had cartridges in his cartridge box. . . . I soon had a motley regiment, white and black, that swore and growled but marched."[57]

Left behind on the battlefield, some of the wounded black soldiers from the 8th USCT, 54th Massachusetts, and 1st North Carolina Colored faced an uncertain fate. A young Georgia cavalryman named William Penniman, who rode over the bloody ground soon after the Federal retreat, wondered why he still heard firing "going on in every direction," which "sounded almost frequent enough to resemble the bark of skirmishers." When he came across a Southern officer, he asked what was going on. "Shooting niggers, Sir," was the chilling reply. "I have tried to make the boys desist but I can't control them." A Georgia footsoldier by the name of James Jordan, writing one day after the battle, admitted that the "men killed some of [the black soldiers] after they fell in our hands wounded." Another Georgian who was present, Joab Roach, wrote that "after the battle the boys went over the battlefield and knoct the most of the wounded negros in the head with lightwood knots." A New Yorker from Barton's brigade who found himself lying near an injured black from the 8th USCT named Brown recalled, "A rebel officer happened to see him, and saying 'Ah, you black rascal, you will not remain here long!' and dismounting from his horse, placed his revolver close to the negro's head, and blew his brains out."[58]

One Olustee historian estimates that some fifty wounded blacks were killed after the fighting had ended, a statistic that may help to explain an act of suicidal bravery recorded by Lieutenant Duren of the 54th Massachusetts: "One of our men a Serg't—on the retreat—was helping along a wounded man—when he was overtaken by reb cavalry—and ordered to surrender, he dropped his comrade [and] bought his gun to his shoulder—but the officer in charge of reb cavalry aimed his revolver at his heart—both fired as one— the Sgt. shot dead—the officer wounded." "It looked sad to see men wounded coming into camp with their arms and equipments on," observed Sergeant Major Jones of the 8th USCT, "so great was their endurance and so determined were they to defend themselves till the death. I saw white troops that were not badly wounded, that had thrown away everything."[59]

Knowledge of the fate that awaited captured comrades may also have inspired an action undertaken by other members of the 54th when they learned that several boxcars filled with (black and white) wounded would be left behind at Baldwin because the locomotive had blown a flue. According to Captain Emilio, "Ropes were attached to the engine and cars; and the Fifty-fourth furnishing the motive-power, they were pushed and dragged over the rails to Camp Finegan, where horses were provided for further progress."[60]

Summing up Olustee, the reporter for the *New York Times* wrote, "The fight was by no means a trivial encounter. It was a battle hotly contested, fought at close range, face to face and foot to foot." Of the 5,500 men whom Seymour parceled into the combat, 1,861 were killed or wounded or went missing. Hardest hit was the 47th New York, in Barton's brigade, which lost 313; next on the list came the 8th USCT, with 310 (it had entered the fight with about 575 in its ranks). Of the two remaining black regiments engaged, 230 men were lost from the 1st North Carolina Colored (out of approximately 600), and 86 from the ranks of the 54th Massachusetts (which had marched into battle with about 495). Total Confederate losses were estimated at 950.[61]

"I think no battle was ever more wretchedly fought," declared Lieutenant Norton of the 8th USCT. "I was going to say planned, but there was no plan." Captain Croft, in temporary command of the 1st North Carolina Colored, was equally dismissive, saying that "the whole force had made an old fashioned Bull Run skedaddle." "I fear the rebels . . . have out-generaled us," Sergeant Stephens of the 54th told the readers of the *Christian Recorder*. "They chose the battle-ground, . . . and managed it so adroitly that no man in the Union Army knew anything about it." He termed the whole engagement a "stupendous ambuscade."[62]

"Our men for the most part fought well, and the darkeys just as well as anyone," wrote a member of the 7th Connecticut. In his summing-up, William Woodlin of the 8th USCT informed the *Anglo-African*,

> They say that, "had it not been for the hairy-backed niggers (our knapsacks being made of calf skin), they would have cut the corps all to pieces." And that this was their intention any one there present could see by their mode of attack, and the flank movements there attempted. The 54th won glory at Fort Wagner, the 8th at Olustee—we dispute not her right to a spoke in the wheel of fame—but we wish her to let ours remain there also, as brothers of a common cause, and fighting for the one grand object, viz.: Unconditional freedom.[63]

Aftermath

"Rumor says that the object [of the Florida expedition] was mainly *political;* to simply make a military demonstration; to ascertain the loyalty of the Floridians; offer them protection, and invite them back to the Union," wrote the *Philadelphia Inquirer's* correspondent. "If that was the principal object, *the expedition is a failure."* Two days after Seymour's battered army returned to Jacksonville, Lyman Stickney offered Treasury Secretary Chase his perspective on the matter. "Since my last a serious disaster to the troops in Florida happened. . . . Gen'l Seymour in command," he wrote. "It was the result of incaution if not rashness akin to his assault on Fort Wagner. I accord to him many high qualities of the soldier, but he is without the just balance of a military commander. The Florida campaign opened so well, I hoped, as it might have been and by proper direction reverse would not befall us. Gen. Seymour too is not in accord with us politically but if he will do the fighting in good style, his copperhead ablations might be pardoned."[64]

The first press barrage of calumny over the Florida fiasco was aimed right at the White House. The opinion voiced by the *New York World* was typical: "Of course, no military purpose took an army into Florida, as the conquest of Florida would do no more to put down the rebellion than would the occupation of Yucatan or Coney Island. The object is political. Florida has been marked out as one of the rotten borough states which are to help make Mr. Lincoln President." Even Lincoln's Secretary of the Navy, Gideon Welles, suspected that the "President has been trying a game himself." Eventually the storm blew over, however, with little lasting damage done to Lincoln's reelection prospects.[65]

Although Stickney was still full of schemes, the wind had gone out of the sails of Florida reconstruction. After Olustee, the number of residents willing to take the U.S. Oath of Allegiance dropped dramatically, and John Hay soon gave up on the project of registering 10 percent of the state's 1860 voter list: "I am very sure that we cannot get the President's 10th," he wrote on March 1. Time was also running out on Salmon P. Chase's quest for the Republican presidential nomination. In early March, the Treasury secretary withdrew his name from consideration, and thereafter his national "machine" slowly fell apart. It was a loss of momentum from which Stickney, for one, would never recover: finding himself shut out of postwar political life in Florida, he ended as barely a footnote in its history.[66]

Of the three black regiments that fought at Olustee, the 54th Massachusetts (Colored) had the shortest stay in Florida. From February to April, it took part in the general defense of Jacksonville; on April 17, its men climbed aboard the steam transport *Cosmopolitan,* and by the next day, they were back at Morris Island, outside Charleston. But the war was not over for this first black regiment raised in the North—not by a long shot.

The 8th USCT remained assigned to Jacksonville's defenses somewhat longer. On April 17, it was moved down the St. John's River to Yellow Bluff, where, according to its regimental history, the men were "set to fortifying that point, and guarding the stream to prevent the enemy from planting torpedoes. In June, Major [Edelmiro] Mayer, of the Seventh Colored, was temporarily assigned to the command of the regiment, and under him, it participated in numerous raids into the surrounding country, destroying a portion of the . . . railroad, and taking some of the enemy's ammunition." The regiment's canine mascot, Lion, came along, though he was a little the worse for wear, having been slightly wounded in a foreleg at Olustee. Still, as Sergeant-Major Jones informed the readers of the *Christian Recorder,* Lion was a "soldier, and has no respect for citizens who may visit the camp and does not hesitate to bite. He attends 'Dress parade,' has musical taste, and shows that he has not been brought up a savage." On August 4, as part of a brigade under Brigadier General William Birney, the 8th was moved to Virginia, where it was soon fully involved in operations against Petersburg and Richmond.[67]

The on-leave Colonel James C. Beecher returned to his beloved 1st North Carolina Colored (now the 35th USCT) in March, arriving in time to guide it through a very active role in the occupation of eastern Florida. Beecher was joined on July 18 by his fiancée, Frances Johnson, and they were married that same evening. She later provided a succinct summary of the post-Olustee service of the 35th. "The weeks succeeding this battle . . . were spent in dislodging the enemy from various small points in the state and holding them until there was no fear of their being retaken," she recorded. "An entire company was taken captive on the steamer *Columbine,* and sent with their captain and lieutenant to Andersonville, Georgia. Those who survived until the close of the war were released." On November 25, the 35th USCT sailed to join another expedition, bound for another field of battle. This time Colonel Beecher would share the fate of his men.[68]

The Battle of Olustee reopened the critical issue of military promotion for blacks, even as the rank and file faced continuing official racism as represented by the pay inequity. A soldier of the 54th who identified himself only as "Venoir" wrote of both matters to the *Anglo-African:*

> We have fought like men; . . . but still we are refused the $13 per month. . . . All we ask is the rights of other soldiers—the liberty of other free men. . . .
>
> Sergeant Stephen A. Swailes, colored, of Co. F, has received his commission as 2nd Lieutenant for this Regiment. . . . We look forward to the day when any colored man, who is competent, shall be assigned to the position that his qualifications call him to. We have sergeants in this Regiment that can handle a company as well as any white man in the army. Will any of them be promoted to a captaincy? We will see.[69]

Chapter Six

"You Are Fighting against Your Master"

——◁◦▷——

Massacre at Fort Pillow, Tennessee, April 12, 1864

THE first word of trouble at Fort Pillow reached Memphis, some fifty miles to the south-southwest, around midday on Tuesday, April 12. The steamer *Platte Valley,* scheduled to make a run up the Mississippi River that would take it past the Union outpost, was allowed to proceed, but only with the gunboat *Silver Cloud* as an escort. A pair of enterprising reporters for competing St. Louis dailies wangled their way aboard the transport, which set out at 5:00 P.M., towing the smaller *Silver Cloud* while boiler repairs were being completed on that vessel.

The two craft were only about three miles below the fort when, at approximately 8:00 A.M., some of the enemy's mounted pickets were sighted on the shore. The *Silver Cloud* boldly steamed toward Fort Pillow, which was set on a steep bluff near a bend in the river; the boat's gunners, certain that Rebels now controlled the fort, opened fire as soon as they came within range, and for the next two hours tried to provoke a response from the garrison. The *Platte Valley* then joined the *Silver Cloud,* and the pair idled in midstream. Passengers crowded the rails of the transport in hopes of catching a glimpse of the fort, but a thick veil of smoke from burning buildings and hay obscured their view. Finally a white flag appeared, and a launch set out from the *Platte Valley* with the two reporters aboard.

The first thing they noticed was bodies scattered "along the river and on the sides of the bluff." The correspondent for the *St. Louis Daily Union* counted fifty or sixty corpses and wondered how many more had floated off in the current. The party was met on the shore by some Confederate officers, who readily agreed to let the men climb the bluff to the fort. Tramping up the steep slope, the writer for the *St. Louis Missouri Democrat* observed that some guns had recently been hauled away from a small redoubt located at the top. He also noticed that the "huts scattered around had been mostly burned up. In one of these were bodies of colored soldiers, partly burned, but whether or not by design I cannot state." The *Daily Union* man asked his guides about the large number of dead black soldiers; he was told that though the officers regretted it, it was impossible for them to "control the *rage* and *indignation* of their soldiers when they find their own slaves fighting against them."

Pillow itself "was a miserably constructed affair," declared the *Daily Union* reporter, who deemed it "surprising the military authorities omit the inspection of such places." His companion quickly spotted a glaring weakness in Pillow's location: "About thirty yards from the fort is a deep ravine, running all along the front, and so steep at the bottom as to be hidden from the fort and not commanded by its guns."

The reporters returned to the *Platte Valley* badly shaken by all they had seen. To the utter disgust of the *Missouri Democrat* writer, several Union officers traveling on the transport invited their Rebel counterparts to dinner. His colleague, meanwhile, could think only about the bodies and destruction. "I have witnessed many revolting results of war," he wrote, "but can assure your readers that the conduct of the rebels, towards our little garrison at Fort Pillow, beggars all description, for fiendish brutality and savage treachery."[1]

No one recorded any details about the moment when Major Lionel F. Booth first stepped ashore at the boat wharf below Fort Pillow. It was March 29, 1864. Not far over the eastern horizon, a demon was loose on the land in the person of Nathan B. Forrest, whose mounted legions moved with wraithlike ease across the middle-Tennessee countryside, striking suddenly and savagely at isolated Federal outposts.

Forrest's men, stirring from their Mississippi lairs in mid-March, slipped northward and were soon chewing up so-called strong points. The garrison at Union City, Tennessee, 475 men strong, surrendered without a fight on March 24; the very next day, other Confederate raiders, led by Forrest himself, appeared outside Paducah, Kentucky. Paducah's white and black Yankee defenders scrambled into a strong earthwork on the western side of the town and stood fast. They beat back one assault, then watched in amazement and relief as the Rebel formations melted away.

This distant threat was a very real concern for the twenty-five-year-old Major Booth. Philadelphia had been his home for twenty of those years, until he decided to seek adventure in the regular army; a fitness evaluation had found him to be a "steady, intelligent and worthy young man." If the later activism of his wife may serve as any measure, it is likely that he looked upon African Americans with a mixture of compassion and interest. In June 1863, Booth (lately promoted from sergeant to captain) joined the 1st Regiment Alabama Siege Artillery (African Descent), organized in western Tennessee and Corinth, Mississippi. The army's new system of naming these black units caught up with the 1st Alabama Siege Artillery on March 11, 1864, when it became the 6th United States Colored Heavy Artillery (USCHA). By this time, Lionel F. Booth had advanced again, from captain to major.

On landing at Fort Pillow, Booth carried orders from Major General Stephen A. Hurlbut, dated Memphis, March 28:

> You will proceed with your own battalion to Fort Pillow and establish your force in garrison of the works there. As you will be . . . the senior officer at that post, you will take command, conferring, however, freely and fully with Major [William F.] Bradford, Thirteenth Tennessee Cavalry, whom you will find a good officer, though not of much experience.
>
> There are two points of land fortified at Fort Pillow, one of which only is now held by our troops. . . . The positions are commanding and can be held by a small force against almost any odds. . . .
>
> I think Forrest's check at Paducah will not dispose him to try the river again, but that he will fall back to [the Tennessee town of] Jackson and thence cross the Tennessee [River]; as soon as this is ascertained I shall withdraw your garrison. Nevertheless, act promptly in

putting the works into perfect order and the post into its strongest defense.[2]

What Booth did not realize was that his superior was placing troops in Fort Pillow in violation of specific orders from Major General William T. Sherman, who needed every man for his Atlanta campaign and to this end had begun decreasing some rear-echelon garrisons and closing outposts that he believed were no longer strategically important. On January 11, 1864, Sherman had informed Hurlbut which posts scattered throughout western and middle Tennessee would be reduced and which eliminated. "Abandon Corinth and Fort Pillow absolutely," Sherman ordered.[3]

About a month after carrying out Sherman's instructions, General Hurlbut quietly reoccupied Fort Pillow, first moving in Major Bradford's detachment of white troops, then Major Booth and his black men. Why this contravention of direct orders? Hurlbut's military record was riddled with financial improprieties and self-serving actions; while there is no hard evidence to prove a direct relationship, there is reason to suppose that he may have been one of many powerful men in the region who took advantage of a lucrative (and illegal) traffic in contraband cotton. With Northern mills' paying up to eighty cents a pound, there was lots of money to be made, and Fort Pillow would have offered a handy distribution point, only a short distance from Hurlbut's Memphis headquarters, yet far enough away not to attract undue attention.

None of this was known to Major Booth as he surveyed his new command. First constructed (and named after one of their own) by Confederate troops in 1861, Fort Pillow had been rendered useless when U. S. Grant flanked it in 1862 by capturing Forts Henry and Donelson. Originally designed to accomodate a garrison of ten thousand, its defensive perimeter had been shortened in 1862 to protect about half that number. This was still too large an area to be held by the troops now assigned to the post, however, so Booth put up an even smaller redoubt on a thirty-acre promontory near the river.

According to Sergeant Henry F. Weaver, a white serving in Company C of the 6th USCHA, "Major Booth, from the time he took command of the post at Fort Pillow, was strengthening the same by throwing up rifle-pits, building [gun] platforms, and making embrasures in the fort for the purpose of working his guns." Booth's blacks built an earthen redan shaped like a "W," with an enclosure of about an acre. Six feet high and six feet thick at their base (tapering to four feet across the top), the earthworks were fronted by a six-foot-deep ditch measuring twelve feet wide. Six cannon were placed inside the redoubt, and additional rifle pits dug some thirty to three hundred yards out either flank. Directly behind the fort was the bluff itself, an extremely steep slope falling a hundred feet down to the river. Just north of the redoubt was a small stream, known alternately as Cold Creek and Coal Creek, which fed into the river from the east.[4]

Booth's redoubt left much to be desired. To begin with, the river side was wide open, with no walls or guns to cover any approach from that quarter (here Booth was counting on fire support from the U.S. Navy river patrols). Then, too, a number of nearby buildings were allowed to remain intact; while they provided quarters for a post hospital and quartermaster offices, they afforded cover for any attackers and could not be targeted by the redoubt's cannon. Further, several trenchlike gullies snaked near the redoubt, and the ground was littered with debris left from the land clearing, offering ample concealment for enemy troops. Most serious of all was the fact that Booth's redoubt was lower than several other knolls within rifle range.

On April 3, the major reported to Hurlbut that everything "seems to be very quiet within a radius of from 30 to 40 miles around, and I do not think any apprehensions need be felt or fears entertained. I think it perfectly safe." Booth's sanguine assessment would prove tragically wrong. The very next day, from the central Tennessee town of Jackson, Major General Nathan B. Forrest sent his superior a status report and his thoughts regarding future plans. His men had been pretty much having their own way against the weak Federal opposition, and "I feel confident of my ability to whip any cavalry they can send against me," Forrest stated. After reviewing some of his immediate supply needs and strategic options, Forrest identified one target that was high on his list: "There is a Federal force of 500 or 600 at Fort Pillow," he indicated, "which I shall attend to in a day or two."[5]

Besides a few civilians, the garrison at Fort Pillow consisted principally of three military units. There was a battalion of some 277 men belonging to the white 13th Tennessee Cavalry, whose ranks contained Tennessee Unionists as well as a handful of former Confederate soldiers. The latter, having changed sides, were derisively dubbed "Tennessee Tories." Another 270 garrison members were contributed by the 6th USCHA, Major Booth's command; many of these were ex-slaves who had been recruited throughout the region. The final portion of Pillow's garrison came from the 2nd U.S. Colored Light Artillery, a total of thirty-five men. This meant there were approximately 582 soldiers present at Fort Pillow—"approximately" because both the 13th and the 6th were still actively recruiting, and there were some in these regiments who were not yet registered on the muster rolls. All in all, the garrison was an explosive mix. As one reporter afterward noted, "The Rebel Tennesseans have about the same bitterness against Tennesseans in the Federal army as against the negroes."[6]

Since most of the blacks in the 6th USCHA were illiterate, only a vague picture emerges from their sparse military records. What is certain is that the racial barriers confronting Tennessee's black soldiers were formidable indeed. The state's leaders, headed by Governor Andrew Johnson, had earlier successfully lobbied to have Tennessee temporarily exempted from the Emancipation Proclamation; when Johnson finally embraced the document, in August 1863, he did so out of his hatred of wealthy Tennessee slave owners, rather than any sincere desire to improve the lot of blacks. With such weak support at the top, it is hardly surprising that many of the state's white citizens—Unionists or not—should have viewed uniformed blacks with animosity and disdain; there is nothing in the historical record to suggest that the attitudes of the pro-Union whites in the 13th Tennessee Cavalry differed markedly from those held by their neighbors serving under Forrest. At Fort Pillow, the two commands were actually physically segregated, the blacks occupying tents within Major Booth's redoubt, the whites living outside those walls.

On the morning of April 12, recalled Sergeant Weaver of the 6th USCHA, "I called the roll of my company soon after daylight, and had gone to the bank of the river, . . . and had not been there long when we heard an uncommon noise and commotion around headquarters, and soon the cry [was] that the rebels were coming." Fort Pillow's outer line of pickets, all from the 13th Tennessee Cavalry, had been struck by the advance elements of a fifteen-hundred-man force that Forrest had sent from Jackson in fulfillment of his promise to "attend to" the outpost.[7]

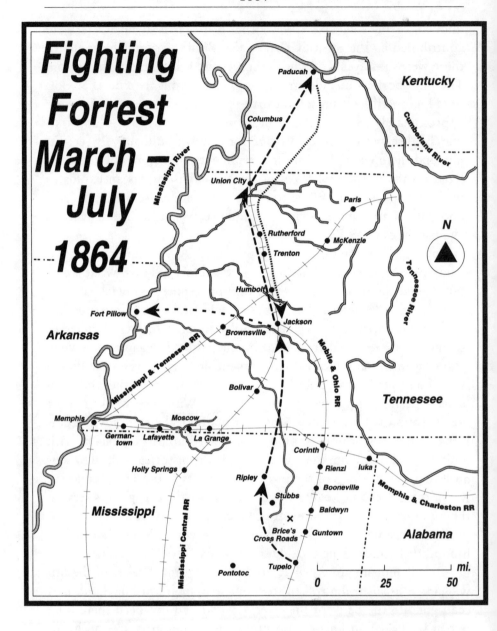

Fighting
Forrest
March –
July
1864

Forrest's command, under the immediate direction of Brigadier General James R. Chalmers, consisted of brigades led by Colonels Tyree H. Bell and Robert McCulloch. According to Chalmers's after-action report, "My orders from General Forrest were to invest the place, and I proceeded to do so." Bell's men were assigned to close on the northern and eastern sides of the fort, while McCulloch's targeted Pillow from the south. Most of the Confederate soldiers had never before faced black soldiers in combat.[8]

As the Rebel troopers pressed the Federal perimeter (Major Booth was holding key portions of the 1862 line), they were met by a furious barrage from the six cannon in Fort Pillow and from the U.S. gunboat *New Era,* stationed on the river. "We fought them right hard during the battle," recalled Private M. Williams of the 6th USCHA, "and killed some of them." James R. Bingham, a civilian who worked at the post store, saw "several negroes wounded, with blood running from their bodies, still engaged [in] loading and firing cannon and muskets cheerfully." Sergeant Weaver, ordered to roll two ten-pounder Parrott guns into position on the south side of Major Booth's redoubt, was soon "firing at the advancing enemy as they came in sight."[9]

Between 9:00 and 10:00 A.M., two things happened that would spell the doom of Fort Pillow. Shortly after nine, a Confederate sniper killed Major Booth. Civilian Hardie N. Revelle claimed to have been "standing not more than 10 paces from Major Booth when he fell, struck in the heart by a musket-bullet." Booth collapsed near the gun being worked by Sergeant Weaver "and was carried away," said the noncom, adding that "command was devolved upon Major Bradford, of the Thirteenth Tennessee Cavalry." (At about this time, probably at Booth's instigation, most of the noncombatants were put on a coal barge and hauled to safety by the *New Era.*) Not long after Major Booth's body was removed, General Forrest himself arrived on the scene.[10]

The Confederate commander had already been riding for many hours, but he immediately undertook a careful survey of the enemy's position, during which circuit he had two horses killed under him and was badly bruised in a fall. A cavalryman he passed during this reconnaissance remembered hearing him say, "There are not many—we must take them." Realizing that the buildings Major Booth had left intact south of the fort offered a sheltered position that he could use to stage troops for an assault, Forrest ordered Chalmers to seize them and to move in along the Cold Creek gully. "The troops responded with alacrity and enthusiasm," reported Chalmers, "and in a short

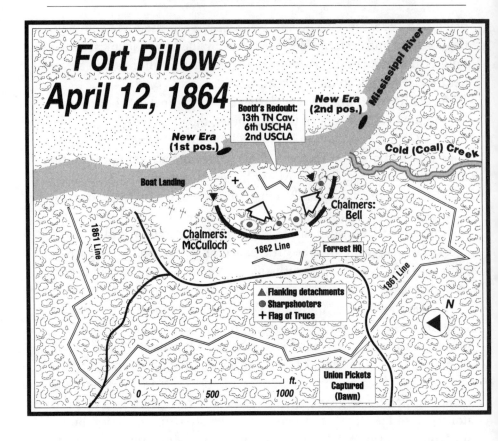

Fort Pillow
April 12, 1864

Booth's Redoubt:
13th TN Cav.
6th USCHA
2nd USCLA

New Era
(2nd pos.)

Mississippi River

New Era
(1st pos.)

Cold (Coal) Creek

Boat Landing

Chalmers:
Bell

Chalmers:
McCulloch

1861 Line

1862 Line

Forrest HQ

1861 Line

N

▲ Flanking detachments
● Sharpshooters
+ Flag of Truce

ft.
0   500   1000

Union Pickets
Captured
(Dawn)

time took possession of all the rifle-pits around the fort, and closed up on all sides within 25 or 30 yards of the outer ditch." Fort Pillow's defenders, both white and black, were now all squeezed together inside Major Booth's ill-sited redoubt.[11]

By 11:00 A.M., Forrest's men controlled the immediate area around the small fort, with his marksmen making it almost certain death for the Yankee artillerymen to show themselves at their guns. Forrest also had two cannon placed on a bluff south of the fort; they opened at midday, forcing the warship to shift to a less advantageous firing position.

Forrest's men spent the next few hours sniping at the Union defenders, who were unable to respond in kind. Reported Forrest's adjutant, Captain Charles W. Anderson, "The width or thickness of the works across the top prevented the garrison from firing down on us, as it could only be done by mounting and exposing themselves to the unerring fire of our sharpshooters." At 3:30 P.M., Forrest sent for-

ward a flag of truce with a message addressed to the fort's commander, thought still to be Major Booth. The missive was typical of the
type of ultimatum Forrest favored in such cases, offering the belea-
guered defenders just two options: surrender or die.

> The conduct of the officers and men garrisoning Fort Pillow has been
> such as to entitle them to being treated as prisoners of war. I demand
> the unconditional surrender of the garrison, promising you that you
> shall be treated as prisoners of war. My men have received a fresh
> supply of ammunition, and from their present position can easily as-
> sault and capture the fort. Should my demand be refused, I cannot be
> responsible for the fate of your command.[12]

"Up to this time," recorded the post's surgeon, "we had not lost in
killed and wounded over 25 to 30 men." The Union reply was a request for an hour's respite to think things over. In one of the many
mysteries of this whole affair, Major Bradford signed the note (as he
would all subsequent ones) with Major Booth's name. Forrest's
scouts now told him they had spotted three Federal steamers approaching, one of which seemed to be "crowded with troops." Forrest promptly rejected Major "Booth"'s plea for a sixty-minute grace
period, instead giving him just twenty to decide. While these negotiations were taking place, according to eyewitness testimony, "the
white men of both sides were bantering each other from their respective positions, while some of the negroes indulged in provoking, im-
pudent jeers."[13]

The scouting reports that moved Forrest to action were only partially correct: two Union steamers did draw near the fort (a third
turned back). However, of the two, one was carrying two batteries of
artillerymen bound for Cairo but was otherwise "entirely defenseless," while the other was running empty. A Union officer aboard the
first boat spotted the truce flag just as its captain was told by the commander of the *New Era* to pass without stopping, which both steamers did. Responding to this perceived menace, Forrest sent flanking
detachments along the riverbank to forestall any landing attempt.[14]

Major "Booth"'s final response to Forrest's ultimatum was terse
and to the point: "I will not surrender." Forrest promptly prepared
his men for the assault. It has been suggested that his failure at Paducah may have compelled him to conquer Fort Pillow, lest his threats

lose their credibility; while he left no testimony either supporting or refuting this point, his methodical preparations certainly demonstrated a firm resolve to take the place by storm. When all was ready, from his command post (uncharacteristically located about four hundred yards behind his front line), Forrest ordered his bugler to sound the "charge."[15]

The Rebels leapt up from their concealed positions and rushed forward. According to a Union officer, the Confederates appeared "as if rising from out of the very earth," whereupon they "received our first fire, wavered, rallied again and finally succeeded in breaking our lines, and in thus gaining possession of the fort." Just minutes after beginning their attack, Forrest's men were atop the parapet and firing down into the masses of blue-coated figures below.[16]

Panic spread among the Union troops, with blacks and whites each later blaming the other for breaking first. What is clear is that while a few Federals stood their ground, most threw down their guns, some to run for the presumed safety of the bluff, others to raise their hands in surrender. No one had lowered the U.S. flag. According to one account, Major Bradford's entire contribution to the final defense of Fort Pillow was to shout, "Boys, save your lives!" before fleeing "down the creek," where he was killed under circumstances that remain appropriately murky.[17]

What came next was a massacre, pure and simple. Corporal William A. Dickey, 13th Tennessee Cavalry, ran from the wall when Forrest's men breasted it. "The rebels followed closely," he recalled, "shooting down all who came in the way, white and black. . . . One rebel came to me and took my percussion caps, saying he had been killing negroes so fast that his own had been exhausted; he added that he was going to shoot some more." According to Confederate Achilles V. Clark, the "slaughter was awful. Words cannot describe the scene. The poor deluded negroes would run up to our men fall upon their knees and with uplifted hands scream for mercy but they were ordered to their feet and then shot down. The whitte men fared but little better." Sergeant Wilbur H. Gaylord of the 6th U.S. Colored Heavy Artillery was wounded as the final assault began, and could not leave the wall. "I should think that 200 rebels passed over the works and passed by me while I lay there. When one rebel noticed that I was alive [he] shot . . . and missed. . . . Just at this time I saw them shoot down 3 black men who were begging for their lives; and who had surrendered." Private George Shaw, also in the 6th, was wounded when he tried to surrender. As the Rebel before him raised his rifle, Shaw heard him say, "Damn you, you are fighting against your master."[18]

Other blacks later told U.S. investigators equally horrifying stories. Private Benjamin Robinson "saw them shoot two white men right by the side of me after they had laid their guns down." Robinson was himself shot, robbed, and stripped. Private Ransom Anderson of Company B testified that he was slashed while lying on the ground after surrendering; from that position he witnessed "Coolie Pride, of the same regiment and company, stabbed by a rebel soldier with a bayonet and the bayonet broken off in his body." Elias Falls of Company A "was ordered with several others to march up the hill, and we were fired upon while thus marching. I was the second man shot while in the hands of the rebel officers, and obeying their commands while marching up the hill."[19]

Forrest and his officers seem to have exercised little positive control over their men during the half hour following the successful assault. A Southern newspaper correspondent related that "Gen. Forrest expected a surrender after entering the fort, and anxiously looked for it, as he witnessed the carnage; but no token was given." Union cavalryman Daniel Stamps was captured after trying to escape down the bluff to the river. "While I was standing at the bottom of the hill," he later testified, "I heard a rebel officer shout out an order of some kind to the men who had taken us, and saw a rebel soldier standing by me. I asked him what the officer had said. . . . It was 'kill the last damn one of them.' The soldier replied to his officer that we had surrendered, that we were prisoners and must not be shot. The officer again replied, seeming crazy with rage that he had not been obeyed, 'I tell you to kill the last God damned one of them.' He then turned and galloped off." Rebel Achilles V. Clark swore that he "with several others tried to stop the butchery and at one time had partially succeeded. But Gen. Forrest ordered them shot down like dogs." If Forrest did let his famous temper overtake him, perhaps the lapse was but a momentary one, for another C.S. soldier, Samuel H. Caldwell, would write to his wife on April 15, "If General Forrest had not run between our men & the Yanks with his pistol and sabre drawn not a man would have been spared." Forrest's General Chalmers similarly claimed to a Federal officer on April 13 that he and Forrest had "stopped the massacre as soon as [we] were able to do so." He further explained that their men "had such a hatred toward the armed negro that they could not be restrained from killing the negroes after they had captured them."[20]

Even after this murderous frenzy had spent itself, however, the ordeal was far from over. At least two of the Tennessee Union soldiers recalled seeing wounded blacks killed as late as the next day. One of the two, James N. Taylor, related that Confederate troops made "2 of the wounded negroes stand upon their feet that they might see them fall again when shot; and shot they were." There were other reports, from both sides, of wounded men being buried alive.[21]

For Forrest, the cost of taking Fort Pillow was 14 killed and 86 wounded. Of the 585 to 605 Federals estimated to have been present that day, nearly half (between 277 and 297) were either killed or fatally wounded. The mortality rate among the black troops was a staggering 64 percent, while the losses among the 13th Tennessee ranged between 31 and 34 percent. Another 226 members of the garrison were taken prisoner; of these, 58 were black and 168 white.

At first, Forrest trumpeted his success. "The victory was complete," he reported on April 15. "The river was dyed with the blood of the slaughtered for 200 yards. . . . It is hoped that these facts will demonstrate to the Northern people that negro soldiers cannot cope with Southerners." What few could have anticipated was the tidal wave of horror and indignation that roiled in response to this action. This was not the first time captured or wounded black soldiers had been killed (nor would it be the last), but never before had such atrocities been on such a large scale, and never so baldly proclaimed as an object lesson.[22]

An official U.S. Army investigation was immediately followed by a congressional examination, vivid testimony from both of which was released to the national press. The report of the Congressional Committee on the Conduct of the War presented all accounts received without qualification, including lurid tales of women and children being shot down. Twenty thousand copies of the proceedings were printed and distributed. "Let Lincoln send a copy of this book to every home," declared a Northern diarist. "It is better than the draft or his greenbacks." Once the North's determination to play the race card became known to the South, the tenor of Confederate coverage changed: no longer a fearsome object lesson, Fort Pillow was now instead cast as a legitimate Rebel victory that had been blown out of all proportion. Those killed, maintained this new Southern line, had died with guns in their hands, fighting to the last. Although strongly urged to institute a policy of retaliation, General Sherman ultimately decided that it would only serve to spin indiscriminate killing out of control. Better, he told Secretary of War Edwin M. Stanton, to "let soldiers affected make their [own] rules as we progress. We will use their own logic against [the enemy] as we have from the beginning of the war."[23]

For America's blacks, word of what had happened at Fort Pillow came as no surprise. "I do not wonder at the conduct and disaster that transpired at Fort Pillow," a black soldier wrote from South Carolina. "I wonder that we have not had more . . . Fort Pillow massacres." An African American clergyman believed that the widespread attention given the incident was crucial if whites were ever to begin to understand the evil of racism. "None but the blacks of the land," he argued, "have heretofore realized the hateful nature of the beast; but now, white men are beginning to feel and to realize what its beauties are."[24]

Perhaps the most profound and immediate impact of Fort Pillow was felt by the black men already in the Union ranks, and by the white officers who commanded them. From Fort Pickering in Memphis, 2nd Lieutenant W. A. Price of the 55th USCT put down his thoughts for New York's *Anglo-African* newspaper:

> While I meditate for a moment on the Fort Pillow massacre my very blood chills within my veins. I often ask myself the question; "Shall we, as officers and men of colored regiments, ever be found with prisoners in our possession?" I can only answer for myself; I would be tempted in such circumstances to mow the infernal rebels to the ground, as I would mow the grass before my scythe. I know not how soon I may be called to share the fate of the gallant officers and men at Fort Pillow. God forbid that such should ever be my lot.[25]

Little could Lieutenant Price know that he and his company would soon cross paths with the fearsome Forrest and his men.

Battle of Brice's Cross Roads, Mississippi, June 10, 1864

Friday, June 10, was a hot, sultry day in northern Mississippi. The sun blazed down on the nearly eight-mile-long column of Federal soldiers plodding eastward on the dirt road leading from Ripley to Guntown. The approximately seventy-nine hundred Yankees were under the command of Brigadier General Samuel D. Sturgis, a West Pointer and Mexican War veteran who had been sent to Memphis by General Sherman with orders to "whip Forrest." Sturgis arrived in that city on April 18 and by the end of the month had his first strike force in the field. He quickly learned that it was one thing to look for Forrest and quite another actually to find him. "My little campaign is over," Sturgis reported to Sherman on May 12, "and, I regret to say, Forrest is still at large."[26]

In the interim, Sherman had begun his long-anticipated Atlanta campaign, traveling with his troops as they marched south from Chattanooga on May 4 and 5. One of his greatest worries was the vulnerable network of rail lines and supply routes needed to sustain the Federal army: it would be disaster for Forrest to sweep into middle Tennessee and wreck the railroads between Nashville and Chattanooga. Sturgis was therefore told to try again. On June 1, he assembled at Lafayette, Tennessee, 3,300 cavalry, 4,800 infantry, and 16 cannon. His purpose was twofold: to wreck as much of the Mobile and Ohio Railroad around Tupelo as possible, and to flush the elusive Forrest into a stand-up fight.

Sturgis's expedition was organized into a cavalry division led by Brigadier General Benjamin H. Grierson, consisting of brigades under colonels George E. Waring and Edward F. Winslow, and an infantry division commanded by Colonel William L. McMillen, containing brigades led by Colonels Alexander Wilkin, George B. Hoge, and Edward Bouton. Bouton's was an all-black outfit, made up of the 55th and 59th USCT and the two-gun Battery F, 2nd U.S. Colored Light Artillery (USCLA).

The 55th had been organized in May 1863, at Corinth, Mississippi, as the 1st Regiment Alabama Infantry (African Descent), becoming a USCT unit in March 1864. Its rank and file were almost all former slaves. Its officers included Lieutenant Eli Babb, a veteran of Bloody Kansas who had fought alongside John Brown. Also wearing shoulder straps in the regiment was 2nd Lieutenant W. A. Price of Company K, who told the *Anglo-African,* "I am not ashamed to be seen out on picket guard with my Company because they are colored men, but on the contrary, am proud that I have the privilege to drill them, instruct them, and educate them, for future benefit." The 55th had something of a zealot in the person of its chaplain, E. R. Pierce, who set up several classes to teach the illiterate ex-slaves to read and cipher. "Our colored troops are doing all the picket duty of Memphis," Pierce wrote to the *Anglo-African* with almost sinful pride. "Better or more loyal men cannot be found in America." Sometimes the harsh realities of slave life placed unusual responsibilities on the officers of black regiments: "I have traveled, many a night, all night in the mud and water, with a squad of men who knew the geography of the country, to get their wives and children," related Lieutenant Price. On May 12, Price commented on the morale of the 55th USCT. "Our men have never been in an engagement, but I have the utmost confidence in their bravery," he said. "They often say, 'O, I wish we could get in a fight! we would make the rebels *get.*'"[27]

The 59th USCT, formerly the 1st Regiment Tennessee Volunteers (African Descent), had mustered in at La Grange, Tennessee, in early June 1863. Its complement of soldiers had been recruited largely in the contraband camps located there and at Bolivar and Jackson. The regiment's commander, Lieutenant Colonel Robert Cowden, would never forget the day the unit was transferred to Memphis and marched into that town. The city's white residents, he recalled, were witness to something they "had never expected to see,—their own former slaves powerfully and lawfully armed for their overthrow. . . . The sight must have burned into their very souls." Sadly, however, the white men serving with the 59th were not themselves free of racism. At first, the regimental color line was drawn below the rank of sergeant, but after a year of training and education, several blacks qualified for the three stripes and were so appointed. The white sergeants who had not by then been raised to lieutenant "were all, at their own request, discharged," noted Cowden. The 59th USCT, like the other black Tennessee regiments, entered the rolls as a garrison outfit, leaving a critical question unanswered. "It had been already abundantly demonstrated that in camp, and as guards on outposts, and provost duty, and wherever tried, the colored man made an excellent, indeed, a *model* soldier," observed Cowden. "But would he stand the test of battle?"[28]

There were a total of nine batteries organized as part of the 2nd U.S. Colored Light Artillery, each consisting of four to six cannon. Batteries C, D, and E were recruited and stationed in Louisiana; Battery B in Virginia; Battery G at Hilton Head, South Carolina; Battery H at Pine Bluff, Arkansas; and Batteries A, F, and I in Tennessee. Two guns from Battery F, Captain Carl A. Lamberg commanding, marched with Bouton's brigade in Sturgis's June expedition.

Members of these units joined a crowd of black soldiers who gathered in Fort Pickering on April 27 to memorialize their comrades killed at Fort Pillow. Mary Elizabeth Weyt Booth, widow of Major Lionel F. Booth, was one of the speakers on this highly charged occasion. According to contemporary accounts, the scene became very emotional, with many USCT men kneeling as they pledged never to forget the atrocity. It was said that some of the soldiers wore medals proclaiming "Remember Fort Pillow!" A number of Memphis residents were assured that the black troops would have their revenge.

Several weeks later, assigned to a field expedition, the black garrison units began to believe that they were finally going to see some combat. But racial stereotyping remained a powerful factor. To ensure successful operations in the enemy's country, General Sturgis was packing more than 200,000 rations, and the assignment to guard the two hundred wagons went to the black soldiers. As Colonel Bouton, commanding the black brigade, reported, "I had the Fifty-fifth U.S. Colored Infantry, Major E[dgar] M. Lowe commanding, distributed through the supply train, some three or four men to each wagon; the train followed by Battery F, Second U.S. Artillery (colored), Capt. C. A. Lamberg commanding; Fifty-ninth U.S. Colored Infantry, Lieut. Col. Robert Cowden commanding, in rear."[29]

On June 10, Sturgis's cavalry headed out of the camp at Stubbs' Plantation shortly after "boots and saddles" sounded at 5:30 A.M. The infantry began moving at around 7:00 A.M., followed by the wagon train with its USCT escort. It had rained during the night, but the day promised to be hot and steamy. The tail of the expedition had traveled about two miles when, noted Colonel Bouton, "I discovered a column of the enemy's cavalry moving parallel with my right flank on a ridge road. . . . I moved with the utmost caution and vigilance, guarding every avenue of approach to the column from that flank." "The regiment [was] strung out the whole length of the [wagon] train," recalled Major Lowe of the 55th. "We marched in this manner until about 10 A.M., when firing was heard at the front, becoming louder and more continuous as we came nearer to it."[30]

The road ahead to Guntown wriggled its way for about eight miles before reaching a four-way intersection on a piece of high ground known as Brice's Cross Roads. Unbeknownst to Sturgis, General Forrest, though badly outnumbered, had decided to attack the Federals, even though his men were widely dispersed throughout the area, some as far as twenty-six miles away. Nevertheless, he had enough of them on hand at daylight to try to seize Brice's Cross Roads before the head of the Union column arrived. This time it was the Yankee riders who were quicker. Colonel Waring's brigade reached that point at 10:00 A.M.; one of his patrols, scouting along the road to Baldwyn, ran into the first of Forrest's men about a mile and a half from the intersection.

Both sides soon began to push troops forward. The initial Federal line took shape about half a mile from Brice's Cross Roads, with the Confederates some two thousand feet east of it. The advantage would lie with whichever side first got enough men in place to launch a successful attack. Forrest had three of his mounted brigades ready by noon, when he ordered his lines forward. At first, only Waring's dismounted cavalry was on hand to meet the assault; though help soon arrived from Winslow's brigade, the combined force was unable to withstand three fierce charges launched by Forrest's men. The last of these charges drove between the two Yankee brigades, compelling the Union battle lines to fall back a quarter of a mile at about 1:30 P.M.

When he realized that the Confederates were going to fight him hard, General Sturgis sent orderlies racing along his strung-out column to hurry the infantry forward. In response, Colonel McMillen set a killing pace. Moving up with the rear of the column, Major Lowe remembered how his troops "passed hundreds . . . of men lying by the side of the road overcome with heat—some even dying from overexertion." "It was a very hot day and we all suffered very much from the heat," recalled Henry Gary of the 55th USCT.[31]

At the crossroads, most of George Hoge's brigade had replaced Waring's exhausted troopers. Wilkin's infantry was just coming into

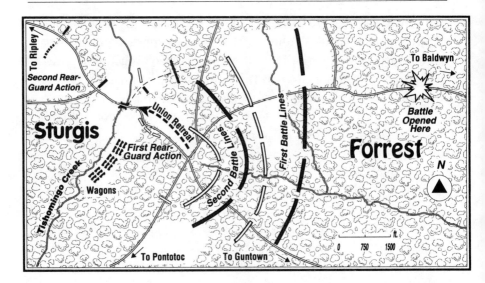

Brice's Cross Roads: June 10, 1864

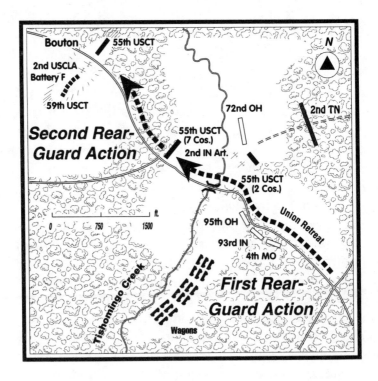

position when, shortly after 2:00 P.M., the Rebels (themselves reinforced) again advanced. For a while it was touch-and-go for both sides as attack was met by counterattack, but then, not long after 2:30 P.M., Sturgis's lines began slowly but surely to unravel.

In his anxiety to get fighting men to the front, General Sturgis forgot about color and sent for the black soldiers as well. When Major Lowe got the word, he decided to pull his scattered command together rather than send it forward piecemeal. Writing after the war and referring to himself in the third person, Lowe stated, "Instead of giving the command, 'Forward! Double-quick; march!' and starting off in a gallop, he halted his leading company and waited until the regiment closed up, and then placing himself in front—his men taking the long, swinging pace that men can stand for hours—we got there in plenty of time to get all the fighting we wanted." Although he instructed the wagon master to halt the supply train, Lowe left no one behind to enforce his orders—a mistake, as it turned out, since the wagons continued to lumber on until they were corralled close behind the main battle line.[32]

By the time the 55th USCT joined Colonel Bouton at a point of high ground about half a mile from Tishomingo Creek, it was clear that things were not going well. Scouting down the hill to the creek, Bouton observed that the Federal left flank failed to cover a trail leading into the rear of the Union position, along which path a Confederate force was even then pushing down. "I went back," Bouton later related, "brought up two companies of the Fifty-fifth, under Captain [Frank M.] Ewing, and posted them in that gap under a heavy fire." It cost the Federals dearly: Rebel musketry slammed into the two companies (B and I), and within ten minutes, virtually every officer was down, either dead or wounded. A short distance away, on the lower slope of the hill, Major Lowe hustled seven more companies into a line of battle to cover what was rapidly becoming a Union retreat. There were some small haystacks nearby that a few of the men used for cover, but they did not manage to screen Private Kinchen Cooper of Company C, who was shot dead at this time.[33]

Back along the ridge, Colonel Bouton now placed the two guns of Battery F, supported on their left by one company of the 55th USCT and on their right by the 59th, which had arrived from the rear. "My instructions," Colonel Cowden noted grimly, "were to hold this position until the entire column had passed securely to the rear, then retire to another position pointed out."[34]

Around this time, Colonel Bouton met his division commander, Colonel McMillen, and showed him the human breakwater his black troops had created to confront the Rebel tide. "That's right," said McMillen. "If you can hold this position until I can go to the rear and form on the next ridge, you can save this entire command. It all depends on you now."[35]

Despite Major Lowe's injunction to stop the supply train, the wagon master brought the vehicles and mules right across the narrow Tishomingo Creek bridge before halting. They were ordered back, but in the panic to reverse course, a wagon overturned on the bridge, causing others to pile up around it and completely block the span. The scene rapidly became a madhouse as fear-crazed teamsters cut terrified animals loose from their traces, infantry files scattered to avoid the tangle, and random Confederate shells set some of the vehicles ablaze.

By now the two companies of the 55th holding the gap had joined the seven on the hillside, which in turn retired to the top of the ridge, where the rest of Bouton's brigade was making its stand. "I want to say . . . that no better fighting was ever done than they did that day," Major Lowe afterward declared. "Every movement that was made was with the same precision as if on dress parade, and every command executed as coolly as at ordinary guard mountings." Captain C. P. Bailey of Company C found the Rebel fire "most galling. . . . Our men were cut down like grass before the scythe." Captain Lamberg's two guns pounded the Confederates as they tried to organize a follow-up attack from near Tishomingo Creek. The roar of the firing so damaged the eardrums of Private Junius Summerville of Company A, in the 59th, that his hearing would still be impaired twenty-five years after the fight.[36]

As the nine companies of the 55th USCT backed up the hill, a Rebel bullet struck Major Lowe, putting him out of action. Command thus devolved to Captain A. T. Reeve, who reported, "Many of the men were nearly exhausted." The regiment briefly held a line in front of the crest of the ridge before being flanked and falling back into alignment with Captain Lamberg's guns. Once more, Confederate troopers began to slip around the Federal right flank. "When I saw that we were unable to protect [Lamberg's] guns, I rode up to him and told him that he would have to move his guns as quick as possible," said Reeve. "He succeeded in moving his guns, leaving, I think, one caisson." It was around this time that Private George Jenkins of Company F was hit by a bullet that passed through his right side and lodged in his left thigh. "I fell like a dead man and fainted away, I reckon," he said. "The enemy advanced and some of them picked me up and laid me by a hole of water so I could drink."[37]

Several of the white regiments that had been partially rallied helped the blacks cover the retreat. The pressure was nearly too much for General Sturgis, who, when Colonel Bouton asked him for assistance, exclaimed, "For God's sake, if Mr. Forrest will let me alone I will let him alone. You have done all you could and more than was expected of you, and now all you can do is to save yourselves." Not yet ready to give up, Bouton ordered the two black regiments to maintain their fighting posture as they fell back; at one point, the colonel even led them in a brief hand-to-hand counterattack against Confederate skirmishers.[38]

A white soldier in the 72nd Ohio would later praise the actions of the USCT units in this phase of the battle:

> During the night of the 10th of June, and the retreat of 31 miles, the only compact organization I saw was the negro regiments, which were much reduced by casualties during the day's fight. They did not straggle, but marched together, and I distinctly remember their solid ranks and the orders of their officers, "Steady, men, steady," several times as I saw them on that awful night. They were kept well together and were the embodiment of all that is praiseworthy of soldiers in retreat.[39]

So heavily pressed was the black rear guard, in fact, that it had to abandon its fatalities. Somewhere along the road to Ripley, a Rebel bullet struck and killed Private Littleton Tucker of Company A, 59th USCT. Tucker's body, recalled the regiment's assistant surgeon, "was left in the road where he fell, as we were too closely pursued [by] overpowering numbers to bury our dead." The rigors of the retreat proved too much for Private Jeff Moreland of Company A, 59th USCT, who stopped his friend Rufus Newborn and asked him to carry his gun for a while. When an equally tired Newborn replied that he couldn't help, Moreland "sat down on a stump and said he could not go any further." Moreland's capture seemed certain, for the enemy was not three hundred yards behind; the exhausted soldier was never again seen by his company.[40]

Not everyone was under command control, and the narrow road soon became a nightmare of wagons and struggling men. Several guns were left at a point where the road led through a particularly difficult swamp, among them Captain Lamberg's two cannon, which the black gunners spiked. In one of the countless rear-guard actions that took place in the course of this long evening, Colonel Cowden of the 59th was wounded in the hip, with command consequently being turned over to Captain Henry W. Johnson. When the head of the retreating column reached Stubbs' Plantation, General Sturgis reformed enough of his cavalry to hold back the Rebel pursuers, who, in spite of Forrest's constant exhortations, were no less exhausted than their quarry.

The Union retreat continued for the next four days, until the weary Federals reached Germantown, Tennessee, where they regrouped. Little more than sketchy images of the black troops in action emerge from these confused days. Captain Henry C. Foster of the 59th, leading men from the 59th and the 55th, was forced to plunder abandoned wagons to get enough ammunition to continue the resistance. Several days into their dispiriting retreat, but now within sight of sanctuary across the Wolf River, Foster spotted a squad of Rebel cavalry moving to cut off his men. "Double-quick, march!" he called out, but the soldiers refused to hurry. "I won't run!" said more than one in the ranks; "I'll be damned if I run," said others. "I at once gave the command, 'Common time, march!'" related Foster, whose men thereby reached safety.[41]

Some other incidents of the retreat were recalled in a letter written to the *Cleveland Leader* from the headquarters of the 59th USCT:

> A corporal in company C, Fifty-ninth, was ordered to surrender. He let his would-be captor come close to him, when he struck him with the butt of his gun.
>
> While the regiment was fighting in a ditch, and the order came to retreat, the color-bearer threw out the flag, designed to jump out and get it, but the rebels rushed for it, and in the struggle one of the boys knocked down the reb who had the flag, with his gun, caught the flag and ran. . . .

One man in a charge threw his antagonist to the ground and pinned him fast, and as he attempted to withdraw his bayonet, it came off his gun, and as he was very busy just then, he left him transfixed to mother earth. . . .

One man had his gun spoiled by a shot. A rebel ordered him to surrender. "Yes, massa," he said. The rebel then loaded his gun, when the colored man jumped on him, took away his gun, and shot him in the mouth.[42]

One of the more harrowing experiences was related by Captain Reeve of the 55th USCT. Separated from the rest of the column, Reeve and some other officers led a group of about 250 men from the 55th and the 59th in the same direction, fighting all along the way. "At Moscow we got out of ammunition," Reeve recollected, "and we scattered through the woods, every man going in for himself. From this point till we reached Germantown the loyal [Confederate] citizens of Tennessee . . . hunted us with bloodhounds as we passed along."[43]

Among the anxious civilians waiting for the return of the black soldiers was Mary Ann Cox, whose son, Everett, was a private in Company B of the 59th. Once a slave on a cotton plantation, she had seen her first husband sold away and lost her second while still in bondage. With her son, she had fled her owner in July 1863 and settled in the contraband camp near Corinth, where young Everett enlisted. She had followed the 59th in its changes of camp, serving the unit as a washerwoman. This time her vigil would be in vain, for Everett had been taken prisoner at Brice's Cross Roads and would be sent to prison in Mobile, Alabama, where he would die. Another Mobile-bound POW was George Jenkins, who had been shot at the start of the Yankee retreat. After lying unattended on the field for some twenty-four hours, he crawled into a log for protection against a summer rainstorm before finally being picked up by a Confederate patrol and dispatched to Mobile's general hospital. Once discharged from treatment, he was assigned to labor battalions until the general surrender, in 1865.

Of the approximately 4,800 men under Forrest in this action, 96 were killed and 396 wounded. Sturgis, who went into the fight with about 7,900 men on hand, lost 223 dead, 394 wounded, and 1,623 missing. Many of the missing either were captured or eventually straggled back to their regiments, but not all: a man named Samuel A. Agnew who lived near Brice's Cross Roads was certain that "a great many negroes were killed. They wore the badge, 'Remember Fort Pillow,' and it was said they carried a black flag. This incensed the Southern soldiers, and they relentlessly shot them down." In this battle, Colonel Bouton's brigade reported casualties of 110 killed, 134 wounded, and 168 missing.[44]

On June 16, Chaplain E. R. Pierce of the 55th USCT, writing from Fort Pickering, reported on the events for the readers of the *Anglo-African*:

> June 1st inst., our regiment received "marching orders," and . . . started down into Mississippi after a large force under the notorious Forrest. . . . They met the foe, and because of double the number of the enemy, were compelled to yield. Our two colored regiments, God bless them! doing most of the fighting. Our lamented friend, Lieut. Price, fell dead at the first fire leading on his men.
>
> Our Major, E. M. Low[e] . . . was wounded in the commencement of the struggle. He entered the contest exclaiming "Remember Fort Pillow, boys!" and well they remember it. They fought with desperation—not as the hireling, who is not elated by success, or mortified at defeat, but true, free men, fighting for their liberties and families. . . .
>
> Our poor boys came in singly and by dozens for four or five days, shoeless, hatless, coatless, and feet so sore they almost had to crawl. The officers stood by their men, and although several could have reached the city to safety, and two or three days sooner, would not leave their men. . . .
>
> I can assure you there is not the least discount on the colored soldiers fighting. They are looked upon by all with pride and joy. They kept themselves supplied with ammunition by emptying the cartridge boxes of white soldiers who had thrown away everything. Our two colored regiments fought the rebel force several hours alone, while the trains and white troops were getting to the rear. They are anxious to go again.[45]

Ironically, Sturgis's defeat had one positive result for the North: it kept Forrest too busy to disrupt Sherman's supply lines. However, it also forced Sherman to divert a number of his units to western Tennessee. "There never will be peace in Tennessee till Forrest is dead," he wired Washington. General Sturgis, for his part, was sacked and sent home to sit out the rest of the war.[46]

There would be one more meeting between the black troops and Forrest, but compared to the fights at Fort Pillow and Brice's Cross Roads, it was a decidedly minor affair. Three USCT infantry regiments (the 59th, 61st, and 68th), brigaded together, would participate in a Federal expedition commanded by Major General Andrew J. Smith that would battle Forrest outside Tupelo on July 14 and 15, 1864. The black units, assigned to rear-guard duties, were in the hot spot as Forrest's riders struck repeatedly at the Federal column marching toward Tupelo. In a continuous series of skirmishes on the day preceding the battle, the USCT regiments successfully fended off the Rebel efforts, at a cost to themselves of eight dead and fifty-four wounded. Reporting on this campaign, Colonel Edward Bouton, commanding the black units, was to note that "the work done by my brigade in rear of column . . . was a severe test of the soldierly qualities and power of endurance of my men." Once again, it was a test that the black soldiers passed with honor.[47]

Chapter Seven

"With Wild, Exultant Cheers"

———◄o►———

Lieutenant Colonel Richard B. Irwin, Assistant Adjutant General,
Department of the Gulf:
The Red River Campaign

After the fall of Port Hudson on the 8th of July, 1863, the forces of the Department of the Gulf . . . were occupied in attempting to carry out the orders of the Government to restore the flag in Texas. . . . [Major] General [Nathaniel P.] Banks was informed . . . that the . . . Texas movement should be made . . . with the least possible delay. . . . The first attempt to [accomplish this] . . . led to the unfortunate expedition to Sabine Pass, in September [1863]. . . . General Banks [next made] . . . the attempt by . . . landing at Brazos Santiago, at the mouth of the Rio Grande. . . . These operations . . . were not satisfactory to the Government. . . . [Instructions were] renewed . . . for the naval and military operation on the Red River; this time it was to be on a larger scale, for [Major General Frederick] Steele was also to advance to the Red River from the line of the Arkansas [River].[1]

Major General Frederick Steele,
Commanding U.S. Forces in Arkansas,
to
Lieutenant General Ulysses S. Grant, Commanding U.S. Forces,
March 10, 1864

... I shall move [from Little Rock] by way of Washington[, Arkansas,] with all my available force to co-operate with Banks.[2]

Major General Frederick Steele,
Commanding U.S. Forces in Arkansas,
to
Brigadier General John M. Thayer,
Commanding U.S. Forces at Fort Smith,
March 17, 1864

... You are directed to co-operate in a movement toward Red River, by way of Arkadelphia and Washington. . . . You will leave only such force at Fort Smith as will safely hold that place, and for this purpose call in such of the outposts as can be evacuated.[3]

Unknown Officer, 2nd Kansas (Colored):
The Camden Expedition

On the 23d of March, 1864, the [Frontier Division] . . . under Gen. Thayer started south from Fort Smith, to form a junction with the forces under Gen. Steele, from Little Rock—all to cooperate with Gen. Banks in the taking of Shreveport.

The weather was rainy, cold and disagreeable, the roads soft and spongy. Numerous mud-holes were found by the enterprising teamsters, and the wagons, sticking fast in them, made our progress slow and difficult. . . . Many places in the road had to be "corduroyed" to render them passable. . . . Often all we had for food was corn meal, ground in hand mills, and the cattle, hogs &c., we killed after camping.[4]

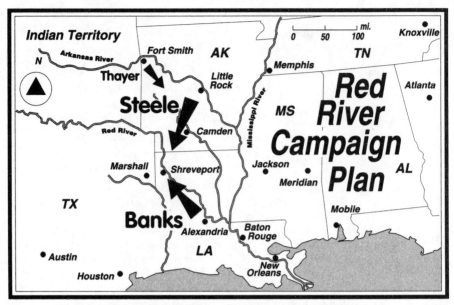

Red River Campaign Plan

Arkansas 1864

Arkansas Expeditionary Force
Maj. Gen. Frederick Steele
Cavalry Division
Brig. Gen. Eugene A. Carr
Third Division
Brig. Gen. Frederick Salomon
Frontier Division
Brig. Gen. John M. Thayer
2nd Brigade: Col. C. W. Adams
1st Kansas (Colored)
Col. James M. Williams
2nd Kansas (Colored)
Col. Samuel J. Crawford

Major General Frederick Steele,
Commanding U.S. Forces in Arkansas,
to
Major General Henry W. Halleck, Chief of Staff,
April 17, 1864
[In the Field, Camden]

The troops from Fort Smith were to have joined me at Arkadelphia. On the 1st instant Thayer changed his route, and all my messengers failed to communicate with him until the 5th, at Rockport. I had crossed the Little Missouri at Elkin's Ferry, and was on high ground, having found the other roads to Camden impassable. A heavy rain fell, raising the Little Missouri so that it could not be forded, and rendered it necessary to corduroy about 5 miles of bottom and lay the pontoon bridges to get Thayer across. He delayed us eight days.[5]

Unknown Officer, 2nd Kansas (Colored):
The Camden Expedition

April 9th.—We crossed the Little Missouri on a pontoon bridge. Here the rebels under [Brigadier General John S.] Marmaduke disputed the passage of the river with Gen. Steele, but were driven away after a sharp contest. The bushes were cut down as if with a knife and the tree[s] badly scarred by bullets and shells. General Steele's army was camped about three miles from the river, and soldiers from both armies were working on the road, which was soft, and needed trees and rails to keep the wagons from going under. We camped with the rear of Gen. Steele's army about two hours after dark, after a continuous march of sixteen days—and long ones at that. We started the next morning [April 10] and found scores of white soldiers on each side of the road, as eager to see the colored soldiers as children to see their first elephant.

At the Prairie de Ann (about ten miles from the river), Gen. Price had made some hasty preparations for a fight; but after seeing Gen. Steele's grand review, he soon "skedaddled." Gen. Steele moved quickly on (as he always seemed to wish to do), without getting hurt or hurting anybody.

April 12th.—We started for Camden and arrived on the 17th, having a fight with the rebels, who made an attack on our rear, just as we were leaving the prairie.[6]

> Major General Frederick Steele,
> Commanding U.S. Forces in Arkansas, to
> Major General Henry W. Halleck, Chief of Staff,
> April 17, 1864
> [*In the Field, Camden*]

Our supplies were nearly exhausted, and so was the country. . . . Everybody said Banks had been repulsed . . . and had fallen back. . . . An immense amount of labor has been expended in fortifying Camden and cutting away forests.[7]

Engagement at Poison Spring, Arkansas, April 18, 1864

> Colonel James M. Williams, 1st Kansas (Colored),
> Commanding Detachment,
> to
> Major General Frederick Steele,
> Commanding U.S. Forces in Arkansas,
> April 24, 1864
> [*In the Field, Camden*]

In obedience to verbal orders received from Brigadier-General Thayer, I left Camden, Ark., on the 17th instant with . . . 500 of the First Kansas Colored Volunteers, commanded by Major [Richard G.] Ward; 50 of the Sixth Kansas Cavalry, commanded by Lieutenant [Robert] Henderson; 75 of the Second Kansas Cavalry, commanded by Lieutenant [Barrett B.] Mitchell; 70 of the Fourteenth Kansas Cavalry, commanded by Lieutenant [Josephus] Utt; one section of the Second Indiana Battery, commanded by Lieutenant [William W.] Haines; in all, 695 men and two guns, with a forage train of 198 wagons.

I proceeded westerly on the Washington road a distance of 18 miles, where I halted the train and dispatched parts of it in different directions to load, 100 wagons, with a large part of the command under Major Ward, being sent 6 miles beyond the camp. These wagons returned to camp at midnight, nearly all loaded with corn. At sunrise

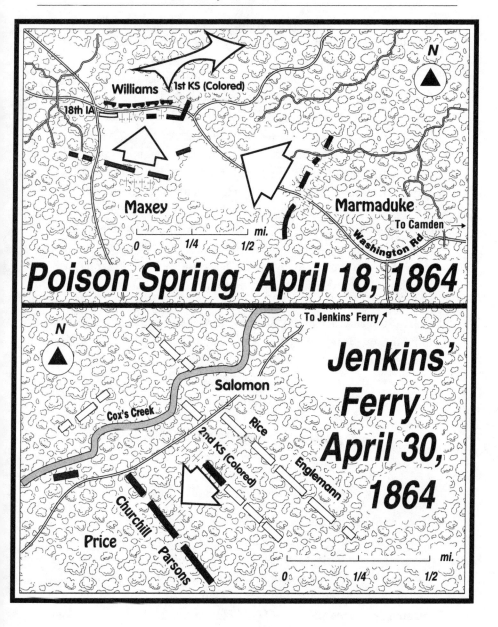

on the 18th, the command started on the return [to Camden], loading
the balance of the train as it proceeded. There being but few wagon
loads of corn to be found at any one place, I was obliged to detach
portions of the command in different directions to load the wagons,

until nearly my whole available force was so employed. At a point known as Cross-Roads, 4 miles east of my camping-ground, I met a re-enforcement of ... 465 men and two howitzers, which, added to my former force, made my whole command consist of 875 infantry, 285 cavalry, and four guns. But the excessive fatigue of the preceding day ... had so worn upon the infantry that fully 100 of the First Kansas (colored) were rendered unfit for duty. ...

At a point 1 mile east of this my advance came upon a picket of the enemy, which was driven back for 1 mile, when a line of the enemy's skirmishers presented itself. Here I halted the train, formed a line of the small force I then had in advance, and ordered that portion of the First Kansas Colored Volunteers which had previously been guarding the rear of the train to the front, and gave orders for the train to be parked as closely as the nature of the ground would permit. I also opened a fire upon the enemy's line from the section of Second Indiana Battery, for the double purpose of ascertaining, if possible, if the enemy had any artillery in position in front, and also to draw in some foraging parties which had previously been dispatched upon either flank of the train.[8]

Major Richard G. Ward, 1st Kansas (Colored),
to
Colonel James M. Williams, 1st Kansas (Colored),
Commanding Detachment,
April 20, 1864
[In the Field, Camden]

Upon arriving [at the head of the train], agreeably to your order, I placed one wing of this regiment on each side of the section of Rabb's battery [2nd Indiana] to support it and awaited further developments. After your cavalry had ascertained the position of the enemy's force on our right flank, and Lieutenant Haines [of Rabb's battery] had planted one of his pieces in a favorable position, I placed [three] companies ... to support it. We had hardly got into position here before our cavalry were forced back upon our line by an overwhelming force of the enemy.[9]

W. P. Hall, 2nd Kansas Cavalry (Co. B):
The Battle of Poison Spring

Our teams moved slowly, scattered along the road, with the escort also scattered, so as to guard the train to the best advantage. Price's cavalry swooped down on us—about seven to one. Col. Williams was a brave and noble fighter, and for two hours made a desperate fight. The [1st Kansas (Colored)] . . . and the detachment of the 2d Kan. Cav., in charge of Lieut. B. B. Mitchell, of Co. K, supported the 2nd Ind. Battery, while the 18th Iowa and the detachments of the 6th and 14th Kan. Cav. supported the two howitzers [at the rear of the train], and did noble fighting.[10]

Colonel James M. Williams, 1st Kansas (Colored),
Commanding Detachment,
to
Major General Frederick Steele,
Commanding U.S. Forces in Arkansas,
April 24, 1864
[In the Field, Camden]

At this moment the enemy opened upon me with two batteries, one of six pieces in front, and one of three pieces on my right flank, pouring in an incessant and well-directed cross-fire of shot and shell. At the same time he advanced his infantry both in front and on my right flank. From the force of the enemy, now for the first time made visible, I saw that I could not hope to defeat him; but still I resolved to defend the train to the last, hoping that re-enforcements would come up from Camden [twelve miles away]. I suffered them to approach within 100 yards of my lines when I opened upon them with musketry charged with buck and ball,* and after a contest of fifteen minutes' duration compelled them to fall back.[11]

---

*A "buck and ball" was a cartridge containing one bullet and three buckshot, devastating at short range.

189

Major Richard G. Ward, 1st Kansas (Colored),
to
Colonel James M. Williams, 1st Kansas (Colored),
Commanding Detachment,
April 20, 1864
[In the Field, Camden]

For about a quarter of an hour it seemed as though the enemy were determined to break my lines and capture the guns, but their attempts were fruitless and they were compelled to fall precipitately back, not, however, before they had disabled more than half of the gunners belonging to the gun on the right. Again they opened their infernal cross-fires with their batteries, and through the smoke I could see them massing their infantry for another attack.[12]

Colonel James M. Williams, 1st Kansas (Colored),
Commanding Detachment,
to
Major General Frederick Steele,
Commanding U.S. Forces in Arkansas,
April 24, 1864
[In the Field, Camden]

Two fresh regiments . . . advanced against my lines, this time with colors flying and continuous cheering, so loud as to drown even the roar of the musketry. Again I suffered them to approach even nearer than before, and opened upon them with buck and ball, their artillery still pouring in a cross-fire of shot and shell over the heads of their infantry, and mine replying with vigor and effect; and for another quarter of an hour the fight raged with desperate fury, and the noise and din of battle of this almost hand-to-hand conflict was the loudest and most terrific it has ever been my lot to listen to. Again were they forced to fall back, and twice during this contest were their colors brought to the ground, but as often raised.[13]

Major Richard G. Ward, 1st Kansas (Colored),
to
Colonel James M. Williams, 1st Kansas (Colored),
Commanding Detachment,
April 20, 1864
[In the Field, Camden]

Three different times the enemy was thus repulsed, and as they were massing for the fourth charge, I informed you that I believed it would be impossible to hold my position without more men on my right and center. You replied that I should have them if they could be spared from other points.[14]

Colonel James M. Williams, 1st Kansas (Colored),
Commanding Detachment,
to
Major General Frederick Steele,
Commanding U.S. Forces in Arkansas,
April 24, 1864
[In the Field, Camden]

. . . It became evident that I could hold my line but little longer. I directed Major Ward to hold that line until I could ride back and form the Eighteenth Iowa in proper form to support the retreat of this advanced line. Meanwhile so many of the gunners having been shot from around their pieces as to leave too few men to serve the guns, I ordered them to retire to the rear of the train. . . . Just as I was starting for the line of the Eighteen Iowa my horse was shot, and caused a delay, . . . [then] I rode to the rear and formed a line of battle facing the direction in which the enemy was advancing. Again did the enemy hurl his columns against the remnant of men which formed my front and right flank, and again were they met as gallantly as before. But my decimated ranks were unable to resist the overpowering force hurled against my line. . . . Major Ward gave the order to retire, which was done in good order, forming and checking the enemy twice before reaching the rear of the train.[15]

W. P. Hall, 2nd Kansas Cavalry (Co. B):
The Battle of Poison Spring

About this time the rebels hoisted their black flag. Col. Williams came up to our command and said: "Boys, do you see the black flag? That means death! We are surrounded. Let every man save himself." He dashed away on his horse.[16]

A. V. Eaton, 18th Iowa (Co. H):
Relief at Poison Spring

When the advance went to pieces of course the train was lost. The mule drivers, artillerymen, cavalry, and what not . . . came rushing back thru the train and the Johnnies after them, shouting like wild Indians, evidently thinking it was all over but the shouting.

If they thought at all they supposed the rear guard had gone back with the mob. But when they ran into that line of 300 guns, that hit them square in the face at short range, they halted and began to take account of things.

After a time they began swarming around our flanks, and to keep from being surrounded we had to fall back and reform. This was done no less than six different times, taking them farther away from the train all the time. The train was really the prize they were after. Thinking, perhaps, they were not interested in the 18th Iowa any more, their fire grew less, and then our Captain made a flank movement and made our "get away."[17]

Colonel James M. Williams, 1st Kansas (Colored),
Commanding Detachment,
to
Major General Frederick Steele,
Commanding U.S. Forces in Arkansas,
April 24, 1864
[In the Field, Camden]

The action commenced at 10 a.m. and terminated at 2 p.m. I was forced to abandon everything to the enemy, and they thereby became possessed of this large train, two 6-pounder guns, and two 12-pounder mountain howitzers. With what force could be collected I made my way to this post, where I arrived at 11 p.m. of the same day.[18]

William Avera, 5th Arkansas Artillery (C.S. Army):
Memoirs

At the battle of Poison Springs . . . [Brigadier General Samuel B.] Maxey[']s Indians* were present. There was several hundred of them. . . . There was some Negro troops with the Yankees and also a considerable number of Negroes who were running away from home. Many Negro soldiers and some of the other negroes was killed and it was with the greatest difficulty that the Indians could be kept from killing every negro prisoner and scalping all dead negroes, and in spite of all, they did kill and scalp some.[19]

Colonel James M. Williams, 1st Kansas (Colored),
Commanding Detachment,
to
Major General Frederick Steele,
Commanding U.S. Forces in Arkansas,
April 24, 1864
[In the Field, Camden]

Many wounded men belonging to the First Kansas Colored Volunteers fell into the hands of the enemy, and I have the most positive assurances from eye-witnesses that they were murdered on the spot.[20]

Brigadier General W. L. Cabel,
Commanding C.S. Army Brigade in Action,
to
Brigadier General Samuel B. Maxey,
Commanding C.S. Army Division in Action
April 20, 1864

The number of killed of the enemy was very great, especially among the negroes. You could track our troops by the dead bodies lying on

---

* "Maxey's Indians" were the 1st and 2nd Regiments of the Second Indian Brigade (C.S. Army).

the ground. . . . Morgan's regiment, which was stationed on the Camden road east of the battle-ground, killed at least 80 negroes [fleeing the fight] and captured 35 prisoners. My whole command captured 62 prisoners—58 white troops and 4 negroes.[21]

Major Richard G. Ward, 1st Kansas (Colored),
to
Colonel James M. Williams, 1st Kansas (Colored),
Commanding Detachment,
April 20, 1864
[In the Field, Camden]

The loss in arms and clothing is quite serious, but from the exhausted state of the men it is strange that as many of them brought in their arms and accouterments as did. . . . We were obliged to bring our wounded away the best we could, as the rebels were seen shooting those that fell into their hands. The men who brought in the wounded were obliged to throw away their arms, but the most who did so waited till they reached the swamps, and then sunk them in the bayous.[22]

A. V. Eaton, 18th Iowa (Co. H):
Relief at Poison Spring

On the second day after [the fight], a detail of the 18th Iowa, under a flag of truce, returned to see if our dead and wounded had been cared for. The dead of the white soldiers had been buried; the colored dead lay where they fell. They took no colored prisoners.[23]

Major Richard G. Ward, 1st Kansas (Colored),
to
Colonel James M. Williams, 1st Kansas (Colored),
Commanding Detachment,
April 20, 1864
[In the Field, Camden]

You will see that I went into action with about 450 enlisted men and 13 officers of the line. Seven out of that gallant 13 were killed or wounded. . . . One hundred and seventeen men are killed and 67 wounded, some of them mortally.[24]

Colonel James M. Williams, 1st Kansas (Colored),
Commanding Detachment,
to
Captain William S. Whitten, Kansas Assistant Adjutant General,
April 24, 1864
[In the Field, Camden]

The conduct of all the troops under my command . . . was character-
ized by true soldierly bearing. . . . The officers and men all evinced the
most heroic spirit, and those that fell died the death of the true soldier.
. . . I have named this engagement the action of "Poison Springs"
from a spring of that name in the vicinity.[25]

A. V. Eaton, 18th Iowa (Co. H):
Relief at Poison Spring

This was Steele's first disaster. Not heeding it, he sent another train
back after supplies, and that also was lost, with a whole brigade of his
army, at the Battle of Marks Mills. Most of his transportation was
now gone, and yet he tarried until the 26th, when Kirby Smith was
knocking at the door of Camden with two divisions of infantry from
Shreveport.[26]

Major General Frederick Steele,
Commanding U.S. Forces in Arkansas,
to
Major General Henry W. Halleck, Chief of Staff,
May 4, 1864
[Headquarters, Little Rock]

The command had been on short rations during the whole campaign.
. . . If we had been supplied at Camden I could have held the place
against Kirby Smith's entire force, but on learning that my communications were effectually interrupted, and that the line of the Arkansas
[River] was threatened by so large a force of the enemy, I decided to
fall back at once.[27]

Unknown Officer, 2nd Kansas (Colored):
The Camden Expedition

The failure of Gen. Banks let loose a large [enemy] army on our comparatively small force . . . and short supplies compelled the evacuation of Camden. This was a new experience for the Army of the Frontier, and filled our hearts with sadness. We crossed the [Ouachita] . . . on the evening of the 26th of April, unmolested, the rear getting over at two o'clock the next morning; destination Little Rock.[28]

Colonel Samuel J. Crawford, 2nd Kansas (Colored),
to
Joseph T. Wilson, Historian,
December 31, 1885

The Second Kansas, afterwards designated as the 83rd United States Colored Troops, was organized at Fort Scott, Kansas, on the 3rd day of October, 1863. . . . The regiment, when organized, was full to the maximum, or nearly so, and composed of active, able-bodied young men. . . .

After remaining in Camden [long enough] . . . to give the victorious rebel armies full time to concentrate upon him[, . . .] General Steele . . . commenced a disgraceful retreat or run back toward Little Rock.

The enemy, under Price and Kirby Smith, followed in close pursuit. . . . The march or retreat was continuous, night and day.[29]

Engagement at Jenkins' Ferry, Arkansas, April 30, 1864

Unknown Officer, 2nd Kansas (Colored):
The Camden Expedition

Our advance reached the Saline river on the 29th of April—a deep narrow stream over which they laid a pontoon bridge. We hoped to be able to cross before the rebels came up; we knew that their great superiority of numbers, and our starving condition and small transportation for wounded men made it necessary that we should now avoid a battle if possible. But fate and General Price decided otherwise. The bridge was in good condition, the army crossing finely, when at 3 p.m. it commenced raining. Soon the ground became soft and spongy. The rain came down in torrents, and baggage wagons and artillery stuck fast in the mud. Occasional volleys of musketry were heard in the rear all the afternoon, together with some artillery fire until late at night. All camped just as night and darkness overtook them, without tents or shelter, exposed to a very severe rain storm. About six thousand of the soldiers were still on the south bank of the river.[30]

Major General Frederick Steele,
Commanding U.S. Forces in Arkansas,
to
Major General Henry W. Halleck, Chief of Staff,
May 4, 1864
[Headquarters, Little Rock]

At daylight on the morning of the 30th, the enemy commenced skirmishing with our pickets. . . . The firing did not become very heavy for several hours. . . . The Saline bottom is 2 miles wide on each side of the river along the Jenkins' Ferry road. The rain continued and many of the wagons became irretrievably stuck in the mud on the east side of the river. . . . While the crossing was going on[, Brigadier] General [Frederick] Salomon was left with his division . . . supported by General Thayer's division of the Army of the Frontier. . . . The fire of the enemy became heavy, and Salomon formed his line of battle in a good position for defense, the right resting perpendicularly on an impassable bayou, and the left, which was protected by a wooded swamp against anything except, perhaps, skirmishers, was thrown back. The reserve was so posted that any part of the line which might be pressed could be promptly re-enforced. About 9 a.m. the enemy made a desperate assault in heavy force upon our line.[31]

Colonel Samuel J. Crawford, 2nd Kansas (Colored),
to
Joseph T. Wilson, Historian,
December 31, 1885

There were but six regiments of us south of the river, with two pieces of artillery. But we were there to stay until a battle was fought. . . .

[The] 2nd Kansas Colored Infantry, commanded by myself, was on the right [of the Union line].

As soon as it was fairly light, the battle began; both lines moving slightly forward until within close range. From the beginning, the crash of musketry was terrific. Our men stood firm against the . . . enemy's infantry, and used their Springfield and Enfield rifles with deadly effect.[32]

Unknown Officer, 2nd Kansas (Colored):
The Camden Expedition

We engaged the enemy for about an hour, advancing our lines considerably. He made several attempts to flank us on the right, but was repulsed each time with loss. Officers passed up and down the lines, cautioning the men to fire low—depressing pieces that ranged too high, and correcting faults of various kind. Soon the rebel fire was not so effective as at first. The leaves and bark fell from the trees, cut off eight or nine feet high. Their fire gradually slackened—wavered—stopped. Soon after this, the rebels opened fire on the center of the regiment, with three pieces of artillery. Then three shots were fired from one gun. These seemed to be the signal for the concentration of the fire of our entire regiment on the [Rebel] battery. Down came the horses, away went the gunners and the infantry supporting, and with wild, exultant cheers we drove them with bullets and bayonets in confusion from the field.[33]

Colonel Samuel J. Crawford, 2nd Kansas (Colored),
to
Joseph T. Wilson, Historian,
December 31, 1885

These orders were executed with a courage and daring seldom equaled by even older troops, and never excelled by a volunteer regiment.

In less than two minutes from the time the charge was ordered, the rebel battery was in our possession, and out of thirty-six horses used in the battery, but two were left standing when we passed the guns.

Most of the artillery-men lay dead and wounded around the battery while the line of infantry support in the rear of the battery fell back in disorder before our bayonets; not, however, until many of them had for the first time felt the effects of cold steel.

The charge, though bloody on both sides, was pre-eminently successful, and my regiment . . . brought away the battery so captured.[34]

Unknown Officer, 2nd Kansas (Colored):
The Camden Expedition

The enemy now massed his forces on our left, and tried repeatedly to flank us; but we had just enough regiments to keep our lines good. . . . For two hours and ten minutes there was a continual roar of musketry!—a hurricane of bullets that might well be called infernal. . . .

The enemy moved back until his right was opposite our left, and then advanced with quick determination, cheering and firing, until they were within fifty yards of our line. Where our soldiers were placed, there were some large "down" trees. These made breastworks, of which they were not slow to avail themselves. The rebels could not stand the storm of bullets, nor face the music of the minie balls, which tore through their ranks in deadly volleys. They were driven like waves before the wind, leaving the field in our possession.[35]

Colonel Samuel J. Crawford, 2nd Kansas (Colored),
to
Joseph T. Wilson, Historian,
December 31, 1885

During the battle my regiment lost in killed and wounded about eighty men, but we were richly rewarded by the achievements of the day. . . .

From this time forward until the close of the war, in so far as the Western army was concerned, we heard no more of the question, "Will they fight?"

The reputation of at least one colored regiment was established, and it stands today, in the estimation of men who served in the Western army, as the equal of any other volunteer regiment.[36]

Unknown Officer, 2nd Kansas (Colored):
The Camden Expedition

It was a question with the soldiers from Little Rock whether the blacks would fight. The 30th of April settled the point with some of the rebels, as well as convinced the white soldiers of our army.

The colored soldiers marched into Little Rock as the captors of the battery. . . . The negroes evinced daring and heroism, bravery and resolution, worthy of veterans; a patient endurance of wounds, fatigue, hunger and hardships worthy of all praise.

We arrived at Little Rock May 4th, as tired and hungry a set of soldiers as ever drew rations.[37]

Major General Frederick Steele,
Commanding U.S. Forces in Arkansas,
to
Major General Henry W. Halleck, Chief of Staff,
May 4, 1864
[Headquarters, Little Rock]

Our troops behaved in all the engagements of this campaign in the most gallant manner. . . . The conduct of the colored troops of my command proves that the African can be made as formidable in battle as a soldier of any other color.[38]

Colonel Samuel W. Crawford, 2nd Kansas (Colored):
Kansas in the Sixties

All things considered, the expedition was disastrous; not from any fault of the troops, but for want of a competent commander. . . . But enough, perhaps, has been said of this disastrous expedition to impress upon the minds of young officers in our army the importance of, first, knowing themselves; and second, qualifying themselves to meet and overcome any and every obstacle in their pathway, real or imaginary. After remaining at Little Rock a few days, General Thayer's division crossed the Arkansas River, and marching back to Fort Smith, went into camp to reflect on the art of war in Arkansas.[39]

Chapter Eight

"On to Richmond!"

———⟨◦⟩———

Expedition from Yorktown, Virginia, against Richmond,
February 6–8, 1864;
Expedition from Yorktown, Virginia, to New Kent C.H.,
March 1–4, 1864

RICHMOND was the object of two offensive actions in the opening quarter of 1864, each born of a scheme more chimerical than real, both representing the initial employment of black troops in a combat role in Virginia. The first was conceived in the always fertile mind of Major General Benjamin F. Butler, commanding the Department of Virginia and North Carolina. The man who had made the "contraband" policy work, who had enlisted the first black troops into U.S. service, and who had unleashed Brigadier General Edward A. Wild on North Carolina was also a connoisseur of military intelligence. Through his various sources (many of which he carefully cultivated), Butler became convinced in late January that only a small portion of the thirty-thousand-man garrison defending Richmond was positioned in such a way as to be able to block any move from the lower Peninsula. A rapid march by a compact strike force could, he reasoned, yield fantastic dividends. Working with Brigadier General Isaac J. Wistar, Butler let his imagination run free. He afterward described his goals as "first and most important . . . to release the large number of [Union] prisoners [of war] there, who would have made a very great addition to our force; and . . . second . . . to capture the Confederate Cabinet and Mr. Jefferson Davis."[1]

On February 5, Wistar assembled his battle group near Williamsburg. It consisted of twenty-two hundred cavalry and four thousand infantry, the latter evenly split among three white and three black regiments. The African American units comprised the 4th, 5th, and 6th USCT, forming a brigade under Colonel Samuel A. Duncan. Despite the anonymous utility of their USCT labels, there was a distinct regional character to each of the black regiments: the 4th had been organized in Baltimore, and the 5th was a product of Ohio's Camp Delaware, while the 6th had formed at Camp William Penn, near Philadelphia.

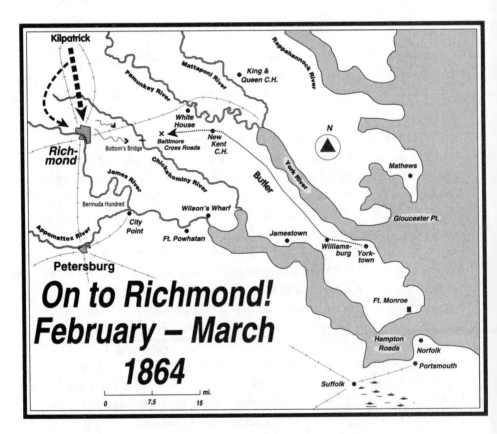

Marching in the ranks of the 6th was a black soldier who identified himself only as "Hard Cracker." "I had just awakened from a nice nap on the morning of the 5th [of February]," he told the *Anglo-African,*

> when the order came, six days rations in knapsacks, and seventy rounds of ammunition. It would be impossible to describe the wild enthusiasm of the men when they received this order. . . . Well, we got ready, and, turning our backs upon our old camp ground, we thought[,] who would live to return[?]
>
> We marched to Williamsburg, and encamped that night upon the battle-field rendered famous by the victory of Union troops over the rebel Gen. Magruder [during McClellan's Peninsula Campaign]. The night was intensely cold, and orders came that no fires should be made. . . . We left Williamsburg at 11 o'clock a.m., marching to New Kent Court House, a distance of 33 miles, arriving at 1 1/2 o'clock a.m., and, I'll assure you, we slept without rocking. Every one felt that we would have a fight before halting, and it would have done your heart good to look down that dark line and noted that stubborn determination to do or die.
>
> We started for Bolton Bridge [i.e., Bottom's Bridge] on the Chickahominy River. We marched to within four miles of the Bridge, and meeting our cavalry, all returned, sadly disappointed I'll assure you. [2]

Reporting this affair to President Lincoln, Butler noted that Wistar's "troops reached Bottom's Bridge, . . . but . . . found a force of the enemy posted there . . . , evidently informed of our intention." Butler's rage soon settled on a captured Union deserter who had been tried, convicted, and sentenced to be shot, only to be reprieved through presidential clemency; he had subsequently escaped and told all to the Rebel authorities.[3]

None of this was known to "Hard Cracker," who reported that the expedition's rear guard "was attacked by the rebels, but was repulsed without loss, arriving safely at camp on the evening of the 10th, without a straggler. Thus ended our first 'On to Richmond!'"[4]

Hardly had the mud dried from this episode when a new scheme was hatched—this one even more fanciful than Butler's notion of storming the Confederate capital with six thousand men. Having taken shape amid the boredom of the Army of the Potomac's sprawling winter encampments around Brandy Station, Virginia, the idea was promoted by a flamboyant, egotistical cavalry division commander by the name of Judson Kilpatrick, and then given a big boost by the lurid stories of suffering told by recent escapees from Richmond's Libby Prison. This was enough for President Lincoln, who summoned the bushy-whiskered Kilpatrick to Washington to brief him about his proposal to take four thousand men on a dash to Richmond, splitting his force so that one group would enter the city from the west while the main body pushed in from the north. Kilpatrick's operation required a cooperative diversion by Butler's men on the Peninsula, which meant that black troops would once more be marching on to Richmond. With Lincoln's backing—and despite opposition from the commander of the Army of the Potomac—the Kilpatrick Raid was set in motion.

A new unit, the 22nd USCT, had joined the three black regiments in the Yorktown area. Its surgeon, James Otis Moore, recalled, "Five & a half o'clock [P.M., March 1,] found us marching toward Richmond. After marching about two hours it began to rain & a darker night I never saw." "It was of course muddy, and a cold drizzling rain had set in," recollected Lieutenant J. H. Goulding of the 6th USCT. "It was dark very early and soon it was black—invisible holes wet our feet; if we tried to get out of the mud a little, invisible trees and stumps ran right into us and received our retreating thanks in language having the merit of force if not of elegance." "It rained, snowed & blew, beside being very cold, mud and slush in abundance," observed Alfred Milo Brigham, an officer in the 4th USCT. Lieutenant Joseph J. Scroggs of the 5th remembered it as "one of the worst nights I ever experienced. We passed through Williamsburg shortly after dark. The citizens kept well within doors. Afraid of the 'nigger' I suppose."[5]

The column of cavalry (one thousand strong) and infantry (two thousand) rested for about an hour at daybreak and then pushed on for New Kent Court House. Here, according to Lieutenant Goulding, after "catching . . . a few minutes sleep, and leaving those who were worn out, we pushed on again, and marched 18 miles further to Baltimore Crossroads, only 16 miles from Richmond." Once more the columns were halted; this time, the men were allowed to get more sleep. By now, according to Surgeon Moore of the 22nd USCT, the "real intent of our hard marching . . . [had] disclosed itself." "It seems our business is to make a diversion in favor of Gen. Kilpatrick who has got in rear of Lee's Army and is 'raiding' around Richmond," explained Lieutenant Scroggs.[6]

It was on the morning of March 3 that Butler's cooperative force met up with the main body of Kilpatrick's expedition. Wrote Lieutenant Scroggs, "Our brigade was drawn up in close column along the roadside to await his coming. We didn't have long to wait." William H. Thomas, a sergeant in the 5th USCT, was among the first to greet the exhausted troopers, with whom he "had a pleasant shaking of the hands." "Some were bare headed," related Lieutenant Goulding of the 6th, "some with slouched grey hats picked up on the way, some with shawls wrapped around them, and one I saw with a very gaily trimmed lady's hat, the ribbons streaming in the wind behind him. . . . The weary nodding riders passed at length, and we guarded their rear back to Yorktown."[7]

Kilpatrick's raid was at once a military failure and a political disaster. Neither element of his two-pronged advance penetrated Richmond's defenses, and on the body of the officer commanding the smaller force, the Rebels found orders targeting Jefferson Davis for assassination. Although the Federal high command vehemently denied that these were official instructions, Confederate newspapers nonetheless had a field day with the information.

Lieutenant Robert N. Verplanck of the 6th USCT summed up the participation of the black regiments in two letters written soon after the expedition ended. "We had very hard marching & some little skirmishing. . . . The army of the Potomac has at last seen colored troops & has received them very well," he declared on March 7. Six days later, he was rather more somber in his assessment: "We have had the toughest kind of time in the mud, rain & dark, did nothing & lost two men from our company who are prisoners in Richmond."[8]

Before the month was out, the four black regiments would take part in further expeditions into King & Queen County and through Mathews and Middlesex counties. Later they would join a small army that was being assembled near Yorktown. "I suppose . . . I shall not be giving aid & comfort to the enemy when I tell you that troops are coming here now from all directions," Lieutenant Verplanck noted on April 17. Next assigned to the staff of Brigadier General Edward W. Hincks, he found himself nearly overwhelmed by the effort needed to organize a black division in what would soon be styled the Army of the James. On May 4, the men bordered transports and early the next day headed up the James River toward Richmond. In a letter written just a few days before they set out, Lieutenant Verplanck had posed the question of the hour: "What can be up?" He closed with the prophetic observation, "The army is glad if there is a prospect of another fight."[9]

Campaign from the Rapidan River to the James River, May 1–June 12, 1864

In the battles it fought throughout 1862 and 1863, the Union's Army of the Potomac had waged a white man's war. Blacks were present in its ranks, as teamsters, quartermaster cooks, and camp servants, but none carried arms. The seeds of change in that regard were planted on January 7, 1864, when Major General Ambrose E. Burnside received orders to reconstitute the Ninth Corps, which had earlier been broken up for garrison service in the West. In a memorandum sent to Secretary of War Edwin M. Stanton on January 26, Burnside agreed to undertake the task but asked that "permission be granted me to organize a division from the colored troops . . . comprised of infantry, artillery, and cavalry." Replied Stanton, "No objection occurs to me in regard to the organization of a division of colored troops."[10]

On March 14, Annapolis, Maryland, was designated the Ninth Corps's assembly point. The far-flung black division taking shape under Brigadier General Edward Ferrero consisted of five full regiments and a sixth partial one. Three of the five (the 19th, 30th, and 39th USCT) had been recruited in Maryland; the fourth (27th USCT) came from Ohio, and the fifth (43rd USCT) from Pennsylvania. Joining these was a detachment from the 30th Regiment Connecticut Infantry (Colored).*

The 43rd was only seven companies full when orders came in April for the men to report to Annapolis. The soldiers marched into Philadelphia, boarded a vessel bound for Baltimore, and from there

*Only four companies of this unit were ever organized; they eventually merged with the 31st USCT.

sailed to the assembly point. "We moved off the boat," Sergeant John C. Brock told the readers of Philadelphia's *Christian Recorder,*

> and we found ourselves on the soil of a state which was once under the despotic sway of slavery, but which we soon hope shall never more allow human bondage to prevail on its borders. After we reached the town, we took up the line of march for our camp, which is about four miles from town. We found the road, as we went out, lined with tents and soldiers, all of which cheered us as we passed. When we got to our camping ground, we found a great many colored troops there.[11]

Others painted quite a different picture of the reception elsewhere given these black troops. In the diary of the 27th USCT's Captain Albert Rogall, a native of Russian Poland who had fought under Kossuth in Hungary, the following entry appears: *"19 Apr.* We left [Camp Delaware] for Annapolis, Md. In Pittsburg[h], Pa., we were stoned by the low people."

When the Ninth Corps was at last ready to join the Army of the Potomac near Brandy Station, Virginia, it was decided that the men would parade through Washington en route. Captain Rogall noted that the troops that left Annapolis on April 24 endured a "long hard march, raining, sleeping in wet, nothing to eat." Nevertheless, on the morning of April 26, the Ninth Corps was encamped on the outskirts of Washington, where the men scraped the mud from their uniforms, shined their buttons, blacked their shoes, and polished their weapons.[12]

The corps formed up at about 11:00 A.M. to begin a slow march down New York Avenue toward the heart of the city. The dense columns pressed on until they reached Fourteenth Street, where a halt was called to allow the long procession to close up. Then the men made the turn south to march past Willard's Hotel. Waiting on a second-floor balcony to review the troops was a small crowd of notables, including the sideburned Burnside and President Abraham Lincoln.

These were the first black troops that Lincoln had ever formally reviewed. Charles Coffin, a reporter for the *Boston Journal,* described the moment as one of "sublime spectacle." "Accoutered, as we were, with a full complement of clothing, etc., and the day being very warm, the march from outside the city until across Long Bridge, without a stop and with cadenced step, was very trying," recalled

Captain James H. Rickard of the 19th USCT, "but not a man left the ranks until the bridge was passed."[13]

Standing across from Willard's was a newspaperman turned hospital attendant named Walt Whitman. The forty-four-year-old poet had come down to watch the procession in hopes of seeing his brother George, in the 51st New York. Lincoln was not wearing a hat, and Whitman thought it odd for the President to have his head uncovered as the black regiments marched below.

According to Coffin, the President acknowledged the African American soldiers with "dignified kindness and courtesy." But the discipline of only a few weeks was not enough to hold the former slaves in line as they recognized the man who had issued the Emancipation Proclamation. "They swing their caps, clap their hands and shout their joy," Coffin wrote. "Long, loud and jubilant are the rejoicings of these redeemed sons of Africa."

"My regiment was the very last in the corps," recalled Lieutenant Colonel H. Seymour Hall of the 43rd USCT. "The constant battalion drill that I had given them the four weeks that I had been in command, and their excellence in the manual of arms, made them appear like veteran soldiers, and the crowd of spectators gave us loud and prolonged applause."[14]

Coffin was not unaware of the irony of "brigades which never have been in battle, for the first time shouldering arms for their country; who till a year ago never had a country, who even now are not American citizens, who are disfranchised—yet they are going out to fight for the flag!"[15]

Military protocol kept the Ninth Corps separate from the Army of the Potomac, as General Burnside ranked Major General George G. Meade, who commanded the army. Grant had Burnside report to him for orders, but for all other purposes, the Ninth Corps was a part of what was to become known as the Overland Campaign. The five Annapolis regiments plus the Connecticut detachment were joined by the 23rd USCT (organized in Virginia), with the whole then being split into two brigades. The First Brigade, led by Colonel Joshua K. Sigfried, contained the 27th, 30th, 39th, and 43rd regiments, while the Second, Colonel Henry G. Thomas commanding, consisted of the 19th and 23rd along with the Connecticut companies.

On May 5 and 6, the Army of the Potomac fought General Robert E. Lee's Army of Northern Virginia west of Fredericksburg, in the region known as the Wilderness. Black troops were assigned a supporting role in this operation, best detailed in a description written by Lieutenant George H. Walcott of the 30th USCT:

We left Manassas Junction, May 4; marched until one o'clock that night; started again next morning, and marched until nine at night; halted until two o'clock [that morning] . . . , then formed again. Crossed Germanna Ford [entering the Wilderness] at eight o'clock A.M. Friday, 6th. Immediately upon crossing were ordered to quickly reinforce [Maj.] Gen. [John] Sedgwick (Sixth Corps), who was hard pressed. We marched up lively, the men singing. It was a frightfully hot march through the woods. It amounted to nothing but to tire us out, for we were ordered back again to the ford. We halted until eleven o'clock at night, when orders came to advance. Passed the entire Sixth Corps; marched up a hill, and formed line of battle. . . . About five o'clock [A.M.] the "Rebs" opened on us, and such a roar of artillery, peals of musketry, and bursting of shells cannot be imagined by one who has not heard it. This battle* lasted half an hour. Gen. Grant sat before his tent, smoking a cigar, as though nothing unusual was transpiring. There were troops enough in front of us, and we lay still all the while, and did not fire a gun. After the battle we were ordered [to move east] to Chancellorsville.[16]

The black troops were now seen for the first time by many of the Army of the Potomac's headquarters staff, one of whom was a Boston patrician named Theodore Lyman. "As I looked at them," he told his abolitionist friends, "my soul was troubled and I would gladly have seen them marched back to Washington. . . . We do not dare trust them in the line of battle. Ah, you may make speeches at home, but here, where it is life or death, we dare not risk it." Lieutenant Freeman S. Bowley of the 30th USCT remembered the blacks' response when some white soldiers jeered them: "One colored soldier, with a clear, mellow voice, raised the song 'Will you, Will you, fight, for de Union?' Instantly the whole line took up the chorus: 'Ah-ha! ah-ha! We'll fight for Uncle Sam!'"[17]

*The "battle" was actually the firing associated with small probing actions as each side tried to fix the position of the other. The major fighting was over after dark on May 6.

Army of the Potomac (Maj. Gen. G. G. Meade)
Ninth Corps (Maj. Gen. A. E. Burnside)
4th Division (Brig. Gen. E. Ferrero)
1st Brigade (Col. J. K. Siegfried)
27th USCT: Lt. Col. Charles J. Wright
30th USCT: Col. Delavan Bates
39th USCT: Col. Ozora P. Stearns
43rd USCT: Lt. Col. H. Seymour Hall
2nd Brigade (Col. H. G. Thomas)
30th CT (Colored) [detachment]: Capt. C. Robinson
19th USCT: Lt. Col. Joseph G. Perkins
23rd USCT: Lt. Col. C. J. Campbell

The Overland Campaign May – June 1864

On the night of May 7, the Army of the Potomac broke contact with Lee's men and began moving toward Spotsylvania Court House. In entering the Wilderness, U. S. Grant severed nearly all communication and supply lines through Brandy Station, so Meade's army controlled only the land it actually occupied. As the "front" pushed farther and farther from the Rapidan River, the rear was left vulnerable to hit-and-run attacks; responsibility for defending this quarter was given to Brigadier General Ferrero's two black brigades, augmented by three white cavalry regiments. This assignment led the blacks to their first combat action in this campaign, near the Alrich Farm, southeast of Chancellorsville.

About midday on May 15, one of Ferrero's cavalry regiments, posted near Piney Branch Church, was attacked by portions of a Confederate cavalry brigade. The outnumbered troopers retreated northward toward the Orange Plank Road, where they formed to protect this important link in the army's supply chain. When General Ferrero arrived from Chancellorsville with the 23rd USCT, the black soldiers, hunched against a pouring rain, advanced against the Confederate cavalry and forced it to withdraw. The regiment's Record of Events contains the following laconic entry for this day: "We . . . had a skirmish with rebel dismounted cavalry, whom we drove back." Anxious to portray the event in the best possible light, Ferrero's report claimed that his men "drove the enemy in perfect rout," though it seems more likely that the Rebels merely disengaged when confronted by a superior force.[18]

The next combat action involving the USCT units occurred on May 19, a few miles west of Salem Church, outside Fredericksburg. General Ferrero put the time at 5:00 P.M. when "an attack was made on my lines . . . by a brigade or more of the enemy's cavalry." Two of the three cavalry regiments that were operating in concert with Ferrero's footsoldiers started this scrap; Lieutenant Bowley of the 30th USCT remembered that the first sprinkle of the little storm came when the "cavalry carbines began to crack at a furious pace." The call went back for infantry, and the 30th USCT came up on the run and was hurriedly ranged into skirmishing order. The white major in charge sought to steady his men by telling them, "Just imagine you are hunting for coons, and keep your eyes open." A voice drawled out of the ranks, "'Pears like 'twas de coons doin' de huntin' dis time." In his account Ferrero noted only, "We held the enemy in check until dark."[19]

Word quickly spread along the army grapevine that the black troops had been up to the job. "Their conduct was above criticism," was how one Pennsylvania soldier put it. By the time a history of the

Army of the Potomac was written, the entry for this fight read, "When Ferrero's division was attacked, his colored troops fought most gallantly." Young Lieutenant Bowley had a narrower view of the affair. As the bullets whizzed around him, he found he had a clear shot at a distant enemy horseman, who appeared to be an officer. "I aimed with great deliberation," Bowley said, "and fired. . . . The rifle . . . kicked spitefully, and gave me the impression that my shoulder had been almost dislocated. And the officer? He did not notice at all, but rode down his line perfectly unconcerned."[20]

The Federal army commenced marching south from Spotsylvania beginning on May 20. Lee's men countered in a series of engagements along the North Anna River from May 23 to May 26, and then the sidestepping continued, leading to some large-scale fighting at Cold Harbor, Virginia, on June 1 and 3. Ironically, even as the daily toll of this bloody combat began to drain the morale and fighting ability of Grant's white soldiers, his black troops were finding increased validation for their participation. Writing to the *Christian Recorder* from Hanover, Virginia, Sergeant John C. Brock of the 43rd USCT explained:

> We have been instrumental in liberating some five hundred of our sisters and brothers from the accursed yoke of human bondage. . . . As several of them remarked to me, it seemed to them like heaven, so greatly did they realize the difference between slavery and freedom. . . .
>
> The slaves tell us that they have been praying for these blessed days for a long time, but now their eyes witness their salvation from that dreadful calamity, slavery, and, what was more than they expected, by their own brethren in arms. What a glorious prospect it is to behold this glorious Army of black men as they march with martial tread over the sacred soil of Virginia![21]

A writer for the *Philadelphia Press* claimed that the black troops in the Overland Campaign "were invariably selected to bring up the rear of the Army of the Potomac, because of their known disinclination for straggling." Yet a glance through the Regimental Order Book of the 43rd USCT suggests that the black regiments may have been no better or worse in this regard than their white counterparts. From Colonel Sigfried's headquarters on May 24 came orders exhorting his

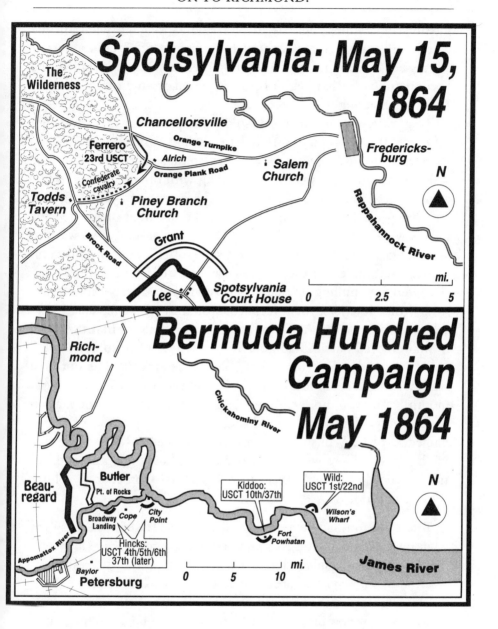

Spotsylvania: May 15, 1864

The Wilderness
Chancellorsville
Orange Turnpike
Ferrero 23rd USCT
Alrich
Orange Plank Road
Salem Church
Fredericks-burg
Confederate cavalry
Todds Tavern
Piney Branch Church
Brock Road
Grant
Lee
Spotsylvania Court House
Rappahannock River
N

mi.
0   2.5   5

Bermuda Hundred Campaign May 1864

Rich-mond
Chickahominy River
Butler
Pt. of Rocks
Kiddoo: USCT 10th/37th
Wild: USCT 1st/22nd
N
Beau-regard
Broadway Landing
Cope
City Point
Wilson's Wharf
Fort Powhatan
Hincks: USCT 4th/5th/6th 37th (later)
Appomattox River
Baylor
Petersburg
James River

mi.
0   5   10

officers to ensure that the "troops in their commands do not straggle on the march," while on May 26, Brigadier General Ferrero railed against the "frequent acts of vandalism . . . perpetuated by stragglers and followers of this army." Three days later, the 43rd's commander,

Lieutenant Colonel Hall, strictly forbade "straggling while on the march and leaving camp without proper authority." Other matters addressed by orders issued during this campaign included the "promiscuous discharging of firearms in and around camp" and the "habit of cheering whilst on drill."[22]

Tragically, the fate of black soldiers captured in this campaign differed little from that suffered by their comrades in the West. Charles Hopkins, a white New Jersey soldier captured during the Wilderness fighting, was marched along with other captives to Orange Court House and placed in the basement of a building that was being used as a holding pen. On the morning of May 9, the POWs were aroused with the cry, "Hey thar you-uns, if yo want to see a nigger hang look 'round right smart." Hopkins and his companions scrambled to the window of their cell, "and sure enough they were just pulling up one of Burnside's black heroes in full uniform," the New Jerseyman recalled. Hopkins, who considered himself one of the "born Abolitionists," muttered aloud that the "soul of that colored patriot had gone to meet the soul of John Brown," and exclaimed, "God bless that colored Veteran!!!" His outburst was met with a set of leveled muskets and the order to "shut up yer mouth!" An even more chilling incident was related in the matter-of-fact entry for May 8 in the diary of a Virginia cavalryman named Byrd C. Willis: "We captured three negro soldiers the first we had seen. They were taken out on the road side and shot, & their bodies left there." According to another Confederate soldier, Westfield Todd,

> Before our army moved out from its lines at Cold Harbor, a negro soldier was captured on the picket line, and brought to the rear. The men were very much inflamed at seeing a negro in arms. . . . The poor creature was almost frightened to death as he looked around on the scowling faces of the curious crowd. He was ashy pale. I do not remember now how the guard happened to give him up, but some noncombatant officer . . . who did not belong to our division, took charge of him and . . . carried him off. I soon after heard the report of a gun, and was told that the negro had been shot in the woods.[23]

On June 13, the Federals marched to the James River, which they crossed on June 14 and 15. Their target was now Petersburg.

Operations on the South Side of the James River, May 4–June 14, 1864

Early on the morning of May 5, even as fighting began in the Wilderness, Major General Benjamin F. Butler's invasion fleet sailed from Hampton Roads. A USCT officer present remembered it as the "grandest sight I ever saw, some thirty steamboats, beside gunboats, monitors, &c, all in one line steaming up the river." A black soldier in the expedition later described the trip for the *Anglo-African:*

> Magnificent scenery is visible up the stream, second to none in this country except the coast of Louisiana, from New Orleans to Baton Rouge. Fine mansions, beautiful fields, and lovely gardens are abundant. . . .
>
> When we were passing Grove's Landing, where stands a house one hundred and ninety-five years old, built by John Smith's men, I heard a concourse singing, "Glory, Glory, Hallelujah! Glory, Glory, Hallelujah! as we go marching 'long." The farther up the river we go the more they seem to rejoice.[24]

A black sergeant nearby was less enamored of the sights: "One I might mention particularly was the ruins of Jamestown, the spot where the curse of slavery was first introduced into the United States. A serpent that has inserted its poisonous fangs into the body of this government, causing it to wither in its bloom."[25]

Butler's primary destination was Bermuda Hundred, a small peninsula formed by the confluence of the James and Appomattox rivers; a landing there would place his troops squarely between Richmond and Petersburg. The assignment to protect his supply line went to Brigadier General Edward W. Hincks's black division, which to this end needed to seize several strategically important points along the James. This was a two-brigade division, with the First under the command of Brigadier General Edward A. Wild, and the Second under Colonel Samuel A. Duncan. Wild's brigade was made up of the 1st (from the District of Columbia), 10th (from Virginia), 22nd (a Camp William Penn regiment), and 37th (from North Carolina) USCT, while Duncan's comprised the 4th, 5th, and 6th USCT.

The black troops were the first of Butler's invasion force to come ashore, with the 1st and 22nd USCT landing at Wilson's Wharf, a commanding bluff on the north bank of the James. According to

Captain Edward Simonton of the 1st, the men were "put to work building intrenchments surrounding the landing, a strong detachment of troops having been thrown out in advance and placed on picket duty. . . . Our main force went into camp within the intrenchments."[26]

A similar operation on the south bank by the 10th and 37th USCT gave the Federals possession of an abandoned Confederate earthwork known as Fort Powhatan. Noted the 10th USCT's Record of Events, "On the 5th [of May] about noon reached Ft. Powhatan where we debarked & proceeded to occupy the place, meeting with no opposition & seeing no enemy except a party of four horsemen who immediately made off. Small detachments of the command scouted about the surrounding country . . . while the main body were engaged in throwing up defenses & cutting away the covering woods."[27]

Before Butler's men reached Bermuda Hundred, the black troops also took control of City Point, a once-thriving supply terminus for Petersburg's trade, located at the mouth of the Appomattox River. Duncan's regiments got this assignment.

As the boat carrying the 5th USCT steamed toward the City Point wharf, Lieutenant Elliott F. Grabill observed a "rebel rag . . . still defiantly flaunting the breezes." "A small detachment of the 5th was immediately landed, surprising and capturing a [Confederate] L[ieutenan]t and thirty men, belonging to the Rebel Signal Corps," recalled Lieutenant Joseph J. Scroggs of the regiment. "We . . . soon tore down the rebel rag and put in its stead on the tall flag staff the *Red, White and Blue,* to be seen away down the river by the long line of transports now coming into sight," related Grabill. "As it was unfolded by the breeze . . . it was greeted by thunderous cheers by our men," added Scroggs.[28]

A member of the 4th USCT who identified himself as "Arnold" recollected that the "colored people, only a few, were running to and fro, so glad were they at the sight of black Yankees. One old man said to a corporal, 'Am dese de Yankees?' 'Yes,' said the corporal. ''Fore God, I'se bin looking for de Yanks dis two yers!'" "Arnold" also recounted the tale of a local planter who was picked up trying to escape to Petersburg with eight slaves. "The morning previous to this he gave a woman . . . nine and thirty [lashes], for saying we were coming, and then had the impudence to ask Col. [Giles W.] Shurtleff, of the 5th, for a guard to protect him. The Colonel could not see it. The gentleman is now [a prisoner] at Point Lookout, Md., and the slave at Fortress Monroe, I hope doing well."[29]

From a Confederate perspective, the Bermuda Hundred Campaign was a miracle of improvised defenses and a tribute to Rebel tenacity. From a Union point of view, Butler's "Operations on the south side of the James River" were a nightmare of missed opportunities, a disaster stemming from that general's lack of combat experience coupled with his troubled relationships with his two principal field commanders, Major Generals Quincy A. Gillmore (Tenth Corps) and William F. "Baldy" Smith (Eighteenth Corps).

The black troops spent the month of May either digging, guarding, or scouting—with two notable exceptions. At noon on May 21, as part of a Rebel effort to cut Butler's supply route, a force of about a hundred riders attacked Fort Powhatan. The black troops there, under Colonel Joseph B. Kiddoo, drove them off, but they returned with reinforcements later in the afternoon. Kiddoo called for help from Brigadier General Wild at Wilson's Wharf and from Brigadier General Hincks at City Point, but by the time it arrived, the Rebels had already withdrawn, this time for good.

A more serious incident took place on May 24, when cavalrymen under Major General Fitzhugh Lee assaulted the black troops holding Wilson's Wharf. An account of this action penned the next day by an officer in the 1st USCT (who identified himself as "M.W.S.") provided all the details:

We have had a fight with Fitzhugh Lee, and whipped him completely. He had 2,000 men. . . . We had about 1,100 men. He came down with cavalry and charged on our pickets, expecting to cut them off, and then surprise the camp. But he "reckoned without his host." The pickets fought him for half an hour and emptied several saddles. In the meantime we, hearing the firing, formed line of battle in the trenches and waited for the pickets to come in. As soon as they were in the works we opened on the rebs. They then sent in a flag of truce demanding an immediate surrender, and promising that we should in such case be treated as prisoners of war; but if we resisted, and attempted to hold the place, he (General Lee) would not be responsible for the consequences. He said it would be impossible for us to hold

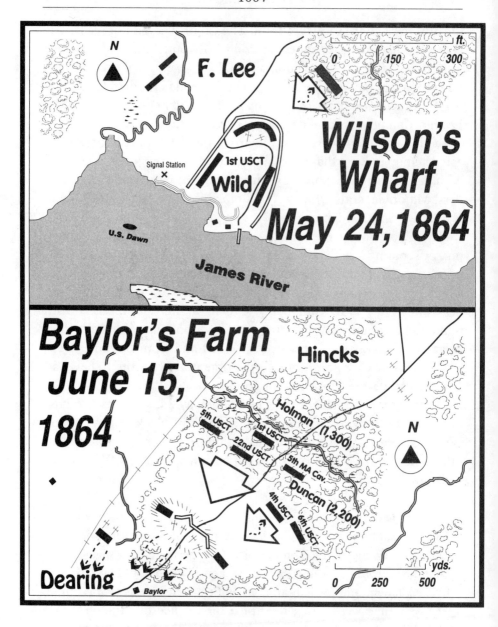

out, as he was determined to take the place. General Wild answered the message, "We will try it." While this parley was going on, the rebels were getting into position, and as soon as the flag was carried back, commenced a very lively firing. We also opened with our artillery, (two 10-pound Parrotts) and, with the assistance of the guns on the steamer *Dawn,* drove the enemy back into the woods.

They then began flank movements on both sides of us, so as to rake our line of works. It therefore became necessary to have the gunboat shift her position, so as to rake the rebs. General Wild sent me off in a small boat with the message, and as the river bank was lined with sharpshooters, I had a very hot sail. . . .

A feint was made on one flank and a charge on the other. They came in with a yell, but our boys gave a louder yell (which must have been heard to be appreciated), and poured so much lead among them that they broke and ran like sheep, leaving numbers of dead and wounded on the field. . . . We lost in our regiment two men killed, one officer and fourteen men wounded, and one man missing. . . .

That the black men will fight is an established fact.

We had a section of the 3d New York volunteer artillery here, and the lieutenant in charge told me, after the fight, that no men in the world could do better than those who supported his gun. . . .

We have taken a number of prisoners, some wounded and some not. We have treated them well, but woe be to them if we find that our missing man has been unfairly dealt with.[30]

By the end of May, most of the Army of the James was stalled before a line of Rebel earthworks stretched across Bermuda Hundred. As U. S. Grant would later put it, Butler's force, "though in a position of great security, was as completely shut off from further operations directly against Richmond as if it had been in a bottle strongly corked." Grant now looked on the Army of the James as a reserve pool for the Army of the Potomac, which had sustained terrible casualties in its marches through Virginia toward the James River. Nearly a full corps was shipped to George Meade in time to fight in the disastrous battles at Cold Harbor on June 1 and 3. None of Butler's black troops were tagged for this operation, but on June 9, two of Hincks's regiments (the 1st and 6th USCT, along with Battery B of the 2nd USCLA), operating out of City Point, took part in a well-conceived though feebly executed effort to capture Petersburg. The operation, under Major General Quincy A. Gillmore, called for three columns simultaneously to converge on the city—white infantry from the northeast, black soldiers from the east, and white cavalry from the south. Gillmore limited his numerically superior footsoldiers to mere probing of the enemy's earthworks, while his cavalry had to withdraw for lack of support. A staff officer with Brigadier General Hincks later voiced the general feeling when he wrote, "Nightfall found all the troops participating in this reconnaissance back in their camps, wondering what the day's work had amounted to."[31]

On June 13, Ulysses S. Grant began to move the Army of the Potomac south from Cold Harbor to cross the James River. The troops that had been "borrowed" from Butler were now returned, with a new mission: to spearhead the all-out assault on Petersburg. Major General William F. Smith was given command of the operation, to which Hincks's black division was assigned. In the early-morning hours of June 15, Hincks's men left their camps near City Point, headed for Petersburg.

Assault on Petersburg, Virginia, June 15, 1864

"Everything is going on splendidly," wrote Lieutenant Robert N. Verplanck on June 14 from the 6th USCT camp near City Point.

> The Army of the Potomac has been crossing the river just below Harrison's Landing all to day and by tomorrow morning will all be over and ready to move on Richmond by the south side. Gen. Smith has come in transports from White House[, Virginia, near Cold Harbor,] and joined Butler before dark this evening. We are all ready to march here and expect to move on Petersburg early tomorrow, to prepare the way for The Army of the Potomac. Gen. Smith will have the command this time & not Gillmore and you may be sure some thing will be done.[32]

Shortly after midnight on June 15, Brigadier General Hincks moved his two brigades to Broadway Landing on the Appomattox River. The first of these was a Provisional Brigade, commanded by Colonel John H. Holman, containing the 1st USCT and half the 5th Regiment Massachusetts Cavalry (Colored),* which was going into action on foot. The Second Brigade, under Duncan, included the 4th, 5th, 6th, and 22nd USCT. Hincks (whose force numbered about thirty-five hundred men) met at 2:00 A.M. with General Smith, who told him to wait near Cope's House for the Federal cavalry, which would lead him to Petersburg.

*Also part of Holman's command was the 10th USCT, then assigned to Fort Powhatan.

"Baldy" Smith was under pressure from Major General Butler to advance quickly, but nothing seemed to be going right. The whole operation had been put together on short notice, with little concern for logistical realities. The new instructions caught many of Smith's troops still in transit from Cold Harbor, with destination orders that had been cut before the Petersburg strike was even set up; consequently, his staff officers had to ride throughout the night of June 14 and well into the early hours of June 15 to round up brigades and divisions that had been landed throughout Bermuda Hundred. The column led by Hincks was one of three aimed at Petersburg, all of which were to have been on their way before dawn. Smith's orders meant that Hincks's men had to wait at Cope's for the cavalry, which finally arrived at 5:00 A.M.

"Orders were given then to fall in; of course we made no delay, knowing duty to be before everything else, a moment before and the column was off," recalled Sergeant Milton M. Holland of the 5th USCT. "We had gone but a short distance before we came upon the ambulance train," noted Sergeant C. R. Douglass in the 5th Massachusetts Cavalry (Colored), "then I knew that some of us were not coming back again." Continued Holland, "About sunrise our advance came in contact with the rebel pickets. . . . Skirmishers were then thrown out in front of the different regiments."[33]

The cavalry riding ahead was stopped at about 6:00 A.M. on the City Point Road near Baylor's Farm; facing the troopers was a line of Confederates in rifle pits backed by four entrenched cannon. Colonel Duncan pronounced the enemy's position "one of very considerable strength, being the crest of rapidly rising ground 300 yards in rear of an exceedingly difficult wood." What made the wood difficult was its width (six hundred yards), its floor (marshy and obstructed by fallen timber), and the fact that it was diagonally traversed by a turnpike and a railroad that would impede any attempted lines of battle.[34]

"Having reported the state of affairs to General Smith, I was ordered to deploy . . . and force a passage," said Hincks. Although Colonel Duncan's report states that his brigade was spread in a single line (left to right: 6th, 4th, 22nd, and 5th USCT), testimony from soldiers who were present suggests that the line was in fact staggered, with the two middle regiments' being well forward of those on either flank. Behind these units was posted Holman's Provisional Brigade. According to Duncan, "The order given to each regimental commander of

221

the first line was to open a heavy fire upon the enemy upon reaching the farther skirt of the wood, to reform the line with all possible dispatch, which would necessarily become much disjointed in passing over such obstructed ground, and then await the order to charge."[35]

Responding to a published letter from a member of the 5th Massachusetts Cavalry (Colored) who claimed full credit for his unit, Sergeant Major Christian A. Fleetwood of the 4th USCT provided the *Anglo-African* with this description of the action:

> Our regiment [4th USCT] was the first to clear the woods and met with a heavy enfilading fire from the rebel work which was discovered on our right. Nevertheless our boys charged at a double quick until our reserve, the *5th Massachusetts Cavalry,* who were *not yet out of the woods,* fired a heavy volley, which took effect upon the rear of our left wing, which, with the fire of the enemy, threw it into confusion. We were then ordered back into the woods to reform, and fell back accordingly, re-formed, and again advanced, in time to lose several more men killed and wounded, before the final capture of the work. . . . It was the 22nd U.S. Colored Troops that took the work when we fell back, and not the 5th Cavalry.[36]

This action, which cost the 4th USCT 120 dead or wounded, resulted in the capture of one of the four Rebel cannon. After noting that a "Serg. Dunwood" of the 22nd USCT had been killed in the charge, a *New York Tribune* reporter wrote that the black soldiers "were very much elated with their success, and talked as much over it as though it had been the capture of Petersburg or Richmond. The Sergeant was sadly buried where he fell, and the boys shouldered their muskets and moved on."[37]

The scrap at Baylor's Farm delayed the Union advance for almost two hours, so it was not until 11:00 A.M. that Hincks's division at last pulled up before Petersburg's main defenses. The black troops, stretched in a line about a mile and a half north from the Jordan Point Road, formed the left wing of Smith's assault formation. The quality of the earthworks confronting these units was perhaps the most impressive aspect of Petersburg's defenses: construction had begun in 1862 under a military engineer named Charles H. Dimmock, who, using a large force of slave labor, had erected a ten-mile belt of imposing works around the city. It took until midday for all of Smith's troops to align themselves before Captain Dimmock's achievement.

Smith then began a personal reconnaissance of the enemy's fortifications that lasted until 3:00 P.M.

While their commander scouted, the assault troops were pummeled by the Rebel artillery. "The situation was everything but a pleasant one to remain in all day, with the scorching sun on the backs of the troops, and the cannons belching forth their murderous missiles," wrote a sergeant-major in the 1st USCT. "The little shells sent every few minutes to greet us were not as large as hornets' nests, but their contents were more annoying," remembered Captain John McMurray of the 6th USCT. "They were filled with little metal bullets as big as hickory nuts, small pieces of broken metal, etc. We had no means of protecting ourselves from them, as when they would burst over our heads, their contents would come down in all directions." Harvey Covell, also in the 6th, recalled, "All were ordered to keep down, but there was not much to shelter us, only small hollows in the

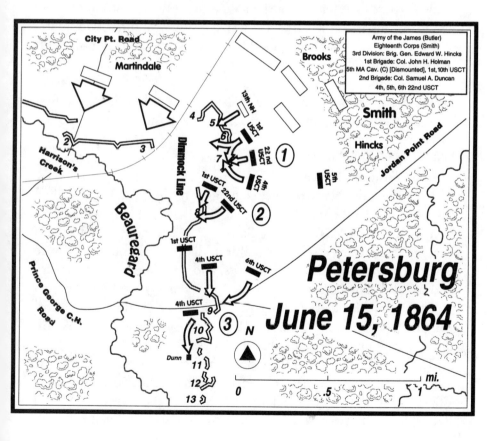

ground, once in a while a small tree." A reporter for the *Boston Daily Advertiser* informed his readers, "Old officers declare that [the] . . . cannonading . . . can be no severer test of a soldier, particularly for green troops, as were Duncan's entire brigade."[38]

"One thing that I must mention which attracted the attention of the whole division," remarked Sergeant Holland of the 5th USCT, "was that brave and daring but strange personage that rides the white charger. We could see him plainly riding up and down the rebel lines, could hear him shouting from the top of his voice to stand, that they had only niggers to contend with."[39]

From his careful inspection, Smith concluded that the Dimmock Line was seriously undermanned. He felt that an attack would succeed if a less dense skirmishing formation was substituted for the standard heavy assault columns, which would only provide fat targets for the enemy's artillery. Smith now rode to each division commander to explain his plan in person, a process that took until 5:00 P.M. Problems with the corps artillery consumed another two hours, and even then it proved impossible to get all the guns into line. Finally, at about 7:00 P.M., the advance began.

By the time the Confederate cannoneers realized that there were no masses of troops behind the thick lines of skirmishers, the first Federals were already filtering into the Rebel positions. Battery 5 fell to white troops from Brooks's division, while elements of the 1st USCT vied with white Union soldiers for the honor of taking the next fortified position, Battery 6.

Now the other black regiments, piling into the fight, began rolling up the Confederate line. The 4th and 22nd USCT, along with a portion of the 1st USCT, overran Battery 7. "The boys made a bold charge," recollected a sergeant-major in the 1st, "although they were exposed to the cross-fire of three forts, and were harassed by infantry and cavalry. They scaled the fort, and the enemy, becoming panic-stricken, ran like deer, leaving three pieces of cannon." Sergeant-Major Fleetwood of the 4th USCT never forgot how the black soldiers "swept like a tornado over the works."[40]

The Rebel batteries were laced together by trenches that now guided the blacks onward. Colonel Joseph B. Kiddoo of the 22nd USCT found a detail of the 1st USCT holding the trenches between Battery 7 and Battery 8; the officer with the detail declined Kiddoo's invitation to form with him for a charge, but agreed to lend fire support. One of the officers participating in Kiddoo's attack was Captain Albert James. "A charge is generally made in line of battle," he wrote, "but on this occasion we were to pass down a ravine or defile only wide enough to admit a company front. Mine being the right company or first in line, I was ordered to lead the charge, and be supported by companies in rear. We started with a yell, bayonets fixed. As we came over the crest of a hill (over which the enemy lay), they poured what might be called or what is called a 'storm of leaden hail' into the head of the column." "My men wavered at first under the hot fire of the enemy," reported Colonel Kiddoo, "but soon, on seeing their colors on the opposite side of the ravine, [they] pushed rapidly up and passed the rifle-pits and fort." Battery 8 now became a Union prize, though Colonel Kiddoo had to fling back a Rebel counterattack to keep it.[41]

The forward momentum passed to other units in Duncan's brigade. Lieutenant Colonel George Rogers of the 4th USCT, having re-formed the regiment after its attack on Battery 7, leap-frogged Kiddoo's men and made for Battery 9. Quoting from Colonel Duncan's report, "As he approached the enemy retired to Battery No. 10, upon which Colonel Rogers immediately charged, driving out the occupants and capturing one gun, with caissons and horses." Right behind the 4th USCT came the 6th, which entered Battery 9 to find it abandoned save for a single dead, teenaged gunner. Captain John McMurray assisted his men in burying the Rebel "as tenderly as though he had been a Union soldier."[42]

McMurray's compassion stood in sharp contrast to the behavior of some of the black troops in this operation. During a roundup of prisoners near captured Battery 6, at least one unarmed Confederate was killed by a USCT man who, according to a member of the 117th New York, "came up to him . . . and ran his bayonet through his heart." Such actions, taken by a few black soldiers, often with the silent complicity of their white officers, represented the reverse side of the Fort Pillow coin.[43]

Battery 10 commanded the rear of Battery 11. With the former in Federal hands, the latter became untenable, so it was quickly evacuated by the Confederates. Smith's men had thus captured nine Dimmock Line batteries, six of which fell to USCT units. June 15 should have been one of the signal victories of the war, for if Petersburg fell, Richmond was doomed. Chaplain William H. Hunter of the 4th

USCT spoke for many of the rank and file—both black and white—when he declared that they all "had a great desire to enter that city on the night of the 15th of June." But it was not to be.[44]

Nearly overwhelmed by the magnitude of his success, Smith suddenly began to fear that a counterattack by the Confederates (who he believed were being heavily reinforced) would cancel out his achievement. But beyond that, his racial prejudices also clearly played a part in his decision to halt all further offensive operations: as he rode the captured lines, he found his exuberant black soldiers camped, their weapons stacked and dinner fires blazing, on the enemy's side of the earthworks. His sharp orders to the men to put out those fires and take up their guns were met by one bewildered infantryman's complaint, "Why, de coffee am about to bile." In a postwar attempt to explain his decision not to press his advantage this night, Smith said that his "white troops were exhausted. . . . [And] my colored troops . . . could barely be kept in order."[45]

Lieutenant Verplanck of Hincks's staff estimated the Union loss at eight hundred, while Lieutenant Grabill of the 5th USCT guessed that the 1st, 4th, 6th, and 22nd USCT lost "from 160 to 200 each in killed and wounded." The only official accounting came from Colonel Duncan, who reported casualties for June 15 of 44 killed, 317 wounded, and 17 missing, for a total of 378. On the plus side of the ledger was a solid sense of accomplishment. "It was rather interesting to see the old veterans of the A[rmy of the] P[otomac] stare when they saw the works we had captured," beamed Lieutenant Covell of the 6th USCT. "The old soldiers would hardly believe that colored troops had done it, but had to do so." Remembering the Southern officer on the white horse who had exhorted his men that they were contending only with "niggers," Sergeant Holland of the 5th USCT observed that Rebel chivalry would no longer be able to "see the nigger part as the man on the white horse presented it."[46]

Smith's failure to follow up his success allowed the Confederates to regroup and patch together a makeshift defensive position that held up against renewed Federal attacks on June 16. There was a breakdown of coordination on the Union side as Army of the Potomac units intermingled with units from the Army of the James, resulting in a day of piecemeal assaults based on no overall plan. The Rebel miracle continued on June 17 and 18; even though the Confederates did lose some ground, in the end they managed to hang on to a stabilized defensive perimeter that kept Petersburg out of Yankee hands.

The black troops played only a small part in the June 16–18 fighting. Those associated with the Army of the Potomac were kept well in the rear to guard supplies and communications, while those under Smith were withdrawn by him early on June 16 for much the same duty. Yet what they had achieved on June 15 would not be forgotten. "It is the day when prejudice died in the entire Army of the U.S. of America," declared the 4th USCT's Chaplain Hunter. "It is the day when it was admitted that colored men were equal to the severest ordeal." Reporter Charles Coffin, who had witnessed the march of the Ninth Corps's black troops through Washington, reached Petersburg in early July and soon after had a disturbing conversation with a Massachusetts officer who loudly wished that there were no black troops in the army, moreover admitting that he believed all blacks were inferior to whites. This prompted Coffin to reflection:

> From my seat . . . I have a full view of the rebel line of works where . . . the colored troops . . . won for themselves a fame which will have a record among the many splendid achievements of the Union army. . . . Without faltering, without flinching, the colored troops of General Hin[c]ks' division moved with the steadiness of veterans upon those formidable works, and carried them at the point of the bayonet. There, at the Dunn house, enclosed by a strong redan, is the hospital [holding] . . . several hundred [black] soldiers . . . torn by shells, by grape, by minie bullets. . . . A few rods distance there is a row of graves, newly made. They who had no home, no country, nothing, have found a home, a country, an inheritance at last upon the battlefield. . . . [What of] their comrades who remain . . . ? The flag that floats above them is not theirs. It means nothing. To us it is . . . the symbol of everything worth living for, but to them it is not the symbol of a vague, undefined, blind hope of something in the future. . . . Standing here upon the ground yet strewn with the wreck of battle— broken muskets, cannon balls, unexploded shells—the scene of their victory, my cheek burns when I recall the words uttered by a Massachusetts captain . . . and remember that our government and the nation are not ready to be just or generous to the colored race.[47]

Assault on the Crater, Petersburg, Virginia, July 30, 1864

On June 19, Lieutenant General Ulysses S. Grant began siege operations at Petersburg. There was some sharp fighting on June 22 and 24 as first the Federals and then the Confederates tried but failed significantly to readjust the shape of the trench lines that were growing between the two armies. Both sides then settled down to an indeterminate period of "static" warfare.

The black regiments in the Army of the James still held some of the forts they had captured on June 15. Despite those soldiers' success that day, serious doubts persisted in the minds of their white commanders regarding their fighting abilities. In a report filed on June 27, Brigadier General Hincks itemized the problems he had had with his command. Battery B, 2nd U.S. Colored Artillery, was, he declared, "inefficient and unserviceable, and . . . the colored gunners were incompetent." The trial use of the 5th Massachusetts Cavalry (Colored) as infantry had also, he felt, been a complete failure. In addition, the two most recently arrived infantry units—the 10th and 37th USCT— were "far from being effective regiments." Hincks concluded, "We should be cautious lest we imperil the success of the project of arming colored men . . . by assuming that the negro is a soldier ready made, rather than that he will make a soldier by patient, persistent, and intelligent drill and instruction." Hincks's comments underscored the prejudice of the commander of the Eighteenth Corps, Major General William F. Smith, who believed that without a strong cadre of white officers to train and lead these men, the "experiment will prove a failure."[48]

Such racist assessments of black troops frequently extended to their punishment as well. In some cases, the white men commanding the USCT regiments seemed to feel that sheer brutality was necessary to keep the soldiers in line. At the end of June, an officer in the 23rd USCT (Burnside's corps) noted in his diary, "A sad affair occurred in Co. 'G' while we were on the march, one of his men refused [to] obey some order of the Capt. when he shot him so that he died in a few moments." Only a few weeks earlier, the same regiment had witnessed the hanging—purposely staged within sight of the Rebel lines—of one of its men, charged with the attempted rape of a white woman. To render the object lesson even more explicit, the body had been left dangling long enough for cameramen to take a series of graphic photographs of it.[49]

Despite these hardships and indignities, black troops soldiered on in the unfolding siege of Petersburg. "Our regiment is now doing picket duty," Alexander Banks of the 1st USCT informed the readers of the *Anglo-African,* "and quietness reigns along the lines, except occasional booming in our rear and from the enemy, the missiles from both sides passing over our heads." The 4th USCT, too, saw its share of front-line service. "I write from within a quarter of a mile of the city," "Arnold" told the *Anglo-African.* "The sharpshooters continue to bang away at each other from morning till night, and finally somebody gets hurt; then the noise and roar of the big guns begin. . . . One not accustomed to this would say it was a general engagement, but not so; for after quiet reigns, perhaps ten or a dozen of our soldiers are found to be wounded, or two or three killed."[50]

Whereas the deadly routine of duty in the trenches and their unceasing labors under the hot July sun soon began to sap the spirit of the white troops, those in the USCT units remained aware of the significance of their presence. "We have seen the fruits of slavery," wrote D. R. Brown of the 31st USCT on July 18, "the desolation and despair of hundreds rushing into our lines, crying and praying for protection." "We know, and the slave knows," added Alexander Banks, "that fighting for the Union is fighting against slavery."[51]

The work was particularly hard for the black soldiers of Brigadier General Edward Ferrero's Ninth Corps division. "We have been marching for the last two weeks from one part to another along the front," Sergeant John C. Brock of the 43rd USCT wrote on July 16,

> engaged in picket and fatigue duty. Our division has built two immense forts. . . . Sometimes they were in the trenches, in very dangerous places, the bullets whistling over and among our troops all day and all night long, while the men were engaged in digging. . . . But notwithstanding all these dangers, the boys shoulder their shovels and picks merrily every day, and go out front to the trenches, ready and willing to do every thing in their power that will lead to the capture and overthrow of the rebel stronghold.[52]

Even as Sergeant Brock was finishing this letter, other Union soldiers were resting on their picks and shovels before one of the most

229

remarkable military engineering achievements of the war. In some of the last convulsive lunges of the June 18 fighting, white units from Burnside's corps had seized a patch of rising ground directly adjacent to a Confederate strongpoint known as Elliott's Salient. The Ninth Corps soldiers dug in and soon established a line of earthworks not four hundred feet from the Rebel defenses—closer together than any other points in the Union and Confederate trenches. It happened that the soldiers in the first Federal unit assigned to duty there, the 48th Pennsylvania, had been recruited among the coal miners of Schuylkill County, and the man commanding the regiment, Lieutenant Colonel Henry Pleasants, was a mining engineer in civilian life. The idea of tunneling under the enemy's fort and blowing it up seems to have occurred simultaneously to the rank and file of the 48th and to several key officers in the regiment's brigade and division.

A successful breaching of the Confederate lines here promised glittering possibilities. The Jerusalem Plank Road ran along a slight ridge roughly parallel to the line of works and only a few hundred yards behind Elliott's Salient; once Federal troops reached that concourse, a quick march would take them to Cemetery Hill in Blandford, where their cannon would dominate Petersburg and the rear of the Confederate front lines.

On June 25, digging commenced into the face of a sheltered ravine about a hundred feet behind the Union line. Over the next weeks, shifts of men from the 48th slowly gouged their way through the red clay soil. The whole endeavor had the enthusiastic blessing of Major General Ambrose Burnside, though only lukewarm approval from the man heading the Army of the Potomac, Major General George G. Meade. Meade's staff, reflecting his ambivalence, was unsupportive of Pleasants's little operation, and refused to provide him with proper tools or measuring instruments.

Pleasants and his men nonetheless managed to make remarkable progress. A way was found surreptitiously to dispose of the excavated dirt; shoring timbers were produced at an abandoned sawmill reactivated by the regiment; specialized digging tools were improvised or borrowed; and the problem of ventilation within the mine was solved with a simple chimney system that exchanged bad air for good.

By July 17, the tunnel extended 511 feet directly beneath the salient, and work was temporarily halted while an examination was undertaken to determine if Confederate countermines posed any danger. Digging soon resumed, and a pair of lateral galleries were run parallel to the enemy line, each stretching an additional thirty-seven to thirty-eight feet. On July 27, the Pennsylvanians began to pack these galleries with four tons of gunpowder.

Even as the engineering problems were being solved, General Burnside pondered the military question. As he later testified to a Congressional Committee, "During the month of July . . . I had made up my mind, in case an assault was to be made by the 9th corps, to put [the black] . . . division in the advance." In other comments, Burnside enumerated his reasons:

I [selected] . . . the Fourth Division . . . inasmuch as that division had not suffered so severely [as the three white divisions], in fact had not been in any general engagement during the campaign, but had frequently been very honorably engaged on the outposts of the army. General Ferrero himself and all his officers expressed to me their utmost confidence in his troops, and especially his confidence in their ability to make a charge, or in other words a dash.

Explaining further to the Committee of Congress, he said, "I had so informed General Ferrero, and, at my suggestion, he submitted to me an opinion as to the formation which would be the most effective in passing over the ground in our front; which formation, after some consideration, I approved, and directed him to drill his troops with a view of making the attack in that way."[53]

Ferrero in turn described the plan approved by Burnside:

The mine was under a considerable fort upon the right. There was a small fort, a short distance, probably six hundred yards to the left, with three or four guns. My idea was to make an assault at the moment of the explosion of the mine between these two points. I wanted to advance one brigade, which was to be the leading brigade, then divide it in two parts, one portion to go to the right and sweep the enemy's lines in that direction, and the other portion to go down the left and sweep the lines in that direction. The other [brigade] . . . of the division [was] . . . to march forward in column, and carry the crest of Cemetery Hill.[54]

Implementation of Ferrero's scheme trickled down the chain of command. Colonel Joshua K. Sigfried, whose First Brigade (27th, 30th, 39th, and 43rd USCT) would lead the attack, recalled that beginning in early July, his men were "daily drilled from two to three hours with a special view of making the assault when the mine should be exploded." His recollection was seconded by statements from officers in three of the brigade's four regiments. Although the commander of the Second Brigade (19th, 23rd, 28th, 29th, and 31st USCT), Colonel Henry G. Thomas, likewise avowed that his men "drilled certain movements to be executed in going and occupying the crest," no similar independent confirmation exists for his statement; in fact, Captain R. K. Beecham, in the 23rd USCT, would later declare, "I am prepared to say from actual knowledge derived from personal experience with the Fourth Division that the only duty assigned to the said division for more than a month before the battle of the Mine was work upon our trenches and fortifications. The Fourth Division during all that time was drilled especially in the use of pick and shovel, and in no other manner." Against this, however, is the word of an officer in the 19th USCT that his colleagues "had expected we were to lead the assault, and had been for several weeks drilling our men with this idea in view, particular attention being paid to charging." It may be that since the most critical maneuvers would be required only of the First Brigade, Sigfried's men underwent special training, while Thomas's did not; it is also possible that since the movements to be made by Thomas's men were standard ones, the officers who carried out the drills never noticed anything out of the ordinary.[55]

Henry G. Thomas was an officer who observed his men carefully. He later described their reaction to the news that they would be leading a major assault:

Any striking event or piece of news was usually eagerly discussed by the white troops, and in the ranks military critics were as plenty and perhaps more voluble than among the officers. Not so with the blacks; important news such as that before us, after the bare announcement, was usually followed by long silence. They sat about in groups, "studying," as they called it. They waited, like the Quakers, for the spirit to move; when the spirit moved, one of their singers would uplift a mighty voice, like a bard of old, in a wild sort of chant. If he did not strike a sympathetic chord in his hearers . . . he would

1. The 1st Regiment South Carolina Infantry (A.D.) on dress parade at ceremonies announcing the Emancipation Proclamation. Of this ceremony, Colonel Thomas W. Higginson remembered: "The day was perfect, and there was nothing but success."

2. The attack of the 54th Regiment Massachusetts Infantry (Colored) on Fort (Battery) Wagner, as drawn by Thomas Nast. "Men all around me would fall and roll down the slope into the ditch," recalled one black soldier. Said another: "Swept down like chaff, still our men went on and on."

3. This engraving, which appeared in the *Illustrated London News,* was based on a drawing made on July 19 by Frank Vizetelly. The artist provided this caption: "The Appearance by the ditch & on the Southern Slope of Battery Wagner, the morning after the assault — The horrible scene that met the eye the morning after the attack beggars description."

4. This illustration from *Harper's Weekly* depicts black troops from Brigadier General Edward A. Wild's African Brigade liberating slaves in eastern North Carolina. In his official report on this December 1863 expedition, Wild estimated that his men freed some twenty-five hundred slaves.

5. Trace of the Jacksonville road not far from the Olustee battlefield in Florida. It was along this route that Federal troops under Brigadier General Truman Seymour advanced to meet Confederates in a combat in which three black regiments, including the 54th Massachusetts (Colored), were heavily engaged.

6. A modern reconstruction of Major Booth's redoubt at Fort Pillow. Confederate troopers under Major General Nathan B. Forrest poured over these walls on the afternoon of April 12, 1864, in one of the most controversial actions involving black troops in the Civil War.

7. The Fort Pillow massacre, as depicted in *Frank Leslie's Illustrated Newspaper*. This was one occasion when even the sensationalist reportage of the day could barely match the awful tales that would be related in eyewitness testimony given before a congressional investigating committee.

8. Officers and men of the 1st USCT. Originally organized in the District of Columbia, the regiment fought at Wilson's Wharf on May 24, took part in the June 15 Petersburg assault, and participated in both Fort Fisher expeditions. In the course of their service, four officers and sixty-seven enlisted men of the 1st USCT were either killed or mortally wounded.

9. Private William H. Johnson, 23rd USCT, executed at Petersburg, Virginia, by U.S. officials on June 20, 1864. According to a dispatch filed by a reporter on the scene: "A Negro named William Johnson was executed this morning . . . in full view of the enemy, for an attempt to violate the person of a young lady at New Kent Court House." Johnson was an ex-slave from Maryland whose service record indicates that he was "killed in the trenches."

10. Men of Company E, 4th USCT, at Fort Lincoln, in the defenses of Washington. This unit participated in operations on the Virginia Peninsula and fought at Petersburg on June 15, 1864, and at New Market Heights on September 29 of the same year. It was also part of the first and second expeditions to Fort Fisher.

11. A sketch by combat artist Alfred Waud shows some of Brigadier General Ferrero's troops moving forward toward the Petersburg crater on July 30, 1864. "They did their duty and that bravely," said a member of the 31st USCT. The artist has exaggerated the sole and heel of one soldier's boots (at lower left) to provide the engraver with some small details.

12. Probably made in October 1864, this sketch by William Waud depicts the work being done on the Dutch Gap canal, near Petersburg. Black troops made up the majority of the labor force used to dig the canal, a task that was accomplished within range of Confederate cannon on Bermuda Hundred and on the north side of the James River. According to a USCT officer: "No day passed without death and wounds in the deepening channel. . . . Fever and ague, and bilious fevers, attacked the working party, and those diseases were aggravated by the cellar-like holes in which the constant fire of the enemy forced the troops to live."

13. Boyd's Landing on the Broad River in South Carolina. The Union troops that landed here fought and were defeated at Honey Hill on November 30, 1864. According to the history of the 55th Regiment Massachusetts Infantry (Colored): "The regiment was at once landed on the muddy bank, near Col. Boyd's deserted mansion, and bivouacked for the night."

14. Trace of the Grahamville road, a short distance below the Confederate earthworks on Honey Hill. Recalled an officer in the 55th Massachusetts (Colored): "The surrounding woods were thickly grown with underbrush, so that infantry movements were very much impeded, and artillery could not be used except in the roadway."

15. The caption of this illustration from *Harper's Weekly* reads: "Marching on! — The Fifty-fifth Massachusetts Colored Regiment singing John Brown's march in the streets of Charleston, February 21, 1865." "Cheers, blessings, prayers, and songs were heard on every side," recalled a soldier in the ranks.

16. Looking toward the Confederate position at Boykins Mill, successfully attacked by elements of the 54th Massachusetts (Colored) on April 18, 1865. The guardrails in the foreground and middle distance mark the edges of a small island that sheltered a squad of black soldiers who provided covering fire while their comrades attacked along an earthen dam (just beyond the left edge of the picture).

17. This simple monument marks the site of the Confederate defenses overrun at Boykins Mill. Another face of the monument (not pictured) honors Lieutenant Edward L. Stevens of the 54th Massachusetts (Colored), one of the last Union officers to die in action in the Civil War.

18. A detail from the 107th USCT, shown in Fort Corcoran in the defenses of Washington. Organized in Kentucky, the regiment took part in operations against Petersburg and participated in both Fort Fisher expeditions.

19. Black troops mustering out in Little Rock in 1865. When an engraving based on this sketch appeared in *Harper's Weekly*, it carried comments from the artist, who said: "Just in from Duvall's Bluff, where they had been stationed, their landing created a furor among the resident colored families. . . . [Some] rushed into the arms of their husbands with an outburst of uncontrollable affection. . . . Children ran about with bundles of blankets or knapsacks for their papas, or begged the privilege of carrying a gun for some sable warrior."

20. A portion of the 5th USCT formed in line on Sandusky Street in Delaware, Ohio. The 5th, organized largely from Ohio's black population, saw action at Petersburg on June 15 and at New Market Heights, where four of its enlisted men won the Medal of Honor.

sing it again and again, altering sometimes the words, more often the music. If his changes met general acceptance, one voice after another would chime in; a rough harmony of three parts would add itself; other groups would join his, and the song would become the song of the command.

The night we learned that we were to lead the charge the news filled them too full for ordinary utterance. . . . They formed circles in their company streets and were sitting on the ground intently and solemnly "studying." At last a heavy voice began to sing,

> *"We-e looks li-ike me-en a-a-marchin' on,*
> *We looks li-ike men-er-war."*

. . . All at once, when his refrain had struck the right response in their hearts, his group took it up, and shortly half a thousand voices were upraised extemporizing a half dissonant middle part and bass. It was a picturesque scene—these dark men, with their white eyes and teeth and full red lips, crouching over a smoldering camp-fire, in dusky shadow, with only the feeble rays of the lanterns of the first sergeants and the lights of the candles dimly showing through the tents. . . . Until we fought the battle of the crater they sang this every night to the exclusion of all other songs.[56]

The tunnel reached the enemy fort on July 17; it took another six days to complete the lateral galleries. Four additional days of labor followed as Pleasants's miners fashioned dry areas to hold the gunpowder, which began to arrive on July 27. By the morning of July 28, Pleasants could report that everything was ready. Worried that the tunnel walls might have been weakened by recent rains, and certain that the Confederates suspected something was up, Pleasants was anxious that the explosion should be set off as soon as possible.

Two days before Pleasants signaled "Ready," a combined Federal infantry-cavalry force had marched over Bermuda Hundred and crossed the James River at Deep Bottom. Its purpose was to disrupt Richmond's still-functioning rail supply lines and to prevent Robert E. Lee from reinforcing a raiding force that was raising hell in the Shenandoah Valley. Although the expedition failed to accomplish its first objective, it succeeded in drawing out so many Rebel units from Petersburg's trenches that by the evening of July 29, only three

Confederate divisions occupied those defensive works. The odds for the Federals at the Cockade City would never be better.

Burnside's real problems began on July 28, when he rode to George Meade's headquarters to tell him that the mine was ready. There he was informed that his plan to let the black troops lead the attack had been rejected. As Meade later explained, "'[Burnside's] colored division [was] . . . a new division, and had never been under fire —had never been tried—and as this was an operation which I knew beforehand was one requiring the best troops, I thought it impolitic to trust it." Meade also wanted the first units over the top to press straight on to Cemetery Hill, instead of fanning left and right as Burnside intended.[57]

After arguing with Meade, who promised to lay the entire matter before General Grant, Burnside went back to his own headquarters to wait for an answer. By now the time for exploding the gunpowder had been set at 3:30 A.M. July 30, so the clock was ticking. At midday on July 29, Burnside convened the three commanders of his white divisions to go over their roles in the forthcoming attack. Still assuming that his original plan was in effect, he did not summon Brigadier General Ferrero, who already knew what to do. Hardly had Burnside begun the briefing, however, when there was a knock on his tent pole announcing the arrival of General Meade and members of his staff. General Grant had sustained Meade's decision, Burnside was told: the black troops were not to lead the attack. Having dropped that bombshell, Meade and company departed.

Burnside thus saw all his careful planning collapse like a house of cards. The assault could not be canceled; it remained only to decide which of the white divisions would lead. This question compelled a frustrating discussion between Burnside and his three subordinates, which kept returning to the obvious conclusion that Ferrero's division was the best qualified. Finally, in a fit of desperation, Burnside had the three officers draw lots from a hat. In this way, the First Division, commanded by Brigadier General James H. Ledlie, was selected to spearhead the assault. A new plan was improvised: Ledlie's men would dash around the crater caused by the explosion and seize Cemetery Hill; the Third Division (under Brigadier General Orlando B. Willcox) would cross behind Ledlie to form a defensive line to the left; and the Second Division (Brigadier General Robert B. Potter, commanding) would do likewise on the right. Only then would Ferrero's men come forward to sweep into Petersburg.

It was perhaps the best plan possible under the circumstances, but otherwise it had terribly little to recommend it. The white troops had all been manning the front lines constantly since June 18; their morale was poor and their combat efficiency low. Brigadier General Ledlie had not performed well over the course of the Overland Campaign, and there were rumblings within his division (unknown to Burnside) that he turned to the bottle when the going got tough. Nevertheless, there was nothing else to be done, so the officers hurried off to prepare for the mine explosion.

The only comprehensive statement as to when the officers of Ferrero's division were told of the new arrangements came from Colonel H. Seymour Hall of the 43rd USCT in the First Brigade (Sigfried's):

> The evening of July 29th our division moved down to the left of the entrance to the covered way leading out to our most advanced line in front of the mined salient of the enemy, and with my regiment in advance, formed . . . in readiness to lead the assault. No hint of change of plans had reached me and General Ferrero does not state when he was informed of it. . . . The commander of our other brigade [Thomas] says that he was not informed of any change till near midnight of July 29th, and as his line officers were apparently in quiet sleep, they were not aroused to be informed of what would do them no service. I did not know of any change till the morning of July 30th.[58]

Soon after dark on July 29, the Ninth Corps troops began to file into their jump-off positions. Joining them as a reserve was a division from the Tenth Corps that would play a minor role in the drama that was about to unfold. Burnside's white troops crowded into the ditches along the jump-off line, filling the communications passages, or covered ways, leading forward, while the black troops massed on the open hillside below the ruins of the Taylor House, not far from an entranceway to the forward trenches. "Around us could be heard the shuffling tread of troops, but it was so dark that nothing could be seen," recalled Lieutenant Freeman S. Bowley of the 30th USCT. "Down on the picket line the rifles were flashing, and over head the bullets hummed with that peculiar droning sound of the nearly spent bullet. Most of us went to sleep as soon as we halted." In the 27th

USCT, Sergeant Joseph H. Payne conducted an impromptu sacred service. "Many professors [of religion] appeared to be greatly stirred up," he averred, "while sinners seemed to be deeply touched and aroused to a sense of their danger and duty. Our prayer meeting was short but not without good and lasting impressions being made upon the hearts and minds of many."[59]

"Before day we were up and ready," remembered Lieutenant Fred A. Chapman in the 29th USCT. "Every one felt the danger awaiting him, and there was unusual silence. All seemed occupied with their own thoughts." Colonel Thomas joined his staff in a soldier's breakfast, "two pieces of hard-tack with a slice of raw, fat salt pork between—not a dainty meal, but solid provender to fight on." All this activity went unnoticed by Lieutenant Charles F. Stinson in the 19th USCT, who had fallen asleep as soon as the regiment halted and was still snoring away, blissfully unaware of his surroundings.[60]

The time appointed for the mine explosion—3:30 A.M.—came and went. Soon it was 4:00 A.M., then 4:30, and still there was only silence. Near the mine entrance, Lieutenant Colonel Pleasants and his tunnel team waited, the tension mounting sharply until, at about 4:15 A.M., someone volunteered to go in and find out what had happened. He quickly returned to report that all three fuse lines had failed at a splice point only a short distance inside the tunnel. Pleasants's man was joined by a second volunteer, and together they relit the fuse and scrambled back out. By now it was about 4:30 A.M; at a time officially reckoned as 4:44 A.M., the sputtering flame at last reached the four tons of gunpowder packed in the galleries beneath Elliott's Salient.

Chaplain Garland H. White, an ex-slave himself, was moving among his flock in the 28th USCT when the explosion went off. "Just at this junction the earth began to shake," he wrote afterward, "as though the hand of God intended a reversal of the laws of nature." Colonel Thomas recalled it as a "dull, heavy thud, not at all startling; it was a heavy, smothered sound, not nearly so distinct as a musket shot." The experience was more vivid for Captain Warren H. Hurd of the 23rd USCT, who watched in awe as a "large black cloud . . . appeared to rise out of the ground." Lieutenant Bowley, 30th USCT, remembered first a "jar of the earth under our feet," followed by a "terrible rumbling." Colonel Hall of the 43rd USCT watched in openmouthed astonishment as the cloud "burst into innumerable

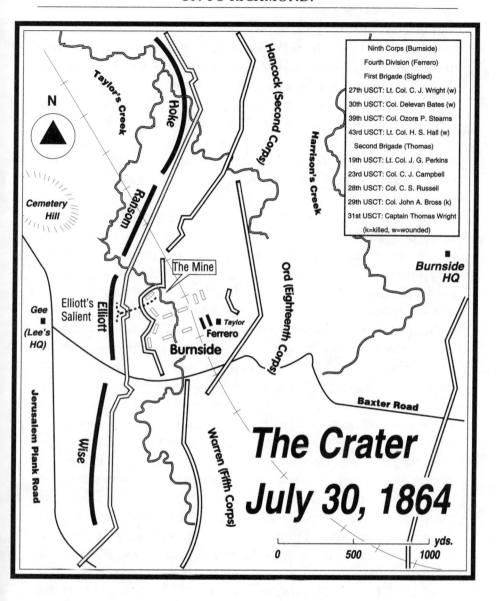

Ninth Corps (Burnside)

Fourth Division (Ferrero)

First Brigade (Sigfried)

27th USCT: Lt. Col. C. J. Wright (w)

30th USCT: Col. Delevan Bates (w)

39th USCT: Col. Ozora P. Stearns

43rd USCT: Lt. Col. H. S. Hall (w)

Second Brigade (Thomas)

19th USCT: Lt. Col. J. G. Perkins

23rd USCT: Col. C. J. Campbell

28th USCT: Col. C. S. Russell

29th USCT: Col. John A. Bross (k)

31st USCT: Captain Thomas Wright

(k=killed, w=wounded)

The Crater

July 30, 1864

fragments and fell in a confused inextricable mass of earth, muskets, cannon, men, an awful debris."[61]

Where there had lately been a redoubt and trenches holding three hundred men, four cannon, and thirty gunners, there was now only a great smoking cavity, 150 to 200 feet long, sixty feet wide, and some thirty feet deep. Cued by the explosion, 110 Federal cannon and fifty-four mortars opened fire along nearly two miles of trench lines. This cannonade, declared Lieutenant Bowley, "was one of the most terrific of the war." Captain James H. Rickard of the 19th USCT was certain that it was this artillery barrage that "made the ground tremble as by an earthquake," a shaking that woke up the sound-sleeping Lieutenant Stinson. It all proved too much for Private Miles Keyes of the 28th USCT, or so thought his comrades: it was to these events that they would later attribute Keyes's contraction of an "unsoundness of mind" that would cause him to end his days in a lunatic asylum near Cincinnati.[62]

About five minutes after the debris stopped raining down, General Ledlie ordered the two brigades of his division to advance, then retired to a nearby aid station for a drink. There he would remain, save for an occasional foray to observe what was happening, for the rest of the battle. Neither of his brigades seems to have been apprised of Burnside's instructions to press toward Cemetery Hill; both stopped in or alongside the great pit, where they began to take cover from the already intense Confederate defensive fire. More men piled in from behind as the two other white divisions dutifully pressed forward. Two brigades of Willcox's division tried to adhere to the plan by swinging left around the crater to secure one of the shoulders of the penetration; they enjoyed some success before the increasingly murderous Rebel rifle and cannon fire drove them to ground. When Potter's division went in on the right, it got mixed in with some of Ledlie's men and shot up by the Confederates who tenaciously held the trenches on that flank.

All of this took perhaps ninety minutes. Back where the black troops were waiting for the order to advance, the soldiers got ready. "The men were ordered to pile their knapsacks, and while doing so we heard the cheers of the second assaulting party, and the brisk musketry fire told us that they were meeting with a desperate resistance," recollected Lieutenant Bowley. Chaplain White was suddenly besieged by individuals asking him to write their loved ones for them and begging him "when pay-day comes, if it ever does come, [to] send what money is due [home]."[63]

Even as the black troops anxiously prepared to enter the covered way, squads of wounded white Union soldiers and captured Confederates began to stumble back through their ranks. "The latter were terribly frightened at the sight of the colored soldiers, and besought their white guards 'not to let the niggers bayonet them,'" noted Lieutenant Bowley. "They could not be pacified, until a colored corporal gave a severely wounded rebel a drink of water from his canteen, and this little act seemed to instantly restore confidence among them." There were some last-minute exhortations by officers to their men, with the colonels commanding the 28th and 29th USCT each vowing to lead their units into Petersburg this day.[64]

Colonel Thomas was lying down with his staff, waiting for the order to advance, when a voice called out near him, "Who commands this brigade?" Thomas rose up. "I do," he said. He found himself facing Lieutenant General Grant, who was mounted and attired in a "broad-brimmed felt hat and the ordinary coat of a private." "Well," Grant said slowly, "why are you not in?" Thomas indicated the still-unmoving files of Sigfried's regiments. "My orders are to follow that brigade," he replied. A thought occurred to him, and he asked, "Will you give me the order to go in now?" "No," said the other after a few moments' reflection, "you keep the orders you have." Grant then rode off. Thomas reckoned it to be some fifteen minutes later when the lines of black men finally began to shuffle forward.[65]

"It seemed forever," wrote Lieutenant Hurd of the 23rd USCT. "The whole [division] . . . filed through a single parallel. . . . We were hindered by officers and orderlies coming to the rear, the parallel being only about six feet wide." As Ferrero approached the trench line from which his men were to debouch, a staff officer who had been sent ahead to scout the situation returned with an alarming description of the chaos ahead. The general appealed his orders to Colonel Charles Loring of Burnside's staff, who told him to halt his men while the directives were confirmed. Loring quickly reappeared and, as Ferrero recalled, "reported that the order was peremptory for me to carry my division through at all hazards." The hasty plan concocted in desperation less than twenty-four hours earlier was now in shambles, with none of the white divisions' having achieved its objective— yet Burnside's mission for the black division remained unchanged. There was one last delay as Colonel Sigfried sought permission from Ferrero to deploy in line of battle instead of in column, a request that was refused. Then, with the 30th USCT leading, the troops of Sigfried's brigade began to move out of the Union trenches and across the no-man's-land toward the crater.[66]

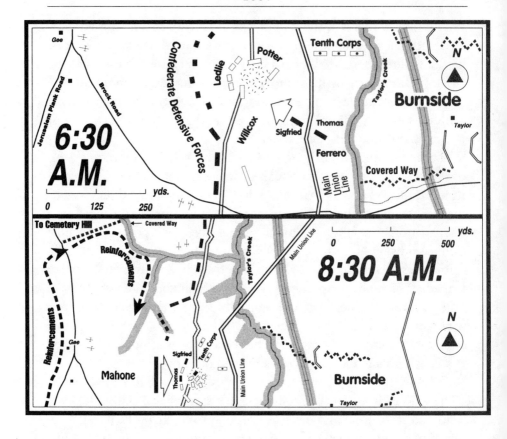

Said Colonel Bates of the 30th, "The appearance of the regimental colors seemed to be the signal for the enemy's batteries, and it was volley after volley of canister and shrapnel they gave us." "Down went our flag," recalled Lieutenant Bowley, "the color-sergeant staining the stars and stripes with his blood. A grape-shot had torn his head in pieces." Behind the 30th, the rest of the brigade spilled into the killing ground—first the 43rd, then the 39th, and finally the 27th USCT. "I well remember the 27th marching in double quick up that approach to the crater and through it, stepping over our dead and wounded," wrote Captain Matthew R. Mitchell. Captain Albert Rogall of the 27th described the enemy fire "tearing the ground in our midst."[67]

Colonel Bates tried to lead his men around to the right of the crater, but Confederate fire pressed the head of his column into the pit. "Push down the line," Bates called out to Captain David E. Proctor, in charge of the leading company. Proctor and his men rushed through and out the other side, where they formed a rough line of battle. Behind them, the 43rd USCT also stumbled into the smoking hole, but Lieutenant Colonel Hall saw at once that the mob inside would make it impossible for his unit to follow the 30th. Although the enemy still held trenches close to the right, Hall spotted a partially sheltered route of approach and personally led his men "along the front of the enemy's intrenchments, so close that some of my officers and men were wounded by the bayonets, others burned by the powder flashes of the foe." Once his regiment was aligned, Hall ordered a charge that plunged his black soldiers into hand-to-hand-combat. "The men killed numbers of the enemy in spite of the efforts of their officers to restrain them," Hall wrote, "and we took prisoners in these intrenchments." (The colonel himself received a severe wound that would knock him out of the action and cost him his right arm.) The 43rd linked up with the 30th on the outside slope of the crater, and the two were then joined by the remaining two regiments of the brigade—or rather, what was left of them, following their deadly passage across no-man's-land and through the disorderly crowd in the pit.[68]

The situation facing these officers and men was a pure nightmare. "The enemy's works on this part of the line was a perfect honeycomb of bomb proofs, trenches, covered ways, sleeping holes, and little alleys running in every direction, and in each hole there appeared one or more rebel soldiers, some ready to 'kill the niggers' when they came in view and some praying for mercy," said Bates. For the next minutes, the black soldiers were occupied with the grim task of clearing out the nearest network of trenches and holes.[69]

It took the four regiments of Ferrero's First Brigade about half an hour to clear the passageway sufficiently for Colonel Thomas to lead his men forward. The 31st USCT was first to rush into the open ground between the lines, followed by the others, with the 19th USCT trailing last. "They did their duty and that bravely," said David R. Brown of the 31st. "While in this work and coming through we were exposed to a heavy cross fire of artillery & musketry," recalled Captain Robert Porter of the 29th USCT. "Here we lost all our line officers." From his place back at the main trench line, Chaplain White of the 28th USCT watched the regimental flag go up and into the enemy's works. "Boys," he cheered to those nearby, "the day is ours, and Petersburg is sure."[70]

Colonel Thomas never had full control of his brigade once the advance began. Two of his regiments got stuck in the confusion of the crater, while one, the 19th USCT, was hung up before it even entered the pit; once stopped, and somewhat sheltered from enemy fire by its walls, the men refused to go forward and could not return across the no-man's-land. Thomas tried to lead the 31st USCT in a charge, but these soldiers remained in the great hole. Their commander, Lieutenant Colonel William E. W. Ross, was hit, along with many of his officers. One of his orderlies, Lieutenant Christopher Pennell, grabbed the brigade guidon and stood at the lip of the pit, calling for the men to follow him, but "in a moment," Thomas wrote, "a musketry fire was focused upon him, whirling him round and round several times before he fell."[71]

The price paid by Sigfried's brigade in cleaning out the works in its immediate vicinity was a heavy one. Colonel Bates was leading a sortie against a pocket of defenders when he was shot in the head and badly wounded. "Bullets came through all the little alleyways, and found victims in the most unexpected places," said Lieutenant Bowley. At one point, the fallen regimental colors of the 30th USCT were picked up by Private William Gray, who was then "struck by a minie ball in the left breast causing almost immediately death." One officer not present to see any of this was Brigadier General Ferrero, who remained back at the Union jump-off trench. His principal contribution to the unfolding events came soon after 8:00 A.M., when he sent an aide forward with orders for Colonels Sigfried and Thomas to follow their original instructions and advance to the Jerusalem Plank Road and Cemetery Hill.[72]

Somehow the two colonels pulled enough of their men together to make the effort: the thin black lines were dressed under fire, and the order to advance was given. As the uneven files lurched ahead, some white units even joined in the attempt. More than three hours had now passed since the gunpowder galleries were ignited. In what proved to be perhaps the greatest failure of this entire operation, the Union Fifth Corps, supporting the Ninth on its left, did not mount enough pressure to prevent Robert E. Lee from pulling three brigades off that front to counterattack at the center. When the black and white battle line began to move forward, it was hit by Confederate troops under Brigadier General William Mahone, who had led his men along the Jerusalem Plank Road from their original positions well south of the breach. These Rebels were highly motivated; some had been recruited right there in Petersburg, and they had been further fired up by grapevine stories that the blacks were giving no quarter. When the gray-clad battle line slammed into the blue-clad one, everything dissolved into a wild melee.

Lieutenant Colonel John A. Bross led the 29th USCT into the attack with a vow to "show the world today that the colored troops are soldiers." Captain Beecham of the 23rd USCT watched as that officer tried to fulfill his promise: "Over this earthwork, with colors flying, Col. Bross led his regiment, and the 23rd, which occupied the second line[; they] had reached and were mounting this rim, when Col. Bross and his regiment received such a concentrated fire from the Confederate line that they were forced back upon us—but the Colonel and his flag and many of his men never came back." Lieutenant Bowley of the 30th USCT watched in horror as the black battle lines bent under the onslaught, then shattered. "For a moment the men moved backward, to the left, firing as they retreated; then the enemy charged with a yell, and poured a volley into their very faces. Instantly the whole body broke, went over the breastworks toward the Union line, or ran down the trenches towards the crater."[73]

This was the end of Ferrero's division as a cohesive fighting force. "My troops came back in very bad order," he later testified. Private Leonard Carter of the 28th USCT, who was a good deal closer to the action than his division commander, remembered that the "confusion became such that officers were separated from their commands, and comrades from each other." Panicked USCT soldiers fled, not caring who might be in their way. A division from the Tenth Corps, assigned to support the assault, was just moving up when the black tide swept over it. "I . . . was among those who were run over by the panic stricken negroes," wrote the colonel of one of the Tenth Corps brigades. "We used our sabers freely on the cowards but could not stop them and were all driven back."[74]

In defense of the black troops, one of the USCT officers later described their ordeal in being exposed under the enemy's heavy fire:

With no attempt at order or organization in either command [Sigfried's or Thomas's], and with panic stricken [white] men spreading alarm as

they flew to the rear, our men, who were in their first engagement, became wild, confused, terror stricken, and, with the veterans of a score of
battles, ran, like the whole army, including myself, at the first Bull Run.
. . . The charge of cowardice can not be proven against our officers or
men, without bringing to lasting disgrace the whole force engaged.[75]

By 10:00 A.M., the entire Union breakthrough had been reduced to
about a thousand disorganized men, both black and white, now
trapped in the crater or next to it. For the moment, the Confederates
(whose fierce counterattacks had cost them dearly) lacked sufficient
manpower to finish things off, but even as they built up strength for
that purpose, they subjected the crater to a pitiless barrage of mortar
and artillery shells, while riflemen targeted anyone who showed himself or tried to run back to the Union lines.

Lieutenant Bowley of the 30th USCT was among those who huddled in the crater. He remembered that the "men were dropping thick
and fast, most of them shot through the head. Every man that was
shot rolled down the steep sides to the bottom, and in places they
were piled up four and five deep." During a brief lull in the storm, the
desperate Federals built up barricades made of dead bodies. "How
we longed for reinforcements," said Captain Hurd of the 23rd USCT.
"It did seem too bad [to have] so many thousand of our men within
a few hundred yds. of us and no effort made for our relief."[76]

A fatal difference of outlook and opinion separated Ambrose
Burnside from George Meade this day, resulting in an almost total
paralysis of the Union high command. Burnside, fully committed to
making the attack a success, sought the best possible intrepretation of
all the field intelligence he was receiving, while Meade, unhappy with
the operation, saw these same data as confirming his dour prognos-
tication. Even while their men were fighting and dying amid the debris of tumbled earth, the two officers were exchanging acrimonious
dispatches. "I wish to know the truth," read one of Meade's communications, "and desire an immediate answer." "I would say that the
latter remark of your note was unofficerlike and ungentlemanly,"
replied Burnside. By about 9:10 A.M., when Burnside felt that the time
had come for the flanking corps to press their fronts, Meade was
ready to shut everything down, and instructed Burnside to pull his
troops out of the cauldron unless he believed there was something to

be gained by leaving them there. This was an admission of failure that Burnside could not make, however, so he allowed matters to run their bloody course, even as the corps commanders on his flanks were being told by Meade, at 9:30, to halt all offensive activity.[77]

By 11:00 A.M., any hope of expanding the assault had dissolved. The situation within the crater now crossed the line from combat to something far worse; in the words of John W. Pratt of the 30th USCT, "We say slaughter for we can call it nothing else—nor can any one who was present say truthfully that it was not." Lieutenant Bowley provided more detail:

> The day was fearfully hot; the wounded were crying for water, and the canteens were empty. A few of our troops held a ditch a few feet in front of the crater and were keeping up a brisk fire. . . . The artillery . . . kept up a constant fire of grape and kept the dirt flying about us. A mortar battery also opened on us, and, after a few shots, they got our range so well that the shells fell directly among us. Many of them did not explode until after they were buried in the earth, and did but little real damage, although the dead men were thrown high in the air; some did not explode at all, but a few burst directly over us, and cut the men down most cruelly. Many of the troops now attempted to make our lines, but, to leave, they had to run up a slope in full view of the enemy, that now surrounded us on three sides; nearly every man who attempted it fell back, riddled with bullets.[78]

In a bitter proof of the racism prevalent throughout the Union ranks, a new and terrible cruelty was inflicted on the black troops caught in the disaster. "It was believed among the whites that the enemy would give no quarter to negroes, or to the whites taken with them, and so to be shut up with blacks in the crater was equal to a doom of death," recalled a New York soldier who was there. "It has been positively asserted that white men bayoneted blacks who fell back into the crater. This was in order to preserve the whites from Confederate vengeance. Men boasted in my presence that blacks had thus been disposed of, particularly when the Confederates came up."[79]

Not until 2:00 P.M. did the Rebels amass enough troops to storm the crater. Among the late arrivals were Alabama men belonging to a brigade commanded by Brigadier General John C. C. Saunders, one of whose soldiers later noted, "Gen. Mahone had told the soldiers of the brigade that negro troops were in possession of the Crater and had come in yelling 'No quarter for the Rebels!' He did not say 'Show no quarter,' but Saunders's men decided that point." These Alabama soldiers, along with others from Virginia, Georgia, North Carolina, and South Carolina, swarmed to the edge of the pit and then down into it. Now the pure killing began. "Within . . . ten minutes," recalled a Virginia soldier, "the whole floor of the trench was strewn with the dead bodies of negroes, in some places in such numbers that it was difficult to make one's way along the trench without stepping on them." "As soon as we got upon them, they threw down their arms to surrender, but were not allowed to do so," said an artilleryman. "I think over two hundred negroes got into our lines, by surrendering & running in, along with the whites, while the fighting was going on. I don't believe that much over half of these ever reached the rear." "I saw the rebs run up and shoot negro prisoners in front of me," recollected a captured Union officer. "One was shot four times."[80]

Horror was piled upon horror. Another Rebel never forgot the sight of a black sergeant begging for his life before two Confederate soldiers, one of whom was beating the man with his ramrod, and the other trying to get a shot at him. "The man with the gun fired it at the negro, but did not seem to seriously injure him, as he only clapped his hand to his hip where he appeared to have been shot, and continued to beg for his life. The man with the ramrod continued to strike the negro therewith, whilst the fellow with the gun deliberately reloaded it, placing its muzzle closer against the stomach of the poor negro, fired, at which the latter fell limp and lifeless at the feet of the two Confederates." Another Southerner avowed that all the blacks would have been killed "had it not been for gen. Mahone who beg our men to Spare them."[81]

"Many a dusky warrior had his brains knocked out with the butt of a musket, or was run thru with a bayonet while vainly imploring for mercy," said Lieutenant Colonel Bates of the 30th USCT. Private Isaac Gaskin of the 29th USCT was one of the "lucky" ones: "After I was made a prisoner," he recalled,

I was shot at by a rebel guard and my cartridge box entirely carried away and my hip severely injured. Just before firing at me he, with an oath, called me a damn nigger, and said if he had known I was a nigger he would have never taken me prisoner, but that I had so much of that damn Yankee blood over my face that he couldn't tell what I was. He said he did not recognize any damn negro as a prisoner of war and that I would never get back to my brother Yankees alive. [82]

Those blacks who managed to be taken alive were corralled in a ravine in the rear of the Rebel lines. Some of their officers, fearing Southern retribution, tore off their unit insignias and denied having any association with them. When Lieutenant Bowley's turn came, he thought of the

black men who had rallied with me in the Crater, and who had died to the last man. Then I told my comrades that I should face the music, and if I died, I should die without denying the brave fellows we had left behind in that trap of death. One of my comrades . . . said, "I'm with you!" and when our names and rank were taken down, we said, "Thirtieth United States Colored Infantry!" and saw the words "negro officer" written opposite our names on the list. [83]

Union losses in this battle were horrific: of the approximately fifteen thousand men engaged from the Ninth Corps, 3,475 were casualties. More were killed, wounded, or missing from the black division than from any of the white ones, even though the latter had already been fighting for fully ninety minutes before the USCT units went in. The official tally of those killed or mortally wounded in Ferrero's division was 209, but a careful examination of pension files and compiled service records reveals that an additional 227 of those previously listed as missing died either in the fighting itself or right afterward. Of the forty-five hundred blacks who battled at the Crater, 1,327 were hit or injured in some way. "I felt like sitting down & weeping on account of our misfortune," wrote one USCT officer. Many of the wounded were transported to City Point, where a nurse named Helen Gilson had established a Colored Hospital Service. [84]

The Confederates' hatred for their black captives was amply demonstrated when the prisoners were paraded through Petersburg on the day after the mine explosion. The officers and men, remembered a lieutenant from the 43rd USCT, "were formed in double file, two officers between four 'niggers'[,] and marched through the principal streets of Petersburg much after the style of a circus." "I was in the third file of officers," recalled Freeman S. Bowley, "and as the head of the column reached the streets of Petersburg we were assailed by a volley of abuse from men, women and children that exceeded anything of the kind that I ever heard." The 43rd USCT officer said some of this abuse was along the lines of, "See the white and nigger equality soldiers!" and "Yanks and niggers sleep in the same bed!" A few blacks were forced to march with untreated wounds. "In many cases the negroes were hardly able to walk," testified an officer in a Maine regiment, "and in such case we were ordered to support them."[85]

The rusty machinery of military protocol was such that it took nearly twenty-four hours for both sides to agree on a truce to bury the dead and succor the wounded. A surprisingly high proportion of the wounded men who were found were black, perhaps because as exslaves they were better at surviving than were whites, or perhaps because they recognized the danger of seeking help behind the Rebel lines. Brigadier General Ferrero finally ventured out of the Federal trenches, entering the no-man's-land only to be pointedly snubbed by Confederate officers, who, in the words of one of them, "were not in the habit of recognizing as our social equals those who associated with negroes."[86]

Among the dead who were identified and buried this day was Henry Heighton, a private in the 29th USCT. Just two weeks earlier, he and his wife had exchanged their last letters. "I feel I am as much enlist[ed] in prayer as ever," Susannah Heighton wrote on July 11, "even more so for I pray for you daily & hourly and hope you will do the same for your self." In his reply, written on July 19, Henry Heighton informed his wife that for "some time I have not been very well, but feel right smart at present." He went on to say, "Remember me . . . that my return may be safe to the bosom of loved ones and that I may be kept in the path of duty and not be led astray by the many snares that beset the path of the soldier in the field." On August 1, Sergeant Charles Greenwell of Company B helped bury his friend. [87]

Colonel Henry G. Thomas was another of those who picked their way slowly through the debris of this battle on August 1. "There is no distinction in color now," Thomas observed of the experience. "The Virginia summer sun has shone two days on these brave men and has turned them all a purplish black." Thomas had hoped to locate the bodies of Lieutenant Pennell and Lieutenant Colonel Bross, but was unable to do so. Swinging wide on his return to the Union lines, he was captured by Confederate pickets and spent some nervous hours waiting for the matter to be straightened out. Less fortunate was Private James Meyers of the 43rd USCT, who according to his military records was "one of the burial party and crossed the lines and was taken prisoner, returned to Co. Apr. 21/65, having been engaged as laborer by Lee's Army up to the surrender."[88]

Sergeant James H. Payne of the 27th USCT had much to say about the battle and the fate of blacks taken prisoner. "Instead of a general effort being made, as was contemplated," he observed, "only a few men were taken in to be slaughtered and taken prisoner, which is the equivalent to death, for no mercy is shown to them when captured, although some still plead that the rebels are treating the colored prisoners very well; but before I can be convinced that this is so, I wish to hear one of the prisoners tell the story." One who did tell his story after the war was Sergeant Rodney Long of the 29th USCT; captured at the crater, he ended up spending seven months in Confederate detention at Danville. "We suffered terribly while in prison," he would recall in 1886, "and most of our men died there." Isaac Gaskin, who survived capture because his bloody face disguised the fact that he was black, also went to Danville. "I never knew what it was to get anything respectable to eat while in prison, and there was not one third enough of the vile stuff that was given us," he said. "I was punished severely on account of my color. Out of 180 colored prisoners taken, only seven survived."[89]

A total of twenty-four Medals of Honor were later awarded to men who fought at the crater, four of them to individuals from Ferrero's division. Colonel Bates of the 30th USCT received one for his gallantry in action, and Lieutenant Andrew Davidson of that same regiment was honored for rallying the men after Bates was wounded. Captain Albert D. Wright of the 43rd USCT received a medal for capturing the enemy's colors, while Sergeant Decatur Dorsey, of the 39th USCT, became the only black so acknowledged in this action for leading his men forward and then helping to rally them after the retreat.

In the wave of shame and frustration that swept through the Union ranks after this fight, the panicked retreat of the black division became the excuse of convenience for the failure of the effort. As a rule, the farther a soldier had been from the actual combat, the more certain he seemed to be that it was the black troops who had doomed the operation. A New York cavalryman who was part of the expedition north of the James wrote to a friend on August 3, "There hasn't any big bouts happened since I last wrote you here, but at Petersburg they have had a stunner and would have done something if it hadn't have been for the nigger troops, but it was too warm for them and they took the back track, leaving a gap open and the Johnnies rushed in and the troops that was on the right and left of it had to fall back to keep from being flanked, you see." "I say put the niggers out of our corps as I do not want to be in the corps they are," declared a man in Burnside's Ninth. For some of the white soldiers who had actually shared the experience, a racist perspective could be tempered by an empathy of mutual suffering. "The slaughter was terrible," recorded one Unionist. "The negroes were piled up in heaps."[90]

The real culprits of the crater were the officers who planned and then directed, or failed to direct, the operation. One veteran who wrote of it afterward concluded, "No battle fought during the war was so discredible to the Union arms as this, and yet in none were the troops actually engaged less deserving of censure."[91]

The findings of a military Court of Inquiry convened in the month of August resulted in Major General Burnside's removal from command of the Ninth Corps. First Division commander Ledlie suffered a similar fate, while only mild reprimands were meted out to divisions commanders Willcox and Ferrero. The three charges against Ferrero were as follows:

> 1. For not having all his troops formed ready for the attack at the prescribed time.
>
> 2. Not going forward with them to the attack.
>
> 3. Being in a bomb proof habitually, where he could not see the operation of his troops, showing by his own order issued while there that he did not know the position of [the] two brigades of his division or whether they had taken Cemetery Hill or not.[92]

"None of the troops, white or colored, are responsible for the action of the Generals," said Chaplain White of the 28th USCT. "I hold that there can be no higher sin in all the world than to blame innocent people for the consequences for which they are not responsible. I care not who it is, whether king or subject, General or private, it makes no difference with me in a point of exposition of truth."[93]

In his comments to Army and congressional investigators, Lieutenant General Grant offered this observation on the Union failure at the crater: "General Burnside wanted to put his colored division in front, and I believe if he had done so it would have been a success. Still I agreed with General Meade as to his objections to that plan. General Meade said that if we put the colored troops in front . . . and it should prove a failure, it would then be said, and very properly, that we were shoving those people ahead to get killed because we did not care anything about them."[94]

For Colonel Henry G. Thomas, the aftermath of the crater had a deeply felt effect on the black troops under his command. In the weeks leading up to the fight, they had sung the song "Like Men of War" all the time. "After that defeat," noted Thomas, "they sang it no more."[95]

Interlude

"This Disgraceful Distinction"

———◇———

THE new year brought no change in the Lincoln administration's policy of pay inequity between black and white soldiers. In a letter written on January 23, 1864, London S. Langley described for the *Anglo-African* how he and other Vermont blacks had been enlisted for the 54th Regiment Massachusetts Infantry (Colored) on the promise that they would receive the "same pay and bounty as the white recruits." They threatened to leave when they learned otherwise, but were persuaded to stay by assurances that the matter would be straightened out when they reached the front. Of course, it never was, and the trusting recruits were stuck. "The boys now feel somewhat down-hearted, but hope for the best, and have *some* faith in the justice of Congress," wrote Langley. "Mr. Editor," he concluded, "may we not hope that Congress, for the sake of the *honor of the country,* and for the sake of the families of a portion of its able and true defenders, will *soon* remove this disgraceful distinction from the military statute of this great nation?"[1]

Langley's plea was that of the volunteer, but there were also black soldiers serving who had been drafted. One in the 6th USCT, who called himself "Bought and Sold," explained his plight to the *Christian Recorder:*

252

I am a soldier, or at least that is what I was drafted for. . . . I could not afford to get a substitute, or I would not be here now and my poor wife at home almost starving. When I was at home I could make a living for her and my two little ones; but now that I am a soldier they must do the best they can or starve. It almost tempts me to desert and run a chance of getting shot, when I read her letters, hoping that I would come to her relief. But what am I to do? It is a shame the way they treat us; our officers tell me now that we are soldiers; that if we were we would get the same pay as the white men; that the government just called us out to dig and drudge. . . . Really I thought I was a soldier, and it made me feel somewhat proud to think that I had a right to fight for Uncle Sam. When I was at Chelton Hill [i.e., Camp William Penn] I felt very patriotic; but my wife's letters have brought my patriotism down to the freezing point, and I don't think it will ever rise again; and it is the case all through the regiment.[2]

To add to their misery, many of the black soldiers' families were denied any sort of local charity. "The wives of the men are, they say, often refused [at] the almshouse for their color, and are reduced to degradation that drives the husbands almost crazy," wrote a USCT officer.[3]

The divisiveness of the pay issue was made clear in another letter, written on August 9 to the *Christian Recorder* by a member of the 32nd USCT, then stationed on Morris Island:

We were mustered in for pay at Hilton Head, and were not offered it till we came to Morris Island, but prior to it were told on company drill that we should prepare ourselves for being paid on a day specified by the colonel, and should come out in good shape on the day that pay would be offered, and we had better take that offered, which would be seven dollars per month,—not that it was any interest to him at all, for he would get his pay if we did not, and to take it, as we could not do any better,—the Government allowed no more for colored troops, and there would be no more appropriated for us. A feeling of despair passed over the whole regiment. There were but few to sign the pay rolls, and those who did a great many of us tried to influence to the contrary, but to no purpose; they, through ignorance, informed the Captain of it, to which he said, if he heard any one say aught against any one that would take, or had taken their pay, he would have him severely punished for it. . . . They try to perpetuate our inferiority, and keep us where we are. This regiment came out just as manfully as any other regiment now in the field; there was no compulsion in our rear at all; we came to have a more legal claim to equality—we responded to the call unhesitatingly,—when we were asked to attend the rally for the preservation of the country, we did not falter, but came up with the expectation that we would be treated accordingly,—though, sad to say, we have been disappointed to some extent in it.[4]

Many black regiments had discipline problems linked directly to the discrepancy in wages. On January 9, 1864, Sergeant William Walker of the 21st USCT was court-martialed on a charge of mutiny stemming from an incident on November 19, 1863, when he led a nonviolent, passive-resistance protest. Vowing not to serve "any longer for seven dollars a month," Walker, along with the men of Company A of the regiment and others, refused to report for duty. After a hurried trial, Walker was found guilty and sentenced to be shot, but because the 21st was part of the ill-fated Union expedition to Florida, the sentence was not carried out until March 1, at Jacksonville. A newsman present wrote that Walker "met his death unflinchingly." Massachusetts Governor John A. Andrew was appalled by the entire affair: "The Government which found no law to *pay* him except as *a nondescript or a contraband,* nevertheless found law enough to *shoot* him as a *soldier,*" he complained to President Lincoln.[5]

Change *was* in the wind, however: a statute of June 15, 1864, equalized the wage scale for all soldiers retroactive to January 1, allowing blacks to collect back pay for 1862 and 1863, provided they had been free as of April 19, 1861. This last provision was a slap in the face for many blacks who had either escaped slavery to enlist or been freed by the Emancipation Proclamation. To get around the requirement, since the government required only the taking of a verbal oath to determine eligibility, the commander of the 54th Massachusetts (Colored) devised a simple statement that sufficed as "proof," asking USCT soldiers to affirm, "You do solemnly swear that you owed no man unrequited labor on or before the 19th day of April,

1861. So help you God." Not until the fall of 1865 would U.S. officials formally remove this stipulation.[6]

For the first time in their war service, the soldiers of the black regiments eagerly awaited the paymaster's arrival. It was a time for rejoicing and celebration. The festivities occasioned by this first honorable payday in the 55th Massachusetts (Colored) were faithfully reported to the *Anglo-African*:

> Doubtless you will have heard before this reaches you, that the 54th and 55th Mass. Regiments have been paid. . . .
>
> Monday, the 10th was the day selected for the celebration. It came, and precisely at 3 o'clock the assembly was sounded, each company issued forth from its street in charge of a non-commissioned officer, and being formed in line . . . , the procession headed by the band marched by the right flank in two wings with a space between, which was occupied by the speakers and officers of the day. After marching a short distance beyond camp the procession turned and proceeded directly to the place of meeting, in front of the Colonel's quarters. . . .
>
> It was a most impressive scene. A regiment of brave men celebrating, in the midst of war, one of the triumphs of peace without arms, in the presence of their officers a band of veteran warriors doing honor by solemn ceremonies to the recognition by government of their citizenship and equality.[7]

Chapter Nine

"I Am Ready to Die for Liberty"

———◆———

Skirmish at Rivers Causeway, South Carolina, July 2, 1864

THE summer of 1864 saw Union forces fully engaged in efforts to hold on to the coastal enclaves at Hilton Head, Port Royal, northeastern Florida, and the mouth of Charleston Harbor. Many of the troops in these areas had been transferred to the Army of the James in Virginia in 1864, leaving only about twenty thousand soldiers spread along the coastline. Outside Charleston, black regiments made up half of the force, with the 54th Regiment Massachusetts Infantry (Colored), the 21st USCT, and the 32nd USCT on Morris Island, while the Folly Island contingent included the 55th Regiment Massachusetts Infantry (Colored) and the 33rd USCT.

Sergeant Joseph H. Barquet of Company H in the 54th Massachusetts (Colored) managed to find some levity in the rough conditions endured by the men. "In a cracker four inches square, you can find a world," Barquet told the readers of the *Anglo-African*. "Out from a little circular hole comes weevils, red ants, and little, tiny butterflies. Here are fresh eggs. Breakfast in this corner. Spider eggs. They are good—all eggs are good. Wash them down with brackish black coffee; no sweetening; the coffee the remnants of three meals. This makes the bones prominent."[1]

256

Sergeant Barquet's bonhomie notwithstanding, the still-unresolved issue of pay continued to sour relations between the black soldiers and their white officers. A low point was reached on June 18, when Private Wallace Baker of the 55th Massachusetts (Colored), having been found guilty of striking a white officer, was executed by firing squad "in presence of the troops on the island." A comrade in the 54th Massachusetts (Colored) avowed that "Baker is one of those men who had become insubordinate from the unjust treatment to which the colored Massachusetts soldiers had been subjected. . . . No man ever met his death with less trepidation than Wallace Baker."[2]

The largest military action of this summer along the South Carolina coast took place on July 2. Believing that the Confederate garrisons throughout the region had been greatly weakened by the reassignment of troops to other fronts, Department of the South commander Major General John G. Foster ordered a three-part advance to exploit the situation. One component, under Brigadier General John P. Hatch, was to move up the North Edisto River, land on Seabrook Island, and cross to John's Island with the intention of disrupting the Charleston and Savannah Railroad. At the same time, Brigadier General William Birney was to lead a smaller command in a landing farther up the same river, with instructions to destroy the C&S Railroad bridge over the South Edisto. A third force, directed by Brigadier General Alexander Schimmelfenning, was simultaneously to test the enemy's defenses on James Island.

The troops assigned to this last operation were the 103rd New York, 33rd USCT, and 55th Massachusetts (Colored). The 33rd, formerly the 1st Regiment South Carolina Infantry (African Descent) and previously commanded by Colonel Thomas W. Higginson,* went into this action led by Major Charles T. Trowbridge. The 55th Massachusetts (Colored) had been organized at Camp Meigs in Readville, Massachusetts, between February and May 1863, around a nucleus of a surplus of recruits intended for the 54th Massachusetts (Colored). Some of its officers had also been initially slated for that "glory" regiment. The 55th had followed the 54th into the Department of the South, but unlike its older sibling, thus far it had seen its service limited to fatigue and outpost duties.

---

*Higginson had commenced an extended sick leave in May.

The James Island defenses protecting Rebel Charleston were anchored on the island's western side by Fort Pemberton and on its eastern flank by a series of redoubts and batteries, one of the most important of which was Fort Lamar. This latter was the target of the expedition, which got off to a false start on the night of June 30. The 55th Massachusetts (Colored) and portions of the 103rd New York had already completed the arduous process of transferring from Folly Island to Long Island when orders came countermanding the movement. "I know not who is responsible for keeping my officers and men rowing between Folly Island and Long Island, depriving them of all rest just as they were about entering upon an expedition," grumbled the commander of the New York regiment. The problem appears to have been a sudden change in personnel at the head of the operation: Colonel William Heine of the 103rd, originally assigned, was placed under arrest, and Colonel Alfred S. Hartwell assumed command after a briefing from Brigadier General Schimmelfenning. "You get over to James Island before daylight," Hartwell was told, "[and] march quickly by the flank to Lamar. They will get one, and, perhaps two discharges of canister into you, and you may lose one or two hundred men." Lieutenant Colonel Charles B. Fox took over the 55th for Hartwell.[3]

The whole operation was under way again by the evening of July 1. This time the tide was low, exposing mud flats that bogged everything down. The 103rd New York crossed first, "many of the men sinking into the mud almost to their armpits." Next came the 33rd USCT, followed by the 55th. Sergeant James M. Trotter of the 55th would later recall "plunging, wading and part of the time almost swimming [before] we got on firm ground." Once on James Island, the 103rd pushed ahead while the 33rd USCT took some time to regroup. According to Sergeant Trotter, "Very soon the crack of the rifle was heard, shot after shot exchanged, so we knew that the Rebel pickets had been encountered." This firing alerted the Confederate cannoneers in Fort Lamar and elsewhere along the line, who now began to shell the area. Shrapnel from one exploding missile shattered the arm of Corporal Thomas J. Brown of Company K in the 55th, eventually necessitating its amputation. Seconds before he was struck, Corporal Brown exclaimed, "My God, how long are they going to keep us under this fire?" Remembered Trotter, "We moved

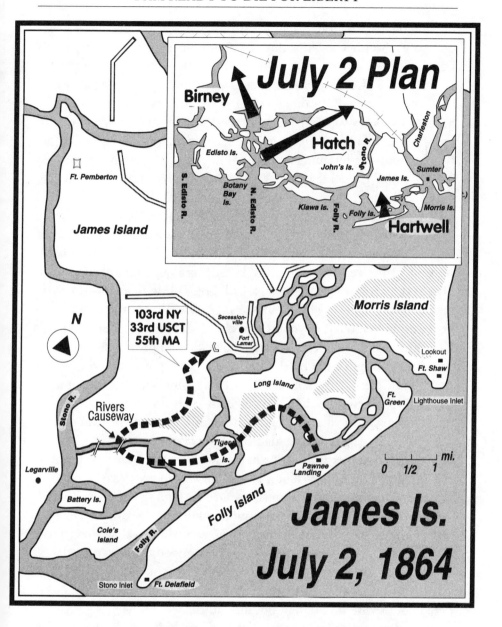

July 2 Plan

Birney

Hatch

Charleston

Edisto Is.

S. Edisto R.

N. Edisto R.

John's Is.

Stono R.

Sumter

Ft. Pemberton

Botany Bay Is.

Kiawa Is.

James Is.

Morris Is.

Folly R.

Folly Is.

James Island

Hartwell

Morris Island

N

Secession-ville

103rd NY
33rd USCT
55th MA

Fort Lamar

Lookout

Ft. Shaw

Long Island

Ft. Green

Lighthouse Inlet

Stono R.

Rivers Causeway

Tiger Is.

Pawnee Landing

0 1/2 1 mi.

Legarville

Folly Island

Battery Is.

James Is.

Cole's Island

Folly R.

July 2, 1864

Stono Inlet Ft. Delafield

forward briskly, day was just beginning to break, and just as we were emerging from a narrow wood, we were opened upon by the enemy from a battery at Rivers Causeway Landing, hitherto unknown to exist to us on Folly, and at first they threw solid shot and shell among the advancing brigade, doing great damage." The Rebels were part of Blake's South Carolina Battery, manning a two-gun outpost of Fort Lamar.[4]

London S. Langley, a member of the 33rd USCT, recorded that these guns "opened a raking fire of grape and canister." "This they hurled among us like hail, scattering death and destruction all around," added Sergeant Trotter. The sudden, surprising pounding, coupled with the fatiguing marches of the past two hot nights, proved too much for the 103rd New York and portions of the 33rd, which, declared Trotter, "became panic-stricken and could not be restrained by their officers and Col. Hartwell from retreating pell mell."[5]

The 55th Massachusetts (Colored) began to deploy into line of battle. "We were then under fire," recollected Sergeant Jordan M. Bobson of the regiment. "As the last company came into line, Col. F[ox] said, forward double quick. Col. Fox said with an adjective, remember fort pillow. This fired the men. We all commenced to yell Fort Pillow. We fixed bayonets and charged without orders I think." "The ground over which we were advancing had previously been rendered most impassable by the Rebels by cutting down and crossing trees," said Sergeant Trotter. "This gave Johnny a great advantage over us, as we could only advance very slowly and men were continually sinking in the marsh. Rapidly they discharged their cannon and our brave boys were falling all along the way."

At one point, Sergeant Bobson reversed his gun to help the rest of the line guide on him. William Russell of Company C cut in front of Bobson just as a round of canister scattered among the men; Russell, Bobson recalled, "stooped just low enough for the canister to take him in the head, so lost his life." As he ran, Corporal William Scott felt one of his shoes coming loose, so he stopped to tighten the laces, whereupon his company commander, Captain Frank Goodwin, "called to me as though he thought I had been shot," Scott remembered. Goodwin did not halt but instead rushed on; he had gone only a slight distance when a spread of canister balls severely wounded him. After struggling against the enemy's entanglements for several minutes, Captain Charles C. Soule took station behind one of the larger men of Company K, "who wore No. 14 shoes, regular beetle-busters, and let him break down the twigs for me." Another canister blast now swept through the ranks, striking down Private Benjamin

Griffin alongside him: "I remember . . . the sickening crash of the canister as it struck his ribs," Soule said.[6]

The closer the men of the 55th got to the enemy battery, the more erratic became the fire directed against them. The yelling, screaming soldiers were still about two hundred yards away when, remarked Sergeant Trotter, "the Rebels broke, jumped on their waiting horses and by the time we had gained the parapet were far down the road." Corporal John J. Johnson was one of the first to clamber up the dirt face of the battery position, but his moment of triumph was cut short when his company commander, Captain William Crane, yelled at him, "Get down, Corporal, they will shoot you." Company F of the regiment, which had been trained to operate cannon, soon had the pieces in working order. A sergeant in the company boasted, "It was my privilege to be the first non-commissioned officer that reached the enemy's guns. . . . I found one of them loaded and fired it, afterwards, loaded it with another charge which the rebels failed to take away and fired that also."[7]

According to London S. Langley of the 33rd USCT, his regiment had started to retreat under orders when the charge of the 55th Massachusetts (Colored) began behind it. "Our Major, who was in command, inferring from the maneuvering of the 55th Mass. that the order to retreat was countermanded, immediately gave the order to 'forward! double-quick!' and away we all rushed toward the fort, arriving there with the 55th Mass." Langley saw a "peculiar fitness in the fact that the Star Spangled Banner of the first colored regiment raised [i.e., the 1st South Carolina (A.D.)], should be the first to float its bright stars and red stripes over the parapet of the captured position."[8]

The history of the 55th claims that that regiment re-formed "and advanced to a heavy hedge, bank, and ditch beyond the fieldwork captured. By this time, however, the Battery Lamar and the whole rebel line were thoroughly aroused; and . . . the advance was stopped." As Sergeant Trotter recalled, "We . . . were too tired to pursue the enemy, besides, we had no support, the other Reg[imen]ts having failed us." For the rest of this hot day, the men of the 55th Massachusetts (Colored) and 33rd USCT hunkered down in their newly won position, under a heavy fire from the enemy; they returned to Coles Island after dark.[9]

The final results of the tripartite Federal advance of July 2 were typical of those of all the operations conducted in this theater during the period following the Confederate evacuation of Fort (Battery) Wagner: well conceived but poorly executed. Deployment of the troops under Brigadier General Hatch was fatally slowed by the heat; when he finally reached his target, Hatch found a line of fully alerted defenders waiting for him. Brigadier General Birney, likewise failing to move promptly and decisively, was also stalemated and had to withdraw.

Union casualties for the James Island phase of this operation were never fully reported. The officer commanding the 103rd New York noted only that the "first fire of the enemy killed 7 of my men and wounded many others." Returns from the 33rd USCT showed six killed and thirteen wounded, though London S. Langley, in his letter to the *Anglo-African,* counted fewer, tallying "four men killed and ten wounded." The price for the 55th Massachusetts (Colored) was logged in the regiment's history as eight men killed and twenty-one wounded; the figures recorded by the state adjutant general for the 55th—"11 killed and 18 wounded"—suggest that three of the wounded later died.[10]

For their courage and coolness under fire, Colonel Hartwell recommended that three of the black sergeants of the 55th be promoted to the rank of 2nd lieutenant. "But the U.S. government has refused so far to muster them because *God did not make them White,*" a 55th man complained to the *Anglo-African.* "No other objection is, or can be offered."[11]

One of the eight killed in the 55th Massachusetts (Colored) was Sergeant Alonzo Boon. "No one's death has made me feel so sad as his," wrote his friend, Sergeant Trotter.

> In truth I loved him. At Readville he could neither read nor write. I spoke to him of the importance of learning, telling him that I would gladly help him, and that when he could read I would recommend him for Sergt. Right manfully he took hold, and before he died he had acted [as] orderly Sergt., and could make out all the papers and [had] written three letters home. He went to James Island with no gun and only side arms. His arm was sore and he could not carry his rifle. But his brave spirit would not rest quiet while his comrades were gone forth to battle. . . . He was wounded by a large grape [shot] in the leg, which was amputated, causing instant death. He was cheerful and

brave to the last. In camp, on the hill-side near to where stands the cannon out of which was hurled the ball that caused his death, he is laid. . . . We have placed a board at his head bearing this inscription:

> Sergeant B.
> lived in
> Boston

> In Memory of
> Sergeant Alonzo Boon
> Died of Wounds
> July 3d, 1864
> As he died to make men holy
> Let us die to make men free.[12]

Action near Flat Rock Creek, Indian Territory, September 16, 1864

Following Major General Steele's ill-fated Camden Expedition, the 1st and 2nd Kansas (Colored) Volunteers marched back to Fort Smith, where, according to their regimental histories, the men spent the next six months "doing heavy escort and fatigue duty." Soon after that, however, some members of the regiments were caught up in the deadly guerrilla war being waged in that region between Union troops and the Confederacy's Indian forces.[13]

In the fall of 1864, the Cherokee Brigadier General Stand Watie convinced the Trans-Mississippi high command to let him undertake a large-scale raid into southeastern Kansas. All the meager military assets of the region were brought together to create a strike force consisting of a Native American brigade (approximately eight hundred men) under Watie and a Texas brigade (about twelve hundred men) under Brigadier General Richard M. Gano. These units left Camp Pike on the morning of September 14, 1864, to march toward a large Federal supply train then en route for Fort Gibson.

At about the same time, a much smaller party of Federals was leaving Fort Gibson on a far more mundane assignment. With the harvest season at hand, groups of field hands with military escorts fanned out to gather in the hay crop. One work gang that had set up its camp fifteen miles west of Fort Gibson was protected by "detachments of the Second Kansas Cavalry and First Kansas Colored

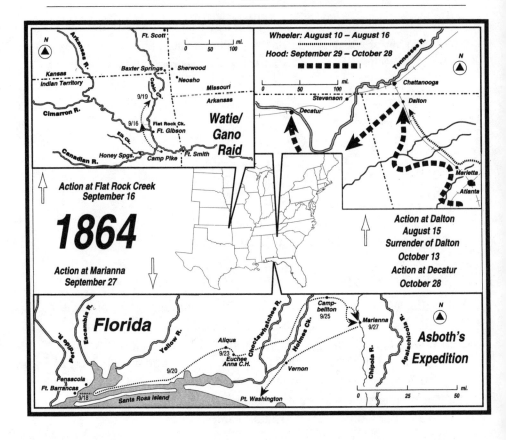

Infantry, amounting in the aggregate to 125 effective men," reported
Captain Edgar A. Barker, who was in charge.[14]

Because a security force of this size was intended only to drive off
small raiding parties, when scouts warned Captain Barker that about
two hundred Rebels were approaching, he immediately posted most
of his men in a small ravine adjacent to Flat Rock Creek—this being,
he felt, "the most advantageous position to repel an attack or protect
the hay." When the Federal officer scouted the enemy's main body, he
was shocked to find it some "1,000 to 1,500 strong," with artillery.
He fell back to the ravine and was soon being hit "from five different
points." Barker's command held out for perhaps thirty minutes, at
which time the Kansas officer led a mounted charge that enabled him
and fifteen others to escape. "The whole force of the enemy then
charged in my camp," he wrote afterward, "capturing all of the white

soldiers remaining there, and killing all the colored soldiers they could find."[15]

According to other accounts, the Union resistance continued for some time after Captain Barker led the mounted breakout, as the black footsoldiers recognized that there would be no quarter given. One survivor, George W. Duval, described as an "intelligent colored soldier of the detachment," held on until sunset, when he slipped into Flat Rock Creek and followed it through the Rebel picket line before escaping out into the prairie. Other black soldiers, hiding in the stream and in a nearby pond, listened helplessly to the "Confederates all around them, . . . pursuing and shooting down their comrades in the most heartless manner." A white trooper in the 2nd Kansas Cavalry named Robert Morris Peck was an eyewitness. "I saw those colored troops when they were killed," he would recollect in 1904, ". . . as were several of our white soldiers."[16]

G. W. Grayson, a Creek chief serving in Stand Watie's brigade, would later write of the events as seen from the other side:

We crossed the Canadian, the Arkansas and the Verdargris rivers after two days march and reached an encampment of negroe hay makers. . . . There appeared to have been a small escort of negro soldiers . . . who for a few minutes after our attack returned our fire. One or two cannon shots of grape from our guns, however, caused a stampede, when we charged the encampment. The defenders disappeared among the thickets and very high weeds that covered the banks of the creek and for a few minutes after reaching the deserted camps it did not appear that there was anything for us to do more than burning the camps and the great ricks of hay that stood about on the field.

Presently, however, some of our men discovered a negro hiding in the high weeds near the creek and shot and killed him. At another point another one was found and shot, and it now appearing that these were to be found hid in the weeds, the men proceeded to hunt them out much as sportsmen do quails. Some of the negroes finding they were about to be discovered, would spring up from the brush and cry out, O! master spare me. But the men were in no spirit to spare the wretched unfortunates and shot them down without mercy. . . . Some of them were found lying in hiding in the creek with barely their noses out of the water and were shot and dragged and thrown out on the bank.

I confess this was sickening to me, but the men were like wild beasts and I was powerless to stop them from this unnecessary butchery.[17]

Of the forty-two men from Company K of the 1st Kansas (Colored) who took part in this engagement, twenty-two were killed and ten captured. According to the Record of Events for the 1st, this represented an "almost total annihilation of K Company." All the hay was burned, and the haymaking equipment destroyed.[18]

On September 19, the Rebels successfully attacked the Union supply train near Cabin Creek. In this fight it was the blue-coated Native Americans, not the blacks, who reaped the harvest of racial hatred, with many of them being massacred after they were left wounded and helpless on the field. The Rebel raiding party returned to Camp Pike, pursued for some small part of the way by a relief force made up mostly of black troops under Colonel James M. Williams.

In one of those fine displays of irony that reveal the thin line between black military service and social action, a sharp skirmish over school integration was taking place in Kansas even as the terrified members of the 1st Kansas (Colored) were trying to escape the slaughter at Flat Rock Creek. When several black families near Indianola, Kansas, attempted to enroll their children in the hitherto all-white school, the white parents immediately withdrew their own offspring from classes, and young blacks trying to cross the color line were physically harassed. A white farmer named Samuel J. Reader thought that such actions were wrong. He asked one of the participants what it was all about, and set the response down in his diary: "He told me that the Darkies coming to school was breaking it up, and thinks they ought to leave, and Mrs. Jones will teach them [separately]. I told him that did not look like a Christian spirit; that it was the prejudice against having them educated, for fear they could not be kept slaves! 'Well,' said he, 'it's not that so much but because they will get SASSY.'"[19]

Indianola was not far from another Kansas town that ninety years later would be the site of a historic legal case in the saga of civil rights in America: *Brown* v. *Topeka Board of Education*.

Action at Marianna, Florida, September 27, 1864

The church bells began to sound soon after the courier arrived, warning that a Yankee raiding force was less than fifteen miles away. There had been rumors for several days that Federal troops were moving in the direction of Marianna, but the news that they were so close still caught many by surprise. Despite the fact that the town was the administrative center of Jackson County, and the site of Confederate headquarters for West Florida, its five hundred inhabitants believed that their relative isolation would protect them. Their luck, like that of so much of the Confederacy, had at last run out.

Colonel A. B. Montgomery commanded the post at Marianna. While other couriers fanned out to summon the few regular mounted units that patrolled the region, local citizens gathered in the church to organize a home defense. About a hundred of these, young people under age sixteen and old men over fifty, grabbed weapons and formed up into what was afterward referred to as the "Cradle and Grave Company."

By 10:00 A.M., the town's defenses were set. In addition to the Home Guard, there were some militiamen from nearby towns, along with a few regular C.S. soldiers who happened to be in the area. A barricade was erected across the Marianna's main street, and several outlying homes were occupied. There was nothing left to do but await the enemy's next move. "I cannot tell the time of waiting," recorded one resident, "for it seemed like an eternity."[20]

On the Waddell Plantation, about eleven miles west of Marianna, an eight-year-old slave named Armstrong Purdee looked with wide-eyed wonder at the road, which was suddenly filled with blue-uniformed men on horseback. One of them signaled to the child, asking if he wanted to come along with them. "Yes, sir," Armstrong said. The white man cleared a stirrup, and when the young slave put a foot into it, he pulled him up behind. "Hold on," he said, "do not fall off."[21]

The riders were part of a Federal expedition of seven hundred men who had left Barrancas, Florida, on September 18 under the command of Brigadier General Alexander Asboth. Restless after spending most of the war policing Union holdings on Florida's western coast, Asboth stretched the intent of standing orders to initiate a raid into the northeastern portion of the state. Not only would it enable him to scatter the Rebel units based in that region, but he could also forage for supplies, liberate slaves, and free the Union prisoners rumored (falsely) to be confined at Marianna.

Asboth's force consisted of three battalions of the 2nd Maine Cavalry, one battalion of the 1st Florida Cavalry, and two companies of mounted infantry from the 82nd and 86th USCT. Colonel L. L. Zulavszky, a fellow refugee from Hungary, led the black units. Both the 82nd and the 86th USCT were Louisiana outfits, originally the 10th and 14th regiments in the Corps d'Afrique. Each had been recruited largely out of the state's slave populations.

Little Armstrong Purdee, who as an adult would practice law in Florida, had no recollection of the black soldiers accompanying the expedition; the huge white Yankees were amazement enough for him. "They did not go around anything," he recalled, "[but] jumped their horses over fallen trees and logs, or anything. They reached the town about 2 or 3 o'clock."[22]

On their arrival, Asboth sent a battalion of the 2nd Maine Cavalry charging down Marianna's narrow main street. Home Guards posted behind the barricade and inside the buildings raked the charging Federals with a fusillade of gunfire that sent them tumbling back in confusion. Asboth next sent a flanking detachment off to the north; once it was in position, he personally led another charge down the main street. The Florida minutemen held Asboth's column at bay for perhaps half an hour, but at last the pressure became too much for the citizen soldiers, and they began to run away.

About thirty mounted Confederates managed to escape Asboth's pincers as the flanking detachment cut off the north side of the town. Everyone else, including Colonel Montgomery, was either killed or captured. There were some ugly moments when word spread among the Federals that Brigadier General Asboth had been shot and badly wounded; a few Home Guards who were holding out in St. Luke's Episcopal Church were dealt with by the brutal expedient of setting the building on fire. Armstrong Purdee, still holding on to the Yankee horseman who had liberated him, would never forget what happened next: "Men were shot down as they came out of the building. I was an eyewitness to the happening at the church."[23]

Colonel Zulavszky filed no report, nor did any of the black soldiers leave any written record, though "L.E.N.," who identified himself as the assistant surgeon of the 2nd Maine Cavalry, wrote:

When the colored troops came up they went into the fight like mad men,—their rallying cry, *Remember Fort Pillow:* giving no quarter, and answering, "Your men give us no quarter when they take us; now it is our turn." A fitting retribution for the barbarities exercised toward them. All who witnessed this engagement say that the negro troops *will fight* and woe to the rebel who is unfortunate as to fall into their hands.[24]

This last statement was echoed in a private letter written by a 2nd Maine trooper named Edwin R. Marson, who said, "We had 200 nigger soldiers with us, it did not make any difference to them about the Rebs surrendering. They would shoot them down, the officers had hard work to stop them from killing all the prisoners." Another Yankee present avowed that the "colored troops dismounted and aided very materially in the fight. Their conduct is commended by all who witnessed it." The Record of Events for Company B of the 82nd USCT confirmed that the men "rec'd many [compliments] for their brave & soldierly conduct."[25]

Accounts of the raid that appeared in Northern newspapers suggested that there were thirty-two Union casualties (including General Asboth), with perhaps a dozen of those being fatalities. Confederate losses, tallied in an edition of the *West Florida News* published soon afterward, were nine killed, sixteen wounded, and fifty-four captured. Local memories of the black troops' actions were especially bitter; as late as the 1950s, a history of Jackson County referred to Asboth and "his blood-thirsty Negroes."[26]

With Asboth out of action, the Federal officers in the field decided to terminate the raid. The expedition took a short cut to the coast to transfer the wounded onto ships, and then the men marched back to Fort Barrancas. Armstrong Purdee wound up at Fort Pickens, where his father finally located him; once reunited, the two went back home.

Action at Saltville, Virginia, October 2, 1864

Captain Charles Francis Adams, Jr., was a proper Bostonian and an Army of the Potomac veteran with the 1st Massachusetts Cavalry. In late 1864, he seized an opportunity to advance and became a major in the 5th Regiment Massachusetts Cavalry (Colored). Writing on November 2 to his father (the U.S. ambassador to Great Britain), young Adams expressed the thinking man's view of African American soldiers on horseback.

> The negro makes a good soldier, particularly in those branches of the service where a high order of intelligence is less required. Negro infantry, properly officered, would I believe be as effective as any in the world. In regard to their efficiency as cavalry I somewhat share your doubt. After all a negro is not the equal of the white man. . . . He has not the mental vigor and energy, he cannot stand up against adversity. . . . He cannot fight for life like a white man. . . . He must and will sleep, no danger from the enemy and no fear of punishment will keep him awake. In infantry, which acts in large masses, these things are of less consequence than in cavalry, but in the service which our cavalry does, where individual intelligence is everything, and single men in every exposed position have only themselves and their own nerve, intelligence and quickness to rely on, it is a very different thing.[27]

Despite such misgivings, seven black cavalry regiments were organized during the Civil War. The 5th USCT Cavalry was still in the process of completing its formation at Camp Nelson, Kentucky, when, in mid-September 1864, six hundred of its recruits were hastily appended to a strike force under Brevet Major General Stephen G. Burbridge, headed into southwestern Virginia to disrupt Confederate salt production. The officer commanding was a Kentucky slave owner whose cautious support of black military enlistment had alienated him from many white Unionists in that border state.

Colonel James F. Wade was given command of the black detachment. "They were mounted on horses that had been . . . drawn with the intention of using them only for the purpose of drilling," reported Colonel James S. Brisbin of the 5th USCT Cavalry. Burbridge's column was already in motion by the time Wade got the assignment, so the black troopers had to hurry to catch up, which they managed to do at Prestonburg, Kentucky.[28]

The African Americans were put in a brigade commanded by Colonel R. W. Ratliff. According to Colonel Brisbin,

> On the march the colored soldiers, as well as their white officers, were made the subject of much ridicule and many insulting remarks by the white troops, and in some instances petty outrages, such as the pulling

off the caps of colored soldiers, stealing their horses, &c., were practiced by the white soldiers. These insults, as well as the jeers and taunts that they would not fight, were borne by the colored soldier patiently, or punished with dignity by their officers, but in no instance did I hear colored soldiers make any reply to insulting language used toward [them] by the white troops.[29]

Burbridge's principal target was Saltville, Virginia, the site of one of the most important salt works in the South. Because it was critical to the preserving of meat, the substance produced here was vital to the Confederate war effort. Although there had been previous attempts to break up this operation, none had succeeded; even now, only the fact that the Union Chief of Staff Henry W. Halleck approved Burbridge's plan allowed that officer to undertake it. His immediate superior, Major General John M. Schofield, went along solely in deference to Halleck's blessing.

Burbridge commanded the main body of about 5,200 men, which included cavalry units from Kentucky, Michigan, and Ohio as well as the 5th USCT Cavalrymen. Two additional cooperating columns were charged with spreading out the Rebel defenses to prevent any concentration from forming against Burbridge. The whole machinery of this campaign had barely begun to function when it started to fall apart. The Confederates opposing the cooperating columns put up a tougher defense than expected, which kept the Federal units from getting into position before Burbridge commenced his final push on Saltville. Then, on October 1, the officers commanding these cooperating columns received new orders from Major General William T. Sherman, calling the whole thing off. The Yankee units immediately began to pull back, allowing the hard-pressed Confederates to converge on Saltville. Tragically, the couriers carrying these same orders to Burbridge failed to contact him until it was too late.

When Burbridge reached Saltville, on October 2, he found a Confederate defensive force waiting in a strong position. The town and its adjacent salt works lay nestled behind some ridges and high ground overlooking the north fork of the Holston River; the Confederate defenses ran along this high ground to the west of the town, then swung north and east to follow Chestnut Ridge, with some troops posted even further north, on Sanders Hill. The defensive array was a real

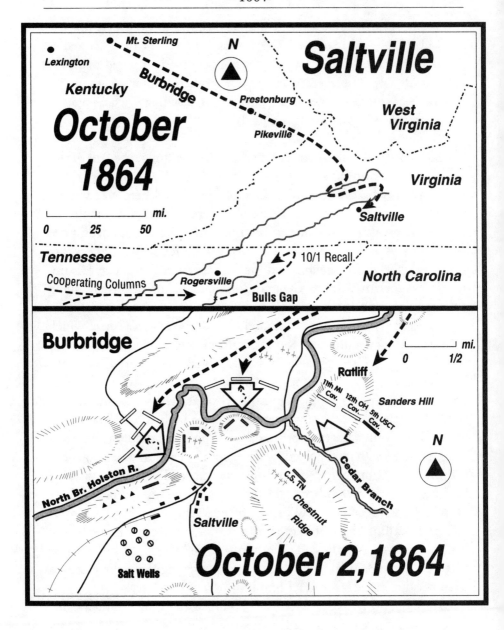

Saltville

October 1864

Lexington
Mt. Sterling
Burbridge
Kentucky
Prestonburg
Pikeville
West Virginia
Virginia
Saltville
N

mi.
0   25   50

Tennessee
10/1 Recall.
North Carolina
Cooperating Columns   Rogersville
Bulls Gap

Burbridge

Ratliff
11th MI Cav.   12th OH Cav.   5th USCT Cav.
Sanders Hill
mi.
0   1/2

North Br. Holston R.
C.S. TN
Cedar Branch
Chestnut Ridge
Saltville
N
Salt Wells

October 2, 1864

hodgepodge, with C.S. Kentucky cavalry units serving alongside Virginia Reserves, Tennessee Cavalry, and local home guards, for a total of about twenty-five hundred men. Stiffening the will of the defenders was the presence of black troops: the Southern specter of armed slaves on a rampage served to inspire these second-rate troops to fight with uncharacteristic fervor.

"Colonel," the officer commanding the Saltville defenses asked the head of a contingent of three hundred of these troops, "my men tell me the Yanks have got a lot of nigger soldiers along. Do you think your reserves will fight niggers?"

"Fight 'em?" the Reserve officer replied. "By God, sir, they'll eat 'em up! No! not eat 'em up! That's too much! By God, sir, we'll cut 'em up!"[30]

On October 2, Brevet Major General Burbridge attacked the Saltville defenses in three places. The two columns advancing from the west made no headway at all, while the third column, Ratliff's brigade, crossed to the north to strike the Rebel forces posted on Sanders Hill. Ratliff dismounted and deployed all three of his regiments in the attack, including the black detachment, which was now down to four hundred men, having lost a hundred to straggling and exhausted mounts and another hundred to horse-holding detail.

"The point to be attacked was the side of a high mountain," reported Colonel Brisbin,

> the rebels being posted about half way up behind rifle-pits made of logs and stones to the height of three feet. . . . The rebels opened upon [Ratliff's brigade] . . . a terrific fire, but the line pressed steadily forward up the steep side of the mount until they found themselves within fifty yards of the enemy. Here Colonel Wade ordered his force to charge, and the negroes rushed upon the works with a yell, and after a desperate struggle carried the entire line, killing and wounding a large number of the enemy and capturing some prisoners.

At one point in the action, the black troopers confronted Rebel Tennesseans, who met the ex-slaves with fierce resistance. Several of the Tennessee officers actually charged the black line singly, armed only with their revolvers, so fanatical was their hatred.[31]

Daylight was disappearing and ammunition running out by the time the weary Federals battled their way to the last ridge line. Believing the tall tales spun by prisoners about the many Confederate reinforcements on their way up, Burbridge decided that the prize was no longer worth the risk. As darkness fell, he ordered a retreat, then turned command of the expedition over to the next ranking officer. With his staff accompanying him, Burbridge rode back into Kentucky.

Many of the Union wounded were left behind in the rapid withdrawal, and a terrible fate awaited some of the abandoned blacks. According to Surgeon William H. Gardner, who remained to tend the casualties, "On Monday morning, October 3, there came to our field hospital several armed men, as I believe soldiers in the Confederate service, and took 5 men, privates, wounded (negroes), and shot them." Fearing this very thing, several horribly wounded black troopers kept up with the forced pace of the retreat: Thomas White remained in the saddle despite having been shot through both hips, and Joseph Green rode along nursing the stump of his just-amputated arm.[32]

Newspaper stories inflated the number of black troops killed at Saltville to 155, while other testimony (given after the war) further embellished the large-scale slaughter of the USCT cavalrymen. The facts suggest that though some of the blacks were indeed murdered, their total number was much smaller than assumed. There were 118 black casualties officially reported at Saltville, but a modern examination of military records has revealed that four of those resulted from clerical or administrative errors, correcting the number to 114. Twenty were known to have been killed in the heavy fighting on Sanders Hill or in the hospital incident reported by Dr. Gardner; another sixty-three were wounded, and thirty-one went missing. Of the wounded, three died of their wounds, while all of the remaining sixty survived. Some of the missing men returned to their regiment in the weeks following the fight, while others are known to have become prisoners of war; just seven suffered unknown fates. Even if all seven were slain in cold blood (and some could have died on Sanders Hill, and their bodies not been found for a time), the total of twelve men murdered, while a damning indictment of the racism faced by African American soldiers, does not constitute a wholesale massacre.

Brevet Major General Burbridge's October expedition to Saltville was a failure, with total casualties of about 350; the only gain the officer could claim was the destruction of "some of the outer salt works." He would return to Saltville that December, this time as a subordinate in an expedition that would at last succeed in wrecking the salt-production facilities. Burbridge would be relieved of his command in January 1865.[33]

Among the small, personal tragedies connected with Burbridge's October campaign was the effect of the death of one black soldier on his wife. On March 25, 1865, Patsey Leach testified as follows:

I am a widow and belonged to Warren Wiley of Woodford County Ky. My husband Julius Leach was a member of Co. D. 5″ U.S.C. Cavalry and was killed at the Salt Works Va. about six months ago. . . . He had only been about a month in the service when he was killed. I was living with aforesaid Wiley when he died. He knew of my husbands enlisting before I did but never said any thing to me about it. From that time he treated me more cruelly than ever whipping me frequently without any cause and insulting me on every occasion. About three weeks after my husband enlisted a Company of Colored Soldiers passed our house and I was there in the garden and looked at them as they passed. My master had been watching me and when the soldiers had gone I went into the kitchen. My master followed me and Knocked me to the floor senseless saying as he did so, "You have been looking at those darned Nigger Soldiers." When I recovered my senses he beat me with a cowhide. When my husband was Killed my master whipped me severely saying my husband had gone into the army to fight against white folks and he my master would let me know that I was foolish to let my husband go he would "take it out of my back," he would "Kill me by piecemeal" and he hoped "that the last one of the nigger soldiers would be Killed". . . . On this and other occasions my master whipped me for no other cause than my husband having enlisted. When he had whipped me he said "never mind God dam you when I am done with you tomorrow you never will live no more." I knew he would carry out his threats so that night . . . I took my babe and traveled . . . to Lexington. I have five children. I left them all with my master . . . but I dare not go near my master knowing he would whip me again.[34]

Action at Dalton, Georgia, August 15, 1864;
Surrender of Dalton, Georgia, October 13, 1864;
Action at Decatur, Alabama, October 28, 1864

"I would prefer to have this a white man's war and provide for the negroes after the time has passed. . . . With my opinion of negroes and my experience, yea prejudice, I cannot trust them yet. Time may change this but I cannot bring myself to trust negroes with arms in positions of danger and trust."[35]

So said William T. Sherman, writing in April 1863. A year's time was not enough for this attitude to change; in May 1864, when his force of approximately 110,000 men began its march on Atlanta, black combat soldiers were not included. The USCT units serving under Sherman's command were assigned to garrisons throughout Tennessee, especially in Memphis, Chattanooga, and Nashville. Sherman's advance depended upon the delivery of supplies via a single railroad line running from Chattanooga to Atlanta; as his men fought their way deeper and deeper into Georgia, protecting this rail link became an increasingly important concern for Sherman, and destroying it a more and more desirable objective for the Rebels battling him.

By the beginning of August, Sherman had led his men to the very gates of Atlanta. The Confederate Army of Tennessee was now commanded by Lieutenant General John B. Hood, a grim, driven man crippled by war wounds, who believed zealously in the doctrine of the offensive. Hood had tried and failed to crush the invaders in a series of fierce battles outside the city; while his men rested and licked their wounds, he kept up the pressure by ordering his cavalry chief, Major General Joseph Wheeler, "to move upon the enemy's line of communications . . . [and] destroy them at various points between Marietta and Chattanooga."[36]

Wheeler began his operation on August 10, leading his four thousand troopers behind Sherman's lines, following the tracks north from Marietta toward Dalton. As the C.S. force approached the latter place on August 14, the Federal officer defending the post pulled his men into a small fort built for just that purpose, and at the same time sent a plea for help to Major General James B. Steedman in Chattanooga. Steedman at once took to the field with a relief force of eighteen hundred men, comprising regiments from Missouri, Indiana, Ohio, and Pennsylvania, as well as one black unit—the 14th USCT.

The 14th had been organized at Gallatin, Tennessee, in late 1863 by Colonel Thomas J. Morgan, a dedicated soldier and a devoutly religious man. His regiment was made up ex-slaves, many of whom had seen previous military service as teamsters, cooks, officers' servants, and the like. During a weeding-out process, Morgan had personally questioned the prospective soldiers about their motivation. As he recollected one of these interviews, "When I told . . . one who wanted to 'fight for freedom,' that he might lose his life, he replied, 'but my people will be free.'"[37]

An example of Morgan's idiosyncratic approach to the ways of command was the manner in which he organized the 14th's companies, grouping his men according to their height. "When the regiment was full," he afterward explained, "the four center companies were all composed of tall men, the flanking companies of men of medium height, while the little men were sandwiched between." However odd his methods may have seemed, they did instill some pride among the rank and file of the 14th, one of whom was H. J. Maxwell. "This Regiment has already won a name," he told the readers of the *Anglo-African,* "and has received the plaudits of all the officers in this Department. They drill well, and go through the evolutions with as much grace and ease as any regiment in the service."[38]

Morgan chafed at the endless number of fatigue assignments given his men, especially in the spring of 1864, as Sherman was preparing his white soldiers for the Atlanta campaign. "I used every means to bring about a change," Morgan wrote, "for I believed that the ultimate status of the negro was to be determined by his conduct on the battle-field. No one doubted that he could work, while many did doubt that he had the courage to stand up and fight like a man." After Sherman put his armies in motion, Morgan (who tagged along for while as a volunteer aide on the staff of Major General Oliver O. Howard) convinced Major General Steedman to include his regiment in any combat operations. Morgan finally got his wish on August 14, when Steedman added the 14th USCT to the Dalton relief force.[39]

The troops were transported on railroad cars to within a short distance of Dalton, where they rested until dawn and then marched forward in battle formation. In the moments before the word to advance was given, one of Morgan's officers told his men, "Boys, some of you may be killed, but remember you are fighting for liberty." To this, one black soldier replied, "I am ready to die for liberty."[40]

Afterward, Major General Steedman would claim that his men had "cleared the town of the enemy," while Wheeler, whose command was about twice the size of Steedman's, would counter that though he had been "attacked by a large force," his loss in this day's action was "trifling." "The fight was short, and not at all severe,"

Morgan stated. "The regiment was all exposed to fire. One private was killed, one lost a leg, and one was wounded in the right hand." Ironically, the dead man was the very one who had vowed to "die for liberty." According to another white officer in the regiment, the heaviest fighting of the day took place in a "limited space among some thickets lining the banks of a small stream, where a few of the enemy's skirmishers found themselves suddenly surrounded, and, refusing to surrender to 'niggers' were all killed." A Rebel officer who watched this fight recalled that his men "fought stubbornly, with the butts of their guns, as they were pushed back off the field." Another Confederate declared that "some of our men surrendered, and . . . were barbarously murdered by some negro troops."[41]

Steedman's footsoldiers were unable to pursue Wheeler's mounted columns, which now continued northward, striking near Knoxville and Nashville before returning to Georgia. They caused a ruckus, and press-ganged about eight hundred men into their ranks, but they did not seriously disrupt Sherman's supply route. A much larger expedition, bent on many of the same objectives, was launched on September 28. It involved just about all that was left of the Army of the Tennessee under its quixotic commander John B. Hood. Forced to abandon Atlanta, Hood had to find a new strategy for moving Sherman out of the Deep South; in a move that remains controversial to this day, he decided to place his entire army astride the Federal supply line.

The Union outposts along that route were not designed to withstand an assault by a major force, with the result that Big Shanty, Acworth, and other stations were gobbled up as Hood's men moved north. On October 13, the Confederates reached Dalton, then being held by eight hundred men, including more than six hundred belonging to the 44th USCT, a Tennessee unit organized at Chattanooga in April 1864. Colonel Lewis Johnson of the 44th, commanding the post, at first rejected the Rebel overtures to surrender, but later in the afternoon, convinced that almost the entire Army of Tennessee was poised to engulf his position, and worried (according to his own testimony) that any resistance would expose his black troops to wanton slaughter, he gave up. "The colored soldiers displayed the greatest anxiety to fight," Johnson reported, "although all could plainly see what an immense force threatened us, and that there was no hope whatever. It grieved me to be compelled to surrender men who showed so much spirit and bravery."[42]

Lieutenant Morris S. Hall of the 44th recalled, "As soon as the terms of surrender were made known my men flocked around me and asked if I thought their lives would be spared or [if] they would be murdered as some they knew at Fort Pillow. Of course I could not answer them positively but quieted their fears as much as possible." There was ample cause for concern: during the surrender negotiations, Colonel Johnson was repeatedly told that a great number of C.S. soldiers were "over anxious to move upon the 'niggers,'" and indeed, many Arkansas troops felt sure that some of their comrades previously captured at Atlanta had been abused by black guards from the 44th. A Tennessee Rebel remembered the captured blacks as being "very insolent," particularly when many of them were immediately put to work tearing up the railroad tracks. "One of the negroes protested against the work as he was a sergeant," an Arkansan recollected, with ominous understatement. "When he had paid the penalty for disobeying orders the rest tore up the road readily and rapidly." Colonel Johnson grimly noted that five of his men who were "unable to keep up with the rest [of the prisoners] on the march" were cut out of the coffle and shot.[43]

The Union officers (jeered by their captors as "white niggers") were separated from the enlisted men, and the latter were marched into Mississippi. Several hundred who managed to escape while en route would eventually make their way back to their regiment in Chattanooga. A Southern correspondent saw the black POWs in an Alabama camp: "Most of them were young fellows," he wrote in late October. "A man with any humanity could not look upon them with any other than feelings of the deepest pity; not on account of any lack of clothes, . . . but all the peculiarities, of right belonging to the race, especially when assembled together in a crowd, were gone. No songs, nor dancing, nor any sign of mirth or gladness, and their manner of getting along in camp showed their utter lack of contrivance peculiar to soldiers." Those who remained in captivity were either put to work in labor gangs or returned to their owners. Colonel Johnson was officially exonerated; he was told that his decision to surrender his men without a fight "was in this instance commendable discretion." Paroled soon after his capture, Johnson rejoined his regiment, and with them would face the Army of Tennessee again before the year was out.[44]

Dalton was but a brief stop for Hood's men, who, directed by the impulses of their commander, marched and countermarched over the next weeks through northwestern Georgia and northeastern Alabama. Hood then determined to forsake worrying Sherman's rail connection to Atlanta in favor of making a strike into middle Tennessee. On October 22, his men began to leave their camps in central Alabama to march toward the Tennessee River, which they had to get across before Federal gunboats could smash their pontoon bridges. Feinting toward the Georgia boundary, Hood abruptly veered his columns westward for Decatur, Alabama, which he believed to be weakly defended. When the first of his men reached that town, on October 26, they were surprised to find a Yankee garrison of three thousand, well dug in, disposed to fight, and backed up by two gunboats. Nevertheless, Hood resolved to force the issue.

His approach to Decatur had not gone unnoticed. In the early hours of October 26, troops in Chattanooga were put into motion. Captain Henry Romeyn of the 14th USCT recalled the confusion of that night, which was "rainy, and in darkness so thick that one could feel it." It was not yet 1:00 A.M. when the men of the regiment waded "toward the railroad, through mud and in darkness so profound that when the guiding lantern was for a moment extinguished," claimed Romeyn, "I could not see the guide marching at my elbow. The first cars available were open racks from which horses had just been unloaded, and into them we were hurried, and stood on our feet the rest of the night. We knew that we were going westward—how far, we did not know." The 14th was just one of several units being rushed to the threatened post.[45]

The troops were carried by train to Stevenson, where new orders extended their journey to Decatur. On reaching this destination, at 4:00 P.M. on October 27, a detachment of a hundred men from the regiment was placed on the north bank of the river, while the remainder crossed the Federal pontoon bridge to help picket the Union left. Colonel Thomas J. Morgan again commanded the 14th. His eccentric way of running the outfit—a mixture of stern military discipline and old-time religion—had created a schism among his officers, with those opposing him rallying around his second in command, Lieutenant Colonel Henry C. Corbin, who was left in charge of the detachment.

As the sun burned off the morning mist on October 28, Corbin detected an opportunity for the black troops to see action. According to Captain Romeyn, also with the detachment, "We saw, 700 yards away on the other bank, a rebel battery busy entrenching. From the top of a tall tree on the bank, it was seen that it had no infantry support; and a plan for its capture, with a rough sketch as seen from the tree top, was carried over to the colonel in the town." It took nearly two hours for this information to be digested and turned into a decision to act; by then, the same spotters had observed Rebel infantry supports moving into a ravine behind the battery. A follow-up message was dispatched "advising abandonment of attempt at capture," but it arrived too late to stop the attack.[46]

At around 10:00 A.M., Lieutenant Colonel Corbin, having been relieved, crossed over the river and rejoined the main body. Shortly before noon, the 14th USCT (numbering perhaps four hundred men) was consolidated within the earthworks, where the troops began to prepare for action. "The men were stripped of all extra load, carrying only gun, accouterments, and canteen of water," reported Colonel Morgan. After filing along a riverbank behind the Federal trenches for a distance of 150 yards, to a point directly before the enemy battery, the troops were marched outside the earthworks and formed into line of battle, while skirmishers were sent ahead to harass the gunners.

Colonel Morgan now indulged in one of those actions that Lieutenant Colonel Corbin felt were dangerously irresponsible. As Corbin described it, "The colonel ordered the regiment to come to 'parade rest' and engaged in prayer. We were in an exposed position. During his time at prayer a number were killed and wounded. . . . I said in no uncertain terms that we were there for other business than prayer, and suggested that we should attend to that business."[47]

When Morgan rebuked Corbin in front of the men, an enmity was born that would eventually result in charges' being preferred by the former officer against the latter. But all that still lay in the future; for the moment, what loomed 780 yards in front of the regiment was a Confederate battery. The colors were shaken loose and the order given to move forward on the double-quick.

"I never saw a prettier piece of work done," related a white Union soldier. "The ground over which the negro troops passed was rolling.

The troops marched with the greatest military precision, not firing a gun, nor halting till they reached the vicinity of the battery, and then they went pell-mell over the breastworks, and in a short time had captured the battery." Morgan had had the foresight to issue files to some of his men, who used them to spike two of the four captured cannon, but before these could be hauled back to the Federal lines, Rebel reinforcements arrived. For a few minutes, the fighting was hand to hand; another Yankee watching from the Decatur defenses remembered it as a "desperate struggle." Morgan ordered his men to fall back, later admitting that a "fleet foot saved the regiment." Men stabbed and clubbed each other as the 14th retreated to the river with Confederates swarming all around. Several blacks who were guarding wounded prisoners had to let them go in order to save themselves. "The affair did not last much more than 20 minutes," observed a Union soldier, ". . . and the colored boys had to fall down along the water's edge under the bank of the river, while the enemy ran along above them and shot down on them."[48]

The spirited defense of Decatur helped convince Lieutenant General Hood to seek easier pickings elsewhere. He raised the siege to move farther west, to Bainbridge, where the low water at Muscle Shoals would keep the Federal gunboats at bay. Still far from over, his meandering journey would bring him face to face with black troops once more in this campaign.

In his report of this action, Colonel Morgan listed one officer and one enlisted man killed, as well as fifty-two wounded and one missing. By any measure, it was a small affair, but it nonetheless had a powerful effect upon the members of the 14th USCT. "The blood of those who fell has hushed the mouths of our Enemies," Morgan told his men, "while the conduct of those who live Elicited praises and cheers from *all* who witnessed it." As the weary regiment returned to the Federal lines after the charge, the white soldiers, recalled a USCT officer, "mounted the parapet and gave it three rousing cheers." The officer would long remember the "glad look" of his black first sergeant, who turned to him and said, "Captain, we've got it at last."[49]

Chapter Ten

"Saved the Colors"

——◇——

O N the night of August 9, 1864, a detail of black soldier volunteers and white officers passed from the northern shoulder of Bermuda Hundred to the point where a loop in the James River had created a tongue of land known as Dutch Gap. Federal military engineers had already staked out a course cutting directly across the peninsula's narrow neck, so almost as soon as they came ashore, the black troops began to dig. Major General Benjamin F. Butler had once again fixed on a scheme, this time a plan to open up a canal across Dutch Gap that would shorten the river route for U.S. gunboats by several miles and in the process bypass several formidable Confederate batteries. All that was required, Butler estimated, was "a cut less than five hundred feet long, sixteen feet deep, and sixty feet wide on the bottom and ninety at the top." After the engineering surveys had been approved by U. S. Grant, Butler quickly acted to implement his idea.[1]

"General Butler," recalled Colonel John W. Ames of the 6th USCT, "in an official order published early in August, 1864, . . . called upon his colored troops for volunteers for a service of extra danger and hard work, promising extra pay for the same." The first night's labor for the men chosen for this duty proved deceptively productive: "The light [top]soil yielded easily, and the progress was plain enough to be seen," noted Ames. In the days following, however, the soldiers encountered what a major of engineers termed a "layer . . . of an in-durated clay and sand, not easily moved by the pick." A brisk if in-accurate shelling by Rebel artillery greeted the new construction at daylight.[2]

An endless procession of mule-drawn carts hauled dirt away as August passed into September. Some Confederate cannon were repo-sitioned and a few mortars brought up to harass the work crews, but the details, drawn almost exclusively from USCT units, soon became adept at scattering for cover whenever spotters observed shells on the way. Said Colonel Ames, "No day passed without death and wounds in the deepening channel. . . . Fever and ague . . . attacked the work-ing party, and those diseases were aggravated by the cellar-like holes in which the constant fire of the enemy forced the troops to live."[3]

The Confederates now began to construct a large fortification on Signal Hill, about a mile from Dutch Gap. Southern officers were confident that once operational, these guns would stop the digging. The new fort would be ready for use by October 6, but not by the Rebels: Ben Butler had a fresh scheme, one that would result in the greatest number of Medals of Honor issued to African Americans in the entire Civil War. The awards would be a bloody byproduct of Butler's naked ambition to be known to history as the man who cap-tured Richmond.

Engagement at New Market Heights, Virginia, September 29, 1864

Throughout the night of September 28, 1864, and well into the next morning, tens of thousands of Union soldiers tramped on dark roads leading north toward the James River. One of the many units on the move was the second battalion of the 45th USCT. "We left front of petersburg in the evening at three o'clock and we marched all night till some of the boys gave out and lay down along the road and some throde their things away," recalled John M. Christy of Company H. The snaking files eventually began to converge into two distinct columns, one aimed for a crossing point known as Aiken's Landing, and the other following a well-worn trail out Jones Neck to Deep Bottom.[4]

The entire force, totaling some 26,600 men, was moving accord-ing to detailed orders from Butler's headquarters that claimed as their primary objective "to get possession of Richmond." Failing that, the Army of the James was to tie down as many Confederate troops as possible in order to prevent them from shifting south to Petersburg, where the Army of the Potomac was about to launch its own offensive. Butler planned to level two heavy blows on the strong Rebel defenses protecting Richmond. His left wing, under Major General Edward O. C. Ord, was to attack the Confederate entrenchments running parallel to the Varina Road, even as the entire Tenth Corps, supplemented by a division from the Eighteenth, all under Major General David B. Birney, debouched from the Union-held pocket at Deep Bottom and, in Butler's words, "endeavor[ed] to carry Newmarket road and the heights adjacent."[5]

The Federals had already twice tried and failed to capture the formidable New Market Heights.* But whereas on each previous occasion the plan had been to flank this strong Confederate position, this time the Union troops were to hit the entrenched line head-on. Butler's extensive instructions did not specify which units were to make the actual attack, but it seems clear enough that on a personal level, he wanted the black troops to be given the task.

Butler would continue to defend his preference long after the war was over. He felt strongly that "from prejudice and ignorance of their good qualities," few military men believed

> that the negroes would fight. . . . This [feeling] . . . was a deep-seated one and spread far and wide, and the negro had not had sufficient opportunity to demonstrate his valor and his staying qualities as a soldier. And the further cry was that the negroes never struck a good blow for their own freedom. Therefore, I determined to put them in position, to demonstrate the fact of the value of the negro as a soldier, . . . and that the experiment should be one of which no man should doubt, if it attained success.[6]

Of the four black brigades that crossed the Deep Bottom pontoon bridge on the night of September 28, only two would play a significant role in the attack itself. Held in reserve was the First Brigade of Brigadier General William Birney's Third Division (Tenth Corps); all of the assault troops belonged to Brigadier General Charles J. Paine's

---

*Several black units had played a minor role in the August expedition to Deep Bottom.

Eighteenth Corps division (temporarily assigned to Birney). Of the three brigades in that command, one, led by Colonel John H. Holman (1st, 22nd, and 37th USCT), would see only slight action, while the other two—Colonel Samuel A. Duncan's (4th and 6th USCT)* and Colonel Alonzo G. Draper's (5th, 36th, and 38th USCT)—were slated for their toughest combat of the war.

Sergeant Major Christian A. Fleetwood of the 4th USCT was a man of few words. "Reg[imental papers] and knapsacks . . . packed away," he noted in his diary on the morning of September 29. "Coffee boiled and line formed." "We were all up at three o'clock [A.M.], took our hot coffee and hard tack and started [in]to [the] field, as the first streaks of dawn were appearing," recalled Lieutenant Colonel Giles W. Shurtleff, commanding the 5th USCT, who had been briefed about the operation only a few hours earlier. "We were told that Grant would be with us, and that it was intended to push straight to Richmond." Even amid the bustle accompanying the mustering of the 6th USCT, Captain John McMurray found time to worry about a man in his company named Emanuel Patterson. The soldier looked sick and said he felt sick, but when McMurray tried to have him excused, the regimental surgeon pronounced him fit for duty. McMurray noted that Patterson "took his place in the company" as the regiment formed.[7]

It was around 4:00 A.M. when Major General Butler rode among the troops. "I told them that this was an attack where I expected them to go over and take a work which would be before them . . . , and that they must take it at all hazards, and that when they were over the parapet into it their war cry should be, 'Remember Fort Pillow.'" ("In contemplating since the results of that day," wrote Captain McMurray in 1916, "I have been led to see the wisdom of God in concealing from man what is before him, as I never saw it before. Had I known when I arose that morning what was in store for my company, for my regiment, within the next two or three hours, I would have been entirely unfitted for the duties of the day.") Then the advance got under way. "All the troops were in motion moving off in various directions to the part assigned them in the day's bloody work," observed Lieutenant Joseph J. Scroggs of the 5th USCT. "The

---

*The 10th USCT was a part of this brigade, but at this time it was on detached service along the James River.

Div[ision] S[harp] S[hooters] were thrown forward . . . and before we had got a mile from camp they had found and engaged the enemy."[8]

Birney's battle plan called for his white regiments to deploy across the northeastern face of the Deep Bottom pocket and engage the enemy's attention, but not to attack; that task was up to the black troops on the left. Tactical control of the assault was assigned to a relatively inexperienced brigadier named Charles A. Paine. Paine, who had yet to direct more than a brigade in action, had never before been entrusted with so much responsibility, and sadly for the men under his command, he was not up to the job. Allowing Duncan's two regiments to deploy in what he would subsequently term a "long skirmish line," he advanced them into the teeth of the enemy's defenses without any immediate support, and before the cooperating white units had gotten into position on their right.

In later years, Colonel Duncan would have proud memories of his troops this day. He vividly recalled seeing them, "in the early gray of the morning, march with steady cadence down into the low grounds in front of Newmarket Heights, when the mists of the morning still hung heavy; saw them disappear, as they entered the fog that enwrapped them like a mantle of death."[9]

After crossing an open field, the attackers entered a small wood through which ran a deceptively steep ravine and creek. Stumbling out of this clutter, the troops then slogged across swampy ground before hitting the first line of enemy entanglements, an abatis of slashing consisting of a belt of chopped-down trees with branches left on and interlaced. A small open space separated the slashing from the next entangling strip, a row of chevaux-de-frise—logs covered with alternating bored holes into which sharpened wooden stakes were inserted in a crisscross pattern. Behind all this lay the enemy earthworks. When the two regiments began their advance, the Rebel defenders were spread along the line at six-foot intervals, but once it became clear that the only threat was coming from two *black* regiments, Southerners started crowding in from the sides. "There were not many men in the reb. line," Brigadier General Paine told his father on October 3, ". . . but where I assaulted there were as many men as the works w'd hold."[10]

The 4th and 6th USCT deployed in two lines of battle, with the 4th leading and the 6th echeloned to the left rear. "Our line is formed just back of a crest or knoll over which we are to charge down upon

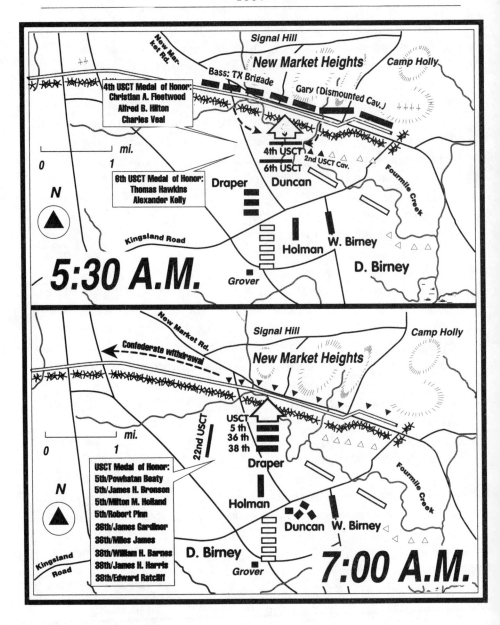

this unknown work," remembered Lieutenant J. H. Goulding of the 6th USCT. "As we clear the top, the ground on either side of us seems broken and woody, while that in our immediate front is smooth and slopes down toward the enemy's line." "Just as we reached this field we could see the first rays of sunlight glinting among the tree tops be-yond the field," observed Captain McMurray, "and noticed a score of Johnnies scampering across the field before us, turning occasion-ally to shoot back at us."[11]

The time was about 5:30 A.M. The black troops had their guns loaded but not capped, to discourage their stopping to fire during the rush to the works. The two regiments pressed across the field, tumbled through the ravine, and scrambled up the other side, where the broken lines were re-formed. Then the double ranks lurched into the slashing. A few individuals found narrow breaks used by the Rebel pickets for passage, but most either began to pull at the obstructions themselves or waited for men with axes to clear them a path. "I know there was a big lot of thinking done by us while we stood there," remembered Captain McMurray. With the Federals bunched up at point-blank range, the Confederates opened fire. "The crash of small arms is terrific," wrote Lieutenant Goulding, "a constant roll with the heavier discharges of artillery breaking in like the bass notes of some mighty organ."[12]

The black soldiers sustained terrible casualties trying to claw through the slashing. "It was slow work," said Captain McMurray, "and every step in our advance exposed us to the murderous fire of the enemy." "With shouts and cries, with deep drawn breath and gasps and choking heart-throbs we plunge on and on, men dropping suddenly or thrown whirling or doubled up as they [are] struck," tes-tified Lieutenant Goulding. As he picked his way through the slash-ing, Captain McMurray found the sickly private, Patterson, lying on the ground. "He was shot in the abdomen," remembered McMurray, "so that his bowels all gushed out, forming a mass larger than my hat, seemingly, which he was holding with his clasped hands to keep them from falling at his feet." The man was doomed to die an ago-nizing death. To the end of his days, McMurray never forgave him-self for not letting Patterson sit this one out.[13]

Somehow, small groups (the 4th and 6th were by now well jum-bled together) managed to break out of the slashing and race toward the frise. A few who climbed through these obstacles were then mired in swampy ground, but a handful did reach the Rebel position, only to be killed or taken prisoner. "The whole line seemed to wilt down under the fearful fire which was then poured into us," wrote

Lieutenant James Henry Wickes of the 4th USCT. "The line was growing too weak and thin to make an assault. It began to waver and fall back."[14]

Lieutenant William Appleton of the 4th USCT and Lieutenant Nathan H. Edgerton of the 6th would receive the Medal of Honor for their conduct in this phase of the action at New Market Heights. Two noncommissioned officers of the 6th also won top honors this day: Sergeant Major Thomas Hawkins kept the regimental flag from capture, while the remaining color of the 6th was saved by Sergeant Alexander Kelly, who also gallantly rallied his men under fire. In addition, three black 4th USCT men would be awarded the Medal of Honor for their bravery here: Sergeant Major Fleetwood, Sergeant Alfred B. Hilton, and Private (later Corporal) Charles Veal.

In his laconic diary entry for this day, Sergeant Fleetwood wrote, "Saved the Colors." Years later, he would have a bit more to say. "When the charge was started our color-guard was complete," he recalled.

> Only one of the twelve came off that field on his feet. . . . Early in the rush one of the sergeants went down, a bullet cutting his flag-staff in two and passing through his body. The other sergeant, Alfred B. Hilton, . . . caught up the other flag and pressed forward with them both. It was a deadly hailstorm of bullets, sweeping men down as hailstones sweep the leaves from the trees and it was not long before he also went down, shot through the leg. As he fell he held up the flags and shouted: "Boys, save the colors!"
>
> Before they could touch the ground, Corporal Charles Veal . . . had seized the blue flag, and I the American flag. . . . It was very evident that there was too much work cut out for our [two] regiments. . . . We struggled through the two lines of abatis, a few getting through the palisades, but it was sheer madness and those of us who were able withdrew as best we could.[15]

Colonel Duncan was down with four wounds, so Colonel Ames of the 6th took over the brigade, his face bloody from a gash across his forehead. "And the going back was worse than the coming up," noted Captain McMurray, "because, to be shot at with your back to the enemy is always more annoying. You feel then utterly helpless." "Reaching the line of our reserves and no commissioned officer being in sight," recounted Sergeant Fleetwood, "I rallied the survivors around the flag, rounding up at first eighty-five men and three non-commissioned officers." Brigadier General Paine later recorded that "Col. Duncan's brigade . . . behaved with great gallantry and met with very severe loss." There were 27 killed, 136 wounded, and 14 missing in the 4th USCT, and 41 dead, 160 injured, and 8 unaccounted for in the 6th. Jubilant Southerners came out of their trenches to plunder the bodies and, by their own admission, finish off some of the badly wounded blacks. Paine's first attack had been a tragic case of too little strength with no support.[16]

General Birney immediately ordered the black troops to make another assault. With Duncan's brigade wrecked, Draper's got the call. Unlike Duncan, who had thinned his troops out in a long line, Draper placed his men in a column with the 5th USCT leading, followed by the 36th and 38th—in formation six companies wide and ten ranks deep. "Shells from the rebel battery were poured in upon us," remembered Lieutenant Colonel Shurtleff of the 5th USCT, "but the fire of the [Union] infantry was withheld. As soon as the whole brigade was uncovered the order was given to 'double quick' and we started on a slow run, with arms at a right shoulder shift, the burnished steel bayonets gleaming in the bright sun." Said Lieutenant Scroggs of that regiment, "A thick jungle in our way deranged our ranks slightly . . . but they pressed forward bravely following their colors." Then came the abatis. Nearby Lieutenant Elliott F. Grabill related how they worked their way "through bushes and trees cut down to prevent approach with hostile intent." All the officers went into this fight dismounted: "The shells were shrieking around so that I was afraid one should tear me to pieces while on horseback," Grabill admitted.[17]

"Within twenty or thirty yards of the rebel line we found a swamp which broke the charge as the men had to wade the run or stream and reform on the bank," Colonel Draper reported. "At this juncture, too, the men generally commenced firing, which made so much confusion that it was impossible to make the orders understood." "Here our progress was arrested and the most murderous fire that I witnessed during the war, opened on us," said Shurtleff. "Our men were falling by the scores," added Draper.[18]

The Rebel musketry began to slacken after thirty long minutes of this pounding. The cause of the diminishment was the startling Union success several miles to the west, closer to Richmond, where Butler's other wing had crossed to the north side of the James, swept aside the Confederates trying to block the Varina Road, and captured the centerpiece of the C.S. defenses, Fort Harrison. Richmond's greatest danger now lay at that contested point: if Butler's Yankees could pour more men through the Fort Harrison breach, the shield of earthworks protecting the capital would be fatally compromised. So unit by unit, the Confederates holding the New Market line were being hustled off to the west, leaving only a screening force behind.

Lieutenant Colonel Shurtleff had by now been hit once in the hand. He checked in with a brigade staff officer and was told that the original orders to advance were still in force. Mustering all his strength, Shurtleff shouted, "Forward double quick," and the tangle of men began to move ahead. Then their commander was down, hit in the thigh. His fight was over.

"The entire brigade took up the shout and went over the rebel works," reported Colonel Draper. "When the brigade were making their final charge, a rebel officer leaped upon the parapet, waved his sword, and shouted, 'Hurrah, my brave men.' Private James Gardiner, Company I, Thirty-sixth U.S. Colored Troops, . . . shot him, and then ran the bayonet through his body to the muzzle." Private Gardiner was one of nine members of Draper's brigade who would be given Medals of Honor for their actions this day. The other soldier in the 36th USCT to be so honored was Corporal Miles James of Company B, who, though his arm had been terribly mutilated by enemy shot, loaded and fired his gun with the other hand while urging his comrades forward. From the ranks of the 38th USCT, Private William H. Barnes was commended for being one of the first to enter the enemy's works, Sergeant Edward Ratcliff for assuming command of his company after the officer in charge was killed, and Sergeant James A. Harris for acting gallantly in the assault.[19]

Four Medals of Honor were given to men of the 5th USCT: Sergeants Powhatan Beaty, James H. Bronson, Milton M. Holland, and Robert Pinn. All were recognized for taking over their respective companies after their officers were killed or wounded. When asked after the war why he had joined up in the first place, Sergeant Pinn said, "I was very eager to become a soldier, in order to prove by my feeble efforts the black man's rights to untrammeled manhood."

Pinn's right arm was severely wounded in this fighting; he would never regain its use.[20]

"The rebels retreated rapidly and we secured but few prisoners," wrote Lieutenant Scroggs. "We carried the [New Market] works but it cost us dearly," declared Lieutenant Grabill. Of the 1,300 men of Draper's brigade, more than 450 were casualties. The 5th USCT lost 28 killed, 185 wounded, and 23 missing; the loss in the 36th was 21 dead and 87 wounded, while that in the 38th was 17 dead and 94 wounded. Command of several of the 5th USCT's companies passed to the black sergeants, who, recalled one of them with pride, "discharged their duties to the entire satisfaction of their superiors."[21]

Major General Butler was among the first to come onto the field after it was all over. "As I rode across the brook and up towards the fort along this line of charge, some eighty feet wide and three or four hundred yards long, there lay in my path [the] . . . dead and wounded of my colored comrades. When I reached the scene of their exploit their ranks broke, but it was to gather around their general. . . . I felt in my heart that the capacity of the negro race for soldiers had then and there been fully settled forever." Writing from his hospital bed, Colonel Duncan told his wife, "Ah! give me the Thunder-heads & Black hearts after all. They fought splendidly that morning, facing the red tempest of death with unflinching heroism."[22]

As most of Birney's units quickly moved after the retreating Confederates, men from the battered black regiments scoured the battlefield. Lieutenant Goulding of the 6th USCT found the color sergeant of the 4th "with both legs shattered by a round shot."

"Have we taken the works?" the wounded man asked.

"Yes, sergeant, we have," Goulding answered. To his surprise, the soldier began to cheer and gesticulate so wildly that the lieutenant feared he would die on the spot. He finally consented to be moved into the shade. When told that it was doubtful he would survive his wounds, the sergeant replied, "Well, I carried my colors up to the works, and I did my duty, didn't I?"[23]

On the march toward Richmond, some of the black troops met a small procession of escaping slaves. When the elder patriarch leading the group recognized that his saviors were African American soldiers, his exultation—and that of the USCT men—knew no bounds. "They cheered," wrote a reporter. "They gathered about the freedman, and

... fairly danced for joy, or cried with delight." He continued, "Men may have their peculiar views about . . . the policy of arming blacks; but he who could stand by and see those soldiers . . . and yet could not share in their joy, and thank God with them that other chains were broken, would have been less than human."[24]

Engagement at Fort Gilmer, Virginia, September 29, 1864

It was about 7:00 A.M. when Butler's Eighteenth Corps stormed Fort Harrison. Great opportunity beckoned, but the loss of a number of key Federal officers in the assault muddled the follow-up actions, allowing the outnumbered Confederates time to reconstitute their defenses. By midday, there was precious little offensive energy remaining in Butler's left wing, and it thus fell to the right wing, just arriving on the field after its victory at New Market Heights, to recover the momentum. The focus of action shifted north along the Rebel line as Major General Birney's route brought his men against Richmond's defenses near the New Market Road.

Birney had been hindered by enemy rear-guard actions, which slowed his pace so much that it took him almost two hours to move one mile along the road. The Tenth Corps commander now had to make a difficult decision. He could press along the New Market Road and strike the enemy's next defensive line, several miles closer to Richmond, which would put him behind the Confederates blocking the Eighteenth Corps; but that would leave at least one enemy stronghold in his rear. Birney opted to reduce that stronghold first, and so began to orient his units to assault it from the north and east.

The target in question was Fort Gilmer. Located about a mile and a half north of Fort Harrison, this five-sided earthwork was screened by a ten-foot moat and two lines of abatis across its northern face, but its eastern face was unprotected. Although the fort boasted just two cannon, its small garrison consisted of veteran troops who would be steadily reinforced throughout any action. It would take a carefully coordinated, maximum effort on Birney's part to crack this tough nut.

The effort that David Birney mounted against Fort Gilmer, however, was neither a carefully coordinated nor a maximum one. The attack from the north began and ended before the one on the east even

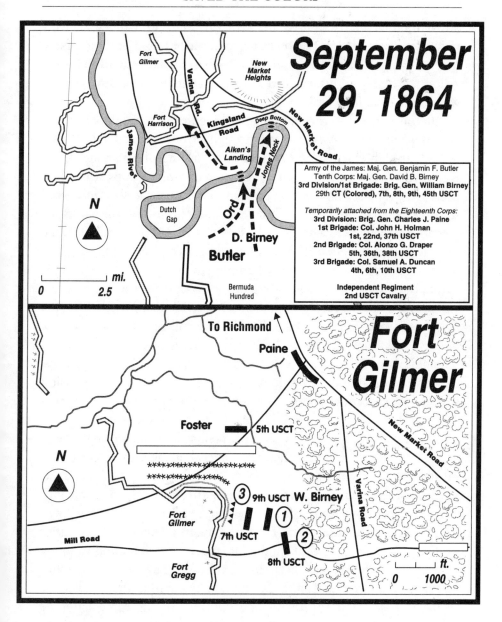

got under way. Brigadier General Robert S. Foster's white division, spread out in a long line as it moved across the broken ground toward Gilmer, was struck by flank fire on its right and directly bombarded from its front, causing the weary Federals (nearly half of Foster's division had already fallen out from exhaustion) to be hammered down and thrown back. Brigadier General Charles J. Paine's black division (still attached to the Tenth Corps), the battered heroes of New Market Heights, stood in reserve, but when Foster organized his division for a second attack, just a single regiment—the 5th USCT—was sent by Paine to assist.

"It was a mad enterprise," remarked Lieutenant Grabill of the 5th, "but it was ordered. We advanced through a front and a cross fire of artillery, through (across) two ravines and slashing of brush and trees. And then we charged through the brigade of white troops which had been badly repulsed and went even beyond the point they had reached." Added Lieutenant Scroggs, "Within one hundred yards of the works the men instinctively halted as if to take breath and that moment saved the remnant of the battalion. The utter hopelessness of succeeding pervaded the mind of every one when they had time to think. . . . I saw the companies one by one commencing on the left rise to their feet, run a few yards, and then as if recollecting themselves, *walk* deliberately from the field." Said Lieutenant Grabill, "We fell back sullenly—we were too exhausted and too proud to run!" Lieutenant Scroggs would never forget the sight of one "Sergeant who had received three different wounds crying because the battalion would not go farther." Foster's white division suffered 35 percent casualties in this failed attempt, while the support effort added another hundred lost to the roster of those from the 5th USCT who had fallen on New Market Heights.[25]

The question of why Brigadier General Paine chose one of his most battered regiments to support Foster when he had three relatively fresh ones on hand has never been answered. His postwar military memoir notes only that a "detachment" of his division "was again engaged the same day." However, a letter he wrote to his father on October 3 suggests that simple inexperience in handling so many men may have been a key factor in his actions: "I had all my divn. but one regt., it was collected the last night & is the first time I have ever seen so much of it together," he admitted. In the same letter he mused, "I don't know whether we sh'd have got Rich'd if we had not been stopped to help the 18th [Corps.]."[26]

The failure of Foster's assault on Fort Gilmer did not prevent the eastern attack from taking place. Under increasing pressure from General Butler to make things happen, Birney, who had moved methodically all morning, suddenly began pressing his subordinates for quick results. It was his older brother, Brigadier General William Birney, who was now expected to deliver. Of the five regiments in his brigade, two were tied down performing rear-echelon duties, which left three available. The 7th USCT was a Maryland unit that had participated in small-scale actions in Florida and South Carolina and been part of the Union expedition to Deep Bottom in August; the 8th USCT had been baptized in battle at Olustee and also taken part in the August Deep Bottom operation; and the 9th USCT, another Maryland regiment, had seen service in South Carolina and at Petersburg.

Like his younger sibling, William Birney was unable to wield his command as a whole and instead committed it piecemeal. His three regiments advanced along Mill Road, debouching from the woods that lined the Varina Road. The first to move was the 9th USCT, commanded by Captain Edwin S. Babcock. According to Babcock's report, "Four . . . companies . . . were deployed forward as skirmishers, . . . the remainder advanced in line of battle. The charge was begun . . . and the regiment was immediately subjected to a very severe artillery fire, enfilading the line on both flanks." Babcock ordered his troops to go to ground while he sought additional instructions; told to renew the attack, he was headed forward when he met his men going the other way. They had already tried to advance again but had been hit with such a storm of grape and canister that they had retreated without orders. Their walk in the sun had cost them seven dead, seventy-nine wounded, and eighteen missing.[27]

Hardly had Babcock's men been repulsed when William Birney sent in the 8th USCT on their left. A small Rebel redoubt known as Fort Gregg was the objective assigned to the 8th's commander. "Gen. Birney . . . ordered me to send four companies, deployed as skirmishers to capture the work," Colonel George E. Wagner remembered. The captain leading this thin line got close to Fort Gregg and then, seeing that he was outnumbered by its defenders, requested further instructions. The courier met Colonel Wagner coming up with four more companies under a direct order from Brigadier General Birney. Wagner estimated that the "enemy had at least ten men behind the works to my one"; he reported this to Birney and waited for a response. "Orders came to remain where I was, to keep up the fire to keep the gunners down, which I did; in fact I could do nothing else," Wagner declared. Of his two hundred men in action this day, he later counted twelve killed and sixty-one wounded.[28]

The third and most tragic scene of this final act of the day's fighting was now played out. The 7th USCT, under Colonel James Shaw, Jr., had formed into line along the Varina Road even as the 8th USCT was ending its mission against Fort Gregg. Shaw was preparing his entire regiment to advance the fifteen hundred yards to Fort Gilmer (over much the same ground already covered by the 9th USCT) when an aide arrived with new instructions from Brigadier General Birney. To his dying day, Colonel Shaw would swear that the orders he now received directed him to reduce his attacking force to just four companies in skirmishing order; for his part, William Birney was equally adamant that the intent of his order was for Shaw to deploy the four skirmishing companies *ahead* of the rest of the regiment. The often vituperative postwar exchange of charges between the two would completely obscure the fact that it would not have mattered whether four, eight, or ten companies were engaged: one regiment, attacking alone, had no chance against Fort Gilmer.

Shaw, according to his recollection, told the aide that as he understood it, his orders had been to attack with his entire regiment. To this the staff officer replied, "Well, *now* the General directs you to send four companies, deployed as skirmishers, to take the work." Shaw called for the senior officer present, Captain Julius A. Weiss, and explained what had to be done. Weiss's response, recorded Shaw, was "What! Take a fort with a skirmish line?" After a moment's cold reflection, he added, "I will try, but it can't be done."[29]

Captain Weiss now led forward Companies C, D, G, and K. "As the party advanced," he recalled, "the enemy's shell and shrapnel were exchanged for grape and canister, followed soon by a lively rattle of musketry." Weiss began his charge with nine officers and about 189 enlisted men; by they time they had covered eleven hundred yards, maybe seventy-seven lay sprawled and bleeding in the Virginia dirt. Still, the rest pressed on. "In a few minutes the ditch of the fort was reached," Weiss remembered. "Some 120 men and officers precipitated themselves into it, many losing their lives at its very edge." According to Lieutenant Robert M. Spinney of that group, "Upon looking about us after getting into the ditch we found there was but one face where the enemy could not touch us, so all the survivors rallied at that face."[30]

"After a short breathing spell," continued Captain Weiss, "men were helped up the exterior slope of the parapet on the shoulders of others, and fifty or sixty being thus disposed an attempt was made to storm the fort. At the signal nearly all rose, but the enemy, lying securely sheltered behind the interior slope, the muzzles of their guns almost touching the storming party, received the latter with a crushing fire, sending many into the ditch below shot through the brain or breast." Incredibly, a second effort was made, followed by a third, but every time a head appeared over the top of the wall, there was a Confederate rifleman ready to blast it down again. Within minutes, nearly half of those who had reached the moat "were writhing in the ditch or resting forever."[31]

Weiss himself was wounded in the first effort. His men, besides being exposed to enemy snipers, also had to weather a lethal torrent of improvised grenades as the defenders lit the fuses of small artillery shells and rolled them into their midst. The USCT soldiers were very much on their own at this point, cut off from direct support and without any hope of relief. The officers agreed that enough was enough, and Lieutenant Spinney raised a white handkerchief on the point of his sword to surrender. Suspicious, the Confederates called for him to come up alone, which he did. They remained skeptical when he explained his mission; only when he stood alone and exposed on top of the wall, beckoning the others to follow, were they finally convinced. The survivors were rushed to the rear. The white officers had hats, watches, and other valuables taken from them, while the blacks were abused, roughed up, and in some cases killed. For the white officers, the future held varying terms in prisoner-of-war camps; for the blacks, there would be labor details for some, a return to slavery for others, and for all, a desperate fight for survival. Almost two thirds of the USCT men taken prisoner this day would die while in C.S. captivity.

As he was helped up the slope and stood for a moment on top of the wall, Captain Weiss looked at the dead black bodies filling the ditch. As he later stated, "It was a time for manly tears." The four companies he had led forward were virtually wiped out. Casualties for the 7th USCT this day were reported as 20 dead, 80 wounded, and 136 missing, but those figures were based on bodies recovered; another officer, taken with Weiss, would put the total of those killed, mortally wounded, or fated to die in prison at 106. It was a terrible waste of life, spent in an attack that never had a chance.[32]

The doomed assault by the four companies of the 7th USCT ended the significant fighting for September 29. General Robert E. Lee counterattacked the next day, but his efforts were repulsed, with the black troops' playing a small role in the action. The Army of the James was now firmly ensconced behind fortified lines, on Richmond's doorstep.

Major General Butler eventually had a special medal created for about two hundred of the black troops who took part in the New Market Heights action. As he described it in his massive postwar autobiography,

> The obverse of the medal shows a bastion fort charged upon by negro soldiers and bears the inscription, "Ferro iis libertas perveniet" ["Freedom will be theirs by the sword"]. The reverse bears the words, "Campaign before Richmond," encircling the words, "Distinguished for Courage," while there was plainly engraved upon the rim, before its presentation, the name of the soldier, his company and his regiment. The medal was suspended by a ribbon of red, white, and blue, attached to the clothing by a strong pin, having in front an oak-leaf with the inscription in plain letters, "Army of the James."

"Since the war," he added in 1892, "I have been fully rewarded by seeing the beaming eye of many a colored comrade as he drew his medal from the innermost recesses of its concealment to show me." Efforts undertaken in the twentieth century to have the Butler Medal officially recognized by the Department of Defense have been unsuccessful. According to a 1981 White House letter, "The Department takes the position that large numbers of unofficial medals were privately issued to members of the Armed Forces of the United States between 1861 and 1865. The Butler Medal was but one of many in this category."[33]

Engagement near the Boydton Plank Road, Virginia, October 27, 1864

The next major initiative involving black troops on the Richmond-Petersburg front was a simultaneous movement by the Army of the James and the Army of the Potomac, intended to turn both flanks of the attenuated Confederate defensive line, that stretched from east of the Rebel capital to southwest of Petersburg. The maneuver planned for the Army of the Potomac was as complicated as any it had attempted. The Confederate lines covered the southern side of the city, then hinged to the southwest, protecting the vital Boydton Plank Road as far as the stream known as Hatcher's Run. The plan as conceived by Major General Meade called for the Ninth Corps to strike the Rebel lines near the hinge, to probe the strength of the position and, if possible, break through. The Fifth Corps moved on the left of the Ninth, ready either to assist if a breach was made or to support the Second Corps, which had to make a long march to get around the enemy flank at Hatcher's Run. At the same time, the cavalry was to swing south and west to cut the lower reaches of the Boydton Plank Road.

The Ninth remained the only corps in the Army of the Potomac that contained any black units. With Burnside long gone, Major General John G. Parke now commanded. Brigadier General Edward Ferrero still led the Third Division, which consisted of a First Brigade under Colonel Delevan Bates and a Second commanded in this action by Colonel Charles S. Russell. The part played by these units was described in an after-action report provided by Brigadier General Ferrero and in a letter written right afterward by Sergeant John C. Brock of the 43rd USCT (Bates's brigade).

Ferrero: My command broke camp on the morning of the 27th [of October] . . . at 3 a.m. and marched, in rear of the First Division of this corps, at 3:30 a.m.[34]

Brock: On last Tuesday [October 25] we were ordered to take six days' rations. . . . Every one thought that a move would be made immediately. . . . All day Wednesday [October 26] the camp was as quiet as usual. . . . On Wednesday evening we went to bed as usual. At two o'clock on Thursday morning a single horseman rode into camp, with a despatch to our commander. Every man was ordered to strike his tent and get ready to march immediately. Soon afterwards long columns of troops commenced to march out past our camp.—In about ten minutes every man was ready to march. But the order to move had not yet arrived, [so] we lay there till broad daylight, before we moved. Meanwhile the 2nd and 5th Corps continued to pass us in one continuous column. Many a man lay there with an anxious heart.

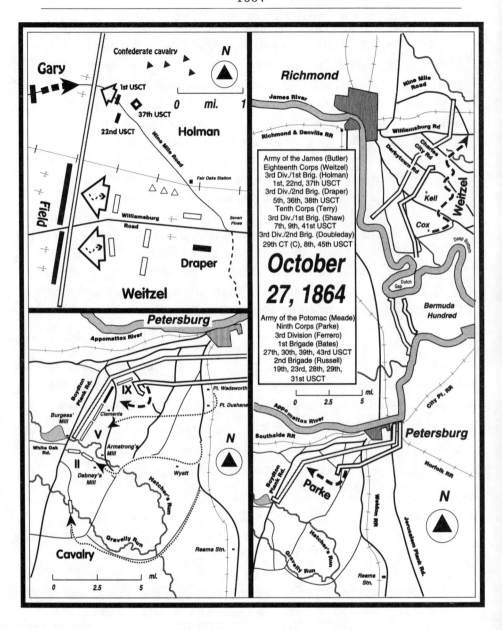

They shook hands with each other, bidding each other farewell, in case they should not meet again. One corporal from the State of Maine handed me a letter, together with his money and watch. "Write to my wife," said he, "in case that anything should happen me." —He was only one out of the many that told me the same thing.[35]

Ferrero: Nothing unusual occurred until we arrived at a point opposite the Clements house, where my command took position on the right of General Wilcox's division—the First Brigade, under command of Colonel Bates, on the left, and the Second Brigade, under command of Colonel Russell, connecting with the Second Division, commanded by General R. B. Potter, at a point near the Hawks house.

Brock: The whole division was soon in motion. . . . We proceeded along slowly and cautiously about a mile before we met any sign of the enemy. "The Johnnies are all gone," says a new recruit. "You will hear from them soon enough," replied an older and wiser soldier. "Hark! what was that," cried one, as the report of musketry was heard in the distance. His companion told him our skirmishers were chasing in the enemy's pickets.

Ferrero: The division was advanced in line of battle through a thick woods covered by a heavy undergrowth until they came within 100 yards of the enemy's line of works, where they were obliged to halt from the obstructions of fallen timber and abatis, which prevented our farther successful advance. Finding it impossible to overcome these impediments, I . . . received orders to fortify my line and make such preparations as to hold this position.

Brock: Our brigade advanced in gallant style, driving the rebels before them all day. Towards night the enemy fell back to his works, where he was found to be strongly fortified. Our boys built breastworks along their line while our skirmishers were busily engaged in watching the enemy.

Ferrero: . . . My division held said line until the morning of the 28th, when, upon the receipt of orders, we fell back to our present camp.

Brock: On Thursday night [October 27] it commenced to rain, and the boys had to take it rough and ready, without tents all night, next morning many of them were dripping wet. Soon after dark, on Thursday night, the rebels attempted to surprise us, but we were not to be caught napping. They found the boys ready and waiting to welcome them with hospitable hands to bloody graves.

On Friday morning [October 28] every one thought that the order of the day would be an attempt to make still further advances, but contrary to every one's expectations we were ordered to fall back. The Second Corps fell back from their position early in the morning, we following soon afterwards.

Now we are in our old camp, where we started from. What good we accomplished we have yet to learn. The loss in our brigade was not very heavy. In our regiment (the 43rd) we had one officer and several men killed, and some 12 or 14 wounded. Fortunate it was that we lost no more, as our regiment was out flanked several times. The most of the men that were lost belonged to Company B—as they were first thrown out as skirmishers, and consequently were most exposed to the enemy's fire.

Ferrero: I have to state that both officers and men of this command behaved with great coolness in carrying out my orders explicitly, and are deserving of great praise for their conduct in this action.

Brock: Of our behavior in this battle, it is spoken of as being very good. . . . The colored soldiers of the 9th Corps, together with their heroic companions of the 18th Corps, have well established the reputation of our soldierly abilities.

In this operation, known both as "Boydton Plank Road" and as "Hatcher's Run," Ferrero's division lost seven killed, sixty-seven wounded, and six missing. The greatest losses were in Sergeant Brock's regiment, which suffered all the killed, nineteen of the wounded, and four of the missing. The operation itself was barren of results.

Engagement near Fair Oaks, Virginia, October 27, 1864

North of the James, the evening of Wednesday, October 26, was filled with anticipation. Reporter Thomas Morris Chester, the only black correspondent covering the war for a white newspaper, recorded that this "night was a lively one, particularly among the colored troops under Col. Holman. The early part was spent in singing, with animating effect, the 'John Brown' song, 'Rally Round the Flag,' the 'Colored Volunteer,' and others of similar import. Never was an army in better spirits, or more confident of a victory."[36]

The plan for the Army of the James was as follows: the Tenth Corps was to press the Rebel lines between the New Market and Darbytown roads while the Eighteenth Corps marched behind to the Williamsburg Road, where it was expected to flank the entire Confederate line. Command of the all-important mobile force was given to Brevet Major General Godfrey Weitzel, who had taken over the Eighteenth Corps for Major General Ord, wounded at Fort Harrison.

Black troops marched with both the Tenth and Eighteenth corps. The two brigades in the Tenth (Colonel Shaw's, consisting of the 7th, 9th, 41st, and 127th USCT; and Colonel Ulysses Doubleday's, the 29th Connecticut (Colored) and 8th and 45th USCT) advanced on the enemy lines near the Kell House, south of the Darbytown Road. Ostensibly, their mission was merely to attract attention away from the movements of the Eighteenth Corps, but in any combat situation, even the most limited action had its perils.

In the diversions undertaken on October 27 and 28 by Shaw's and Doubleday's men, the heaviest burdens fell on the 29th Connecticut (Colored), which lost eleven dead and sixty-nine wounded, and the 7th USCT, which lost one killed and thirty-one wounded, mostly in skirmishing on October 28. Sergeant Alexander H. Newton of the 29th recounted his regiment's actions in the *Anglo-African*:

At 4½ o'clock on the morning of the 27th, the order was, "Fall in! fall in!" along the entire line. Soon the boys were in, and off for the march in light marching order. . . .

We made our way toward the New Market Road, crossed it, shaped our course for the Charles City Road, and halted . . . near the Darbytown Road. We then formed in line of battle, and marched toward White Oak Swamp, where the 29th deployed as advanced skirmishers, the 45th and 8th as supports, the 7th and 9th as reserves, and the rest of the corps toward the right. They did not go far before they met the enemy, and soon drove in their videttes, pursued their pickets, and after a severe fight, succeeded in driving them from their first line of works. They fled to the second line of works, and such tumbling, jumping, and rolling over works I had never seen before. They exclaimed: "The smoked Yanks are after us!" and there we held them for twenty-four hours. . . .

At night we lay under a most terrific storm of rain, shot, shell, grape, and canister, but that only made the boys more eager for the fight, . . . but . . . their orders were only to keep them inside of their works. . . .

About 7 o'clock [A.M., October 28,] we were relieved by the 7th U.S. Colored Troops. About 4 o'clock in the afternoon, the General, having accomplished all that he wanted, ordered us to fall back, and highly complimented the 29th for gallant and brave conduct on the field. We captured a few prisoners, and killed and wounded many.[37]

Weitzel's column meanwhile followed a twisting route over difficult ground. "It was a very hard trip," wrote Lieutenant Grabill of the 5th USCT, "requiring great powers of endurance for the hard marching." "Our progress was slow until about 9:00 A.M. when our pace was suddenly accelerated to the double-quick which was kept up for some time," added Lieutenant Scroggs of the same regiment.[38]

Although there was nothing halfhearted about Major General Butler's objectives for this operation ("If we should have the good fortune to turn the . . . line . . . an attempt may be made to . . . enter Richmond," read his orders), the goals seem to have been less obvious to Major General Weitzel, upon whose resolve everything depended. Weitzel marched beset with anxieties: he suspected that the Tenth Corps and the cavalry were not doing their fair share, he worried about being so distant from the Federal entrenchments, and he feared being cut off. By the time the head of his column finally reached the Williamsburg Road, near the site of the 1862 Battle of Fair Oaks, at about 1:00 P.M. (several hours behind schedule), caution dominated Weitzel's thinking. Ironically, in spite of his slow passage, he had still managed to reach the practical end limit of the Confederate entrenchments ahead of the enemy. But though only a handful of cavalry stood behind the earthworks stretched across the Williamsburg Road, Weitzel hesitated.

He deployed his white troops forward to determine the enemy's strength while he personally scouted the position. Placing one of the two black brigades with him in reserve (Colonel Alonzo Draper's, made up of the 5th, 36th, and 38th USCT), he then instructed Colonel John Holman, commanding the other brigade (consisting of the 1st, 22nd, and 37th USCT), to push north along the Nine Mile

Road "until he should come within sight of the enemy's line, and then to halt and report to corps headquarters."[39]

Holman's brigade had an eventful march. The column had moved no more than a mile when Rebel cavalry was observed and line of battle formed, with the 1st and 22nd USCT south of the road and the 37th north of it. The advance was continued, but when Colonel Holman spotted what he thought was a large body of Rebel cavalry closing on him, he ordered the 37th into a square—a formation better known on the field of Waterloo. It was probably during this movement that Chaplain Henry W. Turner of the 1st USCT stumbled across some Confederate pickets and had what he later described as a "narrow, but merciful escape."[40]

Realizing that the enemy's earthworks across the Nine Mile Road were only lightly manned, Holman now ordered a charge. The 1st USCT went in with a yell to take the position, while on its left, the 22nd, tangled up in underbrush and raked by flank fire, "commenced fleeing to the rear." Colonel Holman was hit, as was the commander of the 22nd, Colonel Joseph B. Kiddoo, who "fell dangerously wounded." The 22nd's failure would later be attributed to two factors: misunderstanding regarding the order to charge and the number of untrained recruits in the regiment's ranks. "They kept firing their muskets while advancing, and in the midst of the excitement broke and ran, causing the worst of confusion," reported an officer. Nevertheless, some of the men of the 22nd did perform well, including Sergeant John Loveday, "who though severely wounded through the leg urged the men on and even dragged himself forward in his zeal to take the rebel position," and Corporal Nathan Stanton, "who carried the colors though shot through the hand [and] would not leave the field . . . until the regiment retreated." The advance of the 1st USCT proceeded through "a severe fire of musketry, grape and canister," which gave the impression that, as Chaplain Turner put it, a "devastating hand had swept among their ranks." The black soldiers briefly held two enemy cannon; though they were unable to haul them away before being forced to withdraw by a Rebel counterattack, they did spike the guns.[41]

Lieutenant Colonel Abial G. Chamberlain led Holman's brigade back to the Williamsburg Road, where at 3:00 P.M. Weitzel had finally launched a tentative push at the enemy lines, only to see it decisively repulsed by just-arrived Confederate reinforcements. Draper's brigade remained in reserve throughout this action. After holding his position until dark, Weitzel ordered a retreat. Lieutenant Grabill summed up the results of the operation when he declared, "The move was a grand fizzle."[42]

Sergeant William H. Thomas of the 5th USCT would never forget the hard marching that miserable October night: "Rain had fallen during the day and the road was flooded with water; this together with the darkness, rendered it almost impossible to get along. And, as the column wound slowly down the road, doubtless, we presented quite a forlorn appearance; as one after another, missing their footing would fall full length in the mud, and then call piteously for a comrade to lend a helping hand, but we bore it patiently."[43]

The heaviest losses among the black troops were concentrated in the 1st and 22nd USCT. The 1st lost twelve killed, ninety-six wounded, and sixteen missing, while the 22nd paid for its inexperience with five dead and forty-five wounded.

The October 27 action marked the last operation undertaken by USCT units as part of an integrated corps. In November, U. S. Grant decided to consolidate all of his black units into the Army of the James, and furthermore entirely to segregate them. The transfer of the Ninth Corps USCT regiments to Butler was followed, on December 3, by the creation of an all-black Twenty-fifth Corps, Army of the James. (Most of the white troops in the Army of the James were meanwhile put into another new organization, the Twenty-fourth Corps.) It was common practice at that time for each corps to be identified by a special insignia; the badge adopted by the Twenty-fifth Corps depicted a diamond within a square.

The correspondent Thomas Morris Chester, whose special beat was with the black troops, reported on some of the immediate effects of this organizational change in a dispatch dated December 6:

> The most remarkable fact about this organization is that the rebels seemed to know just when it went into effect. Day before yesterday the necessary movements towards carrying out the project began, and early yesterday morning the enemy's pickets wanted to know when the "smoked Yankees" were to confront them. It was generally sup-

posed that the Johnnies might be disposed to fire upon these "smoked Yankees," but it is now understood that they will be sufficiently agreeable to bear their presence. This determination was no doubt quickened by the reflection that our colored troops are similarly supplied with weapons, and because the enemy has never known them to hesitate to meet him on any terms which he might feel disposed to offer.[44]

Interlude

"A Practice Justified by No Rule of War"

———◦———

IT was not unusual for either side to interrogate deserters in an effort to glean useful intelligence. When, on the morning of October 12, 1864, Major General Benjamin F. Butler heard that several Rebel deserters were saying that black Union POWs were being used to construct enemy fortifications, he immediately sent a staff officer to get confirmation. The aide reported that three of the men had seen a large number of "colored soldiers, clad in the uniform of the United States," digging trenches, while a fourth had helped escort more than eighty USCT prisoners from Libby Prison to the front, "where they were put to work throwing up intrenchments." With memories of the New Market Heights battlefield fresh in his mind, Butler found this notion intolerable.[1]

Ironically, Butler's own military successes had exacerbated the problem. His Army of the James now occupied stretches of the trench lines that had formerly been part of Richmond's outer defensive ring, and the Confederates were obliged to construct new works to cover the gaps. Even with all available slave labor gangs put to the task, there was not enough manpower to do the job. Robert E. Lee said he needed a thousand additional men, a figure that his engineers upped to almost sixteen hundred. Under official Confederate policy, a slave captured in Union uniform was to be considered a runaway, and either returned to his master or put to work if the owner could not be

310

located. Following these guidelines, Richmond authorities took custody of sixty-eight blacks who had been captured at the crater and added them to the force of slave laborers, along with eighty-two more men from the 5th, 7th, and 30th USCT. But while the C.S. policy offered a legal—or legalistic—justification for using ex-slaves, it provided no sanction for attaching freemen to the fatigue parties. The 5th USCT, for example, had been recruited largely among the free blacks of Ohio and thus contained relatively few ex-slaves; but the men were black, and that was good enough for the provost marshal.

As the U.S. agent for prisoner exchange, General Butler regularly corresponded with Southern officials. The very day he learned that black POWs were working on Richmond's fortifications, Butler fired off a note protesting what he termed "a practice justified by no rule of war" and demanding that it be immediately halted. If he did not receive a prompt, positive response, he vowed, he would put an equal number of Confederate prisoners to work at Dutch Gap "until this practice is stopped." Butler took care to copy U. S. Grant, who quickly approved his "retaliatory measures."[2]

When no Confederate reply was forthcoming, Butler had a squad of captured Rebel soldiers sent to help dig the Dutch Gap canal, which was under long-range fire from Confederate artillery. To further emphasize his point, he assigned men from the 127th USCT to guard the prisoners. "The rebs have too much good sense to provoke in the least their colored custodians," reported Thomas Morris Chester in the *Philadelphia Press*. "It was a curious sight to see the proud sons of the F.F.V.s [i.e., "First Families of Virginia"], who had been accustomed to command negroes wherever they met them, humbly acknowledging the authority of the blackest of the race."[3]

Confederate politicians in Richmond refused to negotiate. Even as General Lee reluctantly ordered the guns trained on Dutch Gap to maintain their harassing fire, directives from the Davis administration promised to escalate the cycle of retaliation should any of the Rebel prisoners be killed. Lee was authorized to communicate directly with U. S. Grant on this matter, which he did on October 19. After repeating the official position of the Confederate government, Lee added that it was not his policy to use such prisoners in labor gangs, further asserting that the "negroes employed upon our fortifications are not allowed to be placed where they will be exposed to [artillery] fire." Those of the captured blacks who were not ex-slaves, Lee had "ordered . . . to be sent into the interior."[4]

Grant, anxious to defuse a very tricky situation, decided that Lee's assurances eliminated the need for any continued retaliation. On October 20, he instructed Butler to move the Rebel laborers from Dutch Gap and immediately to ship them to Northern prison camps. The deep and complex issues that had been raised by the Confederate action and the Union response were definitively swept back under the carpet when Richmond also backed off its threats. Nevertheless, reporter Chester chose to see the standoff as a victory, writing, "General Butler's retaliatory measures, in placing rebel prisoners to work upon the canal, . . . at Dutch Gap, as an offset to the rebels forcing our colored soldiers to work on their fortifications, have had the desired effect."[5]

Chapter Eleven

"Into the Very Mouth of Death"

————◦————

MAJOR General William T. Sherman's March to the Sea began on November 16, 1864, when he led his carefully selected legions east out of Atlanta. An Indiana private named Theodore Upson trudged along the dusty Georgia roads in one of Sherman's long columns. Hardly a day into the march, Upson's regiment came across brutal reminders of the South's "peculiar institution." "We saw a place to day where they used to send the infractory slaves to be punished," the private wrote in his journal. "There were stocks, iron collars with chains on them, several kinds of whips, and a paddle thing with a lot of holes in it. I think that the Darkeys did get whipped all right sometimes."[1]

Sherman had no black troops with him on his march, yet the destructive course undertaken by his men would create conditions that would bring African American soldiers into combat. On November 11, even as he was finishing business in Atlanta, Sherman was finding ways to use the troops posted along the Atlantic seaboard. From Kingston, Georgia, Sherman wired Army Chief of Staff Major General Henry Halleck in Washington, explaining that he "would like to have General Foster to break the Savannah and Charleston road about Pocotaligo about December 1."[2]

Two days later, Halleck wrote to Major General John G. Foster, commanding the Department of the South, to tell him that Sherman

313

expected to reach the coast by the "early part of December, and wishes you, if possible, to cut the Charleston and Savannah Railroad near Pocotaligo about that time." Halleck's letter reached Foster on November 22, but even before it arrived, he had anticipated its contents by asking his most experienced field commander what would be the best route to take in order to cut the railroad. On November 20, with Halleck's request still in transit, Brigadier General John P. Hatch responded to Foster's query by recommending a movement up the Broad River. Hatch also made a passing comment that then seemed of little importance: "I do not know anything about the nature of the country there," he said, "but suppose it as good for operations as any in this section of the country."[3]

Battle of Honey Hill, South Carolina, November 30, 1864

It was a Thanksgiving dinner that Frances Beecher would never forget. The wife of the colonel commanding the 35th USCT was no stranger to the scarce amenities of an isolated post—after all, her wedding had taken place here in occupied Jacksonville in July, and since then she had remained with her husband and his men. The 35th had been one of six infantry regiments garrisoning what was called the District of Florida. The others, most of which had taken part in Gillmore's ill-fated Olustee expedition, had by November been returned to South Carolina or transferred to Virginia.

Mrs. Beecher came from a Connecticut family, so she saw to it that Thanksgiving was celebrated "in New England fashion, feasting on wild turkey shot by one of our men." Like virtually everything else she had experienced in Florida, this Thanksgiving offered up generous helpings of the exotic. "It was the largest and handsomest bird I ever saw," she remembered, "the opalescent plumage being entirely different from that of the tame turkey."[4]

Even as Colonel Beecher and his wife were enjoying their repast, orders were on their way that would dramatically affect their lives. Under the heading "Jacksonville, Fla., November 25, 1864," the directive instructed Beecher to "embark on board the [steamer] *Delaware* to-morrow morning at 3 o'clock, with your regiment rationed and equipped." A small flotilla was already gathering to transport the 35th and 34th USCT, along with a detachment of cavalry and artillery. All these units, under Beecher's overall command, were going to Hilton Head, where the Colonel was to report to Major General Foster for further orders.[5]

Four days earlier, Brigadier General Hatch had learned that he was to take charge of the expeditionary force, bringing with him from Morris Island three of his "best and strongest regiments" and "all the mounted force" he could manage. Hatch's command would constitute a "small division, composed of two brigades, as follows: First Brigade, regiments from Morris Island; Second Brigade, under [Brigadier] General [Edward E.] Potter, composed of parts of nine regiments, from [Hilton Head] . . . , Beaufort, and Florida." In his November 23 reply, Hatch indicated that he had selected the 56th New York and 54th and 55th Massachusetts (Colored) regiments from his command.[6]

John Porter Hatch was a West Point graduate and twice-brevetted veteran of the Mexican war whose Civil War service had yet to reveal any real talent for combat. His failure to move his mounted brigade quickly enough to stop a Rebel railroad raid during the Second Bull Run Campaign in 1862 had cost him his cavalry appointment; shifted to lead an infantry brigade, he had taken it into battle at South Mountain, where he was wounded on September 14, 1862. When he was again ready for active service, he was assigned to a variety of administrative tasks, then moved into the Department of the South to oversee the static warfare on Morris and Folly islands.

Neither of the other two generals commanding in the Department of the South had much more to recommend them. Brigadier General Rufus Saxon's constant efforts on behalf of the black population around Hilton Head had not enhanced his military stature, while the Florida commander, Brigadier General Eliakim P. Scammon, had only just returned from a Confederate POW camp. Major General Foster was himself suffering from an injury received in an accident and remained unfit for an extended field operation, so Hatch was simply the best man available at the time.

When Rear Admiral John A. Dahlgren, commanding the South Atlantic Blockading Squadron, learned of Foster's plans, he resolved that the navy should take part. On November 24, he directed Commander George H. Preble to go to Bay Point and organize a naval battalion made up of Marines, volunteer seamen, and two batteries of howitzers. After four days of drills, Dahlgren's detachment (styled a "Naval Brigade") reported to General Foster.

The troops posted at Hilton Head clambered aboard transports all day long on November 28. The 55th Regiment Massachusetts Infantry (Colored), sailing on the *Mary Boardman,* reached Hilton Head at 2:00 A.M., when the ship was ordered to take on coal at Parris Island. The regimental surgeon, Burt G. Wilder, hoped there would be some action because, as he noted in his diary, the men were "much crowded here." "Orders were issued that the fleet start before daylight on the 29th at a signal light," wrote Captain Luis F. Emilio of the 54th Regiment Massachusetts Infantry (Colored), "but just as anchors were hauled up, a heavy fog came drifting in, preventing much progress." A *New York Times* reporter present noted that this fog was so dense "as [to] almost instantly . . . render it utterly impossible to see shore points, by which alone could the pilots hope to steer clear of the innumerable bars and shoals which beset the route at almost every rod."[7]

The ships under navy control held back until 4:00 A.M., at which time Rear Admiral Dahlgren decided that the heavy mist had lifted enough to "make the attempt." Some of the army vessels, gamely following orders, set off at the signal despite the poor visibility. These ships moved slowly, "sounding carefully all the way," recalled an officer of the 55th Massachusetts (Colored). The fog sowed a harvest of confusion among the army boats, some of which got lost, and others of which ran around. Another portion of the army's flotilla waited until daylight, among them Brigadier General Hatch's headquarters ship.[8]

The canny sailors, though among the last to leave the anchorage, were the first to arrive at the designated landing area, known as Boyd's Neck. "But not a sign of the [army] troops was visible," Dahlgren later reported, "and I began to fear some mistake had been made, when a transport was seen coming up with General Hatch's flag (blue broad pennant)." The time was a little past 8:00 A.M. "In less than half an hour the two batteries of the navy howitzers, with the nine companies of sailors and marines, were landed, formed and advanced under Commander Preble in skirmishing order, guns and men," said Dahlgren.[9]

Two companies of the 54th Massachusetts (Colored) sailed with Brigadier General Hatch. According to Captain Emilio, "The Fifty-

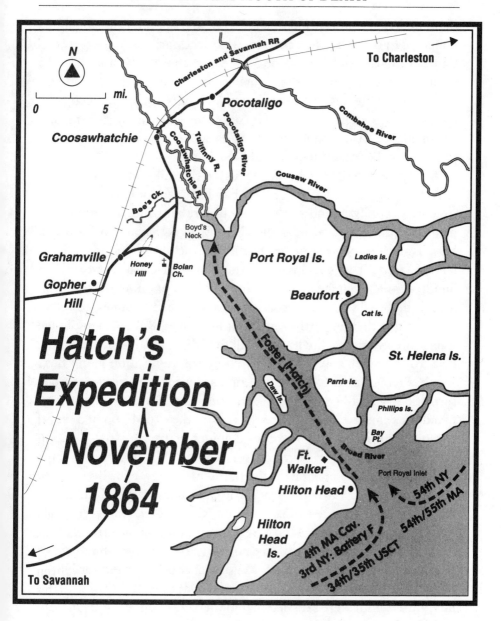

fourth men . . . sprang ashore eagerly, and were the first troops to land. A skirmish line was formed, and advanced without opposition, though several of the enemy's cavalrymen were seen along the edge of the stream. Moving about half a mile, the companies were then halted and disposed to watch the enemy and resist attack." Most of the remainder of the flotilla now began arriving and disgorging its human cargo. "The debarkation was necessarily slow," recorded Captain Charles C. Soule of the 55th Massachusetts (Colored). "The engineers had not arrived with materials to make proper landings. . . . Troops were taken ashore in small boats to scramble up the muddy banks of the marsh. Horses were thrown overboard and swam ashore. A dilapidated plantation wharf was utilized as far as possible by the vessels which could reach it."[10]

Already any hope for a quick thrust to the railroad had been scattered like the fleet by the fog. Foster had intended for his raiding force to march rapidly inland to the town of Grahamville, an antebellum planters' resort located near the Charleston & Savannah Railroad, but it was afternoon before any significant movement began from the landing zone. It was Dahlgren's little Naval Brigade (less than five hundred men) that headed out first. The sailors and Marines followed the Boyd's Landing Road west for about two miles, to its intersection with the north-south-running River Road;* a mounted Rebel force skirmished with them all the while, at River Road falling back to the north toward a prepared defensive position along Bee's Creek. Preble's men followed the riders, setting a pattern of wrong turns that would bedevil the Federals all day. Despite its field commander's admitted ignorance of the region, the expedition had set off without a sufficient number of local guides or even reasonably accurate maps. This poor planning was to cost Hatch's men a day's march, and would precipitate the Battle of Honey Hill. By tracking the Rebels northward, the Naval Brigade missed the Grahamville Road, a short distance to the south on River Road. Dahlgren's men were soon joined by the 32nd USCT, compounding the error.

After a morning and early afternoon of slow buildup, things at last began to happen at the landing. Major General Foster left for Hilton Head at 4:00 P.M., with Rear Admiral Dahlgren following a few hours later; both were satisfied that matters were under control. General Hatch ordered General Potter to move out with as much of his brigade as was on hand, and Potter's men headed along the Boyd's Landing Road toward the River Road at around 4:00 P.M. Hatch was

---

*I use the name Boyd's Landing Road for purposes of convenience only; no such name appears on any period maps. Some maps of the time do, however, designate the north-south artery as the "River Road."

"determined to push forward immediately and attempt to seize the railroad at Grahamville, without waiting the landing of the artillery and the remainder of the infantry." Potter's subsequent odyssey was described by Captain Soule:

General Potter . . . turned to the right after the Naval Brigade and came up with them just as they were halting for supper. Here it was discovered that they were on the wrong road and the column retraced its steps to the first cross road, where the Naval Brigade, thoroughly worn out with the labor of dragging their eight howitzers by hand over the sandy roads, were left for the night, while Generals Hatch and Potter, with the other troops, took the road to the left, on which the advance should have been made at the outset. But bad luck persistently followed the enterprise, for on reaching Bolan's Church,

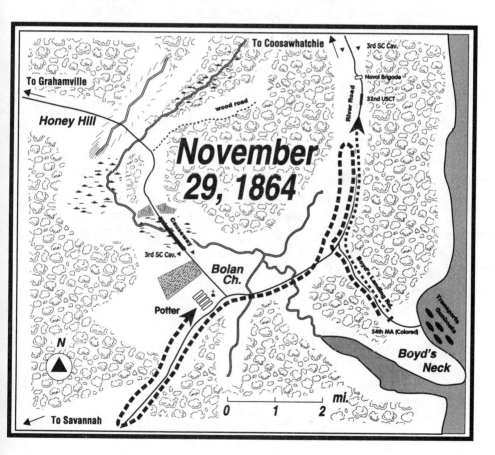

where the Grahamville road turns to the right, and, encountering there the enemy's pickets, the guide persisted in following the direct road toward . . . Savannah. After proceeding on this road four miles without opposition, the guide and the generals became convinced that they had gone astray and countermarched to the church, which they reached at 2 A.M. [November 30], so weary with the night march of fifteen miles that the troops gladly went into bivouac.[11]

November 29 had truly been a day of lost opportunities. When the Federals landed, only a handful of the enemy cavalry opposed them; according to a Rebel artilleryman, "The Charleston & Savannah Railroad was defended by the system of having, at each point likely to be attacked, a small force of artillery, cavalry, and infantry, and trusting to the railroad to rush enough of them together to defend any one point." The area now under direct threat was the responsibility of Colonel Charles J. Colcock, headquartered in Grahamville. In addition to about 250 cavalrymen, he had approximately 175 artillerymen spread along the railroad at strategic locations. Because Colcock was away from headquarters when the first warning messages arrived, and his second-in-command was in Charleston, it fell to Major John Jenkins to spread the alarm. Telegrams requesting immediate assistance were sent off to Charleston and Savannah, and reinforcements were started from those places almost as soon as the messages were received, but everything took time. A picket force of perhaps seventy-five men and a few pieces of artillery were all that stood between Potter's men and the railroad on November 29. Had the slowing fog not been followed by two critical wrong turns that added delay and exhaustion, Foster's raid would have been a success. There was also, however, little sense of real urgency on Hatch's part—a failing for which his men would pay a high price.[12]

Reveille sounded at 5:00 A.M. on November 30 in the camps of the 54th and 55th Massachusetts (Colored) at the Boyd's Neck landing. These troops made up about half of Hatch's Second Brigade, under Colonel Alfred S. Hartwell, who had previously commanded the 55th. Hartwell was a Harvard man, one of those originally slated for the 54th but held over for the sister regiment when the first was filled to capacity. Lieutenant Colonel Charles B. Fox directed the 55th this day, while the eight companies present from the 54th were led by Lieutenant Colonel Henry N. Hooper. Before daylight, Hartwell had ordered forward three regiments of Potter's that were still at the landing: the 56th New York, the 35th USCT, and a portion of the 32nd USCT. A fourth Potter regiment, the 34th USCT, was left behind to secure the beachhead.

The 54th and 55th left their bivouac at about 7:00 A.M. and made good time up the Boyd's Landing Road to the River Road. "Not a hostile sound reached their ears as the men moved at route step," observed Captain Emilio of the 54th, "with only the tinkle, tinkle of pans and cups striking the bayonets for music." Once at the River Road, four companies of the 54th dropped off to relieve the Naval

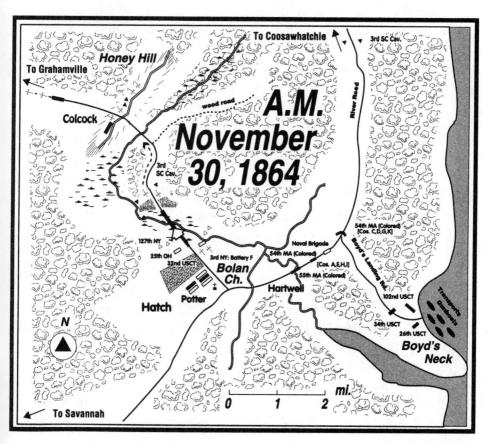

Brigade, which tagged along with Hartwell, the sailors still hauling their little howitzers—two by hand, the rest with horses impressed from local residents.[13]

There were approximately four hundred men in the 55th Massachusetts (Colored) this day. Among them were Robert King, a "brave, handsome lad of eighteen" who carried one of the regiment's flags; Richard Morrison, "who had recently made his escape from that hell of slavery, Kentucky"; and John Posey, of Vincennes, Indiana, who stood five feet eleven inches tall and had brown eyes and black hair. Posey was a steady correspondent with his family and friends back home, a young man proud of what he was accomplishing. "I call myself a rebel router," he wrote, "and in the Confederate country I stay."[14]

"Broken bridges delayed the march," noted the 55th's history, "and at noon the advance had only reached a small, white church, at a cross-roads some three miles from the landing." Not far up the road to Grahamville could be heard musket and cannon fire: Brigadier General Hatch had found a fight.[15]

Potter's troops began to move out of their bivouac around Bolan Church at 8:00 A.M. (At that time there were still more Confederate troops in transit than present on the field.) The 127th New York spread out in skirmishing order, followed in column by the 25th Ohio and an artillery battery. The troops pressed along the Grahamville road for only about half a mile before encountering several Rebel vedettes, who slowly retired across a corduroyed causeway built over a marshy field. Posted on the far side of the causeway were two cannon, which opened fire as soon as the head of the Federal column hove into view. At once the leading units fanned forward into lines of battle, while the battery took a firing position.

The 32nd USCT, marching near the rear, was halted in column so the troops up ahead could be sorted out. The 32nd, another Camp William Penn regiment, had gone straight to Hilton Head after its formation, and served both there and in the Morris Island trenches. Its commander, Colonel George W. Baird, was listening to the firing when Captain William C. Manning of Potter's staff reined up before him. Manning, Baird later recalled, "brought me the order of the Brigade Commander to advance up the causeway to capture or drive away the guns, and added, 'It's going to be close work.'"[16]

Continued Baird,

The order was promptly obeyed; the advance of the double quick was necessarily by the flank along the causeway enfiladed by the two pieces of artillery. . . . Owing, probably, to the shortness of the range the missiles flew just over the heads of those of us who were at the head of the column, but they told with deadly effect at the center and towards the rear. Here the regiment lost . . . a large number of enlisted men killed or wounded. The enemy's artillery was thus driven away and our line advanced.[17]

As the Rebels retreated, they set fire to the open fields on either side of the road, further slowing Potter's march. Covered by skirmishers, men from "the pioneer corps here were advanced . . . to beat out the flames." About thirty minutes were lost in knocking the fire down; by then, the first substantial Confederate reinforcements were arriving up the road, at a line of previously prepared earthworks that roughly followed the crest of Honey Hill. Captain Soule of the 55th described the site:

A substantial open earthwork, pierced for four guns, extended two hundred feet on each side of the road, on the crest of an abrupt slope of about twenty feet. The ground immediately in front of the entrenchments was comparatively open, but at the distance of about one hundred and fifty yards a shallow and sluggish stream, expanding into a swamp with a heavy growth of trees and dense underbrush, ran along the whole Confederate front.[18]

When the Yankee troops tried to get off the narrow dirt track, they were ensnared in what Captain Soule remembered as a "dense jungle of vines and undergrowth." As Potter's men came around a sharp turn in the road, they were immediately exposed to fire from the crest of Honey Hill, and had to go scurrying for cover; in response, their commander began to orient his brigade into some semblance of a line of battle, directing the men to file off to the left of the road, form, and then gingerly feel their way toward the enemy.

By the time the 32nd USCT arrived, said Colonel Baird, the "sound of heavy musketry firing in front was our guide, and spent balls indicated that the infantry of the enemy had been developed." A rough woods road led off toward the northeast, and the 32nd used this to extend itself before moving into line on the right of the 25th Ohio, which Baird found to be "hotly engaged with the enemy." His men were blocked by a morass ringed with thick undergrowth that made further advance impossible, but just beyond it, he could see an "abrupt rise of ground covered with an earth work." His men took cover and opened fire.[19]

The movement of the 32nd was part of a doomed effort on Hatch's part to press the enemy along a broad front. According to the *New York Times* reporter, "As our men advanced they were met by a concentrated fire of musketry from the rifle-pits and the lower part of the fort, and the woods, while from the parapet of the fort they were being mowed down by continuous charges of grape and canister."[20]

Whereas at Olustee, the 35th USCT had had to go into combat without its beloved colonel, this time James C. Beecher was present, riding into battle on his favorite gray horse. The *Times* correspondent could only note with wonder how, despite the pounding, Beecher's black troops "went in with a cheer." Beecher would afterward describe this phase of the action to his wife:

> I was 5th Regt & was ordered up to move through the thicket along the right of the road, flank the battery and charge it. I did so, but the enemy ran the guns off & I came right in front of a strong earth work that nobody knew anything about. A round shot killed poor old gray. I left him & pushed in at head of my column. A round shot struck me across both legs above the knee & upset me. I found no bone broken & pushed on. Then the boys opened fire without orders and the bushes were so thick that the companies were getting mixed. I halted and reformed the companies.[21]

Shortly after noon, at which time the general attack was repulsed and the commander of the 35th USCT bruised, Colonel Hartwell was leading the 54th and 55th Massachusetts (Colored) into action. He had brought them forward from Bolan Church, across the causeway and past the charred field (which Captain Soule saw "still burning fiercely") to the combat zone. There the men rested for about a half hour. David Spears, a sergeant in Company A of the 55th, recalled that while they were waiting, the colonel "gave us our instructions (don't dodge men, step high, shoot low and keep your powder dry)." Above the roar of gunfire, Spears heard someone yelling, "Oh, my left, oh,

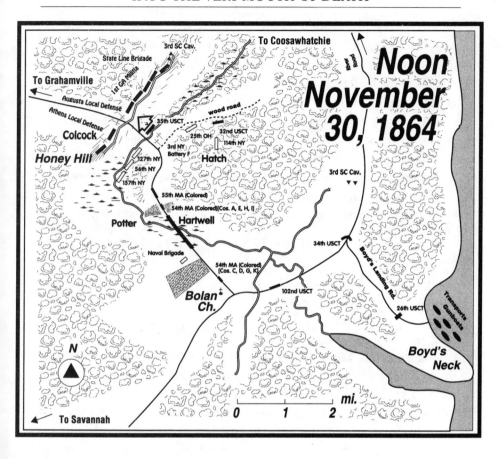

my arm." "Things had begun to get serious then," he recollected, "and Captain Geo[rge] M. Woodward said, there is a mighty rattling among [the] dry bones down there now." Then the men moved up.[22]

The narrow road was already clogged with artillery wagons trying to move forward against the inevitable tide of wounded men and skulkers. As the 55th wriggled its way through, the company files became much disordered by the passage; once clear of the road jam, the men were ordered into a column again, in preparation for an attack. There followed a mixup in the commands that sent three of the companies off into the woods on the right. There was no time to correct the mistake; the 55th would have to go in without those men.

"We fought in a forest dense and marshy and it was almost impossible on this account to maneuver more than half our troops," wrote Sergeant James M. Trotter of the 55th.

The battery on which the 55th charged was situated on a hill on the only road through the wilderness. Between ourselves and this battery, on either side of the road, was an impassable marsh. In passing up this road to the battery, of course, the men could only go by the flank—4 men in a breast. Every shot, therefore, from their guns would mow down nearly a hundred of our brave fellows. It was like rushing into the very mouth of death going up this road facing 7 pieces of death dealing cannon. Col. Hartwell and all of us knew this. But when commanded to charge 'twas not his to refuse, and so waving his hat while his eye looked upon his men, he smiled and cried, "Forward!" The order was promptly obeyed and in we rushed cheering and yelling.[23]

The five companies of the 55th, staggered by the defensive fire, fell back into the woods, where the line was re-formed. Behind them, Lieutenant Colonel Hooper was bringing forward what remained of the 54th Massachusetts (Colored). Besides the two companies posted at the Boyd's Landing Road intersection, he had put two more out picketing near Bolan Church, leaving him with only two companies. His tiny column was nevertheless moving toward the fight when Brigadier General Hatch's chief of staff appeared. According to Hooper, the staff officer "seemed excited, . . . and said but little else than 'Charge! charge!'" When Hooper asked the reasonable question—"Where?"—he was met with a reiteration of the word *"Charge!"*[24]

Hooper decided not to rush ahead. Instead, he moved his two companies off the road to the left, formed a line of battle, and pushed slowly forward. Only the volume of fire told him when he was closing on the Rebel line. He ordered his men to take cover and shoot back, husbanding their ammunition as much as possible.

Even as Hooper was easing up to the front, Colonel Beecher had re-formed the 35th USCT and, lacking any orders to discontinue the attack, was taking his men forward. Remembered Beecher:

I led off by the left flank, the boys starting finely & singing out "follow the command." It was a perfect jungle all laced with grape vines & when I got on the left of the earth work and closed up, I found that another regiment had marched right through mine & cut it off; so that I only had 20 men. I could see the rebel gunners loading. I told the boys to fire on them & raise a yell, hoping to make them think I

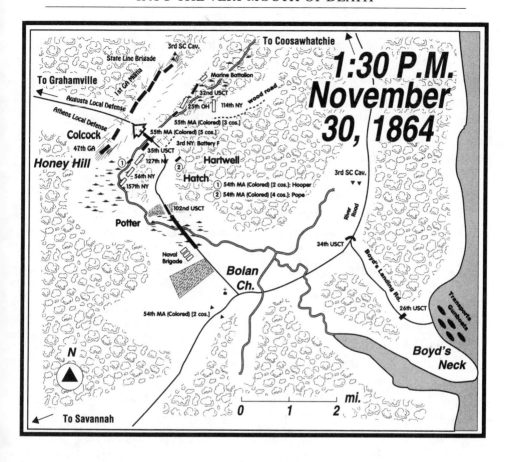

had a force on their flank. We fired & shouted & got a volley or two in return. A rascally bullet hit me just below the groin & ranged down nearly through my thigh. Then I went back with my twenty to the road again, found 35th, 55th, 54th men all mixed together. Went to work to clean up, though the fire of the enemy was very hot. Got hit here with a spent ball in left hand.[25]

Beecher's memory presented these events in a more orderly sequence than they likely occurred: Lieutenant Colonel Hooper recalled seeing Beecher about this time "acting in a dazed sort of way," and he detailed two men to assist him to the rear.[26]

For a second time, the increasingly ragged assault column of the 55th Massachusetts (Colored) now burst from the tree cover to race for the enemy earthworks. Before this attempt, the regiment's color sergeant, Robert King, turned to Corporal Andrew J. Smith and said, "Will you go with me? I am going to carry the flag into the fort or die." "Shot, shell, grape and canister was hurled down the road as thick as hail," recounted Sergeant Trotter. Color Sergeant King was killed, and when the corporal of the color guard, Mathew McFarlan, rushed over to pick up the fallen standard, he was immediately hit in the right elbow, right shoulder, and left leg. "We had nearly reached the muzzles of the guns when [Sergeant King] . . . was killed," remembered Corporal Smith. "I caught him with one hand and the flag with the other when he staggered back. Lieut[enant Thomas F.] Ellsworth, who was commander, screamed at me when he saw the sergeant fall, 'For God's sake, Smith, save the flag!'" Smith did, and carried it throughout the rest of the battle.[27]

Captain William D. Crane of the 55th went into the action as an aide to Colonel Hartwell. Riding near the head of the charging column, he called out, "Come on, men; they are only Georgia militia!" Seconds later, he was struck in the head and killed by a canister ball. Lying close to him was the body of his friend Lieutenant Winthrop P. Boynton, who died leading Company D of the 55th. Although wounded in the hand in the earlier effort to carry the Confederate line, Colonel Hartwell himself led the 55th on horseback in its last attack, yelling to his men, "Follow your colors!" The report filed by the *New York Herald* correspondent told what happened next:

Just as they reached the marsh in front of the turn in the road, and within a short distance of the rebel works, brave Colonel Hartwell's horse, while struggling through the mud, was literally blown in pieces by a discharge of canister. The Colonel was wounded at the same time, and attempted to jump from his horse; but the animal fell on him, pressing him into the mud. At this time he was riding at the side of the column and the men pressed on past. But as they neared the fort they met a murderous fire of grape, canister and bullets at short range. As the numbers of the advance were thinned, the few who survived began to waver, and finally the regiment retreated. In retiring, Lieutenant Ellsworth, with a few men, extricated the Colonel from his perilous position after much delay and by cutting the saddle from his horse. In carrying him away he was again wounded in the side, and advised Lieutenant Ellsworth to leave him behind; but the Lieutenant and a few men brought him from the field without further injury, and he will probably survive.[28]*

The repulse of the second attack by the 55th Massachusetts (Colored) signaled the dramatic high point of the engagement, but the fighting was not yet over, as General Hatch tried to turn the Rebel left. In this movement, the three "lost" companies of the 55th played a supporting role, as did a contingent of Marines from the peripatetic Naval Brigade, which had marched up with the black troops. The four companies of the 54th Massachusetts (Colored) at the Boyd's Landing Road had been relieved and quick-marched to the front, arriving just as the last charge by the 55th was being repulsed. These companies now moved into the center of the Union line, taking position off the right flank of the 35th USCT. "[Fort] Wagner always seemed to me the most terrible of our battles," recollected Color Sergeant Charles W. Lenox of the 54th, "but the musketry at Honey Hill was something fearful."[29]

Nothing came of the attempt to turn the enemy's left. "It was . . . certain that the enemy's position could not be carried," General Hatch reported, "and whilst a moderate fire was kept up, arrangements were commenced for retiring as soon as it became dark." The section of Union artillery that had been pushed closest to the enemy had lost most of its horses, along with a goodly number of officers and cannoneers. Sent to bring off the guns, a detail from the 102nd USCT carried out its orders under covering fire provided by two companies from its regiment. "It is acknowledged without stint on all hands that our regiment maintained the steadiest line of battle and fought with the greatest determination of any troops on the ground," noted a member of the 102nd, formerly the 1st Regiment Michigan Infantry (African Descent). "Many who were wounded quite severely refused to go to the rear, but kept on fighting, while the blood was flowing from their wounds."[30]

"At dusk the retreat commenced," Hatch noted in his report. The 102nd USCT and four of the navy howitzer teams covered the main part of the withdrawal, which was completed by 7:30 P.M. Throughout the day, Bolan Church was a place of desperate activity as surgeons

---

*Lieutenant Thomas F. Ellsworth would later receive the Medal of Honor for his role in saving Hartwell.

worked to patch up the injured so they could be sent to the Boyd's Neck landing. "It would be difficult for you to conceive of the sights and sounds with which the church was soon filled," related a surgeon with the 54th Massachusetts (Colored). "I did not lie down at all but spent the entire night until six next morning in dressing and caring for the wounded," wrote J. Lewis Whitaker, who performed similar duties in the 26th USCT. When the three "lost" companies of the 55th Massachusetts (Colored) fell back to the church at about 10:00 P.M., they found all the supporting troops gone. Twenty wounded Union soldiers still remained inside, so the blacks, after fashioning stretchers out of tent canvas, carried the injured away.[31]

The Confederates who ventured from their earthworks the next morning were appalled by the raw violence done by their firepower. The bodies of the soldiers from the 55th Massachusetts (Colored) and the 35th USCT "lay five deep as dead as a mackerel," observed one of the Rebel gunners. A reporter who had arrived from Savannah "counted some sixty or seventy bodies in a space of about an acre, many of which were horribly mutilated by shells, some with half their heads shot off, and others completely disemboweled." All the Southerners on the scene were convinced that the black troops had been purposely put in front of the white ones; from their racially biased point of view, no other explanation was possible.[32]

"Some think that the generalship displayed was very poor on our side," Sergeant Trotter observed with bland understatement. Captain Soule was a bit more tactful, stating that the "generalship displayed was not equal to the soldierly qualities of the troops engaged. There appears to have been a lack of foresight in the preparations." On the Confederate side, a plucky determination to defend Honey Hill at all costs had been validated when pure circumstance temporarily stranded a contingent of Georgia State Troops in Savannah early on the morning of November 30. Although they were intended for service elsewhere, their commander agreed to waive the usual restriction against these troops' crossing the state line, and most arrived at Honey Hill before the main Federal attack was launched. Their numbers helped extend the Rebel line against the flanking moves, and their firepower assisted in the successful defense.[33]

Confederate losses (there were about 1,500 men on hand at the end of the fight) were between 150 and 200, counting 8 dead.

Brigadier General Hatch tallied 750 casualties, with the greatest number of these (138) coming from the 25th Ohio. The 55th Massachusetts (Colored) was a close second with 137, and the 35th USCT came in third on this doleful list with 114. The 54th Massachusetts (Colored) lost 43 this day, the 32nd USCT 64, and the 102nd USCT 23. Included among the 29 killed in the 55th Massachusetts (Colored) were its color bearer, Sergeant King, the letter-writing John Posey, and Richard Morrison, the ex-slave from Kentucky. "At the time he was killed," said Morrison's friend P. R. Laws, "he had secured about his person the round sum of three hundred and twenty-five dollars, which, no doubt, the rebels considered 'contraband,' and therefore 'confiscated' it."[34]

Confederate sources, proud of their victory, tended to magnify the significance of the action in their postwar writing. Nevertheless, the rail link between Savannah and Charleston did remain open for another two months after this, and when Sherman finally approached the Georgia city, those rails would help evacuate its defenders to South Carolina.

The blacks of the 102nd USCT entered this battle carrying the cross borne by all untested black regiments: the need to prove themselves in combat before the eyes of the white man. In a letter written to the *Anglo-African* soon after the fight, the regiment's black chaplain felt compelled to defend his men:

> The colored regiments engaged in these operations are the 54th and 55th Mass., the 26th, 32d, 33d,* 34th, 35th and 102d U.S. Colored Troops, all of which had been under fire before, except the 32d and ours. "All the fools are not dead yet," for there were some white men here, who were obliged to witness the Battle of Honey Hill, on the 30th of Nov., before they could believe that "niggers would fight just as well as white troops." It is hard to tell which is the more annoying, to have the courage of colored soldiers doubted, or to see intelligent (?) white men make such unaccountable fools of themselves, by expressing those doubts in the face of the fact that not a single colored regiment has ever yet turned tail and run, unless literally overpowered, an assertion that cannot be made truthfully with regard to the white troops in our army.[35]

*Chaplain William Waring erred in his roster of the units engaged: the 33rd USCT was not present at Honey Hill.

Postscript

On December 13, Sherman's men stormed Fort McAllister, south of Savannah, and made contact with Rear Admiral Dahlgren. Seven days later, Savannah's defenders withdrew, and the city itself finally surrendered on December 21. With its occupation, Sherman found the spotlight shining uncomfortably on his policies regarding the blacks who flocked into Savannah seeking freedom and protection, even as their liberator and protector continued to resist all efforts to recruit eligible black males into the U.S. Army. Even a confidential communication from the army chief of staff (who termed the problem the "Inevitable Sambo") and a personal visit from the Secretary of War to explain the Federal policy on blacks were not enough to change Sherman's mind.[36]

Sherman spent the period from late December through early January moving units into place for the next phase of his grand raid—a march through the Carolinas. On January 3, his Seventeenth and Fifteenth corps were transported by water from Savannah to Beaufort. There, for the first time, many of his men came into direct contact with black troops, and witnessed the social experiments that resulted from the ex-slave resettlements. The cultural shock was profound.

The sight of African Americans wearing the same uniform as they proved too much for many of these white soldiers. An Ohio corporal wrote in his diary that "some of the boys would make cute remarks at seeing the negro Sergeants & Corporals with their stripes on, one would say look at that darned nigger he is higher than I am." Even one of the Northern white civilians who had come to Beaufort to work with the black refugees commented that "Sherman and his men are impatient of the darkies, and annoyed to see them pampered, petted, and spoiled, as they have been here. They hustled them out of the way, and the blacks were rather afraid of them."[37]

This feeling was sometimes mutual. Corporal John H. Jenkins of the 55th Massachusetts (Colored) was assigned to Savannah's occupation after Sherman's men left. "I think we will stay here and do garrison duty the rest of our time," he wrote to his wife on January 22, "for Gen. Sherman says he will not fight with our colored troops and I am sure that your Uncle John will not cry, for I have had my share of fighting, so he can take his white men and fight as much as he likes as long as he lets John alone."[38]

Chaplain William Waring of the 102nd USCT, an Ohio free black, saw clearly that despite the prejudices of their commander and rank and file, Sherman's legions were destroying the slave economy, and in so doing, performing a profoundly important act in the cause of African American liberation. Waring penned a long appreciation of Sherman's armies in a letter to the *Anglo-African,* concluding:

> If God, in his infinite wisdom, as we believe, is visiting these Southern people for their wickedness, surely in Sherman's army he has provided an effectual scourge, and to one who thinks ever of the moral features of this great conflict, the thought will suggest itself, as he looks upon this host, how great and heaven-daring must have been the crimes of the people that a merciful God would prepare so terrible a retribution! And involuntarily he will breathe a prayer that the day may speedily come when the loud clang of battle will have hushed, and in its stead the hum of peaceful industry and the songs of a free people float on that morning zephyr.[39]

Chapter Twelve

"Captain, I Am Wounded; What Shall I Do?"

———◁◦▷———

As he spread out his armies for their history-making March to the Sea, Major General William T. Sherman was leaving one big problem unsolved. After ineffectually chasing John B. Hood and the Rebel Army of Tennessee for more than a month following the capture of Atlanta, Sherman had finally decided to stop playing Hood's game. When he departed Atlanta on November 16, he was confident that there were enough troops with Major General George H. Thomas to "successfully cope with Hood should [he] . . . cross the Tennessee [River] northward." Thomas, handed the responsibility for protecting Tennessee in September, had set up his headquarters in Nashville and begun to organize the bits and pieces left by Sherman. Some of these bits were of generous size, such as the two army corps numbering perhaps twenty-two thousand men; others consisted of regiments that had been dispersed along the state's strategic railroad lines. While Sherman could opt not to have black units serving directly under him, Thomas had no such choice.[1]

Although not a racist, Thomas did subscribe to the prevailing white opinion that black soldiers were incapable of combat. He took a dim view of subordinates who agitated outside the chain of command to stop assigning USCT units to fatigue and garrison duties. When Colonel Reuben D. Mussey, the U.S. commissioner for Tennessee black units, complained that the notion "that the negro is to be made a man by first being made a soldier does not seem to be comprehended yet by the commanding generals," Thomas's chief of staff quickly slapped him down. After being informed that such statements "are in violation of the spirit and letter of the regulation of the army," the commissioner was put under arrest until he agreed to make a "proper retraction and apology."[2]

Another officer who incurred Thomas's wrath on this issue was Colonel Thomas J. Morgan of the 14th USCT. Morgan's persistent requests for a combat assignment drew a rebuke from Thomas's assistant adjutant general: "The Major General commanding directs me to say that when you shall have learned cheerfully to perform your duty to the best of your abilities in such position as may be assigned you, then shall you have learned the first lessons of that discipline, which apparently, you are so anxious should be taught your regiment."[3]

Morgan himself recalled a conversation he had with Thomas, during which the major general asked Morgan "if I thought my men would fight. I replied that they would. He said he thought 'they might behind breastworks.' I said they would fight in the open field. He thought not."[4]

Skirmish at Stockade No. 2, Chattanooga & Nashville Railroad, December 2, 1864

On November 20, just four days after Sherman left Atlanta, Hood began his march northward from northwestern Alabama. After crossing the Tennessee River, he directed his forty thousand men around the flank of a twenty-two-thousand-man Federal force posted at Pulaski under Major General John M. Schofield. The next days saw a desperate race as Hood drove his men hard to cut off and destroy Schofield's command. Hood managed to trap Schofield near Spring Hill, but his vague instructions,* coupled with failings on the part of some of his subordinates, allowed the Federals to escape. Enraged by what he felt was a lack of fighting spirit among his troops, Hood ordered a frontal assault the next day on a strongly posted Union rear guard at Franklin. The resulting debacle cost Hood more than six thousand men, including many of his best officers.

---

*Hood had lost the use of one arm at Gettysburg, and his entire right leg had been amputated after Chickamauga, forcing him to take regular quantities of opium to deal with almost constant pain. This may well have had an effect on the clarity of his orders in this instance.

General Thomas was now calling into Nashville every available unit in the state, black or white. On December 1, as Hood's battered but still-dangerous army drew closer, black regiments also moved toward the capital. From western Tennessee, where it had been guarding the railroad, came the 13th USCT under Colonel John A. Hottenstein. Organized in Nashville in late 1863, the 13th, its ranks filled from the area's contraband camps, had spent its entire service protecting the military railroads. Nevertheless, in June 1864, Joseph D. Williams of the 13th could brag to the *Christian Recorder* that his comrades "are the bravest set of men on the Western Continent. They think nothing of routing the guerrillas, that roam at large in the wilds of Tennessee."[5]

Also coming into Nashville from the west was the 12th USCT, which received its orders on December 1. Hood's forces were by now so close that the regiment had to take a roundabout route to its destination. The 12th had been organized in 1863 near the Elk River

Bridge on the Nashville and Chattanooga Railroad, its ranks filled with contraband recruits described by one officer as a real "rag-tag and bobtail." The same man also noted that the recruits nonetheless "showed an aptitude for drill and military duties somewhat surprising, considering their antecedents. . . . From slavery to freedom was itself a grand transition; but to become Union soldiers was a still bigger promotion, exceeding their most sanguine hopes—a privilege estimated at its full value."[6]

Perhaps the most eventful journey to Nashville was made by the black units coming out of Chattanooga. The three regiments there—the 14th, 16th, and 44th USCT—were under the overall command of Colonel Thomas J. Morgan (Thomas's antipathy for whom was evidently superseded by the impending crisis). Morgan's men traveled by rail in detachments, the 16th and most of the 14th going first and arriving in the city on December 1. The follow-up troop shipment, comprising the remainder of the 14th and all of the 44th, was delayed twenty-four hours at Murfreesboro when a supply train derailed. The black soldiers and their white officers resumed traveling early on December 2, the same day Hood's advance elements reached Nashville's outskirts. Rebel cavalry and horse artillery ambushed the troop train near Mill Creek, compelling the black soldiers to fight on foot. It was a bitter déjà vu for Colonel Lewis Johnson of the 44th, who had surrendered most of his regiment to Hood at Dalton on October 13. Now Colonel Johnson led his men along the tracks until they came to one of the blockhouses built for railroad security. Manning Stockade No. 2 were soldiers from the 115th Ohio, who said there was no room inside for the black troops. Forced to put his men in a perimeter defense around the post, Johnson afterward reported, "Three [Rebel] batteries were shelling us terribly, and a heavy musketry fire commenced from all sides." Johnson's men, taking cover among the logs and tree stumps, somehow held out until darkness fell, by which time they were down to four rounds apiece. Their colonel, who feared that "should the place be surrendered or taken by assault a butchery would follow," waited until 3:30 A.M. on December 3 before leading the survivors along the rail bed into Nashville. Fortunately, the Confederate ambush party had also pulled back, so the Union men made the wearying trek without opposition. Of the 307 black troops engaged at Stockade No. 2, 10 were killed in the fight, 40 wounded, and 57 missing. In closing his report, Colonel Johnson observed that his men had marched that night in perfect silence, "determined to die rather than be taken prisoner."[7]

Battle of Nashville, Tennessee, December 15–16, 1864

Throughout the day on Friday, December 2, General Hood settled his army before Nashville, strongly entrenching himself along a series of hills south of the city. His effective strength at this time was around twenty-three thousand men—not enough to assault the Federal earthworks. His strategy was rather to count on pressure from Northern officials to force Major General Thomas to attack *him*.

Although many of Hood's other assumptions verged on pure fantasy, in this instance he was not underestimating the panic his presence would cause in the northern central states, nor miscalculating the long-distance coercion that would be applied to Thomas. When Thomas relayed to Washington his intention to stand pat until his units (especially his cavalry) had been properly equipped and reorganized, Lincoln's military chief of staff quickly complained to Lieutenant General Ulysses S. Grant, who was running all the U.S. armies from his headquarters near Petersburg, Virginia. Grant was soon badgering Thomas with telegrams offering gratuitous advice and bluntly advising him to attack. Despite the pressure, Thomas acted methodically to get everything in order, suffering further delays when a severe ice storm swept over the area, coating the entire landscape in a slippery glaze.

As part of his preparations, Thomas ordered a series of reconnaissances to fix the enemy's positions. The black regiments in Nashville, concentrated on the eastern side of the city, took part in probing actions on December 5, 7, 11, and 13. During the December 5 expedition, a skirmish line of the 14th USCT flushed a rabbit near what everyone supposed were abandoned Rebel rifle pits. As the excited black soldiers shouted and threw stones at the animal, several heads popped up in one of the "unoccupied" holes. The Confederates, all from the 17th Mississippi, were captured. Later asked how they had come to be taken, one of them muttered, "Lookin' at a lot of _____ niggers catch a rabbit." After the December 7 recon, noted the 14th's chaplain, the prompt and disciplined movements of the black troops involved elicited "the highest praise" from all observers.

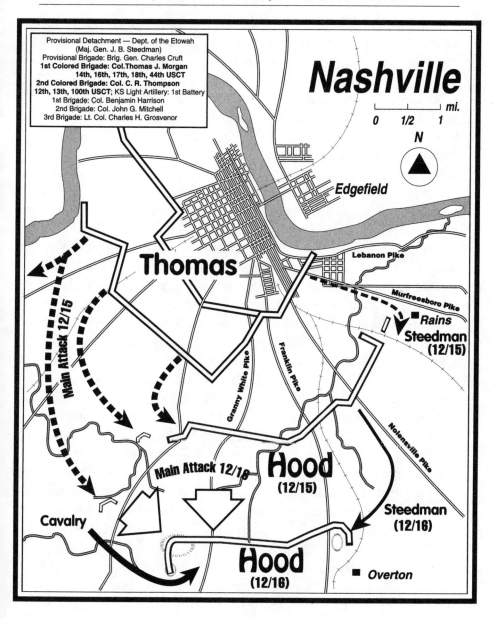

A soldier in the 12th USCT afterward recollected the more sober December 13 affair: "A rail fence between us and the rebel breastworks was laid almost flat to the ground, and we lay on our arms behind it waiting for the order to charge, but were rather glad that it did not come at that time."[8]

The plan developed by General Thomas called for the principal attack to be launched from the Union right, with a large mobile force moving in a grand wheeling action to fall on Hood's left flank. Preceding this assault would be a diversionary attack against the Rebel right. It was to this phase of the operation that the black troops were assigned. The USCT units were all placed in something called the Provisional Detachment (District of the Etowah), under the overall command of Major General James B. Steedman.* In addition to three white brigades, Steedman's detachment included two black ones, the First under Colonel Morgan (consisting of the 14th, 16th, 17th, 18th, and 44th USCT), and the Second led by Colonel Charles R. Thompson (holding the 12th, 13th, and 100th USCT).†

Steedman, a large-framed Pennsylvanian, was a civilian general who had supported Stephen Douglas Democrats in the 1860 presidential election. He had no previous experience with black troops, and soon after the Nashville fight was heard to comment, "I wonder what my Democratic friends . . . would think of me if they knew I was fighting . . . with 'nigger' troops?" True to form, Colonel Morgan rushed to Steedman's headquarters to lobby for front-line service; according to an officer on Steedman's staff, Morgan had previously been told that "if opportunity offered the niggers should have all the fighting they wanted." Again true to form, Morgan was feuding with his subordinates. He was still at odds with Lieutenant Colonel Henry C. Corbin, now commanding the 14th USCT, and had decided that Colonel William B. Gaw, leading the 16th, was a complete coward. On December 14, as Morgan wrote in his report, "Colonel Gaw, by unsoldierly process, succeeded in getting his regiment . . . ordered to a safer place in the rear."9

The time was about 9:00 P.M., December 14, when Morgan was summoned to Steedman's headquarters and briefed on what his role would be. Steedman, recalled Morgan, "said he wished me to open the fight by making a vigorous assault on Hood's right flank. This he explained, was to be a feint, intended to betray Hood into the belief that it was the real attack, and lead him to support his right by weakening his left, where Thomas intended to assault him." When Morgan, who had never before led so many men into combat, asked for

*Spelled Steadman in some accounts.
†Also assigned to Thompson's brigade was the 1st Battery Kansas Light Artillery.

tactical advice, Steedman merely waved him away with the comment, "To-morrow, Colonel, just as soon as you can see how to put your troops in motion, I wish you to begin the fight."[10]

After instructing their men "to have an early breakfast and be ready for serious work at daybreak," Morgan and his adjutant scouted the Rebel position, an appraisal limited to a long-distance examination of the enemy's campfires. These observations, along with information obtained in earlier probes of the area, persuaded Morgan that the Confederates had constructed a spur off their main lines, running in a northeastern direction across the Nashville and Chattanooga Railroad and covered by a ring of rifle pits. Morgan concluded "that if the rifle-pits could be carried and a column pushed well to the rear [of the spur] . . . the ground east of the Nashville and Chattanooga Railroad [would] be given up to us with little loss." What Morgan had missed in the darkness was the small lunette the Rebels had built on the tip of the spur, into which they had put four cannon.[11]

Thursday, December 15: "Camp was astir at 4 A.M.," recalled Captain Henry Romeyn of the 14th USCT, "and breakfast had been eaten long before daybreak. One hundred rounds of ammunition per man and two days' rations were issued, and just as the first grey streaks of dawn appeared, the companies 'fell in,' leaving tents standing." A thick ground fog blanketed the region, and though Morgan's men were ready by 6:30 A.M., another ninety minutes had to pass before General Steedman would release them. While Morgan's USCT regiments marched out the Murfreesboro Pike to get past the spur, one of Steedman's white brigades was to move more directly against the position, and the other black brigade to press it from the east.[12]

At first, everything went according to Morgan's scenario. Three black regiments* formed into three lines of battle: the first, in skirmishing order, from the 14th USCT; the second consisting of the 17th USCT under Colonel William R. Shafter; and the third made up of Colonel Johnson's unlucky 44th USCT. The black troops were supported on their right by a small brigade under Lieutenant Colonel Charles H. Grosvenor. A combat outfit in name only, Grosvenor's

---

*The 16th USCT was guarding the Union pontoon wagons, while the 18th supported the Federal artillery assisting in the attack.

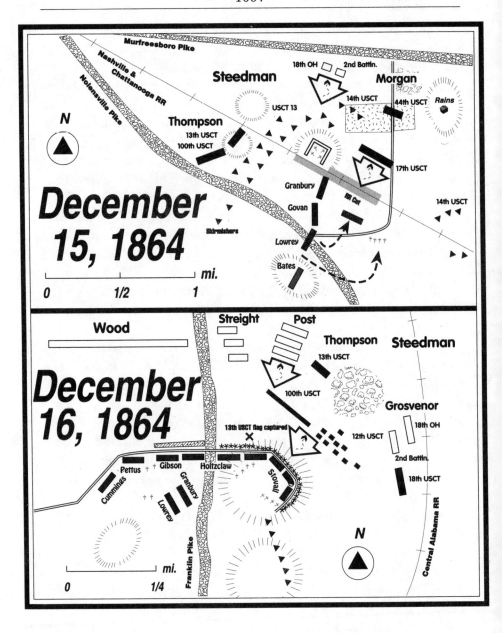

December 15, 1864

Murfreesboro Pike

Nashville & Chattanooga RR

Nolensville Pike

N

Steedman

18th OH   2nd Battln.

Morgan

14th USCT   44th USCT   Rains

Thompson

13th USCT
100th USCT

USCT 13

17th USCT

14th USCT

Granbury

RR Cut

Govan

Skirmishers

Lowrey

Bates

0   1/2   1   mi.

December 16, 1864

Wood

Streight   Post

Thompson   Steedman

13th USCT

100th USCT

Grosvenor

13th USCT flag captured

12th USCT

18th OH

2nd Battln.

18th USCT

Pettus   Gibson   Holtzclaw

Cummings   Granbury   Lowrey   Stovall

Central Alabama RR

Franklin Pike

N

0   1/4   mi.

command comprised three regiments, one of which was detached as
a flank guard, leaving him with the 18th Ohio and a unit culled from
what the colonel would later describe as "new conscripts, convalescents, and bounty jumpers."[13]

When all was ready, Lieutenant Colonel Corbin of the 14th gave the command "Forward!," waving his sword overhead to indicate the advance. According to Captain Romeyn, "Pushing on, the right of the skirmish-line passing through an orchard and cornfield and the left through a field lately cleared of timber and thickly strewn with stumps and piles of brush, over the crest of the slope it had ascended, [the line of battle] found itself on a sloping field . . . and face to face with heavy earthworks on its opposite side, from which, came at once a heavy and deadly fire of both artillery and infantry." The right half of the skirmish line went to ground, while the left trailed off to the south to engage what Romeyn remembered as a "strong force of rebel skirmishers."[14]

It was now time for the 17th USCT to take up the momentum of the advance by sweeping past the enemy's exposed spur. Colonel Shafter's men dutifully moved forward, coming abreast of the silent enemy lunette to their right. Only when these troops got to the railroad line and found their way blocked by a deep ravine did the Rebel cannoneers in the lunette open fire. At the same moment, Confederate infantry and artillery swung out from the entrenched line directly in front of Shafter's men, catching the 17th USCT in a devastating fire from front, right flank, and rear. "It was an awful battle," Shafter wrote to his sister afterward. "We had the negroes in our trap," related a Georgia soldier on the hill, "and when we commenced firing on them, complete demoralization followed. Many jumped into the [railroad] cut and were either killed or captured." In his report, Shafter stated that the 17th USCT had been "soon obliged to fall back, which was done in rather a disorderly manner."[15]

Even as the Rebel fire ripped into Shafter's ranks, Morgan ordered Grosvenor's brigade to launch its supporting attack. Although a portion of the 18th Ohio did actually reach the enemy's main line, the composite regiment, reported Grosvenor, "behaved in the most cowardly and disgraceful manner," and this effort failed. Farther to the west, Thompson's black brigade did little more than engage the Rebel skirmishers.[16]

Morgan's initiative had accomplished none of its tactical objectives. His units all withdrew to the Murfreesboro Pike, though later in the afternoon some of his soldiers occupied the Rains House, where they knocked loopholes in the walls and sniped at the Rebels. Morgan would afterward console himself with the thought that his men had managed to attract Hood's attention, thus making possible Thomas's grand success on the other flank, but he was clearly overstating his accomplishments. The same fog and poor conditions that had held up his advance until 8:00 A.M. caused similar delays on the Union right, with the result that things there did not get under way until 10:00 A.M.; by then, Hood not only was aware of the limited number of troops operating against his right, but also knew that Morgan's effort had failed. With hardly a further thought for the security of his right flank, Hood began shifting troops to his left, where the momentous combat of this day would take place.

"Hood had stubbornly resisted," noted Colonel Morgan of the general events of the day, "but had been gallantly driven back with severe loss." The heaviest casualties among the black troops occurred in Shafter's regiment: the colonel of the 17th USCT reported seventeen of his men killed or mortally wounded and another sixty-seven suffering nonfatal injuries. In the 14th USCT, there were four killed, forty-one wounded, and twenty missing, while the 44th recorded four wounded. "Colored soldiers had fought side by side with white troops," Colonel Morgan enthused of this day's events. "They had assisted each other from the field when wounded, and they lay side by side in death. . . . A new chapter in the history of liberty had been written. It had been shown that marching under a flag of freedom, animated by a love of liberty, even a slave becomes a man and hero."[17]

News of the December 15 Union victory at Nashville reached Washington via telegraph late that same evening. A copy of the message was delivered to Willard's Hotel, where U. S. Grant had gone preparatory to leaving for Nashville, intent on relieving George Thomas of his command for failing to act with enough celerity. The news changed all that. "Push the enemy now," Grant urged in his congratulatory reply, "and give him no rest until he is entirely destroyed." This was precisely what George Thomas meant to do.[18]

On December 16, a cloudy day with showers, Union troops felt their way southward from the Rebel works they had taken the previous day. Even though the Confederates in his front had abandoned their earthworks during the night, it was not until 6:00 A.M., and only after he received orders from General Thomas to do so, that General Steedman moved forward to occupy the enemy trenches he had tried to capture on Thursday. It took Steedman five hours to catch up with the rest of Thomas's army, which was spreading out to confront the new defensive position occupied by Hood's veterans.

Thomas's basic plan for December 16 was a repeat of that for December 15: diversionary actions against the Confederate right, with the main blow delivered against the enemy's left. However, the movements of this day had put the Union Fourth Corps and its aggressive commander, Major General Thomas J. Wood, into position opposite the Rebel right center. Wood, having missed most of the December 15 fighting, was determined to grab a piece of the glory, and on his own, he decided to attack the Rebel right with all his strength, hoping to cut off Hood's retreat. It would not be easy. The Confederate flank was anchored on a piece of high ground known as Overton Hill, or Peach Orchard Hill. As Wood prepared for the attack, his enthusiasm infected General Steedman, who resolved not just to support his effort but also to put some units into the attacking column.

Steedman gave Thompson's brigade the assignment this day; Grosvenor's brigade, which had performed so poorly the previous morning, would support Thompson. There was one difference this time, as Grosvenor had a small black regiment, the 18th USCT, added to his command. Union cannon were rolled into firing positions and began a heavy bombardment of the Rebel position. This artillery barrage lasted until about 2:45 P.M., when General Wood gave the order to attack.

Captain Henry V. Freeman of the 12th USCT took a good look at the Rebel line and was not happy with what he saw. "It was probably their strongest position," he afterward declared. "The slope of the hill was obstructed by tree-tops. The approach was over a ploughed field, the heavy soil of which, clinging to the feet, greatly impeded progress. In front of the Twelfth Colored Regiment of Thompson's brigade was a thicket of trees and underbrush so dense as to be almost impenetrable, constituting a kind of wooded island, in the midst of the cornfield."[19]

Thompson's attack had the 100th and 12th USCT regiments in a first line of battle, supported by the 13th. Captain D. E. Straight of the 100th remembered that as his men watched the preparatory artillery bombardment, it was clearly understood by everyone that the cannonade was "only the prelude to an undertaking more fearful and terrible." A few men brought to their officers or sergeants money or valuables for safekeeping. "This and little talk among themselves showed a settled resolution, to unflinchingly face death in the cause of freedom and nationality," said Straight.[20]

Then, noted Captain Freeman, "one of the batteries gave the signal, and the troops moved to the assault." "On they came in splendid order," observed a Rebel gunner on Overton Hill, "banners flying, mounted officers with drawn swords careening up and down in front of the lines. Then our artillery had its opportunity." "A shell took a file of men from one company, burying itself in the ground at the feet of the company following," recalled Freeman. "Men were falling on all sides." Captain Straight thought that the "air seemed as full of the death-laden missiles as of hail in a driving hailstorm."[21]

One of those hit in the 12th USCT seemed uncertain of the proper conduct for an injured man. "Captain, I am wounded," he called out, "what shall I do?" The enlisted man, whose wounds would prove fatal, was told to lie down as the battle lines advanced ahead. Confederate fire continued to tear into the ranks of the 100th and 12th. "Glancing to the left," said Captain Straight, "I saw the movement by the flank, the soldiers slightly raising the right shoulder toward the fire, as a person will do when beaten by a driving storm; but, tramp, tramp, they sullenly moved along." The heavy thicket through which the 12th had to pass caused problems. The officers opted to make the passage a company at a time; not only did this slow down the 12th and separate it from the 100th, it also caused the men to bunch together as they hurried to catch up. "They were so compact that every shot from Rebel muskets and cannon was telling with fearful effect," said Captain Freeman. "The rebel infantry blazed away at a fearful rate," wrote *New York Times* correspondent Benjamin C. Truman, "and the artillery discharged sixteen shots of canister, which made the assaulting column reel, waver, and almost fall back."[22]

As these two regiments stumbled to a halt, the 13th USCT moved ahead. This was its first battle, and sight of the carnage awaiting them was demoralizing to the raw soldiers. One of the first in the 13th to be hit was Private Alexander Helms, who was caught by a friend as he was spun around by the impact of the bullet, and gently lowered to the ground. "Lord have mercy," Helms groaned as his comrades moved past him. Nearby, Private William Smith was struck in the breast by a minie ball that tore through several layers of clothing before flattening itself and only bruising the stunned soldier. Also advancing with the 13th USCT was Private Newton Tucker, whose family lived in Nashville. During the regiment's march to the front, earlier in the month, as the 13th passed through town without halting, Tucker's wife, Mary, and their two-year-old son had anxiously scanned the files for him. When he at last saw his family, Tucker stopped only long enough to bow to them. Now Newton Tucker hunched against the storm of bullets like everyone else in the regiment.[23]

Helped by the attention drawn to the other two USCT units, and by the efforts of Wood's troops farther to the right, the 13th USCT managed to get closer to the Rebel works than any regiment in action on this flank. Perhaps the unluckiest surviving member of the regiment was Private John Beach, who weighed two hundred pounds and bragged that a "man could bust an inch plank over my head and not faze it." Midway through this charge, Beach was knocked to the ground by a shell that tore off his knapsack and equipments. Although his hip was injured in the fall, Beach got back up to continue forward with his regiment. Once near the enemy's line, targeted by soldiers firing buck and ball charges, he was shot in the head and face. "This so jarred my hard skull & fractured it," Beach later testified, "[that] I fell senseless to the ground." Roused back to consciousness when the regiment began to retreat, Beach lumbered after his comrades, only to be hit a third time, taking a gunshot in the side. Amazingly, he lived to tell this story for many years after the war.[24]

Rebel gunfire also decimated the color guard of the 13th USCT, which carried the standards to within thirty feet of the enemy line. "There were very few negroes who retreated in our front," declared an Alabama soldier on Overton Hill, "and none were at their post when the firing ceased; for we fired as long as there was anything to shoot at." As the shattered ranks of the 13th tumbled back, the adjutant of the 18th Alabama stepped out from behind the breastworks to pick up the regiment's fallen flag. "The bearer was dead, as were nearly all of his comrades," he reported.[25]

Thompson's retreating troops passed by a section of the 14th USCT that had come up to cover them. Captain Henry Romeyn had no trouble tracing their path, as "the ground [was] strewn with dead and wounded as thickly as a farmer's field with sheaves of a more peaceful reaper." Romeyn particularly remembered the sight of the color corporal of the 12th, the only man of it left on his feet, standing beside his color, the staff of which he had driven into the soft ground, and loading and firing. . . . Before many seconds had passed a glancing shot struck the side of his head, and pulling up his flag he drew from beneath the dead [color] sergeant [next to him] the stars and stripes, and with both under one arm, and his musket in the other hand, the blood streaming down his face, he strode proudly back through the supporting line.[26]

The unscheduled attack by General Wood failed to pierce the enemy's line. On the extreme left of the Rebel position, however, long hours of stalemate were broken when Federal infantry captured a key hill, unleashing a Union cavalry sweep into the enemy's rear and instigating a dramatic collapse of the entire Confederate line. A jubilant officer in the 100th USCT wrote in his diary that the "Rebs under Hood are the worst-whipped army that was ever in this part of the U.S."[27]

As the Confederate left flank dissolved into fleeing men, the troops posted on Overton Hill began to withdraw. Along Wood's front, what one officer called a "wave of action" swelled as white and black regiments, without orders, rushed into the emptying Rebel trenches. Reporter Truman watched as one group of USCT men "reached the top [of the hill], and with a yell, went over the works. . . . As soon as the hill was taken, the colored troops pitched after the retreating rebels, chasing them through a valley nearly a mile."[28]

Behind them, scattered in untidy bundles across the slope of Overton Hill, were the black men who had paid the terrible price for Steedman's impulsive decision. The 100th lost 12 killed and 121 wounded, and the 12th, 10 killed and 104 wounded. The 13th suffered most of all, with 55 dead and 166 wounded or missing. Among the 13th's dead was Newton Tucker, who had bowed to his wife and child as his regiment hurried through Nashville in early December. "I never saw him again," Mary Tucker later testified.[29]

On December 17, General Thomas ordered his forces to pursue the remnants of Hood's army. For the next ten days, Billy Yanks and Johnny Rebs alike slogged through a nightmare of hard marches, in abominable weather and with few supplies. "Many of the officers and men were barefoot," reported Colonel Hottenstein of the 13th

USCT, "and never did men display more soldierly qualities than on this march; without shoes and a great time without rations, they performed their duty cheerfully and without murmur." On Christmas Day, Hood's beaten army reached the Tennessee River. A pontoon bridge was finished within twenty-four hours, allowing the weary Rebels to cross over and end their campaign.[30]

There was a pitiful coda to the USCT actions at Nashville. On January 16, 1865, Brigadier General Lorenzo Thomas wrote an angry letter to Colonel R. C. Wood, the Assistant Surgeon General. Investigating a complaint about the care given to wounded black soldiers, Thomas had visited Hospital No. 16, where many such men were housed. The building (which the brigadier termed "unsuitable") had previously been used as a contraband hospital, and was little altered since then, even though most of its patients now wore uniforms. "Words of mine cannot describe the utter filthiness of what I saw," Thomas said. He cited the case of one USCT soldier, whose December 15 leg wound required amputation and whose clothing had not been changed since he was admitted. "Had these men been white soldiers, think you this would have been their condition?" asked Thomas. In Nashville, and other administrative centers, it was painfully clear that the treatment meted out to sick and wounded black soldiers was separate and not equal.[31]

Looking back on their Nashville experiences, some of the white USCT officers were inspired by the record of the black troops. "Who will say that men who fought and suffered as did these colored soldiers have not fairly earned for themselves and their race the freedom which the war gave them?" wondered Captain Freeman in 1888. In concluding his 1885 account of the events at Nashville, Colonel Morgan declared, "I cannot close . . . without expressing the conviction that history has not yet done justice to the share borne by colored soldiers in the war for the Union." Morgan also recalled how, soon after the Federals had seized Overton Hill, Major General Thomas and his staff rode over the bloody ground. Gazing across a muddy field over which black and white bodies lay strewn in the ultimate equality, Thomas had announced, "The question is settled; negro soldiers will fight."[32]

Sergeant Major Daniel W. Atwood, who fought at Nashville in the 100th USCT, believed that the courage and sacrifice of the black troops contributed to more than just a battlefield victory:

It was the first time in the memorable history of the Army of the Cumberland [i.e., Thomas's army] that the blood of black and white men flowed freely together for one common cause for a country's freedom and independence. Each was cheered on to victory by the co-operation of the other, and now, as the result, wherever the flag of our love goes, our hopes may advance, and we may, as a people, with propriety claim political equality with our white fellow-soldier and citizen; and every man that makes his home in our country may, whatever be his complexion or progeny, with propriety, exclaim to the world, "I am an American citizen!" I ask, is there not something in this over which to rejoice and be proud?[33]

Part Four

1865

———◇———

Chapter Thirteen

"Ye's Long Been A-coming"

———◇———

Occupation of Charleston, South Carolina, February 18, 1865

As Major General William T. Sherman plotted his course from Savannah into South Carolina, he decided that a movement toward the interior of that state offered richer possibilities than marching along its coast, where numerous rivers and swamps would heavily favor the defenders. This meant that Sherman's men would bypass the city of Charleston, leaving its fate to the Coast Division.

The two grand wings of Sherman's army began to move on January 13. The left, under Major General Henry W. Slocum, headed north from Savannah, while the right, directed by Major General Oliver Otis Howard, pushed west from Beaufort. Once they had cleared Pocataligo of Rebels, Howard's columns would take a path parallel to Slocum's. The Confederates holding Pocataligo had successfully defied several earlier expeditions mounted by the Department of the South, but this time they abandoned their fortifications (on January 14) and retreated inland. A number of Rebel units still occupied strong points along the coast, and near Charleston, that city's garrison kept up a bold front, though it had been seriously depleted by the transfer of units to the interior.

As Sherman's columns struggled against the wet weather and flooded terrain, other Federals increased the pressure along the seacoast. The

54th Regiment Massachusetts Infantry (Colored), now occupying the former Rebel positions near Pocataligo, witnessed a brand of total war brought by Sherman's men that surprised even hardened veterans such as Lieutenant Colonel Henry N. Hooper, who noted that all "through this country, as far as it can be seen, pillars of black smoke rise. . . . The saying is that 'when Sherman gets through South Carolina, a crow can't fly across the country unless he carries rations with him.'"[1]

Cooperating actions supporting Sherman's movements were mounted from the Charleston area. On February 3, an expeditionary force that included the 55th Regiment Massachusetts Infantry (Colored) was ordered up the South Edisto River, but faulty intelligence resulted in the Federals' taking only a fruitless three-day tramp through the marshland near the river's mouth. The day after this excursion was called off, February 7, the 54th Massachusetts (Colored), in concert with the 102nd USCT, two guns of a New York battery, and two cavalry companies, advanced from Pocataligo toward Charleston, following the railroad. Small groups of the enemy "halted on every bit of rising ground, or on the farther side of swamps, to throw up barricades of fence-rails against a rush of our cavalrymen, and delayed our advance by shelling us with their field-pieces," noted one of the 54th's officers. "But our skirmishers moved on steadily through water, swamp, and heavy under-growth, until their flanks were threatened, when, after exchanging shots, they would retire to new positions." Further delayed by conflicting orders, this Union column made slow progress. [2]

Near Charleston, another foray was ordered, this time against the Rebel lines on James Island, with the 55th Massachusetts (Colored) once again participating. The action, which began on February 10, was described in the diary of the 55th's Captain George T. Garrison:

At sunrise this morning we crossed over (from Cole's Id.) on to James Island, and advancing a short distance upon it[,] remained till near four o'clock watching the movements of the enemy. About this time our skirmish line was ordered to advance, and did so, meeting with some resistance from the rebels. Our regiment, the 144th N.Y. Vols., the 32nd U.S.C.T., and the 54th N.Y. Vols. were ordered up to the support of the skirmish line. We advanced in line of battle half a mile when we came upon a small breast work occupied by the Rebels; here a charge was made upon it by the 32nd U.S.C.T. and 144th N.Y.

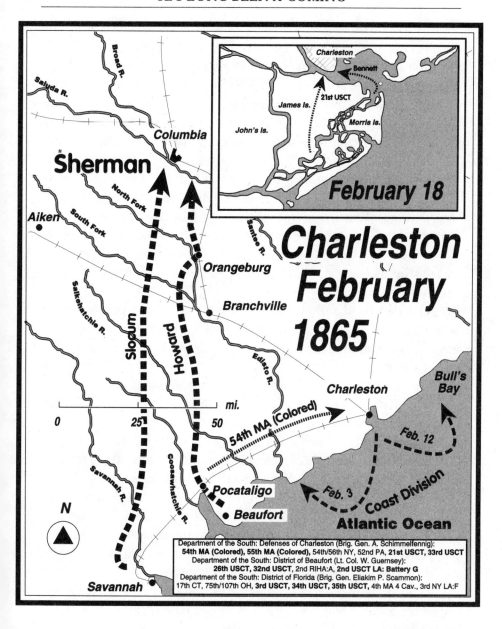

Vols., which resulted in the capture of it, with a loss to us of over thirty men killed and wounded. Some 23 rebel prisoners were captured, many of whom were wounded. The Major commanding the rebels and a lieutenant were captured, both wounded. One man was wounded in our reg't. At dark our forces retired to Cole's Island.[3]

Sherman's armies reached the east-west-running Charleston and Augusta Railroad on February 7, spreading devastation in their path. On the morning of February 12, the first of his troops entered Orangeburg, South Carolina.

In yet another diversionary action, a small expedition set off on transports from Folly Island to threaten the coast north of Charleston. Attempts to land these soldiers at Bull's Bay on February 12, and again on February 16, were frustrated by the weather and by local conditions that limited the movement of the deep-draft Union vessels. Ironically, it was at this time, when most of the forces assigned to the Charleston front were elsewhere, that the city was evacuated by Confederate military authorities. The further Sherman's men penetrated into South Carolina, the more isolated Charleston had become, until officials began to fear it might be cut off entirely; accordingly, on February 14, General P. G. T. Beauregard decided to abandon the city so that its troops could be preserved to fight Sherman. Throughout the night of February 17 and into the morning hours of February 18, Confederate soldiers pulled out of Charleston.

Lieutenant Colonel Augustus G. Bennett, the commander of the 21st USCT (in charge of Morris Island), having been alerted by "intercepted dispatches and the suspicious movements of the enemy," had vigilantly watched all night for signs that the Rebels were gone. As the rising sun burned off a heavy morning fog, it became apparent that the nearest enemy fortifications were unmanned. Several boats, bearing officers and a few enlisted men from the 52nd Pennsylvania, Company M of the 3rd Rhode Island Heavy Artillery, and the 21st USCT, scattered across the harbor, touching at Fort Sumter, Fort Moultrie, and other prominent places to allow the Federals to lower the Stars and Bars and raise the Stars and Stripes.[4]

"Public buildings, stores, warehouses, private dwellings, shipping, etc., were burning and being fired by armed rebels," Bennett noted as he debarked at the Charleston docks. Worried that his small force would be outnumbered by the Confederate rear guard, the USCT officer decided to wait until more friendly troops arrived before entering the town. While he and his party were holding at Mills' Wharf, the Rebel defensive fleet was blown up: "The sight was appalling and awfully grand," recalled Bennett. Shortly after noon, a deputation of civilian leaders met with him to surrender the city and enlist his help in saving it from the flames. Bennett dispatched the few Pennsylvania and Rhode Island companies that were on hand to take control of certain key points and to help fight the fires.[5]

"About 1 o'clock," he recorded, "the 21st U.S.C.T., 900 strong, under the command of Maj. R[ichard] H. Willoughby, made their entry into the city, having crossed over from James Island." Charles Coffin, the reporter for the *Boston Evening Journal,* was there to see the 21st march into town. Many in its ranks, Coffin reminded his readers, "were formerly slaves in the city of Charleston." Employing his usual exuberance, Coffin continued, "With the old flag above them, its fadeless stars and crimson folds waving in the . . . breeze, keeping step to freedom's drum beat, up the grass grown streets, past the slave marts where their wives and children, their brothers and fathers, where they themselves had been sold in the public stables, laying aside their arms, working the fire engines to extinguish the flames, and in the spirit of the redeemer of men, saving that which was lost!"[6]

On February 21, the 55th Massachusetts (Colored) proceeded through Charleston. "Cheers, blessings, prayers, and songs were heard on every side," recalled one of its members. "Men and women crowded to shake hands with men and officers." Six days later, the columns of the 54th Massachusetts (Colored) at last passed into the city, having completed their march from Pocataligo. "We could not but be exultant," wrote an officer of the regiment, "for by day and night, in sunshine and storm, through close combat and far-reaching cannonade, the city and its defenses were the special objects of our endeavor for many months." "On the day we entered that rebellious city," Sergeant John H. W. Collins of Company H told the *Christian Recorder,* "the streets were thronged with women and children of all sizes, colors and grades—the young, the old, the halt, the maimed, and the blind. I saw an old colored woman with a crutch,—for she could not walk without one, having served all her life in bondage,—who, on seeing us, got so happy that she threw down her crutch, and shouted that the year of Jubilee had come." Another black woman presented herself before a pair of newspapermen who watched in amazement as she danced for joy and sang:

Ye's been long a-coming,
Ye's been long a-coming,
Ye's been long a-coming,
For to take de land.[7]

More than a year earlier, Corporal James Henry Gooding of the 54th Massachusetts (Colored)—killed at Andersonville in July—had pointed to the significance of Charleston's fall when he told the readers of the *New Bedford Mercury*, "If the war should end tomorrow, without Charleston being subjugated, our victory would be great, to be sure, but the insurgents would exultingly boast that the first city that sullied the national honor could never be subdued. For the sake of the national honor let Charleston be taken before the war is over."[8]

Assault and Capture of Fort Fisher, North Carolina, January 15, 1865;
Action near Sugar Loaf, North Carolina, February 11, 1865;
Skirmish at Forks Road, North Carolina, February 20, 1865;
Occupation of Wilmington, North Carolina, February 22, 1865

It was shortly after midnight on January 13, 1865, when the long roll sounded to summon the garrison of Fort Fisher to the ramparts. Looking seaward, the officer commanding the Rebel bastion at the mouth of the Cape Fear River could see the distant, flickering lights of a massive Union fleet. This was the second time in less than a month that an amphibious Federal force had descended on Fort Fisher, which kept open the Confederacy's last seaport—Wilmington, North Carolina. The first attempt had come on Christmas Eve, heralded by one of those trademark devices so favored by the officer commanding the Union land forces, Major General Benjamin F. Butler.

Convinced that Fort Fisher's earth-and-log walls would come tumbling down if a large enough explosion occurred nearby, Butler had a 295-ton flat-bottomed boat packed with gunpowder and sent under cover of night to anchor beneath the fort's walls. At 1:46 A.M., the sky brightened as the powder boat went up with a tremendous bang. The detonation was undeniably spectacular, but in the darkness the volunteer crew had positioned the craft nearly six hundred yards north of Fort Fisher before abandoning it, so the blast did little more than frighten the Rebel sentries. At daylight, Union warships began a concentrated bombardment of the fort while the leading elements of Butler's invasion force successfully secured a beachhead nearby. However, the failure of his trick to do the job took all the wind out of Butler's sails, and he soon recalled the troops already landed, told the admiral commanding the fleet that the operation had been canceled, and sailed back to Virginia.

This time, even Benjamin Butler's political power base was not enough to shield him from the repercussions of his failed scheme: the man who had been the highest-ranking U.S. officer actively to promote the combat service of black troops was summarily sacked by Lieutenant General U. S. Grant. In almost the same motion, Grant ordered a new expedition to be mounted against Fort Fisher. The command this time was given to Major General Alfred H. Terry, who eschewed the elaborate designs of his predecessor in favor of a simple, direct approach. As U.S. Navy warships opened fire on Fort Fisher on January 13, the first of some eighty-nine hundred Union infantrymen began to land at the lower end of Myrtle Sound, four miles to the north. The troops came ashore on the Atlantic Ocean side of a relatively narrow peninsula called Federal Point, bounded on the west by the Cape Fear River.

Terry's force comprised two divisions, drawn for the most part from the Army of the James. One of these consisted of black infantry commanded by Brigadier General Charles J. Paine. Paine's First Brigade, led by Colonel John W. Ames, contained the 4th, 6th, 30th, and 39th USCT, while the Second, Colonel Elias Wright commanding, encompassed the 1st, 5th, 10th, 27th, and 37th USCT. The white troops began landing at about 8:45 A.M., and the first of the black soldiers followed about an hour and fifteen minutes later.

"The boats," wrote Colonel Ames,

on approaching the line of surf, threw out small anchors and grapnels, and then let themselves wash shorewards. . . . When the undertow began to recede, one of the sailors jumped into the water and held the boat's stern against the seaward wash, while the armed passengers climbed over the sides into the knee-deep water, carrying knapsacks and the sacred ammunition high up on fixed bayonets, and ran for the shore, chased by the crested advance of the succeeding billow.

"The surf was quite high although the wind was still and I was quite damp, considering that the water was only about knee deep where I leaped from the surf boat—a huge wave followed me up and almost washed me away," recalled the 5th USCT's Lieutenant Elliott F. Grabill. A fellow officer, Lieutenant Joseph A. Scroggs, put it more succinctly: "High surf, all got wet, but none hurt."[9]

The last of Paine's men was ashore by 3:00 P.M. An hour later, their commander led them down the beach in the direction of Fort Fisher, then veered inland with "orders to strike across the peninsula to the Cape Fear River. Our Div. formed a line of battle and started across the peninsula through a laurel marsh," noted Lieutenant Scroggs. "Shortly after dark we emerged from the marsh and our lines were established with our left resting on the Cape Fear river." "Here we worked all night and next day and night and the next day in throwing up strong earthworks—works of great strength stretching from river to ocean," remembered Lieutenant Grabill. "Our first business was to shut off reinforcements from Wilmington by land. This we did effectively."[10]

Worried that a single white division would not be enough to capture Fort Fisher, General Terry drew off one of the two white brigades posted with Paine's men to support his effort, leaving the rear line held by all of his black troops and a single white brigade. Then, on the afternoon of January 15, he began his land attack against Fort Fisher. Henry M. Turner, the black chaplain of the 1st USCT, accompanied some of the assaulting units as a surgeon's aide. "Never had I seen grape and canister used so effectively as the rebels used it on our troops on this occasion," he wrote soon afterward. "At one time I thought they could never stand it, neither do I believe they would have stood, but for the fact that they knew the black troops were in the rear, and if they (the white troops) failed, the colored troops would take the fort and claim the honor."[11]

Even as bitter fighting raged at Fort Fisher, Rebel reinforcements under Major General Robert F. Hoke were making a concerted effort to break through Terry's rear line. Veteran Confederate combat units moved forward at about 4:00 P.M. "My recollection," said a North Carolina officer, "is that we confidently expected to run over the troops in our front and drive them in confusion upon Terry's attacking column."[12]

Reported Brigadier General Paine, "About the time the assault upon Fort Fisher commenced the enemy advanced a strong skirmish line at

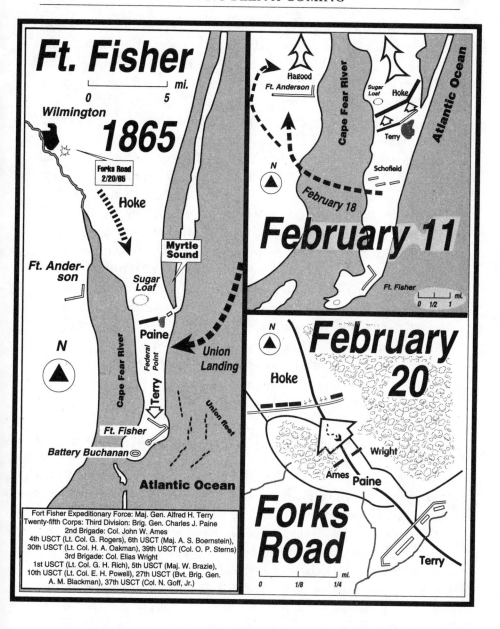

Fort Fisher Expeditionary Force: Maj. Gen. Alfred H. Terry
Twenty-fifth Corps: Third Division: Brig. Gen. Charles J. Paine
2nd Brigade: Col. John W. Ames
4th USCT (Lt. Col. G. Rogers), 6th USCT (Maj. A. S. Boernstein),
30th USCT (Lt. Col. H. A. Oakman), 39th USCT (Col. O. P. Sterns)
3rd Brigade: Col. Elias Wright
1st USCT (Lt. Col. G. H. Rich), 5th USCT (Maj. W. Brazie),
10th USCT (Lt. Col. E. H. Powell), 27th USCT (Bvt. Brig. Gen.
A. M. Blackman), 37th USCT (Col. N. Goff, Jr.)

the double-quick along my entire front. . . . He succeeded in driving back two or three posts held by the white troops toward my right, and occupied their [rifle] pits for a time. The pickets of my division held their ground resolutely." Colonel Ames, who had surrendered to curiosity earlier that day and ventured toward Fisher to watch the attack, came back on the run when he heard gunfire to the north. By the time he drew close to the line, however, the firing had stopped. "This was so reassuring that I slackened my pace as I came among the pines," related Ames, "and, presently, coming upon the idle groups of Negro soldiers lolling about the rear of their unscathed breastworks, I knew, at last, that General Hoke had made no impression upon them."[13]

The combat at Fort Fisher, often hand-to-hand, continued until about 9:00 P.M., when the defenders were finally forced to take refuge in Battery Buchanan, at the tip of the peninsula. So convinced had Terry become of the holding power of Paine's division that he withdrew first the 27th USCT, then all of Wright's brigade, to reinforce the attack. Most of the brigade would return to Paine without seeing any combat, but the 27th would play a part in the capture of Battery Buchanan. "Paine's Divn of Colored Troops did an essential part in the taking of Fort Fisher," declared Lieutenant Grabill, "but as we worked with spade and shovel rather than gun and cartridge, the white troops who did the fighting will get the praise."[14]

Fort Fisher's fall did not conclude the campaign, though it did spell the end of Wilmington's value as a seaport. Because the city remained a strategically important transportation hub, Union planning now turned toward its occupation. General Terry's force of eight thousand fell about five thousand men short of the number needed to accomplish that task, however, so on February 7, the leading elements from Major General John M. Schofield's Twenty-third Corps came up from Nashville. On February 11, Terry's Provisional Corps tested the Confederate defenses across the Federal Point Peninsula.

White soldiers, with the 3rd New Hampshire in advance, pressed the Confederate left, while Colonel Ames's brigade, the 4th USCT leading, probed the Rebel right. James C. Fitzpatrick, the *New York Herald*'s correspondent, reported that Paine's men "pushed the enemy with great gallantry, driving them from every stump and tree where they sought to make a stand. On this part of the line it was a sort of running fight, in which the colored soldiers seemed to pursue their enemy with relentless animosity, driving them at last to the cover of their main works." A captain in the 6th USCT remembered the action this day as a "lively and interesting fight." In Company A of the 6th, the lieutenant in charge was killed, so "the direction devolved to Sergeant Richard Carter (colored), who commanded with great skill and courage until the company was relieved."[15]

The fighting, which Brigadier General Paine classified as a "brisk skirmish," cost the black division two officers and fourteen men killed, and a total of seventy-six wounded. The USCT men, wrote the *New York Times*'s reporter, "behaved well, and secured the respect and admiration of all who witnessed their steadiness and courage." One of Schofield's officers wrote more colloquially that the blacks "fight splendidly. I saw them and our regiment saw it—they all acknowledge that old nigger will fight." The Rebel line probed by Terry's troops proved secure against direct assault, so the emphasis shifted across the Cape Fear River, where, on February 18, Union warships bombarded Fort Anderson while Schofield worked his way around to the west. Finding themselves flanked on that bank, on February 19 the Confederates on both sides of the river commenced a slow withdrawal toward Wilmington.[16]

Terry's troops followed along the Federal Point Road until they came upon the C.S. Major General Hoke's command, dug in a short distance outside Wilmington, near Forks Road. The 5th USCT was ordered forward a little after 3:00 P.M. to develop the enemy's position, with prompt support from other regiments of the brigade. According to an officer in the 5th, the men "were not able to take works manned by 4,500 troops and mounted with six pcs of artillery. . . . I suppose it was fun for Terry but little for us." Brigadier General Paine later reported losses of two killed and fifty-one wounded in this action.

With two Union columns closing on them, it was merely a matter of time before the Confederate defenders began to abandon Wilmington. As soon as this happened—at about 1:00 A.M. on February 22—the Federals moved in and occupied the city. A. G. Jones, adjutant in the 27th USCT, later wrote of this day:

One and a half miles south of Wilmington a strong chain of forts covered the approaches to the city. When we came in sight of the works our columns were halted, stragglers gathered in, ranks dressed, colors unfurled, and away we went for the works, over whose sides we clambered, only to find them deserted. . . . At the outskirts of the city one

363

solitary Union flag in the hands of an aged colored woman greeted our eyes. . . . The streets were thronged with colored people, all in a high state of excitement, shouting, "Glory to de Lord. The blessed day ob salbation am cum. De good Lord bress massa Linkum."[17]

"The frantic demonstrations of the negro population will never die out of my memory," noted a USCT officer. "Their cheers . . . mingled sublimely with the lusty shouts of our brave soldiery that welled up as they caught sight of the 'Old Glory' floating again over the dwellings of the loyal citizens." A reporter recorded the reaction of the local black population to the USCT soldiers: "The men danced in jubilation, the women screamed and went into hysterics then and there, on the sidewalks. And their sable brothers in arms marched past, proud and erect, singing their 'John Brown' hymn, where it was never sung before."[18]

"The march of the Union army through Wilmington will live forever in the memory of the colored people," wrote a USCT soldier who called himself "Solid Shot." John W. Pratt, a black orderly sergeant in the 30th USCT, was another who would never forget Wilmington:

At the appearance of our troops and the old flag the people gathered. I noticed an old man and woman,—both seemed to be lame, shouting and giving God the praise to see this day. They said they had been praying so long, yet they should die without the sight, and they thanked God that the day had come when they were not to be driven to the market to be sold as sheep. The children shouted and clasped their hands. I was indeed speechless. I could do nothing but cry to look at the poor creatures so overjoyed.[19]

The operations against Fort Fisher and Wilmington were the last combat actions for black troops in North Carolina. In his postwar memoir of service, Brigadier General Paine summarized his division's remaining marches as follows: "Upon the approach of Gen'l Sherman's army, my div'n as part of Gen'l Terry's command moved north to join him; and took part in the pursuit of the enemy, until near Raleigh Gen'l Johnston surrendered."[20]

But before they left Wilmington, the black soldiers were to have one more moment of great satisfaction, when they took possession of a slave trader's pen. "The whipping post has been burnt," "Solid Shot" reported, "and the building is being used for a righteous purpose."[21]

Skirmish at East River Bridge, Florida, March 5, 1865; Skirmish at Newport Bridge, Florida, March 5, 1865; Skirmish at Natural Bridge, Florida, March 6, 1865

The 2nd USCT, organized at Arlington, Virginia, between June 20 and November 11, 1863, was sent to Ship Island, near Mississippi, in December of that year. Commissary Sergeant James T. S. Taylor wrote to the Anglo-African *on New Year's Day, 1864, to assure its readers that "all the boys are extremely anxious for a fight. . . . It was quite cheering when we reached the Mississippi river with rebeldom on both sides, seeing thousands who have been made free by the President's Proclamation coming from all parts of the cotton and sugar fields to the river banks with hats and handfuls of oranges for us and cheering us loudly." On February 13, 1864, the 2nd USCT was ordered to Key West, from which posting Company D's first sergeant complained to the* Anglo-African *that some worthy enlisted men were being held back from becoming officers: "Yet the men are kept in the rear of them as far in military life as they were in civil life; but the time is fast approaching when they will have to acknowledge the manhood of the colored man."[22]*

Serious problems simmered in the ranks as the regiment's Florida service entered its third month. "We came out as soldiers . . . to fight for a good cause," declared "a Soldier" in March, "but I am sorry to say that neither the white soldiers, or a majority of our own officers, respect us as soldiers." The anonymous writer went on to cite two incidents of racial violence, one the beating of a black soldier as punishment for a minor infraction, and the other the death of a USCT man at the hands of "friendly" white troops. "This is the kind of treatment we are subject to, and the whole Regiment has resolved that if it continues they will lay down their arms and go to prison, as they would much rather be there than to be treated worse than slaves are in the South," he concluded.[23]

A day later, Sergeant Taylor described the 2nd USCT's arrival at Key West and its march through the town. "Being the first of the colored troops that ever paraded its streets, you may imagine . . . what a galling thing it must have been to the secesh of the town. They looked at us with as much wonder as though it was the first sight they ever beheld, and the last one they ever expected to see in this world," he told the Anglo-African. *Taylor finished his note: "We cannot say much, as yet, for the fighting qualities of the 2d Regiment, but, feeling confident in the drilling given us, and the discipline taught us by our pains-taking Colonel [Benjamin R. Townsend], we believe we will not disgrace him, ourselves, or our country's flag in the day of battle."*[24]

The 2nd USCT took part only in some small actions in 1864. On May 8, Sergeant Taylor wrote to the Anglo-African of a raid to Tampa in late April. *"The boys were entirely successful in surrounding the place,"* he boasted, *"and after two hours fighting the rebels surrendered the entire garrison."* Of special interest to the black soldiers were the blows they struck against slavery: *"The 2d Regiment, in this expedition also, declared perpetual freedom to about 25 contrabands,"* noted Taylor. On July 1, another detachment was sent on a deep penetration raid that lasted more than six weeks. *"Our men were very lucky,"* declared Sergeant H. C. Jones, *"having lost only four men. When the rebs did stand up for a fight our boys brought down nine of them."* This time, however, the blows aimed at enslavement were parried by circumstance. *"Just ahead of our boys there were one hundred or more slaves, chained and being sent out of the way,"* reported Jones. *"Our [white] officers thought [it] best not to follow them, for fear that our force was not strong enough."*[25]

By the end of 1864, with the pay issue at last settled, attention in the 2nd USCT turned toward the lack of black officers. *"Why equal privileges are withheld from one class and not from the other, I am at a loss to conjecture,"* wrote Sergeant Taylor to the Anglo-African. *"Are we still to be deprived of all these rights and privileges which, by our sacrifices, we justly merit? This nation had to be taught some very severe lessons by Providence before they would even let the negro have a musket, and now, not until equal rights are given us as soldiers will the God of all Wisdom lead the nation to a victorious triumph and a lasting peace."*[26]

On February 8, 1865, a newly arrived member of the 2nd USCT praised his regiment in the pages of the Anglo-African. *Isaac L. Dennett averred that his unit "cannot be excelled by any volunteer or reg-*

ular regiment in the service, that is, as far as drill is concerned, their movements being like clock work." He also noted that their service was providing the men with more than mere training as soldiers: "They are striving, with the aid of their officers, to improve themselves in learning. Books can constantly be seen in their hands, and the officers, who are of the right stamp, take great interest in them." Concluded the black soldier, "I pity the rebel regiment that may come in contact with the 2nd Regiment U.S. Colored Infantry, for I fear very few of them would get back to Jeff [Davis]."[27]

The Gulf waters between the grounded ships and the St. Marks Lighthouse were a scene of constant activity as the Union expeditionary force landed on Saturday, March 4, 1865. Some nine hundred men under the command of Brigadier General John Newton came ashore on the Florida Panhandle, just eighteen miles below the state capital. In its intent, this operation was unexceptional—merely a raid, one of many undertaken against Rebel Florida—but in its size, it was well out of the ordinary, with nearly one thousand men participating, instead of the few hundred usual for such actions. Assembling such a force had required virtually all the disposable troops in the Federal District of Key West and Tortugas. Newton's command consisted of a small dismounted detachment of the 2nd Florida Cavalry (U.S.), six companies of the 2nd USCT, and the full complement of the 99th USCT.

The operation's stated goal was a strike on the port facilities in the town of St. Marks, located a few miles up the river of the same name. According to a reporter, "There is no doubt that preparations had been made [by the Confederates] . . . to make St. Marks, in some sort, a compensation for the loss of Wilmington[, North Carolina]." If the rumors heard at district headquarters in Key West were true, General Newton also intended to move on to Tallahassee once he had secured his primary objective. For Newton, who had fought with only modest distinction at Fredericksburg, at Gettysburg, and in Sherman's Atlanta campaign, it was a last chance to win a reputation in the field.[28]

It was not until early on March 5, with the arrival of two navy howitzers, that the black infantry and dismounted white cavalry finally headed toward their first target: the East River Bridge. All the planks

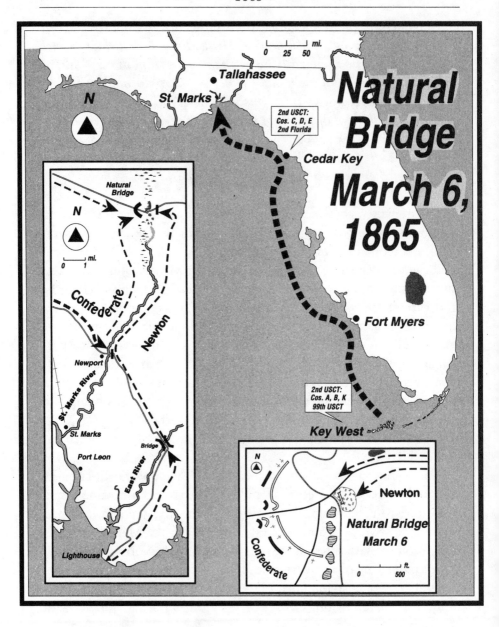

Natural Bridge
March 6, 1865

2nd USCT:
Cos. C, D, E
2nd Florida

2nd USCT:
Cos. A, B, K
99th USCT

Tallahassee
St. Marks
Cedar Key
Fort Myers
Key West

Natural Bridge
Newport
St. Marks River
St. Marks
Port Leon
East River
Bridge
Lighthouse
Confederate
Newton

Newton
Natural Bridge
March 6
Confederate

in the span had been taken up by a small Rebel force dug in there on the opposite bank. Two companies of the 2nd USCT advanced against this force in skirmishing order at about 9:00 A.M. While some of the infantrymen crowded toward the bridge itself, others forded the shallow river to flank the enemy troops. The Confederates fled, in their haste leaving behind a twelve-pounder bronze Napoleon cannon as a prize for the 2nd USCT skirmishers. While no breakdown of losses here was recorded, Confederates at the East River Bridge skirmish claimed to have killed three or four black soldiers.

The 99th USCT had originally been organized as an engineering unit, so the men had little trouble getting the bridge into working order. Newton's columns were soon across the East River and headed for the town of Newport, where the general hoped to cross the St. Marks River and envelop the river port. The tocsin had sounded in Tallahassee on March 4, and within twenty-four hours its defense units were mobilized, including cadets from the Florida Military Institute. Other militia groups, based closer to the landing site, were also coming into line.

When the Yankee troops arrived at Newport, at around 2:00 P.M., they found the bridge partially ablaze and effectively wrecked. An attempt by the white soldiers of the 2nd Florida Cavalry (U.S.) to rush the structure was repulsed. Unable to cross the river here, General Newton continued his march along it after being assured by his local scouts that just a few miles upstream, it dipped abruptly underground to create a solid crossing point known as Natural Bridge. It was to this place that Newton now directed his columns.

Hoping to conceal his destination from the Rebels, the Union general picked a road that was "old and unfrequented." Unfortunately, the estimated distance of five miles to Natural Bridge proved optimistically short, by some three miles. Worse yet, the Confederates evidentally *had* got wind of what Newton was trying to do, since when the Federal vanguard approached the area toward dawn, it found Rebels blocking the way. John Newton decided to wait until daylight to force his passage.[29]

Thus, just at daybreak on March 6, the first wave of Federal troops moved against the Rebels entrenched at Natural Bridge. Companies B and G of the 2nd USCT, under the popular commander Major Benjamin C. Lincoln, drove the Confederate pickets back across Natural Bridge before being checked by heavy fire from the main Southern line on the other side. While Lincoln's men dug in, Newton held back the rest of his command and considered his options. Reports indicated there was a fordable stretch of the river about a mile below Natural Bridge, but on closer examination it proved to be not only impracticable to cross but also already covered by alert enemy troops, who were being continually reinforced. "Nothing now remained to do but to feel the enemy [at Natural Bridge] and ascertain whether or no[t] a passage could be forced," wrote Newton.[30]

By late morning, he had decided on a two-pronged attack, perhaps based on the assumption that he was facing shaky militia units. The plan called for Major Lincoln to lead Companies E, G, and K of the 2nd USCT in a frontal assault while Colonel Townsend took Companies A, B, and H to flank the enemy's right. The 99th USCT, for its part, was to support both wings as a general reserve. The Union attack got under way at about 11:00 A.M.

For a fleeting moment, it seemed as if Newton's gamble might pay off. As Townsend's flanking party approached the Rebel rifle pits, the enemy troops scampered off in a panic. Hardly had Townsend reached the enemy's works, however, when, as Newton later reported, "he encountered a wide and deep slough impassable to troops, and the command reluctantly returned." An even worse fate awaited Major Lincoln and his three 2nd USCT companies, whose advance was targeted by all six Rebel cannon and much of the infantry. Remembered a Confederate cannoneer, "The enemy had a narrow defile to pass through of about forty yards, and all the guns played on this point. We played havoc amongst them, you may be sure." When the Federals reeled back, they carried with them the body of Major Lincoln, who had been mortally wounded in the futile attempt.[31]

Newton now retreated about three hundred yards and set up a defensive line in some pine barrens while he contemplated what to do next. The navy was supposed to be forcing its way up the St. Marks River as far as the site of Port Leon in order to protect his route back to the coast; from there, it was hoped that the vessels could proceed even farther up river to capture a Rebel battery located near St. Marks. The ships had been threading their way very slowly along the unmarked channel and were still a mile or so short of Port Leon when the officer commanding learned that Newton had been blocked at Natural Bridge. That was enough for him: the vessels reversed course and headed back.

It was almost 5:00 P.M. when the Confederates came boiling across Natural Bridge, confident they would catch the Yankee columns strung out in retreat. For once, their confidence was misplaced: Newton had not moved from his strong position in the pine barrens. In his report, he noted that the enemy troops came up against a "perfect line of infantry supported by artillery." He also wrote (taking a bit of literary license) that the "rebels were cut down like grass." Even as the counterattack recoiled, General Newton decided that the navy's withdrawal so imperiled his position that he had no option but to retreat. Leaving eight seriously wounded men behind in a farmhouse, Newton led the rest of his column on a slow march back toward Newport, where he picked up the small cavalry force he had posted to keep the enemy from crossing behind him. At 4:00 A.M., March 7, his men finally reached the lighthouse and there reembarked.* Newton's expedition was at an end, having failed to achieve any of its objectives.[32]

The human cost of this foray (paid mostly by the black troops) was twenty-one killed, eighty-nine wounded, and thirty-eight missing. On the Confederate side, the best estimate of casualties was three killed and twenty-three wounded, three of the latter mortally. If Natural Bridge did not classify as a battle, its carnage was nonetheless pitiable: a Rebel soldier who visited the site after the fight wrote that each of the Federal earthworks

> had dead Negroes enough around, and in it to have made a slave holder rich. I bethought myself to secure a memento of the occasion, . . . I saw what I took to be a dead Negro, with his head on a nice cartridge box that had a broad shoulder strap to it; as I had been wanting just such a box I walked up & gave it a light pull, when the Negro held on to it with his hand and gave a groan I left him to die with his head on it, but afterwards saw the same cartridge box on a member of our company.[33]

On March 16, Isaac L. Dennett wrote to the Anglo-African following the 2nd USCT's return to Key West:

> On Sunday last, the largest funeral ever beheld on this Key, took place. Maj. Lincoln of the 2d U.S. Colored Infantry, Lieut. [Thomas H.] Murphy and Lieut. [Edward] Carrington, were consigned to their graves, followed by those who stood by them on the battle-field. . . .

---

*A portion of one company of the 99th USCT, numbering approximately twenty soldiers, at some point became separated from the main body and was captured by Confederate cavalry near the East River.

Maj. Lincoln stands at the head, and he fell as a brave soldier wishes to fall. In the morning, early, when asked could he take a certain bridge, he replied, "I will try," and at the head of two companies of his own regiment, he charged upon the rebels, who were three times his number, and drove them back, holding the bridge for four hours, till ordered by a superior officer to leave it; and when he saw his noble men at a gun falling, he, with no fear of death, went to it and stood by them. He was struck by a shell, and fell mortally wounded. When told that he must die, he replied, "I am ready." Such men we cannot spare in these trying times, and his loss we deeply feel. . . .

I would not pass over the others who fell on that day. Most of our officers were wounded. Col. Townsend was wounded in the arm while at the head of his men, and I do believe, could he have had his own way, the battle would have been ours. . . . Many of the men are wounded, but desire to get well to try again. Let no one talk ill to me of the courage of the African race. They cannot be beat, and it would send a thrill of pleasure through you to see them charge the arch-fiends on the battle-field. The 2d U.S. Colored Infantry have been tried, and as I remarked I pitied the rebs who should come in contact with them, and I have not been disappointed; for in this late battle, very many of them have bitten the dust. Truly the 2d U.S. Colored Infantry deserve great praise. They are faithful soldiers to a man.[34]

Interlude

"We Want Black Commissioned Officers"

———◄◦►———

THERE was a world of difference between a sergeant and a lieutenant. The former was an enlisted man whose authority did not extend much beyond his regiment, while the latter was recognized as a gentleman who could command units other than his own. Except in the brief instance of the Louisiana Native Guards, U.S. military policy pointedly prohibited the appointment of black line officers. In December 1864, the army's assistant adjutant general posed the key question: "[Are] white officers and men prepared to acknowledge and obey the colored man, or officer, as a military superior? . . . If [not], would not the bestowal of commissions upon colored men introduce in the army, a disturbing element which might be of serious injury to the service?"[1]

Black troops rejected this argument. A sergeant in the 54th Regiment Massachusetts Infantry (Colored) emphatically declared, "We want black commissioned officers; and only because we want men we can understand and who can understand us." By 1864, there was also the matter of invaluable field experience. Writing from Morris Island, the 54th's Corporal James Henry Gooding reflected that there were sergeants in that regiment who "were just as capable of being entrusted with the command of colored troops as those who know nothing of the disposition or feelings of such troops."[2]

It was Massachusetts Governor John A. Andrew who once again stepped forward to press the issue when, in March 1864, he commissioned Sergeant Stephen A. Swails as a lieutenant in the 54th Massachusetts (Colored). Other, similar appointments followed from Andrews's desk later that year, including an order making Sergeant James M. Trotter of the 55th Regiment Massachusetts Infantry (Colored) a second lieutenant. In every case, the War Department blocked the move. In order to become an officer, an enlisted man had to be first mustered out at his lower rank, and then mustered back in at his new, higher one. Following instructions from Washington, the officer commanding the Department of the South refused to muster out Sergeants Swails and Trotter and the other black noncoms slated for promotion. When Trotter was told that his commission was being held up because there was no statute permitting the commissioning of black officers, he could not contain his anger. "Do you know any law that *prohibits* it?" he asked a powerful white friend of the regiment.[3]

By early 1865, the steady performance of key black regiments in the field, growing support for a policy change in high places (not least on the part of former Vice President Hamlin), and continued protests from the soldiers themselves at last broke the barrier. Swails, Trotter, and others were promoted to lieutenant, but as with so many other civil-rights advances, their success merely spawned new conflicts: "There is much feeling in the Regiment among the officers against these promotions of colored men in respect with white officer," wrote Trotter in mid-1865, "but all the best officers are in favor of it."[4]

While black officers still had a long and rocky road yet to travel, filled with switchbacks and detours, they had taken an important first step on the way. As the black chaplain of the 55th Massachusetts (Colored) observed, "The ball does move."[5]

Chapter Fourteen

"Our Errand through the State"

———◇———

Expedition from Georgetown to Camden, South Carolina,
April 5–25, 1865

BY the first of April, the question was no longer *whether* the Confederacy would collapse, but *when*. In southern Virginia, the uneasy stalemate at Petersburg would soon be decisively shattered; farther south, Sherman, having devastating South Carolina, was camped near Goldsboro, North Carolina, waiting to resume his inexorable march on April 10. He was determined that the tattered Rebel army confronting him would not draw sustenance from those sections of the Palmetto State that his men had missed. Just after entering North Carolina, Sherman had informed the officer commanding the Department of the South that the "enemy still has much railroad stock and munitions on the track about Sumterville and Florence, and if you can make up a force of 2,500 men out of your Charleston and Savannah garrisons I want you to reach that road and destroy everything possible and exhaust the country of supplies."[1]

Sherman's letter took a week to reach the officer, who then began concentrating troops at the coastal port of Georgetown. On April 1, Brigadier General Edward E. Potter arrived to take charge of the expedition force, which now, by his estimate, numbered some twenty-seven hundred men. There were six regiments altogether, organized into two brigades, one composed of white troops, the other all black. Colonel Edward N. Hallowell led the black brigade, which contained the 32nd USCT, five companies of the 102nd USCT, and the 54th Regiment Massachusetts Infantry (Colored), this last counting in its ranks 675 officers and men. This would prove to be the final military operation of any significance involving the best-known black regiment to fight in the Civil War.

Day One: Wednesday, April 5

Potter's troops began to march out of Georgetown at 8:00 A.M. There were a lot of sore muscles in the ranks, as most of the men had come directly from occupation duties and were no longer accustomed to spending long hours tramping along dirt roads. Nonetheless, insisted Private Benjamin M. Bond, in Company B of the 54th, the "troops were all in fine spirits, and seemed anxious to have a crack at the Johnnies." First Lieutenant Edward L. Stevens of the regiment made careful note of the "large train of contrabands" that was accompanying the soldiers "for the purpose of getting their families which they had left in Rebbdum." Sergeant John H. W. N. Collins of Company H was nonplussed by the activity, later referring to the whole thing as "our errand through the State."[2]

Lieutenant Colonel Henry N. Hooper, commanding the 54th, reported that the men "marched that day North westerly parallel with the Black River eighteen miles." An approving Lieutenant Stevens thought that the soldiers were "marched with great judgment & celerity, especially considering it was the first day out." "We passed a number of large plantations," observed Private Bond. "Some looked deserted and desolate, while others bore a more thrifty appearance, and brought to mind the former appearance of the once fruitful South." Colonel Hallowell considered the "roads very good." Potter's force camped for the night near Johnson's Swamp.[3]

Potter's movement was quickly communicated to the Black River communities through what one resident called the "flying reports of our scouts." The day before Potter's expedition left, Williamsburg County militia had actually rallied at Potato Ferry, just north of Johnson's Swamp, to launch a preemptive strike on Georgetown. Led by

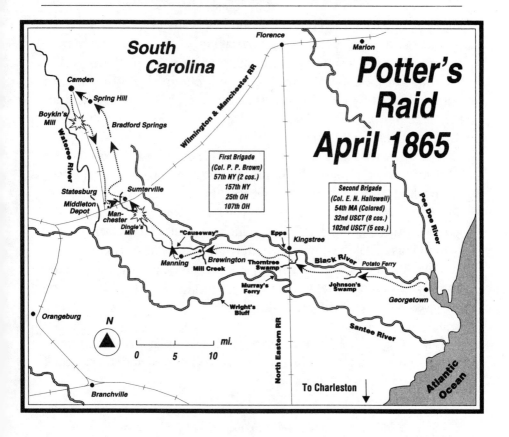

a veteran Confederate officer on convalescent leave, the militia now began to shadow Potter's men, most often trailing along the north bank of the Black River to dispute any attempted crossing. All the river bridges were either burned or partially dismantled.[4]

Tension was running high. "It is doubtful if ever a more contemptible force of cutthroats assembled than Potter's Raiders," declared a later historian of this region. Added another local chronicler, "Soon rumors came to Sumter[ville] of another march from the sea, even more to be dreaded than Sherman's, for armed Negroes made up a large part of Potter's expeditionary force."[5]

Day Two: Thursday, April 6

Lieutenant Stevens was bleary-eyed this morning. "Did not sleep much last night," he scribbled in his journal. "Two or three shots were fired & we turned out a few minutes." The black troops led the infantry and were preceded by a detachment from the 4th Massachusetts Cavalry. From his mounted vantage point, Colonel Hallowell thought the country "more open and rolling" than Monday's, an opinion shared by Lieutenant Stevens. It was what another officer of the 54th described as a "close, warm day," which contributed to "some exhaustion and straggling."[6]

"As we neared Kingstree," reported General Potter, "detachments were sent down to destroy the bridges over the Black River, but the enemy had already done that work." Earlier this day, Lieutenant Stevens's company had come upon a farmhouse whose owner demanded protection as a Unionist. This argument carried little weight with the black soldiers, who "began to slay chickens & take horses," Stevens noted. In a vain attempt to stop the pillaging, a woman in the household flapped a tablecloth like a flag, screaming, "Mr. Officer, see those big men coming in here[!]" Unfazed, Stevens made no effort to halt his troops' actions.[7]

According to the 54th's history, "Camp was made at Thorntree Swamp after a nineteen-mile march with Kingstree across the Black River, seven miles to our right."[8]

Day Three: Friday, April 7

The Union soldiers, black and white, were up before dawn. After a quick breakfast, the men formed into loose files and stood in the dawn prelight waiting for the word of command. Potter gave it at 6:30 A.M., directing his columns through open country to the northwest. As they approached the North Eastern Railroad line, the five companies from the 102nd USCT were diverted toward Kingstree to destroy the Black River bridge. "They exchanged a few shots with the enemy," wrote Colonel Hallowell after their return, "but report no casualties."[9]

"We burned cotton gins & presses," noted Lieutenant Stevens of events this day, "but no dwelling houses." Early in the afternoon, after tramping nine miles, Potter's men came to a crossroads, where Companies A and H of the 54th Massachusetts (Colored) were detached to destroy the Epps Bridge over the Black River. Sergeant

Collins led an advance party consisting of a corporal and fifteen privates. "After advancing about two miles," recollected Collins, "and wading through water and mud, we spied a Johnny sitting upon his horse as a picket. . . . Halting my men for further orders, I received instructions to proceed forward with the utmost caution, and screen my men as much as possible in the woods. The swamp through which we had to pass was waist deep."[10]

When Collins and his party were within seventy-five yards of the picket, they were joined by Second Lieutenant Frederick E. Rogers, then in charge of Company A. Moving roughly parallel with Rogers's men, off to their left, was a platoon from Company H, deployed there by Lieutenant Stevens. "Here was the meanest place I ever saw, black water & black mud," he would remember. Suddenly, Collins, Rogers, and their men were spotted and came under fire from the opposite bank. "Johnny's balls began to fall thick and fast around us," said the sergeant. Captain Charles E. Tucker, commanding the operation, reported that the Union soldiers had "advanced in sight of the bridge and easy musket-range, when the enemy abandoned the temporary works they had improvised from the flooring of the bridge on the opposite side of the river, making quick their retreat and leaving behind the heavy timbering of the work in flames." Tucker, who was mounted on a troublesome horse named Cyclops, rode out into the open to give the fleeing enemy "a bit of my Yankee eloquence and [call] attention to their nervousness in not being able to shoot even old 'Cyclops.'"[11]

"The Lieutenant got wounded in the right arm," wrote Collins. "I had two men [Privates Joseph C. Johnson and Joseph H. White] wounded—one in the right leg, the other in both shoulders; and it appeared to us that the Johnnies had nothing much but *bird-shot* to fire at us, which whizzed about our ears in perfect showers."* Added Stevens, "We retired, as we had found out that the bridge was burned & we had orders not to have an engagement. We marched

---

*Private Johnson's wound, in his left shoulder, while not severe enough to warrant his discharge from the regiment, would affect him for the rest of his life. In testimony given after his death, in 1889, his employer said that Johnson, who before entering military service "was stouter than any man I had working for me," came back "not near the man he was before he went to the army." Private White was hit in the knee; though he later returned to duty, the musket ball remained in his leg and caused him constant pain.

back to the cross-roads, & found the columns had all marched past, & it was about dark." Potter's columns settled down this night near Mill Creek.[12]

Directly ahead of Potter's raiders was the small town of Manning, described by one resident as "quite a pretty little place, with only a few hundred inhabitants. . . . Nearly all the houses in it were built on one long straight street about a mile in length." During an anxious meeting held this evening, the local militia commander admitted that there were not enough men on hand to defend the town against the enemy. It was decided that his unit would join others from the region that were concentrating at Sumterville. "Manning was now left to the mercy of the Federals," lamented a female resident, "and that night many fervent prayers ascended to God from the lonely and defenseless women there, and [for] the safety of the fathers, husbands and sons who had gone forward to await the enemy's coming."[13]

Day Four: Saturday, April 8

On reaching Sumterville, the forty men from the Manning militia became part of a small military force whose makeup was emblematic of the Confederacy's declining fortunes. In addition to the local militia companies, there was a squad drawn from convalescent soldiers, a few cavalrymen separated from their commands by Sherman's march, a couple of artillery officers still recuperating from wounds, and about 120 Kentucky veterans belonging to the so-called Orphan Brigade, which had been sent into this area to protect the railroad stock. There were about 575 men in all, sporting a motley assortment of rifles, muskets, and shotguns and backed up by two antiquated artillery pieces.

"Excitement ran high as scouts galloped back and forth, and rumors flew from mouth to mouth," wrote a later historian. One of the Kentucky soldiers recalled that this scratch force "took up our position in the edge of the town & waited for the enemy. Our line ran through a church yard which was used for a grave yard belonging to a very pretty episcopal church."[14]

On April 8, recounted the history of the 54th Massachusetts, "the column moved over fair roads through a wooded country, with a bright sky overhead, our advance sighting the enemy now and then on the flanks and front." General Potter hoped to cross to the north side of the Black River via a bridge at Brewington Swamp, but when he reached that point, he learned that the span had been burned. Unwilling to take the time to rebuild it, Potter countermarched toward the town of Manning.[15]*

The men were resting at midday when there passed by them an impressive procession of slaves who had fled to the Yankee columns— "I would judge 700 or 800 of them of all ages & both Sexes," Lieutenant Stevens observed. "Little boys & girls of such tender ages, as at home would not be trusted outside the yards, yet these small children Keep up with us marching 20 miles a day. . . . It is Sad & yet encouraging to see the hope in their countenances & their perfect trust in us. What is to become of this Race of uneducated, hopeful, anxious people[?]"[16]

Potter's expedition reached Manning late in the day. Racing ahead of the infantry, the detachment of the 4th Massachusetts Cavalry had cleared the way, though not without cost. "We entered Manningville with a loss of but one man killed, who belonged to the 4th Massachusetts [Cavalry] Regiment," wrote Sergeant Collins. "Manning is a small town, beautiful in appearance," declared Lieutenant Stevens, "[but] I saw scarcely anything of it[, as] we camped in the outskirts of the town." A few white soldiers commandeered the town's newspaper, the *Clarendon Banner,* and turned out a special liberation edition that they called the *Clarendon Banner of Freedom.*[17]

A short distance northwest of Manning, the road crossed a swamp via a mile-long causeway that the Rebels had torched but failed to destroy. Colonel Hallowell now sent some of his men to assist the engineers, and together they labored past midnight to retrieve the floorboards from the swamp where they had been dumped and refit them. Lieutenant Stevens and a detail from the 54th were ordered to move over to the opposite side of the causeway to reinforce the picket line. "We walked over Stringers by moonlight," the officer wrote in his journal. It was a little after 1:30 A.M. on April 9 when the rest of Hallowell's brigade crossed over, marched two miles on, and bivouacked "in readiness for attack."[18]

---

*Referred to by some of his soldiers as Manningville.

From the helpful contrabands, General Potter learned that an enemy force was entrenching somewhere along the road to Sumterville. He, and everyone else in his command, knew that the next day would likely bring a fight.

Day Five: Sunday, April 9

Three miles south of Sumterville, on the Manning road, the Rebel defenders had taken position near Dingle's Mill, where they intended to stop Potter's raid. The road there bridged a broad millpond flanked on either side by a swamp that one soldier described as "wide, dense, and boggy." The men spent part of the morning tearing up the bridge planking, though the span itself could not be pulled down because it rested on large sawed-off tree trunks that had been embedded in the water. The millpond could also be crossed via a causeway that ran atop its dam; this approach was covered by the two cannon, which were emplaced behind a small earthwork with the infantry dispersed to either side, albeit necessarily exposed because the ground was fairly low and flat. On the Manning side of the pond, "the bank of the stream rose up to quite a hill, and the bank and hill were covered with large oak trees." A newfound third cannon had also been brought along, but as it lacked firing primers, no one could get it to work. It was nevertheless put in a very visible position, in the faint hope that the mere sight of it would prove a deterrent.

When there was no sign of the dreaded Yankees by midday, the ladies of Sumterville came out with food for the men. A young militiaman watched in amazement as a convalescent artillery officer working one of the cannon sat on the gun carriage "twirling his glasses and laughingly chatting with his men." It was almost 2:00 P.M. when word spread along the line that the enemy was approaching.[19]

The black soldiers in Hallowell's brigade stood around their breakfast campfires, watching with weary curiosity as the white troops marched past at about 7:00 A.M. "We are extreme rear to-day," noted Lieutenant Stevens as the 54th Massachusetts (Colored) formed up to follow the leader. The regiment's history recorded April 9 as "a rainy morning"; still, from each plantation, "the negroes flocked to the force by [the] hundreds." "The [white] women & children all sat on the piazzas as we pass," added Stevens. "They have a terrible woe-begone expression, & no wonder, for it is a terrible thing [to see] an Invading army full of enthusiasm, part of it, before slaves, eager for revenge on their old masters."[20]

From some of the contrabands, General Potter learned that the "enemy was intrenched at Dingle's Mill with two pieces of artillery commanding the causeway, which serves as a milldam." One of the blacks claimed to know of a plantation road that flanked the Rebel left; Potter ordered Hallowell to take his brigade along that trail, and to turn the enemy's position.[21]

"We filed to the right & went considerable distance, & halted & a Skirmish line was pushed out & found a few pickets," wrote Lieutenant Stevens. What they did not find was a way around the enemy's position—"the guide furnished proving incompetent," explained the regiment's history. By the time the black soldiers countermarched to the main road and hurried toward the front, the fighting was already over. A way had been discovered to get around the enemy's right flank, and the enemy defense force had been routed.[22]

The Rebel pickets at Dingle's Mill were driven in at about 3:00 P.M.; a one-handed gunner serving with the artillery pieces remembered very clearly hearing "the church bells in town ringing for afternoon service" as the shooting began. A small party of Yankee troops poked onto the causeway but scuttled for cover when the two guns barked their defiance. Next, the Federals brought up their own cannon, which soon began to score hits. The young officer commanding one of the Rebel guns was killed when a "shell tore his shoulder out." This long-range exchange of fire lasted for nearly two hours.

When the one-handed gunner glanced to the right and rear of his position, he was shocked to see "several hundred" of the enemy "jumping over the fence into the field a little over a quarter of a mile [away]." The men pivoted their little gun around, but hardly had the weapon been fired once when a volley of shots swept through the battery, killing the officer who had been joking casually and twirling his spectacles only a few hours before. "We were now flanked, vastly out-numbered, and both our officers were killed," said the gunner. The officer commanding the veteran Kentucky troops immediately ordered his men to fall back, and with the most experienced core hustling to the rear, the raw militia scattered, many flinging their guns away in panic.[23]

Although the black soldiers were late getting to the scene of the action, they did not hesitate to proclaim the victory. Private Bond of the 54th Massachusetts (Colored) told the *Christian Recorder* that the "enemy essayed to make a stand, but were soon completely routed by the impetuous onslaught of our troops, with the loss of two pieces of artillery." Sergeant Collins wrote of it as a "short and sharp fight." "Some of the Prisoners we got were old men, some little boys, the cradle & grave," noted Lieutenant Stevens. "The Rebels scattered & took to the woods & swamps."[24]

Continued Potter in his report, "The march was resumed toward Sumterville. The rebels attempted to make another stand, but were easily driven. Our loss in the affair at Dingle's Mill was twenty-six. . . . Sumterville was occupied on the evening of the 9th." Men quickly spread out to wreck the railroad machinery in the town. "We went through the city singing 'Year of Jubilee' & 'John Brown' etc.," recalled Lieutenant Stevens. "Every one was in fine spirits at having gained the railroad without serious opposition," added the 54th's historian, "for the rolling-stock was known to be below on the Camden Branch. Another cause of exultation was the news that Richmond, Mobile, and Selma were in our hands, in honor of which a salute of thirteen shots was fired from the captured guns."[25]*

Day Six: Monday, April 10

It rained a bit overnight, but Lieutenant Stevens was too exhausted to care: "Was very tired last night as we had gone twenty miles before we turned in," he recorded the next day. General Potter remained based in Sumterville this day, though he sent a detachment from the 32nd USCT northward along the tracks to destroy bridges and trestles, and assigned a portion of the 102nd USCT to similar duties south of town. The men of the 54th Massachusetts (Colored) stayed behind in Sumterville and focused their attention on the Rebel property there.[26]

---

*Some of this news was premature: while it was true that Selma had fallen to assault (on April 2), and Richmond had been occupied (on April 3), Mobile would not be taken until April 12.

Stevens took a stroll through the town to view the destruction. "The Stores had been entered, Safes broken open, stores rifled," he said. "There was quite a no. of Drug Stores in Sumter[ville]. . . . There was the greatest conglomeration of Stuff & all sorts of Smells. Medical and other Books were all thrown down together in a confused mass." If Stevens's conscience bothered him, it did not, however, stop him from helping himself to a couple of books that he wanted. Charles E. Briggs, a surgeon in the 54th, visited the Confederate convalescent hospital that had been established in the town's Presbyterian church. "It was somewhat humorous to see the robust, ruddy-complexioned men in the beds," Briggs recounted afterward. "I got the impression that many of the patients, after the fruitless interview with us at the breastworks, had concluded that a hospital bed was the safer place."[27]

The pause in Sumterville would be brief: General Potter's orders had all his men moving again soon after sunrise. This time, their destination was the railroad junction near Manchester.

Day Seven: Tuesday, April 11

The Federal columns were in motion along the railroad by 6:30 A.M. Lieutenant Stevens, whose company led the procession, noted that the "day was warm & the country had little water so we were hot & tired, but were very much refreshed by a good long halt." Shortly before 2:00 P.M., his men reached Manchester station, which had already been visited and burned by the 4th Massachusetts Cavalry. It was here, remembered Sergeant Collins, that the "54th was detailed to go seven miles from the place for the purpose of destroying some trestle-work."[28]

"We marched on sleepers [i.e., railroad ties] with our tired feet," wrote Stevens. "We had but one Short rest in the whole seven miles." Ahead of the men was a major rail intersection known as Wateree Junction, where a scouting party sent ahead under Sergeant Frank M. Welch reported seeing cars, water tanks, and locomotives, at least one of whose engines had its steam up, indicating that it could pull out at any time. Halting his troops and reconnoitering the situation for himself, Hooper saw at once that his men would have to cross an exposed trestle in order to reach the engine. "It was not known whether there was any armed force or not," said the 54th's history, "and it was important to seize the locomotive before it could be reversed and the rolling-stock run back."[29]

Even though the sun had already set, Hooper went ahead with his plan. He first deployed sharpshooters to cover the trestle approach, then detailed eighteen men to rush across the bridge, under the command of Stephen A. Swails. Swails, a New Yorker who had been with the 54th at Fort Wagner and Olustee, had recently received a field promotion to the rank of lieutenant, the first time a black soldier from the regiment had achieved that status.

As the covering party opened fire, Swails led his men forward. "With a loud yell and tremendous cheer the boys charged over the trestle-work . . . , [and] caught the cars," declared Sergeant Collins. "Swails was the first man of all," recorded the 54th's history, "and jumped into the engine cab where, while waving his hat in triumph, he received a shot in his right arm from our sharpshooters, who in the darkness, probably mistook him for the engineer." "The [Rebel] engineer immediately jumped from the train and ran for his life," added Collins. "Nothing could be seen of him but coat-tails and dust."[30]

The rest of the regiment now came up to begin the dangerous job of hooking the cars together so the train could be run back to Manchester. It was while doing this in the dark that, as Collins related, "Sergeant Major [John H.] Wilson and Private Geo. [Jarvis], of Co. A., got mashed by the cars." Around this time, Lieutenant Colonel Hooper learned from a contraband that there were more trains farther down the track, just the other side of a long trestle bridge over the Wateree River. Hooper sent Lieutenant Stevens's company to deal with this Rebel property, along with Captain Charles E. Tucker, who knew how to operate a steam locomotive.[31]

The tramp in the darkness, after a full day of marching, was anything but pleasant for Stevens and his men. "We went over this tressle bridge, forty ft. high in some places," he wrote, "stepping from sleeper to sleeper. It was tiresome to one's head & eyes, as we had to look down so much lest we should make a mis-step which would be about the ruin of us." After successfully negotiating the trestle, Tucker, Stevens, and the enlisted men still had another three miles to go before they reached their prize: three locomotives and thirty-five cars.[32]

The cars were coupled together and one of the engines had its steam up, so Tucker decided they would ride back. The problem came when they reached the Wateree trestle, where they saw that another party from the 54th had set the span afire, supposing the men were going to return by foot. "Knowing that any delay would be dangerous," recalled Tucker, "and that life and death hung in the balance, I crowded on all steam, and we crossed the bridge through flame and smoke in safety, but with not a moment to spare." "It was very dangerous as the train was heavy & the rails snapped off in some places where they had been burned," added Stevens, "but we kept on." One of the 54th's men, Corporal Charles Noe, actually tumbled off the train while it was crossing and was badly injured.[33]

Hooper piled everyone into the cars, intending to ride them back to Manchester. The party started on its way, burning trestles and bridges after crossing them and dropping off cars from time to time to help the straining engine cope with the load. But a short distance outside Manchester, the lead engine blew out its flue, ending their little jaunt and setting everyone back on foot. The engine was then further wrecked by the Federals, and the remaining cars were burned. The men rested for a while, then pushed on, finally rejoining Potter's command at 7:00 A.M., April 12. Displaying a bit of Shermanesque grit, Stevens greatly regretted that they had not run the trains onto the trestles before setting fire to the lot, thereby plunging the engines into the swampy waters. "As it was," he reflected in his journal, "[the engines] were destroyed So that they can't be repaired for months & I hope that [by then] Peace will come to us again."[34]

Throughout this eventful day, the residents of Sumterville reckoned the cost of Potter's raid. "As soon as the Northerners had left," recalled one of them, "all the people of the town went round to each others to find out who were suffering, and how to relieve their needs."

"Most families found themselves without servants, for they are said to have gone with Potter's horde," wrote the county's historian. "Only four Negro men are said to have been left in town: two house carpenters . . . and two preachers. . . .

"Although the occupation by the enemy had not been as terrible as expected, there had been tragedy. Old Mr. Robert Bee was found hanging from the rafters of his attic, tortured and murdered by drunken soldiers."[35]

Day Eight: Wednesday, April 12

"As the rations of bread, sugar, and coffee were exhausted on the 12th," related General Potter, "I sent the wagons and pack-mules to Wright's Bluff, on the Santee [River], to obtain additional supplies." "We have an almost incalculable no. of contrabands," wrote a weary Lieutenant Stevens. "There are not less than 2500 of them. The 32nd U.S.C.T. has been sent to the Santee with the contrabands[, as] they are getting too many for us to guard. . . . I lay down in the sun & got a short nap & after dinner slept till dusk & turned in after Supper & slept till morning— I was extremely tired & was thankful that we did not have to march."[36]

"Our anxiety may be imagined," remembered a Manchester woman, "as we sat . . . watching the smoke arising from the burning depots, dwellings, gin-houses, barns, cotton, etc. in the country around." To add to the tension, it was reported that Mrs. E. C. Campbell's invalid son had been shot by some black troops when he failed to respond quickly enough to their orders. As the county historian later recorded, "His body was left in the dust for a day and a night, while the house was being completely stripped of food, clothing and valuables."[37]

Day Nine: Thursday, April 13

This was a quiet day for the 54th, and for the expedition party as a whole; except for a white regiment's marching thirteen miles to destroy some stores at Statesburg, there was no military action. Rumors circulated that the Confederates were regrouping to fight Potter before he reached Camden. "If so," supposed a suddenly apprehensive Lieutenant Stevens, "we had better be getting back to Georgetown."[38]

The ongoing vandalism practiced in Sumterville by his soldiers continued to bother Stevens, who declared that he wanted "to be away from such Scenes." In this he was not alone: Lieutenant Colonel John S. Cooper of the 107th Ohio railed in his diary about the "gross outrages committed by our colored troops." Today Cooper wrote, "The 54th Mass. seems to be the worst in this business, and they are supported in it by some of the company officers." Private Benjamin M. Bond had a different way of thinking: "Not for a moment did we hesitate to appropriate to our use every luxury which the wealthy Southerners had appropriated for their own special comfort, such as jellies, honey, and preserved fruits," he said. "'Twas the fearless and immortal Sherman, the 'madman' whose name can never die . . . , who first inaugurated . . . this style of fighting the rebels. . . ."[39]

Day Ten: Friday, April 14

Another day of little action for Potter's men in Sumterville: a white regiment patrolled the Statesburg Road, while detachments of the 54th Massachusetts (Colored) scouted other approaches to the town. "Just as we came in to night from our Scout, the wagon train came in [from Wright's Bluff] & Rations are issuing now," wrote Lieutenant Stevens. "There are numerous reports about a heavy Rebel force in the direction of Camden."[40]

Day Eleven: Saturday, April 15

From the information gathered, General Potter determined that the force he had beaten at Dingle's Mill "had been reinforced by two small brigades of cavalry under Major-General [Pierce M. B.] Young and was intrenching at Boykins Mill." Deciding to borrow a tactic from Sherman, he feinted toward Statesburg at 3:00 P.M. and then, once the enemy had moved in that direction, turned onto a side road that led away from the town and connected with the Camden road. His men reached the thoroughfare without any opposition.[41]

Day Twelve: Sunday, April 16

Hallowell's brigade was leading as Potter's men marched "through a hilly and rolling country sparsely settled with poor whites," recorded the 54th's history. Blacks of all ages and sexes continued to swarm to them as the Federal columns passed. "It is a joyful sight to see families & squads strolling across the fields to join their Liberators," said Lieutenant Stevens proudly. "They are welcome & seem to appreciate their freedom." Lieutenant Colonel Cooper of the 107th Ohio, marching in the rear of Potter's column, lacked Stevens's rose-colored view. He described the contrabands as "old crippled men and women, little boys and girls just about to toddle, women in the very agonies of child birth, all moving along, each with 'we t'ings' [i.e., wee things(?)] on their heads." Fed up with crowd-control duties, the harassed officer stopped at one plantation and convinced its slaves that it would be better for them "to remain at home free" than to join the procession.[42]

Mounted Rebels hung on to the head of Potter's columns, keeping up what one officer termed a "running fight all the afternoon." Lewis Clark, a Lebanon, Ohio, laborer and a private in Company C of the 54th Massachusetts (Colored), was killed in one of today's small actions. "Conflicting rumors come of the force at Camden," worried Stevens. "It is estimated from 1 to 5000." Potter's men camped about twelve miles from Camden this night.[43]

Day Thirteen: Monday, April 17

Potter's men were up and on the Camden road by 6:30 A.M., meeting only light enemy opposition. At about 6:00 P.M., when the Federals at last reached the town, the black troops went in first. "Our entry of the town, with the 54th marching in a close order singing 'John Brown's body,' is something that I shall never forget," declared Regimental Surgeon Briggs. According to Sergeant Collins, Potter's men captured "all of the rebel sick and wounded there, numbering at least from three to four hundred men."[44]

The Federals now learned that all the rolling stock collected in Camden had lately been moved south. Having destroyed the trestles near Wateree Junction, Potter knew that the trains must be trapped between him and that point. He was quite certain, however, that the Confederate forces in the area would not let him reach those choice targets unopposed.

Day Fourteen: Tuesday, April 18

Potter's men headed out of Camden at 7:00 A.M., following a route running along the railroad. The five companies of the 102nd USCT proceeded down the tracks, while the remaining troops stuck to a wagon road farther east. After marching seven miles, these units reached Swift Creek, where the Confederates had blocked the wagon-road bridge by pulling up the floor planking and flooding all approaches to the dismantled span. Most of the Rebel troops were waiting on the opposite shore behind a line of earthworks, supported by two cannon posted in a small fort. The railroad bridge, which crossed the swampy ground some three hundred yards west of the wagon road, was covered by enemy riflemen in trenches.

The 32nd USCT tried to cross the creek near the wagon bridge but found the water too deep. An Ohio regiment went eastward along Swift Creek to locate a ford but quickly sent back word that there was no good crossing to be had in that direction. Resolving to probe the enemy's other flank, Potter sent the 54th Massachusetts (Colored) off to the west. With Lieutenant Colonel Hooper leading, the black soldiers moved cautiously along the creek, warily traversing the open plowed fields that bordered the woods of the swamp. "Contrabands stated that the swamp was impassable at any nearer point than . . . Boykin's Mills which were two miles distant," reported Hooper.[45]

The Rebel force at Swift Creek consisted of about 750 men, including the Kentucky veterans who had fought at Dingle's Mill. "Our flanks were protected by an almost impassable swamp," recalled one of these Orphans, "and not withstanding they would constantly bring fresh troops against us in overwhelming numbers, we would drive them back with great loss to them and but small loss to ourselves."[46]

As they pushed toward Boykins Mill, Hooper's men spotted a road that seemed to head in that direction. "Just then," recounted the 54th's regimental history, "[Private Stephen] Warren Morehouse, of Company E, who had been scouting in the woods to the left, came to Major [George] Pope, saying 'Major, there's a lot of Rebs through there in a barn.'" Pope detached Company E and led it through the woods to the place, where his men flushed a squad of Rebels, who scurried across the stream. Leaving the company to watch over this point, Pope hurried to catch up with the main body.[47]

The road did indeed lead the 54th toward Boykins Mill. Off to the left was a substantial millpond corked by a dam located near the mill, below which the creek divided to form a small island. The main road ran directly over this island, crossing one branch of the stream over a bridge and the other at a ford. Here, too, the Rebels had pulled up the planking, leaving the bridge frame held together by stringers. Skirmishers from Company F, commanded by Captain Watson W. Bridge, tried to make their way across the skeletal span but were stopped by a fusillade of gunfire that killed Corporal James

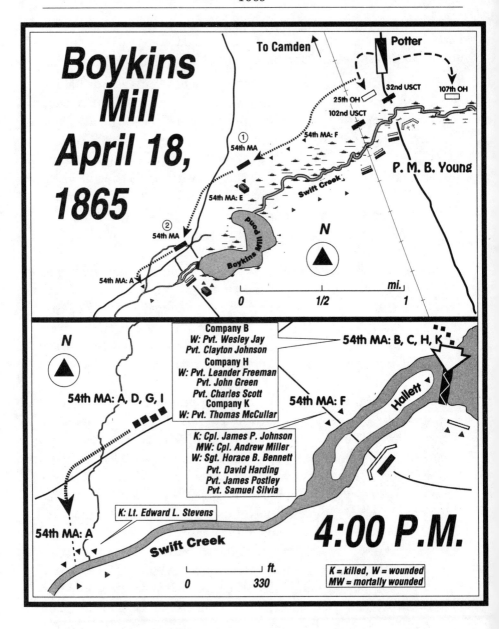

P. Johnson, mortally wounded Corporal Andrew Miller, and wounded four others. Of these last, Sergeant Horace Bennett was struck in the left hip, and Corporal David Harding shot on the inside of the right leg, just below the knee.

Lieutenant Colonel Hooper, having determined that the mill would be his best crossing place, sent Major Pope and four companies farther downstream "under the guidance of an old white-headed negro" to create a diversion. The local guide led Major Pope to a wood road that wriggled down to a ford across Swift Creek. Pope detailed Company A, under Lieutenant Stevens, to move toward the creek and attract the enemy's attention. When Stevens and his men reached the creek bank, he deployed them in the brush lining the stream, intending to fire a volley as soon as everyone was in position. His movements were observed, however, and before he could give the command to fire, a spray of Rebel bullets lashed out from the far bank, one of which struck him in the head and killed him instantly. "He fell partially into the stream," wrote Captain Emilio, the historian of the 54th. "It was a dangerous duty to remove him, but two men were selected from volunteers, who, crawling forward, brought back his body."[48]

At the millpond dam and island, Lieutenant Colonel Hooper kept his men firing at the enemy troops who were posted behind a cotton-bale barricade near the mill. When he learned from Major Pope that the downstream crossing was blocked, he sent a courier back to General Potter to request that one of the artillery pieces be sent up. Once it arrived, he began to prepare his attack. Under a slow covering fire from the cannon, Lieutenant Charles Hallett led a squad of sharpshooters onto the island, where they set up to cover the main attacking column, now slated to go across the top of the dam. The assignment to lead this group went to Lieutenant Lewis Reed. With the sweating Federal gunners working their piece as rapidly as possible, and Hallett's troops keeping the enemy's heads down, Reed and his men, wrote Captain Emilio, "charged across the dike in single file, receiving the enemy's fire, but causing their precipitate retreat." Color Sergeant Charles W. Lenox, ordered to wait under cover, remembered that the men started along the dam with a "rousing cheer . . . and soon were over on the opposite side."[49]

Six enlisted men were wounded in this final phase of the action at Boykins Mill. Two of those six—Privates Leander Freeman of Company H and Thomas McCullar of Company K—were hit in the right ankle, while Private Wesley Jay of Company B caught it in the left arm (the bullet passing through) and Company H's Private John Green had his left elbow struck. The scars borne by Private Clayton Johnson of Company B read like a mini-history of the 54th: he had been wounded in the attack on Fort Wagner by a splinter from an artillery shell, and at Olustee, a tree branch clipped by enemy fire had hit him on the head. Now, in the charge across the dam, Johnson had the little finger of his right hand nipped off by a minie ball. Sadly, the wound received by Private Charles Scott of Company H would eventually result in his death: hospitalized at Charleston after the expedition returned, Scott would contract "country fever" and die on May 1.

Hearing the rapid cannon fire signaling Hooper's attack, Potter also pressed on his front. Another contraband led the 102nd USCT to a rude footbridge, on which the detachment crossed Swift Creek above the millpond.

(One of the Rebels holding the line opposite Potter afterward wrote that the Yankees "had such great numbers that they sent a heavy force some distance off on our right [actually, left] flank to cross the swamp and flank us out of our position.")

The Federal troops quickly reached a nearby railroad station, where they destroyed some supplies. After reassembling his column, Potter pushed on for another three miles before bivouacking for the night.[50]

The bodies of Lieutenant Stevens and Corporal Johnson were buried at Boykins Mill; after the war, both would be reinterred at the Florence National Cemetery, South Carolina. "Lieutenant Stevens was a genial comrade and brave officer," memorialized Captain Emilio. "He must have been the last officer, or one of the very last officers, killed in action during the Rebellion." Stevens was also remembered by Sergeant Collins, who asked the readers of the *Christian Recorder*, "Who will help us mourn his loss—for he fell in defense of the dear old flag?"[51]

On Wednesday, April 19, the Rebels made a feeble stand behind Rafting Creek. Once more, Potter threw out a flanking column that caused the enemy to retreat "in great haste," as he later reported. At Beech Creek, a frontal charge by Ohio and New York troops scattered the enemy. Potter's men spent Thursday, April 20, at Middleton Depot, wrecking or destroying eighteen locomotives and 176 railroad cars, and the next day turned back toward Georgetown. They had just reached Manning when a Rebel courier came forward under a white flag, carrying messages from Major General Sherman proclaiming a general truce. "Cheers without number were given," said the 54th's history, "and congratulations exchanged. Then the Fifty-fourth was brought to a field where the last shots loaded with hostile intent were fired as a salute." "I was too much overcome to talk," recollected Surgeon Briggs, "and was obliged to go off by myself."[52]

It took four more days for Potter's men to get to Georgetown. On April 22, they heard of Lee's surrender at Appomattox Court House, and the very next day, the terrible news that President Lincoln had been assassinated. "Our emotions of joy and hope," wrote Private Bond, "are mingled with the deepest sorrow at the loss of our lamented President, who was so much esteemed and venerated by the community at large." Lieutenant Colonel Hooper's reaction was far less circumspect, as he related to the Massachusetts adjutant general: "[A] cloud settled upon us. We said quietly, 'Now there is no more peace, let us turn back again, load our muskets, and if necessary exterminate the race that can do such things.' Thus we all felt."[53]

Reporting from Beaufort on May 6, General Potter provided an inventory of the Rebel property destroyed during the course of this expedition, and tallied his losses at ten killed, seventy-two wounded, and one missing. Writing from Georgetown on April 20, Private Bond had already given his summary statement to the *Christian Recorder*:

> This is the most agreeable army that we were ever connected with. As we changed our relative position on the march each day, the troops filed on in perfect harmony, as children of one common father: any one could scarcely believe it, unless he were present to witness the unity of feeling among so many men. We are all much gratified to inform the public that we have been instrumental in liberating about six thousand slaves, who, in spite of the President's [Emancipation] Proclamation, might have been kept in bondage for many years to come.[54]

Chapter Fifteen

"The Negro Will Fight & Fight Bravely"

———◁◦▷———

Siege, Assault, and Capture of Fort Blakely, Alabama,
March 27–April 9, 1865

THROUGHOUT the month of February 1865, Major General Edward R. S. Canby assembled a powerful striking force with which he aimed to take control of upper Mobile Bay and advance inland toward Selma and Montgomery, Alabama. His 45,200-man army was organized into the Thirteenth Corps, the Sixteenth Corps, and a smaller corps-sized aggregation in western Florida styled the "Column from Pensacola Bay"—this last commanded by Major General Frederick Steele. Included within Steele's outfit was an all-black division representing nine regiments individually selected from the Vicksburg and Port Hudson districts.

Among these units was the 73rd USCT, which had entered Federal service in 1862 as the 1st Regiment Louisiana Native Guards, and whose bloody baptism of fire at Port Hudson had helped show the country the combat potential of African American soldiers. Soon after that battle, the regiment's small cadre of black officers had been reduced by forced resignations to just one man, Captain Louis A. Snear, described by his commander as having "skin as white as that of any officer in the regiment." Another blow to the men's self-esteem came when they were denied permission to have the battle name "Port Hudson" inscribed on their flag. Just how deeply this rankled the troops was evident as late as the fall of 1864, when a member of the 73rd wrote to the *Anglo-African:*

> The only inscription on the banner of the glorious 73rd is the blood stain of the noble sergeant* who bore it in this fierce assault and the rents made in the struggle of the corporals to obtain the dear rag from the dying man who had rolled himself up in its folds. Regiments which were ridiculed as cowards and vagabonds have "Port Hudson" on their flags. Let us be cautious how we praise the 1st Native Guards; they have it not on their flag. Thank God there were thousands of honest privates in the ranks of the white regiments who will tell the story of the 1st Native Guards![1]

The 73rd was one of three regiments in Brigadier General William A. Pile's First Brigade. The other two, the 82nd and 86th USCT, had both emerged from Brigadier General Daniel Ullmann's Corps d'Afrique. Two former Louisiana regiments of "African Descent," plus the 1st Regiment Mississippi Infantry (A.D.)†—now the 47th, 50th, and 51st USCT—constituted the Second Brigade, under Colonel Hiram Scofield. The Third Brigade, under the charge of Colonel Charles W. Drew, was made up of units previously designated the 10th Regiment Louisiana Infantry (African Descent), the 4th Missouri (Colored), and the 4th Regiment Corps d'Afrique, now known, respectively, as the 48th, 68th, and 76th USCT. Heading the division was Major General Canby's brother-in-law, Brigadier General John P. Hawkins, whose previous service comprised a garrison command and a stint in the army's Commissary Department.

The 76th USCT had the most troubled history of any black unit in this campaign. As members of the 4th Regiment Corps d'Afrique, the men had suffered under a cruel martinet named Augustus Benedict, who meted out severe punishments for minor infractions during his reign as the regiment's second-in-command. In one incident, a soldier was spread-eagled on the ground, and molasses was poured on his

---

*The "noble sergeant" was Anselmas Planciancois.
†150 members of the 1st Regiment Mississippi Infantry (A.D.) fought at Milliken's Bend in 1863.

face, hands, and feet to attract insects. While commanding a portion of the regiment posted to Fort Jackson, below New Orleans, Lieutenant Colonel Benedict flogged two of his men, provoking an angry soldier mob into a brief mutiny for which nine enlisted men were afterward punished by a court-martial board. The same board also dismissed Benedict himself from the service. His immediate superior during this period was Colonel Charles W. Drew, and the next in rank below him Major William Nye. The former officer had been the subject of a letter of censure in which his own superior accused him of physically abusing some of his men, while the latter had conveniently disappeared in the midst of the Fort Jackson mutiny, only to show up again when the trouble was over. Now, as the 76th USCT marched toward the enemy, the regiment was led by Nye, who reported to Drew as brigade commander.

These nine regiments represented the largest single organization of Western black troops ever assigned to a combat role in the Civil War. No longer would these soldiers man remote garrison posts, fend off guerrilla attacks, or join in small hit-and-run actions; instead, they would be a part of a large field army whose first objective was to capture the Rebel citadel of Mobile.

To accomplish this, Canby's strategy posited two cooperating columns, calling for the Thirteenth and Sixteenth corps to move up the eastern side of Mobile Bay while Steele's force (which also included two brigades and some artillery loaned from the Thirteenth Corps) advanced from Pensacola, after feinting toward Montgomery, to link up with them. The initial targets of this operation were two Confederate bastions, Spanish Fort and Fort Blakely. Once these had been reduced, Canby reasoned, it would be relatively easy to approach Mobile from the north, where its defenses were weakest.* The Thirteenth and Sixteenth corps drew Spanish Fort, while Steele's men closed on Blakely.

The first of Steele's troops set out from Pensacola on March 19, with the main body following the next day. Their movement through what was at the best of times rough country was made even more miserable by the weather. The men endured what Steele reported as a "heavy rain . . . which rendered the roads almost impassable. . . . [It] became necessary to corduroy the roads. The streams were higher

---

*Canby had also considered, but rejected as too difficult, the possibility of advancing along the western side of Mobile Bay.

than they had been for many years." Their progress sometimes amounted to as little as two or three miles a day. Remembered the officer commanding the 73rd USCT, "Our wagons actually dropped to their axles while standing in the park and our animals were floundering in mire at the picket lines unable to move until rolled and dragged out by the men."[2]

The expedition had left Pensacola hauling ten days' rations. A few fortuitous forays along the way added slightly to that diminishing larder, but when the head of the column reached Stockton, about twenty-five miles north of Fort Blakely, on March 31, Steele's Federals were hungry. Chaplain George N. Carruthers, with the 51st USCT, later recalled the men's moving "through swamps and forests, part of the time on short rations—even to parched corn and what fresh beef the poor country could afford."[3]

Another chaplain, C. W. Buckley of the 47th USCT, felt that the black troops showed remarkable restraint. "During the march, when hunger or pillage were the only parts of the alternative, hunger was preferred to disobedience of orders," he wrote. Buckley also observed a certain newfound camaraderie between the black and white troops: "During the whole march I have not heard a word of reproach cast upon a colored soldier. . . . All seem to realize that they were marching from victory to victory beneath the same flag—that their arms were alike raised in defense of our endangered liberties."[4]

Steele pushed his columns south from Stockton toward Fort Blakely on April 1, with Hawkins leading. After marching eighteen miles, the black troops were just settling into camp when word came that Yankee cavalry near Blakely needed help. One regiment supported the troopers, while the others took up a line of battle about two and a half miles from the Rebel fort. In the far distance, the USCT men could hear the dull rumble of Federal artillery pounding Spanish Fort, where Canby's two corps had already enclosed the bastion's land side.

The crackle of picket fire came with the dawn on Sunday, April 2. The black troops lined up to await orders, and while standing there received a small amelioration for their growling stomachs: according to an officer with the expedition, "The quartermaster's wagons went round with corn, and two ears and a 'nubbin' were dealt out to each man as rations, providing much merriment."[5]

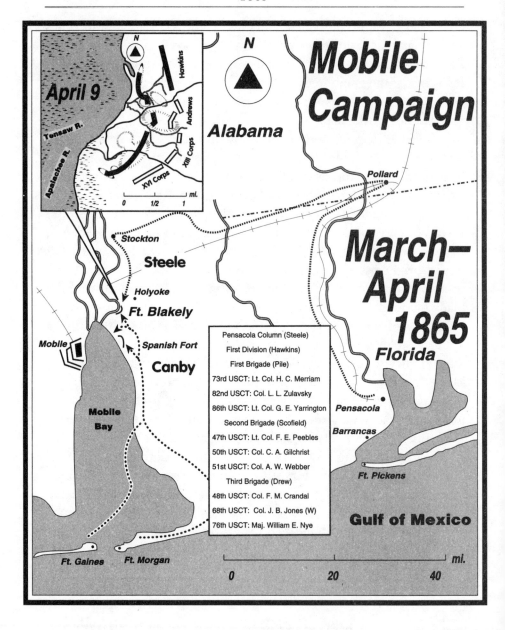

Mobile Campaign

Alabama

Pollard

March–April 1865

Florida

April 9

Hawkins

Andrews

XIII Corps

XVI Corps

Tensaw R.

Apalachee R.

Stockton

Steele

Holyoke

Ft. Blakely

Mobile

Spanish Fort

Canby

Mobile Bay

Pensacola Column (Steele)
First Division (Hawkins)
First Brigade (Pile)
73rd USCT: Lt. Col. H. C. Merriam
82nd USCT: Col. L. L. Zulavsky
86th USCT: Lt. Col. G. E. Yarrington
Second Brigade (Scofield)
47th USCT: Lt. Col. F. E. Peebles
50th USCT: Col. C. A. Gilchrist
51st USCT: Col. A. W. Webber
Third Brigade (Drew)
48th USCT: Col. F. M. Crandal
68th USCT: Col. J. B. Jones (W)
76th USCT: Maj. William E. Nye

Pensacola

Barrancas

Ft. Pickens

Gulf of Mexico

Ft. Gaines   Ft. Morgan

0   20   40   mi.

Hawkins's men now closed up on Fort Blakely. Drew's brigade advanced first, with two companies apiece from the 48th, 68th, and 76th USCT moving ahead. As Drew reported, the movement "was continued for two miles through a thickly wooded and broken country, my skirmishers fighting about half the way. . . . The precision maintained by the line, as well as the bold and steady advance of the skirmishers under a heavy fire, were sufficient, I think, to command the admiration of all." At one point, the battle lines from the 48th USCT breasted a low ridge that brought them into the enemy's cannon range. In no time at all, two shells slammed into the black Federals, mortally wounding two and seriously injuring four more.[6]

Another sharp fight, over a deep ravine about a mile and a half in front of the Confederate left, lasted some three hours and eventually involved twenty-seven different USCT companies. Drew halted his brigade and began entrenching about half a mile from Blakely's outer defenses; soon Pile's brigade connected with his left, while Scofield's formed a reserve. Confederate artillery, overshooting the two advanced brigades, scored some direct hits among Scofield's men, with three shells that exploded amid the 47th USCT proving especially deadly, wounding fifteen men, two of them mortally.

The Rebel officer commanding Mobile's eastern defenses was quick to note the complexion of the first Federal division to challenge Blakely. In his exhortation to the fort's garrison, he declared that "the force of the enemy now in our front is composed principally of negroes, and will not spare any of our men should they gain possession of our works." The position held by some thirty-five hundred Confederates was spread in a rough semicircle about the small town of Blakely, following the curve of a low ridge and a series of small hills whose highest point did not exceed sixty feet. Placed along this line were nine redoubts holding forty artillery pieces. A killing ground had been established in front of the main position, consisting of two slighter lines of entrenchments, each protected by abatis and cleared fields of fire. All the obvious approaches were liberally seeded with deadly land mines, or torpedoes. From end to end, the Blakely lines covered about two and a half miles.[7]

By April 3, Steele had spread his men across Blakely's front, but it took two divisions detached from the Spanish Fort operation to close the circle on the fort's southern side. Siege operations began on April 4, when entrenching tools were distributed. Hawkins's division held the northern third of the Federal lines, and Steele's other division the middle, with the remaining third taken by troops from the Thirteenth and Sixteenth corps. Steele's instructions from Canby were to press the enemy but not to attack until Spanish Fort fell.

401

During the period from April 4 through 8, the principal occupation along the Union lines was digging a constantly expanding network of trenches that zigzagged ever closer to Blakely's outer ring, with batteries placed at key points. "The ground is hard," reported Hawkins on April 8, "and the shovel is a poor instrument without a greater number of picks to assist it." This time, the black soldiers were digging both for their own protection and to hasten the end of the enemy fortress. "[The] behavior of the men when constructing trenches under fire . . . was a convincing proof that the former slaves of the South, cannot be excelled as soldiers," exclaimed the 50th USCT's commander. Forward of this burrowing were the skirmish lines, where the firing, according to the chaplain of the 51st USCT, was "so hot that to show a limb was to lose it." During one scrap, Private Thomas Drayfus of the 68th USCT was shot in the face; his friend Private John H. Jolly never forgot Drayfus's "hollering and cursing about it."[8]

As one officer remembered it, when the heavy siege guns fired over the heads of the black troops, they shouted, "Another through train to Mobile." With the right flank of Hawkins's line resting within range of the Tensaw River, the USCT units also had to endure periodic visits from Rebel warships, whose shelling extracted a human toll.[9]

Sergeant Cassius M. Clay Alexander of the 50th USCT was the only black soldier to produce any account of this operation. His letter appeared in the November 18 issue of the *Anglo-African*:

> We were only ten days on the siege, and had nothing to eat but Parched Corn. But as luck would have it, I crept out of my hole at night and scared one of the Jonnys so bad that he left his rifle pit, gun and accouterments, also one corn dodger and about one pint of buttermilk, all of which I devoured with a will, and returned to my hole safe and sound. After sleeping the remainder of the night, about day I was awakened by our turtlebacks* that were playing with the enemy's works. At that time I forgot myself and poked my head out of my hole, and came very near getting one of Jonny's cough pills. We had to keep our heads down all the time or else run the risk of getting shot. So me and my friend of whom I was speaking had it all that day, shooting at each other. Finally, he got hungry and cried out to me, "Say, Blacky, let's stop and eat some Dinner." I told him, "All right."

*i.e., ironclad monitors

By the time I thought he was done eating, I cried, "Hello, Reb." He answered, "What do you want?" I said, "Are you ready?" "No, not yet," he said. Then I waited for a while. I finally got tired and cried for a chew of tobacco. He then shot at me and said, "Chew that!" I thanked him kindly and commenced exchanging shots with him.[10]

In an unplanned action late on April 8, Union troops captured Spanish Fort's outerworks, forcing all the defenders to evacuate that same night. Almost immediately, Canby began shifting troops to Blakely, with orders for an assault late in the afternoon on April 9. Throughout that morning and into midday, spotters posted in tall trees along the lines reported boatloads of troops moving from Blakely toward Mobile, which led some to conclude that the Rebels were pulling out; in fact, the troops seen were members of the Spanish Fort garrison who had escaped to Blakely by moving along the shore. Meanwhile, Blakely's defenders, convinced that an attack was imminent, had started conserving ammunition. This slower rate of enemy counterfire further contributed to the mistaken impression among the Federals that Blakely was being evacuated.

By now, all three of Hawkins's brigades were holding sections of the front, with Drew on the right, Scofield in the center, and Pile on the left. A little after 3:00 P.M., Brigadier General Pile, eagerly prompted by two of his regimental commanders, pushed forward companies from the 73rd and 86th USCT. The advancing soldiers felt confident that they would quickly capture the enemy's outer defensive line, but it did not turn out that way. Captain Henry Crydenwise, commanding one of the companies, recalled:

About two companies of each regt made the first charge. Cos. B & G of our regt. With a cheer they started forward over logs, brush & fallen trees & soon drove the Rebs from their rifle pits & occupied them themselves. In a moment the captain of Co. G was brought back we fear mortally wounded (though he still lives). A moment more & the Captain of Co. B was brought back wounded in the foot. Then I was ordered to rush forward with my company & place them in the rifle pits from which the Rebs had just been driven, to take command of all our men there & hold the pit at all hazards. Cautioning my men to follow me in one rank & keep close to me, I sprang over our rifle pit & away we went on a hard run for the rebel pits. The Rebs saw us coming & swept the ground with shot, shell & tried to stop our advance, but to no purpose. Onward, still onward we went, down a slope, across a ravine filled with logs, brush, stumps & trees but these we hardly noticed. Then up a little rise & were soon in possession of the desired line. O! My God how the Rebs did sweep that line with those searching, devilish shells & it seemed that nothing could live under such a fire.[11]

Pile's men were pinned down by the heavy fire coming from the supposedly abandoned positions. At around 4:00 P.M., Scofield and Drew sent forward four companies each to support Pile. The entanglements in front of Drew's soldiers were so thick that the black men "took off their coats so as to move more readily through the brush, and charged in their short sleeves." This second small wave was met by what Scofield would later describe as a "withering fire of musketry and of grape and canister" that forced them down. An officer in the 47th USCT wrote that his men "burrowed into the ground with bayonets and some spades which were brought to them by 14 of the members of my company who ran down the ravine to our works, securing their loads and back again in an incredibly short time." Private Andrew Turner, in the 68th USCT, recollected that the "charge was made under a terrible fire from the enemy, the men dashing forward with all their might."[12]

Colonel Drew now sent up more men, a move that resulted only in additional casualties and no added advantage. At one point, the officer in charge of the 68th USCT was importuned by a badly wounded soldier who begged him to take all his unused rifle cartridges and give them "to the boys" on the firing line. In a different sector, another officer with the 68th called for a dozen volunteers to tackle a Rebel strongpoint that was pinning his men down. Private Pless Adams was among the twelve who stepped forward, despite having already been wounded this day; he was shot again in this push, and this time, the wound proved mortal. Seven years later, the officer who had ordered the attack would testify when Adams's mother was prevented from receiving her son's pension by her white neighbors, who swore they would "never assist any damned nigger in getting a pension, so long as pensions are denied to the widows of southern soldiers." Young Adams, declared this officer, "was as good and worthy a soldier as ever drew a bead on a rebel."[13]

The white troops occupying the rest of the Union lines, under orders to mount a 5:30 P.M. assault, remained relatively silent in the interim, so the black men fought their savage little skirmish on the right without any aid from the left. At certain points of this mini-battle, it was later reported that the "din of canister, bullets and hand-grenades prevented a word being heard."[14]

The spiteful combat still flared on portions of Hawkins's front as the appointed hour of 5:30 P.M. approached. Shortly after that time, the white troops, attacking in much larger numbers than had their black counterparts, successfully crossed the minefields, struggled through the entanglements, and hunched through a storm of shot and shell to breach the Rebel lines. According to General Hawkins, once this assault began to succeed, his entire "front, re-enforced with other troops from the rear, went at the works of the enemy, and were soon piling over the parapet, and the rebels confronting us threw down their arms." Captain Crydenwise recalled that the moment the white troops raised the Stars and Stripes over the enemy's fortifications, most of Hawkins's division came forward. "[We] all rushed together for the rebel works," he declared, "& the old 73rd was the first to plant its flag upon that portion of the line captured by the colored troops." Lieutenant Colonel Henry C. Merriam, leading the 73rd, was later awarded the Medal of Honor for "voluntarily and successfully leading his regiment over the works in advance of orders, permission having been given at his own request." Merriam was accompanied in this initiative by his color sergeant, Edward Simon, who was also acknowledged in the official reports.[15]

"The works were strong and well defended by a line of abatis, [with] concealed telegraph wire for throwing [men] down under the range of the guns, and a line of concealed torpedoes," recorded Chaplain Carruthers. A newspaper account said that a "double line of skirmishers preceded the principal line and the whole body, dark as a cloud of wrath, bore down upon the foe." "In Drew's front," wrote an officer with Steele, "several of the confederates, with muskets, remained outside of the works, refused to surrender, and maintained a cool and desperate struggle till they fell. In Scofield's line, the explosion of a single torpedo killed and wounded thirteen men of the Fifty-first regiment." Once his men entered the Rebel works, reported the commander of the 50th USCT, their "enthusiasm . . . was unbounded, and they manifested their joy in every conceivable manner."[16]

Controversy later surrounded the actions of the black troops after they overran the enemy's works. Relatively few prisoners were taken, something that General Hawkins blamed on the Rebels themselves, who, "fearing the conduct of my troops, ran over to where the white troops were entering [their lines, in order to surrender]." Writing home on April 11, however, Lieutenant Walter Chapman of the 51st USCT said differently:

> The rebel line of skirmishers seeing us coming up fell back into their works. As soon as our niggers caught sight of the retreating figures of the rebs the very devil could not hold them. Their eyes glittered like serpents and with yells & howls like hungry wolves, they rushed for the rebel work. The movement was simultaneous, regiment after regiment and line after line took up the cry and started until the whole field was black with darkeys. The rebs were panic-struck, numbers of them jumped into the river and were drowned in attempting to cross, or were shot while swimming. Still others threw down their arms and run for their lives over to the white troops on our left to give themselves up to save being butchered by our niggers. The niggers did not take a prisoner. They killed all they took to a man.[17]

On the Southern side, two firsthand accounts exist of prisoner atrocities. In one, Artilleryman E. W. Tarrant maintained that his gun—the last in the area to discharge its contents—had been overrun by black troops who were "brandishing their guns in great rage, accusing us of having fired upon them after we had surrendered, shooting down Captain Lanier, inspector general of the Mississippi brigade, and clubbing 'Long' Smith of Tarrant's Battery." In the other account, Private Ben H. Bounds, of the 4th Mississippi, claimed that more Confederates had been "slain after the surrender than in the battle." Bounds said he was one of a group of forty to fifty men who were shot at after they gave up; only by keeping a white Union guard between him and the infuriated USCT soldiers did he save himself from being killed. Two Federal officers in the 68th USCT, Captain Fred W. Norwood and Lieutenant Clark Gleason, were reputedly shot this day "in their efforts to save the prisoners." Norwood received a knee wound that left him incapacitated after the war, while Gleason's service record notes that he died on April 11 "of wounds received in action at Blakely, Alabama, April 9."[18]

Testimony refuting such atrocity claims comes from several sources. In a statement written on April 30, the 51st USCT's chaplain declared that "no extravagances were committed beyond those incident to every charge." Samuel M. Quincy, an officer in the 73rd USCT, attested that many of the captured Rebels "fell on their knees expecting Fort Pillow treatment but by the aid of their excellent discipline the troops were restrained." "It is a credible truth," avowed Chaplain Thomas Calahan of the 48th USCT, "that no one was injured by any colored soldier after resistance had ceased." Responding to a white soldier's postwar charge that the blacks had murdered captive Rebels at Fort Blakely, Captain J. L. Coppec of the 47th USCT said, "I can easily see how the report could get abroad that the colored troops had done such a thing, and especially as it was expected that they would do it because of the provocation they had had. But . . . it is a fact that every officer of the colored troops will testify that not a rebel soldier was shot by the darkies after they had surrendered."[19]

The 76th USCT, whose enlisted men had been brutalized by the regiment's former second-in-command, lost two officers killed and three wounded on April 9. Given its clouded history, and the circumstances of this day, this unit seems a likely suspect in any postsurrender incidents that may have occurred. While there was no wholesale massacre of white Rebel prisoners at Fort Blakely, the evidence suggests that a small number of Confederate POWs were probably killed by black soldiers after raising their hands.

Even during the mop-up following Blakely's capture, the fort's passive defenses continued to serve their bloody purpose. Colonel Hiram Scofield was watching a line of Rebel prisoners be hustled past him when one of the black guards stepped on a torpedo. That man, related Scofield, "Private Josias Lewis, Company K, Forty-seventh U.S. Colored Infantry, was . . . severely wounded, losing a leg by the explosion of one of those infernal machines."[20]

Fort Blakely's capture having made Mobile untenable, that city was evacuated on April 10 and occupied on April 12. North of Mobile, a large Federal cavalry force had lately swept into central Alabama, capturing Selma on April 2 and Montgomery ten days later, and in the process rendering the next phase of Canby's plan unnecessary (though it would be carried out anyway). Lieutenant General U. S. Grant later complained that the only problem with Canby's

Mobile Campaign was its timing—it should, he said, have taken place in August 1864, "when [Blakely's] possession by us would have been of great advantage. It finally cost lives to take it when its possession was of no importance, and when, if left alone, it would have within a few days have fallen into our hands without any bloodshed whatever."[21]

The operations of Hawkins's division in the period from March 17 though April 12 cost the black units 48 men killed and 323 wounded. "Of those," observed a white officer who was present during the campaign, "a pretty large proportion were officers." Writing to his parents on April 13 from Blakely, Captain Crydenwise declared, "The Colored Troops in the assault & capture of this place on the 9th done a great thing for the cause & themselves & have again shown that the negro will fight & fight bravely."[22]

Interlude

"Their Enthusiasm Was Said to Be . . . Remarkable"

————‹o›————

ON January 11, 1865, responding to a query from Virginia State Senator Andrew Hunter, General Robert E. Lee set down his thoughts regarding the recruitment of blacks to fight in the Confederate armies. "Do you think," Hunter had asked, "that by a wisely devised plan of judicious selection negro soldiers can be made effective and reliable in maintaining this war in behalf of the Southern States?" "I think," Lee replied, "we must decide whether slavery shall be extinguished by our enemies and the slaves be used against us, or use them ourselves at the risk of the effects which may be produced upon our social institutions. My own opinion is that we should employ them without delay."[1]

Lee's was not the first Southern voice supporting black recruitment; indeed, debate on this issue had begun even as the Confederacy itself was taking shape. In some especially exposed border areas, plantation owners advocated arming selected slaves for local defense. In January 1864, Major General Patrick R. Cleburne had circulated a memorandum within the Army of the Tennessee, urging the "training [of] a large reserve of the most courageous of our slaves," with a guarantee of "freedom within a reasonable time to every slave in the South who shall remain true to the Confederacy."[2]

Cleburne's proposal was firmly rejected by most who heard it, including C.S. President Jefferson Davis. But the continuing decline in

409

the Confederacy's fortunes, and the increasing number of white desertions from its armies, made it inevitable that the idea would resurface. The Confederate Congress began to debate the question in February 1865, but opposition—and a philosophical belief that such matters were best decided on a state level—kept national legislation bottled up in committees. The breakthrough finally came when the Virginia state legislature, on March 4 and 6, issued four joint resolutions authorizing a limited call-up of blacks into armed service. Virginia's act provided a catalyst for the Confederate Congress, which on March 9 gave President Davis the power to call for a levy of troops "to be raised from such classes of the population, irrespective of color, in each State as the proper authorities thereof may determine."[3]

On March 15, the Confederate War Department provided Majors J. W. Pegram and Thomas Turner with full authority "to raise a Company or Companies of Negro soldiers." At the same time, H. C. Scott, a surgeon at one of Richmond's military hospitals, was reported to have "organized from the negro men employed there a very fine looking company for local service." These units may in fact have existed well before they were officially authorized: a report written by Surgeon Scott, dated March 16, notes that some of his men had been attached to Major Pegram's unit on March 11 and had thereafter manned Richmond's earthworks.[4]*

On Wednesday, March 22, a reporter representing the *Richmond Dispatch* checked on the black recruits. The "colored volunteers," he declared, "seemed as happy as larks and expressed their determination to fight the Yankees to the last." Not to be outdone, the *Richmond Examiner* sent a writer to observe the military drills at the black troop barracks located at Twenty-first and Cary streets. "The body numbered some thirty or forty," related the *Examiner*'s man, "and their enthusiasm was said to be something remarkable."[5]

Another edition of the *Examiner* carried a statement from a Virginia free black named John Scott, who enlisted because marauding Yankee cavalry had stolen his canal boat, thus depriving him of his livelihood. "Now I wants to join right away," attested Scott. "I wants

---

*The threat that called out these troops was the presence of most of Sheridan's cavalry corps, which, while marching to Petersburg from the Shenandoah Valley, passed north of Richmond on their way to meet army transports at White House landing.

to fight them Yankees that have treated me so bad. . . . I knows a heap about a gun, just let me git a bead on 'em and I'll bring 'em [down] every pop."[6]

Virginia's Confederate black troops appeared in Capitol Square with the Richmond hospital's local defense unit in a March 23 battalion parade. The Home Guards were lacking uniforms, creating what the *Dispatch*'s newsman called a "marked contrast to the appearance of . . . Major Turner's colored troops, [who were] neatly uniformed, and showing a good soldierly carriage." In its March 27 issue, the *Examiner* supplied a detailed description of Major Turner's unit:

> The company now numbers 35 members, all uniformed and equipped. They are drilled daily for several hours by Lt. Virginius Bossieaux. . . . About a dozen of the recruits are free negroes, who were enlisted of their own free will and choice. Recruits are coming in by ones and twos everyday, and the negroes, being permitted to go out among their friends, are very good recruiting officers. We witnessed a drill of the company on Saturday afternoon [March 25] and the knowledge of the military art they already exhibit was something remarkable. They move with evident pride and satisfaction to themselves. Their quarters . . . are neat, clean, warm and comfortable. Their rations are cooked at the Libby prison.
>
> Major Turner hopes to recruit and equip a command of 80 or 100 in a few weeks and . . . [then] turn them over to Gen. Lee.[7]

In a brief note in its April 3 edition, the *Examiner* assured its readers that the black ranks were "filling up with a gratifying rapidity." Few citizens or soldiers were on hand to be reassured, however, because all during the night of April 2, the Confederate government and military had abandoned Richmond. The hospital Home Guard unit dissolved during that tumultuous period and was never heard of again. Major Turner's little company,* however, left the city in good order to take part in the general Confederate retreat to Amelia Court House.[8]

Assigned to Lieutenant General Richard S. Ewell's command, Turner's company became part of the security force accompanying

---

*The fate of Major Pegram's company is not known. One likely explanation is that Pegram's and Turner's companies merged.

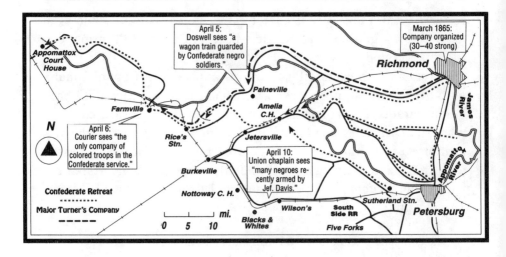

the supply train. These wagons followed the Manchester Pike (which ran parallel to the James River for several miles), then angled down to Powhatan Court House before moving on to Tobaccoville, where they crossed the Appomattox River using the Clementown Bridge. The wagon train and its escort camped for the night near a collection of houses called Paineville, or Paine's Cross Roads.

No Union troops had followed the Confederate forces as they left Richmond, but farther south, Federal pressure was constant and growing. While most of Lee's men rested at Amelia Court House, and others vainly scoured nearby areas for much-needed supplies, hard-marching Federal cavalry placed themselves at Jetersville, across Lee's intended line of march. It was from there, on the morning of April 5, that a mounted strike force swung around to the west to fall on the Rebel wagons parked near Paineville.

R. M. Doswell, a Confederate courier, was making his way through this area when he came upon what he later referred to as a "novel sight"—"a wagon train guarded by Confederate negro soldiers." Continued Doswell:

> When within about one hundred yards of and in the rear of the wagon train, I observed some Union cavalry a short distance away on elevated ground forming to charge and the negro soldiers forming to meet the attack, which was met successfully, the Union cavalry retreating. Not observing the Union cavalry further, I was preparing to

inquire whose wagon train it was. The cavalry charged again, and the negro soldiers surrendered.[9]

The action Doswell witnessed was just a small episode of a much larger strike on Ewell's supply train that resulted in two hundred wagons' being destroyed and three hundred soldiers captured. As the Yankee riders returned to Jetersville, they were heavily attacked by Rebel cavalry, at which time some of the prisoners (both white and black) very likely escaped. Throughout April 5 and 6, Lee retreated to the west along narrow roads leading to Farmville. It was near there, on April 6, that another Rebel courier spotted the remnants of Major Turner's black company:

> Several engineer officers were superintending the construction of a line of rude breastworks, extending about half a mile from the road. Ten or twelve negroes were engaged in the task of pulling down a rail fence; as many more occupied in carrying the rails, one at a time, to the desired spot; and several were busily throwing up the dirt, under the watchful eye of an overseer. The darkeys thus employed all wore good gray uniforms; and I was informed that they belonged to the only company of colored troops in the Confederate service, having been enlisted by Major Turner in Richmond. Their muskets were stacked, and it was evident that they regarded their present employment in no very favorable light.
>
> They did not finish their task, as a courier arriving from the scouting-party brought a . . . message . . . that . . . there was no danger of attack.
>
> Immediately after the receipt of this intelligence, the negro soldiers shouldered their arms and marched from the field under the command of a lieutenant.[10]

The next and final sighting of this unique Confederate unit came the day after Lee surrendered at Appomattox Court House. A chaplain in the 50th Pennsylvania, posted along the South Side Railroad between Petersburg and Wilson's Store, wrote home on April 10, "The first installment of Rebel prisoners, numbering seventeen hundred and seventy, have just passed, under a strong guard. . . . In the squad were many negroes recently armed by Jef. Davis."[11]

That casual observation represents the last record of the Confederacy's only authorized black combat unit.* Apparently none of its members got to Appomattox Court House, for there is no sign of them on the parole lists, nor does Major Turner's name appear anywhere.

In November 1895, U.S. Medal of Honor winner Christian A. Fleetwood gave a talk in Atlanta entitled "The Negro as a Soldier." In his speech, Fleetwood acknowledged the Confederacy's failure to establish policies on arming black freemen and emancipating slaves who enlisted. While it was not his purpose to speculate on what might have been, declared Fleetwood, the "immense addition to [the Confederate] . . . fighting force, the quick recognition of them by Great Britain, to which slavery was the greatest bar, and the fact that the heart of the Negro was with the South but for slavery, and the case stands clear."[12]

---

*The Louisiana Native Guards of 1861–62 were state units that never saw any fighting.

Chapter Sixteen

"Babylon Is Fallen"

———◦———

F OLLOWING the consolidation of the black units in the Virginia theater into the Twenty-fifth Corps, and the subsequent departure of nearly a third of those regiments for Fort Fisher, there remained only two African American divisions outside the Confederate capital in the spring of 1865. From the ten USCT regiments sent to Fort Fisher, some headquarters and commissary details stayed behind. Among their number was Sergeant James H. Payne of the 27th USCT, who on February 16 assured the *Christian Recorder* that at "present our army assumes an attitude of peace and repose, and now all is quiet along the James. . . . But, I presume, one reason for our present tranquil mood is, the fact that the roads are bad, the mud deep, and [there is] a great deal of water in the woods and fields, rendering travel of any kind almost impossible." Sergeant A.D.W. of the 29th Connecticut (Colored) told that same newspaper a month later about the livestock needed to move supplies from the river landing to the front. "The teaming is done on corduroy roads," he said, tongue firmly in cheek, "and if a team should happen to get off the track, good-bye; for only the ears of the mules remain to mark the spot where they disappeared in the mud, and the driver only escapes by some strategic movement."[1]

Early in January, the black soldiers had bidden farewell to Major General Benjamin F. Butler, replaced after fumbling the first assignment to capture Fort Fisher. "Your bravery has won the admiration even of those who would be your masters," he declared to them in parting. "With the bayonet you have unlocked the iron-barred gates of prejudice, opening new fields of freedom, liberty, and equality of right to yourselves and your race forever." Butler's departure garnered mixed reviews from the black rank and file. Private Simon Parker of the 31st USCT praised him as the "man who first entertained the idea of employing colored soldiers," while A.D.W. insisted that the "removal of General Butler brings joy to every soldier in the Army of the James."[2]

As the weather improved, the men were put through their paces. "Company drill in the morning with battalion drill in the afternoon, and dress parade at four P.M., consume nearly the whole of the short spring days," wrote A.D.W. From the 43rd USCT, an anonymous private complained to the *Christian Recorder* about some white officers who routinely employed physical abuse during training. "There are men in this regiment who were born free," he said, "and have been brought up as well as any officer in the 43rd, and will not stand being punched with swords and driven around like dogs."[3]

All these matters were set aside on March 26, however, when the First Division of the Twenty-fifth Corps was marched to a cleared area that served as the parade ground and there lined up to be reviewed by Abraham Lincoln. The men stood patiently from late morning until midafternoon, at which time the President and his entourage finally appeared. Lincoln, mounted on General Grant's horse Cincinnati, rode along the long blue files and was noticeably cheered up by what one aide termed the "manifestation of strength on the part of the splendid Army of the James." Sergeant John C. Brock of the 43rd USCT recalled that "we all looked upon him with that holy awe and reverence which was due him who was the nation's pride, as well as the bondsman's savior." Lincoln's visit contributed to an upsurge of morale that had been building since early in the month, when Corporal Jacob D. Keillies of the 29th Connecticut (Colored) reported that he and his comrades "all seem eager for the day to come when (if this thing is to be fought out) they can pitch in and show to the world that Richmond can and shall be taken, and by them, despite all resistance."[4]

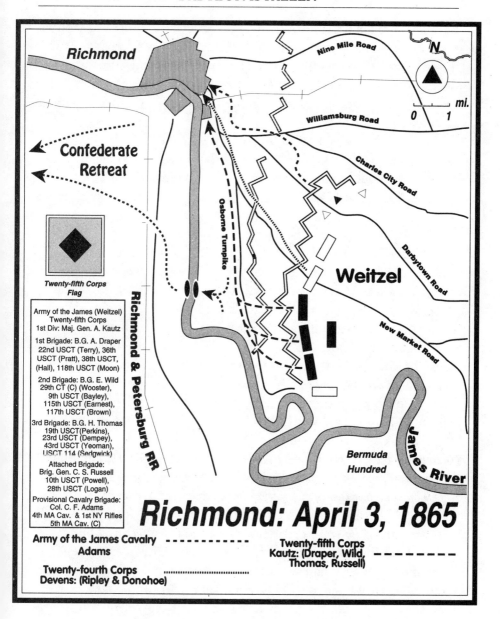

Richmond

Confederate Retreat

Twenty-fifth Corps Flag

Army of the James (Weitzel)
Twenty-fifth Corps
1st Div: Maj. Gen. A. Kautz

1st Brigade: B.G. A. Draper
22nd USCT (Terry), 36th
USCT (Pratt), 38th USCT,
(Hall), 118th USCT (Moon)

2nd Brigade: B.G. E. Wild
29th CT (C) (Wooster),
9th USCT (Bayley),
115th USCT (Earnest),
117th USCT (Brown)

3rd Brigade: B.G. H. Thomas
19th USCT(Perkins),
23rd USCT (Dempey),
43rd USCT (Yeoman),
USCT 114 (Sedgwick)

Attached Brigade:
Brig. Gen. C. S. Russell
10th USCT (Powell),
28th USCT (Logan)

Provisional Cavalry Brigade:
Col. C. F. Adams
4th MA Cav. & 1st NY Rifles
5th MA Cav. (C)

Nine Mile Road

N

Williamsburg Road

mi.
0   1

Charles City Road

Weitzel

Darbytown Road

New Market Road

Richmond & Petersburg RR

Osborne Turnpike

Richmond: April 3, 1865

Bermuda Hundred

James River

Army of the James Cavalry
Adams   – – – – – – – – – – –

Twenty-fifth Corps
Kautz: (Draper, Wild,   – – – – – – – –
Thomas, Russell)

Twenty-fourth Corps   ....
Devens: (Ripley & Donohoe)

Occupation of Richmond, Virginia, April 3, 1865

For the Union troops (black and white) standing watch in the muddy trenches outside Richmond, there was nothing to suggest that Saturday, April 1, was to be any different from the previous days. True, pulses *had* raced a bit faster five days earlier, when three of the five infantry divisions of the Army of the James marched across the river, leaving only an all-white one of the Twenty-fourth Corps and another from the black Twenty-fifth Corps, under Brevet Major General August V. Kautz, to hold the lines. But things had settled down since then.

Also departed was most of the cavalry posted to this sector; detachments from various commands were all that remained. Gone, too, was Army of the James commander Major General Edward O. C. Ord, placing Major General Godfrey Weitzel in charge of all the troops before Richmond. With Brigadier General William Birney's division having headed south, the trenches running from Fort Burnham to the river were held by the infantry brigades of Brevet Brigadier General Alonzo G. Draper (22nd, 36th, 38th, and 118th USCT), Brigadier General Edward A. Wild (29th Connecticut and 9th, 115th, and 117th USCT), Brigadier General Henry G. Thomas (19th, 23rd, 43rd, and 114th USCT), and Brevet Brigadier General Charles S. Russell (10th and 28th USCT).

By April 1, reports received by General Weitzel indicated that some of the Confederate troops manning the Bermuda Hundred peninsula were moving out. Weitzel told the Federal officer in charge there to push out his lines at daylight to investigate. This was done, and though the enemy was still well disposed to fight, the Federals got a good look at what was going on behind the enemy's earthworks. As Weitzel noted, "About 1,400 rebel infantry, 300 cavalry, and a light battery had been seen passing down . . . toward Petersburg."[5]

Deciding that the "enemy were weakening in my front," he readied his two divisions to attack on the morning of Monday, April 3. The arrival of Weitzel's orders found General Kautz tired but eager to carry out the command; his men had been on full alert since April 2, ready to advance had the forces on the Bermuda Hundred probe come up empty-handed. When night fell on April 2, Kautz learned that the "Army of the Potomac had carried the entire Petersburg front, and had captured 12,000 prisoners."[6]*

Surgeon Charles G. Merrill with the 22nd USCT observed that the "Rebels in our front had been exceedingly busy with the spade for

---

*The extent of the Union success at Petersburg, as reported to Kautz, was somewhat exaggerated, but U.S. troops had nonetheless made significant gains in fighting there lasting throughout the day.

one or two days and new works were going up." After dark on April 2, a Confederate brass band "discoursed very sweet music to us from those works; but nobody was beguiled into the belief that they were serenading Jeff. Davis or Gen. Lee." "There was no sound of revelry in our camp that night," recollected Lieutenant Henry C. Clapp of the 23rd USCT. "As we rolled up in our blankets we thought it might be for the last time for many of us." "We did not sleep much that night," added General Kautz, "waiting for the dawn of the day that would give us Richmond."[7]

The first hours of April 3 were filled with dramatic portents. "Early on Monday morning," wrote Sergeant John C. Brock of the 43rd USCT, "we were startled by the heavy explosion of what was, apparently, a magazine; but which, afterwards, proved to be their gunboat, that had been floated down the river and destroyed. There was, also, a great light seen in the direction of Richmond, which led us to suppose there was something more than usual going on. Presently, we heard a succession of heavy reports which was ascertained to be the exploding of shells in the city." General Kautz watched "column after column of fire ascend" amid the "steady glare of the conflagration." Thomas Morris Chester, reporting for the *Philadelphia Press,* was certain that the "immense flames curling up throughout the rebel camps indicated that they were destroying all that could not be taken away."[8]

Kautz wanted to advance his soldiers immediately but was prevented from doing so by a standing order that prohibited night movements into mined areas. He and his men therefore waited for daylight to see where they were stepping. Also sweating it out were the thousand or so cavalrymen still with the Army of the James, who were loosely grouped into a brigade posted on the right flank, near the Darbytown Road. Colonel Charles F. Adams, Jr., commanded this force, which included detachments from the 4th Massachusetts Cavalry and the 1st New York Mounted Rifles as well as most of his own unit, the 5th Regiment Massachusetts Cavalry (Colored). The young colonel had been thrust into his current responsibilities with little preparation and almost no help. "The miscellaneous Brigade of which I had charge was the hardest body to handle of which I had any experience," he said, "being made up of all sorts of detachments and being without any staff or organization." Despite these anxieties,

Adams slept through this night without noting any of the fireworks over Richmond.[9]

Correspondent Chester, for his part, stuck close to the Union forward trenches. "The soldiers along the line gathered upon the breastworks to witness the scene and exchange congratulations," he wrote. It was, he noted, "still dark" when the "Army of the James, or rather that part of it under General Weitzel, was put in motion." The small squads manning the picket lines began to drift forward even as they reported that the enemy positions appeared to be unoccupied. In the camps behind the Union trenches, bugles and drums called the assembly as the regiments (black and white) fell into marching order. According to Sergeant Thomas J. Griffin of the 29th Connecticut (Colored), it was "about 6 o'clock" when the unit "left Fort Burnham . . . , moving against the formidable works of the enemy."[10]*

In the 23rd USCT, the men picked their way "carefully among the thickly planted torpedoes, each marked with a little red tab, in front of the fort." "We were piloted by a Confederate soldier through the lines," recorded Sergeant Griffin, "thus avoiding all danger of the torpedoes, which were laid within five feet of each other, scattered over a large portion of the field through which we were to pass." As the 29th Connecticut (Colored) proceeded, the men drove ahead of them a squad of Rebels who had been ordered by the regiment's commander to "dig up torpedoes that were left in the ground to prevent the progress of the Union army."[11]

Lieutenant Edward J. Bartlett of the 5th Massachusetts (Colored) Cavalry remembered that it was 6:00 A.M. when the vedettes "broke camp and moved out beyond our picket line." These advance parties had ridden only a short distance, however, when the command was given to halt, dismount, and "prepare to fight on foot." The cavalrymen walked only a little way along the road before the order came once again to stop. Behind them, Colonel Adams was "fretting, fuming and chafing" as, "without a staff," he recalled, "I had to get a column in motion." Adams later estimated that it was about seven o'clock before he got his main body moving "at last."[12]

It took some time for the wary infantrymen to pick their way through the belt of Confederate land mines, while groups of Federal

---

*Burnham was also known as Fort Harrison.

pickets that had already eased past this barrier raced ahead. Once clear of the torpedoes, the main columns were formed up to follow the retreating Rebels "as fast as we could go," said an officer in the 43rd USCT. "[Brigadier] Gen. [Charles] Devens's Division held the right, and when we advanced he naturally took the New Market Road," wrote General Kautz, "while the First Division, Twenty-fifth Corps, holding the left to the river, found the river road the natural route to take."[13]*

Reporter Chester kept pace with Kautz's men. "Along the road which the troops marched, or rather double quicked, batches of negroes were gathered together testifying by unmistakable signs their delight at our coming," he noted. "The road was strewed with all kinds of obstacles," related a member of the 29th Connecticut (Colored), "and men were lying all along the distance of seven miles." "The haste of the rebels was evident in guns, camp equipage, telegraph wires, and other army property which they did not have time to burn," observed Chester.[14]

By this time, Colonel Adams had his improvised brigade—consisting principally of his own 5th Massachusetts (Colored) Cavalry—moving briskly along first the Darbytown and then the Charles City Road. "We were alone," reported Lieutenant Bartlett, "a sort of independent army on our own hook." "Finding the enemy's lines deserted and no orders coming I concluded something was up and it was best to push ahead," said Adams. Already some bold riders from the 4th Massachusetts Cavalry, accompanied by two staff officers designated by General Weitzel, had reached Richmond's outskirts, where they were to accept the city's formal surrender, proffered by its mayor.[15]

Devens's white troops, marching along the New Market Road, and Kautz's black soldiers, following the Osborne Road, were on a converging course. Even though the Twenty-fifth Corps had a longer route to take than the Twenty-fourth, General Kautz was certain that the former "would have beaten the latter into the city if Gen. Devens, who was the senior, had not sent his aide to me and directed that [my] . . . Division halt and allow his command to precede it." Devens later reported that when his troops reached the Osborne and New Market crossroads, a portion of Kautz's command "interposed" between the

*The "river road" was the Osborne Road.

main body and its skirmishers. According to Devens, these troops, which he identified as the 36th USCT, were halted to allow his men to pass; other accounts suggest that the rivalry to enter the city first was settled in a less orderly fashion.[16]

"The colored men gave the whites the road," related General Kautz, "but as long as there was room they kept the head of their column abreast of the other, until they reached the narrow streets where there was room for one column only." Exactly when the city limits were passed in this footrace will probably never be known, and claims for the black units' primacy have as much validity as those for the others'. "Brevet Brigadier General Draper's brigade of colored troops, Brevet Major General Kautz's division, were the first infantry to enter Richmond," asserted correspondent Chester. "The gallant 36th U.S. Colored Troops, under Lieutenant Colonel B. F. Pratt, has the honor of being the first regiment." In a letter written on April 24 to the *Boston Commonwealth,* Pratt himself was even more explicit:

> As attempts have repeatedly been made to take from Gen. Draper's brigade of colored troops the credit of being the first to enter the city of Richmond, on the morning of April 3d, and give it to Devens's division of the 24th Corps, I desire to set the facts before you as they are.
>
> Statements published in regard to the cavalry and infantry skirmishers, who were in advance, have been made in such a way as to lead the public to believe that Draper's brigade was not the first in the city; whereas the truth is, the 36th Regt. U.S.C. Infantry, of Gen. Draper's 1st Brigade, 1st Division, 25th Army Corps, was with its colors within the city limits before any other regiment; and the other regiments of the brigade before any other brigade, whether of colored or white troops.[17]

Writing to the *Christian Recorder,* Chaplain Garland H. White of the 28th USCT emphatically proclaimed "that the *colored soldiers of the Army of the James were the first to enter the city of Richmond.* I was with them."[18]

Testifying later before the Congressional Committee on the Conduct of the War, General Weitzel contradicted these accounts:

> When I had got about a quarter of a mile within the city limits, I found that a perfect mob had taken possession of the city, and were

robbing and plundering blacks and whites. . . . It was a perfect pandemonium. I saw the necessity at once of getting some troops in to preserve order, and I sent one of my aides-de-camp back with orders to get the first brigade he could find, and bring it in to act as provost guard. I did not designate any particular brigade, and he brought in . . . one of Genl Devens's. . . . Then, in accordance with instructions, I directed all the rest of my troops to march around the outskirts of the town and take possession of the inner lines of redoubts just outside the city.[19]

Weitzel's testimony notwithstanding, many of the black troops did in fact "march . . . through the city," in the words of General Kautz. The colonel commanding the 29th Connecticut (Colored) personally accompanied his skirmishers to a point from which they could see the seat of the C.S. Government. He then ordered, "Double quick, march," and the "company charged through the main street to the capitol and halted in the square until the rest of the regiment came up." Surgeon Merrill of the 22nd USCT wrote that the black soldiers "marched through the city with banners flying and drums beating." "As we entered the city there was a scene of wild excitement, the burning buildings, the negroes taking anything they found and the white people hiding in their homes, expecting the Yankees to do the most terrible things to them," related an officer in the 43rd USCT. "The delight of the colored population, in welcoming our troops, can neither be expressed nor described," declared Sergeant Brock of the same regiment. "Old men and women, tottering on their canes, would make their way to a Union soldier, catch him by the hand, and exclaim, 'Thank God! honey, that I have lived to see this day!' . . . The young people and children manifested their delight in every possible way."[20]

Leading the infantry procession was the 5th Massachusetts (Colored) Cavalry. "Going through the city we passed thousands of citizens, colored and white, who cheered and cheered us as we rode in triumph along the streets," recalled a trooper named Charles T. Beman. "In the rear of our battalion was a brigade of colored troops, who marched up the street platoon front, with their drums & fife," wrote Lieutenant Bartlett. "It was a grand, triumphal march." The Compiled Service Record for the 9th USCT includes the following notation for Company B: "The Company as part of the 9th Regt. U.S.C.T. entered the city of Richmond on the morning of April 3d 1865. Drums beating, colors flying and men singing the John Brown hymn—Gloria in excelsis!"[21]

In one of the most personally moving events of this historic day, Chaplain White of the 28th USCT came across an "aged woman, . . . inquiring for [one] by the name of Garland H. White, who had been sold from her when a small boy." After questioning her about what she knew of her family history, Chaplain White realized who it was he was speaking with. "I cannot express the joy I felt at this happy meeting of my mother," wrote White, adding, "I have witnessed several such scenes among the other colored regiments."[22]

After setting down some of his impressions of this day for the *Christian Recorder,* Sergeant John C. Brock concluded:

> What a commentary this is on the capture of Richmond! It has been the object we have been trying to obtain through four long years of war. . . . How many thousands have been wounded and slain, in striving to obtain this prize! . . . But, have we not cause to rejoice that this proud city, which has been the cause of all this sorrow, anguish, pain and bloodshed, has fallen; and, with her fall, the wicked cause which she represented. When the history of this ungodly rebellion shall be written, nothing will shine brighter on the pages of the historian, than the heroic firmness, endurance and fortitude, of the gallant armies which struggled over the hills and plains of Virginia for the possession of Richmond.[23]

Occupation of Petersburg, Virginia, April 3, 1865; Appomattox (Virginia) Campaign, March 27–April 9, 1865

A week before Richmond's surrender, on the night of March 27, in a movement calling for great secrecy, white and black troops from the Army of the James left their camps near the capital, their destination unknown. For several days preceding this operation, the units had been pulled out of front-line service and, as Major General Edward O. C. Ord later reported, "placed . . . in camps where they could not be seen or heard." Even as the soldiers marched into the darkness, their encampment fires were kept ablaze, and bandsmen sounded the routine calls. When the men reached the wooden pontoon bridges over the James and Appomattox rivers, they found them "covered with moist straw and compost" to muffle the noise of so many feet.[24]

"Our march proved to be an all-night one," recalled an officer with the 7th USCT, "and the halts were few and short. The night was very dark, and several times the road was lost and we had to retrace our steps. When daylight [on March 28] came we found ourselves behind the Petersburg lines." A full division of black troops joined two white divisions in carrying out this maneuver. Commanded by Brigadier General William Birney, the African American division consisted of brigades led by Colonel James Shaw, Jr. (7th, 109th, and 116th USCT), Colonel Ulysses Doubleday (8th, 41st, 45th, and 127th USCT), and Colonel William W. Woodward (29th and 31st USCT).* As soon as daylight disclosed something of the size and location of the operation, Woodward became convinced that he and his men "were to take a part in . . . the last great struggle for the overthrow of Lee's army."[25]

After several days of heavy fighting in early February, the Union lines at Petersburg stretched from the Appomattox River east of the city to a point southwest of it near the Boydton Plank Road, which represented General Robert E. Lee's last usable wagon supply route. On March 24, Lieutenant General Ulysses S. Grant informed his army commanders of his intention to send the Federal cavalry on a wide western sweep to cut Lee's only rail link south of the Appomattox River, while at the same time the Union infantry took control of the Boydton Plank Road. To free up enough Army of the Potomac units to do this job, however, it would be necessary to bring a number of regiments down from north of the James to replace them. The reason for all the secrecy was to keep Lee from doing the same thing with *his* troops.

On March 29, portions of Birney's black division began to occupy trenches recently vacated by Army of the Potomac soldiers. A chaplain with the 127th USCT recalled that the men "laid down out of doors with no shelter or fire through a cold rainy night." Together with the two white divisions accompanying them, the USCT men held the Union line linking the Sixth Corps with the Second below Hatcher's Run. For some of the black units, this meant combat duty,

---

*Woodward's two other regiments, the 10th and 28th USCT, remained behind. The 10th was posted to City Point and then to the Richmond front, while the 28th appears to have linked up with Draper's brigade near Richmond.

but for most, a shovel and pick were the assigned weapons. The 116th USCT built a small fort in advance of the main Federal line: the 41st USCT scooped rifle pits in the rain; and the 127th USCT sent more than half its strength out on trench-digging duty.[26]

The various elements of Grant's operation all began moving on March 29. The first to make contact with the enemy was the Fifth Corps, which tangled with Rebel defenders along the Quaker Road, at Lewis Farm. Both the cavalry and the Army of the Potomac infantry were in action on March 31, with Sheridan's troopers fighting around Dinwiddie Court House and the footsoldiers (Fifth and Second corps) battling the enemy near the White Oak Road. Neither action was decisive, but in anticipation of a possible breakthrough, Birney's black division was alerted: two of Doubleday's regiments were sent to support one of the white Army of the James divisions, while Colonel Shaw's brigade was "advanced to within a few hundred yards of the rebel works and . . . ordered to form for an attack." When these instructions were subsequently countermanded, the men returned to their trenches, only to spend April 1 under a desultory artillery fire.[27]

At Five Forks, a strategically important road intersection a few miles farther west, Union infantry and cavalry overwhelmed a smaller Rebel force to clear a path to the South Side Railroad. Knowing that this Federal victory would undoubtedly galvanize Lee into a controlled evacuation of Petersburg, U. S. Grant resolved to upset the Confederate applecart by attacking. Early on the morning of April 2, the U.S. Sixth and Ninth corps assaulted the fortified lines in their front. On the eastern side of this perimeter, the effort by the Ninth Corps along the Jerusalem Plank Road failed, but on the western side, the massed Sixth Corps achieved the breakthrough success that had been eluding Federal arms for nearly ten months now.

The other Union corps manning the Petersburg siege lines had been alerted to follow up these efforts. "Early in the morning," reported Colonel Shaw, "heavy firing was heard on our right and we again formed for attack, but the lines of the enemy had been broken by the Sixth Army Corps, . . . and they were deserting the works in our front." In the words of its regimental history, the 116th USCT, placed at the head of Birney's storming column, "moved across the intervening space, being the first to plant the stars and stripes on that portion of rebel defenses in front of Petersburg." Added an officer in the 7th USCT, "Eagerly the men went forward, and pushing through the heavy slashing and abattis in front reached the rebel works to find them abandoned."[28]

Throughout the morning and well into the afternoon, the black division was given no specific assignment but instead was relied upon to act as a general reserve. Some of the regiments met the Sixth Corps soldiers coming down the line after their breakthrough and trailed them back toward Petersburg; another portion of Birney's command was first told to march west to assist the Second Corps, then countermarched back to its starting point.

Near the western side of Petersburg, General Lee had meanwhile patched together a new line of defense running roughly perpendicular to his old one. Situated a few hundred yards to the west of this last-ditch line were two redoubts named Forts Gregg and Whitworth, which Lee now ordered to be held at all costs. Beginning at around 1:00 P.M., these two forts were targeted by the Twenty-fourth Corps in a series of assaults that lasted almost three hours and resulted in the capture of both. The net result of the combat, however, was to exhaust the offensive energy of the Twenty-fourth Corps. The Sixth Corps was also worn out from its exertions this day, while the Ninth Corps was tied down east of the city, and the Fifth and Second were well off to the west. Birney's black division, in contrast, having marched and fought very little since dawn, was both fresh and in position to move against Lee's last line.

An effort was made by Birney to prepare for such an action, which would have brought his men against the enemy's well-fortified Battery 45. According to Lieutenant Colonel James Givin of the 127th USCT, his soldiers "moved up to Battery 45, and formed for charge on right of brigade," in so doing exposing themselves to the enemy's artillery. Chaplain Thomas S. Johnson of the regiment recalled that the "Rebels were throwing grape & canister & shells with great fury." A dumbfounded Colonel Doubleday was told by Birney to place his men "so that the enemy could see them, which was done, and they were consequently exposed for more than an hour to the fire of eleven pieces of artillery." Only the fact that the Confederates were firing solid shot instead of antipersonnel munitions prevented serious casualties among the Union troops. Colonel Woodward later said he was "preparing to advance upon the enemy's works at 6:30 [P.M.], when the order was countermanded. The troops rested for the night, except the party detailed to construct a new line."[29]

Neither Grant's Petersburg report nor his *Personal Memoirs* mentions the actions of the black division on April 2, making it difficult to avoid the conclusion that no one in authority had any intention of using the USCT units in any offensive capacity at all. By the time they formed up near Battery 45, Lee had already received his reinforcements from north of the James, and there is nothing to suggest that a small, division-sized assault would have had the least chance of success; still, there lingers a nagging possibility that a more effective and timely employment of Birney's black division at Petersburg on April 2 might have provided Grant with a knockout blow.

During the night of April 2 and into the early morning hours of April 3, Confederate military forces pulled out of Petersburg and Richmond, following a westward course on the northern side of the Appomattox River. All along the Federal lines, soldiers began to ease forward as dawn arrived. Units from the Ninth Corps, entering Petersburg from the east, had U.S. flags flying from the courthouse steeple by 4:30 A.M.

Lieutenant Colonel Oscar E. Pratt of the 7th USCT (Shaw's brigade) led two companies in skirmishing order into the Cockade City at 6:00 A.M., "amidst the joyous acclamations of its sable citizens." The nearby 8th and 41st USCT (Doubleday's brigade) advanced at about the same time. Colonel Samuel C. Armstrong of the 8th noted that his soldiers received a "most cheering and hearty welcome from the colored inhabitants of the city, whom their presence had made free." As the 41st passed through Petersburg's streets, its commander, Colonel Llewellyn F. Haskill, left "guards to protect all inhabited houses, by order of General Birney." After capturing Battery 45, the 127th USCT, too, crossed over the municipal boundary. "The approach of the Union soldiers was hailed with joy by all the colored population," reported the regiment's chaplain. "They came out in the streets & filled the doors & windows with eager faces. . . . The soldiers partook of the spirit of the occasion and marched well through the city. Some recognized acquaintances who marched along and visited us as they went, others burst out in singing a song of which 'Babylon is fallen, Babylon is fallen,' and 'I'm Going to Occupy the Land' was the chorus."[30]

The only black soldier to publish an account of this morning was Sergeant Major William McCoslin of the 29th USCT (Woodward's

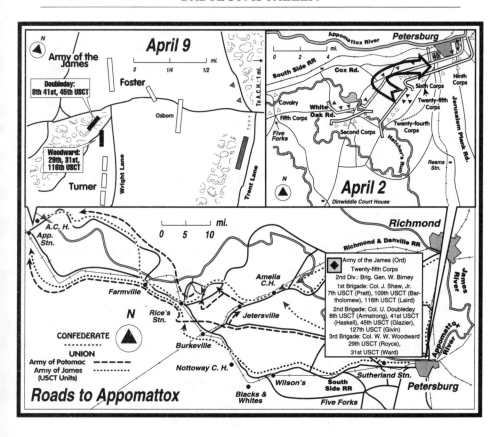

brigade). "We were among the first troops to enter Petersburg," he wrote to the *Anglo-African,* "and the orderly, well-behaved disposition of our command elicited the praise of our officers, and the universal commendations of the people, sobriety and decorum being the order of the day."[31]

The USCT units had only about three hours in which to savor their victory before being marched out the Cox Road to join in the chase after Lee's retreating army. Their route took them along the South Side Railroad, which now became an important link in Grant's supply chain. It had fallen to Birney's division to secure the first stretch of the route, so one by one, the USCT brigades dropped off the line of march. First to stop was Shaw's brigade, which, after tramping some extra miles thanks to a missed turn, set up near Sutherland Station. The two remaining brigades, Doubleday's and Woodward's, covered the track route as far as Wilson's Station, where they waited while the other Union columns raced to overcome Lee's head start. On April 5, Grant's soldiers successfully blocked Lee from turning south through Jetersville, forcing him to move farther and farther west.

It was not until the early afternoon of April 5 that Birney's three brigades, at last relieved of their guard duties, were allowed to rejoin the rest of Grant's columns. "Our march was rapid and devious, being . . . through mud, rain and stones," related Sergeant Major McCoslin. "We had been on short rations for two days and everybody was hungry," an officer in the 7th USCT recorded in his journal entry for April 6. "Our only food was a scanty supply of hard bread and half-cooked beef, without salt."[32]

The end of the day of April 7 found most of the black units near Farmville. Here Lee had moved his diminishing army to the northern side of the Appomattox River as he continued to chart a western course. The river ceased to be an effective barrier near a place called Appomattox Court House, so while the Federal Second and Sixth corps hung on to Lee's heels, Sheridan's cavalry, with hard-marching infantry from the Fifth Corps and the Army of the James trailing close behind, pushed ahead along the southern side of the river to head off the Confederates' escape.

Also on April 7, there were several organizational changes for the black troops. Brigadier General Birney was reassigned to the Petersburg area and left at once for his new posting. Doubleday's brigade was attached to Foster's division of the Twenty-fourth Corps, while Woodward's was appended to Turner's division of the same organization. Shaw's brigade was still coming up: once it arrived, it, too, would join Turner's command. Marching well ahead of the rest of Shaw's men, the 116th USCT was added to Woodward's brigade for the rest of the campaign. The previously segregated Twenty-fourth and Twenty-fifth corps had, for a brief moment in their short histories, become a single integrated outfit.

More than thirty miles passed beneath the feet of the black soldiers as they marched through April 8. By nightfall, they had reached a position near Appomattox Station, where Sheridan's riders had earlier battled with Rebel troops charged with protecting Lee's commissary trains. In the early hours of April 9, the Federal cavalrymen set up roadblocks across the main routes leading west from the village of

Appomattox Court House, where Lee's reduced army was now bivouacked. In a final effort to resume his course toward North Carolina, Lee ordered his infantry to open that route on the morning of April 9. Starting at around 7:00 A.M., Confederate lines of battle moved along the Richmond-Lynchburg Stage Road, shoving Sheridan's horsemen before them. The feisty cavalry commander needed reinforcements to stem this tide, so an urgent call went back for the trailing Yankee infantry to come up on the double-quick.

Foster's white troops (Osborn's brigade) were the first on the scene. Deployed south of the Stage Road, they pushed east as far as the enemy's advanced line of battle before being repulsed and falling back a short distance. Now the rest of the Army of the James began to come onto the field. Foster's other brigades hurried to support Osborn, while Turner's division took station south of Foster. Connecting these divisions were the two black brigades that had reached the battleground—Doubleday's and Woodward's. Doubleday's three regiments (the 127th USCT was off guarding ammunition trains), on orders from Sheridan, moved against some Confederate cavalry. "Early we advanced and our skirmish lines met those of the enemy," wrote Colonel Armstrong of the 8th USCT. "We expected a fight—I never felt more like it. . . . A few bullets whistled around, a few shells passed over." "We rush in, our left in front, a hurrying deployment of two companies of skirmishers," recorded a member of the 41st USCT, "a fine march into a field by the rear rank in our haste." "The rebs gave way," added Armstrong, "all was quiet."[33]

Woodward's brigade was also moving into position on the left of Turner's line. "Skirmishers were deployed on our front, and as we advanced the Confederate skirmishers retired before us," related an officer in the 116th USCT. "After advancing some eight hundred yards the brigade was ordered to halt and form in line of battle. . . . Some eight hundred yards away was the Army of Northern Virginia, with its three lines of battle awaiting us." A short distance south of these positions, the first units of the U.S. Fifth Corps pressed the Rebel lines back toward Appomattox Court House, while to the north, Federal cavalry clashed with some Confederates heading toward Lynchburg. These would prove to be the final combats of the day.[34]

Only the occasional crackle of a skirmisher's rifle disrupted the quiet along the Army of the James's front, as the men waited for *something* to happen. There was talk of a truce; then "other rumors came," said Colonel Armstrong, "and finally it was certain that the cruel war was over. The first inkling I had of it was the continuous cheering of troops on our right. Some staff officers galloped up with the news that Lee was making terms of surrender; the firing ceased. It was impossible to realize that the terrible army of Lee was in existence no longer! The truth was stunning."[35]

"We are a part of the army to which Gen. Lee, the Generalissimo of the C.S.A., has surrendered and have a share in the glory," wrote Chaplain Thomas S. Johnson of the 127th USCT. "Our brigade celebrated the event by firing volleys of musketry in the air," said an officer in the 116th USCT. Wishing his troops had been on hand for some of the sharp fighting of this campaign, Colonel Armstrong "felt a sadness, a feeling that the colored soldiers had not done enough, been sufficiently proved."[36]

With the fact of Lee's surrender confirmed, the thoughts of the men throughout the ranks began to turn to their prospects after the war. For the white soldiers, the focus was inevitably personal, dominated by dreams of returning home to see loved ones. The black soldiers, meanwhile, looked to the future as a continuation of the struggle to achieve the status of fully empowered United States citizens. As Sergeant Major McCoslin of the 29th USCT put it, "We the colored soldiers, have fairly won our rights by loyalty and bravery—shall we obtain them? If they are refused now, we shall *demand* them."[37]

Interlude

"Nothing Has So Shocked Us So Much"

———◄◦►———

THE men of the 41st USCT, who only days before had occupied Richmond, were settled south of Petersburg on the afternoon of April 15 when they learned of President Abraham Lincoln's assassination. "This cast a gloom over our camp," remembered a regimental officer, "and one could see and hear the grief of those poor colored men over his tragic end."[1]

"The news fell upon our company like a thunderbolt," reported an enlisted man in the 11th United States Colored Heavy Artillery. "Heaviness of heart seized them all. Groups discussed the unlikeness of the affair, hoping that some kind paper would bring a contradiction. But none came." "Nothing has so shocked us so much as the death of this patriot and statesman," declared Sergeant Charles H. Davis of the 108th USCT. "He was oppressed Americans' friend, who cherish his name as a household word. His image will be fixed in the hearts of four millions for whom he spoke the word of freedom, and who will mourn for him with great grief."[2]

As plans for the funeral ceremonies were being made in Washington, an order was sent to Major General Weitzel in Richmond, directing him to provide a black regiment for the occasion. According to its unit history, Weitzel chose the 22nd USCT on "account of its excellent discipline and good soldierly qualities." The men received their orders at 5:00 P.M. on April 17 and within an hour were marching toward City Point, finally reaching it just after midnight. At 4:00 A.M. on April 18, they boarded a river transport, which landed them in Washington around noon the next day.[3]

On April 20, the 22nd USCT took position on Pennsylvania Avenue near Sixth Street, in front of the Metropolitan Hotel. There the black soldiers waited until the long funeral cortege that had left the White House on its way to the Capitol drew near. "As the head of the column approached where the 22nd was standing 'at rest,'" wrote a reporter, "the band struck up a dirge, and the regiment immediately moved forward, thereby becoming the head of the procession." Another correspondent thought that the men "appeared to be under the very best discipline, and displayed admirable skill in their various exercises."[4]

Two days after performing this ceremonial duty, the 22nd joined the hunt for John Wilkes Booth. Between April 23 and 27, the black soldiers moved through portions of southern Maryland, often in widely dispersed skirmishing order. Seven miles from Bryantown when they learned of Booth's capture, the men were soon headed back to Petersburg.

On May 6, a black soldier, Sergeant John C. Brock of the 43rd USCT, set down his thoughts on Lincoln's death:

> Thank God! he was permitted to see the fruits of his toil, to see the work he had persevered in so nobly, and arduously, well nigh completed, before he received the summons. . . . He still lives in the hearts of the thousands, yea, millions of those whom he by his love of justice, liberty, and his well known belief in the right of man, redeemed from the curse of slavery, . . . thousands of whom are now in the ranks of the armies of the Union, hurling avenging justice on those who were the cause of this foul rebellion, and whose sworn purpose was to perpetuate human bondage.[5]

Chapter Seventeen

"That Winds Up the War"

———◦———

THE week from December 7 through 14, 1863, saw the organization of the 1st Regiment Missouri Colored Infantry at Benton Barracks, Missouri. This act was a triumph for that state's social radicals, who had managed successfully to navigate through the constantly shifting currents of government policy that more than once had scuttled others' efforts to raise black troops. Because Missouri was a border state, its loyal citizens were exempted from the Emancipation Proclamation, though slaves belonging to pro-Confederacy masters could still be confiscated or forcibly drafted into military service—a distinction that was often ignored by recruiters anxious to fill quotas. So volatile did this issue remain, in fact, that when the initial regiment of Missouri blacks (consisting only of slaves of "disloyal" masters) entered the army, it did so as the "Arkansas Volunteers (Colored)."

By the fall of 1863, the pool of blacks available under the government's policy had diminished to the point where the state's military commander asked permission to recruit the slaves of owners loyal to the Union, suggesting, moreover, that these individuals be financially compensated for their loss. Although President Lincoln refrained from initiating such a policy in Missouri—fearing its impact on upcoming judicial elections—he did proceed with just such a plan in Maryland. Once the Missouri elections went Lincoln's way, he promptly authorized state officials to recruit all blacks, both slave and free. Should the slave of a loyal resident enter the U.S. service, the owner could expect a maximum of three hundred dollars as compensation, but only after filing a deed of manumission and taking an oath of allegiance.

Due to local opposition, the number of conscripts was lower than expected, but eventually enough able-bodied men gathered at the Benton Barracks, near St. Louis, to constitute the 1st Regiment Missouri Colored Infantry. Among those enlisting were David Clark, a house slave for Washington Adams; Allen Stale, a farmer owned by Samuel J. Drysdale; Fleming Humes, who farmed the plantation of Lafayette Humes; and farmer Henry Ellis, for whom compensation would later be claimed by Margaret and Laura Todd. The men not only drilled but also were introduced to reading and writing through special classes given by the officers. In his activity report for December 24, 1863, Brigadier General Lorenzo Thomas recorded the 1st Missouri Colored's strength at 985.

The two men who commanded the regiment throughout its history came to it via different routes. Theodore H. Barrett, described by a reporter in 1865 as "a very young man, a New Yorker by birth, but [one who] has lived in the West the greater part of his life," entered the service as a lieutenant in the 10th Minnesota, subsequently transferred to the 9th Minnesota as a captain, and on December 21, 1863, was appointed colonel of the 1st Missouri Colored. His time with the regiment was repeatedly interrupted, once by an attack of typhoid fever and on other occasions by special duty assignments, causing him to turn much operational control over to his second-in-command. Pennsylvanian David Branson, born in 1840, was living in Mississippi when the conflict began. His pro-Union sentiments did not sit well with the residents of that state, however, so he went north and enlisted as a private in an Illinois regiment. Rising swiftly through the ranks, he served as sergeant, sergeant-major, acting adjutant, and, on his appointment to the 1st Missouri Colored, lieutenant colonel. He was described in 1881 as "possessing a face indicating remarkable courage and activity, and a physique that denotes endurance and a long life."[1]

In late January 1864, the officers and men of the new regiment were ordered to proceed to Cairo, Illinois, whence they were to travel to New Orleans, a trip that would prove anything but routine. The men left Cairo aboard the steamer *Planet*, which, some fifty miles above the Crescent City, struck a riverbank at 5:00 A.M. on February 1. At first Colonel Barrett was assured by the duty officer that the boat had not been seriously damaged; then, half an hour later, the officer returned with word that the vessel was leaking and the pumps had been started. Both men noted that the ship's engines had stopped. Barrett went immediately to the *Planet*'s captain, who insisted that there was no danger since the boat could be safely grounded at any time to keep it from sinking. He explained that he had stopped the engines to reduce the water pressure on the hull while the pumps brought the leaks under control.

By the time Barrett reached the main deck, the *Planet* had noticeably settled in the water. The engines were restarted soon afterward, whereupon the ship, moving sluggishly and with seeming difficulty, nosed toward the shore. It touched the riverbank at about 7:00 A.M. "The water was by this time over some portions of the lower deck," Barrett later reported. "She finally went down about half past 7. Every man in the regiment was saved."[2]

On March 11, the War Department changed the regiment's designation from the 1st Regiment Missouri Colored Infantry to the 62nd United States Colored Troops. The new name did little to help the men overcome the common impression among officers that black units were good only for fatigue duty. In early January, the regiment had been at Baton Rouge, assigned "to demolish certain portions of the works there." By June, Lieutenant Colonel Branson was complaining that the men's "military appearance and efficiency in drill is not improved by continued labor on fortifications." Less than a month later, the same officer, now writing from Morganza, Louisiana, provided his department headquarters with a succinct summary of the problem: "Since the arrival of my command at this place on the 21st day of June, 1864, all men fit for duty not on camp guard or police have been worked eight to ten hours daily on the fortifications except Sundays, one day for review and half a day for muster and inspection. No white troops have been worked on these fortifications during said period except those held as prisoners and undergoing punishment."[3]

It was testament to the dogged persistence of Branson and the officers under him that, following a general inspection, Brigadier General Daniel Ullmann pronounced the 62nd to be the "best under my command." Nonetheless, the exhaustion caused by constant fatigue duty, combined with inadequate sanitation and poor food, exacted a high toll on the regiment. "Scurvy and diseases of a kindred nature prevail," wrote Branson on September 30. "Many men have become permanently disabled from these curses during the past month, and some officers are much impaired in health thereby." Just thirty days earlier, he had reported that since the organization of the regiment, 340 enlisted men had died of disease. Another twenty-nine were so disabled that they had to be discharged; one more had been accidentally killed, and five had deserted. A regiment that had lost a third of its strength in battle would have been considered hard hit, but in the swampy byways of Louisiana, it was merely the cost of doing business.[4]

The 62nd USCT was involved in one small military action during its Louisiana service. On September 6, two hundred men from the regiment, commanded by Major Joseph K. Hudson, along with another two hundred from the 67th USCT, embarked on a one-day expedition from Morganza to Bayou Sara, an effort that proved uneventful. Of far greater import were the orders received later that month transferring the 62nd out of Louisiana.

The regiment's new posting was the island of Brazos Santiago, off the southern Texas coast. This outpost was all that remained of a U.S. effort to control the Rio Grande Valley, an initiative begun in November 1863 with the landing of a modest-sized expeditionary force that managed to extend Union suzerainty upriver as far as Ringgold Barracks. When U.S. planners subsequently decided that there were higher priorities elsewhere, all the Federal posts were abandoned, save Brownsville (about thirty miles inland) and Point Isabel (on the mainland near Brazos Santiago). Less than a year after the Federal retrenchment, Texas Rebels scraped together a three-thousand-man force and recaptured Brownsville. Once again, the Confederacy possessed an invaluable gateway to Mexico for the export of Southern cotton, as well as the importation *into* the South of munitions and medicines.

The United States' land presence near the mouth of the Rio Grande was eventually reduced to a thousand-man garrison on Brazos Santiago. When the 62nd arrived, it joined a force under Colonel Henry M. Day that also included an Illinois regiment and a unit of black engineers, the 81st USCT (New).* There was little to do on

---

*Some USCT units, despite being authorized and having their regimental numbers placed on record, failed to reach minimum strength. These units were often consolidated with others to

Brazos Santiago except keep the island's few buildings in some state of repair, labor on the fortifications, drill, and undertake minor forays along the coast to secure lumber, beef, or similar supplies. Problems of discipline soon developed. On October 29, Lieutenant Colonel Branson issued a general order that addressed one of the common evils of camp life even as it expressed the iron-willed paternalism that informed the relationships of many white commanders toward their black enlisted men:

> Hereafter when any soldier of this command is found to be or have been playing cards he will be placed standing in some prominent position in the camp with book in hand and required then and there to learn a considerable lesson in reading and spelling and if unwilling to learn, he will be compelled by hunger to do so.
>
> When men are found gambling in any way the money at stake will be seized and turned in to the regiment hospital fund. No freed slave who cannot read well has a right to waste the time and opportunity there given him to fit himself for the position of a free citizen.[5]

Still, the disciplinary problems were not limited to the enlisted men, as another of Branson's general orders, this one dated November 9, indicated:

> The Lieutenant Colonel commanding has learned with great regret that several officers of this command have been in the habit of abusing men under their command by striking them with their fists or swords and by kicking them when guilty of very slight offenses. This is as unmanly and unofficer-like, as it is unnecessary. An officer is not fit to command who cannot control his temper sufficiently to avoid the individual application of blows to enforce obedience.[6]

By December 1864, the complement of the Brazos Santiago garrison had been increased through the addition of the 34th Indiana, a veteran white unit that had fought in Grant's Vicksburg campaign. Leaving the island with the Illinois men to join Canby's Mobile expedition, Colonel Day passed command on to Brigadier General

---

form new units with new designations. Rather than let the original number lapse, the bureaucracy would sometimes assign it to the next organizing unit; to minimize confusion, the original USCT regiment was referred to as (Old), and the successor to that designation as (New). The 81st USCT (Old) thus consolidated with the 89th USCT to form the 77th USCT (New), while the 81st USCT (New) was created by the consolidation of the 87th and 95th USCT.

William A. Pile, who himself left soon after, handing over the reins to Colonel Robert B. Jones. Pile tried to have the 62nd (which he described as a "well drilled and disciplined regiment and well fitted for field service") transferred into the division that Brigadier General John P. Hawkins was then organizing for Canby, but without luck. Jones, in his turn, departed the post around April 1865, and command devolved to Colonel Theodore H. Barrett. It would be under Barrett's leadership that the regiment would first see action as a unit, playing a major role in what is generally considered to be the last directed combat of the Civil War.[7]

Skirmishes at Palmito Ranch, Texas, May 12–13, 1865

Reveille came well before sunrise for the 250 men from the 62nd USCT selected for the operation. Every company except Company A had contributed soldiers to the enterprise, and to a man these now stood quietly near the Brazos Santiago landing, each loaded down with a hundred rounds of ammunition and rations enough for five days. Lieutenant Colonel David Branson huddled anxiously with Lieutenant I. B. Rush, acting assistant adjutant general for U.S. forces on the island, pondering a problem that had just cropped up: the steamer assigned to ferry the men across the bay to Point Isabel* had broken down. No one had any idea how long it would take to repair the vessel, so Branson's options were to wait, cancel the operation, or find another way of getting the troops to the mainland. To complicate things even further, there was a storm coming.

Branson soon received new orders from Colonel Barrett, instructing him to return his men to their camp preparatory to crossing to Boca Chica from the southern end of Brazos Santiago. Barrett also authorized Branson to reduce the quantity of rations his men were carrying to three days' worth, and added a pair of six-mule teams to haul surplus supplies and ammunition. Finally, he bulked up the raiding force with fifty white men representing the 2nd Texas Cavalry (U.S.), none of whom were yet mounted. Everyone was to move right after dark.

*Known today as *Port* Isabel, and so called in several contemporary accounts of this action, though its proper name in 1865 was Point Isabel.

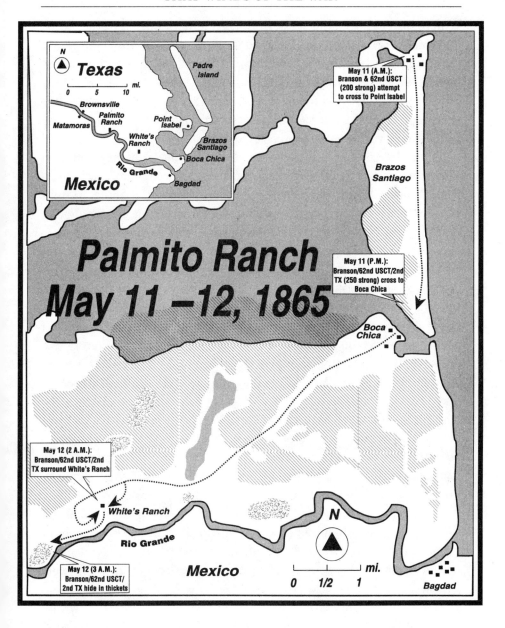

Palmito Ranch
May 11–12, 1865

Texas

Padre Island

Brownsville
Palmito Ranch
Matamoras
Point Isabel
White's Ranch
Brazos Santiago
Boca Chica
Rio Grande
Mexico
Bagdad

May 11 (A.M.): Branson & 62nd USCT (200 strong) attempt to cross to Point Isabel

Brazos Santiago

May 11 (P.M.): Branson/62nd USCT/2nd TX (250 strong) cross to Boca Chica

Boca Chica

May 12 (2 A.M.): Branson/62nd USCT/2nd TX surround White's Ranch

White's Ranch

Rio Grande

Mexico

May 12 (3 A.M.): Branson/62nd USCT/ 2nd TX hide in thickets

Bagdad

The military temperature in this section of the state had quickly gone from hot to cold following the Federal withdrawal to Brazos Santiago in late September 1864. Things were so quiet that in January 1865, a high-ranking U.S. officer arrived hoping to talk the Rebel leaders into capitulating western Texas. When nothing came of this diplomatic offensive, the Federals became even more complacent than they had been before the talks. After all, with the daily news' looking so bad for the Confederacy, Rebel troops in the Rio Grande Valley were deserting in droves, and intelligence received at the Brazos listening post soon suggested that Brownsville and much of the Rio Grande Valley were ripe for the picking.

In the bitter recriminations that followed the fight near Palmito Ranch, an officer in the 34th Indiana would charge that Colonel Barrett's ambitions had played a large part in his decision to initiate a military confrontation, inasmuch as the colonel, according to the Indiana man, wished "to establish for himself some notoriety before the war closed." For the record, Barrett (in the first draft of his after-action report) explained the expedition's purpose as "procuring forage for the command, and also to capture a herd of horses" that he had learned "were grazing not far from Point Isabel, in the direction of Brownsville." Many years after the events of May 12 and 13, Lieutenant Colonel Branson would comment that Barrett had been motivated by the desire "to stop the clamoring of the troops generally, for fresh beef to eat and lumber to build barracks . . . and . . . for horses [to be used by the 2nd Texas Cavalry] to ride while scouting for future supplies."[8]

"The breaking of the steamer's machinery compelled a change of plan," said Branson, "to cross at Boca Chica—night march to camp on [the] Rio Grande, and return via Point Isabel for lumber." The storm made the crossing from the southern end of Brazos Santiago to Boca Chica difficult and hazardous, but no men were lost, and the troops all got over by 9:30 P.M. Members of Company F, Captain Fred E. Miller commanding, took the advance, trailing slowly behind a guide who followed the telegraph right-of-way between Boca Chica and Brownsville. Branson was hoping to surprise a small Rebel outpost at White's Ranch, so he had his men take what he later described as a "long circuitous" route to that objective.[9]

The small column divided as it drew near White's Ranch, with Captain Miller's men marching about three quarters of a mile north before doubling back to close on the ranch from below, while the other Federal soldiers completed the encirclement. Branson, who had notions of scooping up sixty-five Confederate soldiers along with a small herd of horses and cattle, instead discovered "that the enemy had moved camp further up the river to Palmetto Ranch, and now it was too late to get there before daylight."* Still wishing to preserve the element of surprise, the lieutenant colonel ordered his men to find cover "in a thicket and among weeds on the banks of the Rio Grande one mile and a half above White's Ranch." Companies G and H, under Captain Harrison Dubois, kept watch while the rest of the men slept.[10]

Whatever hopes Branson had of keeping his movement a secret were dashed at 5:30 A.M., when, as he reported, "persons on the Mexican shore seeing us started to give the alarm to the rebels." Nevertheless, at 6:00 A.M., he deployed Company F in skirmishing order and continued on toward Palmito Ranch. An hour after getting under way, Captain Miller sent back word that his men had encountered enemy scouts. Branson's small force proceeded around a sharp bend in the river and at noon came up to Palmito Ranch, where the crib proved for the most part empty. Branson would later judge this day's effort "only a partial success," as the enemy was able to clear out before the Union soldiers arrived.[11]

Branson now had to make some serious decisions. His little raiding force was well inside enemy country and several hours from any kind of help. The Rebels knew of his presence, and to add to the tension, Imperial Mexican soldiers were engaging in distinctly threatening movements across the river. Searching the area around Palmito Ranch, Branson's men soon gathered in three prisoners, two horses, four head of cattle, and some rations. At 3:00 P.M., "a considerable force of the enemy appeared," the lieutenant colonel reported. Not wanting to be caught in such an exposed position, he ordered his men to return to White's Ranch. Covering the rear were Captain Miller's men, the captain noting that "the rebel cavalry [was] following closely and skirmishing continually." Once at White's Ranch, Branson sent a report of the day's events and a request for instructions to Colonel Barrett at Brazos Santiago.[12]

Barrett himself arrived at White's Ranch near daybreak, in company with two hundred men from the 34th Indiana, under Lieutenant Colonel Robert G. Morrison. He never explained his decision to reinforce the expedition with the 34th, though it is likely that the black

---

*Although the ranch's name was spelled Palmetto in all contemporary accounts of this action, local usage favored the spelling Palmito, which will therefore be used here in references outside quotations.

troops remaining on Brazos Santiago were too widely scattered on outpost and fatigue duties to be assembled in time. The 34th Indiana was an unfortunate choice, however, as relations between its officers and those of the 62nd USCT were decidedly cool. Much of the Brazos administration was handled by men from the 62nd, who for the most part had few good things to say about the combat-experienced Hoosiers. Typical of these critics was the 62nd's Major Hudson, who later testified that the enlisted men of the 34th "were very lax in discipline. The guard duty was done loosely, and while on duty the soldiers' bearing, as a general state, was unsoldierly." Before the same tribunal, Captain W. C. Durkee complained of men from the 34th "on dress parade doing what they should not, turning their heads and spitting." In their own defense, members of the 34th Indiana denied that the regiment had had any discipline problems while serving on Brazos Santiago. Whichever version may have been closer to the truth, there clearly was an absence of mutual trust and confidence among the two units' officers.[13]

That tension was not to be resolved this day. "Assuming command in person of the forces thus united," reported Colonel Barrett, "I at once ordered an advance to be again made in the direction of Palmetto Ranch, which, upon the retirement of Lieutenant Colonel Branson, had been reoccupied by the rebels." As the 34th Indiana settled down near White's Ranch for some breakfast and coffee, the 62nd USCT began moving. Company F, recorded Captain Miller, "was again deployed in advance and drove the enemy steadily before them as far as Palmetto Ranche." Barrett and Branson, with the 62nd USCT and the unmounted 2nd Texas Cavalry (U.S.), arrived at the ranch at 8:00 A.M. Here, as Branson later related, the "entire command . . . stacked arms and rested, and ate breakfast." After a two-hour break, the soldiers moved slowly toward Brownsville; now the 2nd Texas Cavalry (U.S.) had the advance, with the black soldiers closely following. Around this same time—10:00 A.M.—Colonel Barrett issued orders for the 34th Indiana at White's Ranch to join the main column near Palmito Ranch.[14]

The Rebels harassing Barrett's cautious advance belonged to a detachment under the command of Captain W. N. Robinson, whose members had been spread along the Rio Grande in small outposts. When all gathered together, this body of troopers numbered barely more than sixty, but more were on the way: during the May 12 skirmishing, and as soon as the Federals began moving on May 13, Robinson had sent couriers racing to Brownsville with the news. The senior Confederate officer at that post, when first informed of Branson's advance, had been all for abandoning the place, but his second-in-command, a feisty colonel named John S. "Rip" Ford, would not consider it. "You can retreat and go to hell if you wish," he shouted to his superior officer. "These are my men, and I am going to fight." The time was 11:00 A.M., May 13, when Colonel Ford led about two hundred riders and four pieces of artillery (manned by fifty cannoneers) out to battle the invaders. Because his animals were in poor shape, it took him three hours to reach the Palmito Ranch area.[15]

At the ranch itself, wood smoke curled up into the warm Texas air as flames ate away at the rude barracks built by the Rebel pickets. The structure was burned on Colonel Barrett's orders, along with any supplies that "had escaped destruction the day previous." A short distance to the west, skirmishers from the 2nd Texas Cavalry (U.S.) and the 62nd USCT traded shots with Robinson's men. In a move that suggested that he was seriously considering making a thrust at Brownsville, Colonel Barrett weeded out the slowest-moving elements, ordering the return to Brazos Santiago of a small detail consisting of "all the disabled men, and those not able to make a heavy march, . . . with the wounded men, [prisoners,] horses and cattle."[16]

The surrounding landscape would later be described by a *New York Herald* correspondent as a "vast sandy plain, interspersed here and there with green prairie and Mexican chaparral[. It] is in many places intersected by bayous and lagoons, so that sudden movements . . . would in all likelihood result in . . . surprise." There was no surprise at all, though, when the 34th Indiana reached Palmito Ranch, at around noon. Barrett first provisioned the regiment with rations taken from the 62nd, then ordered Lieutenant Colonel Morrison to advance as far as Palmito Hill. A company of Indiana soldiers relieved Company F of the 62nd, allowing the weary blacks to fall back to the main camp near the hill. The Union forces were now disposed roughly as follows: the 34th Indiana moving along the Brownsville Road, near the river; the 62nd USCT advancing across the open plain to the right of the white regiment; and the small company of the 2nd Texas Cavalry (U.S.) covering the gap between the two.[17]

"Nearly the entire forenoon was spent in skirmishing," Barrett reported. "The enemy, though taking advantage of every favorable position, was everywhere easily driven back. Early in the afternoon a sharp engagement took place, which, being in the chaparral, was attended with comparatively little loss to us." Wounded at this time was Private Henry Ellis of Company D in the 62nd USCT, who later recollected being hit in the right ankle "by a shot from a Confederate soldier lying in the grass, who was [himself] wounded, [and who] raised up and shot me." Ellis was mounted and sent to the rear, the blood visibly streaming from his leg.[18]

Also during this "sharp engagement," Lieutenant Charles A. Jones of the 34th Indiana proposed to ambush some Rebel troopers who were disputing the general advance. After giving Jones permission to attempt his scheme, Colonel Barrett ordered Lieutenant Colonel Branson to bring up a detachment of the 62nd to assist. He failed to inform the Indiana officer of that fact, however, nor was Branson briefed on the plan. As a result, the black troops blundered into the open, thereby scaring off the very Rebels Jones had hoped to catch.

It was approaching 2:00 P.M. when Colonel Barrett made a series of decisions that would doom his expedition once and for all. First he ordered the 34th to return to Palmito Hill, where it was "to encamp and prepare . . . supper." Ninety minutes later, he had the 62nd USCT settle on the right of the 34th, and pulled back the 2nd Texas Cavalry (U.S.) as well. No regular pickets were posted; instead, as Lieutenant Colonel Branson related, "by direction of Colonel Barrett I had placed four or five men on high ground where they could overlook the surrounding country, in order to notify us of the approach of the enemy." Barrett's intention, as he later testified, was to rest the men prior to "moving camp at dark a short distance and marching in the morning at 3 o'clock in the direction of Port Isabel." That plan became moot when, at around 4:00 P.M., as he recounted, "the enemy suddenly appeared in large force, in front [and] on our right flank, and was already attempting to gain our rear, being farther down the river than ourselves, on their left, having already flanked us."[19]

The Rebel Colonel Ford reached the edge of the fighting shortly after 3:00 P.M. Although somewhat unnerved by the number of Yankees opposing him, he nonetheless decided to attack. Combining the men he had brought along with those already on the field under Captain Robinson, Ford had at his disposal a total force of perhaps 360 men.* Two battalions (Robinson's and one under Captain D. W. Wilson) formed his main line, backed by two of the six cannon; these units were placed roughly perpendicular to the Rio Grande, approximately two and a half miles west of Palmito Hill. Two smaller detachments went with a pair of cannon on a wide flanking swing to the north and east. Ford's last two artillery pieces were held in reserve. Once these dispositions were completed, the Confederate colonel rode along his main line exhorting his soldiers before the battle. "Men, we have whipped the enemy in all our previous fights!" he shouted. "We can do it again." The time was shortly after 4:00 P.M. when "Rip" Ford signaled a general advance.[20]

Colonel Barrett was completely surprised by the enemy's aggressiveness. His first impulse was to hustle up some security: "Colonel Morrison," he told the 34th Indiana's commander, "you will put out two companies as skirmishers to cover your front." The requested coverage, about forty-eight in all, spread out into a thin line facing toward Brownsville. The 2nd Texas Cavalry (U.S.) took station to the right of the Indiana skirmishers, while Lieutenant Colonel Branson directed the 62nd USCT into combat formation facing "obliquely to the rear," or parallel to the river.[21]

Even as these maneuvers were being carried out, Colonel Barrett was finding ample reason to quit the place. "With the Rio Grande on our left, a superior force of the enemy in our front, and his flanking force on our right, our situation was at this time extremely critical," he later reflected. The deciding factor came when one of Ford's cannon launched a shell that arched over the plain and hit Palmito Hill. According to Lieutenant Colonel Branson, this first artillery fire produced "some confusion and disorder" in the ranks of the 34th. "Having no artillery to oppose the enemy's six 12-pounder field pieces," said Barrett, "our position became untenable." Turning to the officers near him, the Union colonel said, "Very well then; we will retreat in good order, and good order let it be. Men[,] keep your ranks. They can't hurt you; we'll get out of this yet."[22]

---

*In postwar Northern accounts of this day's action, estimates of the Rebel force range from six hundred to as many as fifteen hundred men. Published Confederate estimates are even less accurate, putting Barrett's command at between eight hundred and sixteen hundred men, when in fact he had only about 450.

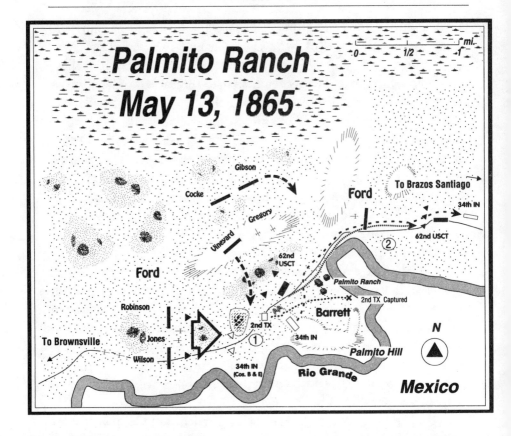

Adding a touch of tragicomic relief to the moment, a commercial steamboat from nearby Bagdad now chugged into view on the river. Ford's nervous gunners, thinking the craft a Yankee gunboat, threw two shells at the vessel, both of which missed. The steamboat was able to identify itself as a nonbelligerent before more shells could be fired.

By the time Barrett decided to retreat, most of the 34th Indiana was already deployed in line of battle on Palmito Hill, save the two companies that had been sent out as skirmishers. The 62nd USCT was in like formation along the foot of the hill, facing north, with the 2nd Texas Cavalry (U.S.) screening its left flank. When Barrett gave the command to fall back, the 34th began to edge over and down Palmito Hill (drawing some cannon fire as it did so), while the 62nd moved eastward by the right flank, with the 2nd Texas trailing after it. Once the 62nd had begun moving, Barrett ordered Branson to throw out a screen toward the enemy's flanking party, so 140 men eased out to provide the necessary protection. Companies E and H, under Captain Dubois, formed a part of this screen. "I found but little trouble in keeping the files dressed and the men in their proper places," Dubois later reported, "although two cannon balls passed through the ranks soon after the retreat was commenced."[23]

There were some tense moments as the paths of the two Union regiments came together on the march toward Palmito Ranch. In his report, Lieutenant Colonel Branson noted, "Some temporary confusion was created by a portion of the Thirty-fourth Indiana breaking through my regiment at double-quick while I was marching in quick time, but order was immediately restored." Testifying later before a tribunal charged with investigating this action, Branson explained that the 62nd had been retreating along the road when the 34th came down off Palmito Hill at a faster gait, its course carrying it around to the western side of the 62nd (i.e., toward the enemy). Since this exposed the Hoosiers to the Rebel artillery, some of them, according to Branson, "broke ranks, and forced their way through my regiment in [the] direction of the river."[24]

Against this account weighed that of Lieutenant Charles A. Jones of the 34th, who claimed it had been the black troops, following direct orders from Branson, who "broke the ranks of the Thirty-fourth Regiment by marching through it." The surgeon of the white regiment, Godfrey Bohrer, would declare twenty years after the fact, "As to the 34th or any of its men breaking through the 62nd with its Colonel[,] I flatly contradict the statement."[25]

Completely forgotten in the confusion were the two companies from the 34th that had been skirmishing with the enemy. In testimony given before the same tribunal that Branson addressed, "Rip" Ford recounted their fate: "They stood as long as they could, until many of them were run over by my cavalry, and nearly all of them were taken prisoners." Also during this phase of the action, many of the 2nd Texas Cavalry (U.S.) hid in the chaparral along the river near Palmito Ranch, where most were captured the next day.[26]

Once the 62nd USCT and the 34th Indiana managed to disentangle themselves, the Federal retreat assumed some semblance of order. The 34th led the way with the supply wagons, while the 62nd followed, covered by a rear-guard screen. The Rebel troopers made a special effort to cut off the Union columns before they reached the sharp bend in the river, but a determined stand by Captain Miller and

Company F of the 62nd provided the rest with the shield they needed to escape.

It took three hours for Barrett's column to reach Boca Chica. During this retreat, discipline in the 34th Indiana broke down to the point where both of the flags carried by the regiment—in normal times, objects of great unit pride—were lost by soldiers too weary, footsore, and demoralized to care. The national flag was hidden in the chaparral, and the state flag taken across the Rio Grande by a soldier who swam to the opposite shore and turned it over to Mexican authorities.

The performance of the 62nd USCT, meanwhile, both in battle and in retreat, drew high praise. "Every attempt of the enemy's cavalry to break this line was repulsed with loss to him, and the entire regiment fell back with precision and in perfect order, under circumstances that would have tested the discipline of the best troops," reported Colonel Barrett. By the time the 62nd reached Boca Chica, at about 8:00 P.M., most of the 34th Indiana had already crossed over to Brazos Santiago. The 62nd, "marching as from dress parade, twenty-eight inch step, music playing," held its position until after 4:00 A.M. on May 14, when it at last followed the Hoosiers across the water.[27]

Among those not reaching camp this night were Fleming Humes of Company D, wounded; Allen Stale of Company I, captured; Wyette Rowlett of Company I, badly wounded in the left hip; and Bill Redman of Company H, also seriously wounded in the left hip. Redman's wound would prove mortal; he would die on June 4 at the Brazos Santiago post hospital, of "wounds received in battle near Palmetto Ranch, Texas, May 13th, 1865." He thus earned the distinction of being the last man to die of wounds received in this final engagement of the Civil War.[28]

Well before the 62nd reached Boca Chica, the Rebel pursuit ran out of steam, many of the jaded horses in Ford's command having broken down due to the rigors of the day's march and the ensuing combat. The final confrontation between the two forces took place somewhere between White's Ranch and Boca Chica, where, according to Colonel Barrett, the "last volley of the war, it is believed, was fired by the Sixty-second U.S. Colored Infantry about sunset." Lieutenant R. B. Foster, in charge of Company I, later claimed the honor of having given the "last command to fire at Confederate troops in this last battle of the war." In an account written in 1883, Lieutenant

Colonel Branson related that he had uttered the final command to cease fire "with probably deeper feeling than [I] ever before gave a military order." Turning to an officer standing next to him, Branson said with a bit of melodramatic finality, "That winds up the war."[29]

If Colonel Barrett undertook this expedition to Palmito Ranch seeking some last wisps of military glory, he was bound to be disappointed: there was none for him there. Afterward, he brought charges against Lieutenant Colonel Morrison of the 34th Indiana for his alleged poor performance during the engagement, but after the evidence of Barrett himself, Branson, and other members of the 62nd USCT was heard, Morrison was found not guilty. In retrospect, it is difficult to absolve Colonel Barrett of his responsibility for the dismal results of the operation: it was his decision to send troops over to the mainland in the first place, and his decision to reinforce Branson's men when they met unexpectedly stubborn opposition at Palmito Ranch on May 12. Barrett's actions on May 13 lacked any sense of objective or mission; rather, they seemed the tentative acts of a man uncertain of his purpose and unwilling (or unable) to commit to a firm course of action.

Although a variety of postwar accounts tallied Union losses at nearly half of those involved in the operation, and Confederate casualties were on a par with Federal, the real numbers are less dramatic. The total among the Rebels, according to Colonel Ford, was "five or six, wounded." In a report written on May 21, Colonel Barrett enumerated his losses as follows: 34th Indiana, seventy-seven captured,* one wounded, one killed; 62nd USCT, two captured, five wounded; and 2nd Texas Cavalry, twenty-two captured, three wounded—making a grand total for Palmito Ranch of 101 captured, nine wounded, and one killed.†

Throughout May 14, the victorious Texas Confederates prowled over the Palmito Ranch battlefield, gathering souvenirs and rounding up groups of Union soldiers. Among those captured was Sergeant David Clark of the 62nd USCT, who heard some cheering behind him shortly after he surrendered. "I was sick," he later related. "It caused me to look around. I saw a United States flag—the Stars and Stripes, very ragged." What Clark saw was the U.S. flag carried by the 34th

---

*Forty-eight of these came from Companies B and E, which was left on the skirmish line while the rest of the command retreated.
†This total was figured before Bill Redman died of his wounds.

Indiana, which had been hidden in the brush, only to be retrieved by the enemy. Mercifully missing from the action this time were any atrocities committed against the black soldiers captured or found wounded on the field; according to Colonel Ford, "There was no disposition to visit upon [the prisoners] a mean spirit of revenge."[30]

The Federal POWs were brought to Brownsville, offered paroles —which they accepted*—and then allowed to return to Brazos Santiago. Before the month was out, all Confederate resistance would end along the Rio Grande, enabling U.S. forces to occupy Brownsville unopposed.

It seems somehow fitting that the last directed combat of the Civil War should have involved black troops: there is something appropriately symbolic in the fact that men who had been legally denied their manhood twenty-nine months earlier by the laws and practice of slavery bore arms in the final battle against that cruel institution. While the engagement may not have been decisive in any way—may have been, in fact, utterly unnecessary—it nevertheless exemplified the willingness of black men to put themselves in harm's way for the sake of their own honor and what they believed would be the future benefits accruing to their race. In the restrained language of his final report on Palmito Ranch, Colonel Barrett said, "The entire operation demonstrated the fact that the negro soldier can march; also that the regiment can keep order in the ranks and be depended upon under trying circumstances."[31]

And perhaps that is praise enough for any fighting unit.

---

*U.S. authorities subsequently declared the paroles invalid and immediately returned the men to duty.

Part Five

1865–1938

Chapter Eighteen

"This Good Work Is Only Begun"

———◦———

LEE'S surrender at Appomattox Court House on April 9 was merely the first in a series of final Confederate military capitulations. At the Bennett House in North Carolina on April 26, General Joseph E. Johnston signed a convention ending the existence of his army. General Richard Taylor eliminated Rebel forces in Alabama, Mississippi, and eastern Louisiana with the stroke of a pen on May 4, at Citronelle, Alabama. The Trans-Mississippi lingered until June 2, when General Edmund Kirby Smith initialed an agreement terminating the Confederacy's last military department. Southern armed forces had ceased to exist, and with them the need for massive U.S. armies; throughout the North, demobilization became the watchword. Veteran units that had fought in the Army of the Potomac, or marched with Sherman to the sea, paraded out in style in Washington on May 25 and 26. Since there were no black units then serving in either of those commands, the only African Americans participating in the Grand Review were contraband laborers whose squads had toiled to build roads for Sherman's legions.

Even as white regiments left the service, virtually every active black unit remained in the field to help occupy the conquered South. There was a certain logic in first mustering out many of the white regiments, simply because their enlistment terms were due to expire before those

455

of their later-arriving black counterparts. Northern white communities were also clamoring for their boys to be brought home, an appeal that few USCT outfits could claim to match because so many had been recruited in the South. (A notable exception was made for "all organizations of colored troops . . . which were enlisted in the Northern States," whose discharges were generally expedited.) A third factor consisted in a certain paternalism on the part of the white planners, who believed that by keeping the mass of untutored ex-slaves in uniform, they were not only providing them with food, shelter, and pay, but also helping to ease their transition into a free society.[1]

Combat-experienced black regiments joined with USCT garrison units to police the peace. Soldiers who had entered Richmond or taken part in the final pursuit of Lee's army now watched over the former Rebel capital as well as Petersburg. Sergeant Alexander H. Newton of the 29th Connecticut (Colored) recalled the sudden abundance of Confederate money, "which was often blown about by the wind as so much worthless waste paper." Troops from the Coast Division and others involved in the Fort Fisher expedition occupied posts throughout North and South Carolina. "Our duty is to let the colored people know that they are free citizens of the United States," wrote a 26th USCT soldier in July from the Palmetto State, "and to protect them as such, and also to prevent their former owners from driving them off the plantations, and cheating them out of their share of the crop, which they are anxious to do."[2]

Other USCT regiments took station along the lower Atlantic Coast and the Gulf of Mexico. "The rebs here seem to die very hard at the idea of having black troops to guard them, but they have been very quiet, and do not have much to say," noted Private William B. Johnson of the 3rd USCT from his Florida post. Still more units assumed occupation duties in Louisiana and up the Mississippi Valley through to Tennessee. An 11th USCHA soldier stationed at Donaldsonville, Louisiana, wrote in early summer that the men had "good quarters to stay in; all that is wanting are the rights of soldiers, justice, liberty and Union."[3]

Throughout the South, the mere presence of armed blacks charged with enforcing the law was a powerful, and often painful, reminder of the great social changes that were underway. "It is very hard," admitted a former Confederate soldier, " . . . to see a white man taken

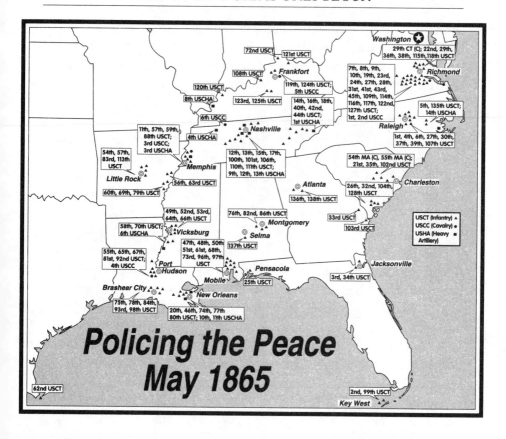

Policing the Peace
May 1865

under guard by one of those black scoundrels." Many Southerners were unprepared to accept the new order. On one occasion, when accompanying his men on a march to occupy a South Carolina village, the officer commanding the 35th USCT was met by a delegation of citizens who implored him "not to bring them niggers into their town." After coldly informing the "welcoming" committee that his detachment consisted of "United States soldiers," the officer carried out his instructions.[4]

Perhaps the most effective weapons used against black occupation troops by white Southerners were false accusations that they were guilty of malicious acts. Too often, Union officers accepted such unsubstantiated complaints and initiated punishment without investigation—a practice that infuriated the black soldiers. After witnessing a member of his regiment being hanged by his thumbs on a fraudulent charge, a private in the 3rd USCT bitterly decried the fact that

"Negro citizens, although they have been the only true and avowed friends of the United States Government in this section of the country, are still compelled to feel that they are black, and the smooth oily tongue of the white planter is enough to condemn any number of them to a tying-up for twenty-four hours."[5]

For many black units, orders in the summer of 1865 required a posting to Texas, where the U.S. Government was amassing a substantial body of troops under Major General Philip H. Sheridan for the fourfold purpose of subduing the Rebel Trans-Mississippi, reestablishing U.S. controls along the troubled Mexican border, guaranteeing political rights for loyal whites and newly freed blacks, and reclaiming the far frontier from Indian tribes.

The first Federals to arrive, in mid-June, were white regiments belonging to the Thirteenth Corps, which took control of the Galveston area and from the Red River inland to Marshall, Texas. The second wave, which followed in late June, comprised Twenty-fifth Corps units shipped from Virginia to Texas (Major General Henry W. Halleck, in charge in Virginia and unhappy about having the all-black corps in his command, had seized on the earliest opportunity to transfer it elsewhere). "Our trip was a very pleasant one," recorded a sergeant in the 29th USCT, "that is, after we had recovered from our sea sickness." The initial leg brought them into Mobile Bay, where supplies were taken on and the men themselves redistributed among the vessels; the next stop came at the mouth of the Mississippi, where the troops again briefly disembarked. Once in Texas, five regiments were stationed at Indianola, and two at Corpus Christi, while the bulk of the corps came ashore at Brazos Santiago.[6]

If the government understood why it was ordering these movements, the men themselves were not so sure. "Frankly," said Sergeant Major Thomas J. Griffin of the 29th Connecticut (Colored), ". . . what we are here for, or why we are here, I, like most of my comrades in arms, am unable to state." The conditions they encountered in Texas were far from those they had left behind in Virginia. "We find Brazos [Santiago] a most undesirable place," wrote a member of Sergeant Griffin's regiment. "There were plenty of fleas and mosquitoes and sand burrs." A soldier in the 45th USCT remembered the island as being "sandy and desolate"; echoing that sentiment, an African American on the headquarters staff of the

USCT in Texas
29th CT (Colored); 5th MA Cavalry (Colored); 1st, 2nd, 3rd USCT (engineers); 1st, 2nd USCT (cavalry); 2nd USCT LA: Battery B; 7th, 8th, 9th, 10th, 19th, 22nd, 23rd, 28th, 29th, 31st, 36th, 38th, 41st, 43rd, 45th, 46th, 47th, 51st, 62nd, 68th, 76th, 80th, 85th, 87th, 95th, 108th, 109th, 114th, 115th, 116th, 117th, 118th, 122nd, 127th USCT

Texas Campaign 1865–1867

Twenty-fifth Corps thought that a "more God-forsaken spot does not [exist] in the wide world." "We are put to considerable inconvenience about water," reported Private S. H. Smother of the 45th USCT. "We have to use condensed water altogether, which is issued to us boiling hot, at the rate of three pints per day."[7]

Perversely, it was an abundance of the wrong *kind* of water that would pose the next obstacle for the black troops on their way to police the U.S.-Mexico border. The Rio Grande flooded unexpectedly, overflowing the low-lying country between Brownsville and the coast. Writing on July 7, Sergeant Griffin described the rugged march: "Following the course of the Rio Grande river, we waded through mud and water, at times knee deep, and in one particular instance, which I am not likely soon to forget, we were obliged to wade for some distance through water waist deep, and at 10 o'clock p.m. on the 5th inst., we entered Brownsville, and are now encamped about two miles from the city."[8]

"The country here is very flat, and is in a wild and uncultivated state," observed Louis T. Wood of the 29th USCT. "There are all kinds of reptiles and venomous insects, and snakes, alligators, lizards, tarantulas, large mosquitoes, scorpions, horned toads, and also wolves." "I came to the front in May, 1864 at Petersburg, and fought at the mine on the 30th of July," declared Sergeant J.C.W. of the same regiment. "Never have I been so displeased with the army as at the present time."[9]

With the U.S. occupation of Texas concentrated along the coastline, the Rio Grande Valley, and several inland population centers, most of the USCT units wound up either guarding the Mexican border or watching the Gulf Coast. These activities, coupled with the service of other black units throughout the South, constituted a source of pride for some in the regiments. "When from Fortress Monroe to the Rio Grande colored pickets can be seen watching the approach of every ship, and the nation intends us to restore peace, order and national tranquillity," wrote Chaplain Garland H. White of the 28th USCT, "the very position we occupy to-day in the army of our country has a voice much louder than the organs of a thousand demoralized cities."[10]

The tasks assigned to the USCT troops in Texas were depressingly similar to those given them during the war. "The officers and men here have been doing incessant and excessive fatigue duty since the organization of the Brigade," complained an officer in the Twenty-fifth Corps. Problems of morale and discipline increased along with time on station. "I have the honor to state that there is a great deal of liquor sold to the enlisted men of this regiment," reported the 43rd USCT's commander in late September, "both while in Brownsville on passes and while there on duty." Illness soon became a deadlier deadly enemy than recalcitrant Rebels: "No set of men in any country ever suffered more severely than we in Texas," avowed the black chaplain of the 28th USCT. "Death has made fearful gaps in every regiment." Another soldier with the Twenty-fifth Corps in Texas was certain that the regiments had "lost many more here than we did in all the battles before Richmond." For his part, the white surgeon of the 41st USCT estimated that "often more than one-half, and sometimes three-fourths, of a regiment were afflicted with scurvy."[11]

Almost as ubiquitous as disease were incidents of violence between white citizens and USCT soldiers, which occurred often enough to prompt General Sheridan to wonder if the government's policy allowing discharged infantrymen to purchase their weapons should be suspended in the case of blacks mustering out in Texas. The attitude of local whites toward them was typified by a newspaper editorial that declared, "The idea of a gallant and high-minded people being ordered and pushed about by an inferior, ignorant race, is shocking to the senses."[12]

For the most part, USCT service in Texas was without significant incident. A notable exception, however, took place on January 5, 1866, when a small party of adventurers claiming to represent the anti-Maximilian Liberal Army seized control of the Mexican town of Bagdad, at the mouth of the Rio Grande. A garrison force from the 108th USCT was posted across the river at Clarksville, Texas. Evidence given at a subsequent Court of Inquiry suggested that some of the USCT soldiers had thrown in their lot with the adventurers, drawn largely by the promise of booty. These men were never identified, nor was their actual number determined. A portion of the Clarksville detachment, under orders, entered Bagdad right after the incident and restored peace until proper Mexican authority could be reestablished.

Throughout this time, the demobilization process unfolded slowly for the troops in Texas, with white soldiers usually waiting at the head of the line. In early January 1866, General Sheridan numbered his Lone Star contingent at 6,500 white soldiers and 19,768 black ones. Sheridan himself had helped to create this imbalance by maintaining that African Americans actually *preferred* military life over civilian status; reports forwarded to him of dissatisfaction in the USCT ranks were often dismissed as coming solely from homesick white officers. It took a direct order from U. S. Grant, in January 1867, to compel Sheridan to muster out the remaining USCT units.

Sheridan's actions began the final phase in the history of black Civil War regiments. On December 20, 1867, in Kentucky, the last of them—the 124th USCT—left the rolls, having been preceded throughout the South by more than a hundred others. Units originally organized by Northern states frequently held formal ceremonies to mark the end of their service, as did the 29th Connecticut (Colored), discharged in Hartford on November 24, 1865. After enjoying a "fine repast, which had been prepared by the white and colored citizens" of the town, the men marched into City Hall beneath a large banner listing their military engagements. There followed a good deal of speech-making, including a tribute by Brevet Major General Joseph Hawley, who had nothing but praise for the men, "for I have seen what you can do." The next day, the soldiers were "paid off, disbanded, and everybody advised by the paymaster to take care of their money, and return to their homes and live the life of peaceable citizens."[13]

Even as the last of the volunteer black regiments ended their record of service, a new service history was beginning. On July 28, 1866, Congress approved an act authorizing the postwar military peace establishment of the United States. To the six cavalry regiments that were already in uniform, the act added four more, "two of which shall be composed of colored men"—what would become the 9th and 10th U.S. Cavalry. That same bill increased the nineteen existing infantry regiments to twenty-seven, of which four were to be black units. Those four were eventually combined into two, creating the 24th and 25th U.S. Infantry and extending the African American military experience into the twentieth century.[14]

On returning home, the black Civil War veterans found that on paper, at least, the world of 1865 was very different from that of 1863. A Marylander in the 39th USCT recalled that when he went to war, what he "left [was] a slave State, with laws existing as black as the nocturnal regions"; now it was a free state, "and every slave at liberty." However, as he pointed out to the *Christian Recorder,* "this good work is only begun, not finished." A comrade in the 35th USCT shared his optimism: "The day is now just beginning to break," he declared, "and the shades of night are gradually disappearing, and the Sun of righteousness [is] shining forth in his beauteous rays on the down-trodden sons of Africa."[15]

The principal issue on every mind was enfranchisement. "We were called in 1863," wrote a member of the 14th USCT, "we came as men, and have stood by the flag of the United States, and now the colored citizens are denied the rights of man." In a petition presented to the citizens of Iowa, members of the 60th USCT proclaimed that "he who is worthy to be trusted with the musket can and ought to be trusted with the ballot." From his post in Texas, the 28th USCT's black chaplain posed the bitterest question of all: "Shall traitors and rebels, who waged war against the general Government be made legal voters at every ballot-box, and we, the National Guard who by the General-in-Chief and War Department were selected to establish a new picket-line on the Rio Grande, to look after the welfare of the whole nation, be deprived of the privilege?" It would take the ratification of the 14th Amendment, in 1868, finally to address this issue.[16]

Education was another matter of major concern to black soldiers. Chaplain Henry Turner of the 1st USCT was adamant on the subject. "It is not natural that a people who have been held as chattel for two hundred years, should thoroughly comprehend the limits of freedom's empire," he wrote. "The scope is too large for minds so untutored to enter upon at once." After praising the learning evidenced by black children at a school run by sympathetic whites in Nashville, a member of the 14th USCT concluded, "So you see that the colored population and friends in this part of the South have got their eyes open, and are beginning to see the light of the brightest day that ever dawned upon an oppressed people." When the soldiers of the 62nd USCT were told that they would be going home to Missouri, they immediately began to raise money to build a school there; the five thousand dollars they collected helped establish the Lincoln Institute in Jefferson City, known today as Lincoln University.[17]

The return of these soldiers to civilian life wrote a complex chapter in this country's postwar history. Many black veterans, especially those in the North, were able to pick up the threads of their earlier lives. Some would rise to positions of prominence on both the local and the national scene: P. B. S. Pinchback, once an officer with the Louisiana Native Guards, briefly served as governor of that state, while Josiah T. Walls, a former slave who had enlisted in the Union army, became a Florida Congressman. For most, however, the postwar path simply led home. Throughout the south, a surprising number of ex-slaves settled in the same areas out of which they had been recruited into the USCT, despite the bitter memories of their bondage. Years afterward, it was not unusual to find former field hands working the land just a few miles from the plantations where they had once toiled at the bidding of white masters.

Some black veterans could look forward to little more than strife and persecution, as Southern whites closed ranks to deny their equality. In a statement written in March 1866, a discharged black soldier from Maryland painted a bleak picture: "The returned colord Solgers are in Many cases beten, and their guns taken from them, we darcent walk out of an evening [but] if we do, and we are Met by Some of these roudies [. . .] that were in the rebbel army[,] they beat us badly." In the most notorious postwar incident involving USCT men, simmering racial antagonisms erupted in rioting that raged throughout Memphis from May 1 to 3, 1866. Ignited by clashes between city police and recently discharged USCT soldiers, the incident became a full-fledged pogrom when white authorities aided and abetted armed gangs in savaging a black shantytown near Fort Pickering. By the time the U.S. occupation officer managed to restore order, forty-six African Americans were dead, five black women had been raped, and a hundred thousand dollars' worth of property (including four churches) lay in ruins.[18]

An effective voice raised after the war on behalf of *all* Union veterans was that of the Grand Army of the Republic, organized in April 1866. In its initial phase, the GAR was broadly supportive of its black membership and an advocate for those members' social rights, with one resolution offered by Missouri's Union vets in August 1866 going so far as to demand that the state promptly extend the election franchise "to black men of the proper age." After this promising beginning, however, the GAR soon entered a period of decline lasting until the early 1880s, when an influx of aging veterans, anxious to secure better pension benefits, succeeded in revitalizing the organization.[19]

A spirit of national conciliation shaped this second phase of the GAR's growth, and the principal losers were the black veterans. In order to establish and maintain posts in the South (where many discharged white Union soldiers had settled), GAR leaders were willing to bend to local mores, which inevitably included a color line. "It is right," declared a white Louisiana GAR delegate in 1891, "that we conform to the social laws and rules that surround us." Opposition within the GAR ranks, both white and black, successfully blocked efforts to establish officially segregated regional posts, but that did not prevent some groups, notably in Maryland and Kentucky, from quietly putting a policy of segregation into practice.[20]

In many ways, the fate of the GAR's black members within that body mirrored their treatment in the larger society. As the nineteenth century drew to a close, the issues of the black community and civil rights were deemed inappropriate for national discussion and relegated to the state level, where, especially in the South, a web of black codes and Jim Crow laws assured the inferior status of African Americans. When America rediscovered its Civil War through a great outpouring of writing that began to appear in the 1880s, it was thought impolitic to say too much about the role played by black soldiers. This was particularly true for mainstream national periodicals such as *Century* magazine, whose celebrated and popular series of articles on the "battles and leaders" of both sides (some written by those leaders themselves) was shaped in such a way as not to offend Southern subscribers. Moreover, the fact that few blacks had taken part in most of the war's major battles made it easy to depreciate their overall role. If *Century*'s editors could not ignore such significant fights as the Battle of the Crater, they could and did pass over other engagements in which black soldiers figured prominently, including Poison Springs, New Market Heights, Fort Gilmer, and Potter's Raid.

A modest exception to this veil of silence was the Military Order of the Loyal Legion of the United States (MOLLUS), an organization of Union veterans dedicated to study and discussion of the war. Many local chapters published the talks given to their groups, and within the hundreds of pages of those reminiscences are a few accounts by white officers who served in black regiments. Also running counter to the national aphonia was a Washington-based newspaper aimed at Northern veterans, the *National Tribune,* which printed letters and articles about combat actions involving black troops. It must be admitted that the perspective presented in both forums was almost always that of a white participant, but nevertheless, a veteran writing in the *National Tribune* in 1887 was astute enough to observe that the "nation seems to be ashamed that [it] gave the slave a chance to strike a blow for himself."[21]

Ultimately, however, neither the MOLLUS papers nor the *National Tribune* had any real national impact. The institutionalized downplaying of black participation was so successful, in fact, that when a popular biography of U. S. Grant appeared in 1928, it could baldly proclaim that the "American negroes are the only people in the history of the world . . . that ever became free without any effort of their own." A "study" undertaken by the U.S. Army War College ten years later concluded that blacks were poor combat material, while a U.S. propaganda film produced during World War II, titled "The Negro

Soldier," extolled armed black involvement in every conflict except the Civil War.[22]

Also forgotten in all this historical amnesia was the nature of the conditions under which USCT units fought. Above and beyond the normal terrors associated with any battle, black troops entering combat faced dangers that put them at a higher risk than their white counterparts. The medical attention given them, for example, was unequal and very often less competent; as one USCT doctor put it, "Very few surgeons will do precisely the same for blacks as they would for white." Added a USCT soldier, "If we have the misfortune of being taken sick, we receive only the *poorest* medical attendance." But if being wounded was bad, being captured was much worse, as black soldiers taken alive could expect either a return to slavery or long imprisonment in appalling conditions. Worst of all, more often than white soldiers, black soldiers were *not* taken alive. One modern historian who examined the wartime totals concluded that "when Confederate troops overran positions held by black soldiers, the number of prisoners they took [alive] was usually far less than when the defenders were white."[23]

Black units were used primarily for garrison duty because of the preconceived notions of most white officers. And when they *were* at last committed to action, they too often entered the fight saddled with the burden of having to prove themselves worthy to their Caucasian comrades. Any misstep during an engagement, or a slip of discipline that would be forgiven a raw white unit, would be held up as proof of a black unit's unreliability, a stain that no amount of blood could wash away. From Port Hudson and Milliken's Bend in 1863 through Fort Blakely in 1865, black troops were ever having to prove anew that they would fight. Of the 178,975 blacks who served in Civil War regiments, 2,870 of the approximately 38,000 who died were combat-related fatalities, while most of the rest succumbed to disease. In the course of the war, black troops took part in some 449 separate fights with the Confederates. The newly instituted Medal of Honor was bestowed on sixteen black soldiers and four black sailors.

Many of those placed in harm's way ended up in secondary theaters of the conflict, often serving under general officers whose abilities did not justify a more significant command. Given the opportunity, and with good leadership, black regiments did well in combat.

In some cases, such as at Port Hudson and New Market Heights, they were deliberately committed to a hopeless task—not for any strategic reason, but solely to test their mettle. While it would be difficult to identify a major engagement in which black soldiers played a crucial role, it is clear that their courage and discipline saved Seymour's army from destruction at Olustee, their steadfastness made possible the Union victory at Fort Fisher, and their combativeness greatly contributed to the Federal capture of Fort Blakely. The best summary of this record of performance came from a trooper in the 5th Regiment Massachusetts Cavalry (Colored), who said, "The colored soldiers in this four years' struggle have proven themselves in every respect to be men."[24]

Also not to be underestimated is the psychological value of black participation in the war. "Rebel Citizens fear them more than they would fear Indians," observed a Union officer after speaking with several Confederate POWs. Writing in the fall of 1863, Abraham Lincoln said, "I know as fully as one can know the opinions of others, that some of the commanders of our armies in the field who have given us our most important successes, believe the emancipation policy, and the use of colored troops, constitute the heaviest blow yet dealt to the rebellion, and that, at least one of those important successes, could not have been achieved when it was, but for the aid of black soldiers."[25]

Even if the country tried to resign the image of the black soldier to the remotest corner of its collective memory, or to forget him entirely, the veterans themselves did not comply by fading quietly away. May 31, 1897, brought the unveiling in Boston of a bronze-relief memorial created by Augustus Saint-Gaudens, depicting Colonel Robert Gould Shaw and twenty-three soldiers of the 54th Massachusetts (Colored). Although the sculptor used black models, the faces of the infantrymen were not intended to be likenesses of actual individuals who served in the regiment. A contingent from the 54th did attend the unveiling ceremony, however, and the moment when they marched past the monument was said to be unforgettable. "They seemed as if returning from the war," Saint-Gaudens wrote, "the troops of bronze marching in the opposite direction, the direction in which they had left for the front, and the young men there represented now showing those veterans the vigor and hope of youth. It was a consecration."[26]

In late June and early July 1938, when the entire nation marked the 75th anniversary of the Battle of Gettysburg, the more than thirteen hundred living Civil War soldiers who participated in the special events counted among their number forty blacks. While none of these latter had actually taken part in that fight, these aged soldiers doubtless all felt they had earned a share of the country's attention. One of those present was Eli George Biddle, wounded at Fort Wagner but now the last living member of the 54th Massachusetts (Colored). In those frail ranks, too, were William Henry Singleton, who had stood with Colonel Beecher and the 35th USCT at Honey Hill; Simpson C. Younger, who as a member of the 27th USCT had helped protect the Federal forces attacking Fort Fisher; George Washington Johnson, who had been with the 2nd Kansas Colored at Jenkins Ferry; and Isaiah Fassett, a survivor of the 9th USCT's effort against Fort Gilmer. Twenty-one other USCT regiments were also represented in this final roll call.

If the fact that the image of the fighting black soldier should have disappeared so completely from the racially biased American culture of the early twentieth century seems in every sense a shame, that it did not linger in the folk tales, songs, poetry, fiction, or visual arts of the American black community is nothing short of a puzzlement. More than twenty years after the war, the black veterans demonstrated the link between their service and their social aspirations when, meeting in a Boston convention, they resolved that it was the "plain duty of the Government . . . to see to it that the colored defenders of its life in its day of peril, and their kindred or race, have the full and equal protection of the laws." Their sacrifices during the war had earned them a place at the table of democracy, and they were determined to occupy it. It was W. E. B. Du Bois who observed that only when the hitherto despised black slave showed that he would fight and die for his beliefs did the "whole nation with one voice [proclaim] him a man and a brother."[27]

One significant African American artistic figure who did not forget the black troops was the poet Paul Laurence Dunbar, whose father, Joshua, served briefly in Company F of the 55th Massachusetts (Colored). In his 1896 collection of verse, *Lyrics of Lowly Life,* Dunbar included a work of eleven stanzas entitled "The Colored Soldiers." Three of those stanzas comprise a fitting epitaph to the combat saga of black troops in the Civil War:

Ah, they rallied to the standard
To uphold it by their might;
None were stronger in the labors,
None were braver in the fight.
From the blazing breach of Wagner
To the plains of Olustee,
They were foremost in the fight
Of the battles of the free.

And at Pillow! God have mercy
On the deeds committed there,
And the souls of those poor victims
Sent to Thee without a prayer.
Let the fullness of Thy pity
O'er the hot wrought spirits sway
Of the gallant colored soldiers
Who fell fighting on that day!

Yes, the Blacks enjoy their freedom,
And they won it dearly, too;
For the life blood of their thousands
Did the southern fields bedew.
In the darkness of their bondage,
In the depths of slavery's night,
Their muskets flashed the dawning,
And they fought their way to light.[28]

Chapter Notes

---◦---

The following sources were used throughout the book and will be referred to in the source note by abbreviated titles, as indicated. Full citations may be found in the bibliography.

Anglo-African (New York black newspaper). Noted as *Anglo*.

Berlin, Ira, Joseph P. Reidy, and Leslie S. Rowland, eds., *Freedom: A Documentary History of Emancipation, 1861–1867*. Noted as *Freedom*.

Christian Recorder (Philadelphia black newspaper). Noted as *Recorder*.

Cornish, Dudley T., *The Sable Arm*. Noted as Cornish.

Emilio, Luis F., *A Brave Black Regiment*. Noted as Emilio.

National Archives: Compiled Service Records of U.S. Colored Troops. Noted as CSR; other National Archives citations given as NA.

National Archives: "The Negro in the Military Service of the United States, 1639–1886." Noted as NMS.

Quarles, Benjamin, *The Negro in the Civil War*. Noted as Quarles.

The War of the Rebellion: A Compilation of Official Records of the Union and Confederate Armies. Noted as OR; assume volume 1 unless otherwise indicated.

Wilson, Joseph T., *The Black Phalanx*. Noted as *Phalanx*.

Chapter 1: "A Liberating Army"

1   Kansas State Historical Society: Williams.
2   *New York Times*, 11/19/62.
3   Kansas State Historical Society: Williams.
4   Quarles, 115. *New York Tribune*, 11/11/62.
5   Blight, *Douglass' Civil War*, 83; Douglass, *Life and Times*, 325.
6   Blight, *Douglass' Civil War*, 99.

7   Quarles, 27.

8   Cornish, 4; Quarles, 29; *The Liberator,* 5/10/61.

9   Rollins, ed., *Black Southerners in Gray,* 2; Quarles, 36.

10   Cornish, 5.

11   *Anglo,* 11/2/61.

12   *Pine & Palm,* 8/3/61.

13   *Pine & Palm,* 2/27/62.

14   *Pine & Palm,* 3/27/62; OR 9:236; *Pine & Palm,* 4/2/62.

15   OR 6:176.

16   *Spies, Scouts and Raiders,* 142; Cornish, 69; OR 3, 516.

17   OR (3) 2:311; ibid., 445.

18   Cornish, 72; *Leavenworth Daily Conservative,* 8/6/62.

19   *Fort Scott Bulletin,* 7/26/62.

20   OR 8:830.

21   Cornish, 35; U.S. Army Generals' Reports of Civil War Service (NA).

22   Cornish, 38; Rose, *Rehearsal,* 145–146.

23   U.S. Army Generals' Reports of Civil War Service (NA).

24   OR (3) 2:196–198.

25   Quarles, 134.

26   McPherson, *Negro's Civil War,* 42; *Anglo,* 9/21/61; *Pacific Appeal,* 6/14/62.

27   Quarles, 145.

28   Westwood, *Black Troops,* 66.

29   Hargrove, *Black Union Soldiers,* 11; Voegeli, *Free but Not Equal,* 99; Foner, *History of Black Americans,* 331; Quarles, 31; Glatthaar, *Forged in Battle,* 30; Southern Historical Collection: Johnson; Scharnhorst, "From Soldier to Saint," 311.

30   Westwood, *Black Troops,* 9.

31   Quarles, 209.

32   *Anglo,* 1/31/63.

Chapter 2: "Will They Fight?"

1   Bowditch, "War Letters," 476; Johnson, "Letters," 220.

2   OR 15:442.

3   Horowitz, "Ben Butler and the Negro," 159; Hollandsworth, *Louisiana Native Guards,* 13; Johnson, "New Orleans under General Butler," 515.

4   Horowitz, "Ben Butler and the Negro," 174; Marshall, ed., *Private and Official Correspondence,* 1:514; 2:125.

5   Marshall, ed., *Private and Official Correspondence,* 2:126.

6   Ibid., 2:148; *Daily Picayune,* 5/27/63; Butler, *Butler's Book,* 491; Berry, "Negro Troops in Blue and Gray," 173.

7   De Forest, *Volunteer's Adventures,* 50–51.

8   Marshall, ed., *Private and Official Correspondence,* 2:328.

9   *Phalanx,* 195; Marshall, ed., *Private and Official Correspondence,* 2:428; *National Anti-Slavery Standard,* 2/14/63.

10   *Phalanx,* 195; Parton, *General Butler,* 517.

11   Hollandsworth, *Louisiana Native Guards,* 27.

12   *L'Union,* 10/16/62; *New York Tribune,* 11/20/62.

13   Marshall, ed., *Private and Official Correspondence,* 2:427; *New Orleans Delta,* 11/7/62.

14   OR 15:170; ibid., 164–165.

15   NA: Record Group 393: Department of the Gulf, Letters Received, 2/23/63; 73rd USCT CSR; Hollandsworth, *Louisiana Native Guards*, 39.
16   *Anglo*, 4/11/63.

Pascagoula Skirmish

17   Daniels, *Diary*.
18   Ibid.; OR 52/1, 61.
19   Daniels, *Diary*.
20   Brown, *Negro in the American Rebellion*, 165.
21   *National Anti-Slavery Standard*, 2/28/63; Hollandsworth, *Louisiana Native Guards*, 43–45.
22   *Freedom*, 323.
23   *Phalanx*, 119.
24   *Daily Picayune*, 5/27/63; U.S. Army Generals' Reports of Civil War Service (NA); Edmunds, *Guns of Port Hudson*, 50.

Port Hudson Assault

25   Hollandsworth, *Louisiana Native Guards*, 50; OR 26/1:498.
26   *Phalanx*, 525; Bosson, *History of the Forty-Second Regiment*, 364.
27   *New York Times*, 6/13/63.
28   Glatthaar, "Civil War through the Eyes of a Sixteen-Year-Old Black Officer," 212.
29   Quarles, 217; Roy, "Our Indebtedness to the Negroes," 8.
30   Hollandsworth, *Louisiana Native Guards*, 52.
31   Bacon, *Among the Cotton Thieves*, 159.
32   *Freedom*, 529.
33   Stanyan, *History of the Eighth New Hampshire Volunteers*, 229; Bacon, *Among the Cotton Thieves*, 161.
34   *Boston Evening Transcript*, 7/20/63; *New York Times*, 6/13/63; Yale Civil War Mss. Collection: Burnham.
35   State Historical Society of Wisconsin: Harding; Duke University: Kinsley; Johns, *Life with the Forty-Ninth Massachusetts*, 255.
36   Hewitt, *Port Hudson*, 175, 177.
37   Hollandsworth, *Louisiana Native Guards*, 78.
38   *Freedom*, 329.

Milliken's Bend Action

39   *Official Records of the Union and Confederate Navies* 25:162, 166.
40   Cornish, 115.
41   Ibid., 118.
42   Ohio Historical Society: Bruner.
43   U.S. Military History Institute: Cornwell, "Dan Caverno"; Ohio Historical Society: Bruner.
44   Pension Files (NA).
45   OR 26/2:15; OR 24/2:469.
46   *National Tribune*, 12/7/05.
47   U.S. Military History Institute: Cornwell, "Dan Caverno."
48   U.S. Military History Institute: Cornwell, "Dan Caverno"; Sears, *Paper of Cyrus Sears*.
49   U.S. Military History Institute: Cornwell, "Dan Caverno."

50   Sears, *Paper of Cyrus Sears,* 9.
51   OR 24/2:467; U.S. Military History Institute: Cornwell, "Dan Caverno."
52   OR (3) 3:453; U.S. Military History Institute: Cornwell, "Dan Caverno."
53   51st USCT CSR.
54   *National Tribune,* 1/13/16; Byers, *Iowa in War Times,* 245; Sears, *Paper of Cyrus Sears,* 10, 14, 15.
55   OR 24/1:102; Sears, *Paper of Cyrus Sears,* 16.
56   *Raleigh Register,* 7/8/63; Blessington, *Campaigns of Walker's Texas Division,* 97; OR 24/1:467; *Confederate Veteran* 8:67.
57   Sears, *Paper of Cyrus Sears,* 18; *National Tribune,* 1/13/16; State Historical Society of Iowa: Henry.
58   Sears, *Paper of Cyrus Sears,* 16.
59   Parrish, *Richard Taylor,* 291.
60   Pension Files (NA).
61   OR 24/2:446.
62   OR (2) 6:21–22.
63   OR (3) 3:452; OR 24/1:106; Bearss, *The Campaign for Vicksburg,* 1183; Southern Historical Collection: Wadley.
64   OR (3) 3:1190.

Interlude: "The Power of Fear"

1   Stampp, *Peculiar Institution,* 141, 146, 211.
2   OR 14:599.
3   Crawford, *Kansas in the Sixties,* 108; Freeman, "Colored Brigade," 401.
4   *Freedom,* 583.
5   OR (2) 6:528.
6   Wiley, *Southern Negroes,* 83.

Chapter 3: "The Old Flag Never Touched the Ground"

1   Duncan, ed., *Blue-Eyed Child,* 339; Higginson, *Army Life,* 216; Duncan, ed., *Blue-Eyed Child,* 339.
2   Higginson, *Army Life,* 216.

Jacksonville Occupation

3   OR 14:423.
4   Higginson, "First Black Regiment," 524.
5   Higginson, *Army Life,* 35–36.
6   *Philadelphia Inquirer,* 4/1/63; Higginson, *Army Life,* 112.
7   *Philadelphia Inquirer,* 4/1/63.
8   Higginson, *Army Life,* 116; King, *Reminiscences,* 56.
9   33rd USCT CSR.
10   Higginson, *Army Life,* 123; Caldwell, *Old Sixth Regiment,* 58.
11   Higginson, *Army Life,* 124–125.
12   Ibid., 126–127.
13   Ibid., 127–128.
14   *Savannah Republican,* 3/25/63.
15   Caldwell, *Old Sixth Regiment,* 60.

16   OR 14:233; Davis, *History of Jacksonville,* 132; Higginson, *Army Life,* 131.
17   Higginson, *Thomas Wentworth Higginson,* 229.

Fort Wagner Assault

18   *Anglo,* 4/4/63; Pearson, *Life of John A. Andrew,* 74.
19   Pearson, *Life of John A. Andrew,* 75.
20   Duncan, ed., *Blue-Eyed Child,* 283, 285, 286.
21   Cornish, 108–109.
22   *Anglo,* 5/9/63; *New Bedford Mercury,* 3/5/63.
23   Emilio, 31–32.
24   Higginson, *Army Life,* 120; West Virginia University: Appleton; Duncan,
        ed., *Blue-Eyed Child,* 356.
25   *Anglo,* 7/6/63; *New Bedford Mercury,* 6/30/63.
26   Duncan, ed., *Blue-Eyed Child,* 343, 348.
27   Duke University: DeVotie; Andrews, *South Reports the Civil War,* 325; *New
        Bedford Mercury,* 8/1/63.
28   Emilio, 62.
29   Appleton, "That Night at Fort Wagner," 12; Emilio, 68.
30   Dahlgren, *Memoir,* 26.
31   Emilio, 72.
32   OR 28/1:13; Eldredge, *Third New Hampshire,* 324.
33   Voris, "Charleston in the Rebellion," 327; Emilio, 73.
34   Little, *Seventh New Hampshire,* 119.
35   James, "Assault on Fort Wagner," 21; Emilio, 77.
36   *New Bedford Mercury,* 8/1/63; Yacovone, ed., *A Voice of Thunder,* 42;
        Appleton, "That Night at Fort Wagner," 12.
37   West Virginia University: Appleton.
38   Wesley, *Ohio Negroes,* 29; Cornell University: Wilder; Emilio, 77.
39   Wise, *Gate of Hell,* 102.
40   Emilio, 79; Library of Congress: Woodson, Douglass.
41   Jones, *Defence of Battery Wagner,* 20–21; *Anglo,* 8/8/63.
42   Library of Congress: Woodson, Douglass; Yacovone, ed., *A Voice of
        Thunder,* 44; Adams, ed., *On the Altar of Freedom,* 40; Furness, "The
        Negro as a Soldier," 473; Wesley, *Ohio Negroes,* 29; Boston Athenaeum:
        Jewett; West Virginia University: Appleton.
43   *National Tribune,* 1/5/93; Appleton: "That Night at Fort Wagner," 13.
44   Appleton, "That Night at Fort Wagner," 13; Williams, *History of the Negro
        Troops,* 197; Quarles, 15; *Anglo,* 8/8/63.
45   *New Bedford Mercury,* 8/1/63; Emilio, 83; *National Tribune,* 1/5/93.
46   Emilio, 84.
47   Ibid.; *National Tribune,* 1/5/93.
48   Appleton, "That Night at Fort Wagner," 14; Yacovone, ed., *A Voice of
        Thunder,* 45; Williams, *History of the Negro Troops,* 197.
49   *Anglo,* 8/8/63; Appleton, "That Night at Fort Wagner," 16.
50   Voris, "Charleston in the Rebellion," 327; Charleston *Mercury,* 8/15/63;
        Emilio, 95; Hagood, *Memoirs,* 143.
51   *New Bedford Mercury,* 8/4/63.
52   Hackett, *Christian Memorials of the War,* 113–114; Schwartz, ed., *Woman
        Doctor's Civil War,* 51.
53   Urwin, "I Want You to Prove Yourselves Men," 51; OR (3) 3:696; Clements
        Library: Schoff Collection, Lincoln; Foner, *History of Black Americans,* 376.

54 *Atlantic Monthly,* 1/64.
55 Hansen, "The 54th Massachusetts," 750.
56 Emilio, 105.
57 *New Bedford Mercury,* 8/1/63.
58 *Anglo,* 8/22/63.
59 *New Bedford Mercury,* 8/21/63, 9/21/63.
60 *Anglo,* 10/24/63; *New Bedford Mercury,* 10/4/63.
61 *Anglo,* 1/2/64.
62 *Recorder,* 1/30/64.

Interlude: "The Question of Pay"

1 Cornish, 184–185.
2 *Anglo,* 8/22/63.
3 *Anglo,* 9/19/63.
4 *New Bedford Mercury,* 12/4/63.

Chapter 4: "The Question That Negroes Will Fight Is Settled"

Wrightsville Skirmish

1 Binder, "Pennsylvania Negro Regiments," 386.
2 Blackett, ed., *Thomas Morris Chester,* 35.
3 Binder," Pennsylvania Negro Regiments," 387.
4 Hoke, *The Great Invasion,* 108.
5 OR 27/2:279.

Mound Plantation Skirmish

6 Grant, *Personal Memoirs* 1: 424–425.
7 Westwood, *Black Troops,* 27.
8 Christ, ed., *Rugged and Sublime,* 77.
9 Bailey, "A Texas Cavalry Raid," 145.
10 Ibid., 143; *Houston Weekly Telegraph,* 8/4/63.
11 *Houston Weekly Telegraph,* 8/4/63.
12 *Official Records of the Union and Confederate Navies* 25:215–216.
13 Bailey, "A Texas Cavalry Raid," 145.
14 Pension Files (NA).
15 *Houston Weekly Telegraph,* 8/4/63.
16 Christ, ed., *Rugged and Sublime,* 77.

Sherwood Skirmish/Cabin Creek and Honey Springs Engagements

17 *Official Military History,* 247.
18 Ibid., 248; Kansas State Historical Society: Graton.
19 Kansas State Historical Society: Graton.
20 *Official Military History,* 248; Kansas State Historical Society: Graton.
21 79th USCT Regimental Papers; Kansas State Historical Society: van Horn.
22 *New York Tribune,* 7/22/63.
23 *National Tribune,* 9/8/04.
24 Ibid.; OR 22/1:449; *National Tribune,* 9/8/04.
25 *National Tribune,* 9/8/04; *New York Tribune,* 7/22/63.
26 Cornish, "Kansas Negro Regiments," 426; *Leavenworth Daily Conservative,* 7/17/63.

Wolf River Bridge Skirmish

27 Cowden, *Brief Sketch,* 38–39.
28 Ibid., 47.
29 Ibid.
30 *OR* 31/1:584.
31 Ibid., 583.
32 Ibid., 584.
33 State Historical Society of Iowa: Riggs; *National Tribune,* 12/18/84; *OR* 31/1:577.

Elizabeth City Expedition

34 *Freedom,* 130, 132.
35 *OR* (3) 3:122.
36 Reid, "General Edward A. Wild," 15.
37 Ibid.
38 Ibid., 15–16; *OR* 18:723.
39 Reid, "General Edward A. Wild," 15–16.
40 *Recorder,* 5/30/63.
41 Ibid., 6/20/63; ibid., 6/27/63.
42 *Freedom,* 493.
43 *Athens* (Ohio) *Messenger,* 2/4/64.
44 Barrett, *Civil War in North Carolina,* 177.
45 *OR* 29/1:911; *New York Times,* 1/9/64.
46 Reprinted in *Charleston Mercury,* 1/5/64.
47 *OR* 29/1:911–912.
48 Ibid., 912; *Athens* (Ohio) *Messenger,* 2/4/64.
49 NMS: Duncan Report; *Athens* (Ohio) *Messenger,* 2/4/64; NMS: Duncan Report.
50 NMS: Duncan Report; *OR* 29/1:913; *Athens* (Ohio) *Messenger,* 2/4/64.
51 Longacre, "Brave Radical Wild," 11.
52 Barrett, *Civil War in North Carolina,* 178–179.
53 Ibid., 180.

Chapter 5: "Amid a Storm of Bullets"

Three Politicians and a General

1 Futch, "Salmon P. Chase," 168.
2 Library of Congress: Chase.
3 *OR* 28/2:129.
4 Ibid., 134; Library of Congress: Chase.
5 *OR* 35/1:276, 279.
6 Futch, "Salmon P. Chase," 178.
7 Ibid., 179.
8 *OR* 35/1:278.

The Forces Gather

9 Norton, *Army Letters,* 196.
10 *Anglo,* 1/23/64.
11 *Brookville Republican,* 2/10/64.
12 *Anglo,* 1/23/64.
13 *New Bedford Mercury,* 2/25/64.

14 Emilio, 148; *Anglo,* 1/23/64.
15 Emilio, 149.
16 Rugoff, *Beechers,* 451–458.
17 OR 35/1:469.

Roads to Olustee

18 West Virginia University: Appleton; *Philadelphia Inquirer,* 2/22/64.
19 *New Bedford Mercury,* 2/22/64.
20 Duren, "Occupation of Jacksonville," 262–287; West Virginia University: Appleton.
21 West Virginia University: Appleton; *New Bedford Mercury,* 2/22/64.
22 *Anglo,* 4/23/64; *Brookville Republican,* 3/9/63.
23 *Brookville Republican,* 3/9/64; 8th USCT CSR.
24 West Virginia University: Appleton; Duren, "Occupation of Jacksonville," 263.
25 *New Bedford Mercury,* 2/22/64.
26 OR 35/1:282.
27 Ibid., 283; ibid., 293; ibid., 277.
28 West Virginia University: Appleton.
29 8th USCT CSR; *Recorder,* 4/16/64; *Brookville Republican,* 3/9/64.
30 Nulty, *Confederate Florida,* 119.
31 OR 35/1:284.
32 Ibid., 286.

Olustee Battle

33 *Recorder,* 4/16/64.
34 *Anglo,* 3/26/64; Emilio, 159.
35 Norton, *Army Letters,* 198; *Recorder,* 4/16/64.
36 *New York Times,* 3/1/64.
37 Norton, *Army Letters,* 198; *Recorder,* 4/16/64; 5/7/64.
38 Norton, *Army Letters,* 198; *Recorder,* 4/16/64.
39 Norton, *Army Letters,* 198; *Anglo,* 4/23/64; *Brookville Republican,* 3/23/64.
40 Norton, *Army Letters,* 198; *Philadelphia Press,* 3/10/64; Norton, *Army Letters,* 198–199; *Brookville Republican,* 3/23/64.
41 *Recorder,* 4/16/64; *Philadelphia Press,* 3/10/64; West Virginia University: Appleton.
42 *Anglo,* 4/23/64; OR 35/1:313–314; ibid., 318.
43 Norton, *Army Letters,* 199, 204; OR 35/1:318.
44 OR 35/1:312.
45 *New York Times,* 3/1/64.
46 *New York Evening Post,* 3/8/64; *Anglo,* 3/26/64; Emilio, 162; *Phalanx,* 269.
47 Emilio, 162–163; *Phalanx,* 269.
48 *New York Tribune,* 3/1/64; Emilio, 163; *Anglo,* 3/26/64.
49 *Xenia* (Ohio) *Torchlight,* 3/16/64.
50 Emilio, 165–166.
51 Pension Files (NA).
52 *Philadelphia Press,* 3/16/64; Vlock and Levitch, *Contraband of War,* 164; *New York Herald,* 3/1/64; United States Military History Institute: Miscellaneous, Wild; *Philadelphia Press,* 3/30/64; Coles, "A Fight, a Licking, and a Footrace," 130; *Phalanx,* 270.
53 *New York Tribune,* 3/1/64.
54 *Anglo,* 3/26/64; United States Military History Institute: Miscellaneous, Wild.
55 *Recorder,* 3/13/64; Duren, "Occupation of Jacksonville," 271; Emilio, 168.

56 Recorder, 4/16/64; Brookville Republican, 3/23/64.
57 Anglo, 3/26/64; West Virginia University: Appleton.
58 Coles, "A Fight, a Licking, and a Footrace," 146–150.
59 Duren, "Occupation of Jacksonville," 286; Recorder, 4/16/64.
60 Emilio, 174.
61 New York Times, 3/1/64.
62 Norton, Army Letters, 202; United States Military History Institute: Miscellaneous, Wild; Recorder, 4/16/64.
63 Bornet, ed., "Connecticut Yankee," 247; Anglo, 4/23/64.

Aftermath

64 Philadelphia Inquirer, 3/8/64; Library of Congress: Chase.
65 Daniels, Prince of Carpetbaggers, 98–99.
66 Coles, "A Fight, a Licking, and a Footrace," 170.
67 Recorder, 5/7/64.
68 Perkins, "Two Years," 536.
69 Anglo, 4/23/64.

Chapter 6: "You Are Fighting against Your Master"

Fort Pillow Massacre

1 St. Louis Daily Union, as reprinted in the Illinois State Journal, 4/19/64; Missouri Democrat, as reprinted in the Philadelphia Inquirer, 4/20/64.
2 OR 32/1:556.
3 Ibid., 179.
4 Ibid., 539.
5 Ibid., 557; ibid., 608–609.
6 Philadelphia Inquirer, 4/20/64.
7 OR 32/1:538.
8 Ibid., 620.
9 McPherson, Negro's Civil War, 218; OR 32/1:521; ibid., 538.
10 OR 32/1:528; ibid., 538.
11 Hurst, Nathan Bedford Forrest, 168; OR 32/1:621.
12 Brooksher, "Betwixt Wind and Water," 68; OR 32/1:594.
13 Cimprich and Mainfort, "Dr. Fitch's Report," 31; Castel, "Fort Pillow Massacre," 40; Williams, ed., Confederate Victories, 33.
14 OR 32/1:573.
15 Ibid., 597.
16 Ibid., 561.
17 Castel, "Fort Pillow Massacre," 43.
18 OR 32/1:523; Cimprich and Mainfort, "Fort Pillow Revisited," 299; OR 32/1:535; McPherson, Negro's Civil War, 220.
19 OR 32/1:519; Ibid., 523.
20 Cimprich and Mainfort, "Fort Pillow Revisited," 302; OR 32/1:531; Cimprich and Mainfort, "Fort Pillow Revisited," 299, 300; OR 32/1:558.
21 OR 32/1:531.
22 Ibid., 610.
23 Williams, "Benjamin Wade," 41–42; Fuchs, An Unerring Fire, 127–128.
24 Litwack, Been in the Storm So Long, 91.
25 Anglo, 5/28/64.

Brice's Cross Roads Battle

26   Bearss, *Forrest,* 5; OR 32/1:698–701.
27   *Anglo,* 5/7/64; ibid., 4/23/64; ibid., 5/28/64.
28   Cowden, *Brief Sketch,* 51–52, 58, 66.
29   OR 39/1:125.
30   OR 39/1:125; *National Tribune,* 12/29/87.
31   *National Tribune,* 12/29/87; Pension Files (NA).
32   *National Tribune,* 12/29/87.
33   OR 39/1:213.
34   Cowden, *Brief Sketch,* 94.
35   Bearss, *Forrest,* 101.
36   *National Tribune,* 12/29/87; Cowden, *Brief Sketch,* 116.
37   OR 39/1:182; Pension Files (NA).
38   OR 39/1:214.
39   *National Tribune,* 3/8/88.
40   Pension Files (NA).
41   Abbott, "Negro in the War of the Rebellion," 379–380.
42   Cleveland *Leader,* as reprinted in *Boston Evening Journal,* 6/28/64.
43   OR 39/1:183.
44   *Confederate Veteran* 8:402.
45   *Anglo,* 7/2/64.
46   Bearss, *Forrest,* 137–138.
47   OR 39/1:303.

Chapter 7: "With Wild, Exultant Cheers"

1   Irwin, "The Red River Campaign," 345–346.
2   OR 34/2:547.
3   Ibid., 638.
4   *Kansas Daily Tribune* (Lawrence), 2/15/66.
5   OR 34/1:661.
6   *Kansas Daily Tribune* (Lawrence), 2/15/66.
7   OR 34/1:661.
8   Ibid., 743–744.
9   Ibid., 751–752.
10   *National Tribune,* 7/2/14.
11   OR 34/1:744–745.
12   Ibid., 751–752.
13   Ibid., 743–744.
14   Ibid., 752–753.
15   Ibid., 745.
16   *National Tribune,* 7/2/14.
17   *National Tribune,* 4/23/25.
18   OR 34/1:746.
19   Cathey, ed., "Extracts from the Memoirs of William Franklin Avera," 107.
20   OR 34/1:746.
21   Ibid., 792.
22   Ibid., 754.
23   *National Tribune,* 4/23/25.
24   OR 34/1:753.
25   *Official Military History of Kansas Regiments,* 252.

26   *National Tribune,* 4/23/25.
27   OR 34/1:668.
28   *Kansas Daily Tribune* (Lawrence), 2/15/66.
29   *Phalanx,* 241.
30   *Kansas Daily Tribune* (Lawrence), 2/15/66.
31   OR 34/1:669.
32   *Phalanx,* 242.
33   *Kansas Daily Tribune* (Lawrence), 2/15/66.
34   *Phalanx,* 242.
35   *Kansas Daily Tribune* (Lawrence), 2/15/66.
36   *Phalanx,* 245.
37   *Kansas Daily Tribune* (Lawrence), 2/15/66.
38   OR 34/1:671.
39   Crawford, *Kansas in the Sixties,* 134.

Chapter 8: "On to Richmond!"

Yorktown Expeditions

1   Butler, *Butler's Book,* 620.
2   *Anglo,* 2/20/64.
3   OR 33:144.
4   *Anglo,* 2/20/64.
5   Duke University: Moore; Goulding, "The Colored Troops," 145; Emory University: Brigham; United States Military History Institute: Civil War Times Illustrated, Scroggs.
6   Goulding, "The Colored Troops," 144; Duke University: Moore; United States Military History Institute: *Civil War Times Illustrated* Collection, Scroggs.
7   United States Military History Institute: *Civil War Times Illustrated* Collection, Scroggs; Library of Congress: Bourne, Thomas; Goulding, "The Colored Troops," 147.
8   Adriance Memorial Library: Verplanck.
9   Ibid.

Rapidan to James River Campaign

10   OR 33:429, 444.
11   *Recorder,* 4/30/64.
12   Ohio Historical Society: Rogall.
13   Trudeau, *Bloody Roads South,* 18–19; Rickard, "Service with Colored Troops," 18.
14   Trudeau, *Bloody Roads South,* 18–19.
15   Hall, "Mine Run to Petersburg," 218.
16   Tyler, *Memorials of Lieut. George H. Walcott,* 78–79.
17   Agassiz, ed., *Meade's Headquarters,* 102; Trudeau, *Bloody Roads South,* 118.
18   23rd USCT CSR; OR 36/1:986.
19   Bowley, *Boy Lieutenant,* 68–70; OR 36/1:987.
20   Bowley, *Boy Lieutenant,* 71; Trudeau, *Bloody Roads South,* 209–210.
21   *Recorder,* 6/18/64.
22   *Philadelphia Press,* 7/1/64; NA: Regimental Papers, 43rd USCT.
23   Styple and Fitzpatrick, eds., *Andersonville Diary and Memoirs of Charles Hopkins,* 59; Virginia State Library: Willis; Trudeau, *Bloody Roads South,* 311–312.

South Side of James River Campaign

24 Emory University: Brigham; *Anglo,* 5/21/64.
25 Redkey, ed., *Grand Army of Black Men,* 104.
26 Simonton, "Campaign Up the James to Petersburg," 482.
27 10th USCT CSR.
28 Oberlin College Archives: Grabill; United States Military History Institute: *Civil War Times Illustrated* Collection, Scroggs.
29 *Anglo,* 5/21/64.
30 *Daily Morning Chronicle,* 5/30/64.
31 OR 36/1:20; Carter, "Fourteen Months' Service," 163.

Petersburg Assault

32 Adriance Memorial Library: Verplanck.
33 Redkey, ed., *Grand Army of Black Men,* 105; *Boston Commonwealth,* 7/15/64.
34 OR 50/1:265.
35 OR 40/1:721; OR 50/1:265–266.
36 *Anglo,* 7/9/64.
37 *New York Tribune,* 6/20/64.
38 *Anglo,* 7/9/64; McMurray, *Recollections,* 34; United States Military History Institute: Harrisburg Civil War Roundtable, Covell; *Boston Daily Advertiser,* 6/21/64.
39 Levstik, ed., "From Slavery to Freedom," 15.
40 *Anglo,* 7/9/64; Fleetwood, *Negro as a Soldier,* 14.
41 United States Military History Institute: Miscellaneous, Burleigh; OR 40/1:725.
42 OR 50/1:265; McMurray, "A Union Officer's Recollections," 169.
43 Jackson and O'Donnell, eds., *Back Home in Oneida,* 142.
44 *Recorder,* 7/16/64.
45 Trudeau, *Last Citadel,* 41.
46 United States Military History Institute: Harrisburg Civil War Roundtable, Covell; Levstik, ed., "From Slavery to Freedom," 15.
47 *Recorder,* 7/16/64; *Boston Evening Journal,* 7/11/64.

Crater Assault

48 OR 40/2:490–491; OR 40/3:27.
49 Private Collections: Hurd.
50 *Anglo,* 8/6/64; ibid., 7/30/64.
51 Ibid., 8/6/64.
52 *Recorder,* 8/6/64.
53 *Report of the Joint Committee,* 14; OR 40/1:58.
54 *Report of the Joint Committee,* 119–120.
55 *Philadelphia Weekly Press,* 10/9/86. Thomas, "Colored Troops at Petersburg," 563; *National Tribune,* 1/20/02; Quarles, 301.
56 Thomas, "Colored Troops at Petersburg," 563–564.
57 Trudeau, *Last Citadel,* 108.
58 Hall, "Mine Run to Petersburg," 221–222.
59 Bowley, "The Petersburg Mine," 29; *Recorder,* 8/20/64.
60 *Memorial of Colonel John A Bross,* 33; Thomas, "Colored Troops at Petersburg," 564.

61 *Recorder,* 8/20/64; Thomas, "Colored Troops at Petersburg," 564; Private
    Collections: Hurd; Bowley, "The Petersburg Mine," 29; Hall, "Mine Run
    to Petersburg," 235.
62 Bowley, *Boy Lieutenant,* 93; Rickard, "Service with Colored Troops," 29;
    Pension Files (NA).
63 *National Tribune,* 11/6/84; *Recorder,* 8/20/64.
64 Bowley, "The Petersburg Mine," 31.
65 Thomas, "Colored Troops at Petersburg," 564.
66 Private Collections: Hurd; *Report of the Joint Committee,* 122.
67 *National Tribune,* 1/30/08; Bowley, *Boy Lieutenant,* 94; United States
    Military History Institute, Miscellaneous, Mitchell; Ohio Historical
    Society: Rogall.
68 *National Tribune,* 10/17/07; Hall, "Mine Run to Petersburg," 224.
69 *National Tribune,* 1/30/08.
70 *Anglo,* 9/17/64; Western Reserve: Palmer, Porter; *Recorder,* 8/20/64.
71 Thomas, "Colored Troops at Petersburg," 564.
72 Bowley, "The Petersburg Mine," 34; Pension Files (NA).
73 *National Tribune,* 11/20/02; Bowley, "The Petersburg Mine," 35.
74 *Report of the Joint Committee,* 122; Pension Files (NA); Cavanaugh and
    Marvel, *Battle of the Crater,* 89.
75 *Cincinnati Daily Commercial,* 8/17/64.
76 Bowley, "The Petersburg Mine," 36; Private Collections: Hurd.
77 Cavanaugh and Marvel, *Battle of the Crater,* 50–51.
78 *Recorder,* 12/24/64; Bowley, "The Petersburg Mine," 37.
79 Kilmer, "Dash into the Crater," 775–776.
80 *Confederate Veteran* 14:178; Seraile, "New York's Black Regiments," 169;
    Robertson, ed., "'The Boy Artillerist,'" 243; Weld, *War Diary and
    Letters,* 354.
81 Duke University: Bernard; Litwack, *Been in the Storm So Long,* 89.
82 *National Tribune,* 10/17/07; Pension Files (NA).
83 Bowley, *Boy Lieutenant,* 100.
84 Glatthaar, *Forged in Battle,* 150.
85 Hall, "Mine Run to Petersburg," 231; Bowley, "The Petersburg Mine," 40;
    40th Congress, "Report on the Treatment of Prisoners," 1075.
86 *Confederate Veteran* 14:26.
87 Pension Files (NA).
88 Thomas, "Colored Troops at Petersburg," 564; Pension Files (NA).
89 *Recorder,* 8/20/64; Pension Files (NA).
90 United States Military History Institute: Gladstone, Hayward; Clements
    Library: Schoff, Bodamer; Boston Public Library: Hesse.
91 Newberry, "Petersburg Mine," 121.
92 OR 40/1:128.
93 *Recorder,* 8/20/64.
94 Trudeau, *Last Citadel,* 125–126.
95 Thomas, "Colored Troops at Petersburg," 564.

Interlude: "This Disgraceful Distinction"

1 *Anglo,* 1/30/64.
2 *Recorder,* 2/20/64.
3 Glatthaar, *Forged in Battle,* 172.
4 *Recorder,* 2/27/64.

5   Westwood, "Cause and Consequence," 230, 233.
6   Glatthaar, *Forged in Battle,* 174.
7   *Anglo,* 11/12/64.

Chapter 9: "I Am Ready to Die for Liberty"
Rivers Causeway Skirmish

1   *Anglo,* 8/6/64.
2   Fox, *Record of the Service,* 29; *Anglo,* 7/9/64.
3   OR 35/1:78; United States Military History Institute: Miscellaneous, Hartwell.
4   OR 35/1:78; Duke University, Kinsley; Cornell University: Wilder; Duke University: Kinsley.
5   *Anglo,* 8/6/64; Duke University: Kinsley.
6   Duke University: Kinsley; Cornell University: Wilder; ibid.
7   Duke University: Kinsley; Cornell University: Wilder; *The Liberator,* 10/4/64.
8   *Anglo,* 8/6/64.
9   Fox, *Record of the Service,* 30; Duke University: Kinsley.
10   OR 35/1:78; *Anglo,* 8/6/64; Bowen, *Massachusetts in the War,* 715.
11   *Anglo,* 8/13/64.
12   Abramowitz, Jack, ed., "A Civil War Letter," 118–119.

Flat Rock Creek Action

13   *Official Military History of Kansas Regiments,* 255.
14   OR 41/1:771.
15   Ibid., 772.
16   Britton, *Civil War on the Border,* 244–245; *National Tribune,* 12/29/04.
17   Baird, ed., *Creek Warrior,* 95–96.
18   79th USCT CSR.
19   Castel, "Civil War Kansas and the Negro," 136.

Marianna Action

20   *Confederate Veteran* 19:484.
21   Schmidt, *Civil War in Florida* 4:2:1201.
22   Ibid.
23   Ibid., 1203.
24   *Whig and Courier,* 10/28/64.
25   Duke University: Manson, Schmidt, *Civil War in Florida* 4:2:1202; 82nd USCT CSR.
26   Stanley, *History of Jackson County,* 190.

Saltville Action

27   Ford, ed., *Cycle of Adams Letters,* 216–217.
28   OR 39/1:557.
29   Ibid., 557.
30   Davis, "Massacre at Saltville," 8.
31   OR 39/1:557.
32   Ibid., 554.
33   Starr, *Union Cavalry in the Civil War,* 558.
34   *Freedom,* 268–269.

Dalton and Decatur Actions

35   Fellman, *Citizen Sherman,* 156.
36   OR 38/3:957.
37   *Phalanx,* 292.
38   Ibid., 292–293; *Anglo,* 5/7/64.
39   *Phalanx,* 296.
40   Ibid., 298.
41   OR 38/2:494; OR 38/3:958; *Phalanx,* 297; *National Tribune,* 7/21/87; Tennessee State Library: Confederate Collection, Allen; Tennessee State Library: Sloan.
42   OR 39/1:719.
43   Bentley Library: Hall; OR 39/1:719; University of Tennessee (Knoxville) Special Collections: Rennolds; Bevens, *Reminiscences,* 41; OR 39/1:721.
44   *New York Times,* 11/10/64; OR 39/1:724.
45   Romeyn, "With Colored Troops," 65.
46   Ibid.
47   Library of Congress: Corbin.
48   *National Tribune,* 9/21/11; ibid., 6/13/12; OR 39/1:715; *National Tribune,* 8/1/12.
49   *Freedom,* 559; Romeyn, "With Colored Troops," 66–67.

Chapter 10: "Saved the Colors"

1   Butler, *Butler's Book,* 744.
2   United States Military History Institute: Coco, Ames; OR 42/1:657.
3   United States Military History Institute: Coco, Ames.

New Market Heights Engagement

4   Pension Files (NA).
5   OR 42/1:1082; Butler, *Butler's Book,* 722.
6   Butler, *Butler's Book,* 742.
7   Library of Congress: Woodson, Fleetwood; Oberlin College Archives: Shurtleff; McMurray, *Recollections,* 51.
8   Butler, *Butler's Book,* 731; McMurray, *Recollections,* 51; United States Military History Institute: *Civil War Times Illustrated* Collection, Scroggs.
9   Furness, "Negro as a Soldier," 483.
10   Richmond National Battlefield Park: Paine.
11   Goulding, "The Colored Troops," 149–151; McMurray, *Recollections,* 51.
12   McMurray, *Recollections,* 52; Goulding, "The Colored Troops," 149.
13   McMurray, *Recollections,* 53; Goulding, "The Colored Troops," 150; McMurray, *Recollections,* 51.
14   Boston Public Library: Wickes.
15   Library of Congress: Woodson, Fleetwood; Ritter, "Congressional Medal of Honor Winners," 135–136.
16   McMurray, *Recollections,* 54; U.S. Army Generals' Reports of Civil War Service (NA).
17   Oberlin College Archives: Shurtleff; United States Military History Institute: *Civil War Times Illustrated* Collection, Scroggs; Oberlin College Archives: Grabill.
18   OR 42/1:819; Oberlin College Archives: Shurtleff; OR 42/1:819.
19   OR 42/1:820.

20 Cooney, ed., "I Was . . . Eager," 281.
21 United States Military History Institute: *Civil War Times Illustrated* Collection, Scroggs; Oberlin College Archives: Grabill; Library of Congress: Bourne, Thomas.
22 Butler, *Butler's Book,* 733; Glatthaar, *Forged in Battle,* 151.
23 Goulding, "The Colored Troops," 151.
24 *Springfield Daily Republican,* 10/12/64.

Fort Gilmer Engagement

25 Oberlin College Archives: Grabill; United States Military History Institute: *Civil War Times Illustrated* Collection, Scroggs.
26 U.S. Army Generals' Reports of Civil War Service (NA); Richmond National Battlefield Park: Paine.
27 OR 42/1:774.
28 Sherman, "Assault on Fort Gilmer," 365–366.
29 Califf, *Record of the Services,* 42.
30 Ibid., 42, 44.
31 Ibid., 43.
32 Ibid., 43.
33 Butler, *Butler's Book,* 743.

Boydton Plank Road Engagement

34 All Ferrero quotes: OR 42/1:592.
35 All Brock quotes: *Carlisle Herald,* 11/25/64.

Fair Oaks Engagement

36 Blackett, ed., *Thomas Morris Chester,* 177.
37 *Anglo,* 11/12/64.
38 Oberlin College Archives: Grabill; United States Military History Institute; *Civil War Times Illustrated* Collection, Scroggs.
39 OR 42/1:814–815.
40 *Recorder,* 12/12/64.
41 OR 42/1:815, 818; NMS: Terry Report; *Recorder,* 12/12/64.
42 Oberlin College Archives: Grabill.
43 Library of Congress: Bourne, Thomas.
44 Blackett, ed., *Thomas Morris Chester,* 202.

Interlude: "A Practice Justified by No Rule of War"

1 OR (2) 7:967–969.
2 Ibid., 967, 969.
3 Blackett, ed., *Thomas Morris Chester,* 165.
4 OR (2), 1011–1012.
5 Blackett, ed., *Thomas Morris Chester,* 165.

Chapter 11: "Into the Very Mouth of Death"

1 Upson, *With Sherman to the Sea,* 135.
2 OR 39/3:740.
3 OR 35/2:328; OR 44:505.

Honey-Hill Battle

4   Perkins, "Two Years," 537.
5   OR 44:547.
6   Ibid., 545; ibid., 525–526.
7   Cornell University: Wilder; Emilio, 237; *New York Times*, 12/9/64.
8   *Official Records of the Union and Confederate Navies* 16:73; Fox, *Record of the Service*, 41.
9   *Official Records of the Union and Confederate Navies* 16:73.
10   Emilio, 238; *Philadelphia Weekly Times*, 5/10/84.
11   OR 44:422; *Philadelphia Weekly Times*, 5/10/84.
12   *National Tribune*, 6/17/15.
13   Emilio, 245.
14   Pension Files (NA); Trudeau, ed., *Voices of the 55th*, 104.
15   Fox, *Record of the Service*, 42.
16   Baird, *32d Regiment*, 2.
17   Ibid.
18   Fox, *Record of the Service*, 42; *Philadelphia Weekly Times*, 5/1/84.
19   Baird, *32d Regiment*, 2–3.
20   *New York Times*, 12/9/64.
21   *New York Times*, 12/9/64; Radcliffe College: Beecher.
22   Cornell University: Wilder.
23   Duke University: Kinsley.
24   Emilio, 245.
25   Radcliffe College: Beecher.
26   Emilio, 250.
27   *National Tribune*, 5/21/29; Duke University: Kinsley; *National Tribune*, 5/21/29.
28   Fox, *Record of the Service*, 42; *New York Herald*, 12/4/64.
29   Emilio, 248.
30   OR 44:423; McRae, *Negroes in Michigan*, 73.
31   OR 44:424; Briggs, *Civil War Surgeon*, 142; Southern Historical Collection: Whitaker.
32   South Carolina Department of Archives and History: Jenkins; Williams, *History of the Negro Troops*, 212.
33   Duke University: Kinsley; Emilio, 252.
34   *Anglo*, 2/4/65.
35   Ibid., 12/31/64.

Postscript

36   OR 44:836.
37   Glatthaar, *March to the Sea*, 55–57.
38   Trudeau, ed., *Voices of the 55th*, 178.
39   *Anglo*, 3/4/65.

Chapter 12: "Captain, I Am Wounded; What Shall I Do?"

1   OR 39/1:583.
2   Record Group 393: Department of the Cumberland Letters Received 1864.
3   Ibid.
4   Morgan, "Reminiscences of Service," 88.

Stockade No. 2 Skirmish

5   *Recorder,* 7/16/64.
6   Freeman, "Colored Brigade," 399–400.
7   OR 45/1:540–541.

Nashville Battle

8   Romeyn, "With Colored Troops," 69; *National Tribune,* 2/13/96.
9   Stone, "Repelling Hood's Invasion," 464; Romeyn, "With Colored Troops,"
       59; OR 45/1:535.
10   Morgan, "Reminiscences of Service," 107–108.
11   OR 45/1:536.
12   *National Tribune,* 8/4/87.
13   OR 45/1:527.
14   *National Tribune,* 8/4/87.
15   Library of Congress: Shafter; *Confederate Veteran* 17:11; OR 45/1:539.
16   OR 45/1:527.
17   Morgan, "Reminiscences of Service," 110–112.
18   Sword, *Embrace an Angry Wind,* 346.
19   Freeman, "Colored Brigade," 415.
20   *National Tribune,* 7/7/87.
21   Freeman, "Colored Brigade," 416; *Confederate Veteran* 12:531; *National
       Tribune,* 7/7/87.
22   Freeman, "Colored Brigade," 416–417; *National Tribune,* 7/7/87; *New York
       Times,* 12/24/64.
23   Pension Files (NA).
24   Ibid.
25   *Confederate Veteran* 13:126.
26   *National Tribune,* 8/4/87; Romeyn, "With Colored Troops," 71.
27   Western Reserve: Lyman.
28   Sword, *Embrace an Angry Wind,* 384; *New York Times,* 12/24/64.
29   Pension Files (NA).
30   OR 45/1:549.
31   Glatthaar, *Forged in Battle,* 194.
32   Freeman, Colored Brigade," 421; Morgan, "Reminiscences of Service," 117;
       Morgan, *Negro in America,* 66.
33   *Anglo,* 4/22/65.

Chapter 13: "Ye's Long Been A-coming"

Charleston Occupation

1   Emilio, 272.
2   Ibid., 272–273.
3   Cornell University: Wilder.
4   *National Tribune,* 11/25/86.
5   Ibid.
6   Ibid., *Boston Evening Journal,* 3/2/65.
7   Fox, *Record of the Service,* 57; Emilio, 284; *Recorder,* 4/15/65; Quarles,
       327–328.
8   *New Bedford Mercury,* 1/21/64.

Fort Fisher Operations/Wilmington Occupation

9   United States Military History Institute: Coco, Ames; Oberlin College Archives: Grabill; United States Military History Institute: *Civil War Times Illustrated* Collection, Scroggs.

10   United States Military History Institute: *Civil War Times Illustrated* Collection, Scroggs; Oberlin College Archives: Grabill.

11   Redkey, ed., "Rocked in the Cradle," 78.

12   Clark, Walter, ed., *Histories* 4:542.

13   OR 46/1:424; United States Military History Institute: Coco, Ames.

14   Oberlin College Archives: Grabill.

15   *New York Herald*, 2/16/65; McMurray, *Recollections*, 72; Bates, *History* 2:945.

16   *New York Times*, 2/17/65; Fonvielle, "Last Rays of Departing Hope," 58.

17   *National Tribune*, 10/18/88.

18   Glatthaar, *Forged in Battle*, 208; *Philadelphia Inquirer*, 2/27/65.

19   *Anglo*, 3/25/65; *Recorder*, 3/25/65.

20   U.S. Army Generals' Reports of Civil War Service (NA).

21   *Anglo*, 3/25/65.

Natural Bridge Skirmish and Related Operations

22   *Anglo*, 1/30/64, 3/19/64.

23   Ibid., 4/2/64.

24   Ibid., 4/2/64, 4/9/64.

25   Ibid., 6/4/64, 9/10/64.

26   Ibid., 2/25/65.

27   Ibid.

28   *Philadelphia Inquirer*, 3/25/65.

29   OR 49/1:60.

30   Ibid.

31   Ibid., 60–61; *Confederate Veteran* 17:220.

32   Schmidt, *Civil War in Florida* 4:2:1321.

33   Ibid., 1327.

34   *Anglo*, 4/1/65.

Interlude: "We Want Black Commissioned Officers"

1   *Freedom*, 304.

2   *The Liberator*, 10/4/64; *New Bedford Mercury*, 1/28/64.

3   Abramowitz, Jack, ed., "A Civil War Letter," 118–119.

4   Duke University: Kinsley.

5   *Anglo*, 8/5/65.

Chapter 14: "Our Errand through the State"

Georgetown to Camden Expedition

1   OR 47/2:804.

2   *Recorder*, 5/27/65; Moore, ed., "The Last Officer," 3; *Recorder*, 5/20/65.

3   NMS: Hooper Report; Moore, ed., "The Last Officer," 3; *Recorder*, 5/27/65; OR 47/1:1036.

4   McGill, *Narrative of Reminiscences*, 215.

5   Boddie, *History of Williamsburg*, 429; Gregorie, *History of Sumter County*, 260.
6   Moore, ed., "The Last Officer," 3; Emilio, 291–299; OR 47/1:1036; Moore, ed., "The Last Officer," 3; Emilio, 291.
7   OR 47/1:1028–1029; Moore, ed., "The Last Officer," 3.
8   Emilio, 291.
9   OR 47/1:1036.
10 Moore, ed., "The Last Officer," 4.
11 *Recorder*, 5/20/64; Emilio, 292–293.
12 *Recorder*, 5/20/64; Moore, ed., "The Last Officer," 4.
13 MRR., "Potter's Raid," 290–291.
14 Kirwan, ed., *Johnny Green*, 193.
15 Emilio, 293.
16 Moore, ed., "The Last Officer," 5.
17 *Recorder*, 5/20/64; Moore, ed., "The Last Officer," 6.
18 Moore, ed., "The Last Officer," 6; Emilio, 294.
19 *Confederate Veteran* 24:549; Gregorie, *History of Sumter County*, 263.
20 Moore, ed., "The Last Officer," 6; Emilio, 294; Moore, ed., "The Last Officer," 6.
21 OR 47/1:1028.
22 Moore, ed., "The Last Officer," 7; Emilio, 294.
23 *Confederate Veteran* 24:549.
24 *Recorder*, 5/27/64; Moore, ed., "The Last Officer," 7.
25 OR 47/1:1029; Moore, ed., "The Last Officer," 7; Emilio, 295.
26 Moore, ed., "The Last Officer," 8.
27 Ibid.; Briggs, *Civil War Surgeon*, 149.
28 Moore, ed., "The Last Officer," 9; *Recorder*, 5/27/64.
29 Moore, ed., "The Last Officer," 9; Emilio, 296.
30 *Recorder*, 5/27/64.
31 Ibid.
32 Moore, ed., "The Last Officer," 10.
33 Emilio, 297; Moore, ed., "The Last Officer," 10.
34 Moore, ed., "The Last Officer," 10.
35 Gregorie, *History of Sumter County*, 266.
36 OR 47/1:1029; Moore, ed., "The Last Officer," 11.
37 Gregorie, *History of Sumter County*, 267.
38 Moore, ed., "The Last Officer," 11.
39 Ibid.; Duke University: Cooper; *Recorder*, 5/27/64.
40 Moore, ed., "The Last Officer," 12.
41 OR 47/1:1029.
42 Emilio, 299; Moore, ed., "The Last Officer," 13; Duke University: Cooper.
43 Emilio, 299–300; Moore, ed., "The Last Officer," 13.
44 Briggs, *Civil War Surgeon*, 149; *Recorder*, 5/20/64.
45 NMS, Hooper Report.
46 Kirwan, ed., *Johnny Green*, 194.
47 Emilio, 302.
48 Ibid., 303.
49 Ibid., 304; Massachusetts Historical Society: Emilio.
50 Kirwan, ed., *Johnny Green*, 194.
51 Emilio, 305; *Recorder*, 5/20/64.
52 OR 47/1:1030; Emilio, 307; Briggs, *Civil War Surgeon*, 153.
53 *Recorder*, 5/27/64; NMS: Hooper Report.
54 *Recorder*, 5/27/64.

Chapter 15: "The Negro Will Fight & Fight Bravely"
Mobile Operations/Fort Blakely Assault

1   Merriam, "The Capture of Mobile," 247; *Anglo*, 9/3/64.
2   OR 49/1:280; Merriam, "The Capture of Mobile," 234.
3   Library of Congress: Carruthers.
4   *Freedom*, 564.
5   Andrews, *History of the Campaign of Mobile*, 123.
6   OR 49/1:295–296.
7   OR 49/2:1188.
8   OR 49/1:286; ibid., 294; Library of Congress: Carruthers; Pension Files (NA).
9   Andrews, *History of the Campaign of Mobile*, 189.
10 *Anglo*, 11/18/65.
11 Emory University: Crydenwise.
12 Andrews, *History of the Campaign of Mobile*, 195; OR 49/1:291; *National Tribune*, 1/5/88; Pension Files (NA).
13 Pension Files (NA).
14 Andrews, *History of the Campaign of Mobile*, 199.
15 OR 49/1:287; Emory University: Crydenwise.
16 Library of Congress: Carruthers; *Daily Missouri Democrat*, 4/26/65; OR 49/1:294.
17 OR 49/1:287; Yale University, Chapman.
18 *Confederate Veteran* 23:457; Bounds, *Ben H. Bounds*, 17–20; Andrews, *History of the Campaign of Mobile*, 201; Clark Gleeson Compiled Service Record (NA).
19 Library of Congress: Carruthers; Library of Congress: Quincy-Wendell-Upsham-Holmes, Quincy; NA: Chaplain's Reports, 48th USCT; *National Tribune*, 1/5/88.
20 OR 49/1:291.
21 Grant, *Personal Memoirs* 2:519.
22 Emory University: Crydenwise.

Interlude: "Their Enthusiasm Was Said to Be . . . Remarkable"

1   OR (4) 3:1008; ibid., 1013.
2   Ruby, "General Patrick Cleburne's Proposal," 201.
3   Stephenson, "The Question of Arming the Slaves," 301–302.
4   *Richmond Daily Dispatch*, 3/18/65; *Richmond Daily Examiner*, 3/18/65.
5   *Richmond Daily Dispatch*, 3/22/65; *Richmond Daily Examiner*, 3/22/65.
6   *Richmond Daily Examiner*, 3/29/65.
7   *Richmond Daily Dispatch*, 3/23/65; *Richmond Daily Dispatch*, 3/27/65.
8   *Richmond Daily Examiner*, 4/3/65.
9   *Confederate Veteran* 23:404.
10 Rollins, ed., *Black Southerners in Gray*, 68.
11 Raup, ed., *Letters from a Pennsylvania Chaplain*, 24.
12 Fleetwood, *Negro as a Soldier*, 6.

Chapter 16: "Babylon Is Fallen"

1   *Recorder*, 2/25/65; ibid., 4/1/65.
2   OR 46/2:71; *Anglo*, 3/4/65; *Recorder*, 4/1/65.

3   *Recorder,* 4/1/65, 1/28/65.
4   Porter, *Campaigning with Grant,* 414; *Recorder,* 5/6/65; *Anglo,* 3/4/65.

Richmond Occupation

5   OR 46/1:1227.
6   Ibid.; *National Tribune,* 5/10/88.
7   Yale University: Merrill; Clapp, *Sketches of Army Life,* 28–29; *National Tribune,* 5/10/88.
8   *Recorder,* 4/29/65; *National Tribune,* 5/10/88; Blackett, ed., *Thomas Morris Chester,* 288.
9   Ford, ed., *Cycle of Adams Letters,* 261.
10   Blackett, ed., *Thomas Morris Chester,* 288; *Anglo,* 4/29/65.
11   Clapp, *Sketches of Army Life,* 29; *Anglo,* 4/29/65; Hill, *Sketch of the 29th Regiment,* 26.
12   Massachusetts Historical Society: Bartlett; Ford, ed., *Cycle of Adams Letters,* 261.
13   Phillips, *Richard and Rhonda,* 62; *National Tribune,* 5/10/88.
14   Blackett, ed., *Thomas Morris Chester,* 289; Hill, *Sketch of the 29th Regiment,* 26.
15   Massachusetts Historical Society: Bartlett; Ford, ed., *Cycle of Adams Letters,* 261.
16   *National Tribune,* 5/10/88.
17   Ibid.; Blackett, ed., *Thomas Morris Chester,* 289; *Anglo,* 5/13/65.
18   *Recorder,* 4/22/65.
19   NMS: Weitzel Testimony.
20   *National Tribune,* 5/10/88; Hill, *Sketch of the 29th Regiment,* 26; Yale University: Merrill; Phillips, *Richard and Rhonda,* 62–63; *Recorder,* 4/29/65.
21   *Anglo,* 4/22/65; Massachusetts Historical Society: Bartlett; 9th USCT CSR.
22   *Recorder,* 4/22/65.
23   Ibid., 4/29/65.

Petersburg Occupation/Appomattox Campaign

24   OR 46/1:1234; ibid., 1160.
25   Califf, *Record of the Services,* 66; OR 46/1:1242.
26   Johnson, ed., "Letters from a Civil War Chaplain," 232.
27   OR 46/1:1235.
28   Ibid.; Kireker, *History of the 116th Regiment,* 15; Califf, *Record of the Services,* 67.
29   OR 46/1:1241; State Historical Society of Wisconsin: Johnson; OR 46/1:1236; ibid., 1243.
30   NMS: Pratt Report; OR 46/1:1237; ibid., 1239; State Historical Society of Wisconsin: Johnson.
31   *Anglo,* 5/13/65.
32   Ibid.; Califf, *Record of the Services,* 69.
33 · Talbot, ed., *Samuel Chapman Armstrong,* 121; Calkins, *Battles of Appomattox Station,* 88.
34   *Phalanx,* 457.
35   Talbot, ed., *Samuel Chapman Armstrong,* 121.
36   State Historical Society of Wisconsin: Johnson; *Phalanx,* 457; Talbot, ed., *Samuel Chapman Armstrong,* 121.
37   *Anglo,* 5/13/65.

Interlude: "Nothing Has So Shocked Us So Much"

1   United States Military History Institute: M.O.L.L.U.S. Collection, Adams.
2   *Anglo,* 5/20/65; ibid., 5/13/65.
3   Bates, *History* 2:992.
4   *Washington Daily Constitutional Union,* 4/20/65; *Washington Daily Intelligencer,* 4/20/65.
5   *Recorder,* 5/6/65.

Chapter 17: "That Winds Up the War"

1   *New York Herald,* 5/29/65; *Grand Army Scout.*
2   *62nd USCT Regimental Papers.*
3   OR 34/3:255; 62nd USCT Regimental Papers.
4   OR 41/2:473; 62nd USCT Regimental Papers.
5   62nd USCT Regimental Papers.
6   Ibid.
7   OR 48/1:964.

Palmito Ranch Skirmishes

8   *New York Times,* 6/18/65; *Supplement to the Official Records* 10:230; *Annual Circular, No. 6.*
9   *Annual Circular, No. 6;* OR 48/1:267.
10 *Annual Circular, No. 6;* OR 48/1:267–268.
11 OR 48/1:268; *Annual Circular, No. 6.*
12 OR 48/1:268; 62nd USCT Regimental Papers.
13 *Supplement to the Official Records* 10:36; ibid., 41.
14 OR 48/1:266; 62nd USCT Regimental Papers; *Supplement to the Official Records* 10:80.
15 Oates, ed., *Rip Ford's Texas,* 389.
16 OR 48/1:266; *Supplement to the Official Records* 10:10.
17 *New York Herald,* 5/29/65.
18 OR 48/1:266; Pension Files (NA).
19 *Supplement to the Official Records* 10:10; ibid., 93; ibid., 11; ibid.
20 Hunt, "There Is Nothing Left to Us," 57.
21 *Supplement to the Official Records* 10:74.
22 OR 48/1:266; *Supplement to the Official Records* 10:81; OR 48/1:266; *Supplement to the Official Records* 10:81.
23 62nd USCT Regimental Papers.
24 OR 48/1:268; *Supplement to the Official Records* 10:81–82.
25 *Supplement to the Official Records* 10:158; *National Tribune,* 10/8/65.
26 *Supplement to the Official Records* 10:185.
27 OR 48/1:269.
28 Pension Files (NA).
29 OR 48/1:267; *National Tribune,* 5/10/83; Branson, "Last Battle of the War," 212.
30 *Supplement to the Official Records* 10:131; Oates, ed., *Rip Ford's Texas,* 395.
31 OR 48/1:269.

Chapter 18: "This Good Work Is Only Begun"

1   OR (3) 5:108.
2   Newton, *Out of the Briars,* 67; *Anglo,* 8/12/65.

3   *Recorder,* 7/8/65; *Anglo,* 8/19/65.
4   Foner, *Reconstruction,* 80; Trowbridge: "Six Months in the Freedman's Bureau," 199.
5   *Recorder,* 10/21/65.
6   *Anglo,* 8/5/65.
7   Ibid., 7/15/65; Newton, *Out of the Briars,* 78; *Recorder,* 7/15/65; *Anglo,* 8/12/65; *Recorder,* 7/15/65.
8   *Anglo,* 8/5/65.
9   Ibid.; ibid.
10 *Recorder,* 11/4/65.
11 Office of the Adjutant General: Returns of the Twenty-fifth Corps (NA); 43rd USCT Regimental Papers; *Recorder,* 10/23/65; *Anglo,* 10/21/65; Hemenway, "Observations on Scurvy," 582.
12 Richter, "It Is Best to Go In Strong-Handed," 131.
13 *Anglo,* 12/16/65.
14 Carroll, ed., *The Black Military Experience,* 39.
15 *Recorder,* 8/26/65; ibid., 5/20/65.
16 *Anglo,* 9/3/65; *Recorder,* 11/18/65; ibid., 10/23/65.
17 *Recorder,* 8/5/65; *Anglo,* 8/25/65.
18 *Freedom,* 805.
19 Primm, "The GAR in Missouri," 363.
20 Davies, "The Problem of Race Segregation," 357.
21 *National Tribune,* 12/29/87.
22 Aptheker, "Negro Casualties in the Civil War," 10.
23 Glatthaar, *Forged in Battle,* 191; *Recorder,* 7/29/65; Hollandsworth, "The Execution of White Officers," 484.
24 *Anglo,* 6/17/65.
25 Glatthaar, *Forged in Battle,* 155; Marcus, "The Shaw Memorial," 8.
26 Hanson, "The 54th Massachusetts Volunteer Black Infantry as a Subject for American Artists," 753.
27 *Boston Evening Transcript,* 8/2/87; Litwack, *Been in the Storm So Long,* 102.
28 Braxton, ed., *Collected Poetry,* 51.

Bibliography

———◄◊►———

Black Regimental/Unit Histories

Annual Circular, No. 6, of the Sixty-Second Regiment United States Colored Infantry. Minerva, Ohio: Weaver Bros.' Steam Printing Works, 1872.

Baird, George W. *The 32d Regiment U.S.C.T. at the Battle of Honey Hill.* N.p., 1889.

Bates, Samuel P. *History of Pennsylvania Volunteers, 1861–5.* 5 vols. Harrisburg, Pa.: B. Singerly, 1869–71.

Burchard, Peter. *One Gallant Rush.* New York: St. Martin's Press, 1965.

Califf, Joseph M. *Record of the Services of the Seventh Regiment, U.S. Colored Troops.* Providence: E. L. Freeman & Co., Printers, 1878.

———. *To the Ex-Members and Friends of the 7th U.S.C.T.* N.p., 1878.

Chenery, William H. *The Fourteenth Regiment Rhode Island Heavy Artillery (Colored).* Providence: Snow & Farnham, 1898.

Cowden, Robert. *A Brief Sketch of the Organization and Services of the Fifty-Ninth Regiment, United States Colored Infantry.* Dayton, Ohio: United Brethren Publishing House, 1883.

Dennett, George M. *History of the Ninth U.S.C. Troops.* Philadelphia: King and Baird, 1866.

Emilio, Luis F. *A Brave Black Regiment: History of the Fifty-Fourth Regiment of Massachusetts Volunteer Infantry.* Boston: Boston Book Company, 1894.

Evans, Ira H. "The United States Colored Troops." In *Revised Roster of Vermont Volunteers . . . during the War of the Rebellion.* Montpelier, Vt.: Press of the Watchman Pub. Co., 1892.

Fox, Charles B. *Record of the Service of the Fifty-Fifth Regiment of Massachusetts Volunteer Infantry.* Cambridge, Mass.: Press of John Wilson and Son, 1868.

Hill, Isaac J. *A Sketch of the 29th Regiment of Connecticut Colored Troops.* Baltimore: Daugherty, Maguire & Co., 1867.

495

Hollandsworth, James G., Jr. *The Louisiana Native Guards.* Baton Rouge: Louisiana State University Press, 1995.

Kireker, Charles. *History of the 116th Regiment U.S.C. Infantry.* Philadelphia: King and Baird, 1866.

Levstik, Frank R. "The Fifth Regiment, United States Colored Troops, 1863–1865." *Northwest Ohio Quarterly* 42, no. 4 (Fall 1970): 86–98.

Luck, Wilbert H. *Journey to Honey Hill.* Washington: Wiluk Press, 1985.

Main, Edwin M. *The Story of the Marches, Battles and Incidents of the Third United States Colored Cavalry.* Louisville: Globe Printing Co., 1908.

Mickley, Jeremiah M. *The Forty-Third Regiment United States Colored Troops.* Gettysburg, Pa.: J. E. Wible, Printer, 1866.

Newton, Alexander H. *Out of the Briars: An Autobiography and Sketch of the Twenty-Ninth Regiment Connecticut Volunteers.* Philadelphia: A.M.E. Book Concern, 1910.

Official Military History of Kansas Regiments During the War for the Suppression of the Great Rebellion. Topeka: J. K. Hudson State Printer, 1896.

Stein, A. H. *History of the Thirty-Seventh Regiment, U.S.C. Infantry.* Philadelphia: King & Baird Printers, 1886.

Steiner, Paul E. *Medical History of a Civil War Regiment: Disease in the Sixty-Fifth United States Colored Infantry.* Clayton, Mo.: Institute of Civil War Studies, 1977.

Wilder, Burt Green. *Fifty-fifth Regiment of the Massachusetts Volunteer Infantry, Colored: June 1863–September 1865.* Brookline, Mass.: The Riverdale Press, 1919.

Other Regimental/Unit Histories

Adamson, A. P. *Brief History of the Thirtieth Georgia Regiment.* Griffin, Ga.: The Mills Printing Co., 1912.

Blessington, J. P. *The Campaigns of Walker's Texas Division.* New York: Lange, Little & Co., 1875.

Bosson, Charles P. *History of the Forty-Second Regiment Infantry, Massachusetts Volunteers.* Boston: Mills, Knight & Co. Printers, 1886.

Caldwell, Charles K. *The Old Sixth Regiment.* New Haven: Tuttle, Morehouse & Taylor Printers, 1875.

Chisman, James A., ed. *76th Regiment Pennsylvania Volunteer Infantry.* Wilmington, N.C.: Broadfoot Publishing Company, 1988.

Clark, Walter, ed. *Histories of the Several Regiments and Battalions from North Carolina.* 4 vols. Goldsboro, N.C.: Nash Brothers Printers, 1904.

Croom, Wendell D. *The War History of Company C, Sixth Georgia Regiment (Infantry).* Fort Valley, Ga.: printed at the "Advertiser" Office, 1879.

Eldredge, Daniel. *The Third New Hampshire and All About It.* Boston: E. B. Stillings and Co., 1893.

Felmly, Bradford K., and John C. Grady. *Suffering to Silence.* Quannah, Tex.: Nortex Press, 1975.

Irwin, Richard B. *History of the Nineteenth Army Corps.* New York: G. P. Putnam's Sons, 1892.

Johns, Henry T. *Life with the Forty-Ninth Massachusetts Volunteers.* Pittsfield, Mass.: published for the Author, 1864.

Little, Henry F. W. *The Seventh Regiment New Hampshire Volunteers in the War of the Rebellion.* Concord, N.H.: Ira C. Evans Printer, 1896.

McGee, B. F. *History of the 72d Indiana Voluntary Infantry.* LaFayette, Ind.: S. Vater & Co., "The Journal," Printers, 1882.

McGrath, Franklin. *The History of the 127th New York Volunteers "Monitors."* N.p., ca. 1898.

Nichols, James M. *Perry's Saints.* Boston: D. Lothrop & Co., 1886.

Stanyan, John M. *A History of the Eighth Regiment of New Hampshire Volunteers.* Concord, N.H.: Ira C. Evans Printer, 1898.

Stevens, William B. *History of the Fiftieth Regiment of Infantry Massachusetts Volunteer Militia.* Boston: Griffith-Stillings Press, 1907.

Wilkinson, Warren. *Mother, May You Never See the Sights I Have Seen.* New York: Harper & Row, 1990.

Personal Narratives/Black Troops

Abbott, Abial R. "The Negro in the War of the Rebellion." In *Military Essays and Recollections, Papers Read before the Commandery of the State of Illinois, Military Order of the Loyal Legion of the United States.* Chicago: The Dial Press, 1899.

Abramowitz, Jack, ed. "A Civil War Letter: James Trotter to Francis J. Garrison." *Midwest Journal* 4 (summer 1952): 117–122.

Adams, Virginia M., ed. *On the Altar of Freedom* [James Henry Gooding letters]. New York: Warner Books, 1992.

Addeman, J. M. "Reminiscences of Two Years with the Colored Troops." In *Personal Narratives of Events in the War of the Rebellion, Being Papers Read before the Rhode Island Soldiers and Sailors Historical Society.* Providence: N. Bangs Williams & Co., 1880–1881.

van Alstyne, Lawrence. *Diary of an Enlisted Man.* New Haven: Tuttle, Morehouse & Taylor Company, 1910.

Appleton, John W. "That Night at Fort Wagner, by One Who Was There." *Putnam's Magazine,* n.s. 4, no. 19 (July 1869): 9–16.

Armstrong, William H. "The Negro as a Soldier." In *War Papers Read before the Indiana Commandery Military Order of the Loyal Legion of the United States.* Indianapolis: published by the Commandery, 1898.

Bangs, I. S. "The Ullman Brigade." In *War Papers Read before the Commandery of the State of Maine, Military Order of the Loyal Legion of the United States.* Portland, Maine: Lafavor-Tower Company, 1902.

Berlin, Ira, Joseph P. Reidy, and Leslie S. Rowland, eds. *Freedom: A Documentary History of Emancipation, 1861–1867.* Series 2, vol. 1. New York: Cambridge University Press, 1982.

Bingham, Millicent Todd, ed. "Key West in the Summer of 1864" [John Augustus Wilder letters]. *Florida Historical Quarterly* 43, no. 3 (January 1965): 262–265.

Birney, William. *General William Birney's Answer to Libels Clandestinely Circulated by James Shaw, Jr., Collector of the Port, Providence, R.I., with a Review of the Military Record of the Said James Shaw, Jr., Late Colonel of the Seventh U.S. Colored Troops.* Washington: n.p., 1878.

Bissell, J. W. "The Western Organization of Colored People for Furnishing Information to U.S. Troops in the South." In *Glimpses of the Nation's Struggle: A Series*

of Papers Read Before the Minnesota Commandery of the Military Order of the Loyal Legion of the United States. St. Paul: St. Paul Book and Stationary Company, 1890.

Blackett, R. J. M., ed. *Thomas Morris Chester: Black Civil War Correspondent.* Baton Rouge: Louisiana State University Press, 1989.

Blassingame, John W., ed. *Slave Testimony.* Baton Rouge: Louisiana State University Press, 1977.

Bowditch, Charles P. "War Letters of Charles P. Bowditch." *Massachusetts Historical Society Proceedings* 57 (1923/24): 414–495.

Bowley, F. S. *A Boy Lieutenant.* Philadelphia: Henry Altemus Company, 1906.

———. "A Dark Night on Picket." *Overland Monthly* 5, no. 6 (1870): 31–37.

———. "The Petersburg Mine: A Paper Prepared and Read before California Commandery of the Military Order of the Loyal Legion of the United States." Wilmington, N.C.: Broadfoot Publishing Company, 1995.

———. "Seven Months in Confederate Military Prisons: A Paper Prepared and Read before California Commandery of the Military Order of the Loyal Legion of the United States." Wilmington, N.C.: Broadfoot Publishing Company, 1995.

Branson, David. "The Last Battle of the War." *The Bivouac: An Independent Military Monthly* 1 (1883): 211–212.

Briggs, Walter De Blois. *Civil War Surgeon in a Colored Regiment.* Berkeley: n.p., 1960.

Browne, Frederick W. "My Service in the U.S. Colored Cavalry." In *Sketches of War History, 1861–1865: Papers Prepared for the Ohio Commandery of the Military Order of the Loyal Legion of the United States.* Privately printed, 1907.

Butler, Benjamin F. *Butler's Book.* Boston: A. M. Thayer & Co., 1892.

———. *Speech of Maj.-Gen. Benj. F. Butler upon the Campaign Before Richmond* [1864]. Boston: Wright & Potter, Printers, 1865.

Carter, Solon A. "Fourteen Months' Service with Colored Troops." In *Civil War Papers Read before the Commandery of the State of Massachusetts, Military Order of the Loyal Legion of the United States.* Boston: published by the Commandery, 1900.

Chetlain, Augustus L. *Recollections of Seventy Years.* Galena, Ill.: Gazette Publishing Company, 1899.

Clapp, Henry S. *Sketches of Army Life in the Sixties.* Newark, Ohio: privately published, n.d.

Connor, Selden. "The Colored Troops." In *War Papers Read before the Commandery of the State of Maine, Military Order of the Loyal Legion of the United States.* Portland, Maine: Lafavor-Tower Company, 1908.

Cooney, Charles F., ed. "I Was . . . Eager to Become a Soldier." *Manuscripts* 26, no. 1 (winter 1974): 280–282.

Crawford, Samuel J. *Kansas in the Sixties.* Chicago: A. C. McClurg & Co., 1911.

Dollard, Robert. *Recollections of the Civil War.* Scotland, S.D.: n.p., 1906.

Douglass, Frederick. *Life and Times of Frederick Douglass.* New York: Gramercy Books, 1993.

Duncan, Russell, ed. *Blue-Eyed Child of Fortune* [Robert Gould Shaw letters]. New York: Avon Books, 1992.

Duren, Charles M. "The Occupation of Jacksonville, February 1864, and the Battle of Olustee." *Florida Historical Quarterly* 32, no. 4 (1953/54): 262–287.

Ellis, Richard N., ed. "The Civil War Letters of an Iowa Family." *Annals of Iowa* 39, no. 8 (spring 1969): 561–586.

Fleetwood, Christian A. *The Negro as a Soldier.* Washington: Prof. George William Crook, 1895.

Ford, Washington Chauncey, ed. *A Cycle of Adams Letters, 1861–1865.* Boston: Houghton Mifflin Company, 1920.

Freeman, Henry V. "A Colored Brigade in the Campaign and Battle of Nashville." In *Military Essays and Recollections: Papers Read before the Commandery of the State of Illinois, Military Order of the Loyal Legion of the United States.* Chicago: A. C. McClurg and Company, 1894.

Glatthaar, Joseph T., ed. "The Civil War Through the Eyes of a Sixteen-Year-Old Black Officer: The Letters of Lieutenant John H. Crowder of the 1st Louisiana Native Guards." *Louisiana History* 35, no. 2 (spring 1994): 201–216.

Goulding, Joseph Hiram. "The Colored Troops in the War of the Rebellion." In *Proceedings of the Reunion Society of Vermont Officers.* Vol. 2, 1886–1905. Burlington, Vt.: Free Press Printing Company, 1906.

Greely, A. W. *Reminiscences of Adventures and Service: A Record of Sixty-Five Years.* New York: Charles Scribner's Sons, 1927.

Hall, H. Seymour. "Mine Run to Petersburg." In *War Talks in Kansas: A Series of Papers Read before the Kansas Commandery of the Military Order of the Loyal Legion of the United States.* Kansas City: Press of the Franklin Hudson Publishing Company, 1906.

Hallowell, N. P. *Selected Letters and Papers of N. P. Hallowell.* Peterborough, N.H.: Richard R. Smith Co., Inc., 1963.

———. *The Meaning of Memorial Day.* Boston: n.p., 1896.

Handy, Moses P. "The Fall of Richmond in 1865." *The American Magazine and Historical Chronicle* (Ann Arbor: Clements Library Associates), autumn–winter 1985–1986.

Hemenway, S. "Observations on Scurvy, and Its Causes among U.S. Colored Troops of the 25th Army Corps, during the Spring and Summer of 1865." *Chicago Medical Examiner* 7, no. 10 (October 1866): 582–586.

Hepworth, George H. *The Whip, Hoe and Sword.* Boston: Walker, Wise and Co., 1864.

Heslin, James J. "A Yankee Soldier in a New York Regiment." *New-York Historical Society Quarterly* 50, no. 2 (April 1966): 109–149.

Higginson, Mary T. *Thomas Wentworth Higginson.* Boston: Houghton Mifflin and Co., 1914.

———, ed. *Letters and Journals of Thomas Wentworth Higginson, 1846–1906.* Boston: Houghton Mifflin Company, 1921.

Higginson, Thomas Wentworth. *Army Life in a Black Regiment.* Boston: Houghton Mifflin and Co., 1870.

———. "Regular and Volunteer Officers." *Atlantic Monthly* 14, no. 84 (1864): 348–357.

———. "Leaves from an Officer's Journal." *Atlantic Monthly* 14, no. 85 (1864): 521–529, 740–748; 15, no. 87 (1865): 65–73.

———. "Up the St. John's River." *Atlantic Monthly* 16, no. 95 (1865): 311–324.

———. "Out on Picket." *Atlantic Monthly* 19, no. 113 (1867): 271–281.

———. "The First Black Regiment." *The Outlook,* July 1898, 521–531.

———. "The Re-occupation of Jacksonville in 1863." In *Civil War Papers Read before the Commandery of the State of Massachusetts, Military Order of the Loyal Legion of the United States.* Boston: published by the Commandery, 1900.

Hobart, Edwin L. *Semi-History of a Boy Veteran*. Denver: n.p., 1909.

James, Garth W. "The Assault on Fort Wagner." In *War Papers: Being Papers Read before the Commandery of the State of Wisconsin, Military Order of the Loyal Legion of the United States*. Milwaukee: published by the Commandery, 1891.

Johnson, Isaac. *Slavery Days in Old Kentucky*. Ogdensburg, N.Y: Republican & Journal Co. Printers, 1901.

Johnson, Mary E., ed. "Letters from a Civil War Chaplain." *Journal of Presbyterian History* 46, no. 3 (September 1968): 219–235.

Knox, Thomas W. *Camp-fire and Cotton-Field: Southern Adventure in Time of War*. New York: Blelock and Company, 1865.

Levstik, Frank R., ed. "From Slavery to Freedom" [Milton M. Holland letters]. *Civil War Times Illustrated* 11, no. 7 (November 1972): 10–15.

Longacre, Edward G. "Brave Radical Wild." *Civil War Times Illustrated* 19, no. 3 (June 1980): 8–19.

———, ed. "Letters from Little Rock of Captain James M. Bowler, 112th United States Colored Troops." *Arkansas Historical Quarterly* 40, no. 3 (Autumn 1981): 235–248.

McMurray, John. *Recollections of a Colored Troop*. Brookville, Pa.: privately printed, 1916.

Marrs, Elijah P. *Life and History of the Rev. Elijah P. Marrs*. Louisville: The Bradley & Gilbert Company, 1885.

Marshall, Jessie A., ed. *Private and Official Correspondence of Gen. Benjamin F. Butler*. 5 vols. Norwood, Mass.: The Plimpton Press, 1917.

Memorial of Colonel John A. Bross, Twenty-Ninth U.S. Colored Troops. Chicago: Tribune Book and Job Office, 1865.

Montgomery, Horace, ed. "A Union Officer's Recollections of the Negro as a Soldier" [John McMurray memoirs]. *Pennsylvania History* 28 (April 1961): 156–186.

Moore, John H., ed. "The Last Officer—April 1865" [Edward L. Stevens journal]. *South Carolina Historical Magazine* 67, no. 1 (January 1966): 1–14.

Morgan, Thomas J. "Reminiscences of Service with Colored Troops in the Army of the Cumberland, 1863–65." In *Personal Narratives of Events in the War of the Rebellion: Being Papers Read before the Rhode Island Soldiers and Sailors Historical Society*. Providence: published by the Society, 1885–1887.

———. *The Negro in America and the Ideal American Republic*. Philadelphia: American Baptist Publication Society, 1898.

Norton, Henry Allyn. "Colored Troops in the War of the Rebellion." In *Glimpses of the Nation's Struggle: A Series of Papers Read before the Minnesota Commandery of the Military Order of the Loyal Legion of the United States*. St. Paul: Review Publishing Co., 1903.

Norton, Oliver Willcox. *Army Letters, 1861–1865*. Chicago: O. L. Deming, 1903.

Offenberg, Richard S., and Robert Rue Parsonage, eds. *The War Letters of Duren F. Kelley, 1862–1865*. New York: Pageant Press, 1967.

Olney, Warren. "Nagging the South: A Paper Prepared and Read before California Commandery of the Military Order of the Loyal Legion of the United States." Wilmington, N.C.: Broadfoot Publishing Company, 1995.

Phillips, Richard C., and Rhonda McConnell Phillips. *Richard and Rhonda, Letters from the Civil War*. Washington: Legation Press, 1981.

Powell, E. Henry. "The Colored Soldier in the War of the Rebellion." In *Vermont War Papers*. Wilmington, N.C.: Broadfoot Publishing Company, 1994.

Putnam, Albert D., ed. *Major General Joseph R. Hawley: Soldier and Editor (1826–1905)*. Hartford: Connecticut Civil War Commission, 1964.

Raup, Hallock F., ed. *Letters from a Pennsylvania Chaplain at the Siege of Petersburg 1865*. London: The Eden Press, 1961.

Redkey, Edwin S., ed. *A Grand Army of Black Men*. New York: Cambridge University Press, 1992.

————, ed. "Rocked in the Cradle of Consternation" [Henry M. Turner letters]. *American Heritage* 31, no. 6 (October/November 1980): 70–79.

————, ed. "They Are Invincible." *Civil War Times Illustrated* 28, no. 2 (April 1989): 32–36.

Rickard, James H. "Service with Colored Troops in Burnside's Corps." In *Personal Narratives of Events in the War of the Rebellion: Being Papers Read before the Rhode Island Soldiers and Sailors Historical Society*. Providence: published by the Society, 1894–1899.

Romeyn, Henry. "With Colored Troops in the Army of the Cumberland." In *War Papers: Being Papers Papers Read before the Commandery of the District of Columbia, Military Order of the Loyal Legion of the United States*. Wilmington, N.C.: Broadfoot Publishing Company, 1993.

Scroggs, Joseph J. "The Earth Shook and Quivered." *Civil War Times Illustrated* 11, no. 8 (November 1972): 30–37.

Sears, Cyrus. *Paper of Cyrus Sears, Late Lieut. Col. of the 49th U.S. Colored Infantry Vols. of African Descent*. Columbus: F. J. Heer Printing Co., 1909.

Shaw, James. "Our Last Campaign and Subsequent Service in Texas." In *Personal Narratives of Events in the War of the Rebellion: Being Papers Read before the Rhode Island Soldiers and Sailors Historical Society*. Providence: published by the Society, 1885–1887.

Sherman, George R. "The Negro As a Soldier." In *Personal Narratives of Events in the War of the Rebellion: Being Papers Read before the Rhode Island Soldiers and Sailors Historical Society*. Providence: published by the Society, 1905–1915.

————. "Assault on Fort Gilmer." In *Personal Narratives of Events in the War of the Rebellion: Being Papers Read before the Rhode Island Soldiers and Sailors Historical Society*. Providence: published by the Society, 1894–1899.

Shewmaker, Kenneth E., and Andrew K. Prinz, eds. "A Yankee in Louisiana" [Henry Rufus Gardner letters]. *Louisiana History* 5, no. 3 (summer 1964): 271–295.

Simonton, Edwin. "The Campaign Up the James to Petersburg." In *Glimpses of the Nation's Struggle: A Series of Papers Read before the Minnesota Commandery of the Military Order of the Loyal Legion of the United States*. St. Paul: Review Publishing Co., 1903.

[Smith, Andrew J.]. *Letters and Memorabilia of Color-Sergeant Andrew J. Smith*. N.p., n.d.

Snider, S. P. "Reminiscences of the War." In *Glimpses of the Nation's Struggle: A Series of Papers Read before the Minnesota Commandery of the Military Order of the Loyal Legion of the United States*. St. Paul: St. Paul Book and Stationery Company, 1890.

Sutherland, George E. "The Negro in the Late War." In *War Papers: Being Papers Read before the Commandery of the State of Wisconsin, Military Order of the Loyal Legion of the United States.* Milwaukee: published by the Commandery, 1891.

Taggart, John H. *Free Military School for Applicants for Commands of Colored Troops.* Philadelphia: King & Baird Printers, 1863.

Talbot, Edith A., ed. *Samuel Chapman Armstrong: A Biographical Study.* New York: Doubleday, Page & Company, 1904.

Taylor, Susie King. *Reminiscences of My Life in Camp with the 33d United States Colored Troops.* Boston: privately printed, 1902.

Thomas, Henry G. "The Colored Troops at Petersburg." In Johnson and Buel, eds., *Battles and Leaders of the Civil War* (1889).

———. "Twenty-two Hours Prisoner of War in Dixie." In *War Papers: Read before the Commandery of the State of Maine, Military Order of the Loyal Legion of the United States.* Portland, Maine: The Thurston Printer, 1898.

Trowbridge, Charles Tyler. "Six Months in the Freedman's Bureau with a Colored Regiment." In *Glimpses of the Nation's Struggle: A Series of Papers Read before the Minnesota Commandery of the Military Order of the Loyal Legion of the United States.* Minneapolis: Aug. Davis Publisher, 1909.

Trudeau, Noah A., ed. *Voices of the 55th.* Dayton, Ohio: Morningside House, Inc., 1996.

Tunnell, Ted, ed. *Carpetbagger from Vermont.* Baton Rouge: Louisiana State University Press, 1989.

Tyler, Charles M. *Memorials of Lieut. George H. Walcott.* Boston: Massachusetts Sabbath School Society, 1865.

Ullmann, Daniel. *Address by Daniel Ullmann, before the Soldiers' and Sailors' Union of the State of New York, on the Organization of Colored Troops and the Regeneration of the South, Delivered at Albany, February 5, 1868.* Washington: n.p., 1868.

Vlock, Laurel F., and Joel A. Levitch. *Contraband of War.* New York: Funk & Wagnall's, 1970.

Weber, John Baptiste. *Autobiography of John B. Weber.* Buffalo: J. W. Clement Co., 1924.

White, Lonnie J., ed. "A Bluecoat's Account of the Camden Expedition." *Arkansas Historical Quarterly* 24, no. 1 (Spring 1965): 82–89.

Yacovone, Donald, ed. *A Voice of Thunder: The Civil War Letters of George E. Stephens.* Chicago: University of Illinois Press, 1996.

Other Personal Narratives

Agassiz, George R., ed. *Meade's Headquarters, 1863–1865: Letters of Colonel Theodore Lyman.* Boston: Atlantic Monthly Press, 1922.

Anderson, John Q., ed. *Campaigning with Parsons' Texas Cavalry Brigade, CSA.* Hillsboro, Tex.: Hill Junior College Press, 1967.

Andrews, W. H. *Footprints of a Regiment.* Atlanta: Longstreet House, 1992.

Ayres, S. C. "The Battle of Nashville, with Personal Recollections of a Field Hospital." In *Sketches of War History, 1861–1865: Papers Prepared for the Ohio Commandery of the Military Order of the Loyal Legion of the United States.* Cincinnati: The Robert Clarke Company, 1903.

Bacon, Edward. *Among the Cotton Thieves.* Detroit: Free Press Steam Book and Job Printing House, 1867.

Baird, W. David, ed. *A Creek Warrior for the Confederacy: The Autobigraphy of Chief G. W. Grayson.* Norman, Okla.: University of Oklahoma Press, 1988.

Bejach, Lois D., ed. "The Journal of a Civil War 'Commando,' DeWitt Clinton Fort." *West Tennessee Society Papers* 2 (1948): 5–32.

Bernard, George S., ed. *War Talks of Confederate Veterans.* Petersburg, Va.: Fenn & Owen, 1892.

Bevens, W. E. *Reminiscences of a Private, Company "G," First Arkansas Regiment Infantry.* N.p., n.d.

Bodnia, George, ed. "Fort Pillow Massacre: Observations of a Minnesotan." *Minnesota History* 43 (spring 1973): 186–190.

Bornet, Vaughn D, ed. "A Connecticut Yankee Fights at Olustee." *Florida Historical Quarterly* 27, no. 3 (January 1949): 237–259.

Bounds, Charles L. *Ben H. Bounds, 1840–1911, Methodist Minister and Prominent Mason, Biography and Highlights from His Early Life and Civil War Memoirs.* Columbus, Ohio: n.p., n.d.

Burbank, Horace H. "The Battle of 'The Crater.'" In *War Papers Read before the Commandery of the State of Maine, Military Order of the Loyal Legion of the United States.* Portland: The Thurston Printer, 1898.

Burns, W. S. "A. J. Smith's Defeat of Forrest at Tupelo." In Johnson and Buel, eds., *Battles and Leaders of the Civil War,* 1889.

Byers, S. H. M. *Iowa in War Times.* Des Moines: W. D. Condit & Co., 1888.

Cathey, Henry, ed. "Extracts from the Memoirs of William Franklin Avera." *Arkansas Historical Quarterly* 22, no. 2 (summer 1963): 99–116.

Chase, Salmon P. *Diary and Correspondence.* New York: Da Capo Press, 1971.

Dahlgren, Madeleine V. *Memoir of John A. Dahlgren.* Boston: James R. Osgood and Company, 1882.

Dana, Charles A. *Recollections of the Civil War.* New York: Boughmans, 1898.

Davis, W. W. H. "The Siege of Morris Island." In *The Annals of the War Written by Leading Participants North and South.* Washington: The Times Publishing Company, 1878.

De Forest, John W. *A Volunteer's Adventures: A Union Captain's Record of the Civil War.* New Haven: Yale University Press, 1946.

Egan, Patrick. "The Florida Campaign with Light Battery C, Third Rhode Island Heavy Artillery." In *Personal Narratives of Events in the War of the Rebellion: Being Papers Read before the Rhode Island Soldiers and Sailors Historical Society.* Providence: published by the Society, 1903–1905.

Fisk, Wilbur. *Anti-Rebel: Civil War Letters.* Croton-on-Hudson, N.Y.: Haddon Craftsman, 1983.

Franklin, John H., ed. *The Diary of James T. Ayers, Civil War Recruiter.* Springfield, Ill.: published by authority of the State of Illinois, 1947.

Frederick, J. V., ed. "War Diary of W. C. Porter." *Arkansas Historical Quarterly* 11, no. 4 (winter 1952): 286–314.

Furness, William E. "The Siege of Fort Wagner." In *Military Essays and Recollections: Papers Read before the Commandery of the State of Illinois, Military Order of the Loyal Legion of the United States.* Chicago: A. C. McClurg and Company, 1891.

———. "The Battle of Olustee, Florida, February 20, 1864." In *Papers of the Military Historical Society of Massachusetts.* Vol. 9, *Operations on the Atlantic Coast 1861–1865.* Boston: The Military Historical Society of Massachusetts, 1912.

Gilchrist, Robert C. *The Confederate Defense of Morris Island*. Charleston: News and Courier Book Presses, 1884.

Gillmore, Quincy A. "The Army before Charleston in 1863." In Johnson and Buel, eds., *Battles and Leaders of the Civil War* (1889).

Grant, Ulysses S. *Personal Memoirs*. 2 vols. New York: Charles L. Webster, 1886.

Hagood, Johnson. *Memoirs of the War of Secession*. Columbia, S.C.: The State Company, 1910.

Hanson, E. Hunn. "Forrest's Defeat of Sturgis at Brice's Cross-Roads." In Johnson and Buel, eds., *Battles and Leaders of the Civil War* (1889).

Harkness, Edson J. "The Expeditions against Fort Fisher and Wilmington." In *Military Essays and Recollections: Papers Read before the Commandery of the State of Illinois, Military Order of the Loyal Legion of the United States*. Chicago: A. C. McClurg and Company, 1894.

Hawley, Joseph R. "The Battle of Olustee, Florida." In Johnson and Buel, eds., *Battles and Leaders of the Civil War* (1889).

Houghton, Charles H. "In the Crater." In Johnson and Buel, eds., *Battles and Leaders of the Civil War* (1889).

Irwin, Richard B. "The Capture of Port Hudson." In Johnson and Buel, eds., *Battles and Leaders of the Civil War* (1889).

———. "The Red River Campaign." In Johnson and Buel, eds., *Battles and Leaders of the Civil War* (1889).

Jackson, Harry F., and Thomas F. O'Donnell, eds. *Back Home in Oneida: Hermon Clarke and His Letters*. Syracuse, N.Y.: Syracuse University Press, 1965.

Johnson, Robert U., and Clarence C. Buel, eds. *Battles and Leaders of the Civil War*. New York: Century Magazine, 1889.

Jones, Charles C. *The Battle of Honey Hill*. Augusta, Ga.: Chronicle Publishing Co., 1885.

———. *The Evacuation of Battery Wagner, and the Battle of Ocean Pond*. Augusta, Ga.: Chronicle Publishing Co., 1888.

———. *Defence of Battery Wagner*. Augusta, Ga.: Chronicle Publishing Co., 1892.

Jones, Samuel. "The Battle of Olustee, or Ocean Pond." In Johnson and Buel, eds., *Battles and Leaders of the Civil War* (1889).

Kilmer, George L. "The Dash into the Crater." *Century* 12 (September 1887).

Kirwan, A. D., ed. *Johnny Green of the Orphan Brigade*. Lexington: The University of Kentucky Press, 1956.

Laas, Virginia Jeans, ed. *Wartime Washington: The Civil War Letters of Elizabeth Blair Lee*. Chicago: University of Illinois Press, 1991.

Langston, John Mercer. *From the Virginia Plantation to the National Capitol*. Hartford: American Publishing Company, 1894.

Lankford, Nelson D., ed. *An Irishman in Dixie*. Columbia, S.C.: University of South Carolina Press, 1988.

Lewis, A. S., ed. *My Dear Parents: The Civil War Seen by an English Union Soldier*. New York: Harcourt Brace Jovanovich, 1982.

"Life in Battery Wagner." *Land We Love* 2, no. 5 (March 1867): 351–355.

Macdonald, Colin F. "The Battle of Brice's Cross Roads." In *Glimpses of the Nation's Struggle: A Series of Papers Read before the Minnesota Commandery of the Military Order of the Loyal Legion of the United States*. Minneapolis: Aug. Davis Publisher, 1909.

Merriam, Henry C. "The Capture of Mobile." In *War Papers Read before the Commandery of the State of Maine, Military Order of the Loyal Legion of the United States*. Portland, Maine: Lafavor-Tower Company, 1908.

M.R.R. "Potter's Raid." In *Our Women in the War*. [Publication information unknown].

Newberry, Walter C. "The Petersburg Mine." In *Military Essays and Recollections: Papers Read before the Commandery of the State of Illinois, Military Order of the Loyal Legion of the United States*. Chicago: The Dial Press, 1899.

Oates, Stephen B., ed. *Rip Ford's Texas*. Austin: University of Texas Press, 1963.

Porter, Horace. *Campaigning with Grant*. New York: Century Co., 1897.

Powell, William H. "The Battle of the Petersburg Crater." In Johnson and Buel, eds., *Battles and Leaders of the Civil War* (1889).

Richards, Channing. "Dealing with Slavery." In *Sketches of War History, 1861–1865: Papers Prepared for the Ohio Commandery of the Military Order of the Loyal Legion of the United States*. Cincinnati: The Robert Clarke Company, 1896.

Ripley, Edward H. "The Occupation of Richmond." In *Personal Recollections of the War of the Rebellion: Addresses Delivered before the Commandery of the State of New York, Military Order of the Loyal Legion of the United States*. New York: G. P. Putnam's Sons, 1907.

Robertson, James I., Jr., ed. "'The Boy Artillerist': Letters of Colonel William Pegram, C.S.A." *Virginia Magazine of History and Biography* 98, no. 2 (April 1990): 221–260.

Root, L. Carroll, ed. "Private Journal of William H. Root, Second Lieutenant, Seventy-Fifth New York Volunteers." *Louisiana Historical Quarterly* 19, no. 3 (July 1936): 637–667.

Schiller, Herbert M., ed. *Autobiography of Major General William F. Smith*. Dayton, Ohio: Morningside House, Inc., 1990.

Schwartz, Gerald, ed. *A Woman Doctor's Civil War*. Columbia, S.C.: University of South Carolina Press, 1984.

Smith, Gustavus W. "The Georgia Militia and the Carolinas." In Johnson and Buel, eds., *Battles and Leaders of the Civil War* (1889).

Stone, Henry. "Repelling Hood's Invasion of Tennessee," In Johnson and Buel, eds., *Battles and Leaders of the Civil War* (1889).

Styple, William B., and John J. Fitzpatrick, eds. *The Andersonville Diary and Memoirs of Charles Hopkins*. Kearny, N.J.: Belle Grove Publishing Co., 1988.

Swift, Lester L., ed. "Captain Dana in Florida: A Narrative of the Seymour Expedition." *Civil War History* 11, no. 3 (September 1965): 245–256.

Upson, Theodore F. *With Sherman to the Sea*. Baton Rouge: Louisiana State University Press, 1943.

Voris, Alvin C. "Charleston in the Rebellion." In *Sketches of War History 1861–1865: Papers Read before the Ohio Commandery of the Military Order of the Loyal Legion of the United States*. Cincinnati: Robert Clarke & Co., 1888.

Weld, Stephen M. *War Diary and Letters*. Boston: Massachusetts Historical Society, 1979.

Yeary, Mamie, comp. *Reminiscences of the Boys in Gray: 1861–1865*. McGregor, Tex.: Smith & Lamar, 1912.

Official Documents

Annual Report of the Adjutant-General of the Commonwealth of Massachusetts for the Year Ending December 31, 1865. Boston: Wright & Potter State Printers, 1866.

Joint Committee on the Conduct of the War, Supplemental Report. Volume 2, Report of Major General J. G. Foster. Washington, 1866.

Official Records of the Union and Confederate Navies in the War of the Rebellion. 30 vols. Washington, 1894–1922.

Reece, J. N., ed. *Report of the Adjutant-General of the State of Illinois (Containing Reports for the Years 1861–66).* Springfield, Ill.: Journal Company Printers and Binders, 1901.

Report of the Adjutant General of the State of Kansas, 1861–65. Topeka: Kansas State Printer, 1896.

Report of Brigadier General Nathaniel B. Baker, Adjutant-General and Act'g Q.M.G. and Act'g as P.M.G. Des Moines: F. W. Palmer State Printer, 1867.

Report of the Joint Committee on the Conduct of the War on the Attack on Petersburg, on the 30th Day of July, 1864. Washington, 1865.

Roster and Record of Iowa Soldiers in the War of the Rebellion, together with Historical Sketches of Volunteer Organizations. Des Moines: E. H. English State Printer, 1908.

Supplement to the Official Records of the Union and Confederate Armies, Wilmington, N.C.: Broadfoot Publishing Company, 1994– .

The War of the Rebellion: A Compilation of Official Records of the Union and Confederate Armies. 128 vols. Washington, 1880–1902.

39th Congress, 2nd Session. House of Representatives Report No. 16: "New Orleans Riots." Washington, 1867.

40th Congress, 3rd Session. House of Representatives Report No. 45: "Report on the Treatment of Prisoners of War by the Rebel Authorities during the War of the Rebellion." Washington, 1869.

44th Congress, 1st Session. Congressional Record: Special Session of the Senate: Debate regarding P. B. S. Pinchback. Washington, 1876.

56th Congress, 1st Session. Senate Document No. 214: "Proceedings of a Court Martial of Lieut. Col. Henry C. Corbin." Washington, 1900.

Secondary Sources

Books

Andrews, C. C. *History of the Campaign of Mobile.* New York: D. Van Nostrand, 1867.

Andrews, J. Cutler. *The South Reports the Civil War.* Pittsburgh: University of Pittsburgh Press, 1985.

Barrett, John G. *The Civil War in North Carolina.* Chapel Hill: University of North Carolina Press, 1963.

Bearss, Edwin C. *Protecting Sherman's Lifeline: The Battles of Brices Cross Roads and Tupelo 1864.* Washington: National Park Service, 1971.

———. *Forrest at Brices's Cross Roads.* Dayton, Ohio: Morningside House, Inc., 1979.

———. *The Campaign for Vicksburg: Unvexed to the Sea.* Dayton, Ohio: Morningside House, Inc., 1986.

———. *Steele's Retreat from Camden.* Little Rock: Pioneer Press, n.d.

———. *Sergeant-Major Hawkins and the Black Heroes of New Market Heights.* N.p., n.d.

Beath, Robert B. *History of the Grand Army of the Republic.* Cincinnati: The Jones Brothers Publishing Co., 1889.

Bergeron, Arthur W., Jr. *Confederate Mobile.* Jackson: University Press of Mississippi, 1991.

Berlin, Ira. "The Black Military Experience, 1861–1867." in Berlin, Ira, Barbara J. Fields, Steven F. Miller, Joseph P. Reidy, and Leslie S. Rowland, eds. *Slaves No More: Three Essays on Emancipation and the Civil War.* New York: Cambridge University Press, 1992.

Berry, Mary F. *Military Necessity and Civil Rights Policy.* Port Washington, N.Y.: National University Publications, 1977.

Bilby, Joseph G. *Forgotten Warriors: New Jersey's African American Soldiers in the Civil War.* Hightstown, N.J.: Longstreet House, 1993.

Blassingame, John W. *The Slave Community.* New York: Oxford University Press, 1972.

———. *Black New Orleans, 1860–1880.* Chicago: University of Chicago Press, 1973.

Blight, David W. *Frederick Douglass' Civil War.* Baton Rouge: Louisiana State University Press, 1989.

Boddie, William W. *History of Williamsburg.* Columbia, S.C.: The State Company, 1923.

Bowen, James L. *Massachusetts in the War, 1861–1864.* Springfield, Mass.: Clark W. Bryan & Co., 1889.

Boyd, Mark F. *The Federal Campaign of 1864 in East Florida.* Tallahassee, Fla.: The Florida Board of Parks and Historic Memorials, n.d.

Bradford, Sarah. *Harriet Tubman: The Moses of Her People.* Bedford, Mass.: Applewood Books, 1886.

Bradshaw, Timothy. *Battery Wagner.* Columbia, S.C.: Celo Book Production Service, 1993.

Braxton, Joanne M., ed. *The Collected Poetry of Paul Laurence Dunbar.* Charlottesville: University Press of Virginia, 1993.

Brewer, James H. *The Confederate Negro.* Durham, N.C.: Duke University Press, 1969.

Britton, Wiley. *The Civil War on the Border.* New York: G. P. Putnam's Sons, 1899.

Brown, William W. *The Negro in the American Rebellion.* Boston: A. G. Brown, 1880.

"The Capture of Fort Pillow." In Johnson and Buel, eds., *Battles and Leaders of the Civil War* (1889).

Calkins, Christopher M. *The Battles of Appomattox Station and Appomattox Court House: April 8–9, 1865.* Lynchburg, Va.: H. E. Howard, 1987.

Carroll, John M., ed. *The Black Military Experience in the American West.* New York: Liveright Publishing, 1973.

Caskey, Willie M. *Secession and Restoration of Louisiana.* New York: Da Capo Press, 1970.

Castel, Albert. *A Frontier State at War: Kansas 1861–1865.* Lawrence, Kans.: Kansas Heritage Press, 1992.

Cavanaugh, Michael A., and William Marvel. *The Battle of the Crater: The Horrid Pit.* Lynchburg, Va.: H. E. Howard Inc., 1989.

Christ, Mark K., ed. *Rugged and Sublime.* Fayetteville, Ark.: University of Arkansas Press, 1994.

Cimprich, John. *Slavery's End in Tennessee, 1861–1865*. University, Ala.: University of Alabama Press, 1985.

Clark, Peter H. *The Black Brigade of Cincinnati*. Cincinnati: Joseph B. Boyd, 1864.

Connelly, Thomas L. *Autumn of Glory: The Army of Tennessee, 1862–1865*. Baton Rouge: Louisiana State University Press, 1971.

Connelley, William E. *Quantrill and the Border Wars*. Cedar Rapids, Iowa: The Torch Press, Publishers, 1910.

Conrad, Earl. *Harriet Tubman*. New York: The Associated Publishers Inc., 1943.

Cornish, Dudley T. *The Sable Arm*. New York: Longmans Green & Co., 1956.

Cunningham, Edward. *The Port Hudson Campaign*. Baton Rouge: Louisiana State University Press, 1963.

Daniels, Jonathan. *Prince of Carpetbaggers*. New York: J. B. Lippincott Company, 1958.

Davis, T. Frederick. *History of Jacksonville, Florida, and Vicinity, 1513 to 1924*. Gainesville, Fla.: University of Florida Press, 1925.

Dearing, Mary R. *Veterans in Politics: The Story of the G.A.R.* Baton Rouge: Louisiana State University Press, 1952.

Denney, Robert E. *Civil War Prisoners & Escapes*. New York: Sterling Publishing Co., 1993.

Dickison, J. J. *Confederate Military History: Florida*. Atlanta: Confederate Publishing Company, 1899.

Drake, Frederick C. *The Empire of the Seas: A Biography of Rear Admiral Robert Wilson Shufeldt, USN*. Honolulu: University of Hawaii Press, 1984.

Durden, Robert F. *The Gray and the Black: The Confederate Debate on Emancipation*. Baton Rouge: Louisiana State University Press, 1965.

Dyer, Frederick H. *A Compendium of the War of the Rebellion*. 2 vols. Des Moines: Dyer Publishing Co., 1908.

Edelstein, Tilden G. *Strange Enthusiasm: A Life of Thomas Wentworth Higginson*. New Haven: Yale University Press, 1968.

Edmonds, David C. *The Guns of Port Hudson*. Lafayette, La.: Arcadiana Press, 1984.

Epple, Jess C. *Battle of Cabin Creek, September 18, 1864*. Muskogee, Okla.: Hoffman Printing Company, 1964.

———. *Honey Springs Depot, Elk Creek, Creek Nation, Indian Territory*. Muskogee, Okla.: Hoffman Printing Company, 1964.

Fellman, Michael. *Citizen Sherman*. New York: Random House, 1995.

"The Florida Expedition," *United States Service Magazine* 2 (1864): 150–157.

Foner, Eric. *Reconstruction: America's Unfinished Revolution 1863–1877*. New York: Harper & Row Publishers, 1988.

Foner, Jack D. *Blacks and the Military in American History*. New York: Prager Publishers, 1974.

Foner, Philip S. *History of Black Americans*. Westport, Conn.: Greenwood Press, 1983.

Fox, Stephen R. *The Guardian of Boston: William Monroe Trotter*. New York: Atheneum, 1970.

Franklin, John H. *The Militant South*. Boston: The Beacon Press, 1956.

Fuchs, Richard L. *An Unerring Fire: The Massacre at Fort Pillow*. Rutherford, N.J.: Fairleigh Dickinson University Press, 1994.

Furness, William E. "The Negro as a Soldier." In *Military Essays and Recollections: Papers Read before the Commandery of the State of Illinois, Military Or-*

der of the Loyal Legion of the United States. Chicago: A. C. McClurg and Company, 1894.

Gerteis, Louis. *From Contraband to Freedmen.* Westport, Conn.: Greenwood Press, 1973.

Gladstone, William A. *United States Colored Troops: 1863–1867.* Gettysburg, Pa.: Thomas Publications, 1990.

———. *Men of Color.* Gettysburg, Pa.: Thomas Publications, 1993.

Glatthaar, Joseph T. *The March to the Sea and Beyond.* New York: New York University Press, 1985.

———. *Forged in Battle.* New York: The Free Press, 1990.

Goodrich, Thomas. *Black Flag: Guerrilla Warfare on the Western Border, 1861–1865.* Bloomington: Indiana University Press, 1995.

Gragg, Rod. *Confederate Goliath.* New York: HarperCollins Publishers, 1991.

Greene, Lorenzo J., Gary R. Kremer, and Antonio F. Holland. *Missouri's Black Heritage.* Columbia, Mo.: University of Missouri Press, 1980.

Gregorie, Anne K. *History of Sumter County, South Carolina.* Sumter, S.C.: Library Board of Sumter County, 1954.

Groom, Winston. *Shrouds of Glory.* New York: The Atlantic Monthly Press, 1995.

Hackett, Horatio B. *Christian Memorials of the War.* Boston: Gould and Lincoln, 1864.

Hargrove, Hondon B. *Black Union Soldiers in the Civil War.* Jefferson, N.C.: McFarland & Company, 1988.

Harrell, John M. *Confederate Military History: Arkansas.* Atlanta: Confederate Publishing Company, 1899.

Hauptman, Laurence M. *The Iroquois in the Civil War.* Syracuse, N.Y.: Syracuse University Press, 1993.

Hearn, Chester F. *Mobile Bay and the Mobile Campaign.* Jefferson, N.C.: McFarland & Company, Inc., 1993.

Hewitt, Lawrence Lee. *Port Hudson: Confederate Bastion on the Mississippi River.* Baton Rouge: Louisiana State University Press, 1987.

Hoke, Jacob. *The Great Invasion.* Dayton, Ohio: W. J. Shuey, 1887.

Hooker, Charles E. *Confederate Military History: Missisippi.* Atlanta: Confederate Publishing Company, 1899.

Horn, Stanley F. *The Decisive Battle of Nashville.* Baton Rouge: Louisiana University Press, 1956.

Howard, Percy. *The Barbarities of the Rebels.* Providence: n.p., 1863.

Howe, Thomas J. *Wasted Valor: The Petersburg Campaign, June 15–18, 1864.* Lynchburg, Va.: H. E. Howard, 1988.

Hurst, Jack. *Nathan Bedford Forrest.* New York: Alfred A. Knopf, 1993.

Johns, John E. *Florida during the Civil War.* Gainesville, Fla.: University of Florida Press, 1963.

Johnson, John. *The Defense of Charleston Harbor.* Charleston: Walker Evans & Cogswell Co., 1890.

Josephy, Alvin M., Jr. *The Civil War in the American West.* New York: Alfred A. Knopf, 1992.

Kennett, Lee. *Marching through Georgia.* New York: HarperCollins Publishers, 1995.

Kerby, Robert L. *Kirby Smith's Confederacy.* New York: Columbia University Press, 1972.

King, Spencer B. *Darien: The Death and Rebirth of a Southern Town.* Macon, Ga.: Mercer University Press, 1981.

Levine, Lawrence W. *Black Culture and Black Consciousness.* New York: Oxford University Press, 1977.

Litwack, Leon F. *Been in the Storm So Long: The Aftermath of Slavery.* New York: Alfred A. Knopf, 1979.

McConnell, Stuart. *Glorious Contentment: The Grand Army of the Republic, 1865–1900.* Chapel Hill: University of North Carolina Press, 1992.

McGill, Samuel D. *Narrative of Reminiscences of Williamsburg County.* Columbia, S.C.: The Bryan Printing Co., 1897.

MacGregor, Morris J., and Bernard C. Nalty, eds. *Blacks in the United States Armed Forces: Basic Documents.* Wilmington, Del.: Scholarly Resources, 1977.

McPherson, James M. *The Negro's Civil War.* New York: Vintage Books, 1965.

McRae, Norman. *Negroes in Michigan during the Civil War.* Lansing, Mich.: Civil War Centennial Observance Commission, 1966.

Maher, Jane. *Biography of Broken Fortunes.* New York: Archon Books, 1986.

Malcaluso, Gregory J. *The Fort Pillow Massacre: The Reason Why.* New York: Vantage Press, 1989.

Martin, Richard A. and Daniel L. Schafer. *Jacksonville's Ordeal by Fire: A Civil War History.* Jacksonville, Fla.: Florida Publishing Company, 1984.

Marvel, William. *The Battles for Saltville: Southwest Virginia in the Civil War.* Lynchburg, Va.: H. E. Howard Inc., 1992.

Maslowski, Peter. *Treason Must Be Made Odious.* Millwood, N.Y.: KTO Press, 1978.

Matson, Dan. "The Colored Man in the Civil War." In *War Sketches and Incidents, as Related by the Companions of the Iowa Commandery Military Order of the Loyal Legion of the United States.* Des Moines: n.p., 1898.

Matter, William D. *If It Takes All Summer: The Battle of Spotsylvania.* Chapel Hill: University of North Carolina Press, 1988.

Mellichamp, Robert E. *Sketch of James Island.* N.p., 1888.

Miller, Lindley. "Marching Song of the First Arkansas." In *The Negro in American History.* Vol. 2, *A Taste of Freedom, 1854–1927.* New York: Encyclopedia Britannica Education Corporation, 1969.

Mitchell, Joseph B. *The Badge of Gallantry.* New York: The Macmillan Company, 1968.

Monaghan, Jay. *Civil War on the Western Border.* New York: Bonanza Books, 1955.

The Monument to Colonel Robert Gould Shaw, 1865–1897. Boston: Houghton Mifflin and Co., 1897.

Nulty, William H. *Confederate Florida: The Road to Olustee.* Tuscaloosa, Ala.: University of Alabama Press, 1990.

Nye, Wilbur S. *Here Come the Rebels!* Baton Rouge: Louisiana University Press, 1965.

O'Connor, Richard. *Sheridan the Inevitable.* Indianapolis: Bobbs-Merrill Company Inc., 1953.

Page, Dave. *Ships versus Shore.* Nashville: Rutledge Hill Press, 1994.

Parrish, T. Michael. *Richard Taylor: Soldier Prince of Dixie.* Chapel Hill: University of North Carolina Press, 1992.

Parton, James. *General Butler in New Orleans.* New York: Mason Brothers, 1864.

Pearson, Henry G. *The Life of John A. Andrew.* Boston: Houghton Mifflin and Co., 1904.

Quarles, Benjamin. *The Negro in the Civil War*. Boston: Little, Brown and Company, 1953.

———. *Frederick Douglass*. New York: Atheneum, 1969.

Rabinowitz, Howard H., ed. *Southern Black Leaders of the Reconstruction Era*. Chicago: University of Illinois Press, 1982.

Ripley, C. Peter. *Slaves and Freedmen in Civil War Louisiana*. Baton Rouge: Louisiana State University Press, 1976.

Rister, Carl C. *Border Command: General Phil Sheridan in the West*. Norman, Okla.: University of Oklahoma Press, 1944.

Roberts, O. M. *Confederate Military History: Texas*. Atlanta: Confederate Publishing Company, 1899.

Robertson, William G. *Back Door to Richmond: The Bermuda Hundred Campaign, April–June 1864*. Newark, Del.: University of Delaware Press, 1987.

Rollin, Frank A. *Life and Public Services of Martin B. Delany*. Boston: Lee and Shepard, 1868.

Rollins, Richard, ed. *Black Southerners in Gray*. Murfreesboro, Tenn.: Southern Heritage Press, 1994.

Rose, Willie Lee Nichols. *Rehearsal for Reconstruction*. Indianapolis: Bobbs-Merrill, 1964.

Royster, Charles. *The Destructive War*. New York: Alfred A. Knopf, 1991.

Rugoff, Milton. *The Beechers*. New York: Harper & Row, 1981.

Schiller, Herbert M. *The Bermuda Hundred Campaign*. Dayton, Ohio: Morningside House, Inc., 1988.

Schmidt, Lewis G. *The Civil War in Florida*. 4 vols. Allentown, Pa.: Lewis G. Schmidt, 1989.

Schoonover, Thomas. *Dollars over Dominion*. Baton Rouge: Louisiana State University Press, 1978.

———, ed. *A Mexican View of America in the 1860s*. Rutherford, N.J.: Fairleigh Dickinson University Press, 1979.

Schouler, William. *A History of Massachusetts in the Civil War*. Boston: E. P. Dutton & Company, 1868.

Simpson, Brooks D., LeRoy P. Graf, and John Muldowny. *Advice after Appomattox: Letters to Andrew Johnson, 1865–1866*. Knoxville: University of Tennessee Press, 1987.

Smith, Steven D., and James B. Legg. *"The Best Ever Occupied . . .": Archaeological Investigations of a Civil War Encampment on Folly Island, South Carolina*. Research Manuscript Series 209. Columbia, S.C.: South Carolina Institute of Archaeology and Anthropology, 1989.

———. *Whom We Would Never More See: History and Archaeology Recover the Lives and Deaths of African American Civil War Soldiers on Folly Island, South Carolina*. Columbia, S.C.: South Carolina Department of Archives & History, 1993.

———. *"Wild's African Brigade in the Siege of Charleston, South Carolina: History and Archaeology."* Unpublished ms., 1994.

Sommers, Richard J. *Richmond Redeemed*. New York: Doubleday & Company, Inc., 1981.

Spencer, Edward. *"Confederate Negro Enlistments."* In *The Annals of the War Written by Leading Participants North and South*. Washington: The Times Publishing Company, 1878.

511

Stampp, Kenneth M. *The Peculiar Institution.* New York: Vintage Books, 1956.

Stanley, J. Randall. *History of Jackson County.* Published under the Auspices of the Jackson County Historical Society, n.d.

Starr, Stephen Z. *The Union Cavalry in the Civil War: The War in the West.* Baton Rouge: Louisiana State University Press, 1985.

Stearns, Frank P. *Cambridge Sketches.* Philadelphia: J. B. Lippincott Company, 1905.

Stockdale, Paul H. *The Death of an Army: The Battle of Nashville and Hood's Retreat.* Murfreesboro, Tenn.: Southern Heritage Press, 1992.

Swinton, William. *Campaigns of the Army of the Potomac.* New York: Charles Scribner's Sons, 1882.

Sword, Wiley. *Embrace an Angry Wind.* New York: HarperCollins Publishers, 1992.

Taylor, Frank H. *Philadelphia in the Civil War 1861–1865.* Philadelphia: n.p., 1913.

Time-Life Books. *The Civil War: Spies, Scouts and Raiders.* Alexandria, Va.: Time-Life Books, 1985.

Trudeau, Noah Andre. *Bloody Roads South.* Boston: Little, Brown and Co., 1989.

———. *The Last Citadel.* Boston: Little, Brown and Co., 1991.

———. *Out of the Storm.* Boston: Little, Brown and Co., 1994.

The Union Army: A History of Military Affairs in the Loyal States 1861–65. Madison, Wisc.: Federal Publishing Company, 1908.

Valuska, David L. *The African American in the Union Navy: 1861–1865.* New York: Garland Publishing Inc., 1993.

Voegeli, V. Jacque. *Free But Not Equal: The Midwest and the Negro During the Civil War.* Chicago: University of Chicago Press, 1967.

Walker, Gary C. *The War in Southwest Virginia.* Roanoke, Va.: Gurtner Graphics & Printing Co., 1985.

Wesley, Charles H. *Ohio Negroes in the Civil War.* Columbus, Ohio: Ohio State University Press, 1962.

West, Richard S., Jr. *Lincoln's Scapegoat General.* Boston: Houghton Mifflin Company, 1965.

Westwood, Howard C. *Black Troops, White Commanders, and Freedmen During the Civil War.* Carbondale, Ill.: Southern Illinois University Press, 1992.

Wiley, Bell I. *Southern Negroes: 1861–1865.* New York: Rinehart & Company, 1938.

Williams, Edward F., ed. *Confederate Victories at Fort Pillow.* Memphis: Nathan Bedford Forrest Trail Committee, 1973.

Williams, George Washington. *A History of the Negro Troops in the War of the Rebellion, 1861–1865.* New York: Harper & Brothers, 1888.

Wills, Brian S. *A Battle from the Start.* New York: HarperCollins, 1992.

Wilson, Joseph T. *The Black Phalanx.* Hartford: American Publishing, 1890.

Winters, John D. *The Civil War in Louisiana.* Baton Rouge: Lousiana State University Press, 1963.

Wise, Stephen R. *Gate of Hell.* Columbia, S.C.: University of South Carolina Press, 1994.

Periodicals

Abbott, Richard H. "Massachusetts and the Recruitment of Southern Negroes, 1863–1865." *Civil War History* 14, no. 3 (September 1968): 197–210.

Aptheker, Herbert. "Negro Casualties in the Civil War." *Journal of Negro History* 32, no. 1 (January 1947): 10–80.

———. "The Negro in the Union Navy." *Journal of Negro History* 32, no. 2 (April 1947): 169–200.

Armstrong, Warren B. "Union Chaplains and the Education of the Freedmen." *Journal of Negro History* 52, no. 2 (April 1967): 104–115.

Atkinson, J. H. "The Action at Prairie De Ann." *Arkansas Historical Quarterly* 19, no. 1 (spring 1960): 36–50.

Axelrod, Stephen G. "Colonel Shaw in American Poetry." *American Quarterly* 24, no. 4 (October 1972): 523–537.

Bailey, Anne J. "A Texas Cavalry Raid: Reaction to Black Soldiers and Contrabands." *Civil War History* 35, no. 2 (June 1989): 138–152.

———. "Was There a Massacre at Poison Spring?" *Military History of the Southwest* 20, no. 2 (fall 1990): 157–168.

Ballard, Michael. "Plymouth North Carolina: A Good Time to Pray." *Civil War Times Illustrated* 25, no. 2 (April 1986): 16–25, 47.

Baltzell, George F. "The Battle of Olustee." *Florida Historical Quarterly* 9, no. 4 (April 1931): 199–223.

Bearss, Edwin C. "Asboth's Expedition up the Alabama and Florida Railroad." *Florida Historical Quarterly* 39, no. 2 (October 1960): 159–166.

———. "Marmaduke Attacks Pine Bluff." *Arkansas Historical Quarterly* 23, no. 4 (winter 1964): 291–313.

———. "General William Steele Fights to Hold On to Northwest Arkansas." *Arkansas Historical Quarterly* 25, no. 1 (spring 1966): 36–93.

———. "McArthur's May Expedition against the Mississippi Central Railroad." *Journal of Mississippi History* 28, no. 1 (February 1966): 1–14.

———. "The Civil War Comes to the Lafourche." *Louisiana Studies* 5, no. 2 (summer 1966): 97–155.

Belz, Herman. "The Freedman's Bureau Act of 1865 and the Principle of No Discrimination According to Color." *Civil War History* 21, no. 3 (September 1975): 197–217.

Bennett, B. Kevin. "The Jacksonville Mutiny." *Civil War History* 38, no. 1 (March 1992): 40–50.

Berfield, Karen. "Fair Treatment of Blacks in the Ranks: Julian Bryant, Martyr for Equality." *Civil War Times Illustrated* 22, no. 2 (April 1983): 36–41.

Bergeron, Arthur W., Jr. "Free Men of Color in Gray." *Civil War History* 32, no. 3 (September 1986): 247–255.

Berry, Mary F. "Negro Troops in Blue and Gray: The Louisiana Native Guards 1861–1863." *Louisiana History* 8, no. 2 (spring 1967): 165–190.

Bigelow, Martha M. "The Significance of Milliken's Bend in the Civil War." *Journal of Negro History* 45, no. 3 (July 1960): 156–163.

Binder, Frederick M. "Pennsylvania Negro Regiments in the Civil War." *Journal of Negro History* 37, no. 4 (October 1952): 383–417.

Blassingame, John W. "The Recruitment of Negro Troops in Maryland." *Maryland Historical Magazine* 58, no. 1 (March 1963): 20–29.

———. "Negro Chaplains in the Civil War." *Negro History Bulletin* 27, no. 1 (October 1963): 23–24.

————. "The Recruitment of Negro Troops in Missouri during the Civil War." *Missouri Historical Review* 58, no. 3 (April 1964): 326–338.

————. "The Union Army As an Educational Institution for Negroes, 1861–1865." *Journal of Negro Education* 34, no. 2 (spring 1965): 152–159.

————. "The Selection of Officers and Non-Commissioned Officers of Negro Troops in the Union Army, 1863–1865." *Negro History Bulletin* 30, no. 1 (January 1967): 8–11.

————. "The Recruitment of Colored Troops in Kentucky, Maryland, and Missouri, 1863–1865." *Historian* 29, no. 4 (August 1967): 533–545.

Blight, David W. "Frederick Douglass and the American Apocalypse." *Civil War History* 31, no. 4 (December 1985): 309–328.

Boyd, Mark F. "The Joint Operation of the Federal Army and Navy near St. Marks, Florida, March 1865." *Florida Historical Quarterly* 29, no. 2 (October 1950): 96–124.

————. "The Battle of Marianna." *Florida Historical Quarterly* 29, no. 4 (April 1951): 225–242.

Bragg, William H. "Victory at Honey Hill: 'A Mere Flicker of Light.'" *Civil War Times Illustrated* 22, no. 9 (January 1984): 12–19.

Brooksher, William R. "Betwixt Wind and Water." *Civil War Times Illustrated* 32, no. 5 (November/December 1993): 64–70.

Castel, Albert. "The Fort Pillow Massacre: A Fresh Examination of the Evidence." *Civil War History* 4, no. 1 (March 1958): 37–50.

————. "Civil War Kansas and the Negro." *Journal of Negro History* 51, no. 2 (April 1966): 125–138.

————. "Jim Lane of Kansas." *Civil War Times Illustrated* 12, no. 1 (April 1973): 23–28.

————. "Fort Pillow: Victory or Massacre?" *American History Illustrated* 9, no. 1 (April 1974): 4–11.

Cimprich, John, and Robert C. Mainfort, Jr. "Fort Pillow Revisited: New Evidence about an Old Controversy." *Civil War History* 28, no. 4 (December 1982): 293–306.

————. "Dr. Fitch's Report on the Fort Pillow Massacre." *Tennessee Historical Quarterly* 45, no. 1 (spring 1985): 27–39.

————. "The Fort Pillow Massacre: A Statistical Note." *Journal of American History* 76, no. 3 (December 1989): 830–837.

[*Confederate Veteran*]. For an extensive listing of articles published in this periodical, please see pages 519–522.

Cornish, Dudley T. "The Union Army as a School for Negroes." *Journal of Negro History* 37, no. 4 (October 1952): 368–382.

————. "Kansas Negro Regiments in the Civil War." *Kansas Historical Quarterly* 20 (May 1953): 417–429.

————. "To Be Recognized as Men." *Military Review* 58, no. 2 (February 1978): 40–55.

Coulter, E. Merton. "Robert Gould Shaw and the Burning of Darien, Georgia." *Civil War History* 5, no. 4 (December 1959): 363–373.

Cowdrey, Albert E. "Slave into Soldier: The Enlistment by the North of Runaway Slaves." *History Today* 20, no. 10 (October 1970): 704–715.

Dabney, Thomas Ewing. "The Butler Regime in Louisiana." *Louisiana Historical Quarterly* 27, no. 2 (April 1944): 487–526.

Davies, Wallace E. "The Problem of Race Segregation in the Grand Army of the Republic." *Journal of Southern History* 13, no. 3 (August 1947): 354–372.

Davis, William C. "The Massacre at Saltville." *Civil War Times Illustrated* 9, no. 10 (February 1971): 4–48.

Dillon, Rodney E. "The Battle of Fort Myers." *Tampa Bay History,* 27–36.

Dodge, Granville M. "The Black Soldier—A Letter from a Friend." *The Crisis—A Record of the Darker Races,* June 1911, 77.

Dyer, Brainerd. "The Treatment of Colored Union Troops by the Confederates, 1861–1865." *Journal of Negro History* 20, no. 3 (July 1935): 273–286.

Everett, Donald E. "Ben Butler and the Louisiana Native Guards, 1861–1862." *Journal of Southern History* 24, no. 2 (May 1958): 202–217.

Ferry, Richard J. "The Battle of Olustee (or Ocean Pond), February 20, 1864." *Blue & Gray Magazine* 3, no. 4 (March 1986): 6–16, 44–61.

Fisher, Mike. "The First Kansas Colored—Massacre at Poison Spring." *Kansas History* 2, no. 2 (summer 1979): 121–128.

———. "Remember Poison Spring." *Missouri Historical Review* 74, no. 3 (April 1980): 323–342.

Fleetwood, Christian A. " . . . To Benefit My Race." *Civil War Times Illustrated* 16, no. 4 (July 1977): 18–19.

Flint, Allen. "Black Responses to Colonel Shaw." *Phylon* 45, no. 3 (fall 1984): 210–219.

Florance, John E. "Morris Island, Victory or Blunder?" *South Carolina Historical Magazine* 55, no. 5 (July 1954): 143–152.

Fonvielle, Chris. "The Last Rays of Departing Hope: The Fall of Wilmington." *Blue & Gray Magazine* 12, no. 2 (December 1994): 10–21, 48–64.

Ford, R. W., ed. "I Fear . . . We Must Go Up." *Civil War Times Illustrated* 25, no. 10 (February 1987): 30–39.

Futch, Ovid L. "Salmon P. Chase and Civil War Politics in Florida." *Florida Historical Quarterly* 32, no. 3 (January 1954): 163–188.

Gauss, John. "Give the Blacks Texas." *Civil War Times Illustrated* 29, no. 2 (May/June 1990): 54–56.

Goldy, James. "The Swamp Angel." *Civil War Times Illustrated* 28, no. 2 (April 1989): 22–27.

Hancock, Marvin J. "The Second Battle of Cabin Creek." *Chronicles of Oklahoma* 39, no. 4 (winter 1961–62): 414–426.

Hansen, Chadwick. "The 54th Massachusetts Volunteer Black Infantry as a Subject for American Artists." *Massachusetts Review* 16 (autumn 1975): 745–759.

Harrington, Fred H. "The Fort Jackson Mutiny." *Journal of Negro History* 27, no. 4 (June 1942): 420–431.

Harrison, Noel G. "A Moment in Black History: May 15, 1864." *Town Hall Cryer* 1, no. 2 (summer 1981).

Hay, Thomas R. "The South and the Arming of the Slaves." *Mississippi Valley Historical Review* 6, no. 1 (1919): 34–73.

Hayne, Paul H. "The Defense of Fort Wagner." *Southern Bivouac,* n.s. 1 (March 1886): 599–608.

Hicken, Victor. "The Record of Illinois' Negro Soldiers in the Civil War." *Illinois State Historical Society Journal* 56, no. 3 (autumn 1963): 529–551.

Hoar, Jay S. "Black Glory: Our Afro-American Civil War Old Soldiery." *Gettysburg Magazine* 2 (January 1990): 125–155.

Hoefer, Jean M. "The Woman 'Moses'" [Harriet Tubman]. *Civil War Times Illustrated* 26, no. 10 (February 1988): 36–41.

Hollandsworth, James G., Jr. "The Execution of White Officers from Black Units by Confederate Forces during the Civil War." *Louisiana History* 35, no. 4 (fall 1994): 475–489.

Horowitz, Murray M. "Ben Butler and the Negro: 'Miracles Are Occurring.'" *Louisiana History* 17, no. 2 (spring 1976): 159–186.

Hubbell, John T. "Abraham Lincoln and the Recruitment of Black Soldiers." *Papers of the Abraham Lincoln Association* 2 (1980): 6–21.

Hudson, Leonne M. "A Confederate Victory at Grahamville: Fighting at Honey Hill." *South Carolina Historical Magazine* 94, no. 1 (January 1993): 19–33.

Johnson, Howard Palmer. "New Orleans under General Butler." *Louisiana Historical Quarterly* 24, no. 2 (April 1941): 434–536.

Johnson, Mary E., ed. "Letters from a Civil War Chaplain." *Journal of Presbyterian History* 46, no. 3 (September 1968): 219–235.

Jones, Howard J., ed. "Letters in Protest of Race Prejudice in the Army During the American Civil War." *Journal of Negro History* 61 (1976): 97–98.

Jordan, John L. "Was There a Massacre at Fort Pillow?" *Tennessee Historical Quarterly* 4, no. 2 (June 1947): 99–133.

Jordan, Weymouth T., and Gerald W. Thomas. "Massacre at Plymouth: April 20, 1864." *North Carolina Historical Review* 72, no. 2 (April 1995): 125–197.

Joshi, Manoj K., and Joseph P. Reidy. "'To Come Forward and Aid in Putting Down This Unholy Rebellion': The Officers of Louisiana's Free Black Native Guard during the Civil War Era." *Southern Studies* 21, no. 3 (fall 1982): 326–342.

Longacre, Edward G. "Black Troops in the Army of the James, 1863–1865." *Military Affairs* 45, no. 1 (February 1981): 1–8.

Lovett, Bobby L. "The Negro's Civil War in Tennessee, 1861–1865." *Journal of Negro History* 41, no. 1 (January 1976): 36–50.

———. "The West Tennessee Colored Troops in Civil War Combat." *West Tennessee Society Papers* 34 (October 1980): 53–70.

Luckett, William W. "Bedford Forrest in the Battle of Brice's Crossroads." *Tennessee Historical Quarterly* 15, no. 2 (June 1956): 99–110.

McConnell, Roland C., ed. "Concerning the Procurement of Negro Troops in the South during the Civil War." *Journal of Negro History* 35, no. 3 (July 1950): 315–319.

McDonald, Harold L. "The Battle of Jenkins' Ferry." *Arkansas Historical Quarterly* 7, no. 1 (1948): 57–67.

McGhee, C. Stuart. "Military Origins of the New South: The Army of the Cumberland and Chattanooga's Freedmen." *Civil War History* 34, no. 4 (December 1988): 323–343.

Maness, Lonnie E. "The Fort Pillow Massacre: Fact or Fiction." *Tennessee Historical Quarterly* 45, no. 4 (winter 1986): 287–315.

Marcus, Lois G. "The Shaw Memorial by Augustus Saint-Gaudens." *Winterthur Portfolio,* 1970, 1–23.

Marvel, William. "The Battle of Saltville: Massacre or Myth?" *Blue & Gray Magazine* 8, no. 6 (August 1991): 10–19, 46–60.

Miller, Robert R. "Arms across the Border: United States Aid to Juarez During the French Intervention in Mexico." *Transaction of the American Philosophical Society* 63, no. 6 (December 1973): 5–61.

Mills, Gary B. "Patriotism Frustrated: The Native Guards of Confederate Nachitoches." *Louisiana History* 18, no. 4 (fall 1977): 437–451.

Murray, Donald M., and Robert M. Rodney. "Colonel Julian E. Bryant: Champion of the Negro Soldier." *Illinois State Historical Society Journal* 51, no. 2 (summer 1963): 257–281.

Nelson, Bernard H. "Confederate Slave Impressment Legislation, 1861–65." *Journal of Negro History* 31, no. 4 (October 1946): 392–410.

Perkins, Frances Beecher. "Two Years with a Colored Regiment." *New England Magazine,* n.s. 17 (January 1898): 533–543.

Popchock, Barry. "A Shower of Stars at New Market Heights." *Civil War Magazine* 46 (August 1994): 30–39.

Preisser, Thomas M. "The Virginia Decision to Use Negro Soldiers in the Civil War, 1864–1865." *Virginia Magazine of History and Biography* 83, no. 1 (January 1975): 98–113.

Primm, James N. "The G.A.R. in Missouri." *Journal of Southern History* 20, no. 3 (August 1954): 356–375.

Proctor, Samuel. "Jacksonville during the Civil War." *Florida Historical Quarterly* 41, no. 4 (April 1963): 343–355.

Redkey, Edwin S. "Black Chaplains in the Union Army." *Civil War History* 33, no. 4 (December 1987): 331–350.

Reid, Richard. "General Edward A. Wild and Civil War Discrimination." *Historical Journal of Massachusetts* 13, no. 1 (January 1985): 14–29.

———. "Raising the African Brigade: Early Black Recruitment in Civil War North Carolina." *North Carolina Historical Review* 70, no. 3 (July 1993): 266–297.

Reid, William G. "Confederate Opponents of Arming the Slaves." *Journal of Mississippi History* 22, no. 4 (October 1960): 249–270.

Richards, Ira D. "The Battle of Poison Spring." *Arkansas Historical Quarterly* 18 (1959): 338–349.

———. "The Engagement at Marks' Mills." *Arkansas Historical Quarterly* 19, no. 1 (spring 1960): 51–60.

———. "The Battle of Jenkins' Ferry." *Arkansas Historical Quarterly* 20, no. 1 (spring 1961): 3–16.

Richter, William L. "'It Is Best to Go In Strong-Handed': Army Occupation of Texas, 1865–1866." *Arizona & the West* 27, no. 2 (summer 1985): 113–142.

———. "'General Phil Sheridan, the Historians, and Reconstruction." *Civil War History* 33, no. 2 (June 1987): 131–154.

Ritter, E. Jay. "Congressional Medal of Honor Winners." *Negro History Bulletin* 26, no. 4 (January 1963): 135–136.

Robbins, Gerald. "The Recruiting and Arming of Negroes in the South Carolina Sea Islands—1862–1865." *Negro History Bulletin* 28, no. 7 (April 1965): 150–167.

Rogge, Robert E. "Devil at the Crossroads." *America's Civil War* 3, no. 3 (September 1990): 42–49.

Roy, Joseph E. "Our Indebtedness to the Negroes for Their Conduct during the War." *New Englander and Yale Review* 51 (November 1889): 353–364.

Ruby, Barbara C. "General Patrick Cleburne's Proposal to Arm Southern Slaves." *Arkansas Historical Quarterly* 30, no. 3 (autumn 1971): 125–140.

Rutherford, Phillip. "Revolt in the Corps d'Afrique." *Civil War Times Illustrated* 24, no. 2 (April 1985): 20–23.

Ryan, James G. "The Memphis Riots of 1866: Terror in a Black Community during Reconstruction." *Journal of Negro History* 62, no. 3 (July 1977): 243–257.

Schafer, Daniel L. "Freedom Was as Close as the River: The Blacks of Northeast Florida and the Civil War." *Civil War Times in St. Augustine,* 1988, 91–116.

Scharnhorst, Gary. "From Soldier to Saint: Robert Gould Shaw and the Rhetoric of Racial Justice." *Civil War History* 34, no. 4 (December 1988): 308–322.

Sealover, Mary S. "Great Grandfather Fought from the Courthouse Steps." *The United Daughters of the Confederacy Magazine* 49, no. 16 (January 1986): 34.

Sellers, John R. "The Union Soldier Meets the Freedman." *Maine Historical Society Quarterly* 33, no. 2 (fall 1993): 88–105.

Seraile, William. "The Struggle to Raise Black Regiments in New York State, 1861–1864." *New-York Historical Society Quarterly* 58, no. 3 (July 1974): 215–233.

Shannon, Fred A. "The Federal Government and the Negro Soldier, 1861–1865." *Journal of Negro History* 11, no. 3 (July 1926): 563–583.

Simpson, Brooks D. "'The Doom of Slavery': Ulysses S. Grant, War Aims, and Emancipation, 1861–1863." *Civil War History* 36, no. 1 (March 1990): 36–56.

Smith, George W. "Carpetbag Imperialism in Florida, 1862–1868." *Florida Historical Quarterly* 27, no. 2 (October 1948): 99–130; 27, no. 3 (January 1949): 260–291.

Smith, John David. "The Recruitment of Negro Soldiers in Kentucky, 1863–1865." *Register of the Kentucky Historical Society* 72, no. 4 (October 1974): 364–390.

Solomon, Irvin D. "Southern Extremities: The Significance of Fort Myers in the Civil War." *Florida Historical Quarterly* 72, no. 2 (October 1993): 129–152.

Sommers, Richard J. "The Dutch Gap Affair: Military Atrocities and the Rights of Negro Soldiers." *Civil War History* 21, no. 1 (March 1975): 51–64.

[*Southern Historical Society Papers*]. For a listing of articles published in this periodical, please see page 522.

Starr, Michael L. "A Pack of Indians and Cowards." *Civil War Times Illustrated* 19, no. 3 (June 1980): 39–46.

Stephenson, N. W. "The Question of Arming the Slaves." *American Historical Review* 18, no. 2 (January 1913): 295–308.

Suderow, Bryce, ed. "The Suffolk Slaughter: 'We Did Not Take Any Prisoners.'" *Civil War Times Illustrated* 23, no. 3 (May 1984): 36–39.

Sword, Wiley. "The Desperation of the Hour." *Blue & Gray Magazine* 11, no. 2 (December 1993): 12–23, 38–58.

Toppin, Edgar A. "Humbly They Served: The Black Brigade in the Defense of Cincinnati." *Journal of Negro History* 48, no. 2 (April 1963): 75–97.

Tucker, Phillip T. "The First Missouri Confederate Brigade's Last Stand at Fort Blakeley on Mobile Bay." *Alabama Review* 42, no. 4 (October 1989): 270–291.

Urwin, Gregory J. W. "I Want You to Prove Yourselves Men." *Civil War Times Illustrated* 28, no. 6 (November/December 1989): 42–51.

Volpe, Vernon L. "Squirrel Hunting for the Union: The Defense of Cincinnati in 1862." *Civil War History* 33, no. 3 (September 1987): 242–255.

Weinert, Richard P. "Olustee—One-Sided Southern Victory." *Civil War Times Illustrated* 1, no. 3 (June 1962): 31–33.

———. "Dickison—the Swamp Fox of Florida." *Civil War Times Illustrated* 5, no. 8 (December 1966): 4–11, 48–50.

Wert, Jeffrey D. "Camp William Penn and the Black Soldier." *Pennsylvania History* 46, no. 4 (October 1979): 335–346.

Wesley, Charles H. "The Employment of Negroes as Soldiers in the Confederate Army." *Journal of Negro History* 4, no. 3 (July 1919): 239–253.

Westwood, Howard C. "Captive Black Union Soldiers in Charleston—What to Do?" *Civil War History* 28, no. 1 (March 1982): 28–44.

Whitfield, Stephen J. "Sacred in History and in Art—The Shaw Memorial." *New England Quarterly* 60, no. 1 (March 1987): 3–27.

Whyte, James H. "Maryland's Negro Regiments—How, Where They Served." *Civil War Times Illustrated* 1, no. 4 (July 1962): 41–43.

Wiley, Bell I. "Billy Yank and the Black Folk." *Journal of Negro History* 36, no. 1 (January 1951): 35–52.

Williams, Harry. "Benjamin Wade and the Atrocity Propaganda of the Civil War." *Ohio State Archeological and Historial Quarterly* 48, no. 1 (January 1939): 33–43.

Williams, Walter. "Again in Chains: Black Soldiers Suffering in Captivity." *Civil War Times Illustrated* 20, no. 2 (May 1981): 36–43.

Articles Published in the Confederate Veteran

Abercrombie, John J. "Battle of Honey Hill." 22, no. 10 (October 1914): 452–456.

["A Comrade"]. "Two of the Six Hundred." 7, no. 9 (September 1899): 415.

Agnew, Samuel A. "Battle of Tishomingo Creek." 8, no. 9 (September 1900): 401–403.

Akin, Mrs. M. F. "Faithful Slave 'Col. Robert.'" 11, no. 10 (October 1903): 470.

"Amos Rucker, the Negro Veteran." 17, no. 10 (October 1909): 496.

Anderson, Charles W. "The True Story of Fort Pillow." 3, no. 11 (November 1895): 322–326.

———. "Col. Wiley M. Reed." 5, no. 3 (March 1897): 101–102.

Ashe, S. A. "Life at Fort Wagner." 35, no. 7 (July 1927): 254–256.

Barnwell, Robert W. "Three Vital Episodes in the Attacks on Charleston." 38, no. 12 (December 1930): 466–469.

Bradwell, I. G. "The Irresponsible Race." 31, no. 4 (April 1923): 132–134.

Breckinridge, G. W. "Story of a Boy Captain." 13, no. 9 (September 1905): 415–416.

Brewer, Theo. F. "Storming of Fort Pillow." 33, no. 12 (December 1925): 459.

Brown, J. J. "The Attack on Fort Johnson." 23, no. 9 (September 1915): 413.

Brown, W. D. "Guntown or Brice's X Roads Fight." 9, no. 12 (December 1901): 556.

Cabell, William L. "Battle of Marks Mills, Ark." 16, no. 5 (May 1908): 233.

Caldwell, J. F. J. "Pensions for Faithful Negroes." 30, no. 2 (February 1922): 77.

Cameron, William L. "The Battles Opposite Mobile." 23, no. 7 (July 1915): 305–308.

Campbell, Mrs. A. A. "The Immortal Six Hundred." 30, no. 6 (July 1922): 216.

Carpenter, N. M. "Flag of the Thirteenth U.S. Infantry." 13, no. 1 (January 1905): 16.

Chambers, H. A. "The Bloody Crater." 31, no. 5 (May 1923): 174–177.

Chapman, Mrs. Fanny B. "The Battle at Marianna, Fla." 19, no. 10 (October 1911): 483–484.

Clark, George. "Alabamians in the Crater Battle." 3, no. 3 (March 1895): 68.

Coleman, Samuel. "Master and His Faithful Slave." 20, no. 9 (September 1912): 410.

"The Confederate Monument at Marianna, Fla." 30, no. 1 (January 1922): 5.

Cook, Henry H. "The Story of the Six Hundred." 5, no. 3 (March 1897): 116–118; 5, no. 4 (April 1897): 148–150; 5, no. 5 (May 1897): 219–220; 6, no. 3 (March 1898): 118–120.

Cullins, G. T. "Who Captured the Negro Flag?" 13, no. 3 (March 1905): 126.

Day, W. A. "Battle of the Crater." 11, no. 8 (August 1903): 355–356.

Dinkins, James. "The Battle of Brice's Crossroads." 33, no. 10 (October 1925): 380–382.

———. "The Capture of Fort Pillow." 33, no. 12 (December 1925): 460–462.

———. "My Old Black Mammy." 34, no. 1 (January 1926): 20–22.

———. "How Forrest Saved the Army of Tennessee." 35, no. 2 (February 1927): 54–56.

Doswell, R. M. "Union Attack on Confederate Negroes." 23, no. 9 (September 1915): 404.

Douglas, C. M. "A Notable Colored Veteran." 2, no. 8 (August 1894): 233.

Draper, Joseph. "Who Fought in the Battle of the Crater?" 8, no. 11 (November 1900): 502.

Etheredge, William H. "Another Story of the Crater Battle." 15, no. 4 (April 1907): 167.

Featherston, John C. "The Battle of the 'Crater' as I Saw It." 14, no. 1 (January 1906): 23; 34, no. 8 (August 1926): 296–298.

———. "Incidents of the Battle of the Crater." 14, no. 3 (March 1906): 107–108.

Flanigan, W. A. "That Fight at Fort Gilmer." 13, no. 3 (March 1905): 123.

"Florida in the War." 22, no. 4 (April 1914): 153–154.

Floyd, N. J. "Concerning Battle of the Crater." 16, no. 4 (April 1908): 159.

Fulkerson, Abram. "Burnside's Controversy with a Prisoner." 1, no. 10 (October 1893): 306.

Garland, W. H. "The Battle of Dingles's Mill, Fla. [S.C.]." 24, no. 12 (December 1916): 549.

Gass, W. T. "A Black Skin, but White Soul." 12, no. 2 (February 1904): 68.

Goodrich, B. G. "Battle of Millican's Bend." 8, no. 2 (February 1900): 67.

Goodwin, G. C. "The Last Battle of the War." 18, no. 7 (July 1910): 324.

Granberry, J. A. H. "That Fort Gilmer Fight." 13, no. 9 (September 1905): 413.

Green, Mrs. T. M. "Pensioning the Old Slaves." 11, no. 3 (March 1903): 108–109.

Hanks, C. J. "Steele's Escape at Jenkins's Ferry." 25, no. 2 (February 1917): 79.

Harley, James A. "The Battle of Olustee." 22, no. 10 (October 1914): 456–457.

Harris, Judge. "Capture of Entire Camp." 11, no. 9 (September 1903): 405.

Harrison, George P. "The Battle of Olustee." 24, no. 8 (August 1916): 344–347.

Heriot, Robert. "Fighting in South Carolina." 30, no. 11 (November 1922): 415.

Hinton, E. H. "The Negro and the South." 15, no. 8 (August 1907): 367–369.

Hord, Henry E. "Brice's X Roads from a Private's View." 12, no. 11 (November 1904): 529–530.

Jones, A. C. "Texas and Arkansas at Fort Harrison." 25, no. 1 (January 1917): 24–25.

Kappa, Omikron. "Something of Slavery as It Existed." 1, no. 6 (June 1893): 171.

Lee, Stephen D. "From Palmetto, Ga., to Defeat at Nashville." 16, no. 6 (June 1908): 257–259.

"Limit to Negro Troops." 13, no. 1 (January 1905): 10.

Lott, Jess B. "Two Boys of the Fifth Texas Regiment." 13, no. 9 (September 1905): 416–417.

McLellan, Alden. "Vivid Reminiscences of War Times." 14, no. 6 (July 1906): 264–266.

McRae, Walter G. "Confederate Prisoners at Morris Island." 29, no. 5 (June 1921): 178–179.

Martin, Charles B. "Jackson's Brigade in Battle of Nashville." 17, no. 1 (January 1909): 11–13.

Martin, Judge. "The Assault upon Fort Gilmer." 13, no. 6 (June 1905): 269–270.

"Massacre of Negroes before Nashville." 9, no. 1 (January 1901): 30–31.

Maxwell, James R. "Lumsden's Battery at Battle of Nashville." 12, no. 10 (October 1904): 484–485.

Moore, James B. "The Attack of Fort Harrison." 13, no. 9 (September 1905): 418–420.

Mosley, T. M. "The Eighth Mississippi Cavalry at Brice's Crossroads." 33, no. 12 (December 1925): 462–463.

Mudd, Joseph A. "The Confederate Negro." 23, no. 9 (September 1915): 411.

Oltrogge, Estelle T. "Battle of Natural Bridge, Florida." 17, no. 1 (January 1909): 21.

Palmer, P. G. "Defeat of Negro Uprising." 26, no. 12 (December 1918): 525.

Perry, H. H. "Assault on Fort Gilmer." 13, no. 9 (September 1905): 413–414.

"Problem of the Negroes." 15, no. 1 (January 1907): 8.

Rastall, John E. "Union Soldier Slave Owners." 7, no. 9 (September 1899): 408.

R. H. A. "Our Faithful Slaves of Old." 9, no. 1 (January 1901): 55–56.

Rice, J. G. "The Battle of Olustee." 22, no. 6 (June 1914): 244–245.

Roberts, Frank S. "Spring Hill–Franklin–Nashville, 1864." 27, no. 2 (February 1919): 58–60.

Robinson, W. P. "Artillery in Battle of the Crater." 19, no. 4 (April 1911): 164–166.

Roche, F. T. "Were Negroes in Our Earlier Wars?" 18, no. 2 (February 1910): 62.

Rogers, George T. "The Crater Battle, 30th July, 1864." 3, no. 1 (January 1895): 12–14.

Sanders, Robert W. "Efforts to Capture Charleston, S.C., and Evacuation of the City." 33, no. 4 (April 1925): 142–143.

Singletary, Don. "The Battle at Brice's Crossroads." 34, no. 8 (August 1926): 293–294.

Smith, Ed. W. "Douglas's Battery in Battle of Nashville." 12, no. 11 (November 1904): 531.

Stephens, A. A. "Siege of Port Hudson." 12, no. 8 (August 1904): 390.

Stewart, William H. "Carnage at 'The Crater,' near Petersburg." 1, no. 2 (February 1893): 41–42.

Stiles, John C. "Confederate States Negro Troops." 23, no. 6 (June 1915): 246–247.

———. "The Devotion of the Slave." 24, no. 2 (January 1916): 52.

———. "The Why of Olustee." 35, no. 4 (April 1927): 130.

Tarrant, E. W. "Siege and Capture of Fort Blakely." 23, no. 10 (October 1915): 457–458.

———. "After the Fall of Fort Blakely." 25, no. 4 (April 1917): 152.

Thrash, A. B. "Vivid Reminiscence of the Crater." 14, no. 11 (November 1906): 508–509.

"Tributes to Faithful Slaves." 8, no. 9 (September 1900): 399.

Tunnell, J. T. "Ector's Brigade in Battle of Nashville." 12, no. 7 (July 1904): 348–353.

Twiggs, H. D. D. "Perilous Adventure at Battery Wagner." 12, no. 3 (March 1904): 104–106.

Vance, P. M. "Incidents of the Crater Battle." 14, no. 4 (April 1906): 178.

White, Joseph F. "Social Conditions in the South During the War between the States." 30, no. 5 (May 1922): 181–184.

Wilson, R. S. "The Battle of Jenkins's Ferry." 18, no. 10 (October 1910): 468.

Wilder, Burt G. "Queries about Rivers Causeway, S.C." 21, no. 12 (December 1913): 590.

Winder, J. R. "Judge Martin's Report Approved." 13, no. 9 (September 1905): 417.

Winston, W. E. "Capturing the Negro Flag." 13, no. 6 (June 1905): 253.

Articles Published in the Southern Historical Society Papers

Baldwin, W. T. "In a Federal Prison." 29 (1901): 229–239.

Baylor, George. "The Army Negro." 31 (1903): 365–369.

Bernard, George S. "The Battle of the Crater." 18 (1890): 3–38.

———. "Great Battle of the Crater." 28 (1900): 204–221.

Buck, Irving A. "A Confederate Plan for Arming the Slaves." 29 (1901): 173–174.

———. "Negroes in Our Army." 31 (1903): 215–228.

Coit, J. C. "The Battle of the Crater, July 30, 1864: Letter from Major J. C. Coit." 10, no. 3 (March 1882): 123–130.

Conyer, Luther. "Last Battle of the War." 24 (1896): 309–315.

Courtenay, William A. "Charles Colcock Jones." 26 (1898): 32–39.

———. "Fragments of War History Relating to the Coast Defense of South Carolina, 1861–'65 and the Hasty Preparations for the Battle of Honey Hill, November 30, 1864." 26 (1898): 62–87.

———. "Heroes of Honey Hill." 26 (1898): 232–241.

Dinkins, James. "The Negroes as Slaves." 35 (1907): 60–68.

Edgington, T. B. "The Race Problem in the South—Was the Fifteenth Amendment a Mistake?" 17 (1889): 21–32.

Etheredge, William H. "Another Story of the Crater Battle." 37 (1909): 203–207.

Featherston, John C. "Graphic Account of Battle of Crater." 33 (1905): 358–374.

———. "Brilliant Page in History of War," 36 (1908): 161–173.

"Field of Blood Was the Crater." 33 (1905): 351–357.

Fitch, C. "Capture of Fort Pillow—Vindication of General Chalmers by a Federal Officer." 7, no. 9 (September 1879): 439–441.

"Fortification and Siege of Port Hudson." 14 (1886): 305–348.

Fulkerson, Abram. "The Prison Experience of a Confederate Soldier." 22 (1894): 127–146.

Johnson, Charles. "Attack on Fort Gilmer, September 29th, 1864." 1, no. 6 (June 1876): 438–442.

Jones, Charles C. "The Battle of Honey Hill." 13 (1885): 355–367.

"A List of Confederate Officers, Prisoners, Who Were Held by Federal Authority on Morris Island, S.C., under Confederate Fire from September 7th to October 21st, 1864." 17 (1889): 34–46.

McMaster, F. W. "The Battle of the Crater, July 30, 1864: Letter from Colonel McMaster." 10, no. 3 (March 1882): 119–123.

Olmstead, Charles H. "Reminiscences of Service in Charleston Harbor in 1863." 11, nos. 2–3 and 4–5 (February–March and April–May 1883): 118–125, 158–171.

Rhett, Claudine. "Morris Island." 12, nos. 7–9 (July–September 1884): 336–342.

Stewart, William H. "The Charge of the Crater." 25 (1897): 77–90.

West, W. C. "The Last Battle of the War." 21 (1893): 226–227.

Manuscripts

Adriance Memorial Library, Poughkeepsie, New York
   Robert Nelson Verplanck Papers

Bentley Library, University of Michigan
   William Baird
   Ludlum C. Drake
   M. S. Hall

Boston Athenaeum
   Richard Henry Lee Jewett Letters

Boston Public Library
   Edwin W. Bearse Diary
   John M. Hawks Diary
   Augustus Hesse Letters
   Edward W. Kinsley Papers
   James A. Litchfield Journal
   Papers of the 43rd Regiment U.S.C.T.
   George W. Piper Letters
   James Henry Wickes Papers

Clements Library, University of Michigan
   Schoff Civil War Collection:
      John A. Bodamer
      Levi B. Downs
      William Elgin
      Benjamin C. Lincoln
      Henry Grimes Marshall
      Charlie and John Moore
      John Pierson

Cornell University Rare Manuscript Collections
   Burt Green Wilder Papers

Duke University
   George S. Bernard Papers
   Asa Biggs Papers
   Samuel H. Brodnax Papers
   John Malachi Bowden Papers
   John E. Bryant Papers
   John Snider Cooper Diary
   Frederick and Sarah (Monroe) Cutler Papers:
      Jacob Saylor
      Harry Wadsworth
   James H. DeVotie Papers
   Eltinge-Lord Family Papers
   John B. Foote Papers
   Samuel Wragg Ferguson Memoir
   Edward W. Kinsley Papers
   Harriet C. Lewis Papers:
      S. S. Watson
   Charles Phineas Lord Papers
   Edwin R. Manson Papers
   James Otis Moore Papers
   Benjamin Pedrick Papers:
      William Pedrick

Robert M. Rodgers Papers
William C. Russel Papers
Hubert Saunders Papers
William Scudder Stryker Papers
Elliot Stephen Welch Papers
Artha Brailsford Wescoat Diary

Emory University, Robert W. Woodruff Library Special Collections
Alfred Milo Brigham Papers
Henry M. Crydenwise Papers
Charles M. Duren Letters
William McFall Letters
William M. Parkinson Papers
Edwin D. Tuttle Letters

Georgia Department of Archives and History
J. M. Jordan Letters (in UDC Collection)
Andrew J. Perkins Letters

Historical Society of Pennsylvania
Free Military School Register/Scrapbook of Clippings

Kansas State Historical Society
Civil War Papers Relating to Individual Units:
1st Kansas Colored
George Brandon Diary
John R. Graton Papers
B. F. van Horn Papers
C. B. Morse Papers:
Lewis Douglass Letter
James Monroe Williams Papers

Library of Congress, Manuscript Division
Nathaniel P. Banks Papers
Samuel Denham Barnes Papers
Black History Collection:
F. W. Browne Autobiography
William O. Bourne Papers:
Robert A. Pinn
William H. Thomas
Benjamin F. Butler Papers
George N. Carruthers Papers
Salmon P. Chase Papers
Henry C. Corbin Papers
Henry Graham Journal
J. M. & Esther Hawkes Papers:
James M. Green Letter
Joseph R. Hawley Papers
Edward W. Kinsley Papers
Miscellaneous Collections:
Thomas J. McKean Papers
Papers of Francisco Morreno
Charles Henry Nichols Papers
Montgomery Family Papers:
Colonel Newton W. Perkins
Orloff Dorman Diary

Quincy-Wendell-Upsham-Holmes Families:
  Samuel Miller Quincy Letters
Roberts Family Papers:
  Junius B. Roberts Letter
William R. Shafter Papers
Robert W. Shufeldt Papers
Homer B. Sprague Papers:
  Diary (1863)
Carter G. Woodson Papers:
  Lewis Douglass Letter
  Christian Fleetwood Letter and Diary

Lincoln University
  Files Relating to the 62nd USCT

Massachusetts Historical Society
  Edward J. Bartlett Papers
  Charles B. Fox Letters
  Warren Goodale Papers
  Edward W. Kinsley Papers
  Massachusetts 54th:
    Luis Emilio Scrapbook
  Massachusetts 55th Volunteers Association of Officers Records

Massachusetts National Guard Supply Depot, Natick
  Military Officer's Records, 54th & 55th Massachusetts

Massachusetts State Library
  A. S. Hartwell Papers

Minnesota Historical Society
  Willoughby Babcock and Family Papers
  Benjamin Densmore and Family Papers
  Thomas Montgomery Letters
  James Peet and Family Papers
  Palemon Smalley Papers

National Archives
  Compiled Service Records, United States Colored Troops
  Department of the Gulf, Letters Received 1863:
    Entry 1756, S. H. Stafford to Wickham Hoffman, February 23, 1863 [R-2, Box 5] (Record Group 393)
  Generals' Papers:
    Daniel Ullmann Papers
  Letters Received from Chaplains of Black Regiments (M619):
    Jeremiah Asher
    John R. Bowles
    C. W. Buckley
    W. W. Eaton
    Selah Merrill
    C. Millerd
    G. A. Rockwood
  "The Negro in the Military Service of the United States, 1639–1886" (M858)
  Records of the Adjutant General's Office:
    Compiled Service Records of Volunteer Union Soldiers (Record Group 94)
  Regimental Books and Papers USCT:
    1st Kansas (Colored); 54th Massachusetts (Colored);

55th Massachusetts (Colored); 1st USCI; 5th USC HA; 16th USCI; 17th USCI; 23rd USCI; 26th USCI; 29th USCI; 30th USCI; 32nd USCI; 43rd USCI; 49th USCI; 50th USCI; 51st USCI; 55th USCI; 59th USCI; 61st USCI; 62nd USCI; 75th USCI; 79th USCI; 82nd USCI; 83rd USCI

Regimental Casualties:
  Iowa Infantry
Pension Records of Volunteer Union Soldiers
Proceedings of General Courts Martial (Record Group 153)
U.S. Army Generals' Reports of Civil War Service, 1864–87:
  David Hunter
  Charles J. Paine
  Isaac F. Shepard
  Henry G. Thomas
  Daniel Ullmann
  Godfrey Weitzel
  Edward A. Wild

New York State Library Manuscripts and Special Collections
  Francis G. Barnes Letters
  Robert Galbraith Letters
  Aaron Ingraham Letters

Oberlin College Archives
  Elliott F. Grabill Papers
  Giles W. & Mary Burton Shurtleff Papers

Ohio Historical Society
  Jacob Bruner Papers
  Albert Rogall Diary

Private Collections
  Warren H. Hurd Collection, courtesy of the descendants of Mary Hurd (Penrose and Sara Hurd Davis, c/o Anne McNair and Kay Sara Orsini, 17 Pinkneyville Road, Sparta, N.J. 07871)

Radcliffe College, Schlesinger Library
  James C. Beecher Papers

Rhode Island Historical Society
  George R. Sherman Papers

Richmond National Battlefield Park
  Charles J. Paine Letters

South Carolina Department of Archives and History
  John Jenkins Papers

Southern Historical Collection, Chapel Hill, North Carolina
  Robert Stuart Finley Papers
  Anne Bachman Hyde Papers
  George H. Johnson Papers
  Andrew McCollam Papers
  Leroy Moncure Nutt Papers
  William Frederick Penniman Reminiscences
  Sarah L. Wadley Journal
  J. Lewis Whitaker Letters

State Historical Society of Iowa
  Robert W. Henry Letters

John L. Matthews Collection
Charles Randall Riggs Collection

State Historical Society of Wisconsin
James M. Bowler Papers
William Fagg Diaries
Frank D. Harding Papers
Harrison Family Papers:
   Samuel A. Harrison
Thomas S. Johnson Papers

Syracuse University
John A. Bogert Papers

Tennessee State Library and Archives
Confederate Collection:
   William Gibbs Allen
   Achilles Clark
W. R. Dyer Pocket Diary
William E. Sloan Diary

United States Military History Institute, Carlisle Barracks
Civil War Miscellaneous Collection:
   Albert A. Brown
   David C. Clapp
   David Cornwell: "Dan Caverno, A True Tale of American Life"
   John M. Eaton
   Luther B. Mesnard
   Matthew R. Mitchell
   Joseph Kibler Nelson: "Recollections of My Early Life," 1909
Civil War Times Illustrated Collection:
   Robert M. Dihel
   Joseph J. Scroggs
   William Seagrave
   Benjamin W. Thompson: "Personal Narrative of Experiences in the Civil War"
Gregory A. Coco Collection:
   John W. Ames
William Gladstone Collection:
   George Blackstone
   Ralph Buckley
   Emmet Crawford
   W. J. Estill
   Aleck M. Hayward
   Ashbel Landon
   B. T. Trail
Harrisburg Civil War Roundtable Collection:
   Harvey Covell
Rudolph Haerle Collection:
   William Campbell
   George Tate
Lewis Leigh Collection:
   Walter S. Gilman
   E. S. Millins
   Charles F. Stinson
   William Trail

Union Folder #1: Union Black Soldier Letters
Willington Wood
Miscellaneous Collections:
  Hattie Burleigh Papers
  John Habberton Papers
  Alfred Hartwell Memoir
  MOLLUS Massachusetts Commandery Autograph Collection
  Edward A. Wild Papers and Correspondence
M.O.L.L.U.S. Collection:
  Silas Adams: "My Observations and Service with the Colored Troops"
Michael P. Musick Collection:
  Asa B. Randall
Pennsylvania "Save the Flag" Collection:
  Thomas Goldsborough
Ronn Palm Collection:
  Adam C. McJunkin
Wiley Sword Collection:
  William R. Shafter

University of Tennessee (Knoxville) Special Collections
Edwin Hansford Rennolds, Sr., Diary and Autobiography

Vermont Historical Society
Rufus Kinsley Papers

Virginia State Library
Bird C. Willis Diary

West Virginia University
John W. M. Appleton Papers

Western Reserve Historical Society Library
Carlos Parson Lyman
William P. Palmer Collection:
  B. F. Moulton
  Robert Porter
  Regimental Papers Folder/1st South Carolina Volunteer Infantry
Bound Reference Material:
  "The Negro Troops"

Yale University, Sterling Library
Walter A. Chapman Papers
Civil War Mss. Collection:
  Walter R. Burnham
  George Cyprian Jarvis
Joe V. Meigs Papers
Charles G. Merrill Papers
Lewis Weld Family Papers

Newspapers

Athens (Ohio) *Messenger*
Boston Commonwealth
Boston Daily Advertiser
Boston Evening Journal
Boston Evening Transcript
Boston Herald

Boston Post
Brookville Republican
Bucks County Intelligencer (Doylestown, Pennsylvania)
Carlisle (Pennsylvania) *Herald*
Charleston Daily Courier
Charleston Mercury
Charleston Sunday-News
Connecticut War Record
The Daily Herald (Newburyport, Massachusetts)
Daily Morning Chronicle (Washington, D.C.)
Daily Picayune (New Orleans)
Daily Sun (Columbus, Georgia)
Davenport Daily Gazette
Grand Army Record
Greenville (South Carolina) *Daily News*
Harper's Weekly
Hartford Courant
Houston Weekly Telegraph
Illinois State Journal
Lancaster (Pennsylvania) *Daily Evening Express*
Lawrence (Kansas)*Daily Tribune*
The Liberator
Memphis Daily Appeal
Montrose (Pennsylvania) *Democrat*
National Anti-Slavery Journal
National Tribune (Washington, D.C.)
New National Era
New Orleans Era
New South (Port Royal, South Carolina)
New York Evening Post
New York Times
New York Tribune
New York World
Our Living and Our Dead
Petersburg Daily Register
Philadelphia Inquirer
Philadelphia Press
Philadelphia Public Ledger
Philadelphia Weekly Times
Quincy Daily Whig & Republican
Raleigh Register
Richmond Daily Dispatch
Richmond Daily Examiner
Springfield Daily Republican

The Union (New Orleans)
Washington Evening Star
Whig & Courier (Bangor, Maine)
Xenia (Ohio) *Torchlight*

Pamphlets

DeMoss, Robert. *The Battle of Honey Springs.* N.p. 1990.

Dissertations/Theses

Berry, Mary Frances. "History of the 73rd and 75th United States Colored Infantry Regiments." M.A. thesis, Howard University, 1962.

Blassingame, John Wesley. "The Organization and Use of Negro Troops in the Union Army, 1863–1865." M.A. thesis, Howard University, 1961.

Bowie, Marilyn Elizabeth. "An Analytical History of the Fourth and Sixth Infantries of the United States Colored Troops in the Civil War." M.A. thesis, Howard University, 1969.

Brown, Robert Benaway. "Guns over the Border: American Aid to the Juarez Goverment During the French Intervention." Ph.D. diss., University of Michigan, 1951.

Coles, David James. "'A Fight, a Licking, and a Footrace': The 1864 Florida Campaign and the Battle of Olustee." M.A. thesis, Florida State University, 1985.

Cook, Curtis Taylor. "The Siege of Port Hudson." M.A. thesis, Louisiana State University, 1934.

Cousins, Phyllis M. "A History of the 33rd United States Colored Troops." M.A. thesis, Howard University, 1961.

Drinkard, Dorothy Lee. "A Regimental History of the Twenty-Ninth Infantry, United States Colored Troops 1864–1865." M.A. thesis, Howard University, 1963.

Gardner, Bettye Jane. "A History of the Third United States Colored Cavalry." M.A. thesis, Howard University, 1964.

Graetz, Robert Bruce. "Triumph and Defeat: The Confederate Victory at Natural Bridge, Florida, March 1865." B.A. thesis, Florida State University, 1986.

Hendricks, George Linton. "Union Army Occupation of the Southern Seaboard, 1861–1865." Ph.D. diss., Columbia University, 1954.

Hunt, Jeffrey W. "There Is Nothing Left to Us but to Fight: The Battle of Palmetto Ranch, Texas." History thesis, University of Texas at Arlington, 1980.

Inniss, Warren A. "The History of the 1st and 7th United States Colored Troops." M.A. thesis, Howard University, 1962.

Richter, William L. "The Army in Texas during Reconstruction, 1865–1870." Ph.D. diss., Louisiana State University, 1970.

Seraile, William. "New York's Black Regiments During the Civil War." Ph.D. diss., City University of New York, 1977.

Whitted, Burma L. "The History of the 8th United States Colored Troops." M.A. thesis, Howard University, 1960.

Whyte, Elise Cornelia S. "History of the Twenty-third and Thirty-eighth Infantry United States Colored Regiments, 1863–1867." M.A. thesis, Howard University, 1963.

Acknowledgments

———◦———

Black troops fought in just about every theater of the Civil War; consequently, my search for materials was wide-ranging. It could not have been accomplished without the extra eyes, minds, and patient determination of a number of researchers who extended my reach into archives all across the country. To each my thanks, and a grateful tip of the hat by here acknowledging them:

Illinois: G. Paul Gerdes; Indiana: Susan H. Truax; Iowa: Jeffrey L. Dawson; Kansas: Julie A. Pope; Minnesota/Wisconsin: James W. Warren, Paula Stuart Warren; Ohio: Mary Christensen, Kella Barnhill; Pennsylvania: Steve L. Zerbe; and Vermont: Ev Grimes.

Principal researcher for this book was Bryce A. Suderow, whose expert ability to negotiate the paperwork maze of the National Archives was of inestimable value (This could not have been accomplished without the assistance as well of the National Archives staff, especially Michael Musick, Mike Meier, Stuart Butler, and Cindy Fox.) In addition to covering the Library of Congress manuscript collection, and tracking down hard-to-find published material, Bryce reviewed hundreds of military records in order to provide me with the revised calculations for the number of black soldiers killed in the Battle of the Crater.

In the course of researching and writing this book, I had the pleasure of crossing paths with many people who were generous with

531

their time and knowledge and with materials in their possession. Thanks here to Edwin C. Bearss, Kathy Dhalle, James G. Hollandsworth, Jr., John Horn, William Marvel, and Lewis G. Schmidt. I also was able to visit a number of manuscript archives and libraries, where I endlessly imposed on the patience of the staffs, all of whom were unfailingly helpful. A special acknowledgment must go to Dr. Richard J. Sommers and his staff at the U.S. Army Military History Institute at the War College, Carlisle Barracks, Pennsylvania.

A real high point in the preparation of this book was having the chance to visit many of the battlefields described, a good number of which are badly marked, if at all. My visits were much enhanced by local experts who gave up parts of their day (often on short notice, and sometimes in inexorable weather) to show me around. Most of these individuals also reviewed portions of my manuscript:

Tour: Bruce Aiken, executive director of the Historic Brownsville Museum (Palmito Ranch).

Tour and manuscript review: Richard H. "Dicky" Ferry (Olustee), Norman A. Nicolson (Fort Blakely), Gregg Potts (Port Hudson), and Stephen R. Wise (Honey Hill and Battery Wagner).

Manuscript review: Mike Andrus (Richmond operations), Jim Bryant (Overland Campaign), Arthur W. Bergeron (Louisiana operations), Chris Calkins (Petersburg and Appomattox operations), Michael A. Cavanaugh (The Crater), David J. Coles (Florida operations), Mike Fraering (Port Hudson), Robert Bruce Graetz (Natural Bridge), Robert E. L. Krick (Richmond operations), Richard Lowe (Milliken's Bend), Donald Pfanz (Overland Campaign), and Edwin S. Redkey (54th Massachusetts actions).

For the final stages of polishing, the manuscript was again entrusted to my friend Christine Malesky, representing the home-office grammar police; from my publisher, Little, Brown, came welcome services of editor Catherine Crawford. A large thanks is also due to my copyeditor, Dorothy Straight, for smoothing the rough edges (there were many) and adding the right word where it was missing.

To everyone involved, my humble thanks for giving their best. All decisions regarding emphasis and presentation of the often conflicting and contradictory evidence were mine to make, and were so made.

Index

Adams, Charles F., 269–270, 419–420, 421
Adams, Pless, 404
A.D.W., 415, 416
Aiken's Landing, Va., 284
Alabama troops (C.S.): infantry (18th Regiment, 347)
Alabama troops (U.S.): heavy artillery (1st Siege Artillery, 158); infantry (1st Regiment African Descent), *see* United States troops: infantry (55th Regiment USCT)
Alexander, Cassius M. Clay, 402–403
Alrich Farm, skirmish at, 211
Amelia Court House, Va., 412
Ames, John W., 283–284, 290, 361–362
Anderson, Charles W., 164
Anderson, Ransom, 167
Andersonville, Ga., 144, 149, 154, 358
Andrew, John A., 71, 92–93, 112, 113, 254, 374
Anglo-African (New York), 11, 17, 71, 72, 73, 85, 89, 92, 126, 152, 169, 171, 180, 203, 215, 222, 229, 252, 255, 256, 262, 277, 305, 331, 333, 365, 366, 371, 397, 402, 429
Annapolis, Md., 206
Appleton, John W. M., 72, 76, 80, 82–83, 85, 129, 133, 135, 138, 150
Appleton, William, 290
Appomattox Court House, Va., 431, 455
Appomattox River, 220, 425, 428, 430

Arkansas troops (U.S.): infantry (1st Regiment African Descent, 98), *see also* United States troops: infantry (46th Regiment USCT)
Arlington, Va., 365
Armstrong, Andrew J., 5–6
Armstrong, Samuel C., 428, 431–432
Army of the James, 206, 219, 228, 285, 305, 416, 424, 431; Twenty-fifth Corps organized, 308
"Arnold" (pseud.), 216, 229
Asboth, Alexander, 267, 268
Athens (Ohio) *Messenger,* 115
Atlantic and Gulf Central Railroad, 137
atrocities: Brice's Cross Roads (June 10, 1864), 179–180; Dalton (August 15, 1864), 278; Flat Rock Creek (September 16, 1864), 265–266; Fort Blakely (April 9, 1865), 406–407; Fort Pillow (April 12, 1864), 167–168; James Island (July 16, 1863), 76; Marianna (September 27, 1864), 268–269; Milliken's Bend (June 7, 1863), 58–59; Mound Plantation (June 29, 1863), 101; Olustee (February 20, 1864), 151; Overland Campaign (May–June 1864), 214; Petersburg (June 15, 1864), 225; Petersburg (July 30, 1864), 245–246; Poison Spring (April 18, 1864), 193–194; Potter's Raid (April 5–25, 1865), 387; Sherwood (May 18, 1863), 103–104; Saltville (October 2, 1864), 274

533

Atwood, Daniel W., 349–350
Avera, William, 193

Babb, Eli, 170
Babcock, Edwin S., 297
Bagdad, Mexico, 461
Bailey, C. P., 176
Bailey, Romanzo C., 144
Baird, George W., 322–323
Baker, Wallace, 257
Baldwin, Fla., 134, 135, 136, 151
Baltimore, Md., 206
Band, Jonathan T., 144
Banks, Alexander, 229
Banks, Nathaniel P., 29, 45, 182, 196;
    enlistment of black troops, 34; purges
    black officers, 33, 45; relieves Butler at
    New Orleans, 29
Barber, Marion, 6
Barber's Station, Fla., 134, 150
Barker, Edgar A., 264
Barnes, William H., 292
Barquet, Joseph H., 90, 256
Barrancas, Fla., 267
Barrett, Theodore H., 437–452; described,
    436
Bartlett, Edward J., 420, 423
Barton, William, 137
Bassett, Chauncey, 28, 37, 43
Bates, Delevan, 240–241, 242, 246, 301
Bates County (Mo.), 3
Baton Rouge, La., 437; battle at, 23
Battery Buchanan, 362
Baxter Springs, Kans., 103, 104
Baylor's Farm, skirmish at, 221, 222
Bayou Lafourche, expedition to, 28–29
Beach, John, 347
Beaty, Powhatan, 292
Beaufort, S.C., 63, 72, 86, 332
Beauregard, P. G. T., 132, 134, 356
Bee, Robert, 387
Beecham, R. K., 232, 243
Beecher, Frances, 154–155, 314
Beecher, James C., 114, 154, 324; battle of
    Honey Hill, 326–327; described, 128
Bell, Tyree H., 162
Beman, Charles T., 423
Benedict, Augustus, 397–398
Bennett, Augustus G., 356–357
Bennett, Horace, 392
Bennett House, N.C., 455
Benton Barracks, 435
Bermuda Hundred, Va., 215, 219, 283, 418
Biddle, Eli George, 468
Biddle, Nicholas, 7
Big Sandy Creek, 37, 40
Bingham, James R., 163
Birney, David B., 285, 296

Birney, William, 154, 257, 262, 297–298,
    425, 427, 430
Black Hawk, U.S.S., 46
black officers, 155, 262, 366, 373–374
Black River, 376–378
black soldiers, combat actions praised, 6–7,
    44–45, 58, 87, 111, 180, 282, 293, 363
Bladensburg, Md., 11
Blunt, James G., 106, 107, 108
Bobson, Jordan M., 260
Boca Chica, Tex., 440, 442, 450
Bogan, Charles, 101
Bogan, Lewis, 101, 102
Bohrer, Godfrey, 449
Bolan Church, 322, 324, 326, 329
Bond, Benjamin M., 376, 384, 395
Boon, Alonzo, 262–263
Booth, Elizabeth Weyt, 172
Booth, John Wilkes, 434
Booth, Lionel F., 157, 159, 160, 172;
    described, 158; killed, 163
Bossieaux, Virginius, 411
Boston, S.S., 64
Boston Commonwealth, 422
Boston Daily Advertiser, 224
Boston Evening Journal, 207–208, 357
Bottom's Bridge, Va., 203
"Bought and Sold" (pseud.), 252–253
Bounds, Ben H., 406
Bourgeau, Alfred, 27
Bouton, Edward, 170, 172, 175, 176, 177,
    180, 181
Bowles, John, 108, 374
Bowley, Freeman S., 210, 211, 235, 236,
    238–239, 242, 243, 244, 245, 247,
    248
Boyd's Neck, S.C., 316
Boydton Plank Road, engagement near,
    300–304
Boykins Mill, skirmish at, 391–394
Boynton, Winthrop P., 328
Bradford, William F., 158, 163, 165–166
Brandy Station, Va., 204
Branson, David, 437–452; described, 436
Brazos Santiago, Tex., 182, 438, 439, 440,
    443, 450, 452, 458
Breckinridge, John C., 23
Brewington Swamp, 381
Brice's Cross Roads, 173; battle of, 170–180
Bridge, Watson W., 392
Briggs, Charles E., 385, 390, 395
Brigham, Alfred Milo, 204
Bright, Daniel, 116, 118
Brisbin, James S., 270–271, 273
Broad River, 314, 316–317
Broadway Landing, Va., 220
Brock, John C., 206, 212, 229, 301–304,
    416, 419, 423, 424, 434

Bronson, James H., 292
Bross, John A., 243
Brown, David R., 229, 241
Brown, John, 13
Brown, Thomas J., 260
Brownsville, Tex., 438, 442, 444, 445, 452, 460
Brown versus the Topeka Board of Education, 266
Bruner, Jacob, 48, 58
Buckley, C. W., 399
Burbridge, Stephen G., 270, 272, 275
Burnside, Ambrose, 208; commands at the Crater, 230–254; North Carolina expedition, 11; organizes black division in the Army of the Potomac, 206
Burnside, S.S., 64
Butler, Benjamin F., 29, 201, 203, 306; Bermuda Hundred campaign, 214–220; contraband policy, 9–10; commands Department of North Carolina, 115; controversy with Phelps, 25; described, 23; Dutch Gap Canal scheme, 283–284; enlistment of black troops, 24–25; operations against Richmond (September 1864), 285–300; prisoner controversy with Robert E. Lee, 310–312; relieved of command in New Orleans, 29; relieved of command following Fort Fisher, 358–359, 416
Butler, Charles, 27
Butler Medal, 300

Cabel, W. L., 193–194
Cabin Creek, Okla., engagement at (July 1–2, 1863), 106–108
Cailloux, Andre, 27, 38, 41–43, 45
Cairo, Ill., 436
Calahan, Thomas, 407
Caldwell, Samuel H., 167–168
Camden, Ark., 195
Camden, S.C., 390
Campbell, J. P., 16
Camp Delaware, 202
Camp Finegan, 132, 135, 152
Camp Meigs, 72, 257
Camp Nelson, 270
Camp Parapet, 25
Camp Pike, 263, 266
Camp Shaw, 136
Camp Strong, 28
Camp William Penn, 125, 126, 141, 143, 202, 215, 322
Canby, Edward R. S., 396
Cape Fear River, 359, 360, 363
Carney, William H., 82, 84–85
Carrington, Edward, 371
Carruthers, George N., 399, 405

Carter, Edward, 27
Carter, Leonard, 243
Carter, Richard, 363
Case, George R., 27, 31
casualties, individual actions: Baylor's Farm (June 15, 1864), 222; Boydton Plank Road (October 27, 1864), 304; Brice's Cross Roads (June 10, 1864), 179–180; Cabin Creek (July 2, 1863), 105; Dalton (August 15, 1864), 278; Decatur (October 28, 1864), 282; East River Bridge (March 5, 1865), 369; Fair Oaks (October 27, 1864), 305, 308; Flat Rock Creek (September 16, 1864), 266; Forks Road (February 20, 1865), 363; Fort Blakely (April 9, 1865), 408; Fort Gilmer (September 29, 1864), 299–300; Fort Pillow (April 12, 1864), 168; Fort Wagner (July 18, 1863), 86; Honey Hill (November 30, 1864), 331; Honey Springs (July 17, 1863), 107–108; Island Mound (October 29, 1862), 6; Jacksonville occupation (March 1863), 70; James Island (July 16, 1863), 75–76; James Island (July 2, 1864), 262; Jenkins' Ferry (April 30, 1864), 199; Marianna (September 27, 1864), 269; Milliken's Bend (June 9, 1863), 58; Natural Bridge (March 6, 1865), 371; Nashville (December 15–16, 1864), 344, 348; New Market Heights (September 29, 1864), 291, 292; Olustee (February 20, 1864), 152; Palmito Ranch (May 12–13, 1865), 451; Pascagoula (April 9, 1863), 32; Petersburg (June 15, 1864), 226; Petersburg (July 30, 1864), 247; Poison Spring (April 18, 1864), 194; Port Hudson (May 27, 1863), 44; Saltville (October 2, 1864), 274; Stockade No. 2 (December 2, 1864), 337–338; Sugar Loaf (February 11, 1865), 363; Wolf River Bridge (December 3–4, 1863), 111; overall totals, 466
Century Magazine, 465
Chalmers, James R., 162, 163–164
Chamberlain, Abial G., 307
Chamberlain, Edwin W., 56
Chambers, John C., 126
Chapman, Fred A., 236
Chapman, Walter, 406
Charleston, S.C., 7, 73, 89; occupation, 353–358
Charleston & Savannah Railroad, 257, 313, 318, 320
Chase, Salmon P., 27, 121–124, 153
Chattanooga & Nashville Railroad, skirmish at Stockade No. 2, 335–338

Chester, Thomas Morris, 304, 308–309, 311, 312, 419, 421, 422
Chestnut Ridge, 273
Chickahominy River, 203
Choctaw, U.S.S., 51, 53, 57
Christian Recorder (Philadelphia), 90, 114, 152, 154, 207, 212, 252–253, 336, 357, 384, 394, 395, 415, 416, 422, 462
Christy, John M., 284
Cincinnati, Ohio, 7
Citronelle, Ala., 455
City Point, Va., 217, 219, 220; capture, 216
Clapp, Henry C., 419
Clarendon Banner, 381
Clarendon Banner of Freedom, 381
Clark, Achilles V., 166, 168
Clark, Charles, 104, 105
Clark, David, 436, 451
Clark, Lewis, 390
Clarksville, Tex., 461
Cleburne, Patrick R., supports enlistment of black troops, 409
Cleveland Leader, 178
Coffin, Charles, 208–209, 227, 357
Colcock, Charles J., 320
Cold Harbor, Va., 212
Coles Island, S.C., 261, 354, 355
Collins, John H. W., 357, 376, 379, 381, 384, 385, 386, 390, 394
Colorado troops: infantry (2nd Regiment, 104, 105)
Colquitt, Alfred, 134, 145
Columbia, Pa., 95
Columbia Bridge, 95
Columbine, S.S., 154
Committee on the Conduct of the War, 168, 231
Confederate States of America, policy toward black soldiers and their white officers, 60–61
Connecticut troops: infantry (6th Regiment, 68, 70, 80, 84); (7th Regiment, 139, 140, 148, 152); (8th Regiment, 10–11); (10th Regiment, 74, 75); (29th Regiment Colored, 461–462; engagement near Fair Oaks, 304–308; Richmond occupation, 417–424; (30th Regiment Colored, 206), *see also* United States troops: infantry (31st Regiment USCT)
contraband policy, 9–10
Cooper, John S., 388, 389
Cooper, Kinchen, 175
Coppec, J. L., 407
Corbin, Henry C., 280–281, 340, 343
Cornwell, David, 48–49, 51, 53, 54–55
Corps d'Afrique, 34, 45, 51, 268, 397; infantry (4th Regiment, 397–398), *see also* United States troops: infantry (76th

Regiment USCT); (10th Regiment), *see* United States troops: infantry (82nd Regiment USCT); (14th Regiment), *see* United States troops: infantry (86th Regiment USCT); (15th Regiment), *see* United States troops: infantry (99th Regiment USCT)
Corpus Christi, Tex., 458
Cosmopolitan, S.S., 154
Couch, Darius, 94
Covell, Harvey, 223–224, 226
Cowden, Robert, 171, 172, 176, 177
Cox, Everett, 179
Cox, Mary Ann, 179
Cox Road, 429
Crane, William D., 261, 328
Crater, The. *See:* Petersburg, Va.
Crawford, Samuel J., 196, 197–199, 200
Crew, Andrew I., 5, 6
Croft, J. S., 148, 152
Crowder, John, 28, 37, 44
Crydenwise, Henry, 403, 405, 408
Curtin, Andrew W., 94, 125

Dahlgren, John A., 77, 315–316, 318, 332
Daily (True) Delta (New Orleans), 29, 37
Dalton, Ga., August 15 action at, 275–278; October 13 surrender at, 278–280
Dana, Charles, 59
Daniels, Nathan W., 28, 31–33, 46
Danville, Va., 248
Darbytown Road, 305, 419
Darien, Ga., destruction of, 73
Davis, Charles H., 433
Davis, Edgard, 27
Davis, Jefferson, 409–410
Davis, Samuel, 6
Day, Henry M., 438
De Bow's Review, 60
Decatur, Ala., action at, 280–282
Deep Bottom, Va., 233, 284
Delhi, La., 102
demobilization of black units, 461–462
Denison, G. S., 27, 29
Dennett, Isaac L., 366–367, 371
Dennis, Elias S., 50, 51
Depass, John, 27
Detiege, Emile, 27
Devens, Charles, 421–422
Dickey, William A., 166
Dickey's Crossing, 5
Dickies Ford, 5
Dimmock, Charles H., 222
Dingle's Mill, S.C., 381; skirmish at, 383–384
Dinwiddie Court House, Va., 426
discipline of black troops, 228
Dodson, Jacob, 7

Dolly, George, 67
Donaldsonville, La., 456
Dorsey, Decatur, 249
Doswell, R. M., 412
Doubleday, Ulysses, 305, 425, 427
Douglass, Charles, 72
Douglass, C. R., 221
Douglass, Frederick, 7; quoted: "Action!
  Action!," 72; "The cry now is for war," 7;
  "I . . . saw in this war the end of slavery,"
  7; "In that terrible battle," 87; "Let the
  slaves . . . be . . . formed into a liberating
  army," 10; "Nothing short of an open
  recognition of the Negro's manhood," 7
Douglass, Lewis, 72, 81, 82, 83
Douglass Monthly, 7
Draper, Alonzo G., 115, 116, 117, 286, 291,
  292, 306, 418
Drayfus, Thomas, 402
Drew, Charles W., 398, 404
Drysdale, Samuel J., 436
Dubois, Harrison, 443, 449
Du Bois, W. E. B., 468
Dubuque (Iowa) Times, 18
Dumas, Francis E., 28, 33
Dunbar, Joshua, 468
Dunbar, Paul Laurence, 468–469
Duncan, Samuel A., 202, 215, 220, 221,
  222, 225, 226, 286, 291, 292
Duren, Charles M., 130, 133, 150, 151
Durkee, W. C., 444
Dutch Gap Canal, 283–284, 311
Duval, George W., 265
Dwight, William, Jr., 38–39, 40–41, 43

Earle, Ethan, 19
East River Bridge, Fla., skirmish at, 368
Eaton, A. V., 192, 194, 195
Eaton, John, 98
Edgerton, Nathan H., 290
Elizabeth City, N.C., occupation by Wild,
  116
Elizabeth City Raid, 115–118
Elk Creek, 106–108
Elliott's Salient, 230
Ellis, Henry, 436, 445
Ellsworth, Thomas F., 328
Ely, Andrew F., 143
Emancipation Proclamation, 18–22, 161,
  254, 435
Emerson, Ralph Waldo, 63, 87
Emilio, Luis F., 76–77, 81, 82, 83–84, 88,
  128, 138, 145, 146, 147, 151, 316, 321,
  393, 394
enlistment efforts in North (1861), 7–8
enlistment efforts in South (1861), 8–9;
  population base, 9–10
Ewell, Richard S., 96, 412

Ewing, Frank M., 175
execution of black soldiers, 228–229, 254,
  257

Falls, Elias, 167
Farmville, Va., 413, 430
Farragut, David, 34–35
Fassett, Isaiah, 468
fatigue duty, 90, 114, 229, 460
Federal Point, 359, 363
Fernandina, Fla., 121, 123
Ferrero, Edward, 206, 211, 212, 301–304;
  commands at the Crater, 231–250
Finegan, Joseph, 132, 134, 136, 145
Finnegass, Henry, 38, 43, 46
Fitzpatrick, James C., 362
Five Civilized Nations, 104
Flat Rock Creek, Okla., action near,
  263–266
Fleetwood, Christian A., 222, 286, 290, 414
Florence, S.C., 88, 394
Florida troops (U.S.): cavalry (1st Regiment,
  268); (2nd Regiment, 367, 369)
Fog, Octave, 27
Follin, Joseph, 27, 45
Folly Island, S.C., 73, 76, 87, 128, 256
Ford, John S. "Rip," 445, 446–447, 449,
  452
Forks Road, skirmish at, 363
Forrest, Nathan B., 110, 157, 161; actions
  at Fort Pillow, 163–169; battle of Brice's
  Cross Roads, 172–180
Fort Africa, 5–6
Fort Anderson, 363
Fort Blakely, siege, assault, and capture,
  396–408
Fort Burnham, 420
Fort Fisher, assault and capture, 358–362
Fort Gibson, 104, 106, 263
Fort Gilmer, engagement at, 294–300
Fort Gregg, 297
Fort Harrison, 294, 420n
Fort Jackson, 31; mutiny at, 398
Fort Lamar, 258, 260
Fort Lincoln, 3
Fort McAllister, 332
Fort Moultrie, 356
Fort Pickens, 121
Fort Pickering, 169, 180
Fort Pike, 31
Fort Pillow, 159–160, 172; massacre at,
  156–169
Fort Powhatan, 217
Fort Pulaski, 77, 123
Fortress Monroe, Va., 217
Fort St. Philip, 31
Fort Scott, 19, 103, 196
Fort Smith, 183, 200

Fort Sumter, 8, 81, 89, 356
Fort Wagner, assault on, 71–86; abandoned by Confederates, 89; battery versus fort, 71n; called Neck Battery, 72; July 11 attack, 73
Foster, Henry C., 178
Foster, John G., 112, 114, 257, 313, 318
Foster, R. B., 450
Foster, Robert S., 295
Foster, Wesley, 49, 58
Fox, Charles B., 258, 260, 321
Franklin, Tenn., 334
Fredericksburg, Va., 209
Freeman, Henry V., 345–346, 349
Freeman, Leander, 393
Freeman, William H. H., 102
Fremont, Charles, 102
Fremont, John C., 16–17
Fribley, Charles W., 125, 142; described, 126; killed, 143
Frick, Jacob G., 95, 97

Gabriel, 9
Gainesville, Fla., 135
Gallatin, Tenn., 276
Gano, Richard M., 263
Gardiner, James, 292
Gardner, Joseph, 5–6
Gardner, William H., 274
Garland, Randall, 104, 105
Garrison, George T., 354
Garrison, William Lloyd, 63
Gary, Henry, 173
Gash, Henry, 6
Gaskin, Isaac, 246–247, 248
Gaw, William B., 340
Gaylord, Wilbur H., 167
General Banks, S.S., 31–32
General Hunter, S.S., 76, 129
Georgetown, S.C., 375, 394, 395
Germantown, Tenn., 178
Gettysburg, Pa., 75th anniversary, 467–468
Gettysburg Campaign, persecution of blacks, 95–96
Gillmore, Quincy A., 73, 77, 85, 89, 123–124, 125, 135, 137, 217, 219
Gilson, Helen, 247
Givin, James, 427
Gleason, Clark, 406
Gooding, James Henry, 72, 73, 74, 80, 83, 86, 89, 92–93, 127, 131, 133, 148–149, 358, 373
Goodrich's Landing, La., 99
Goodwin, Frank, 260
Goulding, J. H., 204, 288, 289, 292
Grabill, Elliott F., 216, 291, 292, 296, 306, 308, 359, 362
Grace, James W., 82

Grahamville, S.C., 318
Grand Army of the Republic, 464
Grand Review, 455
Grant, Ulysses S., 37, 52, 58, 97–98, 209, 239, 251, 311, 338, 344, 359, 408, 425, 461, 465
Graton, John R., 103, 104
Gray, William, 242
Grayson, G. W., 265
Green, John, 393
Green, Joseph, 274
Greenwell, Charles, 248
Grierson, Benjamin H., 170
Griffin, Benjamin, 260
Griffin, Joel R., 118
Griffin, Thomas J., 420, 458, 459
Grimball's Causeway, 75
Grosvenor, Charles H., 341–342, 343, 345
Guntown, Tenn., 173

Haines, William W., 186, 188
Hall, H. Seymour, 208, 213, 235, 236, 241
Hall, Morris, 279
Hall, W. P., 189, 192
Halleck, Henry W., 124, 135, 271, 313, 458
Hallett, Charles, 393
Hallowell, Edward N., 74, 88–89, 128, 147, 149, 376–395
Hamlin, Hannibal, 374
Hampton Roads, Va., 215
"Hard Cracker" (pseud.), 203
Harding, David, 392
Harper's Weekly, 18
Harris, James A., 292
Harris, William, 102
Harrison, William H., 148
Hartwell, Alfred S., 258, 262, 320, 324; battle of Honey Hill, 328–333
Haskill, Llewellyn F., 428
Hatch, Edward, 110
Hatch, John P., 257, 262, 314; commands troops at Honey Hill, 315–333
Hatcher's Run, 301, 425
Hawkins, John P., 399, 405, 440
Hawkins, Thomas, 290
Hawley, Joseph, 137, 140, 462
Hawthorne, Nathaniel, 63
Hay, John, 124, 136–137, 153
Heichold, A. P., 126, 131–132, 133, 136, 142, 150
Heighton, Henry, 248
Heighton, Susannah, 248
Heine, William, 258
Helms, Alexander, 346
Henderson, Robert, 186
Henry, Robert W., 56
Hewett, James C., 81, 82, 147

Higginson, Thomas Wentworth, 63–64, 72–73, 257; U.S. occupation of Jacksonville, 64–71

Hilton, Alfred B., 290

Hilton Head, S.C., 72, 125, 127, 135, 136, 256, 315, 318

Hincks, Edward W., 205, 215, 217, 228

Hoge, George B., 170, 173

Hoke, Robert F., 360

Holland, Milton M., 115, 117, 221, 224, 226, 292

Holman, John H., 220, 286, 306, 307

Holston River, 273

Holt, Joseph, 87

Honey Hill, S.C., battle of, 314–331

Honey Springs, Okla., engagement near, 106–108

Hood, John B., 276, 278, 280, 334, 335, 338, 344

Hooper, Henry N., 147, 150, 321, 326, 328, 354, 376, 385, 386, 391, 393, 395

Hopkins, Charles, 214

Hottenstein, John A., 336, 348

Houston Weekly Telegraph, 100

Howard, Oliver O., 277, 353

Hudson, Joseph K., 438, 444

Humes, Fleming, 436, 450

Humes, Lafayette, 436

Hunter, Andrew, 409

Hunter, David, 60; enlistment of black troops, 14–16

Hunter, Henry H., 49, 58

Hunter, William H., 225, 227

Hurd, Warren H., 236, 239, 244

Hurlbut, Stephen, 111, 158, 159, 160

Illinois troops: cavalry (6th Regiment, 110); (9th Regiment, 110); (10th Regiment, 51)

Indiana troops: artillery (2nd Battery, 186); infantry (34th Regiment, skirmishes at Palmito Ranch, 443–450)

Indianola, Kans., 266

Indianola, Tex., 458

Ingraham, James H., 27, 29

Iowa troops: infantry (18th Regiment, 191); (23rd Regiment, 51, 53; action at Milliken's Bend, 53–57); (26th Regiment, 56)

Irwin, Richard B., 182

Isabelle, Robert H., 33

Island Mound, skirmish at, 3–7

Isle Brevelle, 9

Jackson, Charles, 126

Jackson, Jack ("Big Jack"), 48–49, 54–55, 58

Jackson, Thomas, 147

Jackson, Tenn., 161

Jacksonville, Fla., 136; U.S. occupation (March 10–30, 1863), 64–71; U.S. occupation (beginning February 7, 1864), 129–132

James, Albert, 225

James, Garth W., 80, 81

James, Miles, 292

James Island, S.C., 73, 74, 80, 81; 7/16/63 skirmish, 73–76; 7/2/64 skirmish, 258

James River, 283

Jarvis, George, 386

Jay, Wesley, 393

"J.C.W.," 460

Jenkins, George, 177, 179

Jenkins, John, 320

Jenkins, John H., 332

Jenkins' Ferry, Ark., engagement at, 196–200

Jennison, Charles, 13

Jerusalem Plank Road, 230

Jetersville, Va., 412, 430

Jewett, Richard, 82

Jim Crow Laws, 465

John Adams, S.S., 64, 66, 67

John P. Jackson, U.S.S., 31–32

Johnson, Alexander H., 81

Johnson, Andrew, 161

Johnson, Clayton, 394

Johnson, Frances, 154–155. *See also* Beecher, Frances

Johnson, George Washington, 468

Johnson, Henry, 178

Johnson, James P., 392, 394

Johnson, John J., 260

Johnson, Joseph C., 364, 379

Johnson, Lewis, 278–279, 337–338, 341

Johnson, Thomas S., 427, 432

Johnson, William B., 456

Johnson, William Henry, 10–11

Johnston, Joseph E., 455

Jolly, John H., 402

Jones, A. G., 363

Jones, Charles A., 446, 449

Jones, H. C., 366

Jones, Robert B., 440

Jones, Rufus, 136, 139, 141, 143, 150, 151

Jones, Samuel. *See* Jordan, Samuel

Jones Neck, 284

Jordan, James, 151

Jordan, Samuel, 118

Jordan, Sharper, 49, 58

Jordan Point Road, 222

Kansas troops: artillery (2nd Battery, 103); cavalry (2nd Regiment, 186; action near Flat Rock Creek, 263); (6th Regiment, 106, 186); (9th Regiment, 104); (14th Regiment, 104, 186); infantry (1st

Kansas troops *cont.*
    Regiment Colored, 3, 14; action near Flat Rock Creek, 263–265; Emancipation Proclamation, 19–20; engagement at Cabin Creek, 105; engagement near Honey Springs, 106; engagement at Poison Spring, 186–194; mustered into Federal service, 103), *see also* United States troops: infantry (79th Regiment USCT New); (2nd Regiment Colored, 61, 196; engagement at Jenkins' Ferry, 197–200), *see also* United States troops: infantry (83rd Regiment USCT New)
Kautz, August V., 418, 419–420, 421, 422, 423
Keillies, Jacob D., 416
Kelly, Alexander, 290
Kendrick, Frank A., 110–111
Keyes, Miles, 237
Key West, Fla., 121, 365, 371
Kiddoo, Joseph B., 217, 225, 307
Kilpatrick, Judson, cavalry raid on Richmond, 204–205
King, Robert, 322, 328, 331
King, Susie, 67
King's Ferry, Fla., 135
Kingston, Ga., 313

Lafayette, Tenn., 170
La Grange, Tenn., 171
Lake City, Fla., 134, 138
Lake Providence, La., 47, 50, 58, 101
Lamberg, Carl A., 172, 176, 177
Lane, James H., described, 13; enlistment of black troops, 13–14
Lane, Thomas, 6
Langley, London S., 252, 260, 261, 262
Lanien, Louis D., 27
Lavigne, Victor, 27
Laws, P. R., 331
Leach, Julius, 275
Leach, Patsey, 275
Leavenworth Daily Conservative, 6
Ledlie, James H., 235, 238, 250
Lee, Fitzhugh, 217
Lee, Robert E., 310, 455; supports enlistment of black troops, 409
Lee, Stephen D., 110
Lemons, Captain, 49
Lenox, Charles W., 329, 393
Leonard, James R. W., 126
Lewis, Alcide, 27
Lewis, E., 143
Lewis, James, 27
Lewis, Josias, 407
Lexington, U.S.S., 57
Libby Prison, 204
Lieb, Hermann, 50, 51, 53, 56, 58

Lincoln, Abraham, 204, 207–208, 435–436, 467; decision to enlist black troops, 16–19; Proclamation of Amnesty and Reconstruction, 124; reacts to C.S. threat to execute black soldiers or their white officers, 61; reactions to assassination of, 395, 433–434; reviews black troops, 416
Lincoln, Benjamin C., 369, 370, 371
Lincoln University, Mo., 463
Lion (mascot), 141, 154
Little, W. M., 56
Littlefield, Milton S., 89
Little Rock, Ark., 200
Long, Rodney, 248
Loring, Charles, 239
Louisiana troops (C.S.): infantry (Native Guards, Louisiana Militia, 9, 24); (9th Partisan Ranger Battalion, 41)
Louisiana troops (U.S.): cavalry (1st Regiment, 38); infantry (1st Regiment Native Guards, 27, 28–29, 37, 38, 396; assault on Port Hudson, 41–42), *see also* United States troops: infantry (73rd Regiment USCT); (2nd Regiment Native Guards, 27, 28–29; skirmish at Pascagoula, 31–33), *see also* United States troops: infantry (74th Regiment USCT); (3rd Regiment Native Guards, 27, 28–29, 33, 37, 38; assault on Port Hudson, 41–42), *see also* United States troops: infantry (75th Regiment USCT); (8th Regiment African Descent), *see* United States troops: infantry (47th Regiment USCT); (9th Regiment African Descent, 48, 50, 53; action at Milliken's Bend, 53–58), *see also* United States troops: infantry (63rd Regiment USCT); (10th Regiment African Descent, 397), *see also* United States troops: infantry (48th Regiment USCT); (11th Regiment African Descent, 48, 49, 53; action at Milliken's Bend, 53–58), *see also* United States troops: infantry (49th Regiment USCT); (12th Regiment African Descent), *see* United States troops: infantry (50th Regiment USCT); (13th Regiment African Descent, 53n; action at Milliken's Bend, 53–58)
Loveday, John, 307
Lowe, Edgar M., 172, 173, 175, 176, 180
Lowell, James Russell, 87–88
Lyman, Theodore, 209

McCoslin, William, 428–429, 432
McCullar, Thomas, 393
McCulloch, Henry E., 50, 53, 54, 56, 58
McCulloch, Robert, 162

McFarlan, Mathew, 328
McMillen, William L., 170, 173, 176
McMurray, John, 223, 225, 286, 287, 289, 290
Mahone, William, 242–243, 244, 245, 246
Maine troops: cavalry (2nd Regiment, 267, 268); infantry (8th Regiment, 68, 70)
Mallet, Jules, 27
Manning, William C., 322
Manning, S.C., 379–380, 395
Maple Leaf, S.S., 129, 130
Marianna, Fla., action at, 267–269
Marmaduke, John S., 185
Marshall, Tex., 458
Marson, Edwin R., 269
Mary Boardman, S.S., 316
Massachusetts troops: artillery (6th Battery, 38, 41); cavalry (4th Regiment, 377, 381, 385, 419); (5th Regiment Colored, 270, 467; June 15 Petersburg assault, 220–227; Richmond occupation, 419–424); infantry (2nd Regiment, 71; 42nd Regiment, 37); (52nd Regiment, 37); (54th Regiment Colored, 63, 127–128, 137, 154, 252, 254, 256, 354, 357, 373; assault on Fort Wagner, 71–86; battle of Honey Hill, 315–333; battle of Olustee, 137–151; expedition from Georgetown to Camden, 375–395; occupation of Jacksonville, 129–130); (55th Regiment Colored, 115, 135, 255, 256, 257, 354, 357, 374, 468; battle of Honey Hill, 315–333; Rivers Causeway skirmish, 258–263)
Mathews, William D., 20
Maxey, Samuel B., 193
Maxwell, H. J., 277
Mayer, Edelmiro, 154
Meade, George G., 209, 301; conflict with Burnside at the Crater, 230–251
Medal of Honor, 466; enlisted men: William H. Barnes, 292; Powhatan Beaty, 292; James H. Bronson, 292; William H. Carney, 85; Decatur Dorsey, 249; Christian B. Fleetwood, 290; James Gardiner, 292; James A. Harris, 292; Thomas Hawkins, 290; Alfred B. Hilton, 290; Milton M. Holland, 292; Miles James, 292; Alexander Kelly, 290; Robert Pinn, 292; Edward Ratcliff, 292; Charles Veal, 290; officers: William Appleton, 290; Nathan H. Edgerton, 290; Thomas F. Ellsworth, 329n; Henry C. Merriam, 405
medical treatment, 349
Memphis, Tenn., 169, 171; postwar race riot, 464
Merriam, Henry C., 405
Merrill, Charles G., 418–419, 423
Metropolitan Hotel, 434

Meyers, James, 248
Michigan troops: infantry (1st Regiment Infantry African Descent, 329)
Military Order of the Loyal Legion of the United States, 465
Milledgeville (Ga.) Southern Record, 118
Miller, Andrew, 392
Miller, Fred E., 442, 443, 444, 449
Miller, Matthew M., 55, 56, 59
Milliken's Bend, action at, 46–59
Milwaukee Sentinel, 18
Mississippi troops (C.S.): infantry (4th Regiment, 406); (39th Regiment, 41)
Mississippi troops (U.S.): heavy artillery (1st Regiment African Descent), see United States troops: heavy artillery (6th USCHA); infantry (1st Regiment African Descent, 48, 53, 397; action at Milliken's Bend, 53–58), see also United States troops: infantry (51st Regiment USCT)
Missouri troops (U.S.): infantry (1st Regiment Colored, 435, 436), see also United States troops: infantry (62nd Regiment USCT); (4th Regiment Colored, 397), see also United States troops: infantry (68th Regiment USCT)
Mitchell, Barrett B., 186, 188
Mitchell, Matthew R., 240
Mobile, Ala., 179
Montgomery, A. B., 267, 268
Montgomery, James, 12, 67, 69, 137, 145, 147, 150; described, 72–73
Montgomery, Lucinda, 58
Montieu, Joseph L., 27
Moore, James Otis, 204, 205
Moore, Samuel, 104, 105
Morehouse, Warren, 391
Moreland, Jeff, 177
Morgan, Thomas J., 278, 281, 282, 335, 337, 340, 340–342, 344, 349; described, 276–277
Morris, Morris W., 27
Morris Island, S.C., 74, 78, 80, 88, 127, 134, 154, 256, 315
Morrison, Richard, 322, 331
Morrison, Robert G., 443–452
Moscow, Tenn., 209; skirmish near, 109–111
Moss, Ehurd, 27
Mound Plantation, La., skirmish at, 97–102
Murchison, Abram, 15
Murfreesboro Pike, 343
Murphy, Thomas H., 371
Mussey, Reuben D., 334–335
"M.W.S.," 217
Myrtle Sound, 359

National Intelligencer (Washington), 8
National Tribune (Washington), 465

Native American troops (C.S.): infantry (1st Regiment, 193); (2nd Regiment, 193)
Native American troops (U.S.): infantry (2nd Regiment, 106); (3rd Regiment, 104)
Natural Bridge, Fla., skirmish at, 369–372
Nelson, John A., 27, 38, 43, 46
Neuse River, 11
New Bedford Mercury, 72, 73, 76, 86, 133, 149, 358
New Bern, N.C., 11
Newborn, Rufus, 177
New Era, U.S.S., 163
New Hampshire troops: infantry (3rd Regiment, 362); (7th Regiment, 142)
New Ironsides, U.S.S., 77
New Kent Court House, Va., 203, 204
New Market Heights, Va., engagement at, 284–293
New Market Road, 421
New Orleans, La., 9, 436
New Orleans Era, 44
Newport, Fla., 369
Newport Bridge, Fla., skirmish at, 369
Newton, Alexander H., 305, 456
Newton, John, 367, 369–372
New York, N.Y., 126
New York Herald, 148, 328, 362, 445
New York Times, 40, 45, 115, 140, 152, 316, 324, 346
New York Tribune, 28, 78, 87, 105, 222
New York troops: cavalry (1st Mounted Rifles, 419); infantry (47th Regiment, 148); (48th Regiment, 80, 84); (51st Regiment, 208); (56th Regiment, 315, 321); (70th Regiment, 38); (103rd Regiment, 257; Rivers Causeway skirmish, 258–262); (117th Regiment, 225); (127th Regiment, 322); (144th Regiment, 354); (156th Regiment, 45)
New York World, 153
Nine Mile Road, 307
Noe, Charles, 387
North Carolina troops (U.S.): infantry (1st Regiment Colored, 114, 115, 128, 135, 136, 137, 154; battle of Olustee, 137–151), *see also* United States troops: infantry (35th Regiment USCT); (2nd Regiment Colored, 114), *see also* United States troops: infantry (36th Regiment USCT); (3rd Regiment Colored), *see* United States troops: infantry (37th Regiment USCT)
Norfolk, Va., 115
North Anna River, 212
North Edisto River, 257
Norton, Oliver W., 125–126, 139, 140–141, 142, 143–144, 152
Norwich, U.S.S., 67, 129

Norwood, Fred W., 406
Nye, William, 398

Ohio troops: infantry (18th Regiment, 342, 343); (25th Regiment, 322, 323–324); (72nd Regiment, 177); (107th Regiment, 388); (115th Regiment, 337); (127th Regiment Colored), *see* United States troops: infantry (5th Regiment USCT)
Olustee, Fla., 324; battle of, 137–151
Orangeburg, S.C., 356
Orange Plank Road, 211
Ord, Edward O. C., 285, 424
Orillion, Oscar, 27, 45
Osage River, 3–6
Osborne Road, 421
Ouachita River, 196
Overton Hill, 344, 345, 347, 348, 349

Pacific Appeal (San Francisco), 17
Paducah, Ky., 158
Paine, Charles J., 285–286, 287, 291, 296, 297, 359, 360, 363
Paineville, Va., 412
Palatka, Fla., 69
Palmito Ranch, Tex., 443; skirmishes at, 440–450
Paree, Paul, 27
Parke, John G., 301
Parris Island, S.C., 315
Pascagoula, skirmish at, 32
Patterson, Emanuel, 286, 289
Pawnee Landing (Folly Island), 76
pay issue, 91–93, 155, 252–255
Payne, Joseph H., 236, 248, 415
Peach Orchard Hill, 344
Peck, Robert Morris, 265
Pegram, J. W., 410
Pennell, Christopher, 242
Penniman, William, 151
Pennsylvania troops: infantry (26th Regiment, 10); (27th State Militia, 96); (48th Regiment, 230); (50th Regiment, 413); (52nd Regiment, 356)
Petersburg, Va., 8, 216; June 9 assault, 219; June 15 assault, 220–227; July 30 assault ("The Crater"), 228–251
Phelps, John W., 25, 60
Philadelphia, Pa., 125, 202, 206
Philadelphia Inquirer, 153
Philadelphia Press, 143, 148, 212, 311
Philadelphia Supervisory Committee for Recruiting Colored Regiments, 125
Phillips, Wendell, 63
Pierce, Edward L., 15
Pierce, E. R., 171, 180
Pile, William A., 398, 403, 404, 440
Pinchback, P. B. S., 463

Pine and Palm (Boston), 10
Piney Branch Church, Va., 211
Pinn, Robert, 292
Planciancois, Anselmas, 38, 41, 397n
Planet, S.S., 436–437
Platte Valley, S.S., 156, 157
Pleasants, Henry, 230, 231, 236, 237
Pocotaligo, S.C., 313, 314, 353, 354, 357
Point Isabel, Tex., 438, 440, 446
Point Lookout, Md., 217
Poison Spring, engagement at, 186–194
Pope, George, 82, 391, 393
Porter, David D., 46
Porter, Robert, 241
Port Hudson, La., 26, 27, 34, 396; assault on, 34–44
Port Leon, Fla., 370
Port Royal, S.C., 11, 256
Portsmouth, Va., 115
Posey, John, 322, 331
Potato Ferry, 376
Potter, Edward E., 315, 318, 323, 375–395
Potter, Robert B., 235, 238
Powhatan Court House, Va., 412
Pratt, B. F., 422
Pratt, John W., 245, 364
Pratt, Oscar E., 428
Preble, George H., 315, 318
Prestonburg, Ky., 270
Price, Sterling, 195
Price, W. A., 169, 170, 180
Pride, Coolie, 167
prisoner exchange system, 61–62
prisoners of war, 88, 102, 179, 248, 279, 310–312
Proctor, David E., 240–241
Pulaski, Tenn., 334
Purdee, Armstrong, 267, 268
Putnam, Haldimand S., 80, 85

Quincy, Samuel M., 407

racial confrontation, 332
Rains House, 343
Rapidan River, 211
Rapp, Eugene, 27
Ratcliff, Edward, 292
Ratliff, R. W., 270, 273
Reader, Samuel J., 266
Readville, Mass., 72, 257
Redman, Bill, 450
Red River, 34, 182
Reed, Lewis, 393
Reed, William N., 148
Reeve, A. T., 176, 179
Revelle, Hardie N., 163
Rey, Henry L., 27, 28

Rhode Island troops: heavy artillery (3rd Regiment, 356)
Rhodes, Allen, 6
Richmond, La., 50, 51, 53, 57
Richmond, Va., 204, 410, 411, 433; occupation of, 417–424
Richmond Dispatch, 410, 411
Richmond Examiner, 410, 411
Rickard, James H., 208, 237
Rio Grande, 182, 438–452, 461
Rivers Causeway, 75; skirmish at, 256–263
Roach, Joab, 151
Roanoke Island, N.C., 11
Robinson, Benjamin, 167
Robinson, W. N., 444–445, 447
Rogall, Albert, 207, 240
Rogers, Frederick E., 379
Rogers, George, 225
Romeyn, Henry, 280, 281, 343, 347–348
Ross, William E. W., 242
Rowlett, Wyette, 450
Rush, I. B., 440
Russel, Cabot J., 75, 85, 86
Russell, Charles S., 301, 418
Russell, William, 260
Russell, William Howard, 25
Rust, John D., 68

St. Augustine, Fla., 124
Saint-Gaudens, Augustus, 467
St. John's River, 64, 66, 154
St. Louis, Hyppolite, 27
St. Louis Daily Union, 157
St. Louis Missouri Democrat, 157
St. Marks, Fla., 367, 370
St. Marks River, 369, 370
St. Simon's Island, Ga., 16, 63, 72
Saline River, 196
Salomon, Frederick, 197
Saltville, Va., action at, 269–275
Sanders, Andrew, 104, 105
Sanders, George R., 44
Sanderson, Fla., 134, 139, 150
Sanders Ridge, 273, 274
Saunders, John C. C., 245–246
Sauvenet, Charles, 46
Savannah, Ga., 353
Savannah Republican, 69
Sawyer, Oscar G., 148
Saxton, Rufus, 66, 91, 315; enlistment of black troops, 17–18
Scammon, Eliakim P., 316
Schimmelfennig, Alexander, 257, 258
Schofield, John M., 271, 334
Scofield, Hiram, 397, 404, 407
Scott, Charles, 394
Scott, H. C., 410
Scott, John, 410–411

Scott, William, 144, 260
Scroggs, Joseph J., 204, 216, 286, 292, 296, 306, 360
Seabrook Island, S.C., 257
Seaman, Henry C., 3, 13
Sears, Cyrus, 51, 56, 57
Sedgwick, F. W., 51
Selma, Ala., 62
Sentmanat, Charles, 27
Sepping, Henry, 106
Seymour, Truman, 85, 128, 133–134, 135, 136–137, 142, 148
Shafter, William R., 341, 343
Shaw, Francis G., 72
Shaw, George, 167
Shaw, James, Jr., 298, 425, 429
Shaw, Robert Gould, 63–64, 72, 76–77, 78, 136, 467; killed, 83; martyrdom, 87–88; opinion of James Montgomery, 73; ponders offer to lead 54th Massachusetts Colored, 72; prepares for Wagner assault, 80–81
Sheridan, Philip H., 410n, 426, 430; Texas occupation, 458–461
Sherman, Thomas W., 11
Sherman, William T., 159, 169, 170, 180, 272, 313, 332, 334, 353, 375, 395; opinion of blacks as troops, 275–276
Sherwood, Mo., skirmish near, 103–104
Sholes, A. T., 19
Shurtleff, Giles W., 217, 286, 291
Sigfried, Joshua K., 208, 212–213; commands brigade at the Crater, 232–251
Silver Cloud, U.S.S., 156, 157
Simon, Edward, 405
Simonton, Edward, 216
Simpkins, William H., 80, 81, 86
Simpson, David, 148
Singleton, William Henry, 468
Six Killer, John, 6
Slocum, Henry W., 353
Smith, Aaron, 144
Smith, Andrew J., 181, 328
Smith, Edmund Kirby, 55, 58, 99, 455
Smith, Noah, 126
Smith, William, 346
Smith, William F. "Baldy," 217, 221, 224, 225–226, 228
Smother, S. H., 459
Snear, Louis A., 27, 45, 396
"Solid Shot" (pseud.), 364
Sol Legare's Island, 74
Soule, Charles C., 260, 318, 319–320, 323, 324, 331
South Carolina troops (C.S.): artillery (Blake's Battery, 260)
South Carolina troops (U.S.): infantry (First South Carolina Volunteer Regiment,

15–16); (1st Regiment African Descent, 63, 261; occupation of Jacksonville, 64–71), see also United States troops: infantry (33rd Regiment USCT); (2nd Regiment African Descent, 73; 1st occupation of Jacksonville, 64–70; 2nd occupation of Jacksonville, 133), see also United States troops: infantry (34th Regiment USCT); (3rd Regiment African Descent), see United States troops: infantry (21st Regiment USCT); (4th Regiment African Descent, 89), see also United States troops: infantry (21st Regiment USCT)
South Edisto River, 257, 354
South Mills, N.C., 115
South Side Railroad, 429–430
Spanish Fort, Ala., 398
Spears, David, 324
Spinney, Robert M., 298
Spotsylvania Court House, Va., 211
Spring Hill, Tenn., 334
Stafford, Spencer H., 27, 31, 36, 46
Stale, Allen, 436, 450
Stamps, Daniel, 167
Stanton, Edwin M., 12, 17–18, 59, 62, 91, 94–95, 169, 206
Stanton, Nathan, 307
Starke, Fla., 135
Steedman, James B., 276, 278, 340–341, 344
Steele, Frederick, 182, 183–199, 200, 396
Stephens, George E., 10, 72, 73, 81, 83, 85, 89, 92, 127, 137–138, 145, 147, 149, 150
Sterns, George L., 72, 94–95, 125
Stevens, Edward L., 376–395
Stevenson, Thomas G., 80
Stickney, Lyman D., 122–123, 124, 153
Stinson, Charles F., 236, 237
Stone, Kate, 59
Stono River, 74
Straight, D. E., 346
Strong, George C., 78, 80, 84; death of, 86
Sturgis, Samuel D., 170, 172, 173, 177, 180
Sugar Loaf, action near, 362–363
Sullivan's Island, S.C., 81
Summerville, Junius, 176
Sumterville, S.C., 380, 381, 385, 388
Susquehanna River, 95, 96
Sutherland Station, Va., 429
Suwanee River, 136
Swails, Stephen A., 374, 386
Swift Creek, 390, 394

Talbot, Joseph, 6
Tampa, Fla., 366
Tarrant, E. W., 406
Taylor, James N., 168

Taylor, James T. S., 365
Taylor, Richard, 49–59, 455
Ten Mile Station, Fla., 136
Tennessee troops (U.S.): cavalry (13th Regiment, 158, 161, 163); infantry (1st Regiment African Descent, 109), *see also* United States troops: infantry (59th Regiment USCT); (2nd Regiment African Descent, 109; skirmish at Wolf River Bridge, 110–111), *see also* United States troops: infantry (61st Regiment USCT)
Terry, Alfred H., 359–364
Texas troops (C.S.): cavalry (12th Regiment, 99, 100, 101); (19th Regiment, 99, 100, 101); infantry (20th Regiment, 108); (22nd Regiment, 101); (24th Regiment, 108)
Texas troops (U.S.): cavalry (2nd Regiment, 440, 444, 445, 446, 447)
Thayer, John M., 183, 186
Thibaut, Louis A., 27
Thomas, George H., 336, 338, 344, 345, 348; opinion of blacks as troops, 334–335, 349
Thomas, Henry G., 208, 418; commands brigade at the Crater, 232–251
Thomas, Lewis, 144
Thomas, Lorenzo, 349, 436; enlistment of black troops, 47–48, 59, 98
Thomas, William H., 205, 308
Thompson, Charles R., 340, 345–346
Thoreau, Henry D., 63
Tishomingo Creek, 175, 176
Todd, Laura, 436
Todd, Margaret, 436
Todd, Westfield, 214
Toothman's Mound. *See* Island Mound
Townsend, Benjamin R., 366, 370, 372
Trotter, James M., 258–263, 325–326, 328, 331, 374
Trowbridge, Charles T., 257
Truman, Benjamin C., 346, 348
Tucker, Charles E., 379, 386, 387
Tucker, Littleton, 177
Tucker, Mary, 348
Tucker, Newton, 347, 348
Tupelo, Miss., 181
Turner, Andrew, 404
Turner, Henry W., 307, 360, 463
Turner, Nat, 9
Turner, Thomas, 410, 412

Ullmann, Daniel, 46, 397, 437; enlistment of black troops, 34
Uncas, U.S.S., 67
l'Union (New Orleans), 28
Union City, Tenn., 158

United States Congress: Acts authorizing postwar black units, 462; Direct Tax Law, 122; Second Confiscation Act, 12; Militia Act, 12, 91
United States troops: cavalry (5th Regiment USCT, action at Saltville, 269–275); heavy artillery (6th Regiment, 158, 161), *also known as* Mississippi troops (U.S.): heavy artillery (1st Regiment); light artillery (1st Artillery Battery B, 139); (2nd Colored Artillery, 161; Battery B, 228; June 9 Petersburg assault, 219; Battery F, 170, 172; battle of Brice's Cross Roads, 172–180); infantry (1st Regiment USCT, 114, 115, 215; Fort Fisher operation, 359–364; June 9 Petersburg assault, 219; June 15 Petersburg assault, 220–227; engagement at New Market Heights, 286–300; engagement near Fair Oaks, 304–308); (2nd Regiment USCT, skirmish at Natural Bridge, 365–372); (3rd Regiment USCT, 125, 132); (4th Regiment USCT, 202, 215; Fort Fisher operation, 359–364; Petersburg assault, 220–227; engagement at New Market Heights, 286–300; (5th Regiment USCT, 114, 115, 202, 215, 310; capture of City Point, 216–217; Petersburg assault, 220–227; engagement at New Market Heights, 286–300; engagement near Fair Oaks, 304–308; Fort Fisher operation, 359–364), *also known as* Ohio troops: infantry (127th Regiment Colored); (6th Regiment USCT, 125, 202, 215, 252–253; Fort Fisher operation, 359–364; June 9 Petersburg assault, 219; June 15 Petersburg assault, 220–227; engagement at New Market Heights, 286–300); (7th Regiment USCT, 154, 310; Appomattox campaign, 425–432; engagement at Fort Gilmer, 297; engagement near Fair Oaks, 304–308); (8th Regiment USCT, 125–127, 131–132, 136, 154; Appomattox campaign, 425–432; battle of Olustee, 137–151; engagement at Fort Gilmer, 297; engagement near Fair Oaks, 304–308); (9th Regiment USCT, engagement at Fort Gilmer, 297; engagement near Fair Oaks, 304–308; Richmond occupation, 417–424); (10th Regiment USCT, 215, 220n, 228, 286n; Fort Fisher operation, 359–364; Richmond occupation, 417–424); (12th Regiment USCT, 336–337; battle of Nashville, 340–350); (13th Regiment USCT, 337; battle of Nashville, 340–350); (14th Regiment USCT, 276–277, 338; action at Dalton, 277–278; action at

United States troops *cont.*
  Decatur, 280; battle of Nashville, 340–350; skirmish at Stockade No. 2, 335–338); (16th Regiment USCT, 337; battle of Nashville, 340–350); (17th Regiment USCT, battle of Nashville, 340–350); (18th Regiment USCT, battle of Nashville, 340–350); (19th Regiment USCT, 206, 208; assault on the Crater, 232–251; engagement near the Boydton Plank Road, 301–304; Richmond occupation, 417–424); (21st Regiment USCT, 254, 256, 356), *see also* South Carolina troops (U.S.): infantry (3rd and 4th Regiments African Descent); (22nd Regiment USCT, 204, 215, 433–434; June 15 Petersburg assault, 220–227; engagement at New Market Heights, 286–300; engagement near Fair Oaks, 304–308; Richmond occupation, 417–424); (23rd Regiment USCT, 243; assault on the Crater, 232–251; engagement near the Boydton Plank Road, 301–304; Richmond occupation, 417–424; skirmish near Alrich Farm, 211); (27th Regiment USCT, 206, 208; assault on the Crater, 232–251; engagement near the Boydton Plank Road, 301–304; Fort Fisher operation, 359–364); (28th Regiment USCT, assault on the Crater, 232–251; engagement near the Boydton Plank Road, 301–304; Richmond occupation, 417–424); (29th Regiment USCT, Appomattox campaign, 425–432; assault on the Crater, 232–251; engagement near the Boydton Plank Road, 301–304); (30th Regiment USCT, 206, 208, 310; assault on the Crater, 232–251; engagement near the Boydton Plank Road, 301–304; Fort Fisher operation, 359–364; skirmish near Salem Church, 211–212); (31st Regiment USCT, Appomattox campaign, 425–432; assault on the Crater, 232–251; engagement near the Boydton Plank Road, 301–304); (32nd Regiment USCT, 253, 256, 354; battle of Honey Hill, 315–333; battle of Olustee, 137–151; expedition from Georgetown to Camden, 375–395); (33rd Regiment USCT, 256, 257; Rivers Causeway skirmish, 257–262), *see also* South Carolina troops (U.S.): infantry (1st Regiment African Descent); (34th Regiment USCT, battle of Honey Hill, 321–333), *see also* South Carolina troops (U.S.): infantry (2nd Regiment African Descent); (35th Regiment USCT, 314; battle of Honey Hill, 321–333), *see also*

North Carolina troops (U.S.): infantry (1st Regiment Colored); (36th Regiment USCT, engagement at New Market Heights, 286–300; engagement near Fair Oaks, 304–308; Richmond occupation, 417–424), *see also* North Carolina troops (U.S.): infantry (2nd Regiment Colored); (37th Regiment USCT, 215, 228; engagement at New Market Heights, 286–300; engagement near Fair Oaks, 304–308; Fort Fisher operation, 359–364), *also known as* North Carolina troops (U.S.): infantry (3rd Regiment Colored); (38th Regiment USCT, engagement at New Market Heights, 286–300; engagement near Fair Oaks, 304–308; Richmond occupation, 417–424); (39th Regiment USCT, 206, 208; assault on the Crater, 232–251; engagement near the Boydton Plank Road, 301–304; Fort Fisher operation, 359–364); (41st Regiment USCT, Appomattox campaign, 425–432; engagement near Fair Oaks, 304–308); (43rd Regiment USCT, 206, 208, 212, 416; assault on the Crater, 232–251; engagement near the Boydton Plank Road, 301–304; Richmond occupation, 417–424); (44th Regiment USCT, battle of Nashville, 340–350; skirmish at Stockade No. 2, 335–338; surrender at Dalton, 278–280); (45th Regiment USCT, 284; Appomattox campaign, 425–432; engagement near Fair Oaks, 304–308); (46th Regiment USCT), *see* Arkansas troops (U.S.): infantry (1st Regiment African Descent); (47th Regiment USCT, 397, 399; assault on Fort Blakely, 404–408), *also known as* Louisiana troops: infantry (8th Regiment African Descent); (48th Regiment USCT, 397, 399), *see also* Louisiana troops: infantry (10th Regiment African Descent); (49th Regiment USCT), *see* Louisiana troops: infantry (11th Regiment African Descent); (50th Regiment USCT, 397), *also known as* Louisiana troops: infantry (12th Regiment African Descent); (51st Regiment USCT, 397, 406), *see also* Mississippi troops (U.S.): infantry (1st Regiment African Descent); (55th Regiment USCT, 170, 171; battle of Brice's Cross Roads, 172–180), *also known as* Alabama troops (U.S.): infantry (1st Regiment African Descent); (59th Regiment USCT, 171, 181; battle of Brice's Cross Roads, 172–180), *see also* Tennessee troops (U.S.): infantry (1st

Regiment African Descent); (61st Regiment USCT, 181), *see also* Tennessee troops (U.S.): infantry (2nd Regiment African Descent); (62nd Regiment USCT, 437–452; skirmishes at Palmito Ranch, 440–452), *see also* Missouri troops (U.S.): infantry (1st Regiment Colored); (63rd Regiment USCT), *see* Louisiana troops: infantry (9th Regiment African Descent); (68th Regiment USCT, 181, 397; assault on Fort Blakely, 404–408), *see also* Missouri troops (U.S.): infantry (4th Regiment Colored); (73rd Regiment USCT, 46, 396–397; assault on Fort Blakely, 405–408), *see also* Louisiana troops: infantry (1st Regiment Native Guards); (74th Regiment USCT, 46), *see also* Louisiana troops: infantry (2nd Regiment Native Guards); (75th Regiment USCT, 46), *see also* Louisiana troops: infantry (3rd Regiment Native Guards); (76th Regiment USCT, 397; assault on Fort Blakely, 403–408); (79th Regiment USCT New), *see* Kansas troops: infantry (1st Regiment Colored); (81st Regiment USCT New, 438); (82nd Regiment USCT, 397; action at Marianna, 267–269); (83rd Regiment USCT New), *see* Kansas troops: infantry (2nd Regiment Colored); (86th Regiment USCT, 397; action at Marianna, 268–269; assault on Fort Blakely, 403–408); (99th Regiment USCT, 367–371); (102nd Regiment USCT, 329, 331, 354; battle of Honey Hill, 315–333; battle of Olustee, 137–151; expedition from Georgetown to Camden, 375–395); (108th Regiment USCT, 461); (109th Regiment USCT, Appomattox campaign, 425–432); (114th Regiment USCT, Richmond occupation, 477–484); (115th Regiment USCT, Richmond occupation, 417–424); (116th Regiment USCT, Appomattox campaign, 425–432); (117th Regiment USCT, Richmond occupation, 417–424); (118th Regiment USCT, Richmond occupation, 417–424); (124th Regiment USCT, 461); (127th Regiment USCT, 311; Appomattox campaign, 425–432)
Upson, Theodore, 313
Utt, Josephus, 186

Varina Road, 297
Veal, Charles, 290
"Venoir" (pseud.), 155
Verplanck, Robert N., 205, 220, 226
Vesey, Denmark, 9
Vicksburg, Miss., 8, 47, 58, 102

Vincennes, Ind., 322
Vogelsang, Peter, 75

Wade, James F., 270
Wadley, Sarah, 59
Wagner, George E., 297–298
Wagner, Thomas M., 74
Walcott, George H., 209
Walker, David, 90
Walker, John G., 50, 57
Walker, William, 254
Walls, Josiah T., 463
Ward, Richard G., 3–7, 186, 188–189, 190, 191, 194
Warfield, Charles, 27
Waring, George E., 170, 173
Waring, William, 333
Washington, Edward D., 149–150
Washington, District of Columbia, 207–208, 434
Watie, Stand, 105, 263
Weaver, Henry F., 159, 163
Weiss, Julius A., 298–299
Weitzel, Godfrey, 30, 38, 305, 307, 418, 419–420, 422–423, 433
Welch, Frank M., 385
Welles, Gideon, 153
West Florida News, 269
Wheaton, Horace, 144
Wheeler, Joseph, 276, 278
Whitaker, J. Lewis, 329
White, Garland H., 236, 238, 241–242, 250, 422, 424, 460
White, Joseph H., 379
White, Thomas, 274
White's Ranch, Tex., 442, 443
Whiting, William, 91
Whitman, Walt, 208
Wickes, James Henry, 290
Wild, Edward A., 115, 117–118, 128, 418; described, 113, 215, 217; orders hanging of prisoner, 116
Wilder, Burt G., 316
Wilderness, The, 209
Wiley, Warren, 275
Wilkin, Alexander, 170
Willard's Hotel, 207, 344
Willcox, Orlando B., 235, 238, 250
Williams, George N., 114
Williams, James M., 13, 19–20, 103, 104, 105, 106–108, 186–188, 189, 190, 191, 192–193, 195, 266
Williams, Joseph D., 336
Williams, M., 163
Williams, Preston, 76, 86
Williams, Thomas, 23
Williamsburg, Va., 202, 203, 204
Williamsburg Road, 306, 307

Willis, Byrd C., 214
Willoughby, Richard H., 357
Wilmington, N.C., occupation of, 363–364
Wilson, D. W., 447
Wilson, Henry, 147
Wilson, John H., 386
Wilson, Joseph D., 74–75
Wilson, Joseph T., 27, 128, 145, 148
Wilson's Station, Va., 430
Wilson's Wharf, Va., 215, 217
Winslow, Edward F., 170, 173
Wistar, Isaac J., 201
Wolf River, 179
Wood, Louis T., 460

Wood, R. C., 349
Wood, Thomas J., 345, 348
Woodlin, William P., 131, 137, 142, 143, 152
Woodward, George M., 325
Woodward, William W., 425, 429
Wrightsville, Penn., skirmish at, 95–97

Yazoo River, 47
Yellow Bluff, Fla., 154
Young, Pierce M. B., 389
Younger, Simpson C., 468
Young's Point, La., 47, 50, 51, 58

Zulavszky, L. L., 267

MEN OF COLOR

To Arms! To Arms!

NOW OR NEVER

This is our golden moment! The Government of the United States calls for every Able-bodied Colored Man to enter the Army for the

THREE YEARS' SERVICE!

AND JOIN IN FIGHTING THE

BATTLES OF LIBERTY AND THE UNION

A new era is open to us. For generations we have suffered under the horrors of slavery, outrage and wrong; our manhood has been denied, our citizenship blotted out, our souls seared and burned, our spirits cowed and crushed, and the hopes of the future of our race involved in doubt and darkness. But now our relations to the white race are changed. Now, therefore, is our most precious moment. Let us rush to arms!

FAIL NOW, & OUR RACE IS DOOMED

On this soil of our birth. We must now awake, arise, or be forever fallen. If we value liberty, if we wish to be free in this land, if we love our country, if we love our families, our children, our homes, we must strike now while the country calls; we must rise up in the dignity of our manhood, and show by our own right arms that we are worthy to be freemen. Our enemies have made the country believe that we are craven cowards without soul, without manhood, without the spirit of soldiers. Shall we die with this stigma resting upon our graves? Shall we leave this inheritance of shame to our children? No, a thousand times No! WE WILL Rise! The alternative is upon us. Let us rather die freemen than live to be slaves. What is life without liberty? We say that we have manhood, now is the time to prove it. A nation or a people that cannot fight may be pitied, but cannot be respected. If we would be regarded men, if we would forever

SILENCE THE TONGUE OF CALUMNY

Of Prejudice and Hate, let us Rise Now and Fly to Arms! We have seen what

VALOR AND HEROISM

OUR BROTHERS DISPLAYED AT

PORT HUDSON AND MILLIKEN'S BEND,

Though they are just from the galling, poisoning grasp of slavery, they have startled the World by the most desperate bravery. If they have proved themselves heroes, cannot WE PROVE OURSELVES MEN?

ARE FREEMEN LESS BRAVE THAN SLAVES

[illegible] MEN OF COLOR [illegible] the Englishman the Irishman the Frenchman the German the American have been called to assert their right to freedom and a manly character, by an appeal to the sword. The day that has seen an enslaved race in arms has, in all times, seen their last trial. We now see that

OUR LAST OPPORTUNITY HAS COME

If we are not lower in the scale of humanity than Englishmen, Irishmen, White Americans, and other Races, we can show it now.

MEN OF COLOR, BROTHERS AND FATHERS!

WE APPEAL TO YOU!

[illegible]

STRIKE NOW!

And you are henceforth and forever FREEMEN!